TRIM . . .
but DEADLY
Volume III

TURNER PUBLISHING COMPANY
The Front Line of Military History Books
P.O. Box 3101
Paducah, Kentucky 42002-3101
(502) 443-0121

Copyright © 1993, Turner Publishing Company. All rights reserved.

Destroyer Escort Sailors Association, Volume III was compiled using available information. The Publisher is not responsible for errors or omissions.

Destroyer Escort Sailors Association Staff:

    Samuel L. Saylor, President
    Donald A. Glaser, Executive Administrator
    John P. Cosgrove, National Representative

Library of Congress Catalog
Card Number: 86-51635

ISBN: 978-1-68162-135-7

Volume I and II also available. This book is a limited edition of which this copy is number _____.

Additional books may be purchased from Turner Publishing Company.

Opening page: Courtesy of artist John Charles Roach. Original painting may be viewed at the Destroyer-Escort Museum.

DESTROYER ESCORTS ...

USS Atherton (DE-169) . . . dropping depth charges . . . [after the sinking of the U-853]. (National Archives Photo, Courtesy of Conles D. Payne)

USS Bronstein (DE-189) participating in HunterKiller Operations north of the Azores, Feb. 29, 1944. Lt. Sheldon Kinney, Commanding.

Launching of the USS Roy O. Hale (DE-336) Nov. 20, 1943 at Orange, TX. (Courtesy of George Hollingsworth)

TABLE OF CONTENTS

Commissioning of the USS Roy O. Hale (DE-336), Feb. 3, 1944 at Orange, TX. (Courtesy of George Hollingsworth)

ACKNOWLEDGEMENTS

The publication of this third and final volume of "Trim but Deadly" will mark the completion of one of the more important goals of the Destroyer-Escort Association. Early on, when we first met with the officials of the Turner Publishing Company, we had no idea this project would be so successful. The response from our members and others with an interest in naval history has been magnificent.

Since the publication of Volume II of "Trim but Deadly" another goal of our Association has been successfully completed. Our Destroyer-Escort bronze sculpture is in place within the circle of honor at the Navy Memorial in Washington, D.C. It is there for all to see and to know that the Destroyer-Escort and the men who sailed them did make a difference during the time of their service to our country.

Since the inception of Volume I and continuing through the publication of Volume III, our Association was fortunate to have had the services and dedication from so many shipmates and friends. I wish I could list every name that contributed to the excellence of these volumes. Some names do stand out and I would be remiss if I did not publicly thank them for their efforts. To shipmate John Cosgrove, who was our Editor-in-Chief of the three volumes, I offer my sincere thanks for a job well done. He was our guiding hand in this project. To Don Glaser and his staff, who provides us a functional office through which our business is done, I also offer my sincere thanks. To the members of our Board, past and present, who have given me the guidance to sit at the head of our Association, you have my sincere thanks. To the members of the Destroyer-Escort Sailors Association who, as they always do, give me the help to get any job done, you have my deep appreciation and thanks. To artists, Mike Felish, Tom Freeman, Max Bullock, Crock's Bill Rechin, Don Wilder and John Charles Roach for the beautiful and inspiring work they contributed to all three volumes, I thank them very much. Lastly, I wish to thank the professional staff of Turner Publishing Company for their efforts in seeing that the Destroyer-Escort Sailors Association's three volumes of "Trim but Deadly" are a fitting tribute to the men and ships that served so well in WW II, Korea, Vietnam, and during the interludes between.

Samuel L. Saylor

Samuel L. Saylor, President
Destroyer-Escort Sailors Association

PREFACE

It seems like only yesterday that we were reading final proofs on *Trim but Deadly* and looking forward to seeing in print the first definitive history of the Destroyer-Escort.

We knew then, if not a little before, that the 352-page book was not going to tell the whole story of the DE ship and sailor. At hand was a sufficient stack of photos and stories to fill another book.

Dave Turner, aware of this treasure, suggested that we get Volume Two underway while Volume One was printed and distributed. The story was duplicated as Volume Two was put to bed, which leads directly to the wrapping-up of Volume III. This may be the final volume by Turner Publishing Company but it would appear that the DE story will never be *complete* so long as a DE sailor is around to tell his story, show off his album of snapshots, display precious artifacts and memorabilia—tangible ties to his part in "saving the world."

That's right. "When they were young, they saved the world," wrote Paul Donnelly, a writer of historical significance. History tells us that DE sailors in manning that 563 ship navy, played a major role in restoring peace to a war torn world. They were a special segment of those "ordinary people—American's WWII generation—who lived in an extraordinary time." So well said, Mr. Donnelly.

Destroyer-Escorts were tailor-made for WWII. Many went on to serve in Korea and Vietnam, and a few are operating today in service of foreign nations. What a tribute to the designers and builders! Having been built under wartime secrecy not very much was told about their unique and unequaled ability to combat submarines. Many naval experts decreed that DE's were under-gunned and under-powered Destroyers—and obviously misnamed. The years have proven DE's to be masterfully designed. They captured and/or destroyed German U-boats, helped to win the Battle of the Atlantic, and continued to assume unforeseen assignments and responsibilities, some as APD's, in the Pacific operations.

Special categories and significant characteristics included: a short turning radius, hedgehogs, projectiles fired ahead of the ship, exploding only if they hit a solid object; the best sonar, and a ramming bow—a gigantic piece of steel built into the hull. Fleet doctrine for a sub on the surface was "close and ram." In short, trim *and* deadly. These technical advances were superbly utilized and exercised by crews exhibiting skill, and a patriotic spirit similar to the exemplary standards set by our Founding Fathers.

As I write these words, I recall viewing the parade of Navy vessels marking the 40th anniversary of V-J Day aboard the USS *Enterprise* (CVN-65) in San Francisco Bay. Not a DD nor DE appeared nor ever mentioned. The story of "tough little ships and brave men" was sorely missing in that commemorative ceremony. Later in reporting this event for *DESA News*, I swore that "so long as I could talk or write, the record of DE's and the men who sailed them, would not be forgotten."

It is with much satisfaction now, as we put the finishing touches to this *final* volume, that we have firmly established a proper niche for the Destroyer-Escort in the annals of naval history.

John P. Cosgrove

John P. Cosgrove
USS *Gendreau* (DE-639)

FOREWORD

Rear Admiral Sheldon Kinney

The DE legacy is a story of an astonishingly able, mass-produced vessel that made a critical difference in the successful war at sea in WWII. Importantly, it is the story of the Navy and Coast Guard men who served in these ships, men heroic in combat, long-suffering in endless watches, capable of enduring cruel seas, cold, heat, boredom, waiting, watching, then suddenly rising to amazing capability in crisis.

As you turn page after page of these volumes, the story unfolds for the story of a ship is the individual stories of her men.

In that way I am honored to pen this Foreword responding to the request of John Cosgrove, who said "make this your story." And so, since DEs were the most memorable part of 47 years in Navy uniform, this introduction reflects my DE experience as each of you have yours in the these volumes.

It was a thrilling moment when I experienced my first sight of a DE—USS *Edsall* (DE-129), leader of the class that bears her name. She stood on the building ways in February, 1943, at Orange, Texas, 75% complete. Among the earliest of this new breed she was the first to be build on the Gulf Coast. As the prospective executive officer and navigator, I felt most fortunate as I made my way through the empty compartments and worked from the bilges to the remarkable "open bridge."

The very newness thrilled me. Leaving high school in 1935, Pasadena, CA, to enlist, I served as a seaman in the light cruiser *Omaha*, a signalman in the battleship *New York,* and made my three summer training cruises at the Naval Academy in ships of the same vintage, 1914-1922 construction. Upon graduation in February, 1941, I was assigned to USS *Sturtevant* (DD-240). Same story, an old four-piper. And here was new construction!

The yard in Orange was filled with what amounted to a production line of DE hulls. At very short intervals, launchings were to be quickly followed by keel layings in East, West, Gulf and Great Lakes building yards. This construction of almost 600 DEs, an armada of democracy, American-style, was to prove magnificent tribute to the genius of our shipbuilders. Once launched they were indeed "trim," would they prove "deadly?"

And what of those who would man these new ships? The early commissionings enjoyed a level of experienced and trained personnel that as the war progressed would be steadily thinned. But the quality of men commissioning new DEs never was diluted. Moreover, once through shakedown and off to war the crews fulfilled their responsibilities with an astonishing competence as they rapidly formed a team of true men-o-warsmen.

The commanding officers of Navy DEs were 95% (at least) officers of the Naval Reserve. The ships benefited greatly from the NROTC graduates of the six original units—Harvard, Yale, Georgia Tech, Northwestern, California (Berkeley), Washington and from the Organized Reserve Battalions, American yachtsmen, particularly the New York Yacht Club were greatly in evidence. Often the route to these commands was through the converted yachts, SCs and PCs. The graduates of the newly formed midshipmen programs, V-7 provided a more junior group who in turn worked up to commands. You name the program, and America's officer and enlisted could survive it, profit from it and serve with distinction.

Edsall was launched, commissioned, and we headed down through the cow-pastures on the narrow Sabine River to the sea. My admiration for our chief quartermaster at the wheel, steering a ship of unknown turning characteristics through a series of bends that rivalled a slalom course was unbounded. Up the Mississippi to New Orleans for provisions, ammunition and torpedoes we went, then off to Bermuda for shakedown. There we found ourselves in company with the first DEs from several East Coast building yards, going through the rigorous paces dictated by the shakedown group.

All we DE sailors are indebted to the unique system of education, training and management that prepared us and our ships to join the line of battle; the service schools that converted men from civilian life to competent motor machinist mates, gunners, quartermasters, radiomen, sonarmen, the entire spectrum of the DEs ship's company. The Submarine Chaser Training Center (SCTC) in Miami, was referred to by the Royal Navy as the Yanks' ASW University. Her incomparable Captain E.F. McDaniel led this school on Pier One that was the heart of SC, PC and DE training. The pre-commissioning details at the building yards protected our interests during construction and fitting out. The shakedown groups in both oceans provided a year's experience in one month. All played vital roles that years later as Chief of Naval Education and Training, and Commandant of Midshipmen I would keep in mind.

Shakedown completed we received the usual "availability"—in the Boston Navy Yard for repairs and then undertook trials off Rockland, Maine, where BuShips established the speed and turning characteristics of a new class.

A radio dispatch then caused me first despair, then delight: "Lt. Kinney detached XO USS *Edsall* (despair) Report USS *Edsall* as CO" (delight). Command at sea! For a line officer, the goal.

The first DEs were commanded by career officers, most Naval Academy 1932. They were sent to the SCTC course then to the ASW Navy. Shortly after their DEs were commissioned and organized, they fleeted up to become Escort Squadron (CORTRON) commanders, relieved by their XO. For a lieutenant commissioned two and a half years, this was the chance of a lifetime. (The Coast Guard manned DEs with a much higher percentage of career personnel.)

Looking back, I wonder why no doubt entered my mind that perhaps the assignment was beyond me. The record was there: I had been first lieutenant and gunnery/torpedo officer and top OOD of a destroyer escorting British Convoys transatlantic in the months proceeding and after U.S. entry into the war. We did this with ancient sonar and excellent radars. (Years later in Korea and Vietnam sophisticated systems would cause me to smile at this thought.)

As I said at the change of command ceremony to my skipper the traditional "I relieve you sir" and he was piped over the side, it was a cocky 24 year old that took command.

Following the chief master at arms forward we

passed the double rank of chiefs, quite seasoned. A quiet voice reached my ear with the words "and a little child shall lead them." Excellent corrective therapy for the youngest DE commanding officer.

The months that followed can best be described by "They also serve who only stand and wait." The earliest DEs were required for the training of others. *Edsall* ran daily raids into the Chesapeake with prospective DE crews training at Norfolk before proceeding to commissioning the new ships. The four-stacker *Reuben James* (DD-245), torpedoed on one of our pre-war convoy runs, was in the same division as my destroyer. We lasted only a few months longer. The grounding of the USS *Reuben James* (DE-153) in Key West moved *Edsall* to SCTC as a training ship. A prospective commanding officers course was being conducted at Miami. Every Monday we sailed with PCOs filling the forward crews living compartment, for a one-week mini-cruise. (The good fortune of a week's leave to vacate bunks, was rotated among the crew). There were ASW exercises with "S" Boats at Key West, anchoring drills in the Dry Tortugas, a shoot-off Guantamano, and the high point, liberty in Havana.

While the routine was hardly rigorous, I had a score to settle in the Atlantic, and one in the Pacific, my brother a QM1/c having died on the bridge of the *Arizona*. But my periodic visits to Captain McDaniel were met with his usual (and correct) response that in this war what individuals wanted was secondary to the service needed for them.

It was a response to which I had grown quite familiar when, after *Sturtevant* was sunk, I attended the course at SCTC but was held on as a weapons instructor for six months. (Following the sinking, on the phone to BuPers I gave my choice of duty as PTs—the detailer thought I said PCs!)

In November, 1943, Captain McDaniel relented and had me assigned as PCO of the *Kyne* building in the San Pedro, Californi, area. My last days in Edsall were spent off Key West evaluating a new device called a "Chemical Recorder." We found that at last a device far better than a stopwatch was available to predict the time to drop a depth charge pattern on a contact. It was later to prove so for me in attacking four German U-boats.

The crew gave me the perfect send-off, a request signed by every member (and with the pawprint of Josephine, Ship's Cat1/c) to be transferred to the new ship. After my watch, *Edsall* completed her duty as a teacher and went to war. What a fine band of shipmates.

Train to the West Coast meant a taxi ride across Chicago from one railroad station to the other system. It was there that the Navy intercepted and redirected me to New York. *Kyne* was delayed in construction. Proceed to Port Newark and commission *Bronstein* (DE-189). Skippers were in short supply.

On a dreary December, 1943, day, we commissioned in New York Navy Yard. New ship, new crew. Less experience this time. XO (now a respected Seattle surgeon) had skippered an SC, gunnery officer-armed guard. All others in the wardroom, first sea duty. Crew? Eleven regular Navy. Everyone else had learned their skill in Navy training after enlistment. Disaster? Far from it. On her first mission following shakedown, operating with a hunter/killer group *Bronstein* engaged four German U-boats, three in one night, in which three were sunk, and the fourth so badly damaged that while she managed to reach her base in France, she never fought again. Happily the crew of another escaped their sinking boat, and were welcomed aboard. The concentration was due to Operation Prussia in which the U-boat command attempted to stem the growing bridge of support preparing men, machines, and supplies for the D-day invasion. Unique? No. It was an action repeated in many types of combat by DE crews against enemy ships, aircraft, shore batteries in every theater of war by the exceptional men of the Destroyer-Escorts.

At the time, the ship received little recognition for, as history now reveals communication intelligence had broken the German codes but secrecy of this fact was vital. In 1953 the facts could be made public, and the men of *Bronstein* received the Presidential Unit Citation they had so quickly earned one month after shakedown.

With that award the Chief of Naval Operations, Admiral Robert B. Carney, characterized the engagements as "The most concentrated and successful ASW action by a U.S. Navy ship against U-boats in WWII." It had special meaning for DEs, for as a commander on the staff of the CNO, in 1937 he had played the key role in establishing the operational requirement for "an intermediate or second-line torpedo craft or patrol craft fulfilling somewhere between the subchaser and the modern destroyer." This led directly to the design of the DE. (We DE sailors might disagree with the term "second-line.")

Because of the great endurance of the diesel powered DEs they were preferred in the hunter/killer groups over destroyers because the CVE carriers seldom had to fuel them. Usually a 1630 ton DD was included for a burst of speed. Yet in such a mix in March, 1944, it was *Bronstein* and *Breeman* (DE-104), both diesel/electric, that were ordered detached to proceed, taken aboard in lieu of ammunition and torpedoes, the gold of the Bank Polski (National Treasury of Poland) and carry this treasure across the Atlantic for safe-keeping in the vaults of the Federal Reserve Bank under Liberty Street in New York City.

The remainder of 1944 passed for us in routine fashion—hunter/killer operations, convoys to and through the Med, hours of dull routine interspersed with moments of sheer terror, the average life of a DE

sailor. In September we survived a hurricane that sank a 1830-ton Destroyer.

And with the end of 1944 came the end of my DE commands. Ordered to the Staff of COMDESLANT as ASW officer for Destroyers and Destroyers-Escorts Atlantic, I reported to the flagship *Yosemite* in Casco Bay, Maine. Responsible duties, a good deal of ship-riding, conferring, helping out ships, but without that special satisfaction of serving in a "major combatant" (the smallest- but we were- engenders).

I can speak personally of our ships in the Atlantic and Mediterranean. My knowledge of DEs/APDs in the Pacific is gained only second-hand—but what a record! As I read Admiral Morison's volumes, books like Captain Chester's *A Sailors Odyssey*, and listen to the tales of my fellow skippers of DECOs of WWII and my fellow sailors of DESA, one hears of the capability of the ships and the heroism of the crews. Words can't do justice to the exploits of the *England* in sinking Japanese submarines, the courage of the DEs who committed suicide in attacking the Japanese main body that the CVE force might live, the terror experienced and the courage displayed by DEs in the face of kamikaze attacks during fleet and amphibious operations. I salute you.

And with the war's end, the answer was in, TRIM and DEADLY.

As the demobilization took place my duties took me on visits to the Reserve Fleets, like Green Cove Springs, where both my DEs lay in nests, abandoned. But many continued in the Fleet, particularly radar pickets, Naval Reserve Training ships, and APDs. Some later served other navies and live to the present. During Korea, I visited *Edsall* in the Nationalist Chinese navy, and later *Brownstein/Jose Artgas* of the navy of Uruguay. A last final sight, when our DE historian Dr. Martin Davis and I visited Uruguay and Brazil two years ago on DESA's operation return, *Bronstein/Artigas* was being scrapped, having lived from 1943 to 1990. A remarkable life for a class of ships conceived as quickly built, short life, emergency man-o-war.

And to our DESA shipmates who served in classes built after the war, it was my privilege to observe that you carried on these proud traditions. With eleven commands at sea I watched you through the years, Skipper of 1630-ton DD, 2100-ton DD, Destroyer Leader, Fleet Oiler, Commander PHILBRON 12, Amphibious Force Sixth Fleet, Cruiser-Destroyer Flotilla II, Cruiser-Destroyers Seventh Fleet, and best of all, the 125 ships and 60,000 men of Cruiser/Destroyer Force Pacific Fleet. The DE experience paved the way.

Shipmates ... thank you for sharing my story. When this volume is printed I look forward to reading yours.

Fair winds and following seas,

Sheldon Kinney
Rear Admiral Retired
U.S. Navy

USS Seid (DE-256). (Courtesy of Bonaventure J. Linkus)

SHIPS' HISTORIES

"TRIM BUT DEADLY"
VOLUME III

NOTE: The ships' histories selected reflect for the most part eye-witness reports by DE sailors. These stories were not written, nor polished, by professional historians. They describe scenes as the sailors saw and heard them. Bear in mind that some of these accounts were prepared from notes made years ago, others recently written from memory. These raw notes, with little or no editing, detail life in DEs during exciting times. They describe activities unique in annals of naval history. Some accounts may appear to differ from other stories, even by writers on the same ship. The published impressions reflect the views from different people and from different viewpoints. History is his story.

DE Classification

by Robert J. Martin

In June of 1939 the construction of the Destroyer Escort was envisioned by Commander R.B. Carney, U.S. Navy, who proposed a design of an intermediate second line torpedo ship. Subsequently, in September the War Plans Division of the Bureau of Ships recommended that the plans be drawn for a destroyer escort vessel. Design studies were made and abandoned until January of 1941 when Admiral Stark, Commander in Chief of the U.S. Fleet, requested 50 escort vessels for convoy protection. The building actually began after the lend-lease law was passed on 11 March 1941 which stated, "... the President may, from time to time, when he deems it in the interest of national defense, authorize ... the Secretary of the Navy, or the head of any other department or agency of the government ... To manufacture in arsenals, factories and shipyards ... any defense the President deems vital to the defense of the United States."

Fifty U.S. Navy Four Stack Destroyers were lent to the Royal Navy which was authorized by President Franklin D. Roosevelt. The first of these new ships was laid down at Mare Island Navy Yard in Vallejo, Ca. on 28 February 1942. They were designed to meet British specifications. Some of the escorts were kept for the U.S. Navy with 1,005 ordered and 563 actually built. The remainder were cancelled during WWII with 78 being delivered to England and a few to France.

There were six classes of the Destroyer Escorts because of differences in the armament and powerplant configurations. These were the "short hull" *Evarts* class with 3" guns and GMT-GM Tandem Diesel engines, the *Buckley* class with 3" guns and TE-Turbo-Electric engines, the *Cannon* class with 3" guns and DET-Diesel-Electric-Tandem engines, *Edsall* class with 3" guns and FMR-Fairbanks-Morris Reduction gear engines, the *Rudderow* class with 5" guns and TEV-Turbo-Electric drive, and the *John C. Butler* class with 5" guns and WGT-Westinghouse Geared Turbine powerplant. There were 95 "TE" and "TEV" conversions to APDs.

EVARTS CLASS

The first Destroyer Escort for use by the U.S. Navy was the *USS Brennan (DE-13)*, an *Evarts* class vessel. It was launched on 22 August 1942 at Mare Island Navy Ship Yard with Lt. Cmdr. H. A. Adams, Jr. commanding. There were 97 ships built of this class with 32 going to England before commissioning into the U.S. Navy. The General Motors Tandem Diesel (GMT) was also called the "short hull" DE. The *Evarts* class included DE 5-50, 256-265, 301-307, and 527-530.

This class proved to be unsuccessful and was stricken from the Naval records at the end of WWII.

BUCKLEY CLASS

There were 148 vessels built in the *Buckley* class, 46 going to lend-lease prior to commissioning into the U.S. Navy. They were "long hull" design with a length of 306' compared to its predecessor, the *Evarts* class which was a "short hull" of 289'5". The extra length was because of the needed room for the steam power plants producing 12,000 horsepower. The Turbine-Electric Drive caused the designation of TE class. The first built was the USS *Reuben James* (DE-153) at the Norfolk Navy Yard, commissioned on 1 April 1943 with Lt. Cmdr. F. D. Giambattista commanding. The *Buckley* class had a triple set of torpedo tubes mounted on the first superstructure deck amidships. It had a wide range of armament changes with a conversion of the 3" to 5" guns. Only 11 of the 40 ships slated for the change had this alteration.

Due to the need of more effective anti-aircraft defense, the secondary battery were changed during the war. DE 575-578 were completed with four single Army 40mm guns instead of the torpedo tubes. The guns were placed to the amidships location. Other ships had the change made during overhaul periods with two more 20mm guns added to the stern in tubes, totaling ten 20mm guns.

Fifty TEs were scheduled to be converted to High Speed Transports (APDs) in May of 1944. DE 668-673, being under construction, became APDs. There were 37 that were actually converted. The need for Radar Picket Ships saw five TEs used for this purpose and four others changed to Floating Power-Plants which had large cable reels installed amidships. They were used for supplying power to amphibious landing areas. The Buc*kley* class included DE 53-54, 56-57, 59-60, 62-63, 65-66, 68-70, 153-161, 198-223, 575-578, 633-644, 665-667, 675-683, 693-705, and 789-800.

The *Buckley* class was used by the Navy after the war in active and reserve, being more successful than the *Evarts* class.

CANNON CLASS

There were 72 vessels built in the *Cannon* class of which 66 were commissioned by the U.S. Navy. DE 106-111 were built for Lend-Lease for France. The class looked like the *Buckley* class but had a reduced horsepower because of the Diesel-Electric-Drive (DET). The *USS Levy* (DE-162) was commissioned at the Federal Shipbuilding Co., Newark, NJ on 13 May 1943 with Cmdr. F. W. Schmidt commanding. Program cuts in 1943-44 cut the 252 ships which were initially to be built. Like the other DEs, anti-aircraft batteries were installed with the removal of the amidships torpedo tubes. The *Cannon* class included DE 112-113, 162-197, 739-750, and 763-771.

The Navy considered this class unsatisfactory, and they were sold rather than scrapped.

EDSALL CLASS

The first Destroyer Escort of this class to be launched was the *USS Edsall* (DE-129) on 10 April 1943 with Lt. Cmdr. E. C. Woodward commanding. It was built by the Consolidated Steel Co. in Orange, Tx. The *Edsall* class had 85 ships constructed by Consolidated Steel and Brown Shipbuilding of Houston, Tx. They had a similar appearance to the *Buckley* class with 3" guns, 306' length, high bridge superstructure, and Fairbanks-Morse Diesel engines (FMR). The only ship of this class to have 5" to replace the 3" guns was the *USS Camp* (DE-251). The most famous was probably the *USS Pillsbury* (DE-133) which participated in the 1944 capture of the German submarine U-505 in the Atlantic. The U.S. Coast Guard had 30 of the *Edsall* class during WWII with one lost, the *USS Leopold* (DE-319), having been torpedoed by a German U-boat off Iceland on 9 March 1944 with 28 survivors. The remainder were decommissioned after the war.

Similar to other DE classes, the triple torpedo tubes were replaced by anti-aircraft guns for the *Edsall* class. In 1944 several escorts mounted Army single 40mm guns amidships which were later substituted by power driven 40mm twin guns that were director controlled. For additional firepower, 20mm guns were also mounted on the stern. The *Edsall* class included DE 238-255, 316-338, and 382-401.

At the war's conclusion, 81 "FMRs" were decommissioned and placed in the reserves. Four of them were recommissioned in 1950 for Korean War service. In 1954, 12 of the *Edsall* class were returned to the Navy being converted to Destroyer Escort Radar Picket Ships (DERs).

RUDDEROW CLASS

Seventy-two of this class were built with 22 commissioned as DEs. The remainder became APDs. The *Rudderow* class had turbine-electric-drive (TEV) and a long hull like the *Buckley*. It had two 5"/38 cal guns with an enclosed single mount and a new lower bridge superstructure. The *USS DeLong* (DE-684) was the first built of the class at the Bethlehem Steel Yard in Quincy, Mass. with Lt. Cmdr. R. C. Houston commanding. The *Rudderow* class included DE 224-225, 230-231, 579-589, and 706-709.

The TEVs served in the U.S. Navy reserve fleet after WWII with two being transferred to foreign navies in the 1960s.

JOHN C. BUTLER CLASS

There were 283 of the *Butler* class that were built with 83 completed during WWII. They had a similar appearance to the *Rudderow* class with 5" guns and low bridge superstructure. The first ship of the class was the *USS Edward H. Allen* (DE-531) built by the Boston Navy Shipyard in Boston, Mass. and commissioned on 16 December 1943 with Lt. Cmdr. M. M. Sanford commanding. They were powered by Westinghouse-Geared Turbine engines (WGT). Early armament configuration included two 40mm twin guns plus the 20mm guns for the anti-aircraft battery. Six vessels had one quad 40mm gun aft and one twin 40mm gun forward with two twin 40mm guns amidships in the place of the torpedo tubes. Two ships were built with the quad 40mm gun aft, a twin 40mm gun forward, and no torpedo tubes or other guns. The most famous ship of the class was the *USS Samuel B. Roberts* (DE-413). It was lost during the battle off Samar in October of 1944. The *Butler* class included DE 339-372, 402-424, 438-450, 508-510, and 531-540.

There were four WGTs lost during WWII with 79 remaining on the Navy's list. Six ships were kept active and the remainder placed in the Navy Reserve Fleet. Thirty-two of the *Butler* class were recommissioned for the Korean War.

EVARTS CLASS

General Information

Length Overall	289' 5"
Length at Waterline	283' 6"
Beam	35' 1"
Shaft Horsepower	6,000
Trail Speed	21.5 knots
War Endurance	4,150 miles/12 knots
Displacement	1,436 tons
Complement	15 officers, 183 enlisted
Fuel Capacity	198 tons diesel

Armament

3—3"/50 cal guns- Main Battery
1—twin 40mm gun (DE 13-18, 45) or 1.1" gun
(DE 5-11, 19-44, 47-50, 256-265, 301-307, 527-530)
1—hedgehog
9—20mm single guns
2—depth charge racks
8—"K" gun projectors

BUCKLEY CLASS

General Information

Length overall	306'
Length at Waterline	283' 6"
Beam	36' 9"
Shaft Horsepower	12,000
Trail Speed	23.7 knots
War Endurance	4,940 miles/12 knots
Displacement	1,673 tons
Complement	15 officers, 198 enlisted
Fuel Capacity	350 tons

Armament

3—3"/50 cal guns- Main Battery
1—twin 40mm gun or 1- 1.1" gun
8—20mm guns
1—triple torpedo tube
1—hedgehog
2—depth charge tracks
8—"K" gun projectors

CANNON CLASS

General Information

Length Overall	308'
Length at Waterline	300'
Beam	36' 10"
Shaft Horsepower	6,000
Trail Speed	20.2 knots
War Endurance	10,800 miles/12 knots
Displacement	1,525 tons
Complement	15 officers, 201 enlisted
Fuel Capacity	316 tons

Armament

3—3"/50 cal guns- Main Battery
1—40mm twin gun
1—triple torpedo tube
8—20mm guns
1—hedgehog
2—depth charge tracks
8—"K" gun projectors

EDSALL CLASS

General Information		Armament
Length Overall	306'	3—3"/50 cal guns- Main Battery
Length at Waterline	300'	1—twin 40mm gun
Beam	36' 10"	8—20 mm guns
Shaft Horsepower	6000	1—triple torpedo tube
Trail Speed	20.9 knots	1—hedgehog
War Endurance	5,100 miles/12 knots	2—depth charge tracks
Displacement	1,490 tons	8—"K" gun projector
Complement	8 officers, 201 enlisted	
Fuel Capacity	312 tons	

RUDDEROW CLASS

General Information		Armament
Length Overall	306'	2—5"/38 cal guns- Main Battery
Length at Waterline	300'	2—twin 40mm guns
Beam	36' 11"	1—triple torpedo tube
Shaft Horsepower	12,000	10—20mm guns
Trail Speed	24 knots	1—hedgehog
War Endurance	5,050 miles/12 knots	2—depth charge tracks
Displacement	1,450 tons	8—"K" gun projectors
Complement	12 officers, 192 enlisted	
Fuel Capacity	354.5 tons	

JOHN C. BUTLER CLASS

General Information		Armament
Length Overall	306'	2—5"/38 cal guns- Main Battery
Length at Waterline	300'	2—twin 40mm guns
Beam	36' 10"	1—triple torpedo tube
Shaft Horsepower	12,000	10—20mm guns
Trail Speed	24.15 knots	1—hedgehog
War Endurance	4,650 miles/12 knots	2—depth charge tracks
Displacement	1,600 tons	8—"K" gun projectors
Complement	14 officers, 201 enlisted	
Fuel Capacity	347 tons	

USS Mitchell (DE-43)

USS Durant (DE-389) at Guantanamo, Cuba in 1945.

DE-389 pulling in close to U-Boat 873. The picture was taken from USS Durant (DE-387)—its crew sent the boarding party to take-over the submarine.

DE-181

USS *BAKER* (DE-190)

Submitted by Constantine J. 'Gus' Forkiotis and Frank F. Fry

November 30, 1943:

Crew quarantined - Unit X Bldg 66-3, NTS DE 190 Group Norfolk, VA. As the crew names were formulated the individuals, with their specific rate, were sent to this barracks making up the ship's compliment. Mailing address issued: USS *Baker* DE 190 C/O Fleet Post Office, New York.

December 22, 1943:

Crew was shipped from barracks by train to Brooklyn, NY. Reported aboard USS *Baker* DE-190 in Brooklyn Navy Yard, NY with crew directly from quarantined barracks in Norfolk, VA. Home port designated was Brooklyn, NY.

December 23, 1943:

Commissioned USS *Baker* DE-190 in Brooklyn, NY Navy Yard. Named for Aviation Ensign John Drayton Baker, USNR, who lost his life in the battle of the Coral Sea. Ensign Baker was born in Plainfield, New Jersey 31 May 1915. He enlisted in the Naval Reserve in 1941 and was appointed Naval Aviator 26 August 1941 and commissioned Ensign 18 September 1941. Ensign Baker was reported missing in action 7 May and officially declared dead 8 May 1943. He received the Navy Cross.

The *Baker* 190 was built by the Federal Ship Building and Drydock Company, Kearney, NJ. Displacement 1240 tons; length 306'; beams 36'10"; draft 11' 8"; 3' 3"; triple torpedo tubes; one 40 mm twin gun; 8-20 mm guns; 2 depth charge racks; 8" K gun projectors. Compliment 15 officers with 201 men. Actually had as many as 212 men with some sleeping in hammocks in the forward compartment. Average cost of the Cannon Class was $3,500,000. The *Baker* 190 was launched 18 November 1943 and sponsored by Mrs. Margaret Baker, mother of Ensign Baker, 23 December 1943.

Commissioning:

Captain	Lt. Cmdr. L.B. Lockwood	(Greenwich, Conn.)
Executive	Lt. Cmdr. R.J. Reynolds	(Tobacco Family)
First Lt.	Lt. Norman Hoffman	(became Exec. upon transfer of Lt. Cmdr. R.J. Reynolds)
Captain	Lt. Cmdr. N. Hoffman	(Swampscott, MA, as of June 5, 1944)

(Milton and Dennisport, Mass. Harvard 1934; Veteran and survivor of the ill-fated Oklahoma at Pearl Harbor; stock broker)

Executive	Lt. Fleming	
Damage Control	Lt. Armistead Selden (First Lieutenant)	
Gunnery	Lt. Wilsford (next Executive Officer)	
Communications	Lt. Henry Prickett (College English Professor)	
Sonar	Lt. j.g. Edward	
	Lt. j.g. Harringon	
	Lt. j.g. G.E. Drennan	
	Lt. j.g. H.L. Nelson	
	Ensign Gene M. Willis	
	Ensign A.E. Zipse	
Radar Personnel	J.B. Cusick	RDM 3/c Oklahoma
	Ed Fabryka	RDM 3/c Wm Delaware
	Joe Fitzpatrick	RDM 1/c New Jersey

Radar personnel:	C.J. Forkiotis	RDM 2/c CT
	Al Fraley	RDM 3/c 2/7/89 *
	Art Frosio	RDM 1/c Jersey City, NJ*
	Frank Fray	RDM 3/c Wlm DE
	R.W. Jones	RDM 3/c Anniston, AL
Sonar personnel:	Yurt, Weatherford, Judd, Meyer, Larry Smith,
	and J. Orville Nicholson.
Radio personnel:	Charles J. O'neill, CRM

January 2, 1944:
Started daily trial runs in Long Island Sound.
January 9, 1944:
Started for Bermuda and 'shake down,' scheduled four weeks. One day liberty in Bermuda. Good length of time to familiarize operation of equipment while getting to know each other.
February 7, 1944:
Back in Brooklyn Navy Yard, from Bermuda and shakedown.

February 13, 1944: We missed our scheduled operation to rendezvous with Task Group 21.16 with the Carrier USS *Block Island* (CVE-21) and DEs *Bronstein* 189, *Thomas* 102, *Bostwick* 103, *Breeman* 104, and the destroyer *Corry* (DD-463).

The *Thomas, Bostwick* and *Bronstein,* are known to have sunk two subs in one night on February 29, 1944. Identified at a later date as the U-709 and U-603. March, St. Patrick's Day the *Bronstein* and *Corry* depth charged a third sub to surface. The sub, U-801 was subjected to heavy fire and rammed by the *Corry.*

We joined convoy, UGS-33, as part of the destroyer screen, Escort Div. 48. The other DEs were all Coast Guard manned and part of CortDiv 45 (Escort Division) under *Taffey* 60 (Task Force) and the New York section. Coast Guard DEs; USS *Vance* DE-387; USS *Lansing* DE-388; USS *Durant* DE-389; USS *Calcaterra* DE-390; USS *Chambers* DE-391; USS *Merrill* DE-392. The flag of Commodore E.J. Roland (USCG) was on the USS *Vance* 387. Off Norfolk the remainder of the convoy plus another division under *Taffey* 66 joined together to proceed across the Atlantic.

March 2, 1944: Arrived at Gibraltar where English ships took over the protection screen, and continuation into the Mediterranean. Our division then turned South headed for Casablanca for fuel and provisions.

Due to the fear of failure of the evaporators (making fresh water) and the severe weather, we were restricted from use of water being allowed one 'bucket bath' in the three weeks it took to get to Casablanca. The Captain thought they were not experienced enough to handle any emergency associated with the evaporators.

March 7, 1944: Liberty in Casablanca

Left Casablanca joining with other DEs of Task Force 66 and staged a midnight raid along the French Moroccan Coast to discourage assistance to the German U-boats suspected in that area. It was also suspected that landing parties were being put ashore in that area. The raid, made within the range of shore batteries, went off without mishap and the trip home followed.

March 8, 1944: Rendezvous with the convoy GUS-32 at Gibraltar homeward bound. Ninety six ships were picked up at Gibraltar and delivered to U.S. East Coast Ports.

March 24, 1944: Back in Brooklyn, NY. 72 hours leave. Part of the convoy escorted by Escort Div. 45 went on to Chesapeake Bay area.

April 4, 1944: In Casco Bay, Portland, ME. Had day liberty.

April 13, 1944: Second convoy, Task Force 60, assembled in Hampton Roads (Bay off Norfolk and Chesapeake Bay) began trip to North Africa and into the Mediterranean. Along the way we dropped off merchant ships at varying ports along the coast of North Africa. This was convoy UGS-39 Eastbound. We were on extra precaution since convoy ahead of us ran into some strafing attacks from German aircraft.

On April 20, 1944 convoy UGS-38 was attacked off the coast of Algiers by 21 JU-88s and HE-111s. During this action the USS *Lansdale* (a destroyer) and the USS *Paul Hamilton,* a troopship with 500 soldiers, were sunk and three other merchant ships torpedoed.

The *Bronstein* DE-189 who with the *Breeman* DE-104 were in Dakar on March 20 loaded with 15 tons of gold ($68,000,000) from the Bank of Poland arriving in New York April 3, 1944. The *Bronstein* now joined our CortDiv 48.

April 30, 1944: In the Mediterranean; escorted ship into harbor of Oran and one into Mars El Kabur.

May 1, 1944: Escorted ship into Algiers.

May 2, 1944: Escorted into Bone and Carbone harbors.

May 3, 1944: Tied up at South Carriere, Goulet Du-Lac, Bizerte, Tunisia.

May 4, 1944: Liberty in Bizerte. Many Italian prisoners who were wearing Army sun tans with no insignia. Most happy prisoners. Multitude of them. No fear of attempting escape.

May 7, 1944: Two day liberty into Tunis. About 40 miles. Transportation was hitchhike ride on open Airforce truck, carrying five gallon gas cans. Some sailors spent time with Italian prisoners. Invited to their camp (tent city) at the outskirts of town. Ferryville. Food and bedding in town supplied by Red Cross.

May 11, 1944: Left Bizerte for the States. Task Force 60 Coast Guard Div 45 with USCG *Bibb* 31 as the Flag Ship, USN Div 48, escorting convoy GUS-39.

May 12, 1944: *Bronstein* 189 sank a mine with rifle fire.

May 14, 1944: Just north of Oran, Algeria a German Sub surfaced between the screen of Destroyer Escorts and the merchant ships. The sub was close enough that the large guns could not be depressed enough for use against the sub. Our men were firing hand guns and machine guns at the sub. Two merchant ships were torpedoed, the SS *Waiden* and SS *Fort Fidler.*

They closed off their compartments and survived into port, Oran. A request by our Captain Lockwood to the *Bibb* (command) to at least drop 'embarrasing charge' by all the DEs, was considered and confirmed. Aircraft and other vessels were called to the scene to search out the sub, but it was not confirmed whether the sub was sunk. Division 19, a Destroyer Div. was sent out to search for the submarine.

May 30, 1944: Back in Brooklyn Navy Yard.

June 5, 1944: Began 5 day leave

June 10, 1944: Left Brooklyn for Casco Bay, Portland, Maine.

June 20, 1944: Left Portland, Maine, training and availability.

June 22, 1944: Arrived in Norfolk, Virginia.

June 25, 1944: Left Norfolk, Virginia assigned to USS *Card* CVE-11, a converted aircraft carrier, with the other DEs of Escort Division 48, Task Group 22.10 operating as the screen seeking U-boats. The group included the *Bronstein* 189, *Baker* 190, *Coffman* 191, *Thomas* 102, *Bostwick* 103, *Breeman* 104.

The area of the search stretched to Hamilton, Bermuda; San Juan, Puerto Rico; Horta, Azores; and Reykajavic, Iceland.

July 5, 1944: The USS *Baker* DE-190 was in position two miles on the port beam of the USS *Card.* At seven minutes after seven in the evening the USS *Baker* made sound contact with underwater sound equipment (sonar) and fired off a pattern of Hedge Hogs. At the same time two depth charge attacks were delivered. At 19:31 hours U-233, a 1600 ton minelayer refueler type U-boat, one of Germany's largest, broke the surface with her after torpedo room and after engine room ripped open and flooded. This was the sister ship of the U-234 which surrendered at Portsmouth, New Hampshire shortly after V-E Day with Luftwaffe generals and Jap Hara Kari victims aboard.

1907 - Upon receiving sound contact bearing 135 T distance 100 yards - Streamed Foxer gear - Sounded General Quarters - commenced making runs on sound contact. Lat. 42 39'N and Long. 58 47'W.

1912 - Dropped one full pattern Hedge Hogs and fired K guns.

1916 - Sound gear temporarily out of order. Jarred by explosions of depth charge.

1918 - Regained contact in the lower emergency sound hut, circled and headed towards contact and dropped another full pattern of depth charges and fired K guns.

1925 - Upon surfacing of the German submarine on the Starboard Quarter, the USS *Baker* opened fire with all batteries, expending a massive array of ammunition into the submarine with indications of positive and damaging hits. The *Baker* rode back and forth turning to each side of the ship would be able to fire their guns. This also allowed a short period of time for cooling of guns. Our youngest sailor on the 20mm gun on the stern fired single and short bursts keeping his gun the coolest.

The Submarine had lost steerage way while a continuous stream of fire was directed towards her conning tower. At this point her crew began abandoning their submarine. There were a few attempts of the German sailors to use their forward three inch gun. At least one was killed with a direct hit from our 20 mm gun fire.

Two torpedoes were fired and driven into the submarine's hull causing the actual sinking. At this point the submarine burst into flames and continued smoldering, leaving a black, brown smoke.

My battle station was to man the phones transmitting communications from the Captain to the other ships in the division. Captain Hoffman wished to inform the Commodore, whose flag was aboard the USS *Thomas* DE-102, that we were going to ram the submarine.

A loud voice from the Commodore instructed that his order was to refrain from any ramming of the submarine. It was his intention to bring the submarine into port as a prize catch. At this time the USS *Thomas* was five miles from the scene, steaming towards the scene. This message was relayed to our Captain Hoffman.

The USS *Baker* returned to picking up survivors from the waters. The submarine, meantime was in flames, slowly sinking into the war. The USS *Thomas* on her full steam approach announced to the other ships that she was going to ram the submarine. She continued on her course towards the submarine but literally went over the edge of the deck of the submarine ripping open the bottom of the USS *Thomas*. The submarine had sunk too far into the waters to be capable of any degree of ramming.

1942 - Both ships resumed and continued picking up and rescuing survivors. A total of 69 survivors were rescued. All firing was now ceased.

1945 - The submarine, bright with flame and sending a continuous flow of smoke into the air; battered, wrecked, and beaten from the accuracy of the crews gunfire; leaving debris, oil, and part of her hull and conning tower drifting, was sunk. We rescued ten prisoners, two officers and eight enlisted men; suffering from wounds and exposure.

Captain Hoffman piped over the loudspeaker fair treatment for the prisoners, with immediate medical care as needed; according to the rules of Geneva Conference (Seeing those men in the water seemed to impress those of us on the stern helping them aboard as to how young they looked.)

2020 - Proceeded at standard speed on course 225 T - 225 1/2 P.G.C. 255 P.S.C. towards USS *Card* to discharge prisoners.

2117 - Drew alongside USS *Card* and took lines over from carrier and rigged breeches buoy and established communication.

2121 - First prisoner transferred to USS *Card*.

2139 - Completed transfer of prisoners to carrier. The two officers on board were not transferred due to severe enough injuries. Cut off all lines of USS *Card*; proceeded at full speed to take position on starboard side of guide. Took course 050 T — 050 1/2 P.G.C. 071 P.S.C. — To K and S.

2225 - Changed course B/C to 180 T - 180 1/2 P.G.C., - 207 PSC took station bearing 315 Rel from guide - distance 3000 yds, speed 8 K and S.

2214 - position 42 39' N 58 47' W' Sunset - darkened weather decks.

Note - Submarine sank about 105 miles South East of Sable Island, longitude of Boston.

Resume of Activities with Submarine:

For fourteen minutes U-233 was engulfed in a hail of flying lead, depth charges set shallow, and torpedoes, but these latter had too short a run to allow detonation.

Her chief engineer was decapitated when he came up the after hatch to have a look. One torpedoman was disemboweled when a loose torpedo slid off its tray. The chief's quarters was a shamble from the armor piercing shells.

The U-233 never got off a shot. Her crew abandoned the ship by two's and threes as their boat, down by the stern and with the conning tower on fire, continued to take it. The war was over, 31 were captured, including the skipper, Oberlieutenant Hans Stein, who died the following day from shrapnel wounds.

July 7, 1944: Steaming full speed to Boston, Mass. to deliver prisoners; dry dock the *Thomas* 102 for repairs; and five day R and R. We rammed a whale bending the "sound dome"(which should have been raised under conditions of speed).

The forward compartment into which the sound dome is usually retracted was filling with water since the bent shaft of the sound dome could not be retracted. The compartment was sealed off and water tight.

July 10, 1944: In Boston, orders were changed; sound dome shaft was repaired; the commodore shifted his flag to our ship the USS *Baker* 190 since the repairs to the USS *Thomas* 102 would be longer than expected.

We were off to the Caribbean, with the carrier still on search duty.

Prior to our submarine contact our whole ship was restricted from any future liberty. It seems our ship had received some ice cream from the carrier during a fueling operation.

The Captain and the officers decided to keep the ice cream for themselves without sharing any with the crew members. Someone had taken a large portion of the ice cream under unauthorized status irritating the Captain to the ultimate degree. Signs were posted all over the ship stating no further liberty for anyone on this ship until such time as the culprits who took the ice cream owned up.

The ramming of the submarine by the Commodore after order us not to ram the submarine had infuriated our Captain leaving him very angry at the Commodore.

Now the Commodore is aboard our ship, using the Captain's state room, forcing the Captain to use a small "seacabin" with a bunk and the Loran located outside the C.I.C. and on the wheel deck.

Between the ice cream situation, the ramming situation, and having to deal with the Commodore on a formal basis left our Captain in rather irritated state of emotion.

To top it off - the Commodore chided the Captain even more over the ice cream situation. There were comments as "they must have been hungry enough to devour all that ice cream" to "its unfair to penalize the whole the whole crew for the few that did the stealing."

Eventually the Commodore instructed the Captain to remove the signs and inform the crew there would be liberty for all hands or he would override the Captain's orders.

July 14, 1944: Passing through Mona Passage, Puerto Rico.

July 16, 1944: Submarine contact by carrier based airplane had to be aborted due to USS *Card* engine casualty and dead in the water for about six hours.

July 18, 1944: Entering San Juan, Puerto Rico.

July 24, 1944: Left Puerto Rico heading North East in the Atlantic.

August 16, 1944: In Horta, Azores for fuel. Few hours ashore near the pier.

August 17, 1944: Left Azores.

August 24, 1944: In New York Harbor - channel - degaussing. Testing of men from the fleet for attending V-12 officers training program. Our division had one opening. On to the Navy Yard for upkeep repairs.

September 8, 1944: Left New York for open spaces.

September 10, 1944: In Portland, Maine, Casco Bay, availability.

September 14, 1944: Left Portland 2300 hours due to impending hurricane, heading south. Barometric reading was 28.53, the ship recorded a roll of 62 degrees, we were off the coast of Long Island, New York about 0100 hours listening to the damage ashore in Connecticut (I was on duty).

During this time the small selzen motor that operates the rotor in the antenna on the mast stopped working. We were going to draw straws for the task but Donald "Pappy" Bryant, our electronic expert (and about 40 years old) decided he would be the one. Claimed it was too dangerous for "us" young ones. I still do not know how we could have made it up the mast and back. I also don't know how we would have made out without radar while expected to travel in formation.

Also heard on the radio during this time that two destroyers were sunk in the storm off the coast of Norfolk attempting to make it into the Chesapeake Bay. One of the ships was the D.D. *Warrington*.

September 16, 1944: Arrived in Norfolk, Virginia - extreme weariness.

September 18, 1944: Left Norfolk, headed south for Bermuda to conduct exercises with Escort Div 48, USS *Card*, planes, and friendly submarines.

September 20, 1944: In Bermuda waters. Rough waters during the calm.

September 25, 1944: the *Breeman* suffered engine problems and headed for safe harbor.

October 15, 1944: Terrific gale force storm. Felt worse than recent hurricane. Broke off our starboard fin. Very different roll of ship to the starboard.

October 25, 1944: In Casablanca. Incident of having to use hoses on natives to get to lines to prepare for departure.

October 26, 1944: Left Casablanca headed to New York via Southern route.

November 5, 1944: In Brooklyn Navy Yard, NY.

November 13, 1944: Left for Bermuda. Spent more than one month in training and search for expected Nazi Submarine push.

December 31, 1944: New Year's Eve arrived in New York after two day passage from Bermuda.

January 4, 1945: One section of Escort Division 48 including the *Bronstein* went to Casco Bay for training. Curtailed due to bad weather.

January 11, 1945: With USS *Card* off Nantucket Island and pilot qualification flights.

February 4, 1945: *Baker* 190 and *Bronstein* 189 escorted USS *Card* from Delaware Capes to Norfolk.

February 8, 1945: Escort Div 48 left Norfolk with carrier USS *Bogue*, where she was left at the Ambrose Light Ship, while the DEs continued to Casco Bay.

February 1945: The *Baker* and other DEs, Escort Division 48 operating with the converted flat top carrier USS *Core* CVE-13, Task Unit 22.2.1 screened the North Atlantic. The group encountered one of the worst storms off the coast of Iceland. The winds were of hurricane force and in this region are known as "Iceland Loaf", known for their severity. The wind velocity was up to 95 knots with 35 foot waves pounding the DEs. Rolls of 70 degrees were recorded on several of the vessels.

Before it was over the *Baker* had sustained heavy, but not critical damage. Twelve "Y" frames forward on the portside were sprung from main deck level to the first platform. One expansion joint was cracked and both were leaking. Stanchions and life lines on both port and star board sides were swept away. The depth charge racks were bent and the sound gear smashed, but the ship rode it out and limped into Reytkajavik where minor repairs were made prior to yard overhaul in the States.

The DEs in the unit were USS *Thomas* 102; USS *Bostwick* 103; USS *Bremen* 104; USS *Bronstein* 189; USS *Baker* 190; USS *Coffman* 191. Storm was the loss, overboard, of one of *Coffman* 191. After the storm the seas were still quite treacherous. While on watch the sailor was returning with a pot of coffee from the galley. The search for him was unsuccessful.

There were a total of 12 DEs stretched across an area over 90 miles long looking for a weather reporting German submarine just south of Iceland. The storm was on February 20.

The USS *Core*, the Carrier, reported the winds at 116 knots at which point the anemometer blew away. The carrier was also ordered back to New York while the DEs were on orders to remain on station.

Note: During late March and early April an accumulation of four carriers with some 80 DEs stretched out across the North Atlantic half way between St. John's, Newfoundland and Fayal in the Azores. The ships formed a North-South barrier designated Operation "Teardrop", one of the largest hunter - killer forces assembled. Their duty was to intercept super - Schnorkels (Group SEEWOLF) which was proceeding across the Atlantic to invade America's Eastern Sea Frontier.

Five of the known six submarines were sunk and the sixth surrendered shortly thereafter.

April 1, 1945: Tied up at Pier #90 in New York City. Next to infamous base on Pier #92 with the very cruel Captain and superior officers. You were told to salute a lady if you were confronted - the lady was the Captain's wife. Captain's Mast was to be feared for the slightest infraction. They would line up a group of sailors with no regard to rate, the width of a New York City Street, hand them a big broom and then proceed to have them sweep the city street. (Forkiotis was there awaiting transfer to the *Baker* - no luck had to train to New London.)

Every activity at this base was a form of punishment. It seems one was in error simply because you were ordered to this particular transfer base. The place was exposed by columnist Walter Winchel, who lost his lieutenant commander status in the U.S. Navy because of his revealing the goings on.)

April 4, 1945: Forkiotis reported aboard *Baker* 190 in New London. Many DEs in the harbor tied up abreast of each other.

April 14, 1945: We headed out to sea in search of a submarine off the coast of Norfolk, VA. The search lasted for 22 days and included DEs; DDs; PCs; SCs; and Blimps. The search lasted through May 4, for the *Baker*. The remaining ships continued their search for this submarine. This u-boat got two merchant ships and damaged a third within sight of the Virginia coast.

April 29-30, 1945: The Division was split into two groups. Three DEs worked North of the Norfolk Channel while the other three DEs worked South of the Channel. *Bronstein, Breeman,* and *Baker* were assigned to the Southern Group. The Northern Group made many attacks on a submarine that resulted in a "B" assessment.

May 5, 1945: While at sea we were informed of the impending end of the war in Europe. Orders were immediately issued for transfer of radar personnel and hospital core men, who were badly needed in the Pacific Theater.

We arrived in Brooklyn, New York whereby Forkiotis was transferred from the USS *Baker* DE-190 with orders to Fargo Building, Boston, Mass.

During this time Forkiotis made many attempts to get in touch with the where about of the *Baker* 190. I thought I'd be able to see my shipmates if they pulled into Boston. The only information available was "Daisy Mae." A great personality with a computer memory and knew just where most of the ships or divisions were about. Of course she was the hostess in a large popular night club in Boston. Identification was quite easy, her trade mark was a large daisy flower the size of her head pinned to her hair. Later it was to be found how very accurate her information was.

From May 1945 until October 1945 *Baker* DE-190 operated out of Quonset Point, RI as a plane guard during carrier qualifications.

November 1945: During November and part of December she escorted the captured German Submarine U-977 to various eastern ports as a part of a Victory Loan Drive.

March 4, 1946: USS *Baker* DE-190 went out of commission in reserve.

April 4, 1946: I was formerly discharged from the U.S. Navy (Reserve).

March 29, 1952: *Baker* 109 was transferred to France under the Mutual Defense Assistance Program.

1970: The USS *Baker* DE-190 was sunk in 1970.

Baker received one Battle Star for her action with the U-233.

Additional Details But No Record Of Specific Dates Concerning Life Aboard USS *Baker* DE-190.

On return to New York from our first convoy we were in a severe fog as we approached Ambrose Light House. The radar personnel did their job in calling out the direction, location, and range to the next buoy. Suddenly Captain Lockwood and a few other officers were huddled into the small radar shack. It seems they were treating our information to the bridge rather lightly not truly believing the capabilities of the radar information.

Needless to say that strict attention was paid to the information rendered by the radarman from that point on. We did guide the ship from buoy to buoy all the way in to New York Harbor.

After completion of the two convoy trips Lt. Cmdr. Lockwood, Captain, was succeeded by Lt. Norman Hoffman as our new Skipper. Lt. Fleming was our new Executive Officer.

While leaving the pier in Bayonne, New Jersey, he ordered 1/3 ahead on the engines before/while the lines were being "let go" we pulled part of the pier with us, though it was old and rickety.

While pulling into Newport, Rhode Island we were ordered to tie up along side another DE due to dock space shortage. Since the current was in our favor the Captain ordered all "engines stopped" while we coasted into position alongside the other DE. Needless to say it was too late for the propellers to take hold when the order "all astern full" was issued to avoid damage to the other ship. The two captains could not reach each other from the bridge so the fist - cuffs were avoided.

While at sea we were to practice "mail passing" as well as the use of the "breeches buoy" and "boarding submarines" in preparation for the real occasion. The boarding submarine exercise required that the procre be executed at 1/3rd speed.

During this time the whale boat with thirty eight men is lowered slowly with the stern hitting the water first as the bow is continued in the lowering process. Our Captain ordered 2/3rd speed for the procedure without informing those involved in the whale boat aspect of the procedure. Our thirty-eight men were dumped into the ocean. It took the better part of the day to round up all the men. The currents spread them out rapidly except for those that quickly held hands to remain together. It was also a poor time to find that some of the CO2 canisters did not work to inflate the waist "tube like" life belts. The big "Mae West" jackets worked quite well. Our whale boat was the last to be salvaged and was off at least four miles in the distance.

Another occasion we were to practice "passing mail." This procedure included the use of the "breeches buoy" where by mail, instead of an individual was used as the subject of transfer between ships.

The procedure also included the dropping of the whale boat. First the whale boat, then the breeches buoy, then return to pick up the whale boat. This time the whale boat procedure went off without a hitch and was quite successful.

The Captain decided we did not have to go through all that set up with the lines and alignment for the breeches buoy. He decided we would pull up close enough to the other DE and hand them the mail. It was a good idea but he forgot to order the Davids, which hold the whale boat, to be folded inward within our ship.

As we pulled up close to the other DE, the Davids, which extend outward perpendicular to the ship, knocked out the portside stanchions of the other DEs 20mm gun tub collapsing the gun tub.

During the time of screening the USS *Card* (CVE-11), we often had the duty of "plane guard." The DE rode astern of the carrier and off to the starboard prepared to pick up the pilots in case of being forced to ditch their planes in the landing attempt. The longest we ever counted in the flotation of an airplane was 90 seconds. That was a TBF which held a three man crew. The majority sank just under and within 60 seconds.

There was never a dull moment aboard the USS *Baker* DE-190.

USS *BANGUST* (DE-739)

The USS *Bangust* (DE-739), Flagship of Escort Division 32, conceived by the wartime urgency for submarine defensive measures, constructed by newly trained shipyard personnel and manned by a crew and officers 95 percent Naval Reserve, on October 30, 1943, unfurled her commission pennant. The ceremony took place at the builder's yard, Western Pipe and Steel Company, San Pedro, California where she became the first of 12 ships of her class constructed by that company to join the Naval forces of the rapidly expanding Pacific Fleet.

After a short fitting-out period shakedown and training were commenced under the program outlined and administered by Commander Operational Training Command, Pacific. By December 16 she was deemed ready by CotcPac to join the fighting units of the Pacific Fleet and ordered to the Naval drydocks, San Pedro, California for a final check-over before leaving the continental limits of the United States. This period was completed on January 9, 1944, and the *Bangust* was ready to contribute her share to the war effort.

Arriving in Pearl Harbor January 19, a report was made to Commander Service Force, Pacific Fleet of readiness for duty and the first assignment taking the *Bangust* to Funafuti Atoll, Ellice Islands was received.

For the next two months, operating under the command of Commander Task Group 57.7, the *Bangust* performed various duties in the Marshall and Gilbert area. These assignments included escorting between Majuro, Tarawa, Kwajalein, Eniwetok, Roi, Apamama and Makin, a short tour of duty in Tarawa where Commander Escort Division 32 served as Senior Officer Present Afloat, hunter-killer duties as necessary to keep the Japanese submarine threat at a minimum, participation in the Marshall Islands Operation for which a bronze campaign star was awarded to personnel of the ship, and duty with the Logistic Support Group supporting the Fifth Fleet during the Palau, Yap, Ulithi, Woleai raid of March 30 to April 1. For this latter operation a second bronze star was awarded for wearing on the Asiatic-Pacific Campaign Ribbon.

May 22, 1944, found the *Bangust* at Navy Yard, Pearl Harbor where she remained until June 4, undergoing routine maintenance and overhaul.

Shortly before midnight June 10, while enroute to Roi from Pearl Harbor to join Task Group 16.7, radar contact was established on an unidentified surface contact about sixty miles east of Roi, Kwajalein Atoll, Marshall Islands. Sight contact was made soon after at a range of three thousand yards. The contact, identified as either a small ship or submarine, was challenged immediately but failed to respond and submerged almost at once. Sonar contact was established and on the fourth attack several hits were scored followed by a tremendous underwater explosion. Contact was not regained and at daylight a large oil slick and debris were discovered at the scene of the successful attack. This engagement was assigned a "C" classification by Cominch Committee on Assessments, pending further evidence of destruction.

June 12 was the commencement of a long and unbroken series of operations for this ship with the Logistic Groups supporting the Third and Fifth Fleets in the great Central Pacific counter offensive. Operating first with Admiral Halsey and the Third Fleet, then merely changing task force designations to operate with Admiral Spruance, the *Bangust* successively engaged in the following operations:

(1) *Marianas Operation:*
    (a) Capture and occupation of Saipan (11 June—10 August 1944).
    (b) Battle of Philippines Sea (19—20 June 1944).
    (c) Capture and occupation of Guam (12 July—15 August 1944).
    (d) Capture and occupation of Tinian (12 July—15 August 1944).
(2) *Western Caroline Islands Operation:*
    (a) Capture and occupation of Southern Palau Islands (6 September—14 October 1944)
    (b) Assaults on the Philippine Islands (9—24 September 1944).
(3) *Leyte Operation:*
    (a) Third Fleet Supporting Operations in Okinawa, Luzon and Formosa Attacks.
(4) *Luzon Operation:*
    (a) Third Fleet Supporting Operations in Luzon, Formosa, China Coast and Nansei Shoto Attacks.
(5) *Iwo Jima Operation:*
    (a) Assault and occupation of Iwo Jima (15 February—16 March 1945).
    (b) Fifth Fleet Raids against Honshu and Nansei Shoto (15 February—16 March 1945)
(6) *Okinawa Gunto Operation*
(7) *Third Fleet Air Strikes and Shore Bombardments* against Japan (15 July—15 September 1945).

During this period the *Bangust* successfully survived two tropical typhoons which inflicted considerable damage to many ships of the Pacific Fleet. The first, encountered in December 1944 off the Philippine Islands, resulted in the loss of three destroyers and damage to many other fleet units. The second occurring on June 5-6, 1945 once again found her as a screening unit of Task Group 30.8 employed in replenishing Task Force 38. No major damage or casualties were sustained in either storm although all life rafts, floater nets and other articles were bodily torn from the ship by the force of the wind.

August of 1945 found the *Bangust* still serving with the Logistic Support Group, as a unit of Task Group 30.8 supporting the Fast Carrier Task Force air strikes and bombardments of the Japanese homeland. With the acceptance by Japan of the "Potsdam Declaration Terms" in the middle of August, the *Bangust* was detached from the Logistic Group for the first time since June 1944. During this period she had served effectively and efficiently protecting the tankers, provision ships, fleet tugs, replenishment carriers and other ships necessary to maintain the efficiency of our fighting forces at sea for extended periods. For excellence in tactical ship handling, leadership and devotion to duty during the Okinawa Operation and final assault on the Japanese Empire, Commander C.K. Hutchison, U.S. Navy, Commander Escort Division 32 in this ship, received the Bronze Star Medal.

On August 20 the *Bangust* joined the newly organized Task Group 35.80 for the initial occupation of Sagami Wan and Tokyo Bay. This group was designated as a support group and consisted of various tenders and auxiliary vessels. Orders were received on August 27 placing in effect the entry plan from Commander Third Fleet. Shortly after this the *Bangust* was diverted by further orders from Commander Third Fleet and directed to intercept a surrendering Japanese submarine off northern Honshu. With a prize crew aboard furnished by Commander Submarine Squadron 20, an interception course was set and the following day a rendezvous made with the I-14, one of Japan's newest and largest submarines. The prize crew was exchanged for forty Japanese prisoners of war and on August 29 the *Bangust* entered Sagami Wan in company with her prize.

Tokyo Bay was entered on September 1 and here the *Bangust* remained, with the exception of one short trip to Saipan, until October 2 when orders were received for Escort Division 32 to proceed via Pearl Harbor and San Pedro to the Panama Canal where it would report to the Commander in Chief, U.S. Atlantic Fleet for duty.

On October 2 with homeward bound pennant streamed, the *Bangust* steamed out of Tokyo Bay on a trip which would bring her home to her birthplace in San Pedro just two years and nine campaigns after her commission pennant had first been unfurled.

USS *BARR* (DE-576 and APD-39)
Submitted By A.C. Sovey

The USS *Barr* DE-576 and APD-39 was built at the Bethlehem Hingham Shipyard, Hingham, Massachusetts. She was named for PFC W.W. Barr, a Marine hero who lost his life on Tulagi during the early part of the war.

She was commissioned at Hingham, Massachusetts and after several months of preparations and shakedown cruises she was assigned to a submarine killer group operating in the Atlantic. She was assigned to Task Unit 22.11 operating with the CVE USS *Block Island* and three other destroyer escorts. The other DEs were the USS *Ahrens* DE-575, USS *Buckley* DE-51, and USS *Elmore* DE-686. The Task Unit started out crisscrossing the Atlantic in search of German U-boats. All of the destroyers had many subcontacts but many proved negative.

During daylight hours the USS *Block Island* would launch plans and patrol to a large area for submerged submarine and if located, at night the Task Unit would proceed to that general area hoping to surprise the surfaced subs. These subs had to surface during the night to recharge their batteries, not like the subs of today that can stay submerged for days. Time after time word would come from convoys reporting German U-boats attacking them and if the Task Unit was close to this area it would seek out these subs.

On May 6, 1944 the USS *Buckley* DE-51 made such a surface contact with a German U-boat and a conflict ensued, finally with USS *Buckley* having virtually a hand to hand battle with the surfaced sub they finally were able to overcome the U-boat crew and take aboard the officers and men as German POWs. Damage to the USS *Buckley* resulted in ramming the sub and she was relieved and had to return to the United States for repair.

The USS *Paine* DE-578 relieved the USS *Buckley* and the Task Unit proceeded into Casablanca, French Morroco for supplies and liberty for the crews.

Liberty was unique as this was the first foreign port for most of the crews of the Task Unit. After about five days of being in port, we proceeded out of Casablanca and back up to the sub hunting. There was much speculation aboard the ship as at this particular time was just prior to D-day in France and much talk about us proceeding to the invasion of Europe. However, this was not the case because the ship started crisscrossing the Atlantic again in search of more German U-boats.

About five or six days out of North Africa the Task Unit encountered a major battle with a U-boat. The USS *Block Island* CVE-21 was struck with three torpedoes and the four destroyers went immediately into action. The USS *Barr* made contact with the sub but before she could release her pattern of depth charges she was hit directly in the stern by what the ship officers claimed was an acoustic torpedo.

The USS *Barr* was completely disabled and suffered many casualties. The USS *Block Island,,* at this time, was listing heavily and orders were given to abandon ship. The USS *Ahrens* DE-575 and USS *Paine* DE-578 were ordered to

USS Barr (DE-576)

pick up survivors of the USS *Block Island* and this left the USS *Elmore* DE-686 to protect the remaining group and track down the sub. After several attempts the USS *Elmore* released a pattern of hedge hogs and was able to make contact and eventually sank the U-boat.

After about one and a half hours the USS *Block Island* finally went down and the survivors all picked up. The USS *Block Island* lost six men and incidentally she was the only aircraft carrier sunk during World War II in the Atlantic Ocean.

The USS *Barr* DE-576 lost seventeen men and fifteen wounded. The next morning she was taken in tow by the USS *Elmore* and proceeded back into port, at about four knots with the USS *Paine* and USS *Ahrens* acting as escorts. The two escorts were finally relieved by two French destroyers and later the USS *Barr* was taken in tow by the seaplane tending USS *Humbolt* out of Casablanca harbour. Finally, after several days, she immediately put into dry dock. All the damaged portion of the ship about seventy-five to one hundred feet were removed and a steel plate welded across the stern. She was then taken in tow by a seagoing tug, the USS *Cherokee* AT-66, and was towed all the way back to Boston, Massachusetts for conversion to an Auxiliary Personnel Destroyer (A.P.D.). Enroute to Boston, the convoy she was with encountered a severe hurricane off the coast of the United States mainland. The USS *Barr,* with several other damaged ships, were ordered into Bermuda to seek refuge. After the storm passed, she proceeded to Boston, Massachusetts, for repairs. About three months of repairs and conversions, the ship took several preliminary shakedowns and then back to port to take on supplies and a lot of new personnel. She then proceeded south escorting a supply ship through the Panama Canal and then up to San Francisco to escort another ship to Hawaii.

Upon reaching Hawaii, the ship was then ordered to take aboard an Underwater Demolition Team (U.D.T.-13). With the U.D.T. team aboard, she proceeded to the island of Maui to undergo maneuvers and exercises with other ships. After the exercises at Maui, the ship returned to Pearl Harbor to take on more supplies and equipment. One significant part of supplies taken aboard were about 40,000 pound of T.N.T. This caused a lot of apprehension with the crew as they all wondered what was next. The USS *Barr* finally departed Hawaii with a small convoy consisting of two battlewagons one troop ship and some supply ships. Sailed into Ulithi where, to the amazement of the crew, were hundreds and hundreds of warships all assembled in this atoll. Several days at Ulithi and then the USS *Barr* and U.D.T. team sailed out with another Task Unit. Little did the crew know that was going to be the invasion of Iwo Jima. The USS *Barr* arrived at Iwo Jima three days before D-Day and then did we realized what the U.D.T. team's particular assignment was. Their job was to go into the beach area under cover of darkness and scout out shoreline and areas to be blasted open for the landing craft to be able to discharge the troops ashore. The U.D.T. team from USS *Barr* took heavy fire from the beach but no casualties resulted. After D-Day, the

USS *Barr* was used for fire cover for the Marines and also for enemy aircraft that infiltrated the area. Many close calls were encountered by the USS *Barr* but she managed to escape them all. Many other ships were less fortunate.

After about twenty days at Iwo Jima, the ship was ordered back to Ulithi to be forced into another Task Unit. Enroute from Iwo Jima, the USS *Barr* was ordered by the Fleet Commander to seek out at several miles away the report of a downed U.S. plane. The ship searched the area for several hours, but the results were negative.

Upon returning to Ulithi the USS *Barr* was assigned with another Task Unit to proceed to the invasion of Okinawa. The ship arrived there just one week before D-day and the U.D.T. team performed then many tasks of underwater demolitions of harbours and entries to the beach.

About 105 days total were spent at Okinawa, securing the island and protecting the ship and men within the island. There were many kamikaze attacks at Okinawa and many USS warships and supply ships suffered heavy casualties during this time.

The USS *Barr* had many various tasks to perform. One was to transport— many Filipino crew members from the larger warship such as battlewagons and aircraft carriers. These men had served aboard these ships and aircraft carriers. These men had served aboard these ships as crew members for many years and the USS *Barr* transferred them to Manila Harbour for leave which some had not been home since before the war.

From Manila she proceeded back to Okinawa for more screening and escort duty.

It was shortly after the ship arrived at Okinawa that the first atomic bomb was dropped on Hiroshima, from this time on, word was that the Japanese were ready to surrender.

The USS *Barr* was then ordered with other A.P.D.s to proceed to Japan and assist evacuation of Allied POWs from designated areas along the coast of Japan.

The U.D.T. team and explosives were transferred before we departed and this was a big sign of relief as this constituted a brand new adventure for her crew.

During the several weeks prior to entry into Japan, the USS *Barr* took aboard about 200 British Marines from two British warships that were assembled in this vast armada of ships at sea. Upon entering Japanese waters, the British Marines were let ashore as preliminary occupation forces. The USS *Barr* then proceeded with the USS hospital ship, USS *Benevolence,* to start evacuating Allied POWs. The USS *Barr* went to several areas along the Japanese coast as far north as Sendai and Kamashi, about 600 miles north of Tokyo and several other ports along the coast. The total number of repatriots taken aboard was about 1,135 and transferred to the hospital ship, USS *Benevolence.*

One of the interesting aspects of this operation which should be noted by the crew members was that the USS *Barr* and USS *Reeves* ADP-52 were ordered into inner Tokyo Harbour, a very narrow channel accessible only by smaller warships.

Proceeding the USS *Reeves* by about one-half hour, this ship passed between the small fortress islands with their dummy gun employments and hence the USS *Reeves* moved to a buoy.

Note: The USS *Barr* was then ordered to tie up to the dock in Tokyo thus this ship, the USS *Barr* ADP-39 was the very first U.S. major or minor warship to tie up to any Japanese piers, the goal of the entire U.S. Navy for nearly four years. The USS *Barr* remained there all day.

Taken aboard were several civilians, four missionaries, priests, three women, two young girls, and a very elderly woman that was transferred to the ship on a stretcher.

The USS *Barr* then proceeded back to the general area put all repatriots aboard the hospital ship.

After the liberation of all Allied POWs, the USS *Barr* made one trip to Iwo Jima and then back to Japan to be assigned to the United States Strategic Bomb Survey Unit. The ship then with Army vehicles for transportation purpose was sent to Nagasaki, Japan.

The USS *Barr* remained at Nagasaki for approximately forty-five days with the bomb survey group.

Many pictures were taken of the atomic bomb blast area for those few that had cameras.

Much of the crew was transferred from this point for departure to the States for discharge. New men were assigned to her from other larger ships in the area.

From here the USS *Barr* was ordered to return to the States and arrived on the west coast in December of 1945. She then was taken to Florida and placed in the moth ball fleet. Finally during the 1960s she was taken into the Caribbean Sea and used for maneuvers and she finally was sunk in the Caribbean.

This was a brief story of the USS *Barr* DE-576 and APD-39 and the entire crew. She played her very important part in the war and her crew was very proud of her. She now rests in her watery grave in the Caribbean.

USS *HORACE A. BASS* (APD-124)

The USS *Horace A. Bass* (APD-124) is a high speed transport. She was named after Ensign Horace A. Bass, USNR of Roanoke, Virginia, who lost his life in the Battle of Midway on June 4, 1942. Ensign Bass was one of the gallant fighter pilots protecting our carriers from Japanese air attack at that time.

The *Bass* joined the ranks of the Navy's "light naval units" on December 21, 1944 when her colors and commissioning pennant whipped up the mast through the cold wintery blasts sweeping across the Fore River yards of the Bethlehem Shipbuilding Corporation in Quincy, Mass.

Outfitted in Boston Navy Yard, she departed early in January for an intensive training and shakedown period in Bermuda. 85 percent of her crew of two hundred men and officers had never been to sea previously, but three weeks of strenuous drills, firing practices and anti-submarine training in the rough Atlantic waters brought out a first line team, green but with the fundamentals down pat.

The first taste of sea duty tucked under her belt, the *Bass* put in to Norfolk, VA January 30th for post-shakedown availability. Two weeks later, the ship was ready to join the fighting fleet and sailed from Norfolk to New York where she joined an ammunition ship the following morning.

The *Bass* escorted the USS *Firedrake* (AE-14) to the Panama Canal without incident and on February 22 made the transit to the Pacific. On the following day, she sailed for San Diego in company with the USS *Gosselin* (APD 126) and the USS *Barry* (APD 29), (later sunk in Okinawa) and made port on the 3rd of March. A short overhaul and gunnery exercises off the shores of San Clemente Island occupied a week and then the *Bass* headed west.

With but fueling and provisioning stops at Pearl Harbor, Eniwetok and Ulithi, on April 2nd the ship found itself travelling northwest, screening a convoy headed for Okinawa where the greatest battle of the Pacific was being waged to secure a foothold in the household of Japan.

The initial landings had taken place five days prior to the arrival of the convoy on the 6th of April. Her charges safely in Korama Retto, the *Bass* steamed off Hagushi anchorage when the Japs made their greatest air assault of the war, loosing 371 planes to the guns and planes of the fleet. The *Bass's* first salvo against the foe brought credit for one "Splash" when the forward gunners spotted a Kamikaze plane hurtling towards the transports in the inner anchorage. A burst of 40mm shells shredded the Jap plane before it reached its target.

That day marked the entry of the *Bass* into the most gruelling duty of the war for ships of her type, the picket line. The line was actually a vast armada of destroyer type ships, deployed in a ring around Okinawa and guarding its approaches from sea and air attack. The ships bore the initial brunt of every desperate and calculated attack, suffering the Navy's greatest losses of the war.

To the sailors of the *Bass*, it meant days of patient and alert patrolling sparked by moments and sometimes hours of intense tensions during the numerous general alarms. The Japanese were not sparing their meager reserves of first line planes in the battle for the Nansei Shoto.

On the 10th of April the ship sailed with a convoy for Guam, but was back in two weeks for another tour of duty off Okinawa. In May another convoy to Saipan provided the second and last break in the picket line duty. On the return trip from the Marianas, the *Bass* in company with a DE, a PC and an SC, escorted a convoy of thirty four landing craft to the Okinawa area, where she remained until mid August.

The constant round of patrol and picket line duty began once again. On the morning of June 8th, the *Bass* was steaming off the small island of Ie Shima when an alert lookout spotted four suspicious planes flying in low over the water. Before a general alarm was sounded for the area, the ship had manned its battle stations. There was no question as to the plane's identity when one Jap "Judy" left formation and headed for the bridge of the *Bass*. The alerted gun crews poured lead into the plane as it made a death laden run, deflecting it sufficiently to bring pilot and plane to a watery grave ten yards from the ship's starboard side. A broken high pressure steam line, quickly repaired, was the only damage suffered.

The routine of patrol duty and air raids continued with each day and night bringing the same story of losses to light naval units but more severe damage to the enemy. The campaign was declared secured on the 20th of June but for the *Bass* and her sister ships the fighting off shore continued.

Then came the early morning of July 30th. It was 2 A.M. and a full moon had just emerged from behind a low cloud, casting its yellow rays over the calm waters and silhouetting the semi-circle of picket ships ranged off the west coast of Okinawa from Kiese Shima to Ie Shima. The *Bass* was in the southern whip end, next to Kiese Shima. Sea calm, visibility perfect. The nearest enemy plane was 60 miles away according to the central warning station.

Those on watch saw the plane only when they heard its motor coughing and sputtering on the side away from the moon. It came in from the west, an ancient Jap biplane, armed with death for its pilot and, he intended, for the ship also. Before the guns could be brought to bear, the plane crashed through the superstructure, ripped off the radio antenna and part of a life raft, tumbled over the side and exploded alongside the ship. A wave of concussion swept the *Bass* as the bomb went off and the port side was riddled by bomb fragments.

After the months of duty on the line watching the other ships on all sides being hit, it was as though the law of averages had caught up with the *Bass*. One man was killed, three seriously wounded and ten others received minor injuries.

The holes in the ship's side were rapidly plugged and after transferring wounded personnel to a hospital ship the *Bass* put in to Buckner Bay where she was speedily repaired. On the 14th of August, when the surrender of Japan was still in the rumor stage, the *Bass* headed north with five other APDs to join the Third Fleet off Tokyo.

The APD task unit joined forces with the fueling support group of the Third Fleet on the 16th of August and screened the oilers for the next three days. The surrender of Japan necessitated the formation of an occupation force at sea and on the 19th of August, the *Bass* was assigned to Task Force 31 to take part in the initial occupation of the Tokyo area.

The task force headed by Rear Admiral Badger, included the USS *Iowa*, the USS *San Diego*, fast mine sweeps, transports and a screen of destroyers and APDs. Making over two hundred transfers at sea via breeches buoys, the *Bass* assembled on board prize and demolition crews from the carriers, cruisers and battlewagons of the Third Fleet.

The task force steamed off the shores of Japan for over a week waiting for the Japanese to complete surrender preparations, skirting the edges of the threatening typhoons. On August 27th the USS *Missouri* led the powerful British and American Fleets past the Nipponese shore defenses into Sagami Wan. One day prior to the main body's entry, the *Bass* steamed up Tokyo Bay and dropped anchor off Yokosuka Naval Base on August 29th in company with the advanced force of destroyers, sweeps and battlewagons.

That night orders were received from Admiral Badger to put a prize crew aboard the HIJMS *Nagato* whose big guns overlooked the boat lanes and was considered a potential threat unless neutralized before the scheduled landings at 1000 on the 30th. Prior to seizing the last remaining battleship of the Imperial Navy, a salvage crew from the *Bass* went ahead to insure that a shore cable to the *Nagato* was not a remote booby trap control.

With Captain Thomas J. Flynn, USN, commanding the prize crew aboard, the *Bass* nosed her way through the breakwater of Kokosuka Ko, the great Jap Naval base, and at 0800 was alongside and in control of the last battleship left to the Nipponese navy.

Captain Flynn accepted the surrender from the Japanese Commanding Officer at 0810, the rising sun was struck from the main mast and the American ensign run up. While the prize crew stood guard over the ship, the gunners from the *Bass* inspected the magazines and guns to insure Japanese compliance with the surrender terms. The *Bass* engineers, with the help of interpreters, lighted off the *Nagato's* boilers and set her auxiliary power plant in operation. The *Bass* stayed alongside the *Nagato* acting as Barracks and Headquarters ship for the prize crew until September 5th when she was relieved of that duty.

On the 10th of September the *Bass* moved into the Inner Harbor of Kokosuka Ko assuming the duty as Barracks ship (Flop and Chop House) for the Port Director and his staff, at which task she is still engaged.

The Commanding Officer during the entire wartime career of the *Bass* has been Commander F.W. Kuhn, USN, of Palisades Park, New Jersey.

USS *BLESSMAN* (APD-48)

The USS *Blessman* (APD-48), Destroyer-Transport, was built and commissioned as a destroyer escort, DE-69, at the Bethlehem-Hingham Shipbuilding Yards in Hingham, Massachusetts, at 1500 on 19 September 1943. The ship was placed in commission by Admiral H.T. Smith, USN, and delivered to Lieutenant Commander Joseph A. Gillis, USNR, the ship's first commanding officer, who had as his executive officer, Lt. (jg) Phillip LeBoutillier, Jr., USNR.

Lieutenant Edward Martin Blessman, USN, class of 1931, gave his life to his country and his name to this vessel. Lieutenant Blessman was serving aboard the USS *Marblehead* as naval aviator when he was killed in action during the Battle of the Java Sea in action against Japanese forces. His wife, Helen Malloy Blessman was the sponsor for the ship which bears his name.

After fitting out at the Boston Navy Yard and successfully completing her acceptance trials in Massachusetts Bay, the *Blessman* was ready for her shakedown cruise. On 9 October 1943, the *Blessman* departed Boston for Bermuda and arrived 11 October. Then began the intensive shakedown training which was to ship the ship into fighting shape. Days of gunnery, anti-submarine, engineering, and seamanship exercises operating unit. This period ended when the *Blessman* successfully passed a departure inspection and shoved off for Boston on 5 November.

On 8 November the *Blessman* returned to the Boston Navy Yard for post-shakedown repairs which were completed on 15 November when she departed for New York. She arrived in the New York Navy the next day to await her first war assignment. On 20 November 1943, she sailed from New York as part of Escort Division 19, assigned to escort a fast troop convoy to the United Kingdom. Ten days later after having guided the convoy to the Irish Sea, the *Blessman* tied up at the U.S. Naval Operating Base, Londonderry, Northern Ireland. On 8 December she departed Londonderry to escort another fast transport group to the United States, arriving in New York 20 December 1943.

There followed three more such trips during which no *Blessman* convoyed ship was molested by the German U-Boats packs which were then out in full force in the Atlantic. A chronological summary of these cruisers follows:

Second Cruise departed New York, 9 January 1944, arrived Belfast, Northern Ireland, 19 January, departed Belfast 27 January 1944, arrived in New York, 8 February 1944.

Third Cruise departed New York, 28 February 1944, arrived Swanson, Wales, 9 March 1944, departed Swansea, 13 March 1944, arrived New York, 26 March 1944.

Fourth Cruise departed New York, 6 April 1944, arrived Londonderry, Northern Ireland, 15 April 1944, departed Londonderry, 22 April 1944, arrived New York, 1 May 1944.

The fifth Atlantic cruise of the *Blessman* was her longest and most eventful. She departed New York, 12 May 1944, on what appeared to be another routine escort assignment and arrived at the other end of the "milk run", Londonderry, on 23 May 1944. On 27 May she arrived in Belfast Harbor with her sister ships, *Rich, Bates,* and *Amesbury*. Here at anchor was the major part of the United nations naval power available in the Atlantic. Ships of all types from the United States, Great Britain, France, Norway, and the Netherlands were present. When the *Blessman* joined the armada, all hands know that they were to take part in the Invasion of Western Europe.

On 3 June 1944, the *Blessman* departed Belfast for Baie de la Seine, France, as escort for the Bombardment Group of the European Assault Force. As the task force entered the English Channel it was met by the heavy weather which turned them back and postponed D-Day. Twelve hours later, however, General Eisenhower gave the "go ahead signal" and all ships again turned their bows toward France. Off Portsmouth, the *Blessman* was assigned to screen the USS

Ancon, on which were embarked the commanding generals and admirals who were directing the invasion, and proceeded to the Normandy beaches. The surrounding channel waters swarmed with the thousands of ships, large and small, which were carrying the men who were to liberate Nazi-dominated Europe. Overhead droned flight after flight of bombers on their way to soften up the enemy for the foot soldiers. The dawn of D-Day, 6 June 1944, found the invasion successfully begun and the *Blessman* assigned to the anti-submarine, E Boat screen to seaward.

While the Army was struggling for a foothold, the Navy so completely dominated the Channel that the *Blessman's* task was comparatively easy. Only the vast German laid minefields presented any considerable hazard, and considerable it was too, for the *Blessman's* sister ship USS *Rich* was mined and sunk. The *Blessman* herself on 7 June 1944 came alongside the USS *Susan B. Anthony*, mined and afire. Although the *Anthony* was sinking rapidly, the *Blessman* stayed alongside and removed six officers and thirty-eight enlisted men. As the sinking transport became engulfed in flames, the *Anthony's* commanding officer ordered the *Blessman* away, the last ship to leave as the stricken *Anthony* sank below the surface.

In less than sixty minutes the *Blessman* was on another errand of mercy. This time she came alongside another transport ship to leave as the stricken *Anthony* sank below the surface.

In less than sixty minutes the *Blessman* was on another errand of mercy. This time she came alongside another transport, the SS *Francis C. Harrington*, which had also struck a mine. The crippled ship, which was in no danger of sinking, had twenty-six seriously wounded men in desperate need of medical attention. The *Blessman* quickly effected their transfer and delivered them to a hospital LST for treatment. This ended her active participation in the invasion. Several days and several enemy air attacks and E-boat attacks later, the *Blessman* was detached and returned to Plymouth on 12 June 1944.

Next day she was underway again for New York, arriving there 21 June 1944. On 2 July 1944, the *Blessman* commenced her sixth and last Atlantic cruise. Again, she escorted a troop convoy to the British Isles, arriving in Londonderry, 11 July 1944. She departed for New York on 17 July with a returning convoy of transports loaded with men wounded in the fighting in Normandy. Enroute home, the *Blessman* received word that she was to be converted to a destroyer-transport. This spelled the end of her Atlantic duty.

On 28 July 1944, the *Blessman* entered the Sullivan Drydock and Repair Corporation Yard, Brooklyn, New York, where work was commenced on the conversion job. No longer was the *Blessman's* mission to be an anti-submarine escort. She was to transport small groups of assault specialists to enemy beaches. For this she was equipped with four landing boats, her armament was increased, and her living compartments.

On 6 August 1944, while this work was in progress, Lieutenant Phillip LeBoutillier, Jr., USNR, the ship's executive officer, relieved Lieutenant Commander Gillis, USNR, as commanding Officer. At the same time Lieutenant Thomas H. McCutcheon, USNR, became the executive officer.

On 25 October 1944, the conversion job completed, the *Blessman* departed New York and headed for the war in the Pacific. After a brief shakedown in Norfolk, she passed through the Panama Canal, stopped at San Diego, and San Francisco, and reported at Pearl Harbor for duty with the Pacific Fleet on 27 November 1944.

At Pearl Harbor, Underwater Demolition Team Number 15 reported aboard the *Blessman*. There were the men whose job it was to discover and remove underwater obstacles to amphibious landings. The Navy realized the need for pre-landing information and preparation during the early island hopping campaigns. This job had to be done by someone on the spot, therefore, the Navy organized and trained the underwater demolition teams.

On 11 December 1944, the *Blessman* departed Pearl on the cruise which was to have as its objective the landings in Lingayen Gulf, Luzon. Brief stops at Eniwetok, Saipan, Ulithi, and the Palau Islands, were made before the entire assault force was formed for the invasion. In the powerful force which left Kossol Roads, Palau, on New Year's Day 1945, were battleships, cruisers, carriers, destroyers, destroyer escorts, and destroyer-transports.

As the task force entered Lingayen Gulf on 6 January 1945, they were met by a large group of Japanese kamikaze planes attacking from all directions. When the smoke of the two hour battle had cleared, several ships had been hit and twenty-one planes were destroyed, the *Blessman* had been credited with assisting in the destruction of two of them. Next day the task force returned to the Gulf again, this time unmolested. The demolition team went to work under cover of intense bombardment provided by the heavy ships. The *Blessman* herself covered her swimmers by making the beaches too hot for any enemy bent on bothering the team in its work. So successfully was the job completed that the

Army suffered not a single casualty when they went ashore on 9 January 1945.

Next day the *Blessman* was detached to escort the new empty transports back to Ulithi via Leyte Gulf. Here she rested, re-provisioned, and trained for the next operation which was to take us a stop nearer to Japan.

This next stop was to be Iwo Jima, one of the best defended islands in the world. On 10 February 1945, the *Blessman* departed Ulithi on what proved to be an ill-fated cruise. With other units of the bombarding forces, she arrived at Iwo Jima on 16 February and Underwater Demolition Team Number 15 conducted a preliminary reconnaissance while the heavy ships subjected the Japs to a terrific bombardment. Next day Team #15 went into action again. As the *Blessman* approached the island the Japs, believing her movements to be an indication of the landing of troops, took her under fire. Fortunately she was unharmed and the swimmers were able to complete their job at the cost of one casualty. Next day, 18 February 1945, the process was repeated with no casualties. Her job was finished; she was ordered to withdraw for the night to await the arrival of the Marines who were to land next day.

As she steamed away to join her group, tragedy struck quickly. A low flying Jap bomber appeared out of the black night and dropped two bombs on the speeding ship. One dropped harmlessly over her side, but the other turned her into a flaming holocaust. Ironically, it exploded in the mess hall where her tired men were crowded writing letters home. In that instant forty men stopped writing, never to write again. Twenty-one men of the *Blessman's* crew and nineteen men of UDT #15 were killed. Twenty-three were wounded, one seriously.

For one hundred endless minutes, the stricken ship lay dead in the water. Flames poured fiercely from the gaping hole in her superstructure. Water poured into her riddled hull. All power was lost, emergency pumps had been destroyed. Only bucket brigades were able to be thrown into the battle against the flames, obviously a losing fight. Ammunition began to explode as the fire raced toward the magazines. With enemy planes in the vicinity this looked like the end of the *Blessman*.

Just as destruction had come out of the night before, now help appeared just as suddenly. Fighting hearts in the *Blessman* were relieved to see the USS *Gilmer* (APD-110) come alongside, without regard for her own safety, and provide fire fighting men and equipment. After a two hour battle by the men of both ships, the fires were brought under control and the *Blessman* was saved to fight again.

Next morning, as Marines began their bloody but victorious battle for Iwo, the men of the *Blessman* held burial-at-sea services for these shipmates who were never to sail again:

Arcisz, John Joseph, PhM2c, #606 73 30, USNR
Boyd, Claudie Bert, StM1c, #300 50 17, USN
Dimauro, James Vincent, SC3c, #803 87 95, USNR
Dimeling, Frank Paul, MM2c, #822 19 13, USNR
Goldsborough, Paul Camillus Jr., #256 48 40, MM3c, USNR
Jordan, Harold Patterson, S1c, #951 32 54, USNR
McLeod, Emmett (n), StM2c, #920 84 72, USNR
Novak, Hugo M, SC1c, #625 88 86, USNR
Robertson, Charles Louis, ST2c, #875 04 33, USNR
Rodgers, James Ignatius, MM2c, #817 04 33, USNR
Senedak, Mike (n), S1c, #858 34 09, USNR
Snellenberger, Joseph Roy, EM2c, #850 65 77, USNR
Stiles, Hoyt (n), S1c, #931 39 23, USNR
Thompson, Donald E., S2c, #819 49 13, USNR
Treadway, Harry Preston, Cox. #832 49 96, USNR
Vince, Samuel Francis, SC2c, #825 57 05, USNR
Hawley, Richard William, RM2c, #285 18 87, USNR
Krepps, Ralph Edwin, MM3c, #822 37 29, USNR
Marshall, Sidney (n), SoM2c, #800 18 19, USNR
Sutton, Gordon (n), WT2c, #811 66 63, USNR
Schnabel, Gerald Matthew, MoMM2c, #576 76 00, USNR
Trent, Chester Edward Jr., SC2c, #834 88 10, USNR

Then began the long cruise, made under tow, to Saipan. The *Blessman's* crew lived more like soldiers than sailors on this trip. With all cooking facilities demolished, the crew built a fire place on the fantail and there cooked all their meals, eggs, hash, and beans every.

The repair officers at Saipan thought little of the practicability of restoring the ruined ship. While they were making their estimates, the *Blessman's* crew was busy. In a few days they had made such rapid strides that the repair officers had to revise their estimates. Originally they had decided that the ship's structure was worthless - now, however, they decided that her spirt was invaluable. She was patched and returned to the Mare Island Navy Yard to be placed in fighting trim to return to the war.

For heroic performance the night of 18 February, and for outstanding devotion to duty during the trying days that followed, recommendations for awards were made as follows.

LeBoutillier, Phillip, Jr., Lieutenant USNR
    The Silver Star Medal
Nolan, Walter Ernest Jr., #360 56 73, M1c, USN
    The Silver Star Medal
Kababik, Joseph William, #228 26 71, CBM(PA), USN
    The Navy and Marine Corp Medal
Terrett, Russel Edward, #857 00 29, Cox., USNR
    The Navy and Marine Corp Medal
Parine, Leonard Joseph, #809 96 03, SoM2c, USNR
    The Navy and Marine Corp Medal
Macrander, Melvin "G", #973 10 13, S1c, USNR
    The Navy and Marine Corp Medal
Barron, Albert Bernard, #945 14 16, F1c, USNR
    The Navy and Marine Corp Medal
Coates, Ernest Randolph, Lieutenant, #168210, USN
    Commendation by the Secretary of the Navy
McCutcheon, Thomas Hoyt, Lieutenant #128708, USNR
    Commendation by the Secretary of the navy
Andrews, E.F., Ensign, #328640, USNR
    Commendation by the Secretary of the Navy
McCallum, R.H., Ensign, #339838, USNR
    Commendation by the Secretary of the Navy
Rybski, E., Ensign, #327460, USNR
    Commendation by the Secretary of the Navy

The following named men were awarded the Purple Heart Medal for wounds received as a result of enemy action:

Ainsworth, Edwin Henry, #957 20 72, F1c, USNR
Demi, Leo Alexander, #906 43 16, Bkr2c, USNR
Eastham, Benjamin Burkely, #929 13 51, F2c, USNR
Lawhorn, Claude Elsworth, #845 33 03, F1c, USNR
Schmiedel, Howard Travers, #807 59 ?
Wilson, Jered Herbert, #S65 85
Zwer, Don Orval
Graham, Nicholas Francis, #667 08 75 SC3c, USNR
Edwards, Robert Glenn, #61 57 05,
Hyland, Joseph William #646 86 54, Cox., USNR
Parker, William Herbert, #263 73 34, S1c, USNR

The *Blessman* arrived at Mare Island on 23 April 1945. While the ship was being repaired, her crew took a well-deserved leave. During this period, 21 July 1945, Lieutenant LeBoutillier, Jr., USNR, was relieved as Commanding Officer by Lieutenant Commander Clement O. Davidson, USNR.

As the repair work was being completed it was decided that the *Blessman* was to be the flagship for Underwater Demolition Squadron One of the Pacific Fleet. As such, she departed San Francisco, 11 August 1945, for Oceanside, California, where she was to take aboard the Squadron Commander, Captain Roy D. Williams, USN. Here again the handwriting was on the wall. The men of the *Blessman* know that soon she would be steaming for Japan and the final invasion of the war. She arrived at Oceanside on 14 August 1945, at which time Underwater Demolition Team Number 17 was embarked. The following day Captain Williams hoisted his command pennant aboard his new flagship. This was 15 August 1945, the day hostilities ceased in the Pacific. To the *Blessman* it was a day of preparation for the cruise to Japan. Despite the wars end, landings still had to be made on the Japanese Islands. Next day she departed the United States for a fast run to Japan. Stops were made en route at Pearl Harbor, Eniwetok, Ulithi, Manila, Subic Bay, Lingayen again, Okinawa and then Japan - the end of the long road to victory for all ships of the U.S. Navy.

On 23 September 1945, the *Blessman* entered the harbor at Wakanoura Wan, Honshu, the port for the steel city of Wakayama. Her team #17 charted the landing beaches for the Army which was to occupy the Kobe-Osaka area. Her job done, the *Blessman* lay at anchor on 25 September 1945, and watched the occupation troops go ashore. For the men aboard her that fateful night at Iwo Jima, there was no small portion of satisfaction in this impressive sight.

Several days later orders were received for the *Blessman* to return to the United States and be placed in reserve commission. On 30 September 1945, she steamed seaward, headed for home.

An unnamed admiral commenting on the heavy losses to the light units during the incessant Kamikaze attacks at Okinawa said, "It is always the little ships that deserve the heartiest 'Well Done'. The *Blessman* like hundreds of other light units was such a "little ship".

United States
Hingham, Mass
Boston, Mass
Portland, ME
New York City
Norfolk, VA
San Diego, Calif.
San Pedro, Calif.
Oceanside, Calif.
San Francisco, Calif.
Mare Island, Calif.

Atlantic
Londonderry, Ireland
Belfast, Ireland
Swansea, Wales
Baie de la Seine, Normandy, France
Great Sound, Bermuda,
Cristobal, C.Z.

Pacific
Balboa, C.Z.
Pearl Harbor, Oahu, T.H.
Eniwetok, Marshall Islands
Guam, Marianas Islands
Saipan, Marianas Islands
Iwo Jima, Volcano Islands
Okinawa, Ryukys
Ulithi, Caroline Islands
Kossol Roads, Palau Islands
Leyte, Philippine Islands
Samar, Philippine Islands
Luzon, Philippine Islands
Manila
Subic Bay
San Fernando
Wakanoura Wan, Honshu, Japan

The total distance travelled since the *Blessman* was commissioned is 89,740 miles. More than three times around the world at the equator.

USS *BOWERS* (DE-637)

If true heroism were measured in degrees of adversity faced by men, the crew of the Destroyer Escort USS *Bowers* rose to the highest echelon of the act the morning of April 16, 1945.

Within a matter of minutes, the *Bowers* faced and battled a surprise air attack, and suffered a direct hit from a kamikaze plane which turned the flight deck into an inferno. When the flames were extinguished and the smoke cleared, 49 crewman were dead and another 56 were severely wounded. Most of those wounded would die shortly after.

Despite the devastation, both human and material, the *Bowers* and her men found the strength to undertake a long and exhaustive two-month journey home to Philadelphia, where extensive repairs eventually made the mighty Destroyer Escort seaworthy once again.

The fateful tale of the *Bowers* has seldom been told outside the inner circle of survivors, whose camaraderie and friendships over the years have created a bond and support system only seen in the closest of families.

The sheer devastation alone would merit headlines today. Stories of individual heroism are many. But a statement from Engineering Officer Lt. Ed Davies perhaps explains why the events of April 16 are not more widely known Davies wrote:

"The ship had no heroes. The heroes were dead ... every man did a good job.

The *Bowers* lost 105 of her crew of 200 in the explosions and fire that followed the crashing of a suicide plane through her superstructure. There was little warning of what was to take place in those early morning hours off the coast of Okinawa.

Thirteen days prior, the *Bowers*, under the command of Lt. Commander Charles F. Highfield, was ordered 10 miles north of Kerama Retto on a radar picket station as part of the 7th Fleet of Task Force 54, the Gunfire and Covering Force. The escort came under attack by a single plane on April 6, and successfully shot down the Japanese pilot. The following day a Kate torpedo bomber zeroed in on the *Bowers*, but was quickly shot and sunk in the Pacific.

The next few days were quiet, though battle stations were manned several times after reports that Japanese planes had been spotted in the area. The escort remained off the island of Ie Jima in support of operation on the main beachhead on Okinawa.

In its short but valiant career, the *Bowers* had been credited with shooting down four kamikaze bombers. But single plane attacks would soon be merely a memory for the crew.

In the early morning hours of April 16, four Val-type Japanese bombers pressed an attack on the *Bowers* and several destroyer escorts in the vicinity. The sleeping crew was aroused by an air raid warning at 4:45 a.m.

An hour later a single plane made a strafing attack. The plane was splashed about 700 yards off the port beam and sank immediately. The skies then cleared, although the crew remained on alert following reports that many enemy planes were in the area.

By 8 a.m. the Allied invasion of Ie Jima was under way. All hands on the *Bowers* were at their battle stations with the increase in military action.

At 9:39 a.m. two Vals were spotted flying low and quickly honing in on the *Bowers* and another destroyer escort nearby. Commander Highfield ordered evasive maneuvers. When the planes came within 5,000 yards of the *Bowers*, they split and began attack operations.

The Japanese planes assumed a parallel formation, flying in opposite directions, with one quickly moving directly toward the *Bowers*. One plane was shot down by a nearby destroyer escort. The second plane continued its course, and attacked the port side of the escort.

The pilot turned and flew his Val directly toward the ship. All port side guns opened fire, and witnesses report numerous strikes to the plane. But no flames were seen, and the fuselage remained intact.

The plane attacked in a glide, strafing the decks and injuring at least one *Bowers* crewman with machine gun fire. The pilot managed to weave through the flak and in an evasive move nearly struck the water after veering sharply to avoid hitting the ship.

USS Bowers (DE-637)

Diving in on the ship's port beam, the pilot apparently misjudged his run and not over the *Bowers*, narrowly missing the ship's stack.

The pilot regained control of his Val and circled at a range of about 1,500 feet. Flying at an altitude of only 50 feet, the Japanese flyer moved in a counter-clockwise fashion before taking aim on the ship.

Survivors said it appeared clear the pilot was preparing for a Kamikaze suicide attack on the starboard beam. Commander Highfield grabbed a machine gun and poured a stream of lead into the plane. The crew, meanwhile, was firing tracers and three-inch shells from topside.

But at the last moment of the approaching sweep, the plane veered and struck the bridge of the *Bowers* at a 45-degree angle. The boat was rocked from the impact, and flaming gasoline quickly had the bridge and pilot house area engulfed in flames. Commander Highfield was burned and tossed into the water along with several of the crew. The captain was later rescued and taken to sick bay. Several of the crew were found dead in the water immediately after the attack.

Lt. Commander S.A. Haavik was also injured in the seconds following the explosion and fire, and command rested with Lt. Truman Hinkle, USNR.

When the plane struck the *Bowers*, it was carrying 500 pounds in explosives that the pilot had planned on using to blow the ship out of the water. Fortunately, the explosives ripped loose of the Val seconds before the plane embedded itself into the bridge, glanced off the searchlight and exploded in mid-air off the port side.

Despite the stroke of apparent good luck, the flying shards from the explosion sprayed the ship's topside from stem to stern, cutting down the men on deck and ripping jagged holes in the *Bowers'* frame.

All officers on deck when the kamikaze hit the bridge were killed or wounded, with the exception of Ensign W. Word Jr. In all, 37 were killed instantly, 11 were missing, and 56 were severely wounded. Many of the injured died shortly after.

Minutes after the incident a nearby escort, the *Connolly*, began maneuvering to pick up survivors from the Pacific. Seventeen *Bowers* crewman were rescued, including the captain. Reports from the *Connolly* indicate most survivors had suffered flash burns. The *Connolly* itself came under attack later in the day, but was able to take evasive measures and transport all the wounded to the USS *Swearer* but later transfer to a hospital ship.

Because the deck and its men had been virtually annihilated, help in extinguishing the fires had to come from elsewhere on the ship.

Engineering Officer Lt. Ed Davies was in the forward engine room when the kamikaze hit the *Bowers*. Feeling the jolt from the impact, Davies sent a crewman to the bridge to see if a new speed would be ordered. The crewman returned minutes later, reporting that the entire bridge was gone.

Davies went topside and found only a dazed crew. No officers were in sight. Realizing the confusion and horror on the deck, Davies himself began fighting the fire, which prompted the crew to join in the battle.

During the same period, Lt. Truman B. Hinkle, the ship's damage control officer, rushed to the deck when he realized the *Bowers* was in trouble. He picked up on the work Davies had begun and organized the crew into fire-fighting parties. Hinkle has been credited with instilling a confidence and level-headedness in the crew that was necessary to bring an order to the flaming chaos.

Meanwhile, some of the crew returned to the battle stations that remained after the attack and explosions. Had another Japanese attack ensued during the minutes after the kamikaze hit the *Bowers*, it is likely the ship would not have survived.

Within 45 minutes of Davies' appearance on deck, all fires were under control and the reality of the human and material losses settled in on the survivors.

The remainder of April 16 and the next day were spent assessing damage and getting the *Bowers* seaworthy again. The dead on board were buried at sea, while medical crew worked relentlessly to keep the injured alive.

The wounded were transported under limited power to the hospital ship USS *Hope*.

On April 18 the crew of the *Bowers* assisted in throwing the kamikaze plane overboard. The plane had embedded itself in the deck, and a good deal of work was required to free the ship of this visible reminder of death.

The *Bowers* limped its way to an advance base in the western Pacific, where the repair unit of the Navy ship USS *Nestor* welded a sheet of metal over the gaping wound in the superstructure, making the escort seaworthy enough to tackle the long and arduous journey home to the states.

The *Bowers* suffered more casualties in a single incident than any destroyer escort in World War II. In all, 49 were killed and 56 wounded on the April 16 incident.

The *Bowers* pulled into its berth at the Philadelphia Ship Yard the morning of June 16, exactly two months after being hit thousands of miles and many horrible memories away.

She was reclassified to a high-speed troop transport (APD 40), effective 25 June 1945. She got underway 19 September following conversion for a training cruise to Guantanamo Bay, Cuba. She returned to Philadelphia on 25 October to celebrate the first post-war Navy Day (27 October), then steamed to Green Cove Springs, Florida, where she remained inactive until placed out of commission in reserve, 10 February 1947.

Bowers (APD 40) earned four battle stars and other awards for the operations listed below:

1 Star/Consolidation of Solomon Islands:
    Consolidation of Northern Solomons: 15 Jun; 22 Jun-26 Oct. 1944
1 Star/Western New Guinea Operation:
    Toem-Wakde-Sarmi Area Operation: 20-21 May; 4-6 Jun; 10-13 Jun; 20 Jun 1944
1 Star/Leyte Operation:
    Leyte Landings: 12 Oct-14 Nov; 25-28 Oct 1944
1 Star Okinawa Gunto Operation:
    Assault and Occupation of Okinawa Gunto: 25 Mar-24 Apr 1945
Philippine Republic Presidential Unit Citation Badge:
    12 Oct-14 Nov; 25-28 Oct 1944

USS *BRIGHT* (DE-747)

A train rolls across the country carrying car after car of eager sailors with a common destination - Terminal Island, San Pedro, CA. From Everywhere, USA, with boot camp behind them and specialized Norfolk training fresh in their minds, they are bound for a specific destination - *their ship!*

This nucleus crew, chosen and assembled by the Navy in Norfolk, VA, edges toward its destination, the USS *Bright*. Most of these young sailors have enlisted to defend their country against the enemy.

A mass of iron and steel awaits, her crew is on its way, and she is anticipating their arrival.

Fitted out by the Los Angeles Shipbuilding and Dry Dock Company of the Western Pipe and Steel Company, the USS *Bright* was first christened and launched September 26, 1943, and assigned the number DE-747.

She was sponsored by Mrs. Miriam Engle Bright, widow of Lt. Bright. The ship was commissioned June 30, 1944. She was named in honor of Lieutenant Graham Paul Bright, a 1935 Naval Academy graduate, who was killed on Guam December 10, 1941, three days after the bombing of Pearl Harbor by the Japanese. LCDR William A. McMahan assumed command of the ship.

The *Bright's* shakedown cruise was conducted from San Diego off the California coast and concluded August 22, 1944.

Then on September 19, she sailed from San Diego as an escort for the SS *John B. Floyd* to Hilo, HI, and then to Pearl Harbor.

From October 1 to November 20, she operated out of Pearl Harbor on anti-submarine and gunnery exercises, and then reported for duty with Task Group 12.3

From November 24, 1944, to April 30, 1945, she operated with the TG 12.3, conducting a series of submarine hunter-killer searches near the Hawaii and Marshall Islands. This group was headed by the Kaiser escort carrier USS *Corregidor* (CVE-58). Sometime between November 1944 and April 1945, they encountered a severe typhoon. The *Bright* suffered damage to her #1 gun tub, and the Corregidor almost broke in two from the extremely high waves.

The *Bright* was engaged in (ASW) anti-submarine warfare "Hunter-killer" operations with the USS *Corregidor* and Escort Division 53. This comprised Task Group 12.3. On April 30, 1945, the USS *Bright*, USS *Snyder* (DE-745), and the USS *Hemminger* (DE-746) were ordered from Eniwetok to Saipan for duty in the TF51 (Task Force 51) escort pool. Thus far the *Bright's* missions had been uneventful. From May 5 to May 10, they were assigned as escorts for convoy SOK-1, which consisted of transports and support ships en route to Okinawa. This convoy reached Okinawa on May 10, 1945, and anchored in Hagushi Anchorage, Okinawa, Jima.

On the night of May 9, sonar picked up sounds indicating a submarine. The *Bright* dropped two series of depth charges. Moments later a torpedo was sighted on the port quarter, and it passed about 20 feet off the bow.

A mine was sighted 400 yards off starboard on May 10. The horn-type mine was successfully exploded with rifle fire, with no damage to the ship.

May 11 she took station as a unit of the transport anti-aircraft screen. The screening station was close to Okinawa, and eight miles from Tonechi Jima.

Mother's Day, May 13, had been an uneventful day. The ship was brought to General Quarters at 6:45 P.M. At 7:15 enemy aircraft were reported eight miles away. The crew was not alarmed, for friendly planes were also in the area.

At 7:18 a plane was sighted port side, closing in and flying low, approximately 300 feet above the water. The kamikaze was headed for midship, and when it was within range at about 1000 yards, Robert F. Thomas opened fire with his 20-mm gun, scoring direct hits to the plane's engine and left wing. All guns were trained on the enemy plane, making direct hits.

A.J. Ford captained the 40-mm crew. E.J. Diomedes was director-operator of that gun, which was manned by nine men and two operators. Diomedes is the man who executed that first effective blow.

The pilot was forced to divert from his course to the fantail of the ship. Thomas held his battle station, but his gun then locked up. At about 750 yards, the fighter burst into flames, its port wing falling off. The stub portion of the plane's port wing hit the USS *Bright* at the port depth charge racks, its bomb exploded upon impact. This caused immediate loss of steering, with the rudder jammed hard left. The after-engine room was completely demolished, and both port and starboard depth charge racks were damaged and inoperative, smoke screen generators blown off, the main deck aft buckled and pierced, and three compartments open to the sea. Because of the damage to the rudder, the ship circled helplessly for an hour.

Miraculously only two men were injured, Pete D. Vercolio and Harold E. Crane, Jr. James M. Johnson and Prentiss Marshall are credited with pulling Vercolio from the burning steering engine room. Lt. Fletcher Seymour, Paul Potter, and Mack Paluch are credited for rescuing Crane from the same compartment. Lt. N. Paul operated on Crane and Vercolio on the ward room table, and the two men were then transferred to a hospital ship.

Meanwhile, the men stationed at their guns remained there for two and a half more hours. At 7:24 another kamikaze was sighted and taken under fire by the *Bright* and the *Barr*. This plane was observed to crash.

Gardner Gibson led a work party to repair the steering. Andrew W. Gibson, Jr., worked for a solid week on the "jury rig".

The *Bright* was towed to anchorage at Kerama Retto (called "Frustration Cove"), Ryukyu Islands, for repair. The bomb nose was recovered and indicated it was of the 500-pound variety. She then sailed in a convoy for Ulithi.

On May 31 she was underway from Ulithi to Pearl Harbor via Eniwetok, arriving June 14. From there, she received onward routing to Portland, OR.

It was during her return trip to Portland that Capt. McMahan had two four-leaf clovers painted on her smoke stack, for he indeed felt she was a "lucky" ship to have survived.

From June 23 until September 8, the *Bright* remained in Portland undergoing extensive alterations and battle damage repairs. A new stern was built by the Albina Engine & Machine Works, while the damaged section was cut away at the marine railway at Commercial Iron Works, and the new section was welded into place.

Fully repaired, she sailed to Balboa, Canal Zone, to report to CinCLant, the Atlantic Fleet. Arriving at the Charleston, SC, Navy Yard on September 25, she underwent minor repairs prior to deactivation.

Traveling down the St. John River, she arrived in Green Cove Springs, FL, on October 24 via Jacksonville. The preservation process was completed, and the *Bright* was placed in the Reserve Fleet on April 19, 1946.

The *Lucky Lady* remained in mothballs until November 11, 1950, when she was transferred to France under the Mutual Defense Assistance Program. It is reported that France sold her in 1965.

The *Bright* received the Asiatic-Pacific Campaign Medal and a star for the Okinawa Gunto Operation.

Statistics: Length - 306 feet; Beam - 37 feet; Displacement - 1,240 tons; Speed - 20 knots; Complement - 15 officers, 201 men.

USS *BRISTER* (DE-327)

The USS *Brister* DE-327 was built in Orange, Texas. She was commissioned November 30, 1943 and named Ensign Robert E. Brister. The *Brister* served in the Second World War (see Vol. I of Trim But Deadly page 72). She was decommissioned in 1946 and placed in mothballs at Green Cove Springs, Florida.

At the end of the Korean War in 1955 she was taken out of mothballs and towed to the Charleston Naval Shipyard in South Carolina. There she was rebuilt from the main deck up with aluminum. This was necessary because she was to be outfitted with electronic equipment for radar surveillance which would make her top heavy. Maximum roll with the new superstructure would then be 67.5 degrees.

The *Brister* was recommissioned July 21, 1956 as a DER. She now was a radar picket ship to serve in the North Atlantic as an enemy missile detector to give early warning to North American Allies from Russian attacks. She also made ASW patrols.

The *Brister* patrolled the Atlantic from Miami, Florida to and in the Artic Circle from January until June 1957. Her home port was Goat Island, Newport, Rhode Island. The *Brister* operated with the *Hissem* DER-400, *Joyce* DER-317, *Price* DER-332, and *Kirkpatrick* DER-318.

In June 1957, she received orders to proceed to the Pacific where she was involved in coastal operations off Vietnam. In 1972 she was decommissioned and sold to Taiwan for scrap. Ironically, the *Brister* helped in evacuating over 2,500 prisoners of war from Taiwan after the Second World War. Taiwan ended up being her final resting place.

As a radar picket ship the Port and Starboard sides were enclosed. The Mess Hall and Chief's Quarters were on the Starboard side, and the Engineering Quarters were on the Port side. The old Mess Hall became CIC (Combat Information Center).

In the after section of the ship there was the Junior Officers Quarters and the remaining crew quarters. Between the crew Quarters and Engine room and was located ship's stores, Electronic Shop, Sick Bay, Barber Shop, Yeoman's Office, and After Radar Room.

On the main deck just forward of the Quarter Deck was the Emergency Radio Room and Cook's Quarters.

On the 01 level aft, there was the Airographers Office above which the Height Finder Radar Antenna was mounted. Up forward on the 01 Deck was Radio Central

On the 02 Deck forward was the Captain's Quarters, the Bridge, and Chart Room.

The armament consisted of a 3"50 Fore and Aft, Hedge-hog Rack Forward, Depth Charge Rack Aft, and Quad 20mm.

Rear Admiral George C. Crawford, USN
Commandant of the Sixth Naval District

Captain Herbert J. Pfingstag, USN
Commander Charleston Naval Shipyard

Lieutenant Commander Joseph J. Cote, USN
Commanding Officer USS Brister

Officers of the USS Brister (DER-327)

LCDR Joseph J. Cote, USN	LTJG Howard T. Ross, Jr., USN
Commanding Officer	*Supply Officer*
LT Stephen P. Douglas, Jr., USN	ENS David N. Moore, USNR
Executive Officer	*Communications Officer*
LTJG Henry C. Emmerling, Jr., USN	ENS John C. Bray, Jr., USN
Operations Officer	*Damage Control Assistant*
LTJG Donald J. Schaff, USNR	ENS Eugene H. Vaughan, Jr., USN
Gunnery Officer	*ASW Officer*
LTJG Richard T. Fleming, USNR	ENS Andre N. Abele, USN
CIC Officer	*Assistant CIC Officer*
LTJG James M. Daly, II, USN	ENS Robert W. Beveridge, Jr., USN
First Lieutenant	*Electronics Material Officer*

LTJG James E. O'Brien, USN
Engineering Officer

Chief Petty Officers—USS Brister (DER-327)

Bendel, John (n)	EMC	Holland, Henry N.	HMC
Dear, Sam C.	ETNC	Horba, Michael (n)	GMC
Durrance, Roy S.	ENC	McHone, John F.	ENC
Ellison, Huling A.	ICC	Melton, John R.	RMC
Elmore, James S.	RDC	Metts, George M.	BMC
Firsching, Frank H.	FTC	Redding, Francis M.	ENC
Henninger, LeRoy V.	QMC	Reeb, Karl E.	CSC

USS Brister (DE-327)

Crew of USS Brister (DER-327)

Arruda, Joseph M.	EN2	Durst, Robert J.	RMSN	Lindsey, James A.	FN	Schnabel, George (n)	RDSA
Atkins, Albert G.	RDSA	Edmonds, William J.	EN3	Loggins, Carl E.	SH2	Schneider, Larry w.	ENFN
Bambridge, Jack E.	SN	English, Robert G.	FA	Lucas, Melvin J.	ENDFN	Schnur, Leon H.	RDSA
Barnes, Charles E.	FN	Fairow, Clarence E.	SN	Maier, Leroy C.	BM3	Simms, Michael A.	CS3
Bass, Roy J.	GM2	Fitzpatrick, Joseph J.	SN	Maloney, James M.	RM3	Smith, Charles R.	RD3
Beheler, Willard (n)	RD2	Fox, James E.	GM3	Martin, William E.	EN1	Smith, Francis	RM3
Berry, Minos W.	SH2	Frady, David L.	QMS2	Maxwell, Jack E.	EM1	Smith, Ronald L.	RM3
Bettinger, Robert	RMSN	Gallagher, Eugene J.	ME1	McClintock, Harvey W.	SN	Spitalik, Joseph P., Jr.	FN
Birdsall, Billie L.	SN	Gentzler, Ronald L.	SK3	McGrath, James J., Jr.	RDSA	Sprouse, Kenneth E.	SN
Bogenreif, Orville D.	SN	Goodenough, Walter L.	FP1	McMillon, Burl H.	SN	Standeven, Chas. N., Jr.	FN
Bowen, Clement F.	SN	Gordon, Clifford W.	RM3	Menadue, Thomas D.	SK3	Stearns, James F.	SN
Brice, Ruben P.	SN	Groff, Edward E.	TM2	Mertens, Frank E.	FN	Stitt, Donald E.	EN1
Bruenecke, Otto H.	QM3	Grosso, Andrew V., Jr.	TE3	Michaels, Donald C.	ENFA	Stone, Clyde (n)	TE1
Brown, William E.	SO3	Guida, James S.	DK1	Misamore, Clifford D.	MR2	Stranski, James M.	RM2
Bulaon, Moj A.	SD3	Haas, Harvey (n)	FA	Mitchell, John M.	ET3	Strawser, Paul E.	RD3
Buxton, Marvin D.	FA	Harper, Milton L.	FN	Monaghan, Patrick M.	END3	Summers, Thomas L.	CS3
Bynum, Charles E.	FN	Heeter, Blaine F.	FA	Monette, Lloyd T.	SN	Tadin, George F.	RDSN
Campbell, William T.	FN	Hicks, Larry T.	FN	Morgan, James H.	SN	Testin, Thomas L.	SN
Cantu, Enrique C.	CS3	Hofman, William E.	SN	Morgan, Robert E.	QM1	Thomas, Robert L.	PN3
Carter, Denis W.	EMP2	Hogan, Marion H.	SN	Neville, Thomas A.	SN	Thompson, Joseph B.	EMP3
Cates, Estille (n) Jr.	SN	Hollowell, Morris E.	SN	Nichols, Billy C.	SN	Townson, Roy (n)	TN
Chandler, Robert T.	SN	Horne, Donis (n)	BM1	Nusbaum, Ronald C.	RM3	Tunstall, Frank M.	QMQ3
Cherry, Kyle "B"	EN3	Hotchkiss, Harley W.	YN3	O'Donnell, Joseph D.	RD3	Tyner, Cole B.	DCW2
Chick, Gordon W.	EN3	Hughston, Calvin C.	TN	O'Neill, James A.	SA	Tyree, Eugene W.	SK1
Chitty, John A.	SN	Jackson, Mark W.	SN	Palcak, Edward A.	SN	Uter, Matthew F.	ET1
Clark, Stanville H.	RM1	Johnson, Thomas D.	FA	Phillips, Keneth C.	GM1	Ward, Henry T.	ETSN
Clifton, Robert W., Jr.	EMP3	Jutzi, Eugene K.	IC3	Pitts, Frederick A.	AG3	Weaver, James I.	FN
Cluck, Monroe H.	RM3	Karlson, Roy L.	YN3	Piwonski, Charles J., Jr.	FN	Weidner, Edgar R., Jr.	SK2
Cole, Harold (n)	RDSA	Kimble, Clarence D.	GM3	Plisak, Tadusz F.	RD1	Williams, Sidney (n)	CS1
Collier, William E.	SD1	King, Aris C.	SN	Quigley, George W.	END3	Williamson, Rudolph P.	EN1
Cordero, Juan A.	SA	Kopf, Edward G.	RD3	Quinata, Thomas L.G.	SN	Wills, James D.	FN
Czarnik, Walter S.	SN	Kreitzman, Martin (n)	SO3	Reich, Vincent P.	EN2	Wilmore, Charles A.	GMM3
Davis, Marshall (n)	EN3	Krienke, John W.	ETR3	Ringer, Daniel H.	FN	Wilson, George (n), Jr.	SN
Dennis, Lloyd A.	END2	Land, Robert F.	SO1	Roberson, Roy E.	SN	Wofford, Edward G.	SN
Dobie, William E.	FA	Lane, Arthur S.	EN2	Robinson, William H.	FN	Wolfe, George J.	FN
Doboga, Andrew A.	PN1	Lathan, Robert R.	FN	Roessler, Alfred J.	BM2	Wonsley, Robert (n)	FN
Dorsey, George N.	YN1	Laws, George L.	BMSN	Rogers, "O" "B" J.	BM2	Woodruff, Lyman W.	RD3
Dreher, Julius F.	RD3	Leslie, James S.	FT3	Romans, Charlie F.	FN		
Duffy, Bernard J.	FN	Lind, Robert P.	BT1	Schilk, Joseph C.	FN		

USS *BUNCH* (DE-694)

Kenneth Cecil Bunch—born on 21 January 1919 in Norman County, Minn.—enlisted in the Navy at Des Moines, Iowa, on 9 March 1937, and received his "boot camp" training at San Diego. Rated as seaman 2d class on 9 July 1937, Bunch was transferred to Scouting Squadron (VS) 42 ten days later. He remained in that unit over the years that followed, attaining the rate of radioman 2d class on 16 November 1940. With the extension of his enlistment on 9 March 1941, Bunch was transferred to the Naval Air Station at Norfolk, VA, on 29 August 1941 where, soon thereafter, he joined VS-8, of the incipient *Hornet* (CV-8) Air Group. While in that squadron, he was promoted to the rate of radioman, 1st class, on 1 March 1942.

On 6 June 1942, on the last day of the Battle of Midway, Bunch was flying as radio-gunner for Ens. Don T. Griswold, USNR, in a Douglas SBD-3 "Dauntless," as the *Hornet* air group joined in the attacks on the fleeing Japanese cruisers *Mogami* and *Mikuma*. Antiaircraft fire claimed Griswold's SBD-3, the only plane lost by VS-8 that day, and it crashed, killing both the pilot and his radioman. For his contribution to victory at Midway, the radio-gunner was posthumously awarded the Air Medal.

(DE-694: d. 1,400; l. 306'; b. 36'10"; dr. 9'5: (mean); s. 24 k.; cpl. 186; a. 3 3", 4 1.1", 8 20 mm., 2 dct., 8 dcp., 1 dcp., (hh.); cl. *Buckley*)

Bunch (DE-694) was laid down on 22 February 1943 at Bay City, Mich., by the Defoe Shipbuilding Co.; launched on 29 May 1943; sponsored by Mrs. Kenneth C. Bunch, the widow of the late Radioman 1st Class Bunch; and commissioned at the U.S. Naval Station, New Orleans, LA, on 21 August 1943, Lt. Comdr. Alfred A. Campbell, USNR, in command.

After fitting out, *Bunch* departed Southwest Pass on 12 September 1943. She proceeded via Key West, FL, and carried out her shakedown training out of Bermuda until 15 October, on which date she sailed for Boston. Following post-shakedown availability at the Boston Navy Yard, the ship proceeded via the Cape Cod Canal and Newport, RI, to New York.

On 1 November 1943, *Bunch* commenced her escort work, as she shepherded the New York section of convoy UGS-23 out of coastal waters. That same day, she obtained a sonar contact and attacked with two "hedgehog" patterns on what she later evaluated as a "non-submarine" contact. Released the following day, *Bunch* proceeded to Hampton Roads, reporting soon thereafter to Commander, Task Force (TF) 23 for duty. Over the next eight months, *Bunch* made six round-trip voyages across the Atlantic and back, escorting convoys between New York and Londonderry, interspersing that work with refresher training at Casco Bay, Maine, and availabilities at Boston.

From 28 July to 12 October 1944, *Bunch*—reclassified as APD-79 on 31 July 1944—underwent conversion to a high speed transport at the Naval Frontier Base, Tompkinsville, Staten Island. The yard period was not without incident, though, as during that time, on 8 August 1944, *Bunch* suffered slight damage when she was rammed by the gasoline tanker *Ammonusuc* (AOG-23).

Fitted out as a flagship, she departed New York on 13 October 1944. Steaming first to Hampton Roads, and thence to Annapolis, *Bunch* briefly visited the latter port before she commenced training operations in Chesapeake Bay on 23 October. Between that date and 10 December, *Bunch* trained pre-commissioning crews out of Norfolk; men from 11 other high speed transports received instruction in her during that period.

Following an availability at the St. Helena Annex, *Bunch* then departed the Convoy Escort Piers at the Naval Operating Base, Norfolk, on 20 December 1944. In company with sistership *Hopping* (APD-51), *Bunch* escorted the transports *Anne Arundel* (AP-76), *Dorothea L. Dix* (AP-67) and *Lyon* (AP-20), to the Canal Zone, arriving on Christmas Day 1944. She transited the Panama Canal the following day, reporting for duty to the Commander in Chief, Pacific Fleet, and ultimately reached San Diego on 3 January 1945.

Underway for Pearl Harbor on 9 January 1945, she arrived there on the 15th. *Bunch* then exercised at Maalea Bay, Maui, with Underwater Demolition Teams (UDT) 18 and 21. After embarking UDT-21 at Maalea Bay, *Bunch* sailed for Eniwetok on 14 February, arriving at her destination on the 22d. Fueling from *Gemsbok* (IX-117), the high speed transport sailed the following day in the screen for a convoy, some of which was bound for the Western Carolines, and some for the Philippines.

With the detachment of the Ulithi-bound portion of the convoy on 28 February, *Bunch* screened the remainder to Leyte, arriving on 4 March. After taking on board ammunition and stores, and fueling from *Jaquar* (IX-120), she returned to San Pedro Bay on the 6th. The following day, Comdr. Draper Kauffman, operations officer for Commander, Underwater Demolition Teams, Pacific (ComUDTPac), came on board and briefed UDT-21's officers and men

about what lay ahead. *Bunch's* men, her war diary notes, consequently spent the rest of the day "thumbing through reams of operation(s) orders..."

On 9 March, *Bunch* weighed anchor and stood out for Homonhon Island, Leyte, where she and seven other high speed transports exercised in company with the ComUDTPac flagship *Gilmer* (APD-11) and several LCI(G)s and LCI(M)s. Completing those exercises at 1745, *Bunch* and her sister ships returned to their anchorage where they remained until 13 March.

Designated as flagship for Commander, Underwater Demolition Group "Baker," and of Commander, Task Group (TG) 52.13, Capt. Roy D. Williams, the high speed transport, combat-loaded with a demolition team as were five of her sister ships, was joined by two other high speed transports that carried spare demolition equipment and explosives but did not have embarked teams. She took part in landing rehearsals on the 14th, and, in company with the five high speed transports in her division that had embarked teams, conducted tactical exercises in Leyte Gulf the following morning, after which time TG 52.13 exercised at lowering and recovering the ships' LCPRs off Cabugan Grande Island, in rough seas and a driving rain.

After her men had enjoyed "general recreation and beer parties" at Cabugan Grande Island on the 16th and 17th, *Bunch* and TG 52.13 proceeded to San Pedro Bay. Fueling from *Big Horn* (AO-45) and provisioning from *Hydrus* (AKA-128) on the 18th, the warship embarked five Army observers the same day. After a final conference on the upcoming landings on the 20th, *Bunch* sailed for Kerama Retto on the 21st, screening Transport Group "Easy," Western Islands Attack Force (TG 51.1).

On 26 March 1945, *Bunch* went to general quarters at 0330, as she prepared to enter Transport Area "Easy," five miles west of Kube Shima, in the Kerama Retto group of the Ryukyus. Detached at 0500, *Bunch* and *Hopping* escorted the attack transport *Natrona* (APA-214) to her rendezvous with the control boat, *SC-1328*, in Area "Jig." Released from that task at 0600, *Bunch* and *Hopping* proceeded to stations screening the transport area. Topping off with fuel from the attack cargo ship *Wyandot* (AKA-92) that morning, the warship spent the remainder of the day screening the troopships.

At 0130 the following morning, *Bunch* fired on a single enemy plane, which soon disappeared out of range. Securing from battle stations at 0210, the high speed transport nevertheless remained on the alert; at 0338 she opened fire with her 40-millimeter battery on an enemy plane approaching from the port quarter. Although the ship went to general quarters, no attack developed, and she stood down at 0400. Released from the transport screen later in the day, *Bunch* left TG 52.13's formation early in the first dog watch (1608) for a high speed observation sweep of the objective beaches (White 1, 2, and 3) on Okinawa. Owing to the fact that the waters off the beaches had not yet been swept for mines, and that the heavy fire support units lay on the outer edge of the unswept area, *Bunch* could not close to less than five miles of the objective. She retired from the scene at 1637 to permit the other ships of TG 52.13 to make their individual sweeps.

After spending the night with the fire support night retirement unit, *Bunch* went to general quarters for the dawn alert, at 0555 on 28 March. From her ringside seat, the fast transport observed *Henry A. Wiley* (DM-29) splash two "Vals" (Aichi D3A carrier bombers) and a suicide plane attempt to crash the nearby *Crosley* (APD-87). *Bunch* secured from general quarters at 0655, and after being detached from screening the night retirement group, proceeded to screen the fire support units as they lay off the main invasion beaches. She assumed patrol station R-16 off Mae Shima.

Lookouts sighted enemy planes at extreme range at 2314 on 28 March, off *Bunch's* starboard beam. Going to general quarters at that point, the high speed transport commenced firing on what she identified as a "Betty" (Mitsubishi G4M twin-engined bomber) at 0110 on the 29th; the plane splashed by gunfire from the ships astern, *Bunch* secured from battle stations soon thereafter. Going back to general quarters for the dawn alert at 0525, *Bunch* spotted planes at 0605 but did not fire owing to the extreme range. Action soon came closer to home, however, for just seven minutes later, her lookouts and SL radar operator, picked up a small boat, 2,200 yards off the port bow. *Bunch* went to full speed and altered course to investigate; after establishing the boat's enemy character, she opened fire with .50-caliber, 20- and 40-millimeter batteries, and destroyed it, 500 yards away.

At 0631, *Bunch* detected a second suicide motor boat—later judged to have come from Mae Shima, which was still in the hands of the enemy—bearing down upon the ship. Machine gun fire from the high speed transport stopped the craft dead in the water, however, and its crew jettisoned the explosive charge, which immediately blew up. *Bunch* altered course to pick up the crew of the suicide boat and take them prisoner, but a nearby destroyer "eradicated" both boat and swimmers with a well-placed five-inch burst. After making a report of the incident over the low-frequency voice radio (TBS), *Bunch* resumed her station

patrolling until detached at 0730 to await word to carry out her pre-landing task.

Since a reconnaissance of the "White" beaches had showed that no demolition work would be required, *Bunch* retired to seaward and resumed screening; detached from that at 0645 on 30 March, the high speed transport steamed toward the "Orange" beaches. Lying 5,800 yards off the objective, *Bunch* put her boats in the water at 0905 and retired to a patrol area to await the return of her craft and her swimmers, while LCI(G)s provided close fire support for the unfolding demolition operations. Detonating her charge at 1137, *Bunch* recovered all of her boats at 1225. After standing by for further orders, she then transported passengers from the amphibious command ship *Estes* (AGC-12) to designated high speed transports, whence they would be transferred to ships of the main northern and southern attack forces early the following morning. Completing her assigned task at 1700, she cleared Kerama Retto at 1930 and assumed patrol station R-7.

Steering figure-eight courses, *Bunch* was on screening station soon after the mid watch commenced, at 0117, when she picked up word of an incoming air raid. Reducing her speed to 10 knots to reduce an observable wake, she observed an enemy twin-engined bomber pass along the port side, some 150 yards away. *Bunch* opened fire with her .50-caliber and 40-millimeter gun batteries and went to general quarters but no attack occurred. Ultimately, at 0550, *Bunch* was relieved on station and proceeded with TG 52.13 to transfer a UDT-21 passenger to the attack transport *Mendocino* (APA-100). She steamed thence in company with *Crosley* and *Loy* (APD-56) to Kerama Retto to fuel; once there, *Bunch* topped-off from *Warhawk* (AP-168). She remained at anchor throughout the night, her engines on half-hour standby and an armed watch alerted to keep a lookout for suicide swimmers.

Underway at 0254 on 1 April 1945, *Bunch* cleared the western anchorage at Kerama Retto with TG 52.13, and proceeded east toward the transport area off the northern and southern Hagushi beaches. With the dissolution of the formation at 0500, she steamed to the line of departure to transfer UDT-21 liaison personnel to the "White" beach control vessel, *PC-578*. Passing south of the transport area and north of the LST area, *Bunch* accomplished the transfer at 0616, and then rapidly cleared the area to keep clear of the waves of landing craft forming for the run-in to the beach.

The warship screened the transports for the remainder of the first day of the Okinawa landings, 1 April, and after being relieved of that duty at dawn the following morning, proceeded toward "White" beach to allow Lt. E.P. Clayton, commanding officer of UDT-21, to confer with the beachmaster regarding post-assault demolition needs. Leaving the beachhead area at 1500, *Bunch* then proceeded toward night screening station A-20.

At 1839, around dusk, however, observing a small convoy under attack by five enemy planes, she went to general quarters. *Bunch* took two of them under fire despite the fact that they were just out of range. Once crashed the attack transport *Henrico* (APA-45), the other started a run on *Bunch* but turned away when fired upon by the ship and dropped a bomb at *Dickerson* (APD-21). Missing with its ordnance, however, the same plane returned and crashed *Dickerson*.

The fire was gaining considerable headway as *Bunch* maneuvered to go to help *Dickerson*, but by 1930 was "fairly well under control." Seeing that she was "receiving considerable structural damage" alongside the stricken ship, *Bunch* pulled away, sending a fire and rescue party over, however, in one of her LCPRs. Swimmers from UDT-21, utilizing their rubber boats, had in the meantime rescued many of *Dickerson's* survivors that had gone over the side to escape the flames. *Bunch's* captain credited UDT-21's officers and men as being "instrumental in saving many lives."

Joined by men from *Crosley*, *Bunch's* fire and rescue party succeeded in getting gasoline-driven handy-billies in operation to battle the fires on board *Dickerson*, which had broken out afresh. *Bunch*, which had taken on board the damaged vessel's casualties, passed a towline and three fire hoses across to her, and began to tow her, while men cut away *Dickerson's* boats on her port side to lessen the list. Although the salvagers had again made headway against the fires, they broke out with renewed vigor after the towline and hoses parted. A freshening wind made the matter of getting another hawser across difficult. Eventually, *Arikara* (ATF-98) arrived on the scene, took *Dickerson* in tow and extinguished her fires, and brought her to Kerama Retto. *Bunch's* fire and rescue party returned to their own ship at 0320 on 3 April.

After screening *Arikara* and *Dickerson* to the logistics anchorage at Kerama Retto, *Bunch* transferred the six officers and 55 enlisted men from the damaged high speed transport to *PCE-852* by 1000 on 3 April, for further transfer to a larger ship and hospitalization. She then returned to station A-20 where she operated for the remainder of the day, observing little enemy air activity. *Dickerson*, however, deemed too badly damaged to be restored to service, was taken out to sea and sunk the next day.

Late on the afternoon of 4 April, *Bunch* steamed to the southern anchorage at Kerama Retto, and rendezvoused there with *Gilmer*. On that day, *Bunch* became flagship for all high speed transports present in the Okinawa area, Capt. Williams becoming Commander, TG 52.11. At 1600, she departed Kerama Retto, and rendezvoused with *Estes*, east of Okinawa. Following a conference on board the command ship, *Bunch* screened her for a time until being detached to take screening station A-17, 20 miles south of Mae Shima.

Detached from that duty at 1045 on 5 May, *Bunch* sped to rendezvous with *Estes*, and at 1230 took station in the screen for that command ship, the battleship *West Virginia* (BB-48), and *Arikara*. While screening the Eastern Islands Bombardment Group, *Bunch* operated in *Estes'* vicinity to afford Capt. Williams and his chief of staff, Cdr. Kauffman, a chance to supervise UDT reconnaissance and demolition operations at the eastern islands and in Nakagusuku Wan (later Buckner Bay).

Bunch maintained her duties in the screen into the 6th, until ordered to rendezvous with *Eldorado* (AGC-11) off the western beaches of Okinawa, to transport flag officers for a conference on board that ship. During that conference, *Bunch* remained in the vicinity.

At 1605, the high speed transport received a report of enemy planes in the area; seeing antiaircraft fire blossoming in the sky off her port quarter, *Bunch* spotted a "Zeke" (Mitsubishi A6M5 Type 00 carrier fighter) off her starboard quarter at long range. Her starboard 40-millimeter guns opened up at a range of 700 yards, disintegrated the tail of the "Zeke" and splashed it, 100 yards off the ship's port beam.

After transporting flag officer passengers from *Eldorado* back to *Estes* during the first dog watch, *Bunch* resumed screening. She remained with *Estes* on the 7th, transporting Comdr. Kauffman to that ship at one point in the day and then screening the amphibious command ship during her night retirement. Released from the screen at 1000 on the 8th, she then transported Capt. Williams and his staff to a conference on board Vice Admiral Richmond K. Turner's flagship, *Eldorado*. After fueling from *Saranac* (AO-74), *Bunch* picked up Capt. Williams from *Biscayne* (AGC-18) before taking up a screening station. Warned to expect heavy suicide attacks the following day, *Bunch* delivered staff officers to a conference on board *Panamint* (AGC-13) on the 9th.

The following day, 10 May, with UDT-21 idle and awaiting operational assignment, *Bunch* transferred it to *Appling* (APA-58) to avoid "needless exposure to enemy action" while the ship served as a screening vessel. She operated on auxiliary radar picket station during the day on the 10th.

That same day, having received orders alerting her to her scheduled participation in operations to capture Ie Shima, *Bunch* proceeded to *Panamint* and dropped off Capt. Williams and Comdr. Kauffman for a conference relative to the operation, before she reembarked UDT-21. Planning and preparation for the Ie Shima operation continued on the 12th, and on the 13th, *Bunch* set course for the objective.

She lay off the southern beaches at 0830 on 13 April 1945, so that Capt. Williams could direct the reconnaissance within 6,000 yards of the beach. *Bunch* completed her mission by 1054, when she recovered her boats and men; the latter reported encountering only enemy small arms fire in the course of their work. That night, Williams and his staff attended a conference on board *Panamint* off the Hagushi beaches, Okinawa. Returning the following morning (14 April), *Bunch* and UDT-21 resumed their pre-invasion work at Ie Shima, again encountering small arms fire in so doing; that night, the ship retired to Okinawa, and another conference, that time on board *Eldorado*.

Underway late in the forenoon watch on 15 April, *Bunch* fueled from *Taluga* (AO-62) and then returned to her anchorage off Okinawa. With enemy aircraft reported in the vicinity at 1830, *Bunch* went to battle stations and opened fire with her 5-inch and 40-millimeter battery, helping to splash an enemy plane off the beach. Securing from general quarters at 2000, she manned battle stations an hour later; sporadic enemy air activity kept the ship in that state of readiness until 2220. Japanese attacks on the airfield at Yontan, visible from the ship, continued throughout the night.

Bunch returned to the waters off Ie Shima the following morning, disembarking some of UDT-21's men to the beach control vessel, *PC-1603*, so that they could report to the beachmaster for use by the wave commanders in guiding the assault boats to their respective beaches. She then stood out to screen the transports. At 0811, she went to battle stations as she picked up reports over the TBS of radar picket destroyers to the northwest battling heavy enemy aircraft attacks. At 0935, *Bunch* spotted two "Kates" (Nakajima B5N Type 97 carrier attack planes) approaching the transport area at low speed. One approached from the northeast and *Bunch* took it under fire, and joined the nearby transports in splashing the attacker soon thereafter. Antiaircraft fire drove off the second "Kate" to the south, where a "Corsair" shot it down.

On 17 and 18 April, *Bunch* supported UDT-21's operations, retiring nightly to Okinawa to anchor; on the latter date, enemy shell fire compelled the ship to shift berths out of range, while demolition of the beach proceeded space. Postassault demolition work by UDT-21 occupied the ship on the 19th and 20th, and she wrapped up her work at Ie Shima on the 21st. Considerable enemy air activity occurred in her vicinity during that period, but no Japanese planes came within gun range.

Bunch proceeded to Kerama Retto at the end of the forenoon watch on the 23d; after fueling from *Cuyama* (AO-3), the high speed transport returned to the Hagushi beaches for night screening duties. She patrolled station B-25 on the 24th and into the 25th, until detached at 1400 on the latter day to proceed to rendezvous with *Goodhue* (APA-107) at Kerama Retto. Following that, during which time she received orders covering her departure from the Okinawa area, she anchored off the Hagushi beaches for the night.

At 0700 on 26 April, *Bunch* got underway, and rendezvoused with a convoy off the western beaches of Okinawa, whence she sailed for Ulithi. She escorted this 19-ship convoy of transports to its destination, anchoring at Ulithi at 1305 on 30 April. After provisioning, *Bunch* pushed on for Guam on 1 May, and reached her destination the following morning. From 3 to 17 May, *Bunch*, having debarked UDT-21, enjoyed an availability; ship's work permitting, her crew partook of daily recreation: beer parties, swimming parties, and baseball games.

Bunch sailed for Okinawa on the 19th, and reached Hagushi on the 22d. After an unsuccessful attempt at fueling from *Suamico* (AO-49) on the 23d, *Bunch* remained at anchor off Hagushi until the morning of the 25th, at which time she steamed to Kerama Retto for four days' availability to effect repairs to her sonar, which became inoperable during the voyage from Guam to Okinawa. Receiving orders for her next operation, the assault on Iheya Shima, on the 30th, she proceeded "on duty assigned" at the close of the first watch on the 31st.

Following the postponement of the operations against Iheya Shima, because of foggy weather, *Bunch* fueled from *Enoree* (AO-69) on 1 June, and then briefly screened that ship, returning thence to Hagushi. Underway the following morning, *Bunch* took part, in a standby function, in the assault on Iheya Shima; inclement weather and an excellent combat air patrol (CAP) took care of enemy planes, and *Bunch* remained at anchor during the night and forenoon. The calculated tracks of two approaching typhoons, though, compelled the assault group to get underway and stand out, eventually steaming in the lee of the Motobu peninsula, anchoring in the small bay directly north of that area. While the weather disturbed the wind and sea only slightly, it limited Japanese air activity.

Returning to Iheya Shima with the assault group the following morning, *Bunch* got underway for the northern part of the island, ~~presumably meaning~~, ~~directing her to return whence she had come. Arriving~~, only to receive orders ~~directing her to return whence she had come. Arriving~~ After then remaining at anchor through out the night, *Bunch* carried out a reconnaissance of the northern beaches, finding their gradient to be such that the landing of heavy equipment could be accomplished without any demolition work by the UDTs. Escorting a coastal convoy to Hagushi on 7 June, *Bunch* steamed to Kerama Retto on the 8th, where she fueled from *Brazos* (AO-4).

Assigned next to the assault on Aguni Shima, *Bunch* sailed at 0115 on 9 June; during the passage in the stygian darkness, she heard an enemy plane. Her gun captains showed "excellent judgement" in withholding fire until it was directly overhead, not allowing the Japanese to ride in on the tracers and possibly crash the ship. The landings having been accomplished with little or no resistance, *Bunch* joined *Poe(R)-855* in escorting a small convoy, comprised of *Oak Hill* (LSD-7) and *LST-95*, back to Hagushi.

On 11 June, *Bunch* operated with the survey ship *Pathfinder* (AGS-1) in conducting a reconnaissance of Naha harbor, followed by the necessary charting and demolition operations. During the course of those evolutions the following day, she suffered damage from debris thrown against the ship by her propeller wash in shallow waters, nicking the tip of one screw. She remained anchored the rest of the day in support of the ongoing demolition work at Ie Shima. On the 14th, she fueled from *Chicopee* (AO-34), after which time she proceeded to Kerama Retto for logistics.

Between 15 and 22 June, *Bunch* continued demolition work at Ie Shima. Except for a trip back to Hagushi on the 19th for more explosives, she remained at Ie Shima, at that task, American forces in that area undergoing intermittent air attacks nightly. Excellent smoke coverage left *Bunch* no opportunity to take enemy planes under fire.

Bunch next participated in the assault on Kume Shima on 26 June, the landings taking place in the more sheltered waters on the southeast part of the island. Encountering "no observable enemy opposition," after UDT-21 had guided the LSTs assigned to the operation into the bay, and equipment had been discharged, the high speed transport returned to Hagushi. She then returned to Ie

Shima soon thereafter to complete the demolition work she had begun several days previously.

At 0950 on 1 July 1945, *Bunch* sailed from Okinawa, screening *Auburn* (AGC-10); the following day she exploded a mine, "expending considerable .30 cal. ammunition" in doing so. Making landfall at Saipan at noon on 5 July, *Bunch* received orders from *Auburn* on 9 July to proceed independently to Eniwetok and thence to Pearl Harbor. Reaching Eniwetok the same day, she fueled from *Meredosia* (IX-98) and cleared the Marshalls by the end of the afternoon watch, bound for the Hawaiian Islands.

Reaching Pearl Harbor on the 16th, *Bunch* fueled, took on provisions, and sailed late the following afternoon, proceeding via Maui, where she exchanged demolition gear. She made port at Oceanside, Calif., early on the afternoon of 24 July, where she disembarked UDT-21 and its gear; within an hour, the ship had shifted berths to the Standard Shipbuilding Corp., San Pedro, and commenced a period of yard repairs and an overhaul. The end of the war with Japan in midAugust found *Bunch* in the midst of that yard period.

After fueling, provisioning, and unloading UDT explosives preparatory to sailing for the forward areas, *Bunch* departed San Diego on 6 September with five other APDs. During the voyage to Pearl Harbor, they conducted group tactical exercises, and individual emergency and general drills with ships steaming in regular war cruising condition. At 0130 on 10 September, *Bunch's* air search radar picked up emergency signals, and she altered course to the north-northwest to investigate. She and her sister ships spread out into a scouting line to cover a larger search area; they maintained that routine until Commander, Hawaiian Sea Frontier, informed them that the plane that had been having difficulties had reached base safely. *Bunch* reached Pearl Harbor on the afternoon of 12 September.

The following day, *Bunch* reported to Commander, Mine Force, Pacific (ComMinPac) for duty; soon thereafter, she began loading five LCPRs equipped for shallow water moored minesweeping and embarked men assigned temporary duty in connection with the projected sweeping operations. She sailed on 15 September for Eniwetok, and reached that island on the 22d. Underway on the 23d after fueling from *YO-182*, *Bunch* arrived off Okinawa on the 28th, rendezvousing with *Bibb* (AGC-31) off Buckner Bay, and formed part of a typhoon sortie group. She remained at sea with that group until 1 October, when she dropped anchor in Buckner Bay.

After loading minesweeping cargo and obtaining fuel and stores, *Bunch* sailed for Chinese waters on 6 October. Reaching Shanghai on 10 October, the high speed transport unloaded cargo to be distributed to motor minesweepers (YMS) and minesweepers (AM). She also underwent voyage repairs while her crew enjoyed recreation and liberty in the fabled far eastern city. Underway for Okinawa on 16 October, she returned to Buckner Bay on the 18th.

Over the next several days, *Bunch* assisted in the salvage of ships that had been swept ashore in previous typhoons that had ravaged Okinawa within the past weeks, as well as loaded additional cargo for her return to Shanghai. During this time (19 to 25 October), all of the ship's LCPRs were utilized in the salvage operations, after which time they were again fitted out for moored type minesweeping operations in the Shanghai area. Underway for Shanghai on 26 October, *Bunch* reached her destination on the 28th. She spent the rest of October and the first week of November undergoing voyage repairs alongside *Dixie* (AD-14).

On 8 November 1945, *Bunch* departed Shanghai for Hangchow Bay, whence she operated until 14 November along with three YMSs and two submarine chasers (PC), as a minesweeping and mine disposal unit. During that time, she and her consorts cleared a lane twelve miles long and one mile wide of Japanese mines. The operation netted five of the horned spheres destroyed. After the second day of sweeping, however, the unit abandoned the use of LCPRs as minesweepers because of the wear and tear on the boats; the prevailing four to six knot currents made small boat operations slow and hazardous to the boats. One YMS, *Bunch's* captain wrote in her war diary, could complete sweeping her assigned area in eight hours, covering more than four LCPRs had done in just two days! He concluded that while "the small boat moored minesweepers should be valuable in restricted areas and [in] very shallow water, they would be "impractical and relatively ineffective in water where other and larger vessels can sweep."

Having completed her assigned mission, *Bunch* departed Hangchow Bay on 15 November 1945, and after obtaining onward routing, sailed for Okinawa on the 18th. She reported to Commander, Minecraft, Okinawa on 20 November, at Buckner Bay, and after loading cargo, got underway for Kiirun, Formosa, on the 26th. She reached her destination on the following day, and remained there through the end of the month.

Underway on 1 December 1945 for Shanghai, *Bunch* escorted *YMS-72* to that port for hull repairs. The ships encountered gale force winds and heavy seas en route, but by modifying course and speed accordingly, weathered the voyage successfully. *Bunch* remained at Shanghai until the morning of 6 December, when she sailed to return to Kiirun, steaming in company with six YMSs and one LCS. After making port at her destination on the 9th, she steamed to the naval port of Takao, Formosa, on the 11th. She discharged cargo there until the 12th, when the ship got underway and returned to her former berth at Kiirun.

Bunch put to sea on 16 December, and took up a position off Kiirun Harbor, to render navigational assistance to a group of YMSs sweeping the approaches. During the day, she lay-to, about 20 miles north of the harbor entrance, directing the movements of the sweepers by radar and voice radio. That procedure, *Bunch's* captain reported, permitted minesweeping operations to continue even in periods of reduced visibility.

Completing that task on 18 December, the high speed transport sailed the following morning for Shanghai in company with the minesweepers *Velocity* (AM-128) and *Threat* (AM-124), each with a landing ship in tow *(LC (FF)-45* and *LCS(L)-22*, respectively), *YMS-259* and *LCS(L)-58*. *Bunch* served as convoy guide for the passage, which was undertaken to permit the two craft in tow to receive repairs, and "to return to port for the holiday season those vessels...no longer needed at Kiirun." During the passage, *Threat* spotted a mine; *Bunch* detached *LCS(L)-58* to investigate; the latter sank the mine with gunfire.

Bunch and her charges reached Shanghai on 22 December, and the high speed transport spent the remainder of the month at various buoys at that city, "singing carols and observing holiday routine." On 2 January 1946, *Bunch* got underway, and after fueling from *Kennebec* (AO-36), remained alongside that ship until the following day, when the high speed transport stood downriver, bound for Taichow, China.

During the war, some 1,936 mines had been sown in the East China Sea; quite naturally, in the wake of hostilities a major task remained to be performed, that of sweeping those mines to allow seaborne commerce to resume in the region. As part of that effort, *Bunch* operated with *YMS-338*, *YMS-329*, and *YMS-366* in Taichow Bay, before she shifted her area of operations to Wenchow Bay on 6 January, where she provided those ships with fresh water and fuel; she plotted the minesweeping operations by radar on the 7th and 8th. Returning to Taichow Bay the following morning, *Bunch* and her consorts carried out sweeping operations there until sailing for Hong Kong that afternoon.

Bunch had to take *YMS-366* in tow on 11 January, and brought the crippled minesweeper—that had had difficulty with fuel oil pressure—into Hong Kong on the morning of the 13th. Three days later, the ship unloaded minesweeping gear into an LCM; on the 17th, after fueling from *Kaskaskia* (AO-27), the high speed transport sailed for Okinawa.

Reaching Buckner Bay during the forenoon watch on the 20th, *Bunch* soon began seeing the separation of men who had earned enough "points" for discharge and transferred from the ship to begin the voyage home. After loading minesweeping gear, the high speed transport sailed for Japanese waters on the 25th, reaching Sasebo the following day. Pushing on for Wakayama on the 29th, she reached her destination during the first dog watch on the 30th. Shifting to Kobe on 2 February, *Bunch* embarked eight officer and 75 enlisted passengers for transportation to the United States over the days that preceded her departure on 21 February 1946.

Stopping at Eniwetok only long enough to fuel (27-28 February), and at Pearl Harbor (6-8 March), *Bunch* reached San Francisco at the close of the forenoon watch on 14 March. Steaming to San Diego Bay on the 17th, she ran speed trials on the 18th, and moved to the Naval Repair Base at San Diego on the 20th, where she remained until decommissioned on 31 May 1946. Placed in reserve in July 1947, *Bunch* never returned to active service. Struck from the Naval Vessel Register on 1 April 1964, she was bid upon by Zidell Explorations, Inc., a scrap firm, who desired to defer scrapping, though, so that the ship could be converted to a barge. That particular sale, however, apparently did not go through, and the ship's hulk was sold for scrap subsequently.

Bunch was awarded two battle stars for her World War II service.

USS *CALCATERRA* (DE-390)

Born 7 April 1920 at Escalon, Calif., Herbert A. Calcaterra enlisted in the Navy 14 December 1939. Motor Machinist's Mate First Class Calcaterra was commended 7 July 1942 for his performance as a member of the crew of *Pompano* (SS-181), and was awarded the Silver Star Medal posthumously for conspicuous gallantry as a member of a 3" gun crew until fatally wounded during an action against an armed enemy patrol ship 4 September 1942.

(DE-390: dp. 1,200; l. 306'; b. 36'7"; dr. 8'7"; s. 21 k.; cpl. 186; a. 3 3", 3 21" tt., 8 dcp., 1 dcp.(hh.), 2 dct.; cl. *Edsall*)

Calcaterra (DE-390) was launched 16 August 1943 by Brown Shipbuild-

ing Co., Houston, Tex.; sponsored by Mrs. G.M. Stites; commissioned 17 November 1943, Commander H.J. Wuensch, USCG, in command; and reported to the Atlantic Fleet.

Assigned to the vital duty of escorting convoys between the United States and the Mediterranean, *Calcaterra* made eight round trips between 13 February 1944 and 10 June 1945. The ships she guarded provided the men and equipment which insured the success of the invasions of Italy and southern France. Twice the escort vessel met the challenge of enemy opposition when she depth charged a suspected submarine contact and fired on two aircraft. Her alert action helped prevent damage or loss to the ships under convoy.

On 9 July 1945 *Calcaterra* headed for the Pacific to tackle a new job, but the war ended shortly before her arrival at Pearl Harbor. She lifted passengers back to the west coast, then sailed on to the Atlantic. *Calcaterra* was placed out of commission in reserve at Green Cove Springs, Fla., 1 May 1946.

Reclassified DER-390, 28 October 1954, *Calcaterra* was converted to a radar picket ship at Norfolk and recommissioned 12 September 1955. Based on Newport, the radar picket ship has almost continuously served in the violent weather of the North Atlantic to maintain her link in the extension of the Distant Early Warning system. Except for exercises with the fleet in the Atlantic and Caribbean, and a cruise to Europe (August-October 1958), *Calcaterra* continued this duty through 1960.

Ship's log (approximately 125,000 miles): 12/5/43-1/6/44 Bermuda Shakedown; 1/8/44-1/25/44 Charleston, SC; 1/26/44-1/27/44 Norfolk, VA; 1/29/44-2/3/44 Tampa, FL; 2/8/44-2/10/44 New York (Bayonne, NJ); 2/11/44-2/12/44 Norfolk, VA; 3/3/44-3/7/44 Casablanca; 3/24/44-4/4/44 New York (Bayonne, NJ); 4/5/44-4/8/44 Portland, ME; 4/11/44-4/12/44 Norfolk, VA; 5/3/44-5/11/44 Bizerte; 5/30/44-6/10/44 New York (Bayonne); 6/12/44-6/20/44 Portland, ME; 6/22/44-6/23/44 Norfolk, VA; 7/14/44-7/20/44 Bizerte; 8/4/44-8/19/44 Brooklyn, NY; 8/21/44-8/28/44 Portland, ME; 8/31/44-9/1/44 Norfolk; 9/22/44-9/23/44 Bizerte; 9/23/44-9/27/44 Palermo; 10/18/44-10/28/44 Brooklyn; 10/31/44-11/6/44 Portland, ME; 11/7/44-11/10/44 Staten Island; 11/27/44-12/2/44 Mer El Kibir (Algeria); 12/21/44-1/1/45 Brooklyn; 1/3/44-1/5/45 Montauck LI (Block Island); 1/6/45-1/7/45 Staten Island; 1/28/45-2/11/45 Mer El Kibir (Algeria); 2/19/45-3/2/45 Brooklyn; 3/3/45-3/6/45 Montauck LI (Block Island); 3/25/45-4/2/45 Mer El Kibir (Algeria); 4/21/45-4/27/45 Brooklyn; 4/28/45-5/3/45 Casco Bay, ME; 5/5/45-5/7/45 Staten Island; 5/23/45-6/1/45 Mer El Kibir & Oran; 6/5/45-6/5/45 Azores; 6/10/45-7/5/45 Bayonne, NJ; 7/6/45-7/9/45 Brooklyn; 7/13/45-7/15/45 Guantanimo Bay VI; 7/17/45-7/17/45 Culebra VI; 7/19/45-07/26/45 Cuba; 7/28/45-7/29/45 Coco Solo, PA; 7/29/45-7/29/45 Panama Canal; 8/7/45-8/12/45 San Diego, CA; 8/18/45-9/3/45 Pearl Harbor; 9/19/45-9/11/45 Los Angeles, CA; 9/19/45-9/20/45 Coco Solo, PA; 9/26/45 New York; 5/1/46 Green Cove Springs, FL (Mothballs).

USS *CAVALLARO* (APD-128)

The USS *Cavallaro* APD-128 built in Bay City, MI was commissioned 13 March 1945 in New Orleans, LA. After an eventful trip down the Mississippi River shakedown at Guantanamo Bay, Cuba and short shakedown availability at Norfolk, VA then proceeded her passage through the Panama Canal and reported to the Commander in Chief of the Pacific Fleet on 13 May exactly two months after commission proceeding via San Diego in company with other APDs. She arrived in Pearl Harbor on 30 May and reported to the administrative commander amphibious forces Pacific in the Maui, Oahu area. She received two weeks of special training, departing from Pearl Harbor on 13 June. She acted as escort to a large convoy to Ulithi, Caroline Islands by way of Eniwetok in the Marshall Islands. On arrival in Ulithi she was assigned to escort convoys running between Okinawa and Ulithi. These runs continued for two months without incident except for the seasonal typhoons, characteristic of this area, the almost inevitable air raids at Okinawa and infrequent sound contacts on 25 August 1945. She was assigned duty as escort to the *Auburn* AGC-10 the flagship of Vice Admiral Harry Hill, commander Fifth Amphibious Force. This assignment took her to Manila to prepare for the invasion of the Japanese homeland island of Kyushu, and Honshu. Weighing anchor on the 14th of September. She proceeded with the USS *Auburn* with Gen. Krueger commanding General 6th Army and Vice Admiral Harry Hill aboard to the major Japanese Naval Base at Sasebo having been accomplished on 21st and 22nd. The *Cavallaro* and the *Auburn* proceeded to Nagasaki, Kyushu and Wakayama Honshu upon complete occupation of these areas the *Cavallaro* still escorting the *Auburn* proceeded to Tokyo 6 October 1945. One week later the *Cavallaro* left the *Auburn* and headed for Pearl Harbor where she received orders to return to San Diego for decommissioning and put into the mothball fleet at a later date. She was transferred to the South Korean navy. As of this writing she is still in service.

USS *COOK* (APD-130)

USS *Cook* (APD-130), a high speed transport, was named in honor of Second Lieutenant Andrew Fred Cook Jr., United States Marine Corps Reserve, and Sergeant Dallas Harry Cook, United States Marine Corps. Lieutenant Cook was awarded a Navy Cross for attempting to destroy an enemy machine gun nest on Guadalcanal, Solomon Islands, in which he lost his life. Sergeant Cook's heroic death in his efforts to evacuate comrades from the beach of enemy held Makin Island, was similarly recognized by the award of a Navy Cross.

USS *Cook's* keel was laid May 7, 1944 in the yards of Defoe Shipbuilding Company, Bay City, Michigan, and she was launched August 26 of the same year. A novel feature of the ship's construction was the building of the hull upside down and rolling it over to complete it. On the February 17, 1945 *Cook* departed from the builder's yard for the long trip through the Great Lakes and the Mississippi river to New Orleans. Much of the trip was through heavy winter ice which made progress extremely slow and caused some slight damage. Finally, early in April 1945, the ship arrived at New Orleans, Louisiana, and commenced fitting out at the U.S. Naval Repair Base, Algiers.

On April 25, 1945 USS *Cook* was placed in commission at New Orleans with Lieutenant Commander Drayton N. Hamilton, USNR, of Birmingham, Alabama, as commanding officer. Lieutenant Leonard R. Hardy, USNR, of Highlands, New Jersey, was the executive officer. The next two weeks were spent loading supplies and conducting tests and on May 9, 1945 *Cook* departed from U.S. Naval Frontier Base, Burrwood, Louisiana, for Guantanamo Bay, Cuba, for shakedown.

The shakedown period was a trying one for all hands and audible sigh of relief could be heard when on June 1 *Cook*, now adjudged to be a fighting ship, departed from Guantanamo Bay for Norfolk, Virginia, where she arrived on June 4. After two weeks of amphibious training, shore bombardment and post-

shakedown repairs, *Cook* finally got a taste of the duty for which she was designed. On June 19, 1945 she departed from Norfolk for Colon, Canal Zone, carrying 100 Army passengers. The trip was rough but otherwise uneventful except for the prevalence of sea sickness among the passengers.

After making the transit of the Panama Canal, *Cook* went on to San Diego, California, arriving July 2, 1945. Instead of proceeding immediately to the forward area more training was scheduled and it was not until August 10 that she departed for what was expected to the long awaited trip to the forward area and the war. While anchored off Oceanside, California, taking aboard personnel and gear of Underwater Demolition Team 20, the welcome news was received that hostilities had ceased. On August 16, 1945 *Cook* in company with several other APDs carrying underwater demolition personnel commenced a high speed run to Japan via Pearl Harbor and Eniwetok to participate in the occupation of the enemy homeland. On September 4 USS *Cook* anchored in Tokyo Bay, Japan, off Yokasuka Naval Base.

On September 6, 1946, the executive officer, Lieutenant Commander L.R. Hardy relieved Lieutenant Commander D.N. Hamilton as commanding officer with Lieutenant (jg) John L. Parlette of Dallas, Texas, appointed as acting executive officer. Lieutenant Commander Hamilton stayed aboard as a passenger until USS *Cook* arrived at Okinawa on September 10 and then departed for the United States to return to civilian life along with the first draft of enlisted separatees.

Cook escorted sixteen LSTs back to Tokly Bay where all hands were treated to a too close view of a typhoon which swept the area on the night of September 17-18. Fortunately, the only damage was the loss of a small boat and an anchor. A few days later, *Cook* went to Ominato and later Aomori in northern Honshu.

On September 27, *Cook* finally played an interesting part in the occupation of Japan. On that morning, she steamed into the harbor at Hakodate, Hokkaido, and dropped anchor, the first American ship to enter that harbor. Control was established immediately over all Japanese communication facilities ashore and the ship's and passenger personnel made the necessary reconnaissance of the area for the landing of the occupation forces. The Japanese officials in the area were very peaceful and helpful, making *Cook's* occupation of the city very pleasant and quiet. On October 5 *Cook* was relieved of her position as sole representative of the armed forces of the United States in this area by the Army occupation forces and returned to Yokohama.

On October 18, the most welcome of all dispatches arrived and *Cook* left Yokohama homeward bound via Guam, Eniwetok and Pearl Harbor, arriving at San Diego, California on November 13. Underwater Demolition Team 20 was disembarked at San Diego, and the ship went to San Pedro for repairs.

After remaining at San Pedro for almost two months, on January 5, 1946 USS *Cook* reported to Commandant 11th Naval District for duty transporting enlistd personnel to San Pedro for separation.

On January 25, 1946 USS *Cook* ended her short but active sea-going career and reported to the San Diego Group, 19th Fleet, for inactivation. She is now decommissioned and is in inactive reserve status with the U.S. Pacific Reserve—status date January 1947.

Statistics

Overall Length:	306 feet
Extreme Beam:	37 feet
Trial Displacement:	1,650 tons
Trial Speed:	23.6 knots
Total Accommodations:	12 officers, 192 enlisted
Armament:	(1) 5" 38 cal. (D.P.); (3) twin 40mm anti-aircraft mounts
Stenciled:	June 6, 1949

Andrew Fred Cook Jr. born January 2, 1920 in Alpoca, West Virginia, enlisted in U.S. Marine Corps September 15, 1938, saw service at Parris Island, Quantico, Guantamo, and New River. Serving in the field from May 10, 1942, he was promoted to second lieutenant July 14, 1942. He was killed in action on Guadalcanal November 4, 1942, receiving the Navy Cross for gallantry and self-sacrifice in the action is which he gave his life.

Dallas Harry Cook, his brother, was born May 19, 1921 in Robinette, West Virginia, and enlisted in the U.S. Marine Corps August 14, 1940. After service at Quantico, Guantamo and P.R., he served in the field from February 14, 1942. He was promoted to sergeant May 21, 1942 and was killed in action in the raid on Makin Island August 18, 1942. He was awarded the Navy Cross for the action in which he gave his life with great personal valor.

(APD-139: dp. 1,450; 1. 306'; b. 36'10"; dr. 13"; s. 24 k.; cpl. 256; a. 1 5"; cl. *Crosley*)

Cook (APD-130) was launched August 26, 1944 by Defoe Shipbuilding Company, Bay City, Michigan; sponsored by Mrs. A.F. Cook; and commissioned April 25, 1945, Lieutenant Commander D.N. Hamilton, USNR, in command.

Cook sailed from Norfolk June 19, 1945 for San Diego, arriving July 2. On September 20 she arrived at Tokyo carrying men of underwater demolition teams. After transporting troops to Okinawa, *Cook* reconnoitered Hakodate before its occupation. She sailed home from Yokohama by way of Guam, Eniwetok, and Pearl Harbor, to San Diego arriving November 13. After repairs, she spent the month of January transporting troops along the West Coast. *Cook* was placed out of commission in reserve May 31, 1946, berthed at San Diego.

Cook was recommissioned October 6, 1953, and took part in training and landing exercises off San Diego. She entered Mare Island Naval Shipyard for conversion to an APD flagship between November 28, 1953 and March 15, 1954 and continued training operations out of San Diego until November 19, when she sailed for the Far East. After participating in amphibious exercises on the West Coast of Korea, she operated from January 21, 1955 to May 19 as flagship for Operation "Passage to Freedom," the evacuation of refugees from North Vietnam.

Cook returned to San Diego June 12, 1955, and sailed in various landing and training exercises as primary control vessel or antisubmarine ship. In November she joined in a combined amphibious operation with Canadian forces. Local operations off California, including a period of service as a submarine target vessel, continued until March 21, 1956, when she sailed to Kauai, Hawaii, for an amphibious exercise in which she served as control vessel.

Cook returned to San Diego April 23, 1956 for maintenance antisubmarine exercises, and public orientation cruises, until August 22, 1957 when she departed for a tour of duty in the western Pacific based at Yokosuka. She stood by off Borneo during the Indonesian crisis from December 14-22. Back home in San Diego April 10, 1958, *Cook* participated in operations along the West Coast, including major interservice exercises, and between October 13, 1959 and April 29, 1960 cruised in the Far East once more. Returning to the States, *Cook* operated along the West Coast for the remainder of 1960.

USS COOK (APD-130)

Lt. Cmdr. Drayton N. Hamilton—Birmingham, AL—*Commanding Officer*		
Lt. L. R. Hardy	Highlands, NJ	*Executive Officer*
Lt. Ira J. Horne	Lynn, IN	*Engineering Officer*
Lt. (jg) K. R. Schoettle	Ardmore, PA	*First Lieutenant*
Lt. (jg) R. L. Leeds	Bronxville, NY	*Recognition Officer*
Lt. (jg) J. F. Wright	Syracuse, NY	*Gunnery Officer*
Lt. (jg) W. C. Hearin	Greenville, SC	*Medical Officer*
Lt. (jg) J. D. Lawyer	Hammond, IN	*Supply Officer*
Lt. (jg) J. L. Parlette	Dallas, TX	*Asst. Gunnery Officer*
ENS L. O. Speck	Arlington, NJ	*Com. Officer*
ENS T. O. Edison	Grand Rapids, MI	*Asst. Engr. Officer*
ENS J. M. Hensley	Houston, TX	*CIC & ASW Officer*
ENS J. W. Owens	Moultrie, GA	*Boat Officer*

Chief Petty Officers

Fado, Clarence "J" CMM USN   Hamilton, Andrew L. CEM USN
Dabron, Daniel L. CPhM USN   Phipps, Donald W. CWT USN

USS COOK(APD-130) Crew

* Names may be abbreviated.

		D'Amico, D. A.	QM1c	Gallion, John H.	S1c	Lloyd, Chester A.	S1c
		Dampier, R. C.	S2c	Garrison, C. S.	F1c	Lowery, Max Jr.	FC3c
Adamson, James F.	MM3c	Dancha, George	S1c	Green, Richard R.	S2c	Lucas, George J.	WT3c
Ainsworth, C. P.	EM2c	Dancho, John E.	S2c	Green, Shirley R.	F2c		
		Danielo, Frank	MoM2c	Gregg, Linn E.	MM3c	Martz, Arthur W.	Cox
Baker, Robert F.	RM3c	Davenport, Wm.	S2c	Griffith, Carl M.	S2c	Martin, Arnold F.	S2c
Biddle, John	F1c	Davidson, W. A.	S2c	Gross, Elmer H.	Cox	Masterson, C. J.	S2c
Blenkush, A. J.	RM2c	Davidson, W. P.	S2c			McCants, Elbert	Ck3c
Block, Samuel N.	S2c	Davidson, E., Jr.	S2c	Hamer, B. Jr. "C"	MM2c	McGriff, D. K.	Bkr2c
Boesing, John P.	M1c	Day, Elmo C.	WT2c	Hansen, Robert C.	S1c	McDonald, H. L.	S2c
Bonanni, Frank I.	S1c	DeHaven, R. W.	S1c	Harper, Thomas F.	SC2c	McLong, L.	StM1c
Borkoski, J.B. Jr.	EM3c	Deitz, Daniel D.	S1c	Harris, L.V.	StM2c	Monger, R. Lee	S2c
Brancaccio, G. F.	S2c	Deluca, Albert J.	F2c	Haun, Harold (n)	GM1c	Morgan, H. P.	SM2c
Brady, Kenneth L.	F1c	Demers, Paul L.	BM1c	Havey, A. S. III	F1c	Morris, Charles A.	SoM2c
Brown, Edward O.	S1c	DeMuro, P. J.	EM2c	Hennings, B.A.	EM3c	Motta, Peter G.	S2c
Burchfield, L.H.	S2c	DeShetler, R. A.	MM1c	Herbert, N. W.	S2c	Moy, William L.	SM1c
Burkhardt, Wm. M.	S2c	Dinsmore, A. F.	MM2c	Himes, Brodie L.	EM3c	Muecke, Robert J.	S1c
Burton, Joseph	F2c	Doeringer, G. P.	S1c	Hogan, John P. Jr.	PhM2c	Musgrave, J. Leo	SoM3c
Burke, Acy	S1c	Donahue, R. W.	SK1c	Holland, Delaner	S2c		
Burke, John F.	F2c	Dorio, Frank P.	S1c	Holzapfel, W. C.	S2c	Neff, William R.	F1c
Burns, K. W.	Y1c	Duckett, L.	ST3c	Horn, Andrew	F1c	Newman, Jack M.	MM3c
Bushi, John Jr.	CM3c	Dupree, Donald F.	S2c	Hunsaker, Wm. W.	EM2c	Nickell, F. M.	S1c
		Durbin, Elmer S.	F1c	Hutzler, Carl H.	GM3c	Nuerenberg, R.	GM3c
Campbell, Paul E.	GM3c						
Clark, Elmer Jr.	S2c	Ellis, Orville K.	S2c	Johnson, Warren R.	EM2c	Pabst, Robert F.	WT3c
Clouser, Ruel "E"	WT1c	Ehrlich, R. A.	BM1c	Johnston, Cliff M.	S1c	Paggioli, John E.	RM3c
Colley, Robert F.	S2c			Jones, Ray H.	SoM2c	Papi, Ansel D.	GM3c
Cole, Jack R.	SC3c	Fairley, Bobby Jr.	F1c			Pavlik, Michael M.	EM3c
Cole, James E.	S2c	Faulkenberry, J. Jr.	BM2c	Kennedy, James J.	SF2c	Pfeiffer, Samuel F.	S1c
Cone, Joseph W.	S2c	Fette, Russel J.	F1c	Kenyon, Howard G.	EM2c	Phares, C. W. Sr.	S2c
Conmy, James F.	RM1c	Fine, Alfred	S2c	Klauder, David E.	Cox	Piechuta, Edward	S1c
Cornelius, J. E.	F2c	Fisher, Earl A.	S1c	Krutman, Julius M.	RT3c	Pincley, Robert R.	S2c
Carrello, C. D.	F2c	Fitzpatrick, L.J.	S1c			Polizzi, Thomas J.	MM2c
Cosentino, J. J.	SK3c	Flannery, M. W. Jr.	F2c	Lang, Charles E.	S1c	Pope, Cecil E.	S2c
Creighton, T. Jr.	S2c	Flowers, Wm. M.	F1c	Larrabee, Carl R.	FC3c	Potter, Gordon W.	F1c
Cummings, R. J.	F2c	Flynn, Francis J.	S1c	Lemley, R. C.	S1c	Powers, James A.	S1c
Cunningham, A.	F1c	Forbes, John	S1c	Levan, Robert L.	S2c	Prickett, Wm. Jr.	S2c
Curtis, Cary R.	S2c	Fowler, T. M. Sr.	F2c	Lewis, Harold W.	F1c	Proctor, H. W.	MM3c
Curtis, Robert L.	StM2c	Frazier, George H.	MM1c	Lira, Nichols	B1c	Prunzion, James F.	MM3c
Dale, E. F.	MaM3c	Fritsche, Loren C.	F1c	Livingston, O. Jr.	MM1c		

Ramey, Henry J.	S2c
Register, Robert S.	S2c
Rehfus, John A.	S2c
Rezet, Leon	WT3c
Roberts, Leland E.	S1c
Rocchiccioli, W.M.	SC2c
Romero, Felix	S2c
Rondy, Richard C.	C1c
Rowell, F. L.	StM1c
Rudder, Earl	S2c
Saddler, Wm. P.	F1c
Scala, Anthony J.	S2c
Scherch, Wm. O.	S2c
Scherr, Jerome A.	S2c
Schroeder, Alfred	CM2c
Searles, James A.	S2c
Sherdon, J. A.	EM2c
Sikkema, E. II	F1c
Smith, Kenneth H.	GM3c
Smith, Joseph A.	S1c
Sprong, W. O.	WT2c
Stier, Joseph A.	F1c
Sulham, Joseph	S2c
Suttles, E. C.	S2c
Tuck, Ival L.	SC1c
Variot, Donald F.	Y2c
Vogler, Wm. W.	MM2c
Wagner, Jack L.	S2c
Wheaton, J. C.	S2c
Wilkerson, H. C.	MM1c
Wilkinson, R. M.	SKD2c
Wohl, Lauren L.	C1c
Wood, Irvin H.	S1c
Zweig, George E.	F1c

USS *DECKER* (DE-47)

Submitted by R.L. MacKenzie, CY(AA)

Report of Action: Torpedo Bombers vs CONVOY, protected by Task Force 61, (May 11, 1944)

Action as I saw it:

Red Alert, Man your battle stations - at 2020.

2035 - Escort Vessels commenced laying smokescreen. Very complete and excellent job of screening the convoy with smoke.

2035 - (For exact time get TBS log) - 11 to 30 Foggies reported coming in (direction unknown).

2050 - Enemy planes believed coming in from ahead (Reported over TBS).

2051 - Heard that AA fire was reported from ahead.

2055 - Saw coming in from ahead (5) Torpedo bombers flying very fast in from almost dead ahead cutting diagonally across port bow and veering to starboard. Also saw planes flying by on both port and starboard beam. To the best of my knowledge total or planes attacking numbered from 15 to 20. The planes from port beam followed the first five and cut across the ship from port beam to stbd. quarter. One of these planes dropped a torpedo which left a wake and by rapid and skillful conning by the Captain the ship was turned to port just enough to allow the torpedo to miss the bow by a safe margin of about 20 yards. Of the first wave over the ship, we hit a bomber and its port engine burst into flames and the plane appeared to fall into the sea just this side of the horizon. I understand this was later verified as correct. A third wave of bombers (about 5) came seeming to materialize from the same direction as the second and swept over from port to starboard. A torpedo was headed for the tail of our ship, the ship was turned slightly to the port and it passed through our wake exactly where I would say the FXR was being streamed. Immediately after this another wave came from port bow and separated, two veering abruptly after dropping torpedoes. one of these torpedoes appeared to go directly underneath our fantail, and I believe it either was too deep or was diverted by FXR along with the swinging of the ship. One of these planes was hit in the fuselage by what appeared to me to be 3" shell. It tore a large hole in the fuselage directly in front of the rudder and elevators. Fire broke out but did not seem to continue to burn. However the plane appeared out of control and veered sharply into the darkness to port. Another plane was hit by AA fire and seemed to go down on the horizon to port. A flash of light appeared. I am uncertain if we got this one.

It was steadily getting darker and targets were hard to see. Planes came in individually now and I believe several dropped torpedoes which I did not see. Each time planes came in the AA battery including all guns on the ship appeared to work splendidly and it is my sincere belief as well as those standing near me that only the coming and the fire power saved our ship. The attack was of a most fierce and daring nature. The action (not counting numerous attempts to sneak up on the ship later) took about 35 minutes. It seemed incredible to me how our ship managed to miss being torpedoed as it appeared to me that every plane took a crack at us and most of them circled and came in later for what appeared individual attacks almost simultaneously from both sides. The man on the director, the gunnery officer, the lookouts, and all the men on the guns seemed to do excellent teamwork - not to mention the wonderful job of supervision on the Captains part. Along with all the above I sure believe that we were plenty lucky to survive such an attack. It is also my opinion that the fact that we anticipated the attack in advance and was waiting for them gave the Jerries the surprise of their lives. Also the fact that our very first burst of fire downed one of their planes gave them a shock and put a little respect in their approach after their first daredevil approaches. Secured from GQ at about 0030 leaving Section I at ready guns. Smoke Screen was secured immediately after darkness put an end to its usefulness. Weather conditions helped considerably. Dark overcast. Planes to my very limited knowledge appeared to be very large. Had large crosses on the wings and I believe most of them were probably Messerschmits #210 with maybe a few Junkers thrown in.

This report is based on what I saw. The action was very fast and in twilight to deep dust conditions. Some of the description may be wrong. I've tried to hold myself down to facts as I saw them for entry into the War Diary. I believe I have not exaggerated in any single item but have been if anything conservative. It still seems to me a miracle that so many torpedoes were fired at us and missed by such close margins and also that a DE was able to put up such a battle. I am proud to be part of the crew of this ship, as I consider none better, or more capably officered.

USS *DEEDE* (DE-263)

Submitted by Luther William Norvell (Tex), RM2/c

Deede (DE-263) was launched April 6, 1943 by Boston Navy Yard, sponsored by Mrs. M.B. Deede, mother of Lieutenant (jg) LeRoy Clifford Deede. She was commissioned July 29, 1943, Lieutenant Commander J.W. Whaley in command. Among the crew helping to complete the ship was "Tex" Norvell.

During a six week shakedown cruise in Bermuda she encountered her first hurricane. Following final repairs and training in Boston and Norfolk, she left New York for Pearl Harbor via the Panama Canal, San Diego and San Francisco, arriving November 17, 1943.

On November 26 she departed Pearl Harbor for the invasion of the Gilbert Islands, acting as escort for a convoy to Tarawa and as screening vessel and radar guard ship at Tarawa and Makin Islands. During the campaign the crew was at battle stations several consecutive days and nights, at one point being singled out for special attention by a Betty Bomber. She patrolled off Makin until December 23 and while the area was still under heavy air attack from Japanese bases on Mili Atoll departed for Pearl Harbor.

On December 1, 1943 in Latitude 00000 and Longitude 176 05'W, "bound South for the Equator and the Gilbert Islands," the crew of *Deede* became eligible for the honored title of Trusty Shellbacks. However, due to the urgency of the moment the rite of initiation was not conducted until much, much later. *Deede* departed Pearl Harbor January 29, 1944 as escort for a task force to the Marshall Islands, arriving at Majuro February 3 for

USS Deede (DE-263)

service as harbor pilot and patrol vessel during the occupation of that island. She returned to Pearl Harbor for training exercises February 21 to March 26 after which she acted as escort vessel between Pearl Harbor, Majuro, and Eniwetok Atolls in the Marshalls until May 26.

On June 4, 1944 she sailed from Pearl Harbor for Eniwetok, arriving ten days later. Assigned to the Task Group invading the Marianas Islands, from this base she escorted an oiler task unit which refueled Task Force 53 at sea on June 20 at the close of the Battle of the Philippine Sea, and she escorted Task Force 58 during the raid on the Bonins on June 24. During the Marianas Campaign, the *Deede* was engaged in anti-submarine screening and night bombardment duties at Saipan, Guam and Tinian. While carrying out harassing fire and night illumination assignments against Tinian Town, enemy fire was encountered. Several "straddles" were made by Japanese shore batteries, but no hits were suffered by the *Deede*. On August 27 she departed from Guam, acting as escort to Guadalcanal and Florida Island, British Solomon Islands, by way of Eniwetok. This campaign officially ending September 1.

While engaged as an escort the *Deede* became aware the Sonar was not functioning. The escort became the escorted to a floating dry dock where it was discovered the sound gear was dangling beneath the ship. After repairs and rest at Purvis Bay, Florida Island, *Deede* escorted *Crater* (AK-70) to Guadalcanal and received a new camouflage paint job. On October 2 she joined the escort for a convoy to the Western Carolinas Operation, acting as escort to Ulithi, Kossol Roads and Peleliu.

She continued convoy duty aiding in the occupation of the Palaus until November 12 when she left Kossol Roads for Leyte as sole escort with Kossol Roads/Leyte Convoy #1. In the convoy was a Dutch ammunition ship. Late one afternoon radar picked up an aircraft, the convoy closed ranks but the plane went back into the clouds. Next morning our aircraft carriers passed. On November 17 she departed for Pearl harbor for overhaul and refresher training and two weeks of R&R in the Royal Hawaiian Hotel in Honolulu including a luau with traditional entertainment.

Deede served as escort and target in the training of submarines out of Pearl Harbor until February 6, 1945 when she got underway to escort a convoy of cargo and transport ships to reinforce the operations on Iwo Jima. Upon arrival, February 23, she assumed duties in the anti-submarine screen around the island. She remained on patrol in the Volcano Islands until March 20 when she screened the transports returning the 4th Marines to Pearl Harbor, arriving April 4.

After overhaul at San Francisco and training at San Diego and Pearl Harbor, *Deede* joined the replenishment group for the 3rd Fleet at Ulithi July 21 operating as escort with the Logistics Support Group during the final air raids and bombardments on the Japanese mainland. She served as Communications linking ship between *Benevolence* (AH-13) and *Tranquility* (AH-14) from August 16 to 21, then rejoined the logistics group to enter Tokyo Bay October 2.

Other DEs in immediate support at Tokyo Bay were *Bangust, Joseph E. Connolly, Crowley, William C. Miller, Donaldson, Waterman, Mitchell, Dionne, Leroy, Wilson, Griswold, Lyman, Weaver, Reynolds, Canfield, Willmarth, Lake, Hilbert, Kyne, Lamon, Elden, Gerlson, Cabana,* and *McCrelland.*

After a four day layover in Tokyo Bay she got underway for Pearl Harbor where she served with the Hawaiian Sea Frontier from October 17 to November 19.

After sailing in excess of 175,000 miles, and weathering numerous hurricanes and typhoons, her duties completed, *Deede* arrived at San Francisco November 25, 1945. She was decommissioned there January 9, 1946 and sold June 12, 1947.

Operations Engaged In With Official Dates

1. *Gilbert Islands Operation*-November 13, 1943 to December 8, 1943.
2. *Marshall Islands Operations*-Occupation of Kwajalein and Majuro Atolls, January 29, 1944 to February 8, 1944.
3. *Marianas Operation*-capture and occupation of Saipan, June 11, 1944 to August 10, 1944; First Bonins Raid, June 15, 1944 to June 16, 1944; capture and occupation of Guam, July 12, 1944 to August 15, 1944; capture and occupation of Tinian, July 20, 1944 to August 10, 1944.
4. *Western Caroline Islands Operation*-capture and occupation of the Southern Palau Islands, September 6, 1944 to October 14, 1944.
5. *Leyte Operation-Leyte Landings*, October 10, 1944 to November 29, 1944.
6. *Iwo Jima Operation*-assault and occupation of Iwo Jima, February 15, 1945 to March 16, 1945.
7. *Operations against the Japanese Empire with Task Force 30*-July 29, 1945 to August 15, 1945.

Ports of Call—USS DEEDE (DE-263)

Boston, MA	Saipan, Mariana Islands
Bermuda, B.W.I.	Tinian, Mariana Islands
Norfolk, VA	Guam, Mariana Islands
New York, NY	Guadalcanal
Cristobal, Canal Zone	British Solomon Islands
Balboa, Canal Zone	Purvis Bay, Florida Island, B.S.I.
San Diego, CA	Ulithi, Western Caroline Islands
San Francisco, CA	Pelelieu, Palau Islands
Pearl Harbor, T.H.	Kossol Roads, Palau Islands
Tarawa Gilbert Islands	Leyte, Philippine Islands
Makin, Gilbert Islands	Iwo Jima, Volcano Islands
Majura, Marshall Islands	Tokyo Bay, Honshu Island, Japan
Eniwetok, Marshall Islands	San Francisco, CA

The following alphabetical list of the crew and officers of the USS Deede (DE-263) was taken from a microfilm of the ship's Muster Rolls and reports of changes from July 29, 1943 through December 1, 1945. Following the name is the last rank reported, place of enlistment when given, date first reported aboard, and date of departure when given.

Name	Rank	Place	Dates
Abascal, Joaquin Arsenio	GM3/c disch. from USS *George W. Ingram*	New Haven, CT	9/6/43-11/1/45
Adamson, Augusta H.	CMoMM (AA) hospital	Portsmouth, VA	7/29/43-915/43
Allen, Ethan Laverne	S2/c hospital		4/20/45-5/16/45
Allison, Teddy Junior	S2/c		4/20/45
Amelio, Eugene Andrew	F2/C		4/20/45
Armburst, Marcus Joe	S1/c		4/20/45
Ames, Joseph H.	S1/c, transferred	Springfield, MA	9/28/45-11/18/45
Anderson, Marvin C.	S1/c (Rdm) hospital		2/5/45-5/18/45
Appleton, Charles E. Jr.	MoMM1/c, to USS *Competent*	Memphis, TN	7/29/43-1/17/44
Arnold, John M.	S1/c R/S	Hattisburg, WV	9/28/44-5/16/45
Arnold, William Whitson	RM2/c discharged		6/9/45-9/3/45
Arrance, Larry Dean	S2/c hospital		4/20/45-6/30/45
Arrowsmith, Glen B.	S2/c		4/20/45
Asnes, Bertram Louis	RM2/c (T) R/S	New York, NY	7/29/43-7/7/45
Atchison, Lee (n)	MoMM2/c hospital	St. Louis, MO	7/29/43-11/1/43
Auriemmo, Patrick (n)	F3/c emergency leave 10/10/43, ship sailed short notice, reassigned 11/23/43	Chicago, IL	7/29/43
Babson, Dewitt (n)	COX hospital	Raleigh, NC	7/30/43-6/9/45
Balchitis, Ray John	RdM3/c (T) discharged	Chicago, IL	1/23/44-11/1/45
Barbarino, Salvatore J.	EM3/c to USS *Cascade* (AD-16)	Baltimore, MD	7/30/43-9/9/44
Barber, William Garfield	CMoMM (AA) transferred	Los Angeles, CA	7/29/43-7/20/44
Batcheler, Richard Chester	CMoMM (T) discharged	Philadelphia, PA	7/29/43-11/25/45
Beafore, Louis Joseph	Cox (T)	Clarksburg, VA	9/4/44 from USS *Markab*
Begnaud, Calice (n)	CMoMM R/S enlistment up 1/15/45 re-enlisted 1/16/45	New Orleans, LA	7/29/43-5/16/45
Bennett, Frank Joseph	MoMM3/c school	Philadelphia, PA	7/29/43-1/6/45
Bergen, Charles Francis	MoMM2/c (T)	Philadelphia, PA	7/29/43-
Beshara, Fred	S1/c hospital	Boston, MA	9/28/44-7/17/45
Billingslea, Benjamin F.	St2/c (T) R/S	Detroit, MI	7/29/43-5/16/45
Black, Charles Henry Jr.	S1c R/S	Columbia, SC	7/29/43-5/16/45

Name	Rating	Location	Dates
Blitch, Charles Harry	CCStd (T) discharged	Raleigh, NC	7/29/43-9/21/45
Blomgren, Marshall H.	EM3/c (T) discharged	Chicago, IL	5/10/44-11/25/45
Boldt, Wm. T. Jr.	EM2/c (T)	Minneapolis, MN	5/10/44-
Bond, Howard Richard	EM3/c (T)		6/9/45-
Boone, Vernon Lawrence	S1/c transferred	Jackson, MS	7/29/43-6/30/44
Boone, Vinkley Leroy	S1/c transferred	Jackson, MS	7/29/43-6/30/44
Booth, Allan Lynn	F1/c hospital	Cleveland, OH	5/10/44-7/4/45
Bossard, Harry P.	GM3/c (T)		2/4/45-
Bowden, James L.	F2/c		2/4/45-
Boyd, Walter Henry Jr.	S1/c transferred	Atlanta, GA	7/29/43-5/16/45
Bradsberry, Marion J.	SoM3/c transferred	San Francisco, CA	6/1/44-5/16/45
Brander, Lloyd Joseph	S1/c discharged		4/20/45-10/31/45
Brannegan, Richard (n)	EM3/c (T)	New Haven, CT	5/10/44-
Brennan, Daniel J.	S1/c	Philadelphia, PA	9/28/44-
Brickhouse, Shelton V.	S1/c transferred	Raleigh, NC	7/29/43-6/30/44
Briscoe, Clyde (n)	Ck3/c (T) discharged from USS *Twining* (DD-540)	Little Rock, AR	2/24/44-10/31/45
Brown, Alex (n) Jr.	StM2/c hospital	Raleigh, NC	7/29/43-8/14/43
Brown, John Wilmont	MoMM2/c (T)	Columbia, SC	7/29/43-
Brown, Leon S.	S1/c discharged	Raleigh, NC	9/28/44-11/25/45
Brown, Luther M.	S1c discharged	Huntington, WV	9/28/44-11/2/45
Brown, Robert Dale	S1/c		4/20/45-
Brown, William N.	SoMM3/c (T) school	Cincinnati, OH	1/1/44-6/2/45
Browning, Louis R.	Y2/c (T)		10/26/45-
Bull, John Aaron	Y3/c to USS *Canfield*	Wilmington, DE	7/29/43-9/16/43
Bungert, Joseph Martin	EM2/c (T) discharged	Minneapolis, MN	7/29/43-9/21/45
Burfiend, Odell Francis	S1/c (SM)		12/10/44-
Butler, James Howard	SC2/c (T)		4/20/45-
Button, Lawrence Clair	RdM2/c (T) discharged	San Francisco, CA	1/23/44-11/1/45
Butts, Raymond Henry	MoMM1/c (T),	Albany, NY	7/29/43-
Campbell, Britt (n)	S1/c	Cincinnati, OH	9/28/44-
Campisi, John Robert	MoMM1/c,	Philadelphia, PA	7/29/43-
Carden, Luther I. Jr.	S1/c	Roanoke, VA	9/28/44-
Carlson, Enar L.	SF2/c (T)		5/9/45-
Carter, Paul Frederick	Boatswain (T)	Omaha, NE	7/29/43-9/8/44 R/S
Cauthen, Lewis T.	F1/c discharged	Concord, NC	9/28/43-10/31/45
Cazzell, Billy Eugene	GM2/c (T)	Kansas City, MO	7/29/43-
Cerrato, Ralph W.	F2/c		10/28/45-
Chaves, Victor Manuel	S2/c hospital	New York, NY	7/29/43-1/14/44
Chilton, George T. Jr.	S2/c R/S	Richmond, VA	7/29/43-10/10/43
Claar, William Joseph	GM1/c (T)	Columbus, OH	7/29/43-
Clark, Aubrey J.	GM2/c (T) discharged		2/4/45-11/25/45
Clark, Champ (n)	Y1/c		2/1/45-
Clark, Theodore Vincent	MoMM1/c (T)	New York, NY	7/29/43-
Coburn, Merrick "E"	GM3/c school	Detroit, MI	7/29/43-4/21/44
Cochran, James Arthur	FC2/c (M) school		8/22/43-9/10/44
Coleman, David J. Jr.	StM2/c		10/24/45-
Compton, Harry Richard	Cox to USS *Cascade* (AD-16)	San Francisco, CA	7/29/43-9/8/44
Cox, George Schelley Jr.	SM2/c (T) disch from USS *Canfield*	Houston, TX	1/1/44-11/25/45
Craig, George Rogers	SC2/c (T)	Camp Croft, NC	7/29/43-
Crocker, Doris Lee	S2/c R/S	Columbia, SC	7/29/43-10/10/43
Cullen, Richard Arnult Jr.	SoM1/c (T)		4/30/45-
Cunningham, Jesse S. Jr.	SSML3/c (T)		7/29/43-
Daisey, Waldron Richard	S1/c transferred	Richmond, VA	7/29/43-5/16/45
Daniel, Eddie Lewis	Ck2/c (T)	Columbus, GA	7/29/43-
Deevy, Martin J.	GM1/c (T) school	New York, NY	7/29/43-12/1/44
Demler, Norbert Peter	EM2/c (T) hospital	Milwaukee, WI	9/9/44-5/18/45
Detwiler, Harry Phillips	SC3/c (T), R/S from USS *Canfield*	Richmond, VA	1/1/44-5/16/45
Dickman, Robert F.	F2/c to USS *Cabana* (DE-260)	St. Paul, MN	7/29/43-9/10/44
Diehl, Walter Roy	F1/c from USS *Canfield*	Richmond, VA	1/1/44-
Dobrinski, T. F.Cox	transferred	Boston, MA	7/29/43-5/31/44
Dodson, John Thomas	warrant btswain transferred	Charleston, SC	7/29/43-8/13/43
Drabik, Robert Mathias	MMR3/c,	Toledo, OH	7/29/43-
Drogos, John J.	S1/c leave	Chicago, IL	9/28/44-10/29/45
Dunham, Earle Wilson	RdM2/c school	Boston, MA	11/19/43-4/14/45
Earnest, Melvin Gwin	GM3/c school	Washington, DC	7/29/43-1/6/45
Edismoe, Ordean Arnold	EM2/c (T),	Minneapolis, MN	7/29/43-
Elliott, Edgar Franklin	SM1/c, discharged	San Francisco, CA	11/9/43-9/20/45
Englehart, Edward G.	EM3/c school	Richmond, VA	7/29/43-12/1/44
Ergenbright, Robert F.	EM3/c hospital	Richmond, VA	8/2/43-7/4/45
Erickson, Marvin Juel	S1/c		4/20/45-
Ewer, Basil Allen	F1/c (MoMM)		4/20/45-
Fankhauser, Ralph Kent	Em2/c R/S from USS *Cascade*	Charleston, WV	9/9/44-5/16/45
Farmer, Manor Hollis Jr.	F1/c (MoMM) discharged		4/20/45-10/31/45
Fiene, Warren Edward	EM3/c, transferred	Minneapolis, MN	7/29/43-6/30/44
Fincher, Charles J. Alton	CGM (T) school	Miami, FL	7/29/43-4/14/45
Fletcher, Stacy G. Jr.	F1/c		10/28/45-
Foote, Wilson Harry J.	EM2/c (T)	Los Angeles, CA	3/6/44-
Fowler, Alvin Warney	F1/c (EM)	Omaha, NE	3/6/44-
Fowler, John Paul	EM3/c (T) discharged	Oklahoma City, OK	3/6/44-11/25/45
Fox, Jonathon Henry Jr.	S1/c		4/20/45
Francisco, Stanley D.	S1/c hospital	Los Angeles, CA	9/28/44-5/31/45
Frank, Robert Edward Jr.	EM3/c (T)	Toledo, OH	3/6/44
Freeman, Benjamin Doyle	MoMM3/c (T) discharged	Los Angeles, CA	3/6/44-10/2/45
Frey, Joseph Henry	CY (AA) hospital	New York, NY	7/29/43-4/27/44
Funk, Chester Lemmon	M1/c school	Des Moines, IA	7/29/43-4/14/45
Gamble, Cecil Lee	Cox (T) hospital	Columbia, SC	7/29/43-5/18/45
Genskay, Stanley Wallace	FC2/c (T) disch	Minneapolis, MN	7/29/43-9/26/45
Gerlach, John J. Jr.	SoM2/c (T)		12/8/44-
Girard, Robert Berdette	S1/c R/S	Minneapolis, MN	9/10/44-11/19/45
Goggin, Robert H.	S1/c,	St. Louis, MO	9/28/44-
Good, Walter Clement Jr.	SM3/c trans	Minneapolis, MN	7/29/43-6/30/44
Goodall, Arthur Lloyd	RM3/c (T)		12/8/44-
Goodson, Edward O.	MoMM1/c		12/13/44-5/16/45 R/S
Goodwin, Denzel State	RdM3/c (T)	Colorado	2/5/45-
Gray, Cecil James	RdM2/c (T)		6/13/45-
Griffin, William Harvey	F1/c		4/20/45-
Grossman, Ervin A.	S2/c	Minneapolis, MN	1/144-1/6/44 trans
Gustafson, John Pershing	CPhM (T)		7/2/45-
Hackbarth, John Henry	S1/c		4/20/45-
Haley, Robert Bruce	CEM (PA) school	Newport News, VA	7/29/43-4/14/45
Halweg, Harold Earl	CQM (AA) (T) disch	Minneapolis, MN	7/29/43-9/20/45
Hamersma, Robert Paul	MoMM3/c (T) disch	New York, NY	7/29/43-11/6/45
Hamilton, Robert Melvie	S1/c		4/20/45-no other rec
Hardie, Edward Lyle	S2/c		4/20/45-no other rec
Hardie, James Cloyd	S1/c		4/20/45
Hart, Jack A.	SoM3/c		6/1/45-
Hasting, Hugh Lee	S1/c disch	Spartanburg, SC	7/29/43-11/1/45
Hastings, George William	MoMM3/c (T)	Los Angeles, CA	3/6/44-

Name	Rating	Location	Dates
Hatch, William Phillip Jr.	EM3/c (T)	Boston, MA	3/6/44-
Hatton, James Parnell	MaM3/c discharged		6/19/45-9/20/45
Haught, Andrew Roy	S1/c R/S	Camden, NJ	7/29/43-5/16/45
Havard, James Hiram	EM1/c (T) discharged	Birmingham, AL	7/29/43-11/1/45
Hayes, LeRoy Lee	CM3/c school	Kansas City, MO	7/29/43-3/144
Haynes, Charles Ray	MoMM1/c (T), discharged	Oklahoma City, OK	7/29/43-9/20/45
Henderson, Clive (n)	PhM3/c	Indianapolis, IN	9/4/44-
Henderson, Robert W.	StM1/c discharged	Chicago, IL	11/7/43-11/6/45
Herrick, Edward Lyle	S1/c		4/20/45-
Herrig, Eldon Theodore	S1/c		4/20/45-
Hess, Charles Eldon	RM1/c (T) discharged from USS Cony (DD-508)	Salt Lake City, UT	3/11/44-11/25/45
Higgins, Roy Mead	CY (AA) (T) discharged	Washington, DC	10/6/43-9/3/45
Hileman, Otis Wilbert	F1/c (T) school	Houston, TX	7/29/43-9/20/45
Hill, Jack (n)	SM3/c transferred	Miami, FL	7/29/43-5/31/44
Hinson, Howard Lee	Cox (T)		7/29/43-
Hobrecker, George F.	S1/c		4/20/45-
Hodges, Waylon W.	OS1/c transferred	Pearl Harbor T.H.	7/30/43-10/10/43
Hudson, James Albert	S2/c hospital	Columbia, SC	7/29/43-10/8/43
Hyde, Addison H.	Cox to USS Canfield	St. Louis, MO	7/29/43-1/1/44
Irwin, Frank Willie	S1/c		4/20/45-
Jackson, Robert Winfred	S1/c discharged		4/20/45-10/31/45
Jandrucko, John Peter	F1/c (MoMM)		4/20/45-
Jay, Otis Hidden	PhM3/c hospital	Indianapolis, IN	7/29/43-1/2/44
Johnson, Warren Julian	S1/c		4/20/45-
Joyner, Boykin	St3/c (T) discharged	New York, NY	9/28/44-11/25/45
Kelley, "R" "T"	BM2/c (T)	Nashville, TN	7/29/43-
Kerby, George D.	S1/c (SC)		5/24/45-
Kirby, Jack Dempsey	S2/c R/S	Atlanta, GA	7/29/43-10/10/43
Kornita, John J.	S1/c	Chicago, IL	9/28/44-
Korpics, William (n)	SK3/c (T)	Philadelphia, PA	7/29/43
Kraut, Milton Charles	SF1/c school	Chicago, IL	7/29/43-9/29/44
La Coste, Louis Frank	MoMM2/c (T)	Jacksonville, FL	7/29/43-
Langley, Earnest F.	S2/c, hospital	Hattisburg, MS	9/28/44-1/24/45
Lawrence, Howard F.	F1/c		10/31/45-
Lawson, Ruel Edward	S/c hospital	Camp Croft, SC	7/29/43-5/24/45
Leavitt, Eugene Franklin	S1/c R/S from USS Cascade	St. Louis, MO	9/9/44-5/16/45
Ledwozan, Michael J.	EM1/c (T) R/S	New York, NY	7/29/43-5/16/45
Lee, Harry Ewing	CRT (AA) (T) school	Los Angeles, CA	7/30/43-5/11/45
Levy, David Freeman	F2/c	Boston, MA	8/18/43-
Little, Ben Allen	SoM3/c to USS Cabana	San Francisco, CA	6/1/44-9/11/44
Long, Billy Owen	SC2/c, transferred	Minneapolis, MN	7/30/43-4/14/45
Lowder, Max Howard	RdMc/c (T) R/S	Salt Lake City, UT	1/23/44-5/16/45
Loy, James Henry	F1/c R/S	Los Angeles, CA	7/29/43-5/13/45
Lucero, Manuel Gutierrez	F2/c		5/3/45-
Ludovick, Donald (n)	QM2/c (T)	San Francisco, CA	11/5/43-
Lusk, Edward (n)	F1/c	Chicago, IL	11/5/43-
Macbeth, Robert Gordon	Qm3/c (T)		4/20/45-
Maguire, Paul James	RM3/c (T) R/S	Boston, MA	7/29/43-5/16/44
Mancini, Richard (n)	SC21/c (T)	Albany, NY	10/1/43-
Mandernack, Robert John	RM1/c (T) discharged	Chicago, IL	7/29/43-10/31/45
Marcotti, Jack C.	S1/c	Los Angeles, CA	9/29/44-
Martin, Lewis B.	EM1/c (T) from USS Klondike		10/31/45-
Martinez, John Miranda	SM1/c (T)	Houston, TX	7/29/43-
Mason, Lloyd Henri Jr.	S1/c R/S	Camden, NJ	7/29/43-5/16/45
Mattos, Robert Manuel	MoMM2/c school	Boston, MA	7/29/43-4/1/45
Mawyer, Ralph Amos	CRM (AA) school	Richmond, VA	7/29/43-1/6/45
McDevitt, Thomas F.	F1c (MoMM) discharged		4/20/45-9/20/45
McDonald, Arlen M.	SM2/c R/S	Fargo, ND	7/29/43-9/10/44
McDougall, Stanley Holt	S1/c		4/20/45-
McGehee, Mason R.	BM3/c (T), discharged	Richmond, VA	7/29/43-9/20/45
McGregor, Chester S.	EM3/c school	Milwaukee, WI	7/29/43-4/14/45
McGuffin, Donald S.	SM2/c (T)	Houston, TX	9/29/43-10/15/44
McKissick, Joseph E.	CBM (PA) re-enlistment leave	San Juan, PR	729/43-9/3/43
McMillan, Davis Reams	GM2/c school	Columbia, SC	9/29/43-12/18/44
McPherson, Robert Harold	RM3/c (T)		6/9/45-
Miller, Elliott I.	S2/c		1/1/44-1/16/44
Miller, Guy Francis	S1/c	Harrisburg, PA	9/28/44-
Miller, Ira Leon	CM2/c discharged	Indianapolis, IN	7/29/43-9/3/45
Milteer, Jethro T. Jr.	F1/c		4/20/45-
Mitchell, Leroy (n)	StM2/c R/S	Selma, AL	9/29/43-10/11/43
Mittleman, Marshall E.	EM2/c discharged	Chicago, IL	7/29/43-9/20/45
Mockerman, Theodore I.	PhM3/c to USS Cascade	Kalamazoo, MI	5/28/44-9/23/44
Monger, Samuel Birchell	MoMM1/c (T) R/S	Indianapolis, IN	7/29/43-5/16/45
Moore, George Donald	RdM3/c (T)		6/13/45-
Moore, Robert Dale	QM3/c (T) R/S	Baltimore, MD	7/29/43-5/16/45
Morris, Richard Earl	S2/c R/S		7/29/43-10/10/43
Morton, Allan Roland Jr.	MoMM3/c (T) discharged	Buffalo, NY	7/29/43-9/20/45
Munro, William Elmer	S1/c (RM)		6/14/45-
Musnitsky, Harold (n)	RdM2/c R/S	Philadelphia, PA	7/29/43-4/24/44
Neff, Alfred Parker	SoM3/c school	Richmond, VA	7/29/43-6/2/45
Neitzey, William Albert	BM2/c (T) discharged	Richmond, VA	7/29/43-9/20/45
Nelson, Dennis Darrel	S1/c (RM)		6/14/45-
Newsome, James A. Sr.	S2/c R/S	Atlanta, GA	7/29/43-10/10/43
Newton, Henry (n)	S1/c (T) school	Boston, MA	7/29/43-4/14/45
Nixon, Leroy (n)	StM1/c R/S	Philadelphia, PA	2/23/44-6/30/44
Norman, Edwin (n)	CMoMM (AA) (T) discharged	Jacksonville, FL	7/29/43-9/20/45
Northrup, David Paul	F1/c		4/20/45-
Norvell, Luther William	RM2/c (T)	Dallas, TX	7/29/43-
Nye, Wallace Wesley	S1/c discharged	Washington, DC	7/29/43-10/31/45
Oberlander, Theobold P.	S1/c		4/20/45
O'Brien, Patrick Irwin	S1/c		4/20/45-
O'Brien, William Hubert	EM1/c (T)	Indianapolis, IN	9/29/43-
Oglesby, Walter Leo	MoMM1/c (T) discharged	Raleigh, NC	7/29/43-11/25/45
Oliveira, Eugene (n)	MoMM2/c (T) discharged	Boston, MA	7/29/43-9/20/45
Oliver, Raymond (n)	MoMM2/c (T) discharged	Chattanooga, TN	7/29/43-9/20/45
Orlick, Albert Erving	S1/c R/S	Philadelphia, PA	9/29/43-5/16/45
Orr, David Andrew	S2/c R/S	Washington, DC	9/28/44-5/28/45
Osborne, Donald C.	S2/C	Baltimore, MD	7/29/43-
Osiadlo, John Joseph	F1/c (MoMM)		4/20/45-
Ostermiller, Eugene A.	EM1/c (T) discharged	St. Louis, MO	7/29/43-11/25/45
Otey, Miles Clyde	RdM3/c (T)		6/13/45-

Name	Rating	Home	Dates
Ouellette, Robert Alfred	S1/c to USS *Canfield*	Springfield, MA	7/29/43-1/1/44
Owens, Bruce Carter	GM2/c (T)	Abingdon, VA	7/29/43-
Pace, Walter Roy	F2/c hospital	Spartanburg, SC	7/29/43-2/24/44
Page, Thurman Virdle	S1/c R/S	Chattanooga, TN	7/29/43-6/30/44
Parker, John David	GM3/c, school	Richmond, VA	9/29/43-4/21/44
Patterson, Frank (n)	COX R/S	Birmingham, AL	7/29/43-10/10/43
Paquin, Charles Leon	CPhM (T) R/S	Chicago, IL	5/30/44-7/3/45
Percival, Hubert Douglas	F3/c	Chattanooga, TN	7/29/43-hospital
Perdue, Hyle Wright	S2c R/S	Roanoke, VA	7/29/43-5/16/45
Periandri, Frank Joseph	S1/c R/S	Cleveland, OH	7/29/43-5/16/45
Perry, Robert Lorn	GM2/c school	Springfield, IL	9/29/43-4/14/45
Perugini, Samuel A.	F3/c R/S	Camden, NJ	7/29/43-10/7/43
Petersen, Henry Adolph	F2/c R/S	New York, NY	7/29/43-10/7/43
Phillips, James Armond	MoMM3/c (T) school	Columbia, SC	7/29/43-9/30/44
Phillips, Robert A.	MoMMe/c (T)	Chattanooga, TN	7/29/43-
Pitcher, Elmer Robson	S1/c (RdM)		5/24/45-
Poland, Harold Laverne	S1/c discharged	Cincinnati, OH	7/29/43-9/20/45
Polston, Walser Reedy	BM2/c (T) charged	Raleigh, NC	7/29/43-9/3/45 dis
Ponkos, Rudolph Geogre	RdM2/c school	Albany, NY	7/29/43-4/14/45
Pool, Floyd Taylor	S1c discharged	Dallas, TX	9/4/44-11/1/45
Poole, Jamie Dee	F1/c discharged from USS *George W. Imgram*	Columbia, SC	9/6/43-12/2/45
Powell, Marvin Dean	PhM2/c hospital	Houston, TX	1/6/44-5/26/44
Powers, Ray Warren	S1/c		4/20/45-
Preston, Arthur Marvin	S1/c (SC)		4/20/45
Pritchard, Jack William	Bkr3/c hospital	Albany, NY	7/29/43-5/31/44
Purpus, James Patric	RdM3/c (T)		5/24/45-
Putas, Steve (m)	Sf3/c (T) R/S	Newark, NJ	9/13/43-5/16/45
Quillen, Elbert Matthew	S1/c hospital	Abingdon, VA	7/29/43-9/23/44
Quinn, John Patrick	SoM2/c (T) school	Boston, MA	9/13/43-1/10/44
Randall, Harold F.	RdM2/c discharged	Portland, ME	9/29/43-11/1/45
Rapke, Harold Walter discharged	SoM3/c (T)	Newark, NJ	9/13/43-11/1/45
Raskosky, John Stephen	Y2/c (T), R/S	Newark, NJ	9/13/43-5/16/45
Rasmussen, William A.	GM1/c (T) school	Baltimore, MD	7/29/43-2/5/45
Rauseo, Arthur John	F1/c R/S	Boston, MA	9/13/43-5/31/44
Reed, Edward John	MoMM3/c (T),	New Haven, CT	9/13/43—
Reed, Jack (n)	S1/c R/S	Boston, MA	9/13/43-5/16/45
Reeves, Richard (n)	S1/c R/S	Boston, MA	7/29/43-5/16/45
Rehm, Robert (n)	S1/c R/S	Newark, NJ	9/13/43-5/16/45
Rehmer, Marlan/M.(n)	S1/c R/S	Milwaukee, WI	11/5/43-5/16/45
Renninger, Robert Elmer	EM3/c school	Philadelphia, PA	7/29/43-4/14/45
Repetta, Stephen Charles	S1/c R/S	Boston, MA	9/13/43-5/16/45
Reynolds, Walter Newton	Bkr2/c (T) hospital	Kansas City, MO	11/5/43-6/17/45
Ricciardi, John Thomas	Y3/c R/S from USS *Canfield*	Lowell, MA	5/30/44-5/16/45
Richardson, James E.	S2/c transferred	St. Louis, MO	11/5/43-1/15/44
Riemer, David (n)	MoMM3/c (T)	Chicago, IL	11/5/43-
Rixe, Donald F.	S2/c to USS *Canfield*	Seattle, WA	11/5/43-1/1/44
Rizzo, Samuel William	SM2/c (T) to DE-588	Miami, FL	7/29/43-12/12/44
Robbins, Thomas Harvey	S1/c R/S	San Francisco, CA	11/5/43-6/30/44
Robertson, William C.	S1/c to USS *Cascade*	St. Louis, MO	7/29/43-9/9/44
Robison, Floyd Kenneth	S2/c,	San Francisco, CA	11/5/43-9/2/44
Rogers, Theawell J. H.	RdM3/c died in line of duty 9/10/44	Raleigh, NC	7/29/43-
Roon, Martin Jr.	SM3/c (T)	Newark, NJ	7/29/43-
Roseman, W. William F.	Bkr3/c (T)	Milwaukee, WI	7/29/43-
Rudowski, George (n)	EM2/c to USS *Cascade*	Hazelton, PA	10/1/43-9/4/44
Russell, James Austin	GM3/c school	Louisville, KY	7/29/43-1/6/45
Ryan, Charles Glenn Jr.	RdM3/c (T)		5/24/45-
Sanborn, Herbert M.	S1/c from USS *Cascade*	Detroit, MI	9/9/44
Sauer, Bernard Joseph	F1/c R/S	New York, NY	9/13/43-5/31/44
Schlass, Edward Leo	GM3/c, school	Milwaukee, WI	7/29/43-12/23/44
Schrum, Francis C.	MoMM3/c school	Richmond, VA	9/13/43-9/30/44
Sealscott, Doyle Morris	RT1/c (T) discharged	Indianapolis, IN	7/29/43-9/20/45
Shackleford, Floyd Wm.	S2/c R/S		4/20/45-6/2/45
Shayka, Leo (n)	COX R/S	New York, NY	7/29/43-10/10/43
Sherman, Paul Edward	S1/c leave	Indianapolis, IN	4/20/45-11/14/45
Shernoff, Herbert (n)	RM2/c transferred	New York, NY	7/29/43-7/7/45
Shinault, Charles Mason	F2/c hospital	Richmond, VA	9/13/43-9/29/44
Sidey, John Donald	SoM3/c, V-12	Buffalo, NY	7/27/43-10/1/43
Simon, Sylvan (n)	StM2/c		11/7/45-
Slocomb, Donald Albert	EM3/c school	Boston, MA	9/13/43-12/18/44
Smith, Claud Howard	S2/c		4/20/45-
Smith, Ernest Lester	FC3/c discharged	Houston, TX	7/29/43-9/26/45
Smith, Jesse Fullerton	SC3/c hospital	Philadelphia, PA	7/29/43-10/12/43
Smith, Marvin W.	S2/c hospital	Spartanburg, SC	7/30/43-9/17/43
Smith, Robert Luther	S1c R/S	Nashville, TN	7/29/43-6/2/45
Snider, Wallace Kay	S1/c (Y) hospital		4/20/45-7/7/45
Spalding, Charles Stuart	EM3/c school	New York, NY	7/29/43-12/1/44
Spanish, Joseph	S1/c	Albany,NY	9/30/43-
Spedalere, Basil Anthony	F1/c R/S	Baltimore, MD	9//25/43-5/25/45
Stafford, Howard W.	COX (T)	Harrisburg, PA	7/29/43-
Staugh, Sydney R.	S2/c to USS *Tranquility*	Pittsburg, PA	7/29/43-7/24/45
Stegmoyer, John R.	S1/c from USS *Markab*	Harrisburg, PA	9/4/44-
Stephenson, Stanley E.	F1/c		10/28/45-
Stewart, Russell Alie	Cox	Richmond, VA	7/30/43-
Stockwell, David Wm.	S1/c discharged	Albany, NY	7/29/43-9/20/45
Strader, Don Smith	QM1/c (T)	Columbus, OH	7/29/43-
Stults, William Wesley	RdM3/c (T)		5/24/45
Summers, Clarence E.	F1/c		4/20/45-
Sundstrom, Lowell W.	SKD1/c		5/24/45-
Swallow, Francis F.	BM2/c (T)	Springfield, IL	7/29/43-
Talley, Granville Hartwell	S2/c R/S	Raleigh, NC	7/29/43-10/10/43
Tarter, Walter Robert	S2/c R/S		4/20/45-5/24/45
Taylor, William Leander	F1/c R/S	Harrisburg, PA	7/29/43-5/31/44
Techiera, Joseph Edmund	SSMB3/c hospital	Boston, MA	7/29/43-7/15/45
Tew, Miles Casey Jr.	Cox school	Raleigh, NC	7/29/43-5/1/44
Thomas, Warren Laverne	MoMM3/c (T) R/S	Raleigh, NC	7/29/43-4/16/45

Thomas, William Charlie	RM2/c (T)	Richmond, VA	7/29/43-
Thornton, Thomas B.	SoM2/c school	Roanoke, VA	7/29/43-9/10/44
Treshow, Michael Jr.	Y3/c (T)		4/20/45-
Toraya, Mateas (n)	CPhM (PA) transferred	Washington, DC	7/29/43-5/30/44
Wagner, Theophil T.	S1/c		4/20/45-
Wageman, Robert A.	RdM3/c (T)	Milwaukee, WI	2/23/44-
Wahl, Benny R.	SSML3/c (T)	San Antonio, TX	9/28/44-
Walker, Earl Reuben	SoM3/c school	Richmond, VA	7/29/43-2/1/45
Walker, Vernon LeRoy	S2/c	Des Moines, IA	7/29/43-
Wall, Jesse M.	S1/c	Spartanburg, SC	9/28/44-
Warner, Francis Eugene	RT2/c (T)		6/9/45-
Watson, Dryefuss O'Neal	EM3/c discharged	Jacksonville, FL	7/30/43-9/20/45
Webber, Walter George	S1/c		4/20/45-
Weiland, George Elmer	SK2/c (T) transferred	New York, NY	7/29/43-9/20/45
Welden, Robert Edwin	F1/c	Camden, NJ	7/29/43-
Wendt, William Edward	EM3/c school	Milwaukee, WI	7/29/43-7/20/44
Wessig, William John	F1/c discharged	Los Angeles, CA	7/29/43-11/25/45
Whalen, Henry Lawrence	S1/c		4/20/45-
Wheadon, Leo Lee	S1/c		4/20/45-
Whitt, Lawrence Albert	S1/c R/S	Abingdon, VA	7/29/43-5/16/45
Wieland, A. Wm. A.	RM3/c R/S	Milwaukee, WI	7/29/43-3/9/44
Wille, Henry George	RT2/c (T)		6/9/45-
Williams, Charles Tyrone	S2/c (SC) hospital		4/20/45-5/18/45
Williams, Robert Eldren	S1/c		4/20/45-
Williams, Sylvester Agee	Ck1/c R/S	Mare Island, CA	7/30/43-3/26/44
Willis, Erville Hanneford	BM1/c	San Diego, CA	7/29/43-9/15/43
	enlistment up, re-enlisted 4 years 9/16/43-2/1/45 to USS Hutchins (DD-476)		
Willis, Jack (n)	SoM2/c school	Wilkes Barre, PA	7/29/43-9/30/44
Wilson, Don (n)	BM1/c (T) to USS Canfield	Little Rock, AR	7/29/43-1/1/44
Winston, Calvin Roland	S2/c to USS Canfield	Richmond, VA	7/29/43-1/1/44
Witt, Samuel Raymond	SK1/c R/S	New York, NY	7/29/43-5/16/45
Woerner, William C.	S2/c to USS Canfield	Philadelphia, PA	7/29/43-1/1/44
Wolf, Franklin A.	GM3/c (T) from USS Detroit		10/26/45
Wolf, Frederick S. Jr.	CEM (AA) discharged	New York, NY	7/29/43-11/25/45
Wright, Oliver (n) Jr.	EM3/c (T)		6/9/45-
Yantko, Edward Michael	SoM3/c (T)		6/1/45-
Yantz, Peter John	F1/c R/S	New York, NY	9/25/43-5/31/44
Yeager, Noble Dale	GM1/c (T)	Des Moines, IA	7/29/43-
Young, Howard Jr.	PhM3/c R/S		6/1/45-11/10/45

Officers

Acheson, David C.	Lt (jg) (DE-217)	6/13/45-9/25/45 from USS Coolbaugh
Bartlett, Edward Lewis	Ensign	4/29/45-
Bates, Thomas F.	Ensign	8/20/43-8/30/43
Bender, James Joseph	Ensign	4/29/45-
Bertleson, Chad M.	Ensign	4/30/44 Temp Duty
Brozier, Burton G.	Ensign	8/20/43-8/30/43
Camp, James Daubney	Lieut (TD)	7/29/43-
Carter, Paul F.		came aboard 7/29/43 promoted to boatswain and transferred 9/8/44
Davis, William M.	Ensign	1/2/43-
Dodson, John T.		came aboard 7/29/43 promoted to boatswain and transferred 8/13/45
Fellows, Byron W.	Lt. (jg)	9/20/45
Green, William P.	Lt.	9/10/45-11/25/45 discharged
Grimes, Alan P.	Lt. (jg)	7/29/43-5/4/45 transferred
Harrigan, Lawrence P.	Ensign	7/29/43-
Holliday, Alexander R.	Ensign	7/29,43-9/26/43 to USS Ganther
Johnson, Howard F.	Ensign	3/9/44-reassigned
Kelsen, Knut Arthur	Lt. (jg)	6/8/45-10/26/45

Larick, Roy R. Jr.	Ensign	7/29/43-
Lebherz, Robert W. Jr.	Lt. (jg)	4/6/45 TD Div Radar Ofcr
Ludemann, Berthold A.	Ensign	8/2/43 TD
Livingston, Marshall E.	Lt. (jg)	7/29/43 off and on 3/45
Mahoney, Donal M.	Lt. (jg)	12/10/44-5/14/45 FURAS
Maxwell, Murdock M.	Lt. (Lt. Cmdr. TD)	1/1/45 7/29/43-10/27/45 discharged
Moody, Muller P.	Lt.	7/29/43-9/13/45
Mulholland, Sidney C. Jr.	Ensign	7/29/43-9/13/45
Peery, James H.	Lt.	7/29/45-9/20/45 discharged
Relf, George O. Jr.	Ensign	9/25/43-5/14/45
Senrick, James F.	Ensign	11/1/45-
Sinn, Herbert C. Jr.	Lt. (jg)	5/28/44-11/25/45 discharged
Smith, Joseph M.	Lt. (jg)	10/19/45-11/3/45 discharged
Soule, Frank F. Jr.	Lt. (jg)	10/1/43-11/21/43 school
Stephenson, Eldred C.	Ensign	9/19/44-
Wagner, Jay W.	Ensign	10/2/44-5/8/45 to USS Crouter (DE-11)
Whaley, James W.	Lt. CO (CO)	7/29/43-
Wilson, Waldron E.	Ensign	11/25/43-12/30/43
Zajec, John M.	Lt. (jg)	5/27/44-8/20/44 3/31/45-4/6/45

Commander Escort Division Sixteen
USS Deede (DE-263) Flagship (Temporary) November 22, 1943

Bull, John A	Y2/c	Wilmington, DE
Darby, Jefferson, OD	StM2/c	Chicago, IL
Love, Lee R.	RM3/c	Baltimore, Md
Powers, Edward P.	SM3/c	Springfield, IL

Officers

Tedders, Fondville L.	Cmdr relieved 12/31/43 by
Cleland, John B. Jr.	Cmdr promoted to rank of captain 10/13/44 Staff transferred 1/18/44 to USS William C. Miller (Flagship) October 31, 1944
Zito, Paul F.	Lt. is noted as being on staff of Commander Escort Division then aboard Deede.

Only two of several times Deede acted as temporary Flagship.

USS *DONEFF* (DE-49)

To offest constant enemy aerial and sub-surface attacks on it's fleet units, the U.S. Navy fostered the speedy mass production of hard hitting destroyer escorts. Throughout World War II, in ever theater, these bantam-sized battlers depth charged pig boats, peppered Axis planes, rescued downed fliers by the score. Merchantmen and fleet ships alike developed profound respect for their DE running mates, and the men of grit who sailed them.

Destroyer Escort No. 49 was paid for by Lend-Lease Administration funds, launched at the Philadelphia Navy Yard on July 24, 1942, and promptly handed over to Great Britian. After serving effectively as a unit of the Royal Navy she was reallocated to the United States in early 1943, and renamed in honor of Ensign John Lincoln Doneff, USN. Hero Doneff was killed in enemy action 30 November 1942 during the titanic land-air-sea struggle for the Solomons. USS *Doneff* (DE-49) was duly commissioned at Philadelphia 10 June 1943.

Captained by Lt. Commander Louis C. Mabley, USNR, the short-hulled type (289 ft. 5 in.) DE went southeast in the Atlantic, dropped anchor at Bermuda on 29 June 1943. For a month Skipper Mabley put his new command and the sailors who were to man her through their nautical paces.

Doneff gunners peppered towed sleeves, conducted structural firing tests with three 3-inch .50 caliber guns. Below decks, *Doneff* machinists eagerly studied the diesel-electric engines. Continuous drills and tactical maneuvers were the order of the day. Shakedown terminated 23 July and a seasoned destroyer escort *Doneff* sped northwest to Philadelphia.

Upon arrival two days later, the *Doneff* went into the Navy Yard for a thorough post-shakedown overhaul where minor defects encountered during the preliminaries were eradicated. Declared ready for sea, the ship stored and provisioned, steamed to Norfolk on 17 August for a week's lay-over, then nosed south on the 24th. At night on 30 August the *Doneff* slipped through the Panama Canal locks and into the Pacific Ocean.

Pausing overnight at San Diego, the *Doneff* moved up to San Pedro and made that Californian port her base for the next month. She tested and trained in sunlit Pacific waters off San Pedro, until 27 September, when Skipper Mabley conned her out of the Bay, set her course for desolate Adak in the Aleutians.

With its blasts that sometimes reached velocities well above 100 knots and which roll unbelievably gigantic seas of 50 to 70 feet from trough to crest, the North Pacific was the global war's most rugged theater from the climatic stand-point, a storm-lashed proving ground for both ships and men. Amid the barren crag and tundra of Attu Island, American troops had succeeded in ousting the firmly-implanted Japs three weeks of arduous of bayonet-and-butt conflict. Into this theater plowed USS *Doneff* on the 6th of October, 1943. Into her log would be entered fifteen months of Alaskan duty.

Convoy escort work comprised most the *Doneff's* North Pacific tour of duty, the trim DE tagging along with gaunt, cargo-rich merchant ships as they shuttled from one port to another along the Aleutian chain. To *Doneff* sailors, names like Kodiak, Dutch Harbor, Adak, Amchitka, Shemya, Kiska, Chernovski and Attu grew as familiar as those of home town streets.

In late April and early May 1944, and again in August of that same year destroyer escort *Doneff* served under the Commander, Fleet Air Wing Four, acting as plane guardship for Navy planes which hammered installations in the Northern Kuriles. While the *Doneff* was working with ComFairWing Four, on 18 May 1944, a Nip twin-engined bomber pounced on her, dropped two near-miss bombs and darted away to safety.

Twice in 1944 the command of USS *Doneff* changed hands. Lt. Commander R. P. Baruch, USNR relieved Commanding Officer in January 1941. Lt. Commander Thomas A. Graham, USNR in turn took over from him, in June 1944.

1945 saw the long-awaited shift in scenery. Destroyer *Doneff* had seen her last of war in an ice-box as she jubilantly stood out of Adak 13 January 1945. Thawing as she sailed, the *Doneff* wended her way south to Mare Island in San Francisco Bay. Six days later she arrived at the Mare Island Navy Yard and was soon resting on keel blocks in drydock. To the tune of rattlinghammers and hissing acetylene torches she was given a thorough overhaul, restored to her peak of fighting trim. *Doneff* churned out beneath the Golden Gate Bridge on 3rd March, completed passage to Hawaii on the 8th.

Twelve days of exercising ensued, whereupon the DE left for reconquered Guam on the Marianas, on 20 March. *Doneff* stopped in at Eniwetok in the Marshall Islands 26 March to top off with fuel, checked in at Guam's Apra Harbor on the 31st.

Operating out of Guam for the following two and one-half months, the destroyer escort shepherded convoys, teamed with scout planes to locate "ditched" pilots. Intermittently she patrolled off the entrance to Apra Harbor, her sonar tuned to intercept enemy midget submarines reported in the area. When the battleship *Maryland* journeyed to Eniwetok in the latter part of April, the *Doneff* went along as her escort, later received a commendation from the dreadnought's Captain.

Detached from Guam in mid-June, the *Doneff* took up station at neighboring Saipan. Supply ships and transports chaperoned from Saipan, southeast to Eniwetok and northwest to captured Okinawa and Iwo Jima during the summer months. 10 August found the *Doneff* riding gun guard on zig zagging convoy of Okinawa bound troopships. Suddenly the word was passed through the night that a man had toppled from a transport in to the inky waters. Escort *Doneff* began probing in the pitch darkness, hauled the groggy unfortunate of the sea in thirty minutes.

All rumors of Japanese peace feelers ended on 15 August. To the ships of the fleet went the electrifying "cease offensive operations" message. It was no longer a rumor but an actuality. Destroyer escort *Doneff* participated in the highlight of her career in the feverish days which followed, when she was ordered to accompany the veteran destroyer *Mayrant* and submarine APOGON to the enemy's oft-bombed citadel of Marcus.

Marcus Island and its 2700-strong garrison comprised the last point of resistance in the Central Pacific. To effect the surrender, *Mayrant* and company arrived off the Islands beaches at 1330 on 27 August 1945. No signs of life were visible other than the prescribed Japanese signals, i.e., the Rising Sun Flag flying together with a white one. Destroyer *Mayrant* dispatched a motor whale boat which went skimming ashore through the surf. It returned with three Jap officers and the Islands deputy chief Lt. Commander Nakamura.

While the *Doneff* lay to her guns were primed for any emergency, the Nips parleyed for two years with Commodore Vernon F. Grant aboard the *Mayrant*. Solemnly the conference talked of mine fields in the waters surrounding Marcus,

USS Edmonds (DE-406)

USS Eugene E. Elmore (DE-686)

so which there were reputed to be none: mine fields as such which the Japs agreed to mark; the critical health situation on the island; and a host of items to mark; the critical health situations on the island; and a host of items coincidant to the surrender of Marcus military organization. At the end of the session Lt. Commander Nakamura presented the commander a gift of musk-melons, was himself given a carton of American cigarettes. Up went the Stars and Strips over Marcus Island.

Two more Saipan to Marcus trips were made during September and, on the 24th of that month the *Doneff* made the 8 hour jaunt to Guam, left 1 October to cover mopping-up operations at Truk in the Carolines. Four days of patrolling off the Atoll ended on the morning of 7 October, when the *Doneff* back-tracked to Guam. Four days of taking on food and supplies at Guam prepared the *Doneff* for the long voyage home.

Doneff weighed anchor in Apra Harbor on 12 October and cut a swatch across peaceful Pacific swells to San Pedro, via Pearl Harbor. Lt. Commander Graham left his vessel in the hands of Lt. Stewart B. Hobbs at Terminal Island, San Pedro. There the Navy placed destroyer escort *Doneff* out of commission 22 December, 1945. Struck her off its registry 21st January 1946.

This information was supplied by: Department of The Navy, Office of Public Relations, Washington, D.C.

The following information is supplied by Henry Pfeifer Bkr. 2/c.

On returning from Bermuda the thrust bearing on the starboard main propulsion shaft burned out.

While in the North Pacific Seaman *Painter* was lost overboard while carrying his tray of chow to his aft quarters.

The ship was painted a two-tone light and dark gray while in San Pedro before going to the North Pacific.

USS *EDMONDS* (DE-406)

A Message From Rear Admiral T. L. Sprague, Commander Escort Carrier Group To All Ships and Units Under His Command

"To the Officers and Men of the Escort Carriers and to the kin of those who were lost"

This Task Group has participated in one of the decisive battles of this war. The aircraft of these carriers not only have met and defeated enemy attacks in the air but they have turned back a large enemy fleet composed of his most modern ships.

The intrepid courage, skill and fighting spirit of the pilots and air crewmen were superb. Never have fighting men had a greater task and never have fighting men performed their duty with greater determination and distinction.

The seamanlike handling of the vessels, the brilliant offensive and defensive work of the screen, the cool accuracy of the gunners, the sustained and imperturbable handling of planes on deck, the calm singleness of purpose of the re-arming and gasoline details, the prompt and efficient action of the damage control parties and the engineers - all contributed to turning the tide of battle to victory. Against such teamwork the enemy could not prevail.

I am proud to have been privileged to be present and observe your achievements. May God bless everyone of you and may be citizens of your country forever remember and be thankful for your courage.

To the mothers, fathers, sisters and brothers, wives, and sons and daughters of those who were lost I say, 'Do not be sad; be comforted and inspired in the thought that the victory for which these men so freely and courageously gave their lives has contributed immeasurably to the final defeat of the enemy'."

The USS *Edmonds* (DE-406) was one of the ship operating under the command of Rear Admiral Sprague during the first invasion of the Philippine Islands at Leyte Gulf and during the subsequent naval engagement off Surigao Straits.

I am proud to make this message available to every Officer and Man serving with me on the *Edmonds*.

J.S. Burrows, Jr., Lt. Comdr., USNR, Commanding Officer.

USS *EUGENE E. ELMORE* (DE-686)

Eugene E. Elmore, born 30 June 1900 in Americus, Georgia, graduated from the Naval Academy in 1922, and served in a number of ships as well as ashore before reporting 25 October 1940 to Quincy (CA-39). Lieutenant Commander Elmore was killed in action when his ship was sunk 9 August 1942 in the Battle of Savo Island.

(DE-686: dp. 1,450; l. 306'1 b. 37'; dr. 9.8"; s. 24 k." cpl. 186; a. 25'', 3 21'' tt., 8 dcp., 1 dcp. (hh.), 2 dct.; cl. Rudderow)

Eugene E. Elmore (DE-686) was launched 23 December 1943 by Bethlehem Steel Co., Quincy, Mass.; sponsored by Mrs. Eugene E. Elmore, widow of Lt. Commander Elmore; and commissioned 4 February 1944, Lt. Commander G.L. Conkey in command.

On 22 April 1944 at Norfolk, *Eugene E. Elmore* joined the antisubmarine group formed around Block Island (CVE-21), and sailed for Casablanca to provide cover for convoys moving across the mid-Atlantic. During the return passage, on 29 May, Block Island was torpedoed as was the escort *Barr* (DE-576). *Ahrens* (DE-575), dead in the water rescuing Block Island survivors, made a submarine contact, and directed *Eugene E. Elmore* to the target, U-549. *Eugene E. Elmore* sank the German Submarine in 31° 13' N., 23°03' W., then stood by *Barr* throughout the night, next day taking off her wounded and many of her crew members. She took *Barr* in tow for Casablanca, and was relieved of her tow one day before reaching port 2 June.

Eugene E. Elmore returned to New York City 13 June 1944, and during the next 4-1/2 months made two voyages escorting convoys to the Mediterranean. On 3 November she got underway from New York for the South Pacific, arriving at Hollandia 11 December to join the 7th Fleet. She cleared Hollandia 30 December, and at Biak joined the escort of a convoy bound with reinforcements and supplies for newly invaded Lingayen Gulf. Arriving 12 January 1945, *Eugene E. Elmore* joined the ships providing antiaircraft fire to protect the assault shipping for 2 days, then sailed to San Pedro Bay to prepare for the landings at Subic Bay 29 January.

The escort vessel continued to operate out of San Pedro Bay, supporting the continuing liberation of the Philippines by escorting convoys from Biak, the Palaus, Ulithi, and New Guinea. Between 13 July 1945 and 22 August, she twice escorted convoys from the Philippines to Okinawa, and on 3 September arrived off Okinawa once more for occupation duty. In October she escorted transport carrying men to Jinsen, Korea, and on 15 October, sailed from Okinawa for San Diego, arriving 5 November. There she was decommissioned and placed in reserve 31 May 1946. She is now struck from the Navy Register. She was sold for scrap in May 1969.

Eugene E. Elmore received four battle stars for World War II service.

USS *FAIR* (DE-35)

Victor Norman Fair Jr. born August 15, 1921 in Lincoln County, North Carolina, enlisted in the Naval Reserve August 15, 1940, and was commissioned ensign March 14, 1941. Serving in *Gregory* (APD-3), Lieutenant (jg) Fair was wounded when his ship was sunk by Japanese gunfire in the Solomons on September 5, 1942, and died four days later.

(DE-35: dp. 1,140; l. 289'5"; b. 35'1"; dr. *'3"; s. 21 k.; cpl. 156; a. 3"3"; cl. Evarts)

Fair (DE-35) was launched July 27, 1943 by Mare Island Navy Yard; sponsored by Mrs. V.N. Fair Jr., widow of Lieutenant (jg) Fair; and commissioned October 23, 1943, Lieutenant D.S. Crocker, USNR, in command.

Fair escorted a convoy from San Francisco to Pearl Harbor, where she arrived January 9, 1944. She put to sea nine days later to conduct an anti-submarine patrol off Tarawa, and late on February 4 joined *Charrette* (DD-581) to develop a contact previously made by the destroyer. Attacks by both ships led to the sinking in the early morning of February 5 of I-21. *Fair* returned to Pearl Harbor February 17, and sailed February 25 for Majuro, where from March 5 to June 12, she patrolled the entrance to the lagoon, and escorted ships to and from

ocean rendezvous and to Roi-Namur. On June 14, she arrived at Eniwetok with three oilers, and for the next two weeks, screened them in the fueling area off the Marianas as they fueled ships serving in the assault and capture of Saipan. The escort vessel served on patrol out of Eniwetok between July 1 and 14, 1944, then returned to screen the logistics group during the assaults on Tinian and Guam. She returned to Pearl Harbor August 31 for a brief overhaul and to take part in training operations. On October 13 *Fair* was back at Eniwetok for duty escorting convoys to Ulithi until January 19, 1945. She continued her escort duty from Eniwetok to Manus, Guam, and Guadalcanal, until March 24, when she arrived at Ulithi to stage for the assault on Okinawa.

Guarding a convoy composed primarily of LSTs, *Fair* put out from Ulithi March 27, 1945, and after the initial assault April 1, put into Kerama Retto. On April 6, before getting underway for Saipan with unladen transports, she fired on the massive wave of kamikaze planes which attacked shipping off the island, splashing one. After her voyage to Saipan, *Fair* patrolled off Chimu Wan, Okinawa, until May 12, then screened the transport area, firing on attacking aircraft and suicide boats for 10 days. Her next assignment was a convoy escort voyage to Saipan and Guam, returning to Okinawa June 10 for local escort duty and patrol.

Fair cleared Okinawa July 5, 1945 for a West Coast overhaul. She was decommissioned at Portland, Oregon, November 17, 1945, and transferred to the Army May 20, 1947.

Fair received five Battle Stars for World War II service.

USS *FARQUHAR* (DE-139)

(De-139: dp. 1,200; l. 306"; b. 36'7"; dr. 8'7"; s. 21 k.; cpl. 186; a. 3 3", 3 21" tt., 8 dep., 1 dep. (hh.), 2 dct.; cl. Edsall)

The second *Farquhar* (DE-139) was launched February 13, 1943 by Consolidated Steel Corp., Ltd., Orange, Texas; sponsored by Miss S.B. Garton, great-granddaughter of Admiral Farquhar; and commissioned August 5, 1943, Lieutenant Commander L.E. Roseberg, USNR, in command.

Farquhar arrived at Norfolk, VA, October 3, 1943, and next day sailed on the first of three convoy escort voyages to Casablanca. She returned from each to New York for replenishment and repairs before joining a new convoy at Norfolk. On April 3, 1944, she sailed for Casablanca once more, this time in a hunter-killer group formed around *Core* (CVE-13). The group guarded the passage of a convoy, hunting submarines in the general area through which the convoy sailed.

USS Farquhar (DE-139)

Returning to New New York June 9, 1944, *Farquhar* trained in antisubmarine warfare at Bermuda with the *Wake Island* (CVE-65) hunter-killer group, then sailed on the Casablanca convoy route once more. Homeward bound, on August 2 she went to the rescue of *Fiske* (DE-143) who had been torpedoed while away from the group searching for a previously sighted target, and arrived in time to rescue 186 survivors. These she took into Argentia for medical attention and clothing, then on to Boston, where they were landed. In September, she began patrols and convoy escort duty in the South Atlantic with the *Mission Bay* (CVE-59) hunter-killer group. She voyaged from Bahia, Brazil, to Dakar, French West Africa, and Capetown, Union of South Africa, and during a submarine hunt off the Cape Verde Islands on September 30, made a contact against which she and her sisters operated six days, finally sighting a large oil slick, but no other evidence of a sunken submarine.

During training exercises off Cuba in December 1944 *Farquhar* rescued 10 aviators from life rafts after their patrol bomber splashed, and while in Florida waters as plane guard for carriers conducting operations to qualify aviators, rescued a downed pilot February 3, 1945. She returned to Guantanamo Bay for training with the Mission Bay group later in February, and with it arrived at Argentia April 3 for hunter-killer operations in the North Atlantic. While bound for New York May 6, she made a sonar contact, very close, early in the morning. Just five minutes after it was reported, she dropped 13 depth charges, set shallow, and both she and her sisters could make no further contact with the target. Post-war evaluation revealed that she had been the last American ship to sink a submarine in the Atlantic in World War II, sending U-881 to the bottom.

Farquhar prepared at Boston and Guantanamo Bay for duty in the Pacific, and arrived at Pearl Harbor August 8, 1945. Escort duty took her to Eniwetok September 5, and on September 10 she sailed in company with *Hyman* (DD-732) to receive the surrender of Ponape. There she served as station ship for several months, then sailed from Kwajalein early in January 1946 for the East Coast. She was decommissioned and placed in reserve at Green Cove Springs, Florida June 14, 1946.

Farquhar received one Battle Star for World War II service.

USS *FECHTELER* (DE-157) & USS *LANING* (DE-159)

Both ships made identical, Buckley class, built at Norfolk Navy Yard, Portsmouth, Virginia. 306 feet long 36 feet and 10 inches wide at the beam, crew of 215 seamen, shakedown cruise Bermuda. *Fechteler* was launched April 22, 1943. Sponsored by Miss Joan S. Fechteler, commissioned July 1, 1943. *Laning* was launched July 4, 1943. Sponsored by Mrs. Mable C. Laning, commissioned August 1, 1943. Typical destroyer escorts.

From September 8th to the 31st of December 1943 these two ships helped escort two convoys OT "Oil Torch" fast-tanker convoys from the Caribbean Sea, Curacao to the Mediterranean Sea, Bizerta and Algiers and back with an average of eight tankers each. Sailed at 32 day intervals, these convoys supplied armies in the Italian Campaign with much needed gasoline and oil products. Encountered German submarines near the strait of Gibraltar and while at Algiers both ships searched all night for a U-Boat that torpedoed a British destroyer. DE 157 and DE 159 worked together as a team and would tie up along side of each other at sea ports, where you saw one you usually saw the other.

In January of 1944 the two ships parted ways, separated went on different voyages but in April they met again. *Fechteler* under command of skipper Lt. Calvart B. Gill and *Laning* under command of skipper Lt. Cmdr. E. Arthur Shuman, Jr. Ships met at Hampton Roads Norfolk, Virginia to help escort convoy "UGS-38", more than 100 ships, believed to be the largest convoy to ever cross the Atlantic Ocean.

Convoy "UGS-38" from the United States to Gibraltar and the Mediterranean Sea and becomes "GUS-38" homeward bound. Same convoy eastward and westward. Convoy consisted of eighty-five merchant vessels, two navy tankers, two coast guard cutters, *Duane* and *Taney*, twelve United States destroyer escorts, *Joseph E. Campbell* DE 70, *Chase* DE 158, *Falgout* DE 324, *Fechteler* DE 157, *Fessenden* DE 142, *Fiske* DE 143, *Laning* DE 159, *Lowe* DE 325, *Menges* DE 320, *Mosley* DE 321, *Newell* DE 322, *Pride* DE 323. Escorted by Task Force 66, flagship USCGC *Taney*, the sole survivor of 101 vessel of the Pearl Harbor attack, Commodore Commander, W.H. Duvall.

Convoy "UGS-38" departed Norfolk April 3rd, smooth slow sailing for two weeks. It was early spring, beautiful weather, plenty of sunshine, sight was spectacular, ocean water blue and clam, waves from ships gave the flying fish a chance to fly across decks of DEs, some landing on decks. Saw many schools of porpoises jumping out of the water in complete unison as if they were being drilled like sailors on a parade field in boot-camp, even better. This voyage across

the Atlantic was peaceful and enjoyable, the watch, four hours on and eight hours off wasn't bad, even the food was good.

What a beautiful sight, seeing all those different types of ships sailing the same way in column after column with all the escorts ships around them. Ships carrying troops and all kinds of materials that took weeks even months to make or build in defense plants, ocean looked as if it was covered with ships. During this period of time no one on board could imagine what lay ahead, German aircrafts and submarines.

Another convoy "UGS-37" was crossing the Atlantic ahead of convoy "UGS-38" by nine days and on April 11, 1944 "UGS-37" was attacked by German aircraft in the Mediterranean near the coast of North Africa, Cape Bengut 42 miles east of Algiers was called "Torpedo Junction". The USS *Holder* DE 401 was hit by a torpedo that damaged her bow, she stayed afloat and was towed to port. This same fate lay ahead for convoy "UGS-38".

Naval war in the Mediterranean Sea during the prolonged Anzio deadlock which lasted from January until June 1944. Allied convoy escorts had fought life-and-death battles on that sea-going road which entered the Mediterranean through the Straits of Gibraltar, trailed along the coast of North Africa. These battles did not make front page news but they were all part and parcel of the effort that loosened the Nazi grip on Italy and southern Europe. Typical was the onslaught on convoy "UGS-37", "UGS-38", "GUS-38" which sank allied cargoes, killed allied sailors and cost the navy three hard fighting war ships, the USS *Holder*, USS *Lansdale* and USS *Fechteler*.

The enemy knew well when UGS convoy was coming. In order to avoid mine fields in the approaches to Gibraltar, convoys had to pass the Strait in daylight, and for 40 miles their course lay within sight of the Barbary coast where Axis spies and coast watchers were thick as fleas, the stretch of 110 miles from Europa point to Alboran Island was usually traversed at night, after which the convoy closed the Algerian coast about 25 miles west of Oran and hugged the shore for 180 miles to Algiers. Their progress along shore was signaled by bonfires on the beaches and in the hills, kindled by degenerate descendants of Barbary corsairs in Axis pay.

During 1944, Mediterranean Convoys encountered some of the toughest air versus surface battles of the entire war. In April the German air offensive grew more intense. It was aimed at the big UGS convoys, principal means of supplying Allied campaign in Italy, of building up for the invasion of southern France, and carrying material to India and Russia. Destruction or diminution of these convoys was of such vital importance that Marshal Goering (in charge of all of German aircraft) used all resources that he could spare from the Italian and Russian fronts and all the tactical ingenuity he could muster. These efforts long persisted, despite heavy losses.

The planes used in these attacks, based on airfields in southern France and on Bordeaux, were not numerous, amounting to about 140 JU-88s, HE-111s, DO-217s carrying torpedoes, bombs and controlled glide-bombs. Owing to the recent improvement in antiaircraft fire of allied escorts and of the Naval Armed Guards in merchant ships, the Luftwaffe attacked only at night or in twilight. For that purpose, elaborate, too elaborate tactics were worked out. Each convoy from the time it passed Alboran Island was shadowed by long-range planes. Who reported its course, speed and strength and the next step was to dispatch the tactical reconnaissance, two planes, flying low, laid the launch pointer, a line of acetylene float lights some 60 miles long, pointing toward the spot where the convoy was to meet its death near North Africa coast. There, bonfires burning by Axis spies to aid in finding convoy.

British aircraft (Beaufighters) stationed at airfields near Algiers to scout ahead of convoy for German planes and to engage them and help protect ships under attack. Convoy "UGS-38" was relying on these aircrafts to help in case of an attack. Radio communication between British aircraft and convoy escort ships were worked out, everything in readiness.

Morning of April 19, 1944 "UGS-38" was entering the Strait of Gibraltar, another great sight to behold. Sunny day, sea gulls flying all around ships. A gigantic rock sticking up out of water, a British seaport called the Rock of Gibraltar, on the European point of Spain. This port is in the future for the crew members of the *Fechteler* and *Laning* but not scheduled.

"UGS-38" passed the Rock peaceful without any trouble from all the German submarines lurking in these waters, too many DEs for the U-Boats to make a move. The most German submarines in the Mediterranean Sea, eighteen in March of 1944, most of these slipped in through the Strait underneath convoy ships entering the Mediterranean.

Convoy "UGS-38" grows larger after entering the Mediterranean, more escorts, the veteran destroyer USS *Lansdale* DD 426, same ship was part of the escorts of convoy "UGS-37" now joins convoy "UGS-38". The Dutch cruiser

HNMS *Heemskerck*. A ship partly built and completed in London in 1940 after its hull being towed from Holland just prior to its invasion by the Nazi, now a part of "UGS-38". Two British minesweepers, HMS *Speed* and HMS *Sustain*, also three submarines and a tugboat HMS *Vagrant* was a part of the convoy. Which grew to 109 vessels, ships from horizon to horizon, could not see them all from any direction.

Afternoon of April 19th "UGS-38" was cruising slow, about 6 to 8 knots, weather still beautiful, convoy in ten columns with three British submarines 600 yards on port beam, escorts surrounding convoy. All escorts were given gunnery doctrine for this area in the event of an air attack by the enemy during darkness. Doctrine, directs escorts to fire machine guns only at seen targets. All ships were well drilled to encounter enemy aircraft expected next day April 20th.

April 20, 1944 the onslaught on convoy "UGS-38". Hitler's 55th birthday, Goering was going to try to sink the largest convoy ever to sail across the Atlantic. Was this going to be Hitler's birthday present from Goering?

The day began with regular chores aboard ship, weather pleasant. Young sailor's life seem to be safe and secure but anxiety among the crew. Feeling of uncertain, it was as if everyone knew something big, something great was going to happen. Goering had his aircraft ready to fly across the Mediterranean to attack convoy "UGS-38" near North Africa coast (Torpedo Junction) where they would find bonfires to aid them. The British had their aircraft at Algiers to help protect the convoy and all of the American and British escort ships were ready for the onslaught.

The sun was setting, evening shadows were growing longer, dusk dark was approaching, no smoke screen were laid. GQ rang, boatswain mate blew his whistle over the loud speakers and said all hands man your battle stations. Tension was growing strong among the ship's crew. Suddenly excitement began when two British aircraft were flying over convoy, traveling east from aft to forward. At first some thought they were German planes, then realized they were friendly scout planes. Just as they flew out of sight the onslaught began.

The battle was on, about 30 German planes came flying from dead ahead just above the water. Darkness began as the enemy aircraft flew in quickly like a flight of bats. Escort ships open fire, enemy aircraft dropping torpedoes, ship SS *Paul Hamilton* blew up like an atomic bomb. German planes being shot down by machine gun fire from escort ships. USS *Lansdale* was torpedoed and sinking but she did not give up without a good fight. Her brave crew were still firing their guns while ship was sinking. More planes being shot down, some hit and had to leave battle. A dog fight between a British and a German plane was observed over the convoy. Three merchant ships hit by torpedoes, SS *Samite* and SS *Stephen F. Austin* damaged, towed to port. SS *Royal Star* damaged, sunk next day. Six German planes shot down, five damaged. Just as the battle came to an end, darkness had fallen but there was another plane flying high over head, *Fechteler* firing at plane 3 inch shells were bursting near plane, then cease-fire was given. It was a British Beaufighter plane, almost shot down by a mistake of identification. Looking back at the battle scene as the convoy sailed on, you could see a silhouette of a cloud formation against the sky that looked like the clouds of an atomic bomb explosion where *Paul Hamilton* blew up.

Rescue operation was outstanding and deserve the highest praise. The quick and determined action of the tug *Vagrant* and the USS *Menges* which picked up two German aviators that had been shot down, also rescued survivors of the USS *Lansdale* which had been torpedoed and sunk. All the escorts ships of convoy "UGS-38" deserve credit for outstanding action against the enemy.

Next day April 21st, after observing convoy five ships had been lost but convoy still consisted of over 100 ships, this twilight, escort ships laid down smoke screen to hide convoy in case of another enemy air attack. Convoy "UGS-38" made its destination. Escort ships tied up in port of Bizerta April 22nd. As escorts made their way in and around sunken ships that littered the harbor, some of the sunken ships were laying on their sides, some their mast was sticking up out of the water, as many as nineteen was counted, it looked like there were more.

During World War Two, every ship building country in the world had mass productions in all shipyards. More ships were being manufactured than were sunk, 2,882 merchant ships and 175 warships of the Allies was sunk by German submarines alone. Great Britain lost the most, she also had the largest navy, Royal Navy in 1939. The United States lost most of their navy by the Japs attack on Pearl Harbor, December 7, 1941 but under the leadership of Secretary of the Navy, Frank Knox the United States by 1944 had built the world's largest navy. While convoy escorts were tied up in port of Bizerta, crew members were doing their work on deck, someone noticed all escort ships had their American flags flying at half mast in honor of Secretary Knox who had suffered a heart attack and died April 28, 1944 at age 70. He was buried with full military honors at Arlington National Cemetery. Flags on every U.S. Navy ship flew at half mast for three days.

The next convoy of task force 66 was a 106 ship Mediterranean to USA convoy "GUS38." DEs surround convoy at Bizerta and headed west for the long journey back home. The Germans were not through with trying to sink ships of the convoy. German's Admiral Doenitz was going to send his U-Boats to attack convoy before it could get out of the Mediterranean Sea.

Morning of May 3rd in this area where the Mediterranean bottle narrows into a neck, the Nazi enemy was ready and waiting for "GUS-38" and in the early hours a torpedo from U-Boat 371 crashed into USS *Menges* carried away both propellers and rudders and wrecked the after compartments. She stayed afloat and was towed to port. Commodore Cmdr. Duvall ordered two DEs to hunt down her assailant.

USS *Pride* and USS *Joseph E. Campbell* picked up the submarine's contact near USS *Menges*, HMS *Blankney* and HMS *Sustain* also French DEs *L'Alcyon* and *Senegalais* joined the hunt. For 24 hours the U-Boat evaded the search team. Finally on May 4th the desperate submarine came to the surface and torpedoed French DE *Senegalais*, she stayed afloat. U-Boat was hit with fire arms from escort ships, some shouting Germans were glimpsed in the water. Nazi sailors were picked up, some went down with their submarine.

May 5th, a date that will bond the crews of the USS *Fechteler* (DE-15) and USS *Laning* (DE-159) together forever. One of the escorts for westbound convoy "GUS-38". The *Fechteler* Captain Lt., C.B. Gill plotted on with the slow ship-train which took an evasive course after the submarine attack on USS *Menges*. The convoy swung southward toward Oran, then headed west. Early in the morning on May 5th it was approaching the island of Alboran, a Spanish flyspeck in the center of the Mediterranean's bottleneck. Here German submarine U-Boat 967 was trying to get within range of convoy ships to try to torpedo them. Captain of the submarine knew it was going to be his last chance to sink a ship or ships of the convoy before it would leave the Mediterranean Sea that day, so the attack plan was underway.

Destroyer Escort USS *Laning*, Captain Lt. Cmdr., E. Arthur Shuman, Jr. made sonar contact with a strange vessel 13 miles distant. Presently the "pip" disappeared, the vessel had submerged. The submarine alarm was flashed and the convoy made several course-changes, maneuvering to evade ambush.

Fechteler covering a sector between the convoy and the sub's reported position, was swinging right to follow a new course. *Fechteler* was between the submarine and a large ship, either a troopship or a hospital ship. The captain of the submarine fired his torpedo probably at the large ship. Some of the crew members of the *Fechteler* believes that Captain Gill maneuvered the *Fechteler* between the U-Boat and the large ship in order to save it, where the loss of life would have been much greater.

The *Fechteler* was still turning when she was rocked by a thunderclap explosion. On the topside men were thrown from their footing on the bridge and at gun mounts. In the compartments below decks engineers and firemen were hurled against bulkheads or pitched into a jungle of shattered machines. Water spouted in through the smashed hull, and the Destroyer Escort wallowed in helpless disablement.

Heroes, every able-bodied sailor aboard the *Fechteler* helped rescue all the wounded, Captain Gill saw that every injured man was put into the whaleboat or on life rafts, after all hands had abandoned ship. The water surrounded the sinking vessel was full of sailors waiting to be rescued. The USS *Laning* started picking up some of the survivors and before rescue efforts could get underway *Laning* was ordered to stop and go search for the submarine.

USS *Mosley* dropped extra life rafts to *Fechteler* survivors while they were in the water swimming trying to find anything that was afloat to hold on to, as they watched their ship sinking, what a horrible experience, knowing their fellow shipmates were going down with their ship. Some 186 survivors were picked up by the USS *Laning* and a rescue tug. The ship now broken in the middle cracked as the bow and stern came together in a perpendicular rise 125 feet above water. The vessel held that position for 5 minutes and sank, following a violent explosion. The rest of *Fechteler's* crew either perished in the torpedo blast or went down with the wreckage.

Captain Shuman of the USS *Laning* (DE-159), there is not enough words of thanks or praises for this man who was so courageous to stop his ship dead still in the water, a setting target subject to be torpedoed at any moment during the rescue operations, for the survivors of the *Fechteler*. All crew members of the *Laning* contributed to the effort of helping save lives that moonlight morning. During the rescue operation the submarine surfaced, reason unknown, and was spotted by a boatswain mate of the *Laning*, the sub then submerged.

Fechteler survivors appreciate the *Laning* crew for rescuing them while endangering their own lives, how survivors were given everything from the *Laning* ship's canteen, tooth brushes, razors, candy etc. Even loaning their shoes, clothes and blankets. Gave survivors their peacoats to ward off the chill while transferring them to Gibraltar. Treating and given medical aid to the wounded sailors. One of *Fechteler* survivors, Malichi Rich was seriously wounded. His foot was cut open like a sardine can, said Robert Jones one of the crew members of the *Laning* who helped with medical aid to the injured survivors. These two ex-sailors would meet again 46 years later at a ship reunion.

Willis Walker one of the *Fechteler* survivors made this statement. The USS *Fechteler* (DE-157) was honored, she was just a small insignificant ship in a big war. Built in just a few weeks, minimal cost and just another unit in a large navy, they probably used cheap champagne to christen her. With just a few seasoned Navy men, "Old Salts" and some 200 sparsely trained rookies, we were soon pressed into convoy duty on seas filled with German U-Boats. During the eleven months of her life we did many missions for the war effort. Our ship got some real tough duty assignments. We soon realized that our ship and its crew were expendable. This did not discourage us but caused us to give total effort to the cause of freedom.

On May 5, 1944 our ship the USS *Fechteler* (DE-157) and her crew received the highest honor given any U.S. Navy ship and crew. As the USS *Laning* (DE-159) sailed out of the port of Gibraltar after unloading *Fechteler* survivors which she saw standing on the deck of a merchant ship, she was at quarters, her flag was "dipped" saluting our ship and her crew.

The Blue-jacket Manual states "The National Flag is never dipped except in answer to the dip of a merchant ship". We who observed this salute know it was for us and not the merchant ship. We were honored by our peers. As the *Laning* sailed out of sight sailors of both ships wondered if this would be the last relations between two ships and their crews.

Mediterranean Sea, war zone, battlefield for the convoy of "UGS-38" time it entered the Strait of Gibraltar until "GUS-38" exited the Strait. Here is the final tally sheet of the battles of task force 66.

Eight ships torpedoed, 1 blown into bits, 3 sunk, 4 towed to port. Five ships torpedoed by German aircraft. USS *Lansdale* (DD-426), sunk, 47 killed. M/V *Paul Hamilton* exploded, 580 killed. M/V *Royal Star* sunk. M/V *Samite* towed. M/V *Stephen F. Austin* towed. Three ships torpedoed by German submarines. USS *Menges* DE 320 towed, 31 killed. French DE *Senegalais* towed. USS *Fechteler* DE 157 sunk, 29 killed. 11 German aircraft hit by firearms, 6 shot down, 5 damaged. 1 U-Boat sunk, U-371, 49 Germans captured, 2 pilots, 47 seamen. More than 700 casualties.

Thanks to the "Desa News," now DE Ship Reunions are easier to formulate. Survivors of the USS *Fechteler* for a few short years have held their reunions on May 5th the anniversary date of the ship's sinking. The 1990 ship reunion (46th anniversary) Pigeon Forge, Tennessee was an historical event. Their guest was former crew members of their sister ship the USS *Laning* and Captain E. Arthur Shuman, Jr. and wife Polly were special guests. Captain Shuman spoke at the banquet, everyone in attendance was honored by his presence. While he was at the ship reunion, he won a ship model of the sinking of the USS *Fechteler*. The model was made by the talented Curtis Toombs a survivor of the *Fechteler* who is a big help at all reunions.

The first ship reunion of the USS *Laning* (DE-159) was hosted by Jim and Kate Graham, August 17-19, 1990, Lawrenceburg, Tennessee. Their guests were former crew members of their sister ship the USS *Fechteler*. A great time was had by all in attendance. Jim and Kate went all out to show everyone a good time. There were welcome signs throughout the town for visitors of both ships. The banquet supper, was held on Jim's birthday with a huge cake with the picture of

the USS *Laning* (DE-159) on it made of cake icing. At the last ship reunions, it was agreed by both ships' crews to combine ship reunions into one reunion and to hold them on May 5th each year. So "May 5th" which bonded the *Fechteler* and *Laning* crew in 1944, that same bond will continue for years to come.

In closing this story, findings were in history books, National Archives, ship histories and from crew members of both ships.

USS *FISKE* (DE-143)

August 2, 1944	
Task Group 22.6:	USS *Wake Island* (CVE-65)
Hunter-Killer Group:	USS *Douglas L. Howard* (DE-138)
	USS *Farquhar* (DE-139)
	USS *J.R.Y. Blakely* (DE-140)
	USS *Hill* (DE-141)
	USS *Fessenden* (DE-142)
	USS *Fiske* (DE-143)

Howard and *Fiske* were detached to investigate and attack surfaced U-Boat, sighted ten miles on the Task Group's port beam. Contact was made by both vessels almost simultaneously. Both were turning in for an attack, when *Howard's* foxing gear was blown up, and *Fiske* was struck by a torpedo amidship, causing her to break in two. Bow and stern up ended, bow sank immediately. *Farquhar* picked up survivors, including 50 badly wounded, 30 were killed. *Howard* then made several hedgehog and depth charge attacks, on the 'decoy' sub and the 'shooter' sub, with no results. These attacks were delayed until survivors in water could be picked up by *Farquhar*. *Fiske* was 1000 yards from *Howard* when hit. Later, *Howard* sank *Fiske* stern section with 3 inch 50 gunfire.

USS *FLAHERTY* (DE-135)

The USS *Flaherty* (DE-135) was named for Ensign Francis X. Flaherty, USNR, of Charlotte, Michigan, who gave his life at Pearl Harbor on Dec. 7, 1941, where he held a flash light while the men of his turret escaped from the heavily damaged *Oklahoma*. The *Flaherty* was built at Orange, TX and commissioned June 26, 1943. The officers and men of her original crew had been thoroughly trained at the Sub Chaser Training Center, Miami, Florida and at the Naval Training School, Norfolk, VA, but the real training took place at Bermuda on the shakedown cruise during which many hours were spent practicing operations so necessary for a naval ship—breeches buoy, fueling at sea, anchoring, mooring to a pier, battle stations, and various gunnery exercises.

Proceeding to Charleston, SC for a period in the Navy Yard, The *Flaherty* commenced her duties which from then until this time have taken her to many United States and foreign ports. To list a few: Orange, TX; Galveston, New Orleans; Charleston; Norfolk; New York; Portland; Southampton, England; Porte Del Gade, and Horta, Azores; Guantanamo Bay, Cuba; and Argentia, Newfoundland.

During the fall and winter of 1943 the *Flaherty* made several convoy runs to Casablanca; then in March 1944 she, with the other ships of Escort Division Four, joined the escort carrier *Guadalcanal* (CVE-60) to make up a sub killer group whose duty it was to seek out and destroy enemy submarines.

USS Flaherty (DE-135)

And this they did on their first trip. Depth charges and gun fire from the DDs accounted for the U-515 which was sunk April 9, 1944, and some days later the planes from the carrier accounted for the U-68 from which the *Flaherty* picked up a section of a torpedo for study.

The next trip was, however, by far the most historic and unusual anti-submarine patrol of the war. Nearly out of fuel after an extensive search for submarines off the coast of French West Africa the Task Group was headed for Casablanca when on Sunday, June 4, 1944, the U-505 was brought to the surface by depth charges from the *Chatelain* and subsequently saved from scuttling by heroic salvage parties from the *Pillsbury* and *Guadalcanal*; later she was towed to Bermuda for study by Naval experts. For this exploit the Task Group later received the Presidential Unit Citation.

Another trip during the summer netted no submarines; and the winter months, with the submarine menace at a low ebb found the *Flaherty* at Guantanamo Bay, Cuba for training with the Division, and later in Miami, Florida and Jacksonville, Florida training pilots in carrier landings with the other ships of the division and the Guadalcanal.

In preparation for increased sub activity which was expected in the spring of 1945 the ship left Jacksonville in April and with nearly 50 other DEs and with several escort carriers joined a patrol designed to eliminate the subs. And in this the *Flaherty* played a major role; for on April 24, 1945 after her sister ship the *F.C. Davis* had been sunk by an enemy torpedo the *Flaherty* with other DEs carried on a day long attack on the U-546; the *Flaherty* forced it to the surface herself and took aboard several crew members and the captain as prisoners of war.

The ship was then sent to Mayport, Florida to operate with the Solomons CVE-67 training pilots in carrier landings. Now the *Flaherty* is at the Charleston Navy Yard, undergoing a yard availability. Upon completion of this availability the ship will proceed to Green Cove Springs, where she will be put out of commission, fleet reserve.

NOTE: After 19 years in the moth ball fleet, the *Flaherty* was scrapped in January 1965.

USS *FOGG* (DE-57)

It was the last of April, 1943.

Destroyer Escort Training School, Norfolk, VA, that was the destination on our orders. We came from all over the country, Alaska and Canada. Naval Operations Base, they called it now, but it was the old Naval Training Station to some of us who had survived "boot camp" there! Almost everyone's first question, What is a destroyer escort? It didn't take long to find out. Sleek, trim, maneuverable, a lot of firepower and could turn in its own length. Little did we know during those first days that on March 20, the USS *Fogg* (DE-57), had been launched and she would be our next duty station.

The Advanced Ship's Company party was sent to Hingham Shipyards, in Fore River, MA, We had our first look at the real thing, and there was a unanimous feeling, she's something special. During the next weeks of receiving stores, equipment and overseeing installation. A number of the crew, when off duty would go over in the yards and learn various skills and trades. Once certified by a Naval inspector you could do piece work and get extra funds, even a nickname or two. Butts was tagged to a West Virginian, because he burned the backside of two workers on the deck above him who were taking a smoke. Millimeter Mike wore a 20mm dummy projectile around his neck on a chain. Each day she came more to life, with additional crew arriving. The big day came on July 3, 1943, and she was commissioned the USS *Fogg* (DE-57), of the United States Navy.

Shakedown was at Guantanamo Bay, Cuba. All of the armament was tested day and night. Two 3.50" forward and one aft, at No. 4 position. 4 20mm, torpedo tubes and a British 1.1 Pom Pom at No. 3 mount amidships. On one occasion, during AA practice, a talker, on a 20mm, failed to call a "dummy run" as the plane towing an aerial target sleeve approached, and his gunner opened fire, the *only* gun to open fire. Cease fire was immediately called, as the target sleeve drifted down to the water. On recovery there were three holes in the sleeve and the cable severed about 50 feet in front of the sleeve. The gunner was presented with a piece of the sleeve but from then on he was called "dummy run" which he didn't mind unless they left off the run. Then there was the electrician's mate who always had a pleasant "glow" on until they found the glass covers on the lights were filled with Vodka, invisible to the eye. When he wanted a snort, he simply changed a light bulb. He became Ivan. There was "Blowtorch," a metalsmith, "Skivvies," a signalman, Peppers, a cook, "Champ", a fleet boxing champ who already had 12 years of service and the usual "Tex," "Doc," "Keys," "Slim," "Rocky," and many others, but they all had a story to tell of the one who answered to it.

Shakedown behind them, the *Fogg* made several coastal runs off the east coast and on September 18, 1943, Comdr. H.T. Chase, became Flag Officer and Commander of ComDesCortDiv., 12 and the *Fogg* became Flag Ship. First convoy duty began Oct. 13, 1943, from New York, with empty tankers to the Dutch West Indies port of Aruba and Curacao, and full tankers taken on to Algiers in North Africa. One of the signalmen had been at the U.S. Navy Hydrographic Office, in Suitland, Md., and had had a hand in printing the original invasion maps for North Africa, in early 1943, and pointed out many landmarks for the crew. Every ship had one and it was in Algiers we found our scrounger. A tall rangey kid from Rockport, Ill., who could find and get anything. He had so many stories he used it didn't take long to tag him with "Bull."

The *Fogg* returned to New York by way of Curacao and Trinidad arriving back in the States on December 4, 1943. During the next three weeks she was given a new look. The torpedo tubes and 20mm guns were replaced with 4 mounts of twin 40mm guns and the 1.1. PomPom was replaced with a quad 40MM gun. A Hedgehog Battery was also installed between the superstructure and No. 2 gunmount. During a firing sequence check by Navy Yard personnel a dummy round was left in place and was fired over the bow into the Navy yard. No one was injured but a lot of people scattered in all directions. As one worker said, "I'll go home with wet pants tonight."

The day after Christmas, 1943, Escort Division 12, was again at sea. The *Fogg* with the USS *Foss*, USS *Fox*, USS *George W. Ingram* and the USS *Ira Jefferies*, made six trips across the North Atlantic to Ireland, and return. The North Atlantic was a constant upheaval of sea, waves and pounding walls of water. One lookout from Kalamazoo, Mich., who could see the big ones coming, would holler "DUCK", and it was not long before he had the nickname "Duck." One of the best orders to be heard on these crossings was, "Air Bedding." That meant the weather was good enough to bring all bedding topside, drape it over the railing, and get the "stink" out from being closed up below decks during the rough weather.

Returning August 20, 1944, from the 6th crossing she left on Sept. 12, 1944, to escort a convoy to Cherbourg, France, returning, after a port of call at Portsmouth, England, on Oct. 9, 1944 returning to New York.

After a brief overhaul, and special training, she sailed on November 6, 1944, to escort what had to be the slowest moving convoy in Naval History. It was made up of barges with cranes and yard equipment, flat barges, dry dock sections, all under tow, along with the usual supply ships and oil tankers. All of this became docking facilities at Cherbourg, France.

On the return trip, with a convoy of mostly empty ships, at a position of 42°22" North and 18°41" East, on December 20, 1944, a quiet, sunlit, almost perfect weather day was shattered with the rumble of an explosion. An LST in the outside starboard column of the convoy reported an explosion in their engine room. Called to general quarters with *Fogg* withdrew from its escort position to assess the situation and lend assistance. As the *Fogg* was completing its final turn to draw alongside, she was hit in the stern by a torpedo. Aware now of the presence of a submarine the convoy changed speed and direction, and the remaining escorts began tactical anti-submarine maneuvers.

The *Fogg* began to settle at the stern, but the watertight bulkheads held tight at No. 2 engine room. Remaining at battle stations, those of the crew, who could use cutting torches, and those who could be spared, set about lightening the load at the stern. Depth charges were released from the racks, the racks cut away and anything else that could be dumped.

The LCI 419, returned from the convoy to the side of the *Fogg,* and for two days the crew fought to save their ship but on December 22, 1944, when the stern sheared off, the wounded and all but a skeleton were taken off by the LCI 419.

Rejoining the convoy, the crews were placed aboard the USS *Mattole*, AO-11, a fleet oiler, on December 23, 1944. Crews Quarters were limited so the crew of the *Fogg* spent the first night on deck huddled under canvas where ever they could find shelter from the wind. They ate their meals on deck during Christmas Eve and had a big Christmas dinner in the mess hall Christmas Day but very little time to eat it in because of the *Mattole's* watch schedule.

Christmas Day, in the afternoon, one of the *Fogg's* signalman obtained permission to send the survivors list, by blinker light, to the acting flag ship, and on completion of the list, added, "Is there someway we can put back aboard our DE's and feel at ease and at home." Before long the *Ingram* was spotted coming along side and survivors were divided up and put aboard the remaining DEs. On the *Ingram* survivors were embraced by the crew, given Red Cross packages for the first time, and most took their first showers. In a matter of a few short hours the survivors were part of a crew, a very special crew, as was any crew who put to sea on a DE. The crew of the *Ingram* even took a collection among themselves and divided it up among the survivors, so they could buy what they wanted at ship's store. The grim faces of the survivors gave away to smiles as they became part of a crew and had a DE deck under their feet.

January 14, 1945, the *Ingram* entered New York Harbor, with the survivors standing amidship as the "Lady with the Torch," came into view. Through each and everyone of them the feeling swelled, the tears came. As they realized, as no other person can, that we made it back, we are home. Thanks Be to God, we made it.

No nicknames came out of these last events, just names whose memories will always be there. DE's were special ships, with special crews and a special duty like no other in the whole U.S. Navy.

USS *THOMAS J. GARY* (DE/DER-326)

Thomas Jones Gary-born on 16 September 1922 in Texas City, TX. Enlisted in Navy on 30 September 1940. When the Japanese attacked Pearl Harbor on 7 December 1941, Seaman 2nd Class Gary was on board *California* (BB-44). During the raid, the battleship suffered torpedo and bomb hits which caused extensive fires and flooding. After he had rescued three or four wounded men from closed and burning compartments in the ship, Seaman Gary continued his efforts to save others until he lost his own life. He was posthumously commended by the Secretary of the Navy for his courageous action and disregard for personal safety in assisting his endangered crewmates.

Gary (DE-61) (q.v.) and *Gary* (DE-326) were named for Seaman 2nd Class Thomas Jones Gary. The latter was renamed *Thomas J. Gary* on 1 January 1945.

(DE-326: dp. 1,200 (est.); 1. 306'; b. 36'7"; dr. 12'8; s. 21.2 k. (tl.); cpl. 216; a. 3-3", 6-40mm., 10-20mm., 2 dct., 8dcp., 1 dcp. (hh.); cl. Edsall)

Gary (DE-326) was laid down on 15 June 1943 at Orange, TX, by the Consolidated Steel Corp.; launched on 21 August 1943; sponsored by Mrs. Willie Mae Gary, mother of Seaman 2d Class Gary; and commissioned on 27 November 1943, Lt. Comdr. William H. Harrison, USNR, in command.

Following shakedown exercises out of Bermuda and post-shakedown overhaul at Charlestown, *Gary* reported to the Command Caribbean Sea Frontier at Guantanamo for temporary duty on 5 February 1944. She was detached from that command on 9 March and set her course for the Straits of Gibraltar, escorting the first of many transatlantic convoys. Until May of 1945, *Thomas J. Gary* operated as an escort vessel in the Atlantic, safely screening eight convoys from the east coast to ports in the Mediterranean and the United Kingdom and back to the United States. While on the east coast between patrols, *Gary* trained off the coast of Maine and out of Guantanamo Bay, Cuba, and conducted antisubmarine warfare exercises out of New London. During June of 1944, she was assigned to the Navy Fleet Sound School.

In December 1944, she detached from the homebound convoy she was escorting from British ports to aid *Huron* (PF-19) which had collided with a merchantman. On the 9th, she took on board more than 100 Coast Guardsmen from the badly damaged patrol escort vessel and then screened her as she was towed to Bermuda.

While the ship was moored at Boston on 1 January 1945, her name was expanded to *Thomas J. Gary*. She completed her last Atlantic convoy upon her arrival at New York on 7 May and spent the remainder of the month preparing for service in the Pacific. Following refresher training in the Caribbean, she departed waters off the coast of Haiti on 22 June; steamed, via the Panama Canal, to the west coast; and departed San Diego on 12 July with a convoy bound for Hawaii. She arrived at Pearl Harbor on 20 July to begin repairs and training.

On 1 August, she departed Oahu with Escort Division 57 and steamed for Saipan. After a brief stop at Eniwetok, she was rerouted to Guam and arrived at Apra Harbor on the 13th. The same day, she again got underway; this time with Carrier Division 27. As the force steamed toward the Philippines, word of Japan's surrender reached the ship.

Following her arrival at San Pedro Bay on 17 August, *Thomas J. Gary* remained in port until the 29th when she departed Leyte to screen the aircraft carriers of Task Group (TG) 77.1 during their passage to Korea.

En route, the task group was diverted to Formosa. With Commander Escort Division 57 embarked, *Thomas J. Gary* was designated to liberate allied prisoners of war who had been held on that island. On 3 September, she embarked 19 Marines from *Block Island* (CVE-106) charged with arranging the details of the evacuation of the POWs. Her division commander was also responsible for making the preliminary arrangements for the occupation of Formosa.

Before dawn on 5 September off the coast of Formosa, *Thomas J. Gary* and *Kretchmer* (DE-329) were detached from the escort carrier task group. The destroyer escorts were without navigational guides to indicate the location of mines in waters surrounding the island. Despite the signing of the peace some days before, resistance from die-hard Japanese was a distinct possibility.

At 0718, as the two ships approached the waters most apt to be mined, every precaution was taken to minimize damage and casualties, should the ships strike a mine. The American sailors maintained a state of readiness to repel possible attack. *Thomas J. Gary* with her sister ship 500 yards astern, threaded he way at 9 knots through the unknown and dangerous waters. Four Combat Air patrol planes provided cover, and two anti-mine sweep planes from the carriers relayed word of the sightings of possible mines as the destroyer escorts picked their way through the hazardous approaches to Kiirun, making frequent changes of course to avoid sonar contacts which exhibited a suspicious similarity to those made by mines. One mile north of Kiirun Island, she rendezvoused with a small Japanese tug, where a Japanese harbor pilot pointed out the dock to be used.

The ships maintained a condition of modified general quarters and stationed armed guards on shore. A detail headed by *Thomas J. Gary's* communications officer took over the Japanese radio station to insure reliable communications between the task group and Japanese authorities in Kiirun for the duration of the evacuation operation. Finally, at 1630, a train arrived bearing allied prisoners of war who were quickly transferred to the waiting destroyer escorts.

At 1800, provided now with a Japanese pilot and Japanese charts of the minefields in the vicinity of Kiirun, *Thomas J. Gary* got underway. Her commanding officer later dryly reported: "Our outbound route did not coincide with the one used inbound since we discovered that our inbound track crossed several minefields." That night, she rendezvoused with the carriers and transferred the newly freed POWs to the larger ships.

On the 6th, *Thomas J. Gary*, joined by other DEs, returned to Kiirun to transport additional POWs. After transferring most of her passengers to *Block Island* (CVE-100), she got underway for Manila; and, on the 9th, she arrived at Manila to discharge the last 50 of her POWs.

Later in the month, she steamed on to the Ryukyus with the escort carrier group; and she operated out of Okinawa into October conducting exercises in the East China Sea. On 19 October, while at sea with the escort carrier group, she struck a submerged log which caused considerable damage to her starboard propeller. Slowed to 13 knots, she was forced to leave formation and put in at Saipan on 23 November for repairs.

She next operated in the Philippines into the new year with calls at Hong Kong and Okinawa. She departed Singapore on 8 April 1946 and set her course via the Suez Canal for the Mediterranean where she spent much of May visiting European ports. On 29 May, she arrived at Charleston to commence drydocking and preservation procedures. On 25 September, tug *Nancy Moran* towed the destroyer escort from Charlestown and headed for Green Cove Springs, Florida. She was decommissioned there on 7 March 1947 and placed in reserve.

On 24 July 1956, she was delivered to the Philadelphia Naval Shipyard for conversion to a radar picket escort ship; and on 1 November 1956 she was redesignated DER-326.

She was recommissioned on 2 August 1957 and spent the remainder of the year in training exercises out of Newport, RI, and Guantanamo Bay, Cuba. On 30 December, she departed Newport and began duties on the Atlantic Barrier, a part of the North American Defense Command. Operating out of Newport, she completed 12 radar picket assignments in the next year and one-half, breaking the routine duty with a visit to Belgium and the United Kingdom in August 1958.

In July 1959, *Thomas J. Gary* entered the Boston Navy Yard for overhaul. She remained there until 30 October when she got underway for refresher training in waters off the coast of Cuba. On 20 December, she resumed for her former duties in the Atlantic alternating North Atlantic Barrier and Contiguous Radar Coverage System Assignments.

Early in 1961, she varied radar picket duties with participation in Operation "Springboard;" and, in May, she steamed off Bermuda participating in Operation "Lantbex." In August, she completed a Dew Line assignment in the northeastern Atlantic with a visit to Scotland and finished out the year in overhaul at Boston.

Thomas J. Gary next set her course for Guantanamo for refresher training; then on 10 July 1962, she steamed from Newport for now familiar North Atlantic picket deployment. Between picket assignments, she put in at Greenock and at Wilhemshaven for well-earned recreation for all hands. Shortly after her return to Newport on 22 October, she was called upon to conduct patrols in support of the Cuban Quarantine. Relieved of her patrol station off Key West on 29 November, she returned to Newport for availability and a welcome holiday in homeport.

She filled the opening months of 1963 with radar picket duty out of Key West as Southern Tip Picket, and two tours as Sonar School Ship at Key West. In April, a period of tender availability was cut short for *Thomas J. Gary* when she was called upon to take part in the unproductive search for the submarine *Thresher* (SSN-593) lost off the Atlantic Coast. She resumed Southern Tip Picket duties in July, and she returned to Newport late in August. On 24 September, she arrived at Boston for overhaul and trials which occupied the remainder of the year.

She opened 1964 with operations in the Caribbean including refresher training and participation in Operation "Springboard." She spent March undergoing availability at Newport and, during April and May, patrolled on picket station off Florida, with time out in May for a good will visit to Fall River, Mass. on Armed Forces Day. She continued picket duties for the rest of the year breaking her routine with gunnery exercises off the Virginia Capes and a visit to the Naval Academy in October.

After participating in the annual exercise Operation "Springboard" again in 1965, she resumed picket duties and, on 30 June, phased out the Southern Tip Picket Station where she had spent so much of her post-World War II career. On 13 September, she departed Newport for a nine-month deployment in the Pacific which took her through the Panama Canal later that month and included support for Operation "Deepfreeze," a scientific expedition to the Antarctic. In March 1966, she departed New Zealand, visited Adelaide and Perth, Australia, and steamed via the Suez Canal, to the Mediterranean. Her ports of call in that ancient sea and the eastern Atlantic included Barcelona, Bremen, Copenhagen, Gothenburg, and Edinburgh. She returned to Newport on 21 May 1966.

Thomas J. Gary again got underway from Newport on 24 August and set course, via the Panama Canal and Pago Pago, the Dunedin, New Zealand, her replenishment port during her participation in Operation "Deepfreeze". Manning her station midway between McMurdo Sound and New Zealand, *Thomas J. Gary* acted as logistics headquarters for Operation "Deepfreeze" and stood ready to provide search and rescue for downed fliers. She remained in southern waters through the end of 1966.

In March, she called at Perth, Australia; then she set her course on the 23d for the Suez Canal. She called a European ports and returned to Newport on 24 May. On 1 July, her home port was officially changed to Key West. After her arrival there on 9 July, she helped to test experimental equipment during Operation "Combat Keel" late in the year. On 12 December, she returned to Key West for a period of upkeep.

In 1968, she operated out of Key West; conducted refresher training out of Guantanamo; and, in August, participated in support operations for the practice firing of Polaris missiles by nuclear submarine *Daniel Webster* (SSBN-626). Later in the year, she conducted special operations in the Bahamas and acted as school ship for the Fleet Sonar School at Key West.

She continued operations in the Caribbean and off Florida into 1969. In July, she began a special four month deployment during which she conducted intelligence support activities for antisubmarine forces in the Atlantic and earned a Navy Unit Commendation. She visited the Canary Islands and Malta before returning to Key West late in October.

After participating in Operation "Springboard" off Puerto Rico early in 1970, she got underway on 1 April and steamed across the Atlantic for operations which took her to Spain, Denmark, Germany and the British Isles. On this deployment, she helped to develop new techniques and tactics in the antisubmarine warfare in such as exemplary manner that she was awarded another Navy Unit Commendation. She returned to Key West on 7 September and operated out of that port into 1972 providing surveillance in support of the Atlantic Fleet. Departing Key West on 14 January 1972, she visited Wilhemshaven; then returned via Senegal, to the United States. Back in Key West in March, she resumed local operations out of that port which she continued well into 1973.

In September 1973, she began preparations for the transfer to the Tunisian government. That month, 33 members of a Tunisian turnover team came on board for training. On 12 October, she got underway from Charleston and crossed the Atlantic, stopping briefly at Ponta Delgada and Palma de Mallorca before arriving at Bizerte on 21 October. The next day, *Thomas J. Gary* was decommissioned in ceremonies at the Quai d'Honneur, Bizerte; and, moments later, the ship was commissioned by the Tunisian Navy as the *President Bourgiba* (E-7). Her name was struck from the Navy list that same day.

USS *GEORGE* (DE-697)

George (DE-697) was laid down 22 May 1943 by the Defoe Shipbuilding Company, Bay City, Michigan; launched 14 August 1943; and commissioned at New Orleans, Louisiana, 20 November 1943 Lieutenant Commander J.E. Page in command.

George sailed from Boston 11 January 1944 to Noumea, New Caledonia, where she arrived 19 February. Until the spring of 1944 *George* escorted transports to the Admiralities, the New Hebrides, and the Solomons during consolidation operations in the Solomons. On 16 May she sailed from Florida Island, Solomons, in a hunter-killer group with *England* (DE-635) and *Raby* (DE-698) on what was to become one of the most successful antisubmarine actions in the Pacific War. During this patrol from 19 to 31 May the three-ship

team sank six Japanese submarines (I-16, RO-106, RO-104, RO-116, RO-108, and RO-105) in waters north of the Bismarck Archipelago—a truly remarkable achievement. *George* arrived Manus 4 June after this feat, and during the next three months she conducted antisubmarine patrols and escorted merchantmen to the New Hebrides, the Solomons, and the Marshalls. After serving briefly as stationship at Funafuti, Ellice Islands, she steamed to Australia, arriving Sydney 12 October.

After returning to Purvis Bay, Florida Island, 28 October, *George* resumed antisubmarine patrols and escorted convoys to New Guinea, Manus, Guam and Saipan. During the liberation of the Philippines, she escorted ships from Guam to Iwo Jima during the invasion and occupation of that embattled island. In addition she served as air-sea rescue station, and on 18 April 1945 she rescued three survivors from a B-29 forced to ditch off Iwo Jima. During the summer of 1945, she made two escort voyages to Okinawa; and, after the Japanese surrender, she delivered surrender terms 12 September to the Japanese garrison stationed in Truk, Carolines. She departed Guam 18 September and sailed for the United States, where she arrived San Pedro, California, 5 October.

Between 10 March 1946 and 9 April 1947 *George* deployed with the 7th Fleet in the Western Pacific. From 1947 to 1951 she served with Escort Division 31, attached to the Fleet Sonar School at Pearl Harbor. *George* moved to San Diego in 1951 and served there until undergoing overhaul at Pearl Harbor in the spring 1953. Following return to San Diego in September 1953, she sailed for Sasebo, Japan, 10 November. She returned to San Diego 25 June 1954, and for more than a year she operated out of San Diego along the coast of southern California.

George sailed on her next WestPac cruise 4 October 1955. She operated out of Guam for more than two months and conducted surveillances of the Carolines, Marianas, Bonin and Volcano Islands before reaching Yokosuka, Japan, 17 January 1956. On 10 March she sailed for the West Coast, arriving San Diego 31 March. Subsequently, she resumed operations out of San Diego, highlighted by an October 1956 cruise to British Columbia. On 3 January 1957 she again sailed to join the 7th Fleet, the force for peace in the Far East. After steaming to New Zealand and Japan, she served as station ship at Hong Kong; and operated out of Guam on island surveillance patrols in the Marianas. Departing Guam 10 June she returned to San Diego 7 July. On 18 September 1957 *George* was assigned to duty as a reserve training ship out of San Francisco. She decommissioned at San Francisco 8 October 1958 and entered the Pacific Reserve Fleet at Stockton, California.

George received two Battle Stars for World War II service.

USS *GUSTAFSON* (DE-182)

The USS *Gustafson* is, in comparison to some mighty warships of the Navy, both small and young. Nevertheless, like her older sisters, she has in her own way contributed in some measure to the final victory which is now ours, and we are confident that should she be called upon, she will be able to maintain the peace which cost us so much to buy.

When, on 24 August 1943, eight officers and twenty-four men were brought together for the first time, the "Gus" was but a name, a number, and a few large hunks of steel. It was then the ground work was laid for the organization that would in two months take the ship to sea. This nucleus crew spent a month at the Naval Training Center, Miami, Florida, in getting to know each other, and getting to know the DE. The next stop was Norfolk for some, where they were joined by the remainder of the ship's company and where the "getting-to-know-each-other-and-the-ship" process was continued on a large scale. The rest travelled to Newark, New Jersey, where the name and number were beginning to look like a ship, to commence work with Commander Herman Reich, USNR, the Commanding Officer. The Executive Officer, Lt. Comdr. Ambrose Ely Chambers, USNR, put the crew hopefully through an extensive training program during which time a continuous stream of news regarding the progress in the building yard was received and which served to keep hopes and expectations high.

November 1st, 1943, marked the end of the preliminaries. The crew assembled from all directions to go aboard for the first time and at noon the 182 became a full-fledged fledgling of the U.S. Navy - USS *Gustafson* (DE-182). Hectic days followed in the Navy Yard, NY, in preparation for the maiden voyage to Bermuda where the real work was to start. Somehow it was ready to sail at the appointed hour — the work finished an no bones broken, and on 14 November the "Gus" set sail for Bermuda and shakedown. As she went through the gates Captain Reich was heard to remark (for the benefit of Executive Officer and Navigator Chambers, whose home is New York) "We may not get there on time but I'll bet we get back in a hell of a hurry!"

Part one of this prophecy was fulfilled. The *Gus* was unable to make a landfall because of heavy fog and after a night of steaming back and forth outside the gate, she was given permission to enter the next morning.

Shakedown is easy to define. It means just what is says but for the uninitiated it may be defined as a period of time, usually as short as possible, during which a training group gives many, usually as many as possible and sometimes more, opportunities to the ship to conduct — there the term is used somewhat loosely — various exercises after first making sure that the ship is not sent to sea unless it is sufficiently rough to give it and everyone aboard a shake-up. If you live through it you are ready to face the enemy in combat.

The *Gus* profited greatly, in spite of the usual difficulties which are familiar to all her kind. She was now more than a fledgling, she had her wings.

On 17 December, she left Great Sound and headed home to New York to freshen up for her first assignment. It is to be noted here that a new record was set for Bermuda to Ambrose Light Ship on the return voyage - well, almost. The entire crew needed a rest, but since we were fortunate enough to remain in New York until 0900 on 1 January 1944, they probably didn't get one.

1944

Upon completion of the post-shake-down availability in the Navy Yard, the *Gus* received it's first assignment to active duty as a member of the U.S. Fleet. To a crew eager to get into the thick of the fight, it turned out to be a disappointment. The *Gus* was ordered to Key West, Fla., the headquarters for the Fleet's extensive A.S.W. training program. It was feared that she would be forgotten and passed over, such was not the case. Instead, a very profitable month was spent in extensive training with a group of Marine torpedo planes, a new phase in the Key West Air Station program.

This was brought to a close when the *Gus* was ordered to join a West-bound convoy in the Gulf — destination Galveston, Texas, and return to New York.

On 20 February, she joined the big time, setting sail for Recife, Brazil, thence to Capetown, S.A., and Carachi, India in company with the USS *Mission Bay* (CVE-59), USS *Trumpeter* (DE-180) and USS *Straub* (DE-181), the latter two being members of her division. It was while en route to Recife that Commander Reich received orders to turn over the command to Lt. Commander Chambers. Transfer of command was affected during a 20 hour stop-over in Recife and the *Gus* proceeded under her new Skipper. Lt. Fred T. Mays, Jr., acceding to the position of Executive Officer. It was a hasty good-bye to a man known to the crew a short time, nevertheless, those who served under him will remember Little Herman as a very able Captain, competent ship handler, and a generally likeable guy.

The second leg of this long trip was interrupted abruptly by orders sending the three DEs into Rio de Janeiro, Brazil, leaving the baby flattops to continue on their own. At Rio de Janeiro, the DEs joined the cruiser USS *Memphis* (CL-13), and the destroyer USS *Winslow* (DD-357), setting sail for Montevideo, Uruguay on 13 March. It was a disappointment to all that because of our very short time in Rio none were able to see the "town." This disappointment was only mometary and dissolved when the group was informed to it's mission. The task force set sail on the eve of the Argentine revolution. Once again plans were abruptly changed. The revolution was consummated the day before our scheduled entry into the capital city of Uruguay, with the result that the group was sidetracked into Rio Grande do Sul, Brazil.

Three days were spent in this small city, during which time Holiday Routine was declared by the Mayor and the DEs got their first taste of Brazilian hospitality — augmented by a large quantity of good scotch at the British Club.

Next stop for the three escorts was Salvador, Bahia, Brazil's fourth largest

USS Gustafson (DE-182)

city lying about halfway between Rio de Janeiro and Recife. Here ten days were spent getting things ship shape, trying to learn the language, buying up huge quantities of what proved to be ersatz Channel #5, and arguing with taxi drivers. During that ten days something was learned of the Brazilian way of life and of the ways of Bahia. Next to the incomparable Rio, it became the *Gus's* favorite city. That meant it will be seen later, that it ranked above Recife.

On 28 March, the *Straub, Trumpeter* and *Gustafson* set sail for a mid-ocean rendezvous with the USS *Solomons* (CVE-67) to commence the work which was to occupy the *Gus* steadily until 22 November. For the next eight months, the *Straub* and *Gustafson*, as steady customers, took on the job of escorting CVE's assisted by various other DEs of Division 18 and 24 (included were the *Trumpeter*, USS *Christopher* (DE-100), USS *Alger* (DE-101), USS *Marts* (DE-174) and USS *Micka* (DE-176). This "hunter-killer-group," as it is known, paraded back and forth over the entire South Atlantic - from Uruguay and Capetown, north to Dakar, and Trinidad — once achieving the doubtful distinction of crossing the Equator seven times in 24 hours — in an unending search for enemy submarines, broken only by hurried trips to Recife and Bahia, once to Rio for an eight hour stopover, to load supplies, fuel and ammunition.

This constant searching was rewarded on 15 June, when the group caught an enemy supply sub on the surface at 05° West Longitude, 25° South Latitude. Attacked by the carrier planes resulted in a kill in near-record time of seven minutes, from first run. Survivors were recovered and the group proceeded homeward, sporting a "Well Done" from Admiral Ingersoll, Commander-in-Chief, U.S. Atlantic Fleet. However, to the disgust of all hands, no Battle Star was authorized for this engagement. This victory was not without its price however. Two F4F planes, and two TBF planes were lost in the protracted search and final attack — ten men. It need not be said that the loss on one man is a high price to pay, almost too high, but victory does not come cheap. On another occasion the *Gus* was instrumental in saving the lives of two airmen whose plane crashed in a night take-off. Alert ship-handling and the daring of her crew who went into the waters when enemy subs were known to be in the area, succeeded in bringing two survivors aboard. The pilot never was able to get out of the plane and went down with it.

On 22 August, the *Solomons* was replaced by the USS *Tripoli* (CVE-64) and the search continued. About the end of September, a good contact was made on an enemy sub and resulted in a probable kill. No survivors were taken nor was the enemy ever seen, but indications are that he broke up under water.

The hunter-killer-group activities drew to a close with the departure of the *Tripoli* about 15 November, and the *Gus* spent three weeks cleaning up and resting up in Recife and Bahia, where she went into dry dock.

On 22 November, the *Gus* set sail for a rendezvous with the USS *Omaha* (CL-4), (light cruiser), the transport *General M.C. Meigs,* one Brazilian cruiser and two Brazilian destroyers. The *Gus* was to relieve the *Omaha* as commander of that task force while she refueled in Recife. The group was transporting Brazilian Expeditionary Forces who were to join the Allies in Italy. The rendezvous was affected, but in passing the orders, the *Gus* was caught in the stern of the cruiser, and her screw did a good job of hacking a great tear in the *Gus's* bow, and also, serious damage to the left forward shaft of the cruiser. Both ships carried on to the completion of their respective missions however, at which time the *Gus* went into dry dock at Bahia, and the *Omaha* to New York. The Board of Investigation ruled that in view of the construction of the two ships and the high speed at which the maneuver took place (20 knots-top speed for the *Gus),* a collision was inevitable. Orders forbade reducing the speed of the task force. Both skippers were commended on their ship-handling ability in avoiding further damages and in their ability to carry out their assigned tasks in spite of the damage incurred.

This accident provided the excuse for which she had been looking, on 21 December, the *Gus* was ordered to New York for repairs in the Navy Yard, once again just in time for Christmas.

The *Gus* was now an old hand, a veteran, and could look with pride on her first year of duty. She had made an enviable record of performance and continuous duty with the Fourth Fleet. The leaves that were forthcoming had been well earned — doubly welcome at the Christmas season, so for a month the *Gus* was put into the capable, if hurried, hands of the Navy Yard while her crew caught up on life at home and in the city of New York.

1945

On 15 January, the crew, feeling like new men after their visit home, came back aboard to begin a New Year on a new *Gus.* For changed indeed she was, from the *Gus* they had left but three weeks before. The Navy Yard had gone to work in earnest. They tore off the flying bridge and reassembled it with new fire control

equipment. The insides of the chart house were pulled out to make room for the installation of a new C.I.C. New guns were added on the fantail and in general the *Gus's* face was lifted. The result was an even sleeker better looking ship. A week was devoted to loading her up again with stores of all kinds and on 22 January, she set sail for Key West once again.

This time, she was not to be lightly brushed off and relegated to the unhappy position of playing school teacher, for on board was equipment with which even the experts were unfamiliar. She received great attention while being put through her paces — experts watched, the crew wondered, and both tried to understand, until it was felt she was ready to take on her duties once again, better equipped than ever in men and material.

Orders were received to report back to Commander FOURTH FLEET and on 17 February she set sail for Trinidad, where a slow convoy was picked up, destination Recife. The *Gus* arrived in Recife in time to see the rest of her division steaming gaily towards Rio on a tour of large South American ports. Better things were in store for the *Gus* and she was ordered back to New York within four days to be detached from the FOURTH FLEET.

After a week in New York, she then proceeded to Casco Bay, Maine, the home of U.S. ATLANTIC FLEET destroyers for an intensive refresher training period. Exercises of all kinds and inspections of every variety were held to find out whether or not she was capable of performing her task and the *Gus* came through with flying colors. Originally intended as a two week period, it was a month before the training was finally completed. This delay was due to an interruption caused by a sub scare off Boston, during which the *Gus* in company with the *Micka* and two Coast Guard frigates joined the search. During the hunt, good contact was made on a submarine, and repeated attacks resulted in underwater explosions, classified as definite damage and possible sinking of the sub.

Then followed a sub hunt off Cape Hatteras during which two subs were sunk in areas adjacent to that in which the *Gustafson* was engaged with the rest of Division 24 (*Micka, Straub, Trumpeter*). Two weeks were occupied with the Fleet Sub Training Command in New London, CT. It was during this period that VE-Day came to the Allies in Europe. Thankful we were for it - but thoughts turned immediately to the Pacific for there was still a war to be won there in spite of the victory achieved over the Nazi.

On 15 May she was ordered to Norfolk and on the 18th shoved off for Oran, North Africa with what turned out to be the next to last convoy of the Atlantic War. Three days out of Gibraltar the word was received that lights in the Atlantic could once again be lit, and that the necessity for convoy work having been removed, escort duty in the Atlantic was at an end.

The return trip was made by way of the Azores but only a few hours were spent there. The *Gus* parted company from her group and on 15 June arrived at the Navy Yard, Charleston, South Carolina.

Here, once again the *Gus* underwent extensive remodeling. Torpedo Tubes, Smoke Screen Generator, and single 20mm, were replaced with new twin 40mm, new smoke maker with twin 20mm, the latest thing. All this is in preparation for a voyage to the home-waters of the fearsome kamikaze.

Refreshed by another leave, and hopeful of a quick end to the Pacific War, the crew returned aboard and shoved off for Guantanamo Bay, Cuba for a second shakedown.

If anything, this period of training was even more intensive than that provided at Bermuda, but the *Gus* was an old hand now and she came through in great shape. When she left for the Panama Canal on 24 July, she was unsatisfactory in no department and was able to boast very good to excellent marks in several phases of the training.

By 27 July, she was through the canal on on her way to San Diego for a few last minute repairs, and supplies, and one last fling in the States. On 9 August, the *Gus* set sail for Pearl Harbor and not without signs of trepidation. The Navy's war in the Pacific was not easy and the crew knew only too well the part she might play in it, and the fact that she might not return. The *Gus* could not know that even before she reached Hawaii, the Japanese would quit. But quit they did on 14 August, and the war was at an end.

Since that time the *Gus* has been available for utility service to Destroyers U.S. Pacific Fleet and Submarines, U.S. Pacific Fleet, taking life easy and generally getting settled down to a peace-time existence. At present, she has just completed her second weather patrol north of Hawaii during which Christmas was spent at sea, the first Christmas in three years that she has not managed to get home, but life has been good to her and she does not complain. This New Year brings with it the fulfillment of the hope that has been in her heart as it has been in every ship of the Navy, every person in the world.

Since V-J Day, the changes have been many. Captain Chambers who was promoted to commander this fall, has been relieved by Lt. T.H. Dyer, who became executive officer following the departure of Lt. F.T. Mays. Even now, the *Gus* is waiting the arrival of Lt. Lanier W. Pratt, who will relieve him as captain. So with all aboard from apprentice seaman to captain, they are returning home to take up where they left off two, three and four years ago. Many have spent more than two years on the *Gus*, others not so long. One and all, the *Gustafson* is at once glad to see them returning home, but saddened at this parting of the ways. To those who are leaving, *Gus* says, "So long, good luck and good sailing - to those who remain, here's hoping you keep up the good work."

1946

The *Gus* returned to the States in February, and was decommissioned in Green Cove Springs, Florida on 26 June.

Not until after the war (1954) did investigators learn, through captured German records, that the *Gustafson* had sank the U-857, commanded by Oberlieutenant Zur See Rudolf Premauer, on 7 April 1945, almost within range of Boston Light.

DE-182 was transferred to the Royal Netherlands Navy in 1950. Was put into service as Hr. Ms. frigate *Van Ewijck* Number F 808. William van Ewijck, 1645-May 1684 was captain of the Admiralty at Amsterdam; served under Admiral De Ruyter in 1672-1764. He was killed in a fight against French men-of-war in 1684. *Van Ewijck* served in Den Helder in 1950-1955. In April 1956 she was put in reserve. On 5 June 1962, she returned to service in the Dutch Antilles and was scrapped in early 1968.

Former crew members of *Gustafson* hold an annual "GREASY GUS REUNION," the first was in Toledo, Ohio in August 1946, the forty-fifth in August 1990 in Salisbury, North Carolina.

USS *HANNA* (DE-449)

Commissioned 27 January 1945 at New York Navy Yard, Brooklyn, NY.

Named in honor of William T. Hanna, USMC, killed 9 October 1942 at Guadalcanal. Sponsored by his mother Mrs. William P. Hanna.

Lt. Commander Means Johnston, Jr. in command. Class - "John C. Butler". Guns - two 5 inch.

After shakedown out of Bermuda and Guantanamo Bay, *Hanna* returned to New York 24 March 1945. Departing New York 9 April she escorted *Akutan* (AE-13) to Cristobal, Canal Zone. Then sailed via San Diego arriving Pearl Harbor 4 May. After more intensive training and various escort missions in Hawaiian waters *Hanna* sailed 9 June for Eniwetok where she took up duty with Marshall-Gilberts Surface Patrol and Escort Group. This duty continued until 28 September after the Japanese surrender. Then she and the U.S. prize Tachibana Maru formed the task unit to evacuate Japanese soldiers and sailors from Wake Island. Embarking 700 passengers they reached Tokyo 12 October. The U.S.

Navy crew was withdrawn; the United States ensign hauled down; and Tachibana Maru turned over to the Japanese.

Departing Tokyo 24 October 1945, *Hanna* returned to Eniwetok and then sailed to Guam, where she took up duty as air-sea rescue and weather reporting ship. She continued this important task until her return to the States, where she was decommissioned at San Diego 31 May 1946 and joined the Pacific Reserve Fleet.

Hanna was recommissioned at San Diego 27 December 1950. Lt. Commander C.W. Ward in command to augment Navy strength in the Korean conflict.

Once more an active unit of the Pacific Fleet, *Hanna* served with Escort Squadron 9 until 16 April 1951 when she sailed for the Western Pacific. Here she served as patrol ship in the Formosa Straits. In June 1951 *Hanna* joined Task Force 95 for blockading and escort duties off the west coast of Korea. In August, while on shore bombardment mission in Wonsan Harbor *Hanna* was instrumental in silencing enemy shore batteries after a duel lasting more than 2 hours. During the ensuing months *Hanna* served gallantly, operating with the Blockading and Escort Forces of Task Force 95. She was part of the anti-submarine and anti-aircraft screen for our aircraft carriers launching repeated strikes against the Communists. In early November 1951 *Hanna* was detached for the United States, reaching San Diego 26 November for overhaul.

Three months later *Hanna* returned to the Western Pacific and resumed her shore bombardment missions in addition to escorting damaged vessels and investigation of fishing craft. She returned to San Diego 9 June 1953. After operations off the California coast *Hanna* departed 19 November for an island-hopping cruise of the Central Pacific, returning to San Diego 6 June 1954.

Between 9 November 1954 and 28 June 1957 *Hanna* made three more deployments to the Western Pacific. On her last deployment *Hanna* took up patrolling the Central Carolines, Northern Marianas, the Bonins and the Volcano Islands. In addition she participated in a rescue mission involving the Chinese Nationalist merchantman S.S. *Ping Tung* that had run aground on Yokoate Shima, an island of the Ryukyu chain.

Hanna's home port was changed to Long Beach 26 November 1957 and she was designated a Naval Reserve Training Ship. She commenced the first of her reserve training cruises 6 February 1958 to Manzanillo, Mexico, and from that date until 27 August 1959 made 18 such cruises in addition to numerous weekend cruises. *Hanna* decommissioned at Mare Island 11 December 1959 and joined the Pacific Reserve Fleet. *Hanna* received five stars for Korean service.

USS *HERZOG* (DE-178)

The USS *Herzog* (DE-178) was commissioned on 6 October 1943 with Lt. Comdr. J. C. Toft commanding. She was built by Federal Shipbuilding

USS Hanna (DE-449)

& Drydock Co., Newark, NJ. After a shakedown cruise out of Bermuda, *Herzog* steamed from New York on 29 November 1943 on her first escort mission. She accompanied the USS *Ariel* (AF-22) to the West Indies.

On 18 December 1943, *Herzog* was a part of an escort mission protecting a merchant convoy through the treacherous Caribbean passages arriving at the Canal Zone on 27 December. Later, she served as an escort vessel between Recife, Brazil, and Trinidad.

Herzog joined the Task Group 41.6 on 14 April 1944 patrolling the South Atlantic for German submarines with the escort carrier USS *Solomons* (CVE-67). On 15 June, *Herzog* was detached to pick up survivors from a U-boat sunk by aircraft, then rejoined the group arriving in Recife on 23 June 1944.

USS *Herzog* (DE-178) was placed out of commission and loaned to the Brazilian navy under lend-lease on 1 August 1944. She served Brazil as *Beberibe* (D-23), and on 30 June 1953 was permanently transferred to their navy register under the Mutual Defense Assistance Program.

USS *HOLDER* (DE-401)

Submitted by Edmond J. Anusczyk SM2/c

This is the story of the USS *Holder* (DE-401) as I had lived it. For many years I wouldn't talk about it and the mere smell of diesel fuel brings back memories of that fateful day.

Let's begin with November or December 1943. I had just finished Signal School in Newport, Rhode Island. Only the top few exceptional men received the 3rd Class Signalman rating. Some of my friends were being separated from our group by going to the Armed Guard, Merchant Marine, others to the Amphibious Force and still others to various ships. I parted Newport Naval Station in December 1943 for Norfolk Naval Station, Virginia as a seaman second class, Communication Division Signalman.

Here we went through intensive training in Fire and Damage Control, Ship and Plane Recognition. This is where I prided myself. For I loved planes going back to when I was a little boy. It didn't take long to learn friendly and enemy planes. We even had an opportunity to go out into the Atlantic on a destroyer training ship for a day just to get the feel of it. You must remember, we were raw recruits who probably had never sailed on a ship or even been away from home for any length of time.

We were still in the dark as to what would become of us and what our duties would be in the near future.

Suddenly, one day, the orders came - "Pack your gear. We're moving out." You talk about packing your hammock and seabag full of clothes in such a way as to be able to get the whole thing on your shoulder and lug it some distance to a waiting truck. Sailors were dropping them while others helped each other carrying the pack.

We were wheeled to the railroad station, destination unknown. Everybody had their own thoughts and speculations. As for myself, I had no ideas whatsoever. We rode for some time with no clues of a sign anywhere. We finally came to a station and as we were passing through slowly, a sign appeared- Cincinnati! Rumors were flying again. Great Lakes? West Coast?

I don't know how long it took for this was now January 1944 when we arrived in Houston, Texas, Brown Shipyard. I could hardly believe my eyes. In 1924, I was born 75 miles away in a town called Brenham. My Grandmother and Aunt were still living right here in Houston. I never had seen them because my parents and I left for New Bedford, Massachusetts in 1926. What a strange quirk of fate. Before the saga of the USS *Holder* ends, there will be other surprises.

I went aboard the USS *Holder* (DE-401), my new home. I met *Crouch* (SM1/c) from Virginia, I believe, and Johnson with a rating like me.

The ship was commissioned January 18, 1944. I was issued a pneumatic tube for a life jacket. I hated it because I couldn't trust it.

Anyways, I got liberty and visited my relatives. I shall always remember this. Just like that, we pull out in the middle of the night and tied up in San Jacinto, Texas to load ammunition. From there, it was on to Galveston, Texas to start our shakedown cruises.

Day after day, sometimes two and three times, we practice running to our stations for General Quarters, man overboard, boat drill, fire drill and abandon ship drill. We even ran into a beauty of a storm out in the Gulf. Naturally, the sailors began yakking but this shall prove how necessary it was to shave time off each drill.

Our next stop in February or March, was Bermuda. More shakedowns and more drills and depth charge runs.

On one such day, it was fairly rough and we were practicing lowering and raising our boat in and out of the water when a wave flipped the boat. Two of our men were heading aft and disappeared under the ship. Our skipper had presence of mind to halt the engines. The two sailors popped up aft of the stern and were saved.

While it is true, we were young, clumsy and still learning, this is the time to straighten out all the errors, so that we would be ready for the real test.

Here, I would like to say to those who criticized us, I wonder what they were like when they started but better still-how would they stand the test under fire?

To me, Storming Norman does not mean a violent man but a man who is persistent that his men be as ready as they could possibly be for any eventuality. I salute General Schwarzkopf for this. For I understand what he wanted to accomplish and that is to save lives just as our captain demanded of us on the USS *Holder*. This also will prove itself at the appropriate time.

Enough of this, we left Bermuda in March and arrived Charleston Navy Yard, South Carolina. Here, they outfitted our guns, gun tubs and made several other changes. We were ready!

We leave for Norfolk, Virginia and arrive amidst an armada of ships of all descriptions laying in wait. Captains are holding meetings. The place is buzzing with activity. Something big is coming.

As I think back to that day, I can still see the flashing lights of the buoys-red-green-white at different intervals. The water was quiet. We were pulling out. It is March 28, 1944 at night. How can one forget an evening like that?

We reached the open sea. Ships as far as the eye can see. Little did I realize that this could be one of the largest convoys to be assembled and I was part of it. I understand ships came from New York to join us. We were on our way. I counted 145 ships including 12 LSTs. The Navy tanker USS *Chicopee* (AO-34) was here. There were 16 DEs and 6 DDs-old four pipers as escorts. I can remember a small part of the escorts-USS *Stanton* (DE-247), USS *Price* (DE-332), USS *Strickland* (DE-333), USS *Forster* (DE-334), USS *Daniel* (DE-335), USS *Hissem* (DE-400) and USS *Holder* (DE-401).

I perfected my Morse Code by light, my semaphore by flags and I knew how to use the flagbag for flaghoist. I was as ready as I could possibly be. The opportunity came to take the test. I passed with flying colors and became Signalman Third Class.

The convoy could only move as fast as the slowest ship. A few days out and a whale was being a little stubborn in staying clear of us but he soon left us. Two days from Gibraltar, Spanish ships began to show up and getting in our way. Our interpreter had trouble conveying the message in Spanish to move out of the way. I noticed that they had what looked like high-powered radios aboard judging by the array of antennae wiring strung up. They finally got the idea and left. I often wondered - did they notify our adversaries of our position?

The USS *Price* left us escorting the LSTs towards the Azores. Perhaps for the Great D-Day that was coming.

The British cruiser *Delhi* met us near Gibraltar. She stayed awhile and then left. In the Mediterannean, the USS *Nevada* (BB-36) met us and she too stayed for awhile and then steamed off in the direction of the European coast.

April 11, 1944 A.M.

I had the watch 8 to 12 this morning. I don't know when but I saw something flash on the horizon on the port side. Looking through the long glass, it looked to me to be a Messerschmitt ME-109 lazily circling. I immediately reported the sighting to the O.O.D. He said to keep an eye on it. After a fashion, it left and I reported same. 12o'clock came, I told my relief which is the usual procedure when being relieved, of anything happening on the watch. I went below still thinking about the plane.

April 11, 1944 P.M.

I am back for my 8 to 12 watch on the bridge. As usual, I check my codes and lights for this period for ships, planes and submarines. I took my usual walk around the bridge with my binoculars looking at the water and the horizon. About 11:25 P.M., a flare drops dead ahead. I told the O.O.D. that it is not one of ours because of its peculiar color. He said "Could you have made a mistake?" I said, "I have double-checked all codes and it is not ours. We don't have that color flare." The O.O.D. called for General Quarters. About 11:32 P.M. I was standing forward, port side, when flares began dropping one after the other on the starboard side. The O.O.D. saw it too. I heard the engine of a plane coming towards us. I ran to the starboard side and threw myself down to the deck. Suddenly, there was a hell of an explosion-bright red- I went up into the air. I don't know how high. I was cut on the forehead. I was kind of groggy. My life jacket that I hated, was torn. It only took a split-second for the *Holder* to sink and settle and then listed slightly. Johnson called the pharmacist and he cleaned my forehead. I was pretty well set after that.

I looked around, there was debris everywhere. We were hit amidship and laying dead in the water. A merchant ship headed toward us. Somebody yelled to warn him. I signaled him and he turned away. Another bore down on us. Order was given to fire a warning shot. She veered away but an escort opened up on us and as quickly stopped. The captain gave an order to ask an escort to come alongside and take our wounded. Again, I got on the light and signaled the closest escort and he acknowledged our call for help. They came alongside and the process began with them receiving the wounded. Signalman 1/c Crouch asked me if I wanted to go aboard the other ship and I told him no. Someone said that our gunners knocked the undercarriage of one plane onto our stern. I'll tell you one thing about this crew, they were superb. Before, during and after the hit, the crew went about their duties unselfishly.

Our wounded were being taken off safely. They will go on to Bizerte. The fire was being taken care of by fire and damage control. The smell of diesel was everywhere. What seemed like an eternity, ended in a few minutes with damage control keeping us afloat. Our water-tight integrity held. When I had time to think about what had transpired, my knees began to shake. I can't believe the things we were able to do under these conditions. I think back to all those drills and how clumsy we were and how young this crew was, in one fleeting instance, we grew up and did the things that had to be done without question. Everybody did their share.

One sailor got the Silver Star and the captain got the Legion of Merit.

A British tug came out and had us in tow to Algiers by morning.

We went directly to the drydock. The workers threw logs into the water around the ship and placed them against our sides so as to keep us upright when the water was drained.

There was a gaping hole in our side. Compartments B1, B2 and B3 had been damaged. Yes, water-tight integrity had saved the ship from going to the bottom. Drills paid off!

Pictures were taken from every angle of the hole.

Now, there was the nasty job of taking the dead out for burial. The engineers were wiped out. Lt. Tyler was the only officer killed.

While in drydock, we had a few air raids. One night a balloon went up in flames. Nothing serious.

I remember a little boy was living under one of the boats on the dock near our ship. He spoke English quite well. He had lost both his parents. He was fed, clothed and washed by some of the crew that kind of adopted him. I believe one of the servicemen did adopt him.

Our crew was moved to the naval base while repairs were being done.

Twenty-two days later, the USS Me*nges* (DE-320) was hit astern by a torpedo from a submarine. Later, the USS *Lansdale* DD was hit by a torpedo just like us. They say she went down in 28 seconds.

On one liberty from the base, I went looking for the Polish families living in the area. I came upon a jeep with some soldiers drawing water from a well into cans. Lo and behold, one of the soldiers was from my hometown in Acushnet, Massachusetts and lived a couple of streets away from me. I promised him that as soon as I got home, I would tell his parents, which I did.

Our ship was patched up and it was off to Oran under tow. We came alongside the French DD *Epervier*. It was in tough shape but still under command. Other ships here-*Vulcan* (Sopa) senior officer present afloat. DDs *NiBlack, Gleaves, Edison, Ludlow, Earle* and the French BB *Loraine.*

Our crew was sent out to the range. We fired a 20mm at a moving target towed by a spitfire. The British soldier in charge told me I did very good.

I got the word that I would be part of the skeleton crew on the *Holder* going back to the States. This would make me the Signalman, 20mm gunner, lookout and part-time quartermaster on the wheel. I don't know if this is good or bad. In the end, it turned out alright.

We left Oran under tow by the USS *Choctaw* (ATR-70) and met a convoy of ships. We were placed in the 6th column and last ship. One day out and flares started to drop, but they were too far away.

When we reached the Atlantic Ocean, received word that the carrier *Block Island* was being attacked. I understand some of our DDs or DEs went south to assist.

Being on the Bridge, I am able to pick up a lot of information. Some may be true and others not. Scuttlebutt is quite rampant at times, like the reporting of 30 submarines laying in wait somewhere between us and New York.

I noticed that the water was as smooth as glass. A welcome sight. I don't think we could take too much if it became rough.

June 9, 1944

The Statue of Liberty appeared. I am not ashamed to say that there were tears in my eyes. Slowly, we inched our way to 33rd Street Pier, Brooklyn. I left the USS *Holder* never to see her again. I didn't know what happened to her until I read "All Hands" Magazine, telling how *Holder* was made a part of the USS *Menges*.

USS *Holder* (DE-401) got a second chance. Not too many ships can boast of such an opportunity. The *Holder* lived on.

I can't end this story here for there is one more surprise to this ending. To shorten this, I received a 30 day survivor leave. When I got back, I reported to the USS *Panamint* (AGC-13) for commissioning and assignment.

We left Bayonne, New Jersey and ended up on the other side of the United States in Mare Island, San Francisco, California. Actually it was Vallejo that was closest.

Well, we had liberty and somehow took a bus to Sacramento where I took a trolley and ended up at a place called the Greystone Lodge. Saturday nights, they had dancing. I would say that was a very good reason for being there. For 50¢, you received a place to sleep for the weekend and breakfast on Sunday. The hostess at the Greystone Lodge offered me a ride to the bus terminal on one such Sunday so that I could get back to my ship. She began questioning me about a battle in the Mediterranean Sea. At first, I was concerned about her asking such questions because this was war time. The motto was "Loose lips, sink ships." I pressed her for more details. It was only then that I realized that she was telling me about the USS *Holder*. With this info, I admitted that I had been on the *Holder*. Another surprise, she told me her husband was Lt. Tyler. I couldn't believe my ears. Out of the way and by mere chance, perhaps 10 million to 1 shot—I find a person whose husband was the only officer killed aboard our ship—amazing! She invited me to her home for Christmas dinner. I met her parents, her two children, Gordon and Kent and saw a picture of Lt. Tyler and pictures of the USS *Holder* being built at Brown Shipyard, Houston, Texas. Truly amazing! This was quite an evening for all of us.

Sometime later, I received a check for $5.35. My share from the commissary on the USS *Holder*. We had put in $5.00 a piece when our store began aboard the ship.

Yes, this is the story of the USS *Holder* (DE-401) as I had seen it. Others from our ship and other ships that were in the area should be able to provide other perspectives and details as to what they saw and were doing in this time frame.

USS *HOLT* (DE-706)

Arriving in New Orleans in early summer 1944, I was impressed by the gleaming new ship tied up across the river at the Algiers Naval Station. So impressed that my foot slipped on the narrow walkway along the river side of the barge we had to cross to pick up the LCVP for the trip across the river—splash seabag and sailor hit the muddy water simultaneously! Both were quickly and unceremoniously hauled aboard the LCVP and smarting under the salty words of the Coxswain, reported aboard the receiving station without further incident. A few days later this young sailor was assigned to the gleaming new ship whose beauty caused the fall into the Mississippi River—the USS *Holt* (DE 706).

Holt's early days in commission were similar to countless other Destroyer Escorts loading supplies and ammunition, then off to Bermuda for a month of intensive underway training and shakedown, followed by Navy Yard availability at the Charleston Navy Yard, Boston, Massachusetts.

Holt was named in honor of LT(JG) William Mack Holt, an Idaho lad who lost his life in an air engagement over Guadalcanal in August 1942. The ship bearing his name was built by the DeFoe Shipbuilding Co., Bay City, Michigan, and was a turbo-electric drive vessel of the RUDDEROW Class. The basic hull, without mast, was towed through Saginaw Bay, Lake Huron, through the Mackinac Strait into Lake Michigan, down to Chicago, through the Chicago ship canal, Illinois River, and then down the Mississippi to New Orleans where her armament was installed, her mast stepped and she completed fitting out prior to commissioning on 9 June 1944.

After yard availability, *Holt* had several coastwise escort duties, including going to the aid of the SS *George Ade* which was torpedoed off the Georgia coast. This involved spending three days in rough seas caused by the passage of a hurricane that skirted the eastern seaboard. A Coast Guard tug took the SS *George Ade* in tow and *Holt* along with other DEs made an unsuccessful effort to locate the German sub.

Following duty as a school ship for DE crews, conducting classified underwater testing at Pautexent River, additional coastwise escort duty, checking out submarine reports, and another period of yard availability, *Holt* was assigned as an escort, along with the rest of CORT DIV 74, for a European-bound convoy, UGS56.

Much to everyone's surprise, CORT DIV 74 was detached from the convoy and proceeded to New York where some state-of-the-art gear was installed and we picked up a large supply of charts for the Pacific Ocean area. Although the information was classified, all hands knew full well we were leaving the liberty ports of the east coast and heading for God-only-knew where.

Transiting the Panama Canal, *Holt* made fuel and provision stops at Galapogas Island, where all hands enjoyed the turtles, Bora Bora, where the officers enjoyed the club, and joined the 7th Fleet in Hollandia, New Guinea. Hardly had we anchored in Hollandia, when the word to get underway for escort duty to Leyte was received. November and December, 1944 were spent escorting amphibious craft; on harbor entrance ASW patrol and at General Quarters for air attack in the southern Philippine Islands.

Holt was in the screen escorting a slow tow (4 knots) of tugs with barges and assorted small craft from Leyte to Mindoro Island. We departed Leyte prior to the landings on Mindoro and arrived there after the invasion. The strike force passed us en route then passed us again as they retired. Our little convoy was carrying the material needed to establish a PT base at Mindoro. All the way up and most of the way back, the group was harassed by Japanese planes. Some got close enough for *Holt's* guns to splash them.

After Mindoro, came a succession of amphibious escort and fire support assignments—Lingayen Gulf, Port Legaspi, Borneo, and then a series of convoys to Okinawa.

On 21 June 1945, *Holt* received an unglamorous but interesting assignment—delivering mail and passengers in the Philippine Islands. Leaving Leyte, *Holt* in rapid succession visited Cebu City, Zamboanga, Puerto Princesa, Iloilo, and Panay, returning to Leyte on 24 June. No time for liberty but then we hadn't had liberty since Panama the prior October.

As the war came to a close, *Holt* was assigned to escort duty for submarines in and out of Subic Bay. This was followed by endless days of ASW training and war games with 7th Fleet submarines. *Holt's* last duty with the 7th Fleet was a two-week weather patrol in the Philippine Sea. Returning to Guiuan Roads, Samar in mid-December 1945, *Holt*, along with the rest of CORT DIV 74, was ordered home.

Departing Samar 18 December, *Holt* refueled at Eniwetok on Christmas Day and arrived Pearl Harbor New Year's Eve. After three days of R & R, *Holt* departed for San Francisco, arriving there 9 January 1946. CORT DIV 74 was dissolved and *Holt* languished in San Francisco until March when she steamed to San Diego where she was decommissioned 2 July 1946 and placed in the reserve fleet. Sometime between 1946 and 1962, *Holt* was towed to the reserve fleet at Stockton, California. In late 1962, she was towed to Seattle for a survey, then towed to Portland, Oregon where a civilian contractor overhauled the ship from stem to stern, prepatory to loaning the ship to the Republic of Korea.

On 19 June, 1963 the USS *Holt* was recommissioned as the ROKS *Chungnam* (DE 73) and turned over to the South Korean Navy under the Military Assistance Program. On 15 November, 1974 *Holt* was sold to the South Korean government and her name was stricken from the list of U.S. Naval Vessels.

Holt was officially credited with shooting down four Japanese aircraft and received two battle stars for the Asiatic-Pacific operations. Her skipper, Victor Blue, descended from a line of distinguished Naval officers. His brother was killed in an early South Pacific action. Captain Blue was driven by a desire to engage the enemy. His first priority was refuel, replenish, and re-arm then report "Ready For Sea." Despite this authoritarian approach, *Holt* was a happy ship. Eighty percent of the crew were under 25 years old and only a handful had prior sea duty. Her crew worked hard and when the opportunity presented itself—played hard.

There were 200 men and 12 officers on board. There are 211 other stories about *Holt*.

USS *HERBERT C. JONES* (DE-137)

Submitted by Glen Theodore Kettelhut

The USS *Herbert C. Jones* (DE-137) was placed in commission on July 21, 1943, at Orange, Texas, with Lieutenant Commander Alfred W. Gardes, Jr.,

USN, as commanding officer. The period from this date to September 16, 1943, was taken up with outfittings, shakedown at Bermuda and post shakedown availability at Navy Yard, Charleston, SC.

On September 17th, the *Jones* arrived at Navy Yard, Washington, DC where equipment was installed under the supervision of engineers from the Naval Research Laboratory for investigation of the method of control used by the Germans for their glider bomb. The installation was completed on September 30, 1943, and after conducting tests in Chesapeake Bay, the *Jones,* in company with the USS *Frederick C. Davis* (DE-136), which had been similarly equipped, sailed from Norfolk, VA on October 7, 1943, for the Mediterranean Sea with orders to report to the Commander Naval Forces, Northwest African Waters, for temporary duty.

On October 14th the *Jones* arrived at Gibraltar where she fueled and received orders to proceed to Algiers, Algeria.

On arrival at Algiers on October 16th, while laying to in the harbor awaiting a berth assignment, the *Jones* was rammed by the British submarine HMS *Universal* due to a failure of the submarine steering gear. The bow of the submarine pierced the side of the *Jones,* cutting a hole about nine feet by three feet which required four days alongside a tender to repair. The only compartment that was flooded contained all the supplies for the Ship's Service Store, which proved very difficult to replace.

The *Jones* and the USS *Frederick C. Davis* were formed into Task Group 80.2, of which Lieutenant Commander Alfred W. Gardes, Jr. USN, was Task Group commander. From October 21st until the end of 1943 these ships were used primarily as additional escorts to convoys, principally along the coast of North Africa, particularly between Cape Tenes and Bizerte, as it was in this area that it was considered most likely that the glider bomb would be encountered. During this period several trips were made with combat loaded convoy to Naples, Italy.

On the evening of November 6th, while acting as an additional escort to convoy KMF-25A, the *Jones* participated in its first "star" engagement. At 1803 the convoy was attacked by German aircraft in a dusk attack. The raid was primarily by torpedo aircraft, although three glider bombs were observed and three radio signals were intercepted, showing that the bombs were most likely radio controlled and giving us the frequency of the control carrier wave.

At 1818 a torpedo plane identified as an HE-111 coming in on the port bow was taken under fire. It released its torpedo, then burst into flames and crashed into the sea. The torpedo was successfully evaded.

The USS *Beatty* (DD-640) was sunk by a torpedo during this engagement.

The second engagement the *Jones* participated in was on November 26th while acting as additional escort to convoy KMF-26. Although the engagement lasted two hours and was considered as one of the heaviest air attacks on any convoy, no engagement star was ever awarded for this action, although it was recommended by the Command Naval Forces, Northwest African Waters that one be awarded. At 1651 a German bomber sneaked in low over the convoy and dropped a bomb, narrowly missing a transport. The ready gun crew on the 40mm gun of the *Jones* opened fire on the plane as it crossed our stern. This was the first gun in the convoy to open fire. The plane was seen to start smoking and later crash into the water about three miles from the ship.

This attack was followed up by two waves of planes carrying glider bombs. We were able to confirm the findings in regard to frequencies used to control the bombs and make recordings of several of the signals. Attempts were made to jam the control signals with the equipment on board. It is felt that the results of the attack, one ship hit in two hours indicates success even though the equipment was not really adequate.

The bombing attack was followed by a torpedo attack at dusk, one plane attacking the *Jones*. The plane was shot down just after releasing its torpedo, and the torpedo was successfully evaded. The attack ended about 1900.

Early in December a powerful jamming set was installed in the *Jones* and the *Davis*. This more or less marked the end of the "investigational" period and the beginning of the "protective" period as our mission now was to attempt the jamming of control signals rather than investigate them.

On December 7, 1943, Lieutenant Commander Alfred W. Gardes, Jr., USN, was relieved of command by Lieutenant Commander Rufus A. Soule, III, USNR, the then executive officer.

January 13, 1944, Task Group 80.2 arrived at Naples, Italy, and reported to the Commander Amphibious Force, Eighth Fleet, for temporary duty which proved to be for the landing at Anzio, Italy. The *Jones* sailed from

USS Herbert C. Jones (DE-137)

Naples Bay at 0430 the morning of January 21st at the head of a convoy of LCTs, the first ships to sail for the invasion. At the time of the actual landing, 0200 on January 22nd, the *Jones* was part of the outer anti-submarine screen, moving in to the transport and fire support areas just at daybreak. Our mission was to provide anti-submarine and glider bomb protection to the cruisers and destroyers providing fire support, and to the ships in the transport area.

It is a matter of record that during the first twelve weeks after the landing the beachhead was raided by enemy aircraft 277 times. The vast majority of these raids occurred during the first two months. Although many of the raids were on the beachhead itself, the shipping in the area came in for its share. The raids occurred at all hours of the day and night, being made by the light of flares and even by moonlight. All types of attacks were made, including low level bombing, diving bombing, glider bombs and torpedo attacks. In addition to these raids a German railroad gun approximately an eleven inch gun, would drop shells into the area for about a half hour daily. This gun was never located until captured when the Army finally broke through at Cassino and moved up through Italy.

The *Jones* was in the immediate area for the first seventeen consecutive days and for a total of forty out of the first sixty-four days. The other twenty-four days were utilized in replenishing rest and recreation at Capri, and a two day anti-submarine search in the Tyrrhenian Sea.

On the night of January 23rd two dive bomber attacks were made on the *Jones*. Both resulted in close misses, but no damage was received.

On the evening of February 15th two near misses from glider bombs severely shook the ship and caused considerable damage to the hull, but the *Jones* remained on station for two days after the event, and emergency repairs were effected in Naples on February 19th.

Although the *Jones'* primary mission was anti-submarine and glider bomb protection, the ships of Task Group 80.2 provided another very valuable service. Until the Army was firmly established and was able to set up its radar stations, the warnings of air attacks were given by the ships, mainly British fighter director cruisers. Because of the proximity of hills and the nearness of the German airfields, many raids were not detected until the actual attack had developed. By utilizing some of the equipment and special personnel who had been placed on board in connection with our particular mission, the *Jones* and the *Davis* were able to predict raids and even the type of raid with considerable accuracy.

On March 31st the *Jones* arrived in Oran, Algeria, for a fifteen day tender availability, the first since leaving the United States. From October 7th, the day of sailing from the United States until March 31st the *Jones* had been underway seventy percent of the time.

During the availability at Oran, Algeria, Lieutenant Commander Rufus A. Soule, III, USNR, the commanding officer, was presented the Legion of Merit Medal.

The *Jones* was used as an additional escort to convoys between Oran and Bizerte during the last two weeks of April. The two east bound convoys escorted were the only ones in this area that did not undergo attacks during the months of April, which was fortunate as this duty had been assigned with the intention of giving the *Jones* a needed rest.

The *Jones* was back at Anzio on May 5th and from then until June 13th, which time was spent alternating between Anzio and Naples. The Anzio area had quieted down considerably since leaving it in March although there were still occasional air raids, primarily mine laying raids. Plots were kept of the location of these mines as well as possible, and very little damage was caused by them. The "Anzio Express," the eleven inch railroad gun, continued to drop shells into the area. The actual damage caused by the Anzio Express was very slight, but considerable difficulty was met keeping the merchant ships from weighing anchor and moving out during the shelling, thus slowing up the unloading.

June 13th the *Jones* sailed from Anzio and joined a convoy to Civita Vecchia, Italy, the first convoy to move north of Anzio following the breakthrough and advance of the Fifth Army.

June 19th the *Jones* sailed from Civita Vecchia to Oran, Algeria, joining a convoy off Bizerte as additional escort to Oran.

The month of July and the first of August were spent escorting, mostly between Oran and Naples. As this was the "buildup" period for the invasion of southern France, there was a great deal of shipping to be convoyed.

On August 7th the *Jones* sailed from Naples to Taranto, Italy, in preparation for the invasion. Sailing from Taranto on August 13th with a convoy of ten troop transports escorted by six French destroyers and destroyer escorts and the *Jones,* the convoy arrived in the assault area on August 16th, D-day plus one.

The *Jones* was assigned for anti-submarine and glider bomb protection in the area off San Raphael, France, where we remained until September 19th. Because of excellent air coverage there was very little enemy activity in the area. Only six glider bomb signals were intercepted, but no bombs were sighted. Only once did an enemy aircraft come close enough for this ship to open fire, and then the range was too great for any success.

Although the glider bomb was not used to any extent during this invasion, it was considered to be a constant threat and therefore necessary to keep the *Jones* and the *Davis* in the area for protection.

On September 19th the *Jones* sailed from San Raphael to Oran with orders to be prepared to join a convoy on October 1st as additional escort from Oran to the United States.

October 1st the *Jones* sailed from Oran and joined convoy GUS-53 as additional escort. After an uneventful trip we arrived at the Navy Yard, New York, on October 18th for thirty days availability and a much needed rest.

Following this availability the *Jones* was assigned to Escort Division Nine, which was operating with an escort carrier as an anti-submarine killer group. The *Jones* joined the group in December 1944. At that time German submarine activity was at an all time low, so the group conducted training exercises off Guantanamo Bay, Cuba, and carrier qualification for aviators off Jacksonville, Florida, being at all times on twenty-four hour notice for anti-submarine work in case of increased submarine activity.

On February 15th, 1945, the group sailed from Guantanamo Bay, Cuba, for a spot in the middle of the Atlantic Ocean on what we thought was to be an anti-submarine hunt. However, it proved to be for the purpose of providing air coverage for the ships returning President Roosevelt and his party to the United States from the Yalta conference.

This trip was followed by a short training period at Bermuda, followed by ten days availability in the Navy Yard, New York.

On March 27th, the entire task group sailed from Norfolk, Virginia, for anti-submarine operations in the North Atlantic. Several killer groups were sent up at the same time to set up barriers against several German submarines known to be attempting to reach our east coast. The operation lasted until May 12th and proved to be very successful. Although several submarines were sunk, our particular task group had the misfortune to be in just the wrong end of the barrier. It was on this operation that the USS *Frederick C. Davis* (DE-136) which had participated with the *Jones* in the various operations in the Mediterranean, was sunk by a torpedo from a German submarine.

The group arrived in New York on May 14th and remained on forty-eight hours notice for anti-submarine operations throughout the uncertain period after V-E Day.

On May 24th the group sailed from New York, the carrier and three destroyer escorts for Quonset, and the other three destroyer escorts, including the *Jones,* for New London to provide services for submarine training. The group was alerted on May 29th on what proved to be a false submarine report.

June 5th, 1945, the task group was dissolved and on June 7th the ships of the division sailed for Navy yards to prepare to proceed to the Pacific Oceans.

June 28th the *Jones* sailed from New York for the Pacific, stopping at Guantanamo Bay for two weeks refresher training. On July 20th we passed through the Panama Canal and proceeded to San Diego, California, for supplies and voyage repairs, sailing on August 2nd for Pearl Harbor.

The *Jones* was in Pearl Harbor when the announcement was made that Japan had accepted the Allied surrender terms. It was very appropriate that the *Jones* should be there inasmuch as Ensign Herbert C. Jones, USNR, for whom the ship was named, was killed and was posthumously awarded the Congressional Medal of Honor for his work in the attack on Pearl Harbor on December 7th, 1941.

After a short training period the *Jones* sailed for Eniwetok and was assigned to duty in the Marshalls-Gilberts Area. On September 10, 1945, the *Jones* relieved the USS *Levy* (DE-162) as station ship at Wake Island, where we remained, except for logistics until October 25th.

Commander Rufus A. Soule, III, USNR, was relieved of command by Lieutenant Paul D. Bartlett, Jr., USNR, on November 8, 1945.

For the period from October 25th to date, the *Jones* has been participating in air-sea patrol duty at Eniwetok Atoll, Marshall Islands. Lt. Comdr. C.S. Livingston USN relieved Lt. Paul B. Bartlett Jr., USNR as commanding officer at Pearl Harbor January 1946.

As this written, it is anticipated that the *Jones* will be returned to the United States shortly after the first of the coming year and placed in the Atlantic Reserve Fleet.

The *Herbert C. Jones* returned to Pearl Harbor in January 1946, sailed on to the States and on through the Panama Canal up to New York for repairs at the Brooklyn, NY Navy Yard.

The journey ended at Green Cove Springs, Florida on the St. Johns River where the *Herbert C. Jones* (DE-137) was decommissioned in 1946.

USS *KEITH* (DE-241)

Submitted by Robert C. Sweitzer Torpedoman 1st Class.

August 4, 1942 keel was laid for the *Keith* at Brown Ship Building Co. Houston, Texas.

July 19, 1943 ship was commissioned. A month before, Lt. Drayton

Cockran and other officers and petty officers arrived, getting acquainted with the ship. Executive officer Lt. Jack Rinn was in Norfolk, VA with the rest of the crew.

July 14, 1943 ship was completed.

July 19, 1943 ship was commissioned. After a few days and three railroad cars of supplies were loaded, the ship got underway.

July 23, 1943 she took on fuel and ammunition and headed for sea. A hurricane came up. Winds of one hundred thirty miles an hour pounded this new ship and her crew. What a great start for a great ship. This was the first of many storms the ship was to endure.

Sept. 14, 1943, after shakedown and gunnery practice, she was ready for duty. Orders came for the *Keith* to join the convoy. An anxious crew watched as the lights of Virginia Beach faded away, not knowing what lie ahead with all the U boats, Wolf Packs and Surface raiders.

Oct. 2, 1943 Straight of Gibraltar and the Mediterranean Sea. The first convoy was over.

Oct. 8, 1943 left for home with returning convoy.

The USS *Keith* made a few more of these trips but did not see the enemy.

Feb. 22, 1944 went in Brooklyn Navy Yard for a new sonar gear.

March 15, 1944 sailed on her first offensive task group operations with the USS *Tripoli.*

April 4, 1944 crossed the equator.

April 5, 1944 pulled into Recife, Brazil.

April 6, 1944 left for the United States. Had a few plane crashes and picked up survivors.

Nothing happened until April 19, 1944. TBFs sighted U-Boat on surface and attacked but no kills. Two escorts searched but could get no contact.

After more of this duty, more contacts, more rough weather, Atlantic style. Cutting through ice, the ship was in sorry shape. It needed repairs and a new paint job. This time it got a camouflage job.

April 3, 1945 found the USS *Keith* underway with her sister ships and the USS *Core.* Gunnery and anti-submarine exercises lasted until April 13th.

April 13, 1945 went to Bermuda and met with twelve DEs and the USS *Brogue.* We formed a barrier one hundred miles long, with air coverage. The purpose was to intercept U-Boats reported heading for the United States.

April 23, 1945 we made contact with submarine but lost it. Near dawn the USS *Keith* investigated a radar contact which proved to be a U.S. frigate. At 8:40 a.m., the *Frederick C. Davis* was torpedoed and sunk with great loss of life. At 10:30 a.m. the *Keith* arrived at the scene. Contact was held for several attacks. At 6:39 p.m., the U-546 surfaced and was fired on by the *Keith* and other ships. The submarine sank, leaving thirty-three survivors swimming in the cold Atlantic Ocean. Four of these were picked up by the USS *Keith.*

May 4, 1945, a plane from the USS *Brogue* saw and attacked a U-boat on the surface and left a large oil slick, but no contact was made.

May 8, 1945, USS *Ward* made a sonar contact. The USS *Keith* and the USS *Otterstetter* were sent to assist but no positive results. Shortly after this, the barrier was broken up and ships were sent to intercept surrendering U boats. On the last day, the sea got rough. Water slammed over the bow, tore loose the gun shield and made a large hole in the deck. Mattresses were used to keep out most of the water. This is life aboard a D.E.

May 19, 1945, the USS *Keith* steamed out of New York bound for Boston to have her engine completely overhauled and torpedo tubes removed. More anti-aircraft guns were installed and a new dark blue paint job, after which he was ready for the Pacific Ocean.

July 31, 1945, we got more ammunition and ten days later arrived at Pearl Harbor. The duty now was to assist planes in distress, send weather reports and investigate suspicious objects in the water.

During her twenty-six months of commissioned service, the USS *Keith* has steamed two hundred and fifty thousand miles and visited many ports.

The manner in which she served her country and the weathering of many gales and high seas of the North Atlantic, give credit not only to her designer and builders but to the men who have served aboard her as well.

She was decommissioned on September 20, 1946.

USS *CHARLES J. KIMMEL* (DE-584)

Feel no remorse about her. She had her sad and happy days on the oceans and seas of the world. We shared her bad times, the hurricanes and typhoons, and we fought her enemies from foreign lands, under the sea and in the air. She was a ship of combat born in war and now destined to die in a time of peace. But these past happenings never put her down...

She was once our home and school. A gallant protector of our seagoing

USS Keith (DE-241)

family. Her guns are silent now and her war years are finished. We all survived the ordeals thrust upon her by endless patrols and battle missions in campaigns of long ago. Now she moves silently outbound under cable tow. No longer the escort leader with sister ships in screen, protecting convoys of ships destined for zones of combat. Her orders are final. For this is the last outbound voyage. The wind and sea gently ride along with her and we remember in the calm of the morning mist how her colors once looked two-blocked at the fore. Perhaps she too can hear voices from the past...A faraway command by her captain "All ahead full, come right to zero-nine zero"...or..."God bless this ship and all who sail in her"...by the mother of her namesake. Surely, we remember voices of her long departed crew, seabags in hand..."Permission to leave the ship, sir"...in her final port of call. These were the sounds of the sailors who once shared her sealife.

Now she moves forward slowly rising and falling on the deep Pacific tide. The cable tow is hauled in by her lonely companion—a small Navy tug in the final escort to nowhere. Her greatest times are past but yet she remains proudly undefeated, for she was never sold for scrap or trades away to a foreign shore. They kept her afloat for this last voyage as a target ship for the new Navy and its modern combat frigates. The C.J.K. will now serve a final purpose for the ships who were designed to follow her.

She waits for the fired salvos. The signal is given and the deadly inbound missiles of the frigates that track her smash into her topside. She accepts this final end, this last naval goodbye, knowing no enemy ever touched her or those who sailed in her. This is the warriors way to die! She slowly rolls on her side. The explosive fires leap up and cover her bridge and torpedo deck. Her 5" turret forward tears itself from its mount of twisted steel. Smoke rises from her broken hull compartments and then her smashed stern explodes as a second salvo screams into her. Tons of water enter the sinking tomb as she slips beneath the waves. The bow slowly rises vertically for the descent into oblivion. The morning sunlight reflects on the grey hull number...five eight four...is seen-but only for quick moment. Then she is gone...forever...in 400 fathoms.

One can almost hear the voices from the deep...Welcome *Charles J. Kimmel*...You are alone on the final voyage but your crew will not forget you. You once shared in their dreams and survival and so you will always be part of their lives-as long as sailors remember the war that created you."

Old friend DE584! You know our final salute is for you...and also for us. We would like to think that there will never be another ship or crew like we once were. You will always be in our thoughts. Thank you... goodbye brave destroyer escort...farewell!

Raymond Doolan, SM3/c USNR
USS *Charles J. Kimmel*
DE-548 WWII 1944-1946

June 15, 1957 News Item:

The Destroyer Escort USS *C.J. Kimmel* DE-584 was stricken from the naval decommissioned list and towed 35 miles west of Oceanside, California. She was sunk as a target test vessel by U.S. Naval frigates utilizing ship to ship guided missile weapon systems. The test was a success.

USS *LEWIS* (DE-535)

Submitted by John C. Butler (WGT) Class Destroyer Escort

General Information	*Armament*
Length Overall 306'-0"	2-5"/38 cal guns-Main Battery
Length at Waterline 300"-0"	2-Twin 40mm guns
Beam 36'-10"	1-Triple Torpedo Tube
Shaft Horsepower 12,000	10-20mm guns
Trail Speed 24.15 Knots	1-Hedgehog
War Endurance 4,650 Mi./12 Knots	2-Depth Charge Tracks
Displacement 1,600 Tons	8-"K" gun projectors
Complement 14 Officers 201 Men	World War II
Fuel Capacity 347 Tons	

Commanding Officers

Lt. Cmdr. R.H. Stevens, USNR, Sept. 5, 1944 to Dec. 26, 1944
Lt. Cmdr. F.A. Reece Jr., USNR, Dec. 26, 1944 to Sept. 5, 1945
Lt. Cmdr. G.A. Waller, USNR, Sept. 5, 1945 to Dec. 16, 1945
Lt. (jg) J.A. Newell, USNR, Dec. 16, 1945 to March 22, 1946
Lt. Cmdr. J.M. Gunn, USNR, March 22, 1946 to May 31, 1946

Atlantic Fleet from November 8, 1944 to November 18, 1944
Pacific Fleet from November 18, 1944
5th Fleet from January 4, 1945 to January 12, 1945
3rd Fleet from January 12, 1945 to February 1, 1945
5th Fleet from February 1, 1945 to July 2, 1945
9th Fleet from July 2, 1945 to October 15, 1945
19th Fleet from October 1945 to Inactivation

The USS *Lewis* was built by the Charleston Navy Yard, Boston, Massachusetts; her keel having been laid on November 3, 1943. The ship was launched March 23, 1944, and christened USS *Lewis* in honor of Ensign Victor Alan Lewis.

USNR, who was declared missing in action on June 4, 1942, in the Battle of Midway. He was attached to the USS *Hornet* as a member of the famed Torpedo Squadron 8.

At the launching ceremonies Mrs. Serena V. Lewis, the mother of the man for whom the ship was named, acted as the official sponsor. The *Lewis* was placed in commission on September 5, 1944, by rear Admiral Theobald, First Naval District, with Lieutenant Commander R.H. Stevens, USN, as her first commanding officer.

The *Lewis* departed Boston September 28, 1944 en route to Bermuda for shakedown training. While on shakedown training the *Lewis* made contact with an enemy submarine and attacked with depth charges until all contact was lost. It was never known if the sub was sunk or escaped. No oil slicks or debris were found.

The *Lewis* returned to Boston on October 31, 1944 and remained anchored until November 9, 1944 when she sailed to Casco Bay, ME to join a group of ships being formed for assignment to the Asiatic-Pacific Theater. The *Lewis* was attached to the Atlantic Fleet from November 8, 1944 until November 18, 1944.

She left Casco Bay, Maine in Task Unit 27.7 for the Pacific War Theatre on November 10, serving as escort with USS *Henry A. Wilery* (DM-29) for USS *Texas* and *Arkansas*. USS *Missouri*, *Wake Island*, *Shamrock Bay*, *Hank* and *John W. Weeks* joined Task Unit 27.7 on November 12, 1944. The *Lewis* served as a Rescue/Anti Submarine screening ship and rescued a downed pilot en route to Panama. After passing through the Panama Canal, the group remained overnight at Panama City. The *Missouri* was so big she barely made it through the canal, taking chunks of concrete from the walls of the canal as she passed through.

The convoy departed for Pearl Harbor via San Diego and San Francisco on November 19, 1944 and the *Lewis* was transferred to the 3rd Fleet. More ships joined the convoy at both stops. The entire Armada arrived at Pearl Harbor on December 13, 1944.

Shortly after arrival in Pearl Harbor a Board of Inquiry was conducted to determine if Lieutenant Commander Stevens should remain as commanding officer of the *Lewis*. The Board recommended that he be relieved of command. As a result Lieutenant Commander F.A. Reece Jr. Commanding Officer of the *Silverstein* (DE-534) was transferred to the *Lewis* as the new skipper. The *Silverstein* had run aground entering Pearl Harbor and was laid up for repairs. The *Lewis* crew spent Christmas Eve at Pearl Harbor and on December 26, 1944 sailed for Eniwetok with merchant convoy PD 220-T. She arrived Eniwetok on January 4 and sailed the same day for Ulithi with USS *Fortune* and USS *Grady* forming Task Unit 96.3.12. Arrived Ulithi January 10, 1945.

On January 12 at about 0700 an ammunition ship was reported torpedoed in Ulithi Anchorage. *Lewis* joined the general area search, for the offending submarine, and departed with Task Unit 30.18.14 consisting of five AOs and five DEs en route to rendezvous with Task Unit 30.8.12 and Task Group 30.7. Rendezvous was effected on January 14 when *Lewis* was detached to report to commanding officer USS *Anzio* as Commander Task Force Group 30.7. The combined units rendezvoused with Task Force 38 and Commander 3rd Fleet on January 23 northeast of Luzon. On the same date Task Group 30.7 was ordered back to conduct ASW operations north of Yap Island. There were unfortunately no contacts, and the group returned to Ulithi Anchorage on January 27.

On February 1 *Lewis*, *Silverstein*, *Howard F. Clark* and *Raymond* joined Task Unit 50.7,2 with Commander Escort Division 64 with *Lewis* as Task Unit Commander. This task unit was a special anti-submarine force under direct control of Commander 5th Fleet, assigned to the Logistic Support Force (TG 50.8) until such time as the Commander 5th Fleet issued further orders. Sailed for Eniwetok on February 1 to join Task Group 50.8 and operated as the anti-submarine screen of that task group during the capture and occupation of Iwo

Jima, and servicing Task Force 58 during raids on the Empire of Japan. The unit left for Ulithi on March 21, arriving on March 27. She operated as part of the screen for TG 50.8 throughout the Okinawa Campaign. *Lewis* reported to Commander Task Force 94 on July 2 in compliance with the commander 3rd Fleet Dispatch #280034. From September 15, 1945 she operated as escort for several Ulithi-Okinawa convoys and as a radar, anti-submarine vessel at Ulithi.

On June 5, 1945 the *Lewis* while assigned to anti-submarine screening for the USS *Jefferson*, ran into a very strong typhoon (named "Viper") along with other ships of the 3rd Fleet. The *Lewis* got into "chains" losing all rudder control and barely missed crashing into another ship. At the peak of the storm *Lewis* heeled over from 45 degrees to 67 degrees. Men below deck were walking on the bulkheads half the time. Crew members off watch lay below in their sacks lashing themselves in so they wouldn't be thrown out. Several depth charges broke loose on the fantail. The charges were set on safe so they wouldn't explode but all that weight rolling around could cause a lot of damage. The ships mast was really taking a beating and the skipper was concerned that it would snap!

When the *Lewis* reached the center or "eye" of the typhoon the sea became relatively calm with an eerie silence. Two members of the torpedo gang rushed out on deck and secured the depth charges while deck hands scoured the ship securing anything that had come loose or broken. All hands went back inside and water tight doors were shut and secured.

Then the *Lewis* steamed into the other side of the storm. She was now taking water through the ventilators and the crew's quarters had a foot of water sloshing over lockers etc. The storm finally subsided and the crew survived without serious injury. Other ships were seriously damaged and several CVEs lost aircraft. The *Lewis's* screws were badly bent from either something she hit during the storm or from the sheer force of the "Viper" and had to proceed to Ulithi for floating dry dock repairs. On October 27, 1945 the *Lewis* was dispatched from Guam to Gaferut Island to pick up a Marine who had drowned off the coral reefs of the island. A rescue party in the ships whale boat went through a narrow channel in the coral reef and brought the body to the ship. The *Lewis* returned to Guam with the body.

While on air/sea rescue duty the *Lewis* rescued several pilots who had to "ditch" their aircraft at sea. During the period January 10, 1945 through November 5, 1945 the *Lewis* served with the 3rd and 5th Fleets where she participated as a carrier force screening ship, anti-submarine screening ship and performed air/sea rescue operations. She took part in the Luzon Operation, 3rd Fleet China coast attacks, Formosa attack, Nansei Shoto attack, raids on Japan, Iwo Jima Operation, Leyte Gulf Operation, and the Okinawa Gunto operations. The *Lewis* ceased offensive action on August 15, 1945.

The *Lewis* departed Pearl Harbor November 18, 1945 flying her "going home" pennant with over 100 Marine passengers on board. She arrived in San Pedro, CA on November 23, 1945. The *Lewis* was then assigned to the 9th Fleet, until her decommissioning on May 31, 1946. The ship was inactivated at San Diego on September 17, 1946.

The *Lewis* earned the following medals during her Asiatic-Pacific assignment: American Area Campaign, Asiatic-Pacific Campaign, Philippine Liberation, and World War II Victory.

The USS *Lewis* earned three (3) Battle Stars on the Asiatic-Pacific Area Service ribbon for participating in the following operations during World War II: one star for Luzon Operation-3rd Fleet supporting operations, China Coast attacks, January 12, 16, 1945-Formosa attacks, January 3, 4, 9, 15, 21, 1945-Nansei Shoto attacks, January 22, 1945; one star for Iwo Jima Operation-assault and occupation of Iwo Jima, February 15-March 16, 1945; one star for Okinawa Gunto Operation-assault and occupation of Okinawa Gunto, March 24 to June 30, 1945; 5th and 3rd Fleet raids in support of Okinawa Gunto Operation, March 17 to June 11, 1945.

The *Lewis* also earned the Navy Occupation Service Medal for her services in the occupied Asiatic-Pacific areas, after the Japanese surrender, for the period of September 8 to 10, 1945.

By directive dated January 1947, the USS *Lewis* was to remain out of commission, in reserve, attached to the U.S. Pacific Reserve fleet, berthed in San Diego.

Korea (1950s)

In the fall of 1951, the Lewis was towed from San Diego to Mare Island where reactivation conversion and modernization was completed. This conversion and modernization involved installation of new and better anti-submarine warfare equipment which necessitated the removal of the entire heavy machine (20mm and 40mm mounts) battery, the triple-tube torpedo mount and the single fixed hedgehog mount. An extraordinary battery of 14 K-gun depth charge throwers were installed to supplement the two stern depth charge racks; two fully stabilized and trainable hedgehog projectors were mounted forward of the bridge. A short second mast (mainmast) was added for future electronic countermeasures equipment installation. The *Lewis* retained her original two enclosed 5"/38 caliber gun mounts forward and aft and so was nicknamed "Two Gun Louie."

On March 28, 1952, the *Lewis* was recommissioned at the U.S. Naval Shipyard, Mare Island, Vallejo, California, with Lieutenant Commander Gordon S. Hawkins as her commanding officer. On May 8, 1952 the *Lewis* reported to the U.S. Pacific Fleet Cruiser Destroyer Force for operational and administrative control, and underwent shakedown training near San Diego. Almost immediately after successfully completing shake-down training in July 1952, the *Lewis* joined Escort Division 92 which also included the USS *Marsh* (DE-699), the USS *Vammen* (DE-644) and the USS *Naifeh* (DE-352). From July 19 through most of August 1952, the division of ships were en route to the Korean Theatre of Operations with a stop over for training at Pearl Harbor and shorter stops at Midway Island, Yokosuka and Sasebo, Japan.

The *Lewis* reported to the Commander United Nations Blockade and Escort Force for operational control on August 21, 1952. Her first assignment was blockade patrol on Aug. 21, 1952. Her first assignment was blockade patrol on the East Coast of North Korea. In the months of August and September the *Lewis* completed twenty-three consecutive days of gun fire support inside the harbor of enemy-held Wonsan. During that period the *Lewis* fired 1,116 rounds of five inch ammunition, silencing communist shore batteries and inflicting heavy damage, and was herself taken under fire on four occasions.

Her other duties included bombardment of shore targets, driving fishing boats ashore, protecting friendly troops stationed on islands in the harbor, providing friendly troops stationed on islands in the harbor, providing gun fire support for United Nations Minesweepers, sinking drifting mines, and providing rescue and communication facilities for Naval and Air Force air craft operating in that area. Duty in Wonsan was relieved by two trips to Sasebo for upkeep and recreation.

After escorting the mine-damaged destroyer USS *Barton* (DD-722) to Sasebo, Japan and completing an upkeep period there, the *Lewis* returned to the East Coast of North Korea, and on October 11, 1952 the commanding officer assumed the duties of Commander Central Patrol Element until relieved on October 16, 1952. While on blockade duty south of Hungnam as a unit of the Central Patrol Element the ship was engaged in a running gun duel with a communist battery of three heavy caliber weapons believed to be radar controlled, involving eighty-four rounds of highly accurate enemy artillery fire. The *Lewis* retaliated with two hundred fourteen rounds in a forty-eight minute engagement and scored a direct hit on one gun before the communists ceased fire.

While operating off Wonsan, North Korea in the period from October 16 to October 21, 1952, the *Lewis* rescued wounded Navy pilot Lieutenant (jg) W.G. Moore, USN who had ditched his F9F-2 Panther jet in the waters of the inner harbor after being hit by enemy anti-aircraft fire. The *Lewis* was maneuvered along side Moore; crew members brought the injured pilot on on board and administered first aid within ten minutes of the crash. Lieutenant (jg) Moore was later transferred to the Cruiser USS *Toledo* for further medical treatment.

During this period and while serving as flagship for the commander of the Wonsan Task Element the *Lewis* coordinated search and rescue missions which resulted in the rescue of two pilots downed behind enemy lines.

On October 21, 1952 the *Lewis* was furnishing gunfire support for two Republic of Korea Minesweepers operating in Wonson Harbor when they were taken under fire by four to six enemy guns. The *Lewis* moved in to the aid of the ROK ships returning the fire, and while laying a smoke screen to cover their withdrawal was hit by two 75mm shells. The first shell exploded in the forward fireroom, killing seven men and knocking the fireroom out of action. The second shell pierced the main deck causing minor damage from shrapnel and slightly wounding one man.

Killed aboard the *Lewis* were: Richard E. Brower, boilerman first class, Canton, OH; James Crossman, fireman, Weaver, SD; Raymond E. Remers, boilerman first class, Honolulu, HI; George Schofield, fireman, Fair Oaks, PA; David D. Schmit, chief boilerman, Long Beach, CA; Floyd Sneed, fireman, Batesville, AR; and Arnold W. Karlin, boilerman third class, Marion, OR.

Returning the enemy fire, the *Lewis* spread a smoke screen to protect the small Korean vessels. After the engagement the *Lewis* steamed away under one boiler and signaled it did not need assistance.

Upon being relieved the *Lewis* proceeded to Sasebo, Japan for an upkeep period and battle damage repairs. Special Memorial Services were held on on board on October 27, 1952 for those crew members killed in action.

After a short upkeep period the *Lewis* continued patrol and blockade duties

in a less dangerous area since only one boiler remained. The *Lewis* concluded her Western Pacific tour of duty patrolling the sea defense zone off the coast of South Korea from November 2 to November 10, 1952. When relieved the ship returned to the United States with other units of Escort Division 92.

While in the Korean Theater the *Lewis* steamed a total of 14,000 miles on blockade patrol. Alert lookouts won steak dinners and Christmas leave for spotting four large drifting mines which were sunk by small arms fire. The ship fired 1,559 rounds of five inch ammunition. Her guns destroyed ten supply warehouses, three troop shelters and many boxcars and trucks. Heavy damage was inflicted on three supply dumps and four gun emplacements and 70 observed personnel casualties were caused among enemy labor forces and troops. A total of 196 rounds were fired at the *Lewis* by Communist shore batteries in seven different actions; she scored direct hits on three firing guns while so engaged. On returning to fully operational status, the *Lewis* was under the operational control of Commander Cruiser-Destroyer, U.S. Pacific Fleet.

Since the Korean War, the *Lewis* alternated between local operation in the San Diego area and overseas tours to the Western Pacific. The 1956-1957 cruise covered a six-month period from August to February. The trip began with visits to New Zealand and Australia. Following this the *Lewis* and other U.S. ships joined with the forces of the Philippines, Pakistan, Australian, British, New Zealand, and Thai navies in "Operation Albatross." Among the many ports of call during the cruise were Manila, Yokosuka, Auckland, Darwin, Pearl Harbor, and Hong Kong. Upon returning to San Diego, the *Lewis* again commenced local operations.

Towards the end of September, the *Lewis* departed Conus once again for duty in the Western Pacific with a five day visit in Brisbane, Australia. November saw the ship in Guam where she was assigned to the operational control of Commander Naval Force, Marianas for island surveillance patrols and search and rescue work. The following two and half months were spent visiting islands in the Caroline, Marianas, and Volcanic groups, and conducting several SAR missions. During this time the *Lewis* was assigned to Escort Squadron Three after the decommissioning of Escort Nine.

Leaving Guam in mid-January 1958, the *Lewis* steamed to Hong Kong and thence to Yokosuka, Japan. While in the Yokosuka area she participated with the units of the U.S. Pacific Fleet and Canadian Forces in Operation Rex 58 Juliett. Departing Yokosuka in mid-February the *Lewis* returned to Conus stopping briefly at Midway and Pearl Harbor to refuel. The *Lewis* arrived in San Diego in early March where she was assigned local upkeep and operations prior to entering the San Francisco Naval Shipyard at Hunter's Point, San Francisco, CA in early May. Upon completion of the two and half month scheduled overhaul the *Lewis* returned to her homeport of San Diego, undergoing refresher training exercises.

On October 4, 1958, Lieutenant Commander D.E. Packard, USN relieved Lieutenant Commander H.L. Cravens, USN as commanding officer prior to departure from San Diego to her new homeport of Guam, Marianas Islands. Upon the *Lewis* arrival in Guam on November 1, 1958, the ship commenced island surveillance and search and rescue operations under the operational control of Commander Naval Forces Marianas while remaining a unit of Escort Squadron Three. While homeported at Guam, the *Lewis* made continual patrols conducting island surveillance of the Trust Territories Island in the Caroline and Bonin Volcano groups insuring their security and welfare.

Two trips to Yokosuka, Japan and a trip through the Philippines to Hong Kong were made during the first year at Guam. On December 2, 1959, Lieutenant Commander D.L. Banks, Jr. relieved Commander D.E. Packard as commanding officer in a ceremony at Apra Harbor, Guam.

In November 1959, the *Lewis* was assigned as the escort ship for "Project Nekton." A project supervised by the Office of Naval Research that used the Bathyscaphe "Trieste" to explore the depths near Guam. The Trieste was a self contained, diving craft capable of carrying two men to the bottom of the deepest valleys of the sea. The *Lewis* carried a large number of technicians on each diving expedition, and used her depth finding gear to determine the actual diving site. In her search for the deepest point of the Chanllenger Deep in January 1960, the *Lewis* recorded the greatest depth ever found. At this position, the Trieste submerged for her successful descent to the bottom on January 23, 1960, 35,800 feet below the surface.

The *Lewis* departed from Guam on February 1, 1960 and headed back to the United States and inactivation at the U.S. Naval Shipyard, Mare Island, Vallejo, California. At dawn on February 22, 1960, the ship steamed under the Golden Gate Bridge flying a homeward bound pennant one hundred thirty four feet long, a foot for each man who had been aboard at least a year.

On May 27, 1960, the commissioning Pennant was once again hauled down as the *Lewis* joined the Mare Island Group, Pacific Reserve Fleet.

Lt. Cmdr. D.L. Banks Jr., USN Commanding Officer
Lt. Cmdr. J.E. Myrick, USN Executive Officer
Lt. (jg) G.V.V. Barnes Jr., USNR Engineering Officer
Lt. (jg) D.T. Linch, USN Gunnery Officer
Lt. (jg) P.H. Partridge, USNR Operations Officer
Ensign R.D. Kindwall, SC, USNR Supply Officer

On December 22, 1965, the Chief of Naval Operations, based on findings of a Navy Board of Inspection and Survey, recommended the disposal of the *Lewis*. On December 28, 1965 the Secretary of the Navy declared the *Lewis* unfit for further Naval service and directed that she be stricken from the Naval Vessel Register as of January 1, 1966, pursuant to Title 10 USC 7304. Subsequently, on March 18, 1966 the Honorable Graeme C. Bannerman, Assistant Secretary of the Navy (Installation and Logistics) authorized the Chief of Naval Operations to dispose of the *Lewis* as a target to destruction as provided by Title 10, USC 7306, in accordance with a request from Commander First Fleet. The *Lewis* was towed to sea and sunk as a target late March 1966.

She served her skippers, crews and nation well ...

Prepared by: Elmer A. Sailer TM2/c USS *Lewis* (WWII).

Contributors: CDR Gordon S. Hawkins (50s); Gerry Graf (50s); Dave Martinsen (50s); Jim McComb (50s); Chris Nielsen (50s); Keith C. King (50s); Lawrence G. Raasch (WWII); Fred C. Lewis (WWII); Robert Green (WWII); Fleming Jensen (50s); John H.D. Williams (50s).

Sources: USS Lewis War Cruising Records, WWII; Destroyer Escorts of WWII; The Floating Dry Dock (Destroyer Escort Sailors Association).

USS *LOWE* (DE-325)

Lowe (DE-325) was laid down by Consolidated Steel Corp., Orange, Tex., 24 May 1943; launched 28 July 1943; and commissioned 22 November 1943, Comdr. Reginald H. French, USCG, in command. After a shakedown cruise to Bermuda, *Lowe* reported for convoy duty 2 February 1944 and departed Charleston, SC, escorting convoy UGS-32 to Casablanca, French Morocco, and back. On her second such assignment, *Lowe* went into action 20 April when her convoy came under tenacious enemy air attack off the north African coast. Simultaneously, two high-speed wakes made directly for the starboard side of the ship. She evaded the torpedoes by a hard right turn which enabled her to escape between the oncoming warheads. *Lowe* continued convoy escort service making a total of 12 Atlantic crossings until 5 March 1945 when she joined TG 22.14, an exclusively Coast Guard "killer" group, with the specific mission of finding and destroying an enemy submarine operating due east of Newfoundland. While steaming in search of the enemy 18 March 100 miles east of Halifax, *Lowe* made sonar contact and attacked with two patters of hedgehogs. The depth charge attacks with those of other ships of the group brought an oil slick and large amounts of debris to the surface. The submarine was still on the bottom the following day when *Lowe* reestablished sound contact. Postwar investigation verified the destruction of U-866 by this group; *Lowe* received credit for the kill, and her commanding officer and four other crew members received awards for their part in the action. While serving with TG 22.14 3 May, *Lowe* rescued the crew of the foundered Newfoundland schooner *Mary Duffitt* and her guns sank the hulk, which was a menace to navigation.

Commencing 6 July, the ship assumed duties as a training vessel at Norfolk, VA, departing only to participate in the Navy Day observance at Washington, D.C., 24 October. Departing the Capital 1 November offloaded ammunition at Yorktown, and 30 December arrived at St. John's River, Fla, headquarters of the Florida Group, 16th Fleet, U.S. Atlantic Fleet, where she decommissioned 1 May 1946 and entered the Reserve Fleet. Recommissioned 20 July 1951 as USCGC *Lowe* (WDE-425), saw service as a weather ship in the Atlantic and Pacific Oceans. She decommissioned a second time 1 June 1945 at the Todd Shipyard, Long Beach, CA. She saw extended duty with the North American Air Defense Command as a unit of the seaward extension of the DEW line, eventually completing 67 tours as a picket vessel. While on station 20 February 1962, was an emergency rescue line for Lt. Col. John Glenn's three-orbit space mission. At the disestablishment of the Radar Barrier 30 June 1965, *Lowe* sailed for the Western Pacific and joined the 7th Fleet 5 August. Taking station off the coast of Vietnam 15 August, was assigned the task of preventing seaborne infiltration of enemy elements of the south of that country as a part of Operation "Market Time." In early September 1965, returned to her new homeport, Guam, for a period of rest and upkeep. She rejoined TF-115 off Vietnam 22 November and

resumed "Market Time" surveillance. When not a unit of TF-115, *Lowe* served as a unit of the Taiwan Patrol Force or as station ship Hong Kong. This pattern of duty continue until 20 September 1968 when decommissioned at Guam. Struck 23 September *Lowe* began stripping in preparation for being sold for scrapping.

USS *LYMAN* (DE-302)

February 19, 1944-at noon this date the USS *Lyman*, escort destroyer Number Three Zero Two was commissioned at the Mare Island Navy Yard in Vallejo, California. The crew stood in the rain for the ceremonies.

March 4, 1944-the *Lyman* gets underway from Mare Island en route to San Diego for her initial shakedown cruise. The shakedown lasts one month and three days. The green crew is made into a seagoing crew. We operate out of San Diego, the liberty here is fair but not as good as Frisco or surrounding towns.

April 7, 1944-we leave San Diego for the last time en route to Mare Island. The ship goes into drydock and the crew goes on 48 hour liberties, some of the West Coasters get leave.

April 20, 1944-we leave Mare Island for the last time and go to Finger Pier at Treasure Island. Frisco is the liberty and recreation center.

April 23, 1944-*Lyman* gets underway for the Hawaiian Islands. Last look at fog blanketed Golden Gate Bridge for a year and a half.

May 1, 1944-arrive at Pearl Harbor. We stayed at Pearl for three months and 20 days. Engaged in submarine maneuvers and did some escorting down by the Marshalls. Honolulu is all day time liberty. The whiskey is no good, the women are very business like and impersonal. Navy torpedo juice is better than the whiskey, anyway it's stronger.

August 20, 1944-underway from Pearl Harbor en route to forward Pacific areas.

August 30, 1944-arrived at Roi Island in the Marshall group, stayed here a few hours and got underway for Kwajalein in the same group.

September 1, 1944-left Kwajalein Island. From Kwajalein to Manus Island in the Admiralty Group the *Lyman* crosses the equator. The Polywogs (non-equator crossers) are initiated by the shellbacks (men who have crossed the equator before). This includes the miserable ceremony of his Majesty King Neptune, royal ruler of the raging main. All Polywogs are well flogged by his majesties courtmen. The *Lyman* has also crossed the 180th Meridian which makes its crew members of the Order of the Golden Dragon. Good time was had by all ... shellbacks ...

September 7, 1944-we arrived at Manus Island.

September 15, 1944-the *Lyman* is underway for her first invasion, the Palau Islands. Two of these islands are invaded by the 1st Marine Division, the 81st Army Infantry Division and the mighty 3rd Fleet. We spent 45 days on the Palau picket-line. The island battles are bloody, the Jap airforce isn't much, our airforce is plenty potent. A pilot hits the silk near our station one day when his shot-up plane fails him. It was the first parachute jump I ever saw and it was a peach. The Japs in caves are bad. Banzai attacks are frequent, many are our casualties before we take the island. The island is bright red at night being lit up with flame throwers and artillery flares. The chow aboard gets down to rice and beans. We finally leave this place and get underway for the Russel Islands in the Solomons.

October 30, 1944-arrive in the Russell Islands escorting the 1st Marine Division. Here we move around a bit and wind up in Port Purvis in the Solomon Islands. Get liberty at Tulagi Island.

November 4, 1944-we leave Port Purvis underway for Manus Island.

November 7, 1944-we arrive in Manus. On the 10th day of this month the ammunition ship *Mount Hood* explodes. The cause is unknown, the biggest explosion I ever saw. The entire crew of the *Mount Hood* is killed with the exception of about a dozen men on the beach. Shrapnel is thrown for miles, we only get a small hole in our ship but the D.E. alongside is hit twice and one man aboard her is killed. We were scheduled to go alongside a tender that morning, this same tender was badly damaged by the explosion, for some reason that day we didn't go. The lucky lady gets her name.

November 14, 1944-we leave Manus Island.

November 17, 1944-we arrive at our new operating base, Ulithi Atolls in the western Caroline Islands.

November 29, 1944-we leave Ulithi.

December 4, 1944-we arrive at Eniwetok in the Marshall Islands.

December 8, 1944-we are back at Ulithi after a fast trip to Eniwetok. On about November 18 the tanker *Missisanewa* is sunk by midget subs that slipped through the anti-submarine nets in Ulithi. All anti-submarine craft in the harbor attack. We attack a position where air bubbles are spotted, damage is undetermined. All of the midgets are accounted for and no more of our ships are hit.

December 16, 1944-we get underway from Ulithi en route to Philippine Sea. We are operating with the 3rd Fleet which routes the Jap navy in this area. Also during the Philippine Operation, we hit a typhoon in the Philippines, pretty rough; and the destroyers *Spence, Hull* and *Monaghan* are sunk with almost all lives lost.

December 22, 1944-we leave the Philippines and go to Guam for fleet replenishments.

December 24, 1944-we arrive at Guam.

December 25, 1944-we spend Christmas Day at Guam, the liberty party gets two cans of beer each. We spend the day pillaging caves and finding scores of Jap skeletons. Some of the boys take bones back for souvenirs, but the officer of the deck says no. On this Christmas Day, I am 9,000 miles from home.

December 26, 1944-we leave Guam en route to Ulithi.

December 27, 1944-we arrive at Ulithi.

December 30, 1944-we get underway again and this time we are going back out to the Philippine area.

January 8, 1945-after operating in the Philippine area we again start back to Guam.

January 12, 1945-we arrived in Guam, stay overnight and start back to Ulithi.

January 14, 1945-we arrive in Ulithi, go alongside a tender (ice cream) and we stay in port for a month.

February 8, 1945-we get underway for the Bonins area, there is to be an invasion.

February 19, 1945-this is D-Day at Iwo Jima. The 5th Fleet with the 2nd and 3rd Marines do the job. The Iwo Jima Battle is the bloodiest in the Pacific and two hours after landings there are 2.000 casualties on this eight mile strip of coral.

February 21, 1945-we leave the Iwo Jima area en route to Guam.

February 23, 1945-arrive at Guam. Here we hold services for our chief boats, W.M. Smith, Chief Boatswains Mate USN. He was lost over the side at Iwo Jima while fueling in rough weather.

February 25, 1945-we leave Guam and start back to the Bonins.

March 4. 1945-after operating with the 5th Fleet at Iwo Jima, we finally start back to Ulithi.

March 6, 1945-we were expecting a rest but were ordered to Manus Island, we cross the equator again and let the Polywogs have it.

March 9, 1945-we arrive at Manus, the British Fleet has taken over everything here including the liberty island.

March 10, 1945-we leave Manus en route to Ulithi.

March 13, 1945-we leave again with tankers but when one breaks we are picked to escort it back to Ulithi. We finally all get mail!

March 15, 1945-back in Ulithi with the first mail in over 45 days.

March 22, 1945-we leave Ulithi with the 5th Fleet en route to the Southern Islands of Japan, the Ryukus.

March 26, 1945-we arrive in the Okinawa area. This invasion is quite a show. The picket line is hell, and proves to be the bloodiest spot of all. This island is invaded by the 10th Army, and the 3rd, 4th, and 6th Marine Divisions with the 5th Fleet. Destroyers, Destroyer Escorts, and Patrol Craft man the picket line against Jap aircraft. This line is the first line of defense against the Jap suicide planes that are so widely used in this campaign. They bear the brunt of the kamazike. The Navy takes more casualties in this operation than the Army and Marine Corps combined. (There are no fox holes in the ocean.)

March 28, 1945-we leave the Okinawa area for Ulithi.

April 1, 1945-we arrive in Ulithi.

April 3, 1945-we go back to the Okinawa area.

April 6, 1945-we arrive at rendezvous point in Okinawa area.

April 16, 1945 we go to Guam with a carrier tonight (Good Dope).

April 19, 1945-we arrive at Guam.

April 20, 1945-left Guam to proceed north to Okinawa.

April 23, 1945-we arrive at point of rendezvous at Okinawa.

April 25, 1945-we get an excellent contact tonight with the sound gear. We attack with depth charges, damage undetermined.

May 7, 1945-we start back to Ulithi.

May 11, 1945-we arrive in Ulithi.

May 13, 1945-we go into a floating dry dock for repairs, here we scrape the bottom of the ship. (ugh).

May 20, 1945-we leave Ulithi en route to Okinawa again.

May 24, 1945-we arrive at point of rendezvous with the fleet.

June 5, 1945-we are trying to outrun a typhoon, instead we run into one worse than the first. The wind is blowing at a speed of 138 knots. The waves are like mountains and are beating the devil out of us, this is the worst I have ever seen. We take a 70° roll and the ship is twisting and turning like a bronco. The cruiser

Pittsburgh loses her bow, some of the ships lose men over the side. We lose two life rafts and get banged up a bit. Lord, if I ever get out of this, I'll write home every night.

June 6, 1945-the typhoon is over and we are ordered back to Ulithi.

June 11, 1945-we arrive in Ulithi and stay for 22 days.

July 3, 1945-we form into a task group and get underway for Japanese waters. This is to be a naval raid against Japan.

July 8, 1945-a fleet tug breaks down and we are ordered to take her to Saipan. We stay at Saipan overnight and start back out to meet the Fleet.

July 27, 1945-we are off the coast of Japan with the 3rd Fleet which is raiding Japan. Carrier planes and bombardment are really giving the Japs hell. The Jap air force is not very active and the 3rd Fleet bombs and bombards almost at will. On this date we are to escort a carrier to Guam.

July 30, 1945-we arrive at Guam.

August 1, 1945-we leave Guam to proceed to the 3rd Fleet.

August 4, 1945-we arrive at rendezvous. The 3rd Fleet is on Japan's doorstep. The tankers are a hundred miles from Tokyo. Maybe this is pre-invasion.

August 13, 1945-we leave for Ulithi with tankers.

August 15, 1945-the Japs have surrendered (Glory Be) the crew raises the devil. Two cans of beer for each man at chow and then back to the old routine.

August 19, 1945-we arrive in Ulithi after a 46 day cruise. During this stay in port the captain is relieved by Lt. Cmdr. John D. Lawson. Two days before we arrived at Ulithi, E.P. LaFlamme Yeoman Second Class died and was buried at sea. He was one of the best liked men on the ship and his death was a shock to all.

August 24, 1945-we leave for Jap waters with units of the 3rd Fleet. We will be among the first to enter Japanese waters.

August 29, 1945-we get orders today to proceed to Tokyo Bay with a fleet tanker

August 30, 1945-we enter Tokyo Bay with us are two Jap subs that have surfaced and surrendered. We stay in Tokyo Bay for a few days, we are here when the surrender is signed on the *Missouri* which is sitting off our starboard bow. The city of Yokohama is off our port quarter. The great 3rd Fleet sits in Tokyo Bay and the war is officially over. We were the first destroyer escort to enter Tokyo Bay.

September 3, 1945-we are ordered back out to sea with a tanker, when we arrive at rendezvous point we are ordered to Leyte, Philippine Islands with three ammunition ships.

September 10, 1945-we arrive at Leyte, here we get the best liberty we've had since we left Pearl Harbor.

September 13, 1945-tonight, right after the movies a message was received by radio ordering our ship to Ulithi, Pearl Harbor, and the West Coast for decommissioning. On September 14, we get underway for home ... Finis ...

In this diary I have attempted to put down a general outline of where the *Lyman* has been and what she has done. In her year and a half in the Pacific she took part in three invasions and one major naval raid. From the time she went into commission she was underway 20 out of every 24 hours. Of course it was impossible to put down everything we saw or did, every general quarters or every depth charge. But it covers in general our voyage.

Palau, Iwo Jima, Okinawa, Japanese Homeland Raid
Philippine Islands

Officers

Wilson, J.W., Lt. Cmdr.	Freeman, D.B., Lt. (jg)
Lawson, J.D., Lt. Cmdr	Lineburg, G.W., Lt. (jg)
Young, P.S., Lt.	Bowman, H.S., Ens. (SC)
Magill, D.M., Lt.	Watkins, A.C., Lt. (jg)
Charbonnett, W.H., Lt.	Doar, W.T., Ens.
Price, R.M., Lt.	Spitzer, W.A., Ens.
Michaelsen, J.C., Lt.	Helfgott, S.L., Ens.
Miller, I.E., Lt. (jg)	

USS *MASON* (DE-529)

Ensign Newton Henry Mason was born December 24, 1918, at New York City, and died as a result of enemy action in the Asiatic Area (Coral Sea), the presumptive date of his death being May 9, 1943. He was officially reported missing in action May 8, 1942, when the plane of which he was pilot failed to return from an engagement with the enemy in the Coral Sea.

Ensign Mason enlisted in the United States Naval Reserve as a Seaman

USS Mason (DE-529)

Second Class, at New York City, on November 7, 1940, for a period of four years, his enlistment terminating on February 9, 1941, to accept appointment as Aviation Cadet. In an enlisted status, he was assigned to active duty for elimination flight training at the United States Naval Reserve Aviation Base, Floyd Bennet Field, Brooklyn, New York, on November 15, 1940, and on February 6, 1941, transferred to the United States Naval Air Station, Jacksonville, Florida.

Ensign Mason accepted his appointment and executed the oath of Office as Aviation Air Cadet in the United States Naval Reserve on February 10, 1941, to rank from February 1, 1941, and designated naval Aviator (Heavier-than-air) on August 18, 1941, and was promoted to the rank of Ensign of Sept. 3, 1941, to rank from July 16, 1941.

Ensign mason began his training as an officer February 10, 1941, at the Naval Air Station, Jacksonville, Florida, from which he was detached July 9, 1941, and assigned to the Naval Air Station at Miami, Florida, for active duty undergoing training, reporting July 11, 1941. From September 3, 1941, he was in active duty status other than training and was assigned to Advanced Carrier Training Group, Pacific Fleet, for temporary active duty involving flying under training and further assigned to Fighting Squadron Three for active duty involving flying.

Ensign Mason was awarded the American Defense Service Medal (Fleet Clasp), 1939-1941, and the Distinguished Flying Cross with the following citation:

"For extraordinary achievement in aerial combat as pilot of a fighter plane in action against enemy Japanese forces in the Battle of the Coral Sea on May 7-8, 1942. With utter disregard for his own personal safety, Ensign Mason zealously engaged enemy Japanese aircraft, this contributing materially to the defense of our forces. In this action, he gallantly gave up his life in the service of his country."

Built at the Boston Navy Yard, the USS *Mason* was launched on November 17, 1943. The *Mason* was sponsored by Mrs. David N. Mason of Scarsdale, NY, mother of the late Ensign Newton Henry Mason, USNR, hero pilot of the Battle of the Coral Sea. The destroyer escort was named in honor of Ensign Mason.

Following her shakedown cruise which took her to Bermuda in May, the *Mason* saw her first convoy duty the next month through submarine-infested waters between Charleston, SC, and Bermuda. From July 1944 to April 1945, the *Mason* was on convoy duty between this country and Europe. She crossed the Atlantic six times, making two trips to England, three to Oran, Algeria and one to Belfast, Northern Ireland.

While numerous undersea contacts were made on these voyages, the *Mason* was never the target for German torpedoes and never had the opportunity of sinking a Nazi Submarine. On one occasion, as the escorts of Task Force 64 entered the approaches to the Straits of Gibraltar, there were several calls to general quarters aboard the *Mason* following reports that one ship traveling in convoy some 60 miles ahead had been torpedoed. Additional air coverage was provided for the *Mason* and other ships of the convoy. She later proceeded to Oran without incident.

While on convoy duty with Task Force 64 in January 1945, en route from Oran to new York, the *Mason* suffered minor damage when she collided with a wooden derelict, probably a barge. She proceeded to Bermuda for emergency repairs.

While enroute between New York and Norfolk, VA, in early April 1945, the *Mason* was the locale for Navy motion picture photographers in shooting scenes for *The Negro Sailor*, a film recently released for public showing.

The *Mason* was the first Naval vessel with a predominantly African-American crew. Under the command of Lieutenant Commander William M. Blackford, USNR, of Seattle, WA, the *Mason* crew initially consisted of 160 African Americans and 44 Caucasian Americans.

Destroyer escort vessels like the *Mason* are larger than corvettes, but smaller than destroyers. They are designed for escort or convoy duty, weigh 1300 tons, and are about 300 feet in length.

The USS *Mason* was de-commissioned by the Navy as of October 16, 1945.

USS *McCALLA* (DD-488)
Submitted by Ira W. Wells GM2/c

USS *McCalla* commissioned 27 May 1942 Kearnay, NJ. Reported to Com. So. Pac. 28 Sept. 1942 Noumea, New Caledonia. Ten battlestars from the South Pacific to the 3rd Fleet operations against Japan 10 July to August 1945. *McCalla* sunk 1 heavy cruiser, 2 destroyers, 40 landing craft, 8 air craft and damaged 1 submarine. Rescued 197 Duncan crew, captured 3 Jap sailors in the Cape Esperance Second Savo Battle. Went to Dunedin South Island New Zealand for two weeks R&R in May 1943.

In a collision with USS *Patterson* (DD-393), 29 Sept. 1943, *McCalla's* bow was heavily damaged. While enroute to Mare Island, CA for repairs rescued 868 survivors of the torpedoed troop ship SS *Cape San Juan* and delivered them to the Fiji Islands. *McCalla* was overhauled in Portland, OR August 1945 to January 1946, then decommissioned in Charleston, SC May 1946 and transferred to the Turkish Navy.

USS *MENGES* (DE-320)

Herbert Hugo Menges, born in Louisville, KY Jan. 20, 1917, enlisted in the Naval Reserve as seaman second class at Robertson, MO July 3, 1939. Appointed naval aviator July 24, 1940, he was assigned to Squadron 6 on *Enterprise* (CV-6) Nov. 28, 1940. Ensign Menges was killed during the Japanese attack on Pearl Harbor Dec. 7, 1941.

(DE-320: dp. 1,200; l. 306'; b. 36'7"; s. 21 k.; cpl. 186; a. 3 3'; 2 40mm., 8 20mm., 2 dct., 8 dcp., 1 dcp. (h.h.), 3 21" tt; cl. *Edsall*)

Menges (DE-320) was laid down by Consolidated Steel Corp., Orange, TX, March 22, 1943; launched June 15, 1943, sponsored by Mrs. Charles Menges, mother of the late Ensign Menges; and commissioned Oct. 26, 1943, Lt. Comdr. Frank M. McCade, USCG, in command.

After shakedown off Bermuda, Menges spent January 1944 on schoolship duty in the lower Chesapeake Bay. On January 26, she got underway from Norfolk for New York City. She departed January 31 for Europe on the first trip of three months of convoy escort operations.

On the night of April 20, her convoy, UGS-38, while off the coast of Algiers enroute to the east coast, was attacked by 30 German torpedo bombers. After splashing one of the planes, *Menges* rescued 137 survivors of the *Lansdale* (DD-426), sunk by an aircraft torpedo, and two German flyers.

On May 3, *Menges* was 15.5 miles astern of the convoy chasing down a radar contact when she was hit at 0118 by an acoustic torpedo from U-371. The U-boat was sunk the next day by *Joseph E. Campbell* (DE-70) and *Pride* (DE-323). The explosion was so violent that the aft third of the ship was destroyed with 31 men killed an 25 wounded. However, Commander McCabe properly refused to give the order to "abandon ship" as long as there was chance of saving her. In addition, several of the crewmembers heroically jumped astride torpedoes loosened in the blast to disarm them. *Menges*, thanks to such creditable action, remained afloat.

Four hours later, Menges was taken in tow by HMS *Aspirant* and reached Bougie, Algeria, that same day to debark her dead and wounded. The escort ship, with temporary repairs made, got underway from Oran, Algeria, June 23 under tow of *Carib* (AT-82) for New York, arriving July 22.

From August 14-31 the stern of *Holder* (DE-401), whose forward two-thirds had been shot away by submarine torpedoing in the Mediterranean April 11, was welded to the remaining two-thirds of *Menges*. The "new ship" came out of drydock at the New York Navy Yard for shakedown from September 26 to October 20 in Casco Bay, ME.

On November 15, *Menges* steamed in convoy CU-47 from New York for Europe, arriving in Plymouth, England, the 26th. She spent the next months again on Atlantic convoy duty before joining *Pride*, *Mosley* (DE-321) and *Lowe* (DE-325) late in February 1945 to form the only hunter-killer group in the North Atlantic to be manned completely by Coast Guard personnel. On March 18, *Menges* assisted *Lowe* in sinking U-866, their first target. She continued anti-submarine sweep and patrol operations until Germany surrendered May 7.

On May 30 she escorted her last convoy to Europe, CU-73, arriving Cheshire, England, June 8. *Menges* arrived back at new York the 21st for duty as training ship for the US Coast Guard Academy, with two cadet cruises to the West Indies before arriving New London, CT, September 7.

Three days later she departed for the Cape Cod area, arriving Boston, MA the 17th. By Navy Day, October 27, Menges was moored at Fall River, below Boston.

The escort ship moved on to Green Cove Springs, FL, for assignment in March 1946 to the 16th (Inactive Reserve) Fleet. *Menges* decommissioned in January 1947 and entered the berthing area in the St. Johns River to spend the next 15 years there in reserve. By Jan. 1, 1962, she was berthed at Orange, TX, in the Atlantic Reserve Fleet, where she remained into 1969.

Menges received two battle stars for World War II service.

USS *EARL K. OLSEN* (DE-765)

The USS *Earl K. Olsen* (DE-765) was launched on February 13, 1944, and sponsored by Mrs. H.E. Olsen, mother of Lieutenant Commander Earl K. Olsen, who was lost during enemy action off the Solomon Islands in 1942. She was commissioned at Tampa, Florida, on 10 April 1944, for inclusion as a unit of Escort Division 35, U.S. Atlantic Fleet.

Following commissioning, limited training and structural firing tests were conducted off Tampa and Key West. The *Olsen* was then ordered to Bermuda, B.W.I., on 2 May 1944 to undergo shakedown training exercises. On completion of the training period, 31 May 1944, orders were received to proceed to Navy Yard, Boston, Massachusetts for post-shakedown availability. Subsequent to this availability the ship was assigned as an A.S.W. school ship at Key West, Florida, where operations were commenced 25 June, 1944.

During the period of 25 June, 1944 to 25 August, 1944, the activities of this vessel consisted of operations as a Sound School Ship, a short upkeep period, and refresher training exercises at Casco Bay, Maine. On 25 August, 1944, the vessel reported for duty to Escort Division 35, U.S. Atlantic Fleet, was engaged in the escorting of C.U. and U.C. convoys for the duration of hostilities in the European Theatre.

Beginning with the first Trans-Atlantic convoy to arrive in Cherbourg, France, CU-37, the *Olsen* assisted in escorting a total of six convoys to various European ports, including Cherbourg, Plymouth, Southampton, Portsmouth, England, and Cardiff, Wales.

Convoys escorted by the *Olsen* included: CU-37 from Boston, Massachusetts to Cherbourg, France; UC-37 from Plymouth, England to New York, New York; CU-43 from New York to Plymouth, England; UC-43 from Plymouth to New York; CU-49 from New York to Cardiff, Wales; UC-49 from Cardiff to New York; CU-55 from Boston to Plymouth; UC-55 from Portsmouth to New York; CU-61 from Boston to Southhampton; UC-61

USS Menges (DE-320)

from Plymouth to New York; CU-67 from New York to Cardiff, Wales, and UC-67 from Cardiff to New York. The European War came to an end while the *Olsen* was moored in Cardiff waiting to escort convoy UC-67 back to the States. Although numerous depth charge patterns were dropped by the *Olsen*, at no time during the above mentioned escorting were any of the convoys threatened by confirmed enemy action, and no convoyed vessels were lost from any cause.

During the escorting of convoy CU-61 the *Olsen* engaged in the rescue of survivors of the collision between U.S.A.T.J.W. *McAndrew* and F.N.S. *Bearn*. This action occurred in latitude 41° 54' North, 36° 0 West in the early morning hours of 13 March 1945. Seventy-three men were lost from both ships, of which the USS *Roche* (DE-197) rescued eleven, and the *Olsen*. The rescue of personnel was made hazardous by the conditions of wind and sea. One enlisted man from the *Olsen*, received the Navy and Marine Corps Medal while five others received letters of commendation for service above and beyond the normal call of duty. The *Olsen* escorted the two crippled ships into Penta Delgada Azores, before proceeding to Southampton as per Admiralty orders.

Following completion of escort work in the Atlantic the *Olsen* was granted fifteen days availability in Navy Yard New York, Bayonne Annex, for armament improvements. With Escort Division 35 she next proceeded to Guantanamo Bay, Cuba for a period of refresher training.

On completion of training, the division was ordered to proceed to the Panama Canal. Transit of the Canal was made on the 28 of June, and Escort Division 35 proceeded to San Diego, California, arriving there on 7 July 1945. Upon arrival at San Diego, the flag of Commander Escort Division 35 was hoisted on the *Olsen*.

From San Diego the *Olsen*, in company with USS *Thornhill* (DE-175), got underway for Pearl Harbor. Entrance to Pearl was effected on 19 July, 1945. Here again more extensive training was completed. The division finally departed for the forward areas on 6 August 1945, having been assigned to Commander Third Amphibious Force, arriving first at Eniwetok Atoll in the Marshall Islands Group, on 14 August 1945. The following day as hostilities with Japan ceased the USS *Clinton* (APA-144) was taken under escort to Guam. From here the *Olsen* proceeded successively to Ulithi, Leyte, Legaspi, and Manila, PI, escorting APs, AKs and LSTs. At Manila, Task Unit 33.11.1, LST Echelon 4, was picked up for escort to Tokyo Bay, Japan. The Task Unit arrived off Yokohama September 12, a few days after official surrender.

Though the *Olsen* never fired a gun in action (but was long on firing training), it did enter Tokyo Bay with its guns blazing. A Japanese floating mine was sunk a few miles off Kannon Saki at the entrance to the bay. A total of three LST groups were escorted to the Tokyo Bay area from the Philippine Islands without mishap. During the course of these operations the *Olsen* sank four floating mines by 20 mm gunfire, one detonated.

The decline in amphibious force activities in the forward area and the subsequent deactivation of the Third Amphibious Force, found the *Olsen* moored in the Tokyo Bay area where she reported to the Commander Philippine Sea Frontier on 24 November 1945, finally arriving in Manila on December 1945.

By directive dated September 1946, USS *Earl K. Olsen* (DE-765) was to be transferred to the Sixth Naval District to train Naval Reserves.

USS *Earl K. Olsen* earned the Navy Occupation Service Medal, Pacific for the periods of 11 to 20 September 1945; 5 to 26 October 1945; and 16 to 27 November 1945.

Statistics

Overall Length	300 feet
Beam	36 feet
Displacement	1,400 tons
Speed	25 knots plus
Restencilled	June 1951

April 1944
10   Ship commissioned at Tampa Shipbuilding Co. yard, Tampa, Florida, under command of Lt. Cdr. Winfield F. DeLong.
19   Underway for Edgmont Key, Florida.
21   Returned to Tampa.
30   Departed Tampa enroute to Bermuda for shakedown cruise.

May 1944
6   Arrived Great Sound Anchorage, Bermuda, for scheduled exercises.

June 1944
1   Departed Hamilton, Bermuda, enroute to Boston, Mass., Navy Yard for repairs and alterations.
3   Arrived Boston Navy Yard.
21   Departed Boston Navy Yard enroute to Key West, Florida, to act as SONAR school ship.
26   Arrived Key West, Florida.

August 1944
13   Departed Key West, Florida, enroute to Portland, Maine (Casco Bay).
16   Arrived Portland, Maine.
24   Departed Portland, Maine, enroute to Boston, Mass.
25   Arrived Boston, Mass.
28   Departed Boston enroute to Cherbourg, France (Convoy CU-37).

September 1944
8   Arrived Cherbourg, France. Departed Cherbourg enroute to Utah Beach, Normandy. Departed Utah Beach enroute to Cherbourg. Arrived Cherbourg.
10   Departed Cherbourg enroute to Plymouth, England.

12 Departed Plymouth enroute to New York (Convoy UC-37).
23 Arrived Brooklyn Navy Yard.

October 1944
4 Departed Brooklyn Navy Yard enroute to Basco Bay, Maine, to conduct ASW/AA exercises.
6 Arrived Casco Bay, Maine.
10 Departed Caco Bay enroute to New York to await formation of convoy.
11 Departed New York enroute to Plymouth, England, as escort for convoy (CU-43).
25 Arrived Plymouth, England.

November 1944
1 Departed Plymouth enroute to New York (Convoy UC-43)
12 Arrived Brooklyn Navy Yard.

December 1944
1 Departed New York enroute to Cardiff, Wales (Convoy CU-49).
12 Arrived Cardiff having escorted Bristol Channel section of the convoy.
15 Departed Cardiff enroute to the anchorage at Milford haven, Wales.
17 Departed Milford Haven enroute for Brooklyn Navy Yard, Convoy UC-49, numerous submarine contacts…no attacks.
27 Arrived Brooklyn Navy Yard.

January 1945
7 Departed Brooklyn Navy Yard enroute to Casco Bay, Maine, for exercises.
8 Arrived Casco Bay
16 Departed Casco Bay enroute to Boston, Mass.
18 Departed Boston to rendezvous with "Able" section of convoy (CU-55).
20 Rendezvous with "Able" section of convoy (CU-55) enroute to Plymouth, England.

February 1945
1 Departed Plymouth, England, escorting ships to Portsmouth, England. 2200…collided with HMS *Cowl*, T238. Damaged aft port beam…damaged depth charge racks…hull punctured and strained…taking on water in several isolated compartments…no immediate repairs required.
2 Departed Portsmouth to rendezvous with "Able" section of convoy. British destroyer torpedoed.
3 Delivered convoy to escorts; returned to Plymouth.
4 Anchored in St. Helens Road, Portsmouth, England.
6 Departed Portsmouth enroute to U.S. escorting convoy (UC-55). Rough passage.
18 Moored Brooklyn Navy Yard.

March 1945
1 Departed Brooklyn Navy Yard enroute to Fort Pond Bay, Long Island, NY.
4 Returned to Pier 35 New York to await formation of convoy.
7 Departed New York enroute to Southampton, ENG (Convoy CU-61).
13 French Aircraft Carrier FNS *Bearn* collided with USAT *J.W. McAndrew* (41 54'N. 36 00'E.) causing considerable damage to both ships and the loss of 73 troops. Standing by to pick up survivors, USS *Roche* (DE-197) rescued 11 men. Vince Brennan (Coxswain) rescued two men, Pvt. Aubrey R. Daily and Pvt. Oscar M. Butler; failed in an attempt to rescue a third; was awarded the Navy/Marine Corps Medal. Four other men aboard the *Olsen*, Dorman J. McDonald, (MoMM3c1), Carlos J. Acosta (MOMM3c1), Salvatore Barbuto (S1c), and James W. Kelly (S1c), were given letters of Commendation. Enroute to Ponta Delgada, Azores, with survivors, in escort with damaged ships.
17 Arrived Ponta Delgada. Departed Ponta Delgada enroute to Southampton, England.
22 Arrived Southampton, England.
24 Departed Southampton enroute to New York.
26 Encountered two Spanish fishing boats with high powered radios operating in a restricted zone. Dry-run attack and warned them away.

April 1945
3 Arrived Brooklyn Navy Yard.
9 Departed Brooklyn Navy Yard enroute to Casco Bay, Maine.
10 Arrived Casco Bay conducting scheduled exercises.
21 Departed Portland, Maine, enroute to New York.
22 Arrived Pier 35, New York, to await formation of convoy.
24 Departed New York enroute to Cardiff, Wales, (Convoy CU-67).

May 1945
4 Arrived Cardiff, Wales
9 Departed Queen Elizabeth Basin via locks, standing off Cardiff. Anchored in Barry Roads, Wales. Underway to Cardiff.
13 Departed Cardiff enroute to New York (Convoy UC-67).
24 Moored at Brooklyn Navy Yard Annex, Bayonne, New Jersey.

June 1945
8 Departed Bayonne enroute to Virgin Islands in company with - USS *Cates* (DE-763), USS *Gandy* (DE-764), USS *Slater* (DE-766), USS *Ebert* (DE-768), and USS *Burrows* (DE-105), all comprising COMCORT Div. 35.
12 Arrived Culebra Islands in Virgin Islands to conduct shore bombardment.
13 Departed Culebra Island enroute to Guantanamo Bay, Cuba.
14 Anchored in Guantanamo Bay.
24 Completed scheduled exercises, departed for Gonaives, Haiti.
25 Departed Haiti enroute to Panama Canal.
27 Arrived Colon, Canal Zone, moored to pier at Coco Solo Naval Base.
28 Underway for Panama Canal. Entered Canal, passed through locks, departed Canal enroute to San Diego, California.

July 1945
7 Arrived Naval Repair Base, San Diego, CA.
12 Departed San Diego enroute to Pearl Harbor in company with USS *Burrows* (DE-105), USS *Thornhill* (DE-175). Olsen made flagship COMCORT Div. 35.
19 Arrived Pearl Harbor for extensive training.

August 1945
6 Departed Pearl Harbor enroute to Eniwetok, Marshall Islands, in company with USS *Gandy* (DE-764), USS *Fitch* (DMS-25), USS *Ebert* (DE-768), USS *Slater* (DE-766), and USS *Burrows* (DE-105). Olsen still flagship of COMCORT Div. 35.
11 Crossed International Dateline.
13 Arrived Eniwetok, Marshall Islands.
15 Departed Eniwetok enroute to Guam, Marshall Islands. 1115-Official word—War is over.
18 Arrived Apra, Guam, in company with USS *Clinton* (APA-123).
26 Departed Guam enroute to Ulithi Atoll, Carolines. Assigned to THIRD FLEET.
27 Arrived Ulithi; underway for Leyte, Philippine Islands.
30 Arrived San Pedro Bay, Leyte.
31 Departed Leyte enroute to Manila Bay…orders changes…enroute to Legaspi, Luzon, PI.

September 1945
1 Arrived Legaspi, Luzon. Underway enroute to Manila in escort of LST.
3 Arrived Manila Bay; refueled. Underway to Tokyo Bay, Japan. Escorting second amphibious invasion. Escorting (APs, AKs, & LSTs) as TASK UNIT 33. 11. 1, LST ECHELON 4.
12 Arrived Tokyo Bay; anchored off Yokohama.
19 Departed Yokohama enroute to Leyte Gulf, P.I., escorting 30 LSTs.
26 Arrived San Pedro Bay, Leyte Gulf.

October 1945
1 Underway enroute to Manila.
4 Arrived Manila to await formation of convoy.
8 Departed Manila enroute to Otaru, Hokkaido, Japan, escorting 45 LSTs. Ordered to take shelter in Subic Bay due to bad weather.
9 Underway for Otaru.
16 Orders changed…enroute to Tokyo.

18   Arrived Tokyo Bay; anchored off Yokohama.
25   Departed Tokyo Bay enroute to San Pedro Bay, PI.

November 1945
2   Arrived San Pedro Bay.
9   Departed San Pedro Bay enroute to Tokyo Bay.
17   Anchored inner harbor, Yokohama.
18   Anchored in Yokosuka, Japan.
26   Departed Yokosuka enroute to Manila, under command of Commander Philippine Sea Frontier.

December 1945
1   Arrived Manila Bay
6   Departed Manila Bay to Culion Leper Colony, Calamaines, PI.
7   Arrived Culion; anchored in Coron Bay.
8   Departed Culion Bay enroute to Manila Bay.
9   Moored in Manila Bay.
13   Departed Manila Bay enroute to Subic Bay to act as escort for submarines. Anchored in Subic Bay.
15   Departed Subic Bay escorting 7 submarines to Luzon, PI, in company with USS *Slater* (DE-766).
16   Arrived Linguyan Gulf; anchored in San Fernando Bay. Departed Linguyan Gulf, escorting subs to Luzon.
18   Arrived Casiguran Sound. Departed enroute to Legaspi.
19   Arrived Legaspi, Albay Gulf, Luzon.
20   Departed Legaspi enroute to Subic Bay, Luzon.
22   Arrived Subic Bay.

January 1946
2   Departed Subic Bay enroute to Manila
7   Arrived Subic Bay.
27   Returned to Manila; ordered to return to the U.S.
28   Departed Manila enroute to Samar to rendezvous with other ships of the division.
30   Arrived Samar.
31   Departed Samar enroute to Pearl Harbor in company with USS *Cates* (DE-763), USS *Ebert* (DE-768), USS *Slater* (DE-766), USS *Burrows* (DE-105) and USS *Gandy* (DE-764).

February 1946
13   Arrived Pearl Harbor
17   Departed Pearl Harbor, enroute to San Pedro, California.
23   Arrived San Pedro, CA.

March 1946
10   Departed San Pedro, CA, enroute to Norfolk, VA.
26   Arrived Norfolk, VA.

April 1946
11   Departed Norfolk, VA enroute to Green Cove Springs, Florida.
13   Arrived Green Cove Springs, FL for decommissioning.

June 1946
17   Placed out of commission in reserve at Green Cove Springs, FL.

December 1946
13   Towed to Tampa, FL, for use as a Naval Reserve Training ship.

November 1950
21   Recommissioned for Korean War Service.

January 1951
17   Arrived Charleston, South Carolina, for Naval Reserve Training (Caribbean, France, Spain, and Portugal).

July 1953
18   Arrived Philadelphia, PA, for Naval Reserve Training and Fleet ASW exercises.

November 1957
20   Deactivated.

February 1958
28   Placed out of commission in reserve at Philadelphia, PA.

August 1972
1   Stricken from U.S. Navy list of ships and scrapped.

USS *O'TOOLE* (DE-527)

Chronology of the USS *O'Toole* (DE-527) commissioned 22 January 1944 at the Boston Navy Yard in Boston, MA - decommissioned Charleston Navy Yard, SC. 18 October 1945. During her short lived career the *O'Toole* operated in the Atlantic on several convoy escort missions under TG27.5, TF. 64, TG60.11 and TG23.2.

September 1943, keel of *O'Toole* was laid down on the 25th of September.

November 1943, launched on the 2nd at Boston Navy Yard, Mass.

January 1944, commissioned on the 22nd as the USS *O'Toole* (DE-527) by Mrs. J.A. O'Toole, mother of John Albert O'Toole, killed in action in November 1942 during an assault on Fedhala, Morocco. Lt. Comdr. Enzensperger Jr. was placed in command. Proceeded to Bermuda for a shakedown cruise and returned to Boston on its completion. After minor repairs departed Boston and sailed South to serve as a training ship at the Fleet Sonar School in Key West, FL.

July 1944, departed Key West and sailed North to Casco Bay, ME, then on to Norfolk, VA to escort the USS *Tripoli*, CVE-64 to Recife, Brazil.

August 1944, on the return voyage, escorted the USS *Solomons* (CVE-67) back to Norfolk and arrived there on the 28th.

September 1944, on the 9th of September the *O'Toole* stood out of New York awaiting her first Trans-Atlantic convoy. Departed on the 19th, acting as a communication liaison ship between CTG 27.5 and Convoy NY-119, shepherded a small craft convoy to the Azores, thence to Falmouth, England.

October 1944, arrived in Falmouth, England on the 18th. Departed Falmouth and arrived at Plymouth England on the 22nd. November 1944, departed Plymouth, England on the 8th, sailed through the Irish Sea and arrived Reykjavik, Iceland to serve as an escort to the USS *Abanaki*, (ATF-96). Departed Iceland proceeded to Halifax, Novia Scotia and then to New York Harbor.

December 1944, departed New York on the 5th of December and arrived in Portland, ME on the 7th. Departed Portland, ME on the 15th and sailed South to Norfolk, VA arriving there on 17th. On the 19th proceeded to Oran, Algeria in North Africa as part of Task Force 64.

February 1945, after a short stay in Oran, departed and proceeded back to New York arriving there on the 2nd of February 1945. As the Flagship for Task Group 60.11 the *O'Toole* left New York on the 14th and arrived in Norfolk on the 16th. March 1945, departed Norfolk for Mer-El-Kebir, Algeria arriving there on the 5th. Departed North Africa on the 13th, arriving in Bayonne, NJ on the 30th.

April 1945, departed Bayonne, NJ and arrived in New London, CT on the 11th. On the 18th departed Norfolk, VA as part of Task Troup 60.11 and sailed to the Mediterranean Sea bound for Oran. Arrived there on May 4th.

May 1945, the *O'Toole* was enroute home when the war in Europe ended. Arrived New York on May 23rd. May 8, 1945 was VE-Day.

July 1945, the *O'Toole* operated off the New England coast until mid-July when she proceeded to Miami, FL for a brief tour as a school ship.

September 1945, September 2nd, 1945 VJ-Day. The *O'Toole* proceeded to the Charleston Navy Yard, SC for inactivation.

October 1945, USS *O'Toole* (DE-527) was decommissioned on the 18th of October. November 1945, the USS *O'Toole* was struck from the Navy's list of ships in November 1945.

March 1946, the *O'Toole* was scrapped in March 1946.

USS *RICH* (DE-695)

The first reunion of the USS *Rich* (DE-695) was held at Myrtle Beach, SC on June 6, 7, and 8th. Fifteen survivors attended, four officers and 11 enlisted men were present. It had been 47 years since the USS *Rich* sank in the Normandy invasion.

The story of the USS *Rich* began in Bay City, Michigan where the ship was launched, being built by the DeFoe Shipbuilding Company. A skeleton crew manned the *Rich* down the Mississippi River to New Orleans, Louisiana.

The future crew members were in Destroyer Escort Training School at Norfolk, VA. Upon completion of school, they were routed to Port Of Algiers at the 12th Naval District in New Orleans, LA. There they would go on board the new sleek destroyer escort for sea duty. The commissioning date was October 1, 1943. The ship was sponsored by Mrs. Margorie E. Rich, widow of the namesake, Lieutenant (Junior Grade) Ralph McMaster Rich, USNR, who was awarded the Navy

Cross for heroic action while piloting a plane of the famed Torpedo Squadron Six in the Battle of Midway. Lt. Rich was a native of Denmark, South Carolina.

A green crew took the ship on shake-down cruise to Bermuda, but their indoctrination was hastened by extremely rough weather enroute. Following a period of post shake-down repairs, the *Rich* escorted a transport to Argentina, Newfoundland, for its first assignment.

Further convoy duty took the *Rich* to Panama, but by the beginning of 1944 the destroyer escort seemed destined for regular North Atlantic convoy duty. All the trips were from New York to Northern Ireland (Londonberry) where the vessel laid over to wait for the convoys to unload and then return to the States with them. This routine continued through the winter and spring.

On May 10, 1944, the *Rich* left on what appeared to be the usual run to the United Kingdom. Upon arrival off Northern Ireland; the vessel was, in the past, sent to Londonberry to await trip back. But, the convoy sailed on the return trip without the *Rich*, she was diverted to take part in the invasion.

The *Rich* departed with orders to proceed to Plymouth, England experiencing rough seas through the Irish Seas; she reached port on the English Coast June 4, 1944. More armament was added and the vessel would be assigned as the protective ship for the Battleship USS *Nevada* (BB 36).

Steaming in the vanguard of a powerful echelon of American ships, the *Rich* got underway from Plymouth, England, on June 5, 1944, and by dawn of next day was leading the USS *Nevada* (BB 36) into the Normandy channel, which had been swept for mines. As the *Nevada* was guided into bombardment position, the *Rich* remained on destructive salvos into the beach. A few shells from enemy shore batteries were coming over, none very close.

On June 7, the USS *Meredith* (DD 726) a new 2200 ton destroyer on her maiden voyage struck a mine close by the *Rich* and was enveloped in a mass of flames. At this point the *Rich* had to make a decision whether to go along side the burning vessel or remain on station. The *Rich* elected to protect the heavy fire support ships by laying down a smoke screen. Another destroyer escort, the USS *Bates* maneuvered into position to render assistance to the *Meredith*. During the *Rich's* smoke screening operation; the vessel was approximately 4.8 kilometers off shore. Enemy planes were coming over; however not doing any considerable damage. The *Meredith* had been abandoned and later sank.

On the morning of June 8th, the commanding officer went down to the wardroom, leaving the bridge for the first time since leaving Plymouth. He stopped to shave. The lather on his face had scarcely set when orders were received by visual dispatch from GR 1258, Admiral Deyer directed the *Rich* to proceed to vicinity of Fire Support Station No. 5 to standby the USS *Glennon* (DD 840) which had struck a mine. The time was approximate 0845 on June 8th. As the *Rich* slowly came along side the USS *Glennon*, suddenly a heavy explosion shook the *Rich* and staggered personnel and severing some 30 feet of the *Rich's* fantail completely. The *Rich* had gotten into a mine field and three German underwater magnetic mines, each containing 1600 pounds of TNT, exploded in rapid succession literally blowing the DE to pieces.

From a nearby PT boat, United Press War Correspondent, Robert Miller wrote the following eye witness account of the *Rich*. Invasion Ship Groans Farewell To Dying Crew: Announcement of the Allied Naval losses in the invasion of France permitted Robert Miller to release and reveal the following dispatch of how one of them went down.

USS *PETERSON* (DE-152)

The USS *Peterson* (DE-152) was laid down by Consolidated Steel Corp., Orange, TX on 28 February 1943, and launched 15 May 1943 with Lt. Comdr. Richard F. Rea, USCG, commanding. On 2 December 1943, *Peterson* commenced her maiden voyage from New York to Casablanca, French Morocco returning to New York on 18 January 1944. She was then assigned to duty in Northern Europe making ten voyages to British and French ports. With other escorts of Division 22, *Peterson* steamed from New York on 1 March 1944 to screen a oiler convoy to Londonderry, Ireland. The USS *Leopold* (DE-319) was sunk by a submarine on this convoy. On 28 March 1944, she joined the USS *Gandy* (DE-764) and the USS *Joyce* (DE-317) in rescuing survivors of the torpedoed *Pan Pennsylvania*. The escorts engaged and subsequently sunk the attacking U-boat. At 1345 hours *Joyce* picked up the enemy on her sonar and began a depth charge attack as the remaining survivors were boarding the *Peterson*. The U-boat surfaced while *Gandy* opened fire. The submarine returned fire until rammed with a glancing blow by *Gandy*. *Peterson* commenced firing to lay open the conning tower and fired two depth charges at close range from her starboard "K" guns as she passed alongside the enemy sub. At 1409 hours the U-boat surrendered with the crew abandoning the ship. *Joyce* picked up the crew of *U-550* while their vessel sank at 1430 hours.

Peterson made three more convoy voyage to Londonderry with successive

voyages from New York to Plymouth, England (6 October-5 November 1944). She was then assigned to the Pacific on 4 June 1945 with Escort Division 22. She arrived at Pearl Harbor 16 July 1945 and reported to Commander Amphibious Group 8 and Commander Transport Squadron 18 for duty. On 31 August 1945, she joined a LST convoy sailing to Wakayama, Japan where she assumed patrol in the Inland Sea until 29 October 1945 when she returned to Jacksonville, FL on 14 January 1946 where she was deactivated. *Peterson* received one battle star for WWII service.

Peterson was recommissioned on 2 May 1952 with five years of service with Escort Squadron 10. In August of 1957, she played a vital role in the first successful recovery of a missile nose cone fired from Cape Canaveral on a Jupiter missile.

USS *PRESLEY* (DE-371)

Sam Davis Presley, born at Carthage, Mississippi, 17 December 1918, enlisted in the Navy 7 November 1939. On 30 September 1942 he became Aviation Machinist's Mate first class. He received the Navy Cross for extraordinary heroism during the Battle of the Santa Cruz Islands, 26 October 1942. As his first ship *Enterprise,* came under sustained enemy air attack, Aviation Machinist's Mate First Class Presley voluntarily abandoned the shelter of his normal battle station. Climbing into a plane parked on the flight deck, he manned the flexible guns in the rear cockpit and commenced an effective fire against the attacking aircraft. As the battle continued, a bomb explosion blew the plane overboard. AM 1 Presley was listed as "missing in action," and presumed dead 27 October 1943.

(DE-371): dp. 1,745 (f.); l. 306'0"; b. 36'7"; dr. 13'4"; s. 24 k.; cpl. 222; a. 2 5", 6 40mm., 2 dct., 8 dcp., 1 dcp. (hh.), 3 21" tt.; cl. John C. Butler

Presley (DE-371) was laid down by the Consolidated Steel Corporation, Ltd., Orange, Texas, 6 June 1944; launched 19 August 1944; sponsored by Mrs. Willie Lynn Presley; and commissioned 7 November 1944, Lt. Cmdr. Richard S. Paret, USNR, in command.

After shakedown off Bermuda, *Presley* transited the Panama Canal 24 January 1945 and proceeded to Pearl Harbor for further training. She arrived at Noumea 22 March, and departed 3 May to escort a group of transports to Leyte Gulf. She subsequently touched at Manus, Saipan, and Ulithi before making two trips to Okinawa. The end of the war found her anchored in Ulithi Harbor.

On 19 September *Presley* proceeded to Guam for duty, making two trips to Truk where she served as harbor patrol and station ship pending the occupation of that enemy post by the U.S. forces. On 5 November the ship was ordered to the United States to be placed in inactive status.

Presley decommissioned 20 June 1946 and joined the Pacific Reserve Fleet berthed at San Diego. She was struck from the Naval Register 30 June 1968.

USS *WILLIAM T. POWELL* (DE-123)

William T. Powell (DE-213) was laid down on 26 August 1943 at Charleston, SC by the Charleston Navy Yard; launched on 27 November 1943; commissioned on 28 March 1944, Lt. James L. Davenport, USNR, in command.

William T. Powell got underway from Charleston on 18 April, bound for Bermuda. At 1541 on 20 April, the ships' search radar disclosed a contact. Seven minutes later, *William T. Powell* went to headquarters as lookouts noted a submarine running on the surface. The destroyer escort charged ahead of flank speed and challenged the submarine, only to be informed that the stranger was *Pomfret* (SS-391). All hands very disappointed when sub turned out to be friendly, noted Comdr. Adams. Underway for the Canal Zone on 9 June, *William T. Powell* test-fired her new 40-millimeter battery en route and reached Cristobal, Canal Zone, at 1147 on 11 June. She sortied from Hampton Roads on 10 July in the screen of Convoy UGS-48. At 0029 on 1 August 1914, *William T. Powell* received a TBS message from the task force commander, Capt. C.M. Hoffman, in Moffett (DD-362), to man battle stations in anticipation of an enemy air attack. Radar picked up the enemy attackers at 90 miles away; HMS *Delhi*—a British antiaircraft cruiser—commenced the action at 0058, firing by radar control. At 0105, lookouts in *William T. Powell* spotted flares close aboard on the port side of the convoy; but the gunners were cautioned not to fire. With enemy planes within range, the convoy opened up; mounted 21 in *William T. Powell* glimpsed an enemy bomber, and fired a four-round burst; The firing lasted only a minute. *William T. Powell* ceased fire at 0016.

The defense of UGS-48 was a successful one; the enemy did not claim any of the ships. After seeing all ships of UGS-48 safely to their Mediterranean destination, *William T. Powell* served with TF-62. *William T. Powell* resumed operations from Argentina on 4 January 1945 and continued them through the end of the month. During the closing weeks of the European war, *William T. Powell* patrolled shallow water approaches, for 12 convoys in submarine-infested waters. Released from the 12th Fleet and the Western Approaches

Command on 24 May 1945, the destroyer escort soon sailed for home, entering the Brown Shipbuilding Co. Inc. yard in Houston, TX, on 15 June for conversion to a radar picket ship. However, while she was in the yard for alterations, Japan capitulated in Mid-August. The destroyer escort subsequently returned to the Norfolk and Casco Bay operating areas in early June and July before visiting Bar Harbor, Maine, for 4th of July celebrations.

For the next 11 years, *William T. Powell* operated off the eastern seaboard of the United States ranging from Casco Bay to Cape Henry to Key West and into the West Indies and Guantanamo Bay. During that period, the ship underwent several changes of the status and two reclassifications. On 5 November 1948, she was assigned to the 4th Naval District and homeport at the Philadelphia Naval Shipyard to serve as a Naval Reserve Training (NRT) ship. On 18 March 1949, the warship was reclassified DE-213 on 1 December 1954 and continued training duty until September 1957. *William T. Powell* was placed out of commission, in reserve, at Philadelphia on 17 January 1958. Struck from the Navy list on 1 November 1965, *William T. Powell* was sold on 3 October 1966 to the North American Smelting Co. Wilmington, Del, and was scrapped. Although she participated in the defense of Convoy UGS-48 on 1 August 1944, and was in proximity to enemy forces.

William T. Powell inexplicably received no Battle Stars for that action.

USS RICHEY (DE-385)

Submitted by Arthur P. McNamara

The USS *Richey* (DE-385), a Coast Guard manned Destroyer Escort was commissioned into the United States Navy on October 30, 1943. This ship was named in honor of Ensign Joseph Lee Richey, USNR, born on June 8, 1920 at Barnard, Missouri and who died on December 7, 1941 as the result of a Japanese attack in the Hawaiian area while on active duty, attached to the Observation Squadron Two of the battleship, USS *California*.

The *Richey* was built by the Brown Shipbuilding Company of Houston, Texas. Sailing from Texas, early in November of 1943, the *Richey* headed for Bermuda where it underwent a shakedown cruise for a month. Having passed all necessary requirements and qualifications, the *Richey* was then assigned to the Atlantic Fleet where she escorted convoys to Africa, Ireland, England and France. Altogether, the *Richey* made sixteen safe crossings of the submarine infested waters of both the Mediterranean Sea and the Atlantic Ocean.

Early in April of 1945, while on escort duty in the Atlantic, this ship participated in the rescuing of survivors from the SS *Nashbulk* and the SS *St. Mihiel*. These two ships, both tankers carrying high octane gasoline collided in mid-ocean causing a tremendous fire in which scores perished. Thirty two men, more than half of the number of survivors, were picked up by this vessel alone, from the fire swept seas. John F. Collins, Motor Machinists Mate, first class, who was assigned to a repair party, upon seeing three men in the water about 100 yards from the ship, jumped in the oil covered water and swam to their assistance. He kept them together and in a composed state until the ship was maneuvered close enough for rescue operations. The men were very tried and full of oil, and were swimming in different directions when first sighted. They probably would have been missed had not Collins kept them together, and for this heroic action. Collins was awarded the Navy and Marine Corps Medal by the Commander in Chief of the U.S. Atlantic Fleet.

The *Richey* had just returned to New York from France when the final surrender of Germany was announced. This ship underwent an extensive overhaul and immediately was ordered to the Pacific Theatre of War. Before reaching the Aleutian Islands, stopovers were made at such places as Cuba and the Canal Zone.

The first week in July, the *Richey* reported to the Northern Pacific Fleet at Adak, AK. Since that time, this ship has operated from the Aleutian area as part of the Ninth Fleet, which constantly harassed the Kurile Islands by bombardment of its shores.

When capitulation of Japan came, the *Richey* was then assigned to the Fourth Fleet, under Admiral Frank Jack Fletcher, which on September 8, 1945, occupied the Japanese Naval Base at Ominato, Northern Honshu, Japan.

The *Richey* has covered many miles, visiting many ports in many countries. On Oct. 27. 1945, fifty two of the original crew are still aboard.

Lieutenant R.J. Auge, Commanding Officer
Lieutenant C.R. Sparrow, Executive Officer
Lieutenant (jg) J.T. McHugh, Gunnery Officer
Lieutenant (jg) W.M. Boykin, Jr., Pay and Supply Officer
Lieutenant (jg) V.A. Eilman, Communications Officer
Lieutenant (jg) L.M. Dalton, Engineer Officer
Lieutenant (jg) L.C. Ernst, Assistant Engineering Officer
Ensign A.C. Pearce, First Lieutenant

Enlisted Men Attached to the USS Richey (DE-385)

Acampara, George, S1c	Forte, John A., S1c	Lyons, Henry N., S1c	Sanitate, James, S1c
Adesso, Patsy, Cox.	Fraley, Eugene E., So(M)3c	Mahle, Jack C., S1c	Saroniero, Michael L. MM2c (EM)
Alexander, Vernard T., S1c	Fricker, Daniel A, EM3c	Mallory, Edgar H., S1c	Scheuermann, Andrew E., Jr., RM3
Baltus, Robert C., MoMM2	Gautier, Francis A., S1c	Marak, Victor R., MoMM3c	Simpson, Robert, SoM3c
Bandy, Kenneth M., EM3c	Gay, Carl C., S1c	Marks, Donald L., MM2c	Slavinsky, Albert T., S1c
Beechick, Paul, S1c	Gillette, William A., BM1c	Martin, Jack C., CY1	Small, Harold L., StM2c
Bennett, Charles, S2c	Green, James E., BM2c	McDonagh, Martin F., S1c	Smith, Arthur E., MoMM2c
Bentkowski, Fred, S1c	Hagstrom, Hugo J., GM3c	McNamara, Arthur D., RdM2c	Smith, George A., S2c
Bernath, Frank W., RdM3c	Hansen, Gerald H., CM2c	Menachem, Jack, SoM3c	Steele, Monty R., S1c
Biggs, Robert D., S2c	Harnan, Edward P., S1c	Miller, Virgil A., F1c (MoMM)	Stevens, George J., GM3c
Bodine, Joseph J., S1c	Harris, James O., S1c	Moore, Charles T., PM2c	Stutzman, Richard L., S1c
Bowman, Russel A., RdM2	Haven, James A., RM1c	Neal, Raymond H., S1c	Swenson, Lowell C., S1c
Brown, Robert, S1c	Hays, Otto A., St1c	Nelson, Joseph "B", Jr., MoMM3c	Taddeo, Chester C., S1c
Bubser, Robert A., S1c	Hebert, Eugene D., RM2c	Neumen, Walter J., MoMM2c	Tanguay, Robert V., S1c
Calimano, Joseph A., Jr., MoMM2	Heimlich, Frederick J., Y3c	Newman, Norman "H", S1c	Thompson, John E., S1c
Caro, Nunzio, SC1c	Hines, Ellis R., S1c	Nichols, Samuel E., CSK	Tobin, Thomas J., FCO2c
Chapman, Raymond J., MoMM3c	Holmes, Lowell D., QM3c	Okun, Irving, FC3c	Trutt, Earl K., Jr., MoMM2c
Chuba, Joseph A., GM2c	Hostler, Alfred W., Jr., RM1c	Olson, Donald A., S1c	Turner, Troy C., GM2c
Cicci, Domenic J., GM3c	Indovina, Anthony J., SC3c	Orlansky, Morton, S1c (SM)	Tyler, Roger C., Jr., SoM2c
Coleman, Wiliam T., EM3c	Israel, Richard D., S1c	Ostrander, Clark W., F2c	Udovich, Anton J., MoMM2c
Collins, John F., MoMM1c	Jackson, Patrick W., CPhM	Packey, Charles J., Jr. S2c	Valentine, Lloyd M., Cox.
Cordy, Robert L., S1c	Jamison, Ralph F., S1c	Parsons, Robert C., CM3c	Vavreck, Joseph B., MoMM2c
Couch, Robert J., SoM2c	Jaworski, Clarence C., E1c	Petersen, Laurence C., Cox.	Veronica, Robert G., S1c
Daish, Alvin, S2c	Jennings, Sidney W., Cox.	Pfeiffer, Edward F., RdM3c	Vreeland, Milton R., Y2c
Dalton, Edward J., CGM	Jose, Douglas S., CRM	Piantedosi, Alfred, S1c	Wagoner, Robert B., S1c (Rdm)
Dato, Anthony, F1c (EM)	Kenny, Leo F., S1c	Pieta, Andrew J., MoMM3c	Wallace, Joseph L., Jr., S2c
Day, Alfred Z., S2c	Kling, Frank E., SoM3c	Pinkowski, Eugene T., S2c	Warren, Marshall Jr., S1c
Delaney, Joseph M., F1c	Knobel, Edward D., S1c(SM)	Pisula, Tony J., S1c	Watt, George G., E1c (MoMM)
Dimond, Oscar M., Jr., SSML2c	Konrad, Henry R., F1c(MoMM)	Potter, Curtis L., S2c	Weller, Gerald S., RM3c
Diventi, Benedict C., MoMM3c	Kowalewski, Alexander S., GM3c	Presley, Frederick A., Jr., RM3c	Weyl, Paul J., EM2c
Dofer, Helmuth, MoMM1c	Kratzer, Gerald L., S1c	Rainer, John C., Jr., S1c	Wogberg, Volmer L., MoMM3c (RT)
Druker, Emanuel, MoMM1c	Lasker, Carl A., SSML3c	Ratizff, Eldred "D," CGM	Young, Jack L., S1c
Dwyer, Patrick J., MoMM3c	LeBianc, Walter P., S1c	Rich, James A., F1c	Zambernardi, Lawrence D., F1c
Egan, William J., Cox.	Lewis, Richard B., MoMM2c	Ritch, James, S1c	
Evans, William R., S1c	Light, Mark H., SC2c	Roaf, George M., S2c	

USS *SEDERSTROM* (DE-31)
From the Captain's War Diary

March 21, 1945-at 0553 underway as part of T.U. 52.1.1 Support Carrier Unit #1 en route Ulithi to Okinawa. Captain V.D. Long, USN ComDesRon 6, in USS *Bagley* (DD-386) as screen commander, designated as CTU 52.1.12. Task Unit 52.1.12 consists of the following destroyers and destroyer escorts: USS *Bagley* (DD-386), USS *Patterson* (DD-392), USS *Ingraham* (DD-694), USS *Hart* (DD-594), USS *Richard M. Rowell* (DE-403), USS *Dennis* (DE-405), USS *O'Flaherty* (DE-340), USS *Richard S. Bull* (DE-402), USS *Fleming* (DE-32) and USS *Sederstrom* (DE-31) with Commander C.A. Kunz, USNR, ComCortDiv-31 on board. CTU 52.1.1, Rear Admiral CAF Sprague, USN, in USS *Fanshaw Bay* (CVE-70 (Guide and Convoy Commodore). Rear Admiral Durgin, USN, in USS *Makin Island* (CVE-93) is CTG 52.1. Escort carriers designated as Task Unit 52.1.1 are: USS *Fanshaw Bay* (CVE-70), USS *Makin Island* (CVE-93), USS *Lunga Point* (CVE-94), USS *Natoma Bay* (CVE-62) and USS *Sangamon* (CVE-26).

March 24, 1945-at 1300 arrived in operating area off the southern tip of Okinawa Island.

March 25, 1945-1210, while maneuvering alongside USS *Sangamon* (CVE-26) to fuel, this vessel was swept against a 40mm gun shield, below and outboard of the flight deck, port side aft, causing the following damage to the signal bridge area on starboard side of this vessel: Section of bulwark between frames 47-61; one watertight door; one 24" searchlight, frame #51; one group of fighting lights, frame #59; one three foot section grab rail, frame 51-55, damaged beyond salvage.

(Because the flow of water between the two hulls flows faster than the water flowing on the seaward sides, the water pressure between the hulls is reduced thereby having the effect of drawing the ships in toward each other. The USN perfected this manner of refueling whereas the Royal Navy and others transferred fuel by trailing the supply ship. In hindsight it appears it was not a prudent decision to direct us to come alongside the *Sangamon* with a following sea and wind when rudder control is substantially reduced.)

March 26, 1945-0605 detached from T.U. 52.1.1 by TBS Order of CTU 52.1.1, directing this ship to join T.U. 52.1.2 for duty. 0632 this vessel joined T.U. 52.1.2. Task Unit 52.1.2 designated as Support Carrier Unit Two, consists of following ships: USS *Marcus Island* (CVE-77), USS *Saginaw Bay* (CVE-82), USS *Sargent Bay* (CVE-83), USS *Rudyard Bay* (CVE-81), USS *Petrof Bay* (CVE-80), USS *Tulagi* (CVE-72), USS *Wake Island* (CVE-65), USS *Capps* (DD-550), USS *Evans* (DD-552), USS *John D. Henley* (DD-533), USS *Boyd* (DD-554), USS *Bradford* (DD-554), USS *William Sieverling* (DD-441), USS *Ulvert M. Moore* (DE-442), USS *Kendall C. Campbell* (DE-443), USS *Goss* (DE-444), USS *Tisdale* (DE-33), USS *Eisele* (DE-34, USS *Fleming* (DE-32) and this vessel with Commander C.A. Kunz, USNR, ComCortDiv-31 aboard. Rear Admiral F.B. Stump, USN, as OTC and CTU 52.1.2 in USS *Marcus Island*. Screen Commander is Captain G.P. Hunter, USN, in USS *Capps*.

(NOTE: Skipper of the *Ulvert M. Moore* was Franklin D. Roosevelt, Jr.)

March 30, 1945-0715 maneuvering to standby to refuel from USS *Escalante* (AO-70). 0845 alongside USS *Escalante* (AO-70), port side to, for fueling. 0948 secured from fueling having received 46,180 gals. diesel oil. 1014 cast off lines, maneuvering to take station #11 of a 13 ship screen.

March 31, 1945-1606 USS *Fleming*, USS *Tisdale*, USS *Eisele* and this vessel detached from T.U. 52.1.2 and ordered to report to CTU 52.1.1. 1610 reported to CTU 52.1.1, ordered to take screening station #4 of 11 ship circular screen. T.U. 52.1.1 composed of the following ships: USS *Fanshaw Bay* (CVE-70), USS *Savo Island* (CVE-72), USS *Lunga Point* (CVE-90), USS *Sangamon* (CVE-26), USS *Anzio* (CVE-57), USS *Natoma Bay* (CVE-62), USS *Patterson* (DD-392), USS *Ingraham* (DD-694), USS *Eisele* (DE-34), USS *Bagley* (DD-386), USS *Fleming* (DE-32), USS *Richard S. Bull* (DE-402), USS *Hart* (DD-594), USS *Robert F. Keller* (DE-419), USS *Melvin R. Nawman* (DE-416), USS *Tisdale* (DE-33), USS *Oliver Mitchell* (DE-417), USS *Lowry* (DD-770) USS *Tabberer* (DE-418), and this vessel. Rear Admiral CAF Sprague, USN, in USS *Fanshaw Bay* (OTC and CTU 52.1.1). Screen Commander is Captain V.D. Long, USN, in USS *Bagley*, This T.U. designated as Support Carrier Unit #1.

April 1, 1945-at 0515 USS *Natoma Bay* (CVE-62), USS *Robert F. Keller* (DE-419) and USS *Tabberer* (DE-418) left Task Unit to carry out duty assigned.

At 0705 USS *Sangamon* (CVE-26), USS *Fleming* (DE-32), USS *Tisdale* (DE-33), USS *Eisele* (DE-34) and this vessel detached from T.U. 52.1.1 to report to TU 52.1.3.

At 0830 joined T.U. 52.1.3, designated as Support Carrier Unit #3, consisting of the following ships: USS *Suwanee* (CVE-27), USS *Chenango* (CVE-28), USS *Sangamon* (CVE-26), USS *Santee* (CVE-29), USS *Fullam* (DD-474), USS *Guest* (DD-482), USS *Metcalf* (DD-595), USS *Drexler* (DD-741), USS *Massey* (DD-778), USS *Fleming* (DE-32), USS *Tisdale* (DE-33), USS *Eisele* (DE-34), USS *John C. Butler* (DE-339), USS *Edmonds* (DE-406) and this vessel. OTC and CTU 52.1.3 is Rear Admiral W.D. Sample, USN, in USS *Suwannee*. Screen Commander is Captain J.C. Daniel, USN, in USS *Fullam*. Commander C.A. Kunz, USNR, ComCortDiv-31 aboard this vessel.

April 2, 1945-at 1237 aircraft of USS *Chenango* crashed into water 400 yards on port bow of this vessel. Proceeding to pick up pilot. 1242, pilot aboard, Ensign R.T. Wright, USNR, suffering from exhaustion, put in charge of pharmacist mate.

At 1847 joined T.U. 52.1.1, designated as Support Carrier Unit #1, consisting of the following ships: USS *Fanshaw Bay* (CVE-70), USS *Savo Island* (CVE-78), USS *Steamer Bay* (CVE-87), USS *Makin Island* (CVE-93), USS *Natoma Bay* (CVE-62), USS *Bagley* (DD-386), USS *Lowry* (DD-770), USS *Ingraham* (DD-694), USS *Hart* (DD-594), USS *Richard S. Bull* (DE-402), USS *Richard M. Rowell* (DE-403), USS *Fleming* (DE-32), USS *Eisele* (DE-34) and this vessel with Commander C.A. Kunz, USNR, ComCortDiv-31 on board.

At 2302 the USS *Savo Island* (CVE-78), USS *Richard M. Rowell* (DE-403) and the USS *Hart* (DD-594) were detached to proceed on duty assigned.

April 3, 1945-at 0645 USS *Lunga Point* (CVE-94), USS *Patterson* (DD-392), USS *Oliver Mitchel* (DE-417) and USS *Melvin R. Nawman* (DE-416) joined T.U. #52.1.1.

At 1514 USS *Fleming* (DE-32) detached from T.U. 52.1.1 to report to T.U. 52.1.3.

At 1538 USS *Anzio* (CVE-57) and USS *Tabberer* (DE-418) joined T.U. 52.1.1.

At 1816 this vessel detached from T.U. 52.1.1 and ordered to report to T.U. 52.1.3 for duty.

At 1844 joined T.U. 52.1.3, designated as Support Carrier Unit #3, consisting of the following ships: USS *Suwannee* (CVE-29), USS *Chenango* (CVE-28), USS *Sangamon* (CVE-26), USS *Santee* (CVE-29), USS *Fullam* (DD-474), USS *Edmonds* (DE-406), USS *Massey* (DD-778), USS *John C. Butler* (DE-339), USS *Metcalf* (DD-595), USS *Eisele* (DE-34), USS *Guest* (DD-472), USS *Fleming* (DE-32), USS *Tisdale* (DE-33), USS *Drexler* (DD-741) and this vessel with Commander C.A. Kunz, USNR, on board.

April 4, 1945-at 1620 alongside, port side to, USS *Sangamon* (CVE-26) for fueling.

At 1652 cast off all lines and cleared USS *Sangamon* to permit flight operations. Received 2,900 gallons of diesel oil.

April 5, 1945-at 0700 carriers commenced fueling escorts. At 1305 TBF plane crashed in water. At 1309 USS *Drexler* (DD-741) recovered plane crew.

At 1540 fueling operations completed.

April 6, 1945-at 1503 USS *Tisdale* (DE-33) alongside for transfer of officer. At 1510 transfer completed.

At 1512 this vessel with Commander C.A. Kunz, USNR, ComCortDiv-31 on board, and the USS *Eisele* (DE-34) were detached from T.U. 52.1.3 and proceeded to join T.U. 52.1.1.

At 1521 reported for duty to T.U. 52.1.1. Ordered to take screening station #3. T.U. 52.1.1 consists of USS *Fanshaw Bay* (CVE-70), USS *Lunga Point* (CVE-94), USS *Makin Island* (CVE-93), USS *Steamer Bay* (CVE-67), USS *Anzio* (CVE-57), USS *Natoma Bay* (CVE-62), USS *Bagley* (CVE-386), USS *Robert F. Keller* (DE-419), USS *Patterson* (DD-392), USS *Lawrence C. Taylor* (DE-415), USS *Helm* (DD-388), USS *Lowry* (DD-770), USS *Tabberer* (DE-418) USS *Ingraham* (DD-694), USS *Eisele* (DE-34) and this vessel.

April 7, 1945-at 0647 joined fueling group consisting of USS *Guadalupe* (AO-32), USS *Monongahela* (AO-42) and USS *Cimmarron* (AO-22).

At 0846 sighted mine bearing 048 degrees true, distance 1500 yards.

At 0850 commenced firing 20mm guns at mine.

At 0851 exploded mine by 20mm fire after 23 seconds firing, expending 30 rounds of 20mm AA ammunition.

At 0958 alongside, port side to, USS *Guadalupe* (AO-32) for fueling.

At 1056 completed fueling, having received 36,624 gallons diesel oil.

At 1343 USS *Shamrock Bay* (CVE-84), USS *Richard M. Rowell* (DE-403), and the USS *Richard S. Bull* (DE-402) reported to this Task Unit for duty.

At 1546 fueling exercises for Task Unit completed; fueling group departed.

April 8 1945-at 0914 USS *Ingraham* (DD-694) and USS *Lowry* (DD-770) joined T.U. 52.1.1.

At 0925 USS *Kendall C. Campbell* (DE-443) joined T.U.

At 1421 this vessel and the USS *Eisele* (DE-34) detached to proceed and rendezvous with T.U. 52.1.3.

At 1740 reported for duty to CTU 52.1.3. T.U. consists of the following ships: USS *Suwanee* (CVE-27), USS *Sangamon* (CVE-26), USS *Santee* (CVE-29), USS *Chenango* (CVE-28), USS *Fullam* (DD-474), USS *Drexler* (DD-741), USS *Edmonds* (DE-406), USS *Massey* (DD-778), USS *John C. Butler* (DE-339), USS *Metcalf* (DD-595), USS *Guest* (DD-472), USS *Eisele* (DE-34), and this vessel.

April 9, 1945-at 1217 fire broke out on flight deck of USS *Chenango* (CVE-28) after plane crashed into planes on forward part of flight deck.

At 1219 course changed to 090 degrees T., this ship steaming 400 yards on port quarter of USS *Chenango* standing by to assist in any way.

At 1504 USS *Chenango* returning to Task Unit, this vessel and the USS *Guest* (DD-472) screening her.

At 1650 USS *Fleming* (DE-32) and USS *Tisdale* (DE-33) joined this T.U.

April 10, 1945-at 1900 detached by CTU 52.1.3 with USS *Suwannee* (CVE-27), USS *Massey* (DD-778), and USS *Eisele* (DE-34) to proceed to Keramo Retto. Screen Commander is Commander C.A. Kunz, USNR, ComCortDiv-31 in this vessel.

April 11, 1945-at 0805 arrived off channel entrance, Keramo Retto. At 1619 underway to rejoin T.U. 52.1.3, maneuvering to clear harbor.

At 1735 USS *Suwannee* clear of channel, anti-submarine screen formed, consisting of this vessel with Commander C.A. Kunz, USNR, ComCortDiv-31 as screen commander aboard, the USS *Eisele* (DE-34) and USS *Massey* (DD-778).

At 2310 joined Task Unit 52.1.3 and this vessel assigned station #3.

April 12, 1945-at 0922 enemy aircraft shot down by carrier aircraft; sighted parachute falling at 065 degrees T., distance five miles. Ordered to investigate by OTC. 0937 sighted parachute in water. 0952 retrieved empty Japanese parachute.

At 1626 alongside USS *Housatonic* (AO-35) for fueling while underway.

At 1650 cast off all lines and cleared USS *Housatonic* to permit change of course.

At 1812 alongside USS *Housatonic* to resume fueling.

At 1836 completed fueling, having received 12,773 gallons diesel oil.

At 2045 USS *Eisele* (DE-34) detached and directed to relieve USS *Tisdale* (DE-33) as escort for USS *Santee* (CVE-29) en route Keramo Retto.

At 2130 USS *Tisdale* rejoined T.U. 52.1.3

April 13, 1945-at 2020 USS *Chenango* (CVE-28), USS *Guest* (DD-472), USS *Tisdale* (DE-33) and this vessel with ComCortDiv-31 aboard were detached from T.U. 52.1.3. Proceeding to Keramo Retto; ComCortDiv-31 is screen commander.

April 14, 1945-at 0620 USS *Natoma Bay* (CVE-62) and the USS *Richard M. Rowell* (DE-403) joined this formation.

At 0824 entering Ko Harbor, Keramo Retto.

At 1910 USS *Chenango* and USS *Natoma Bay* clear of channel, anti-submarine screen formed, consisting of this vessel with Commander C.A. Kunz, USNR, ComCortDiv-31 as screen commander aboard the USS *Tisdale*, USS *Guest* and the USS *Richard M. Rowell*.

April 15, 1945-at 0510 USS *Natoma Bay* and USS *Richard M. Rowell* left this unit to rejoin T.U. 52.1.1.

At 0732 rejoined T.U. 52.1.3 and this vessel assigned station #7.

At 1025 assumed station as plane guard; sonar gear out of commission.

At 1100 half-masted colors during memorial services for F.D. Roosevelt, late commander-in-chief, U.S. Navy.

(*NOTE:* The radio room had received a message directed to the captain of the USS *Ulvert M. Moore* (DE-442), Franklin D. Roosevelt, Jr. We were unable to decode this message. Upon learning of the death of the President, we assumed the message was to inform the President's son of his father's demise.)

April 16, 1945-at 0635 USS *Sangamon* (CVE-26) and following escorts, USS *Fleming* (DE-32), USS *Eisele* (DE-34) and USS *Drexler* (DD-741) rejoined this Task Unit.

At 1706 USS *Fleming* detached from T.U. 52.1.3, proceeding to join T.U. 52.1.1.

At 2100 USS *Eisele*, USS *Tisdale* and this vessel detached from T.U. 52.1.3, proceeding to Okinawa Island, Nansei Shoto to report to CTG 51.5 for duty.

April 17, 1945-steaming underway in accordance with CTU 52.1.3 visual message of April 16, 1945, proceeding to Okinawa Island with USS *Eisele* (DE-34) and USS *Tisdale* (DE-33), to report to CTG 51.5 for duty. This vessel with Commander C.A. Kunz, USNR, ComCortDiv-31, OTC, aboard designated as guide.

At 0803 entered Hagushi Anchorage, Okinawa, proceeding independently to anchor in berth H-162.

At 1634 underway in accordance with CTG 51.5 visual message, directing this vessel to proceed to Kerama Retto and report to CTG 51.15.

At 1819 entering Kaikyo Passage, Kerama Retto, proceeding to anchor in berth K-46.

At 2103 went to General Quarters. 2110 enemy planes overhead, was fired on by other ships in harbor. 2240 secured from General Quarters.

April 18, 1945-anchored in berth K-46, Kerama Retto.

At 0818 alongside USS *Bowers* (DE-637) in berth K-47, Kerama Retto, to obtain spare parts for sonar gear.

(*NOTE:* The *Bowers* was a mess having been hit by a suicide that crashed directly into the pilot house. There was substantial loss of life amongst those whose GQ stations were in the super-structure and along the port side. There were many personnel wounded as well.)

At 1426 anchored in berth K-41.

April 19, 1945-anchored in berth K-41, Kaikyo Anchorage, Kerama Retto, affecting repairs to sonar gear.

At 1410 anchored in berth K-24, Kerama Retto.

(*NOTE:* It was the evening of the 19th that we received work via signal light to be on the alert for Japs swimming to and boarding the ship. We learned that Japs had boarded a cruiser and were caught down in the crew's quarters knifing the sailors. Small arms were issued top-side personnel on watch. Becoming bored with no action, debris that would float was tossed off the bow and fired on as it drifted by the ship. I heard that the Signal gang obtained a 30 caliber machine gun and started firing it from the starboard signal bridge directly over the captain's cabin. "Big Joe" decided that was enough.)

April 20, 1945-anchored in berth K-24 affecting repairs to sonar gear.

At 1404 underway in accordance with CTG 51.5 visual message en route Kerama Retto to Okinawa. Sonar gear repaired.

At 1538 off Hagushi Beach Anchorage, Okinawa. Reported to CTG 51.5 for duty.

At 1613 received orders from CTG 51.5 to take patrol station Baker 27, 14 miles from Point Bolo, Okinawa.

At 1710 on station B-27.

At 1843 Air Flash Red at Kerama Retto. Went to General Quarters, enemy planes in vicinity.

April 21, 1945-steaming underway in accordance with CTG 51.5 verbal order of April 20, 1945, patrolling station Baker 27 off Okinawa.

At 0955 ordered to relieve USS *Revenge* (AM-110) on patrol station Baker-15 off Okinawa Island.

At 1015 on patrol station Baker-15.

At 2050 went to General Quarters, enemy aircraft in vicinity.

At 2155 secured from General Quarters.

April 22, 1945-steaming underway in accordance with CTG 5115 verbal order of April 21, 1945, patrolling station Baker-15, off Okinawa Island.

At 1805 sounded General Quarters, enemy aircraft in vicinity.

At 1830 enemy aircraft reported bearing 310 T., distance 35 miles.

At 1900 unidentified aircraft bearing 310 T., distance 17 miles, closing.

At 1924 four enemy aircraft sighted, bearing 245 T., elevation 25 closing on our port bow. 1926 all guns commenced firing. Enemy aircraft split into two groups on port bow. One plane crossed bow port to starboard, turned down starboard side, circled stern to port, headed for bridge of this vessel, crossed this vessel vicinity of mast to starboard bow showering gasoline on bridge of this vessel and forecastle. The plane banked sharply and crashed into water 10 feet off starboard bow, showering additional gasoline and bits of metal on bridge and forecastle. The two-engine plane, identified as Frances, received numerous hits from gunfire of this vessel and had both engines aflame when it hit the water.

At 1929 ceased firing, man reported overboard from 20mm gun #5. During attack this vessel maneuvered vigorously using full rudder and flank speed to bring as many guns as possible to bear on targets. Total ammunition expended: 44 rounds 3"/50 caliber; 485 rounds 1.1"/74 AA; 1430 rounds 20mm.

The escorts in the stations Baker-14 and Baker-16 reported shooting down two and one planes respectively from the group of eight planes attacking this vessel.

At 1948 man sighted in water off starboard bow. 1950 man recovered aboard, identified as O. McDermitt, 832 47 40, S1c, USNR. This man reported passing through gasoline and debris from crashed plane while he was afloat in water.

At 2010 resumed patrol Baker-15.

At 2035 secured from General Quarters, all enemy planes clear of area.

(*NOTE:* It appears that of the four planes that headed toward the *Sederstrom*, our gunners hit #1 which veered away to the north aflame and disappeared from the radar screen, possibly splashed. Meanwhile planes #3 and #4 came down the port side. Both were fired upon and #3, trailing smoke, faded from the radar screen, possibly splashed, whereas #4, also hit by us, was splashed by the USS *Stern* (DE-187) patrolling Baker-16. The above covers plane #2. Of the four aircraft in the other group, two were definitely splashed by the Seusens in Baker-14. One plane out of this group veered back toward the *Sederstrom* and was spotted and fired upon by the #1 20mm gun crew. This plane then veered away from the ship. This action was pictured by a drawing on a logarithmic scale chart by our executive officer, Phil Dana. It appears that the *Sederstrom* accounted for three splashed but the powers-to-be decided to credit us with only one kill.)

April 23, 1945-at 0030 enemy aircraft bearing 215 T., distance seven miles, this vessel went to General Quarters. At 0055 secured from General Quarters, all enemy aircraft clear of area.

April 24, 1945-at 1515 maneuvering to pick up wing section from plane. At 1529 wing section brought aboard, identified by markings as part of Japanese aircraft. This was later identified as wing section from Baka bomb.

At 1615 recovered red conical buoy considered a hindrance to navigation.

April 25, 1945-at 0944 relieved on station B-15 by USS *Finnegan* (DE-307), proceeding as ordered by CTG 51.5 TBS message to fuel from USS *Suamico* (AO-49). At 1125 alongside USS *Suamico* (AO-49); commenced fueling at 1128. At 1155 fueling completed; all lines vast off, proceeding on various courses to patrol station C-24 in accordance with orders of CTG 51.5 TBS message. At 1228 on station Charlie-24.

April 26, 1945-at 0355 unidentified aircraft in vicinity, closest approach to this vessel 21 miles.

April 27, 1945-at 1230 received verbal orders from CTG 51.5 to proceed to station Killer One when relieved by USS *Skirmish* (AM-303). Proceeding as necessary to reach station Killer One. At 1505 relieved USS *Carlson* (DE-9) in vicinity Killer One. At 1655 USS *Baker* (DE-642) joined this vessel as part of Killer Group One. At 2340 unidentified aircraft reports near transport area, Okinawa, Air Flash Red, control Green at Okinawa.

April 28, 1945-at 0011 unidentified aircraft in area, sounded General Quarters. At 0132 unidentified aircraft clear of immediate vicinity, secured from General Quarters. At 1725 unidentified aircraft in close vicinity, sounded General Quarters. At 1730 unidentified aircraft believed to have passed overhead at high altitude, vapor trails sighted. At 1745 unidentified aircraft clear of immediate area, secured from General Quarters. At 1840 exercised at General Quarters, unidentified aircraft in area. At 2044 three unidentified aircraft 100 T., distance 12 miles, closing. Changed course to 060 T., to unmask battery. Observed explosion to starboard, distance five miles. 2051 proceeding to scene of explosion. At 2059 CIC reports ship in vicinity of explosion maintaining course and speed, apparently undamaged; returning to station. At 2355 no enemy aircraft in vicinity, secured from General Quarters.

April 29, 1945-USS *Baker* (DE-642) is other patrolling vessel of Killer One. At 0450 departed patrol station Killer One in accordance with CTG 51.5 verbal order, en route Kerama Retto for provisioning and fueling. At 0600 entered Kaikyo Anchorage. Fueling and provisioning as directed. At 1425 underway as directed to take station B-45, anti-submarine screen off Kerama Retto. At 1500 on station B-4, relieved USS *Oberrander* (DE-344). At 1858 unidentified aircraft in vicinity. Went to General Quarters. At 1947 unidentified aircraft clear of vicinity. Secured from General Quarters.

April 30, 1945-at 0240 enemy aircraft in vicinity. Sounded General Quarters. At 0325 enemy aircraft clear of vicinity. Secured from General Quarters. At 2203 enemy aircraft in area to northward. At 2300 enemy aircraft clear of area; closest approach to this vessel, 16 miles.

May 1, 1945-0349 to 0400 many unidentified aircraft in vicinity. Closest approach to this vessel 1.5 miles. Altitude of plane very high, not observed visually. 0400 observed large explosion inside anchorage at Kerama Retto. Reports identify vessel hit as the USS *Terror* (CM-5). 0455 no unidentified aircraft in vicinity. Many reports received throughout balance of day of unidentified aircraft, but none picked up by this ship's radar.

May 2, 1945-a quiet day for a change. No enemy air action.

May 3, 1945-relieved on station by USS *Stern* (DE-187). Proceeding as directed to fuel from USS *Saranac* (AO-74). 1125 fueling completed and proceeding to Hagushi Anchorage, Okinawa. 1835 to 1953 many unidentified aircraft in vicinity, this vessel at General Quarters. Closest approach to this vessel 24 miles. 1955 unidentified aircraft clear of vicinity; secured from General Quarters.

May 4, 1945-anchored in berth H-82, Hagushi Beach Anchorage, Okinawa. 0202 unidentified aircraft approaching area; went to General Quarters. 0202 to 0448 unidentified aircraft in vicinity; all ships in harbor made smoke during raid. Closest approach to this vessel—directly overhead at very high altitude. Enemy aircraft dropped bombs in vicinity of airfield on Okinawa. 0455 secured from General Quarters. 0752 enemy aircraft approaching area, this vessel underway to form anti-aircraft screen for transport area. 0846 observed enemy plane under fire make a vertical dive hitting USS *Birmingham* (CA-62). 0920 enemy aircraft clear of vicinity; secured from General Quarters. 1125 proceeding to anchor in berth 154.

May 5, 1945-anchored as before. 0215 to 0442 unidentified aircraft in vicinity, none sighted by this vessel. 0442 secured from General Quarters, unidentified aircraft clear of vicinity. 1132 underway as escort for USS LST-678 en route Hagushi Anchorage to Nakagusuku Wan (east side of Okinawa). 1850 duty completed, anchored in berth B-208, Nakagusuku Wan. 1945 proceeding to relieve USS *Riddle* (DE-185) in patrol station 153.

May 6, 1945-patrolling station 153. 0218 to 0422 enemy aircraft in vicinity, this vessel at General Quarters. Aircraft directly overhead but not observed by this vessel due to cloud cover. 0430 secured from GQ. 0530 off entrance to Nakagusuka Wan to rendezvous with USS *Pondera* (APA-19) and on station at 0720 escorting USS *Pondera* to Hagushi Anchorage. 1005 arrived at point "elder," escort duty completed and proceeding to Hagushi anchorage. 1240 anchored in berth H-110 awaiting orders. 1454 underway proceeding to station C-27. 1525 relieved USS *Daniel T. Griffin* (APD-38) on station C-27.

May 7, 1945-0205 to 0507 unidentified aircraft in vicinity, closest approach to this vessel, seven miles, not observed visually. This vessel at General Quarters. Secured from GQ at 0335.

May 8, 1945-1345 relieved on station by USS SC-1313 this vessel proceeding to report to CTG 51.5 in Hagushi Anchorage. 1428 proceeding to close USS *Enoree* (AO-69) to fuel. 1745 alongside AO-69, commenced fueling at 1801. 1817 fueling completed having received 15,110 gals. diesel oil, 1,000 gals. lube oil and received dry provisions. 1830 proceeding to station B-30 and on station at 1922.

May 9, 1945-1836 enemy aircraft reported by radar in area; distance 55 miles, bearing 340 degrees T. 1854 aircraft closed to 10 miles, bearing 280 degrees T; went to GQ. 1856 enemy aircraft seen to make suicide dive on USS *Oberrender* (DE-344), 1917 several enemy aircraft reported in vicinity. 1945 enemy aircraft clear of vicinity; secured from GQ. 2000-ordered to take station A-35-A arriving on station at 2047. Commander C.A. Kunz, USNR, ComCortDiv-31, aboard this vessel is sector commander of Sector "G."

May 10, 1945-0005 to 0103 unidentified aircraft in vicinity, closest approach 30 miles, not observed visually. From 0210 to 0442 aircraft periodically directly overhead at 10,000 feet. Secured from GQ at 0442. 1212 relieved on station by USS *Farenholt* (DD-491); proceeding to transport area to rendezvous with USS *Arkansas* (BB-33) and USS *Hudson* (DD-475) and screen USS *Arkansas* out of area en route to Guam. This vessel to detach prior to arrival Guam and return to Okinawa.

May 11, 1945-1400 detached and proceeding independently to Hagushi Anchorage. 1631 sighted British Task Force composed of 21 ships including the carriers HMS *Victorious* and HMS *Indomitable*. This vessel replied to challenge from British aircraft. 1810 made preparations for firing exercises and released target balloon. 1811 commenced firing. 1818 ceased firing; balloon punctured.

May 12, 1945-1125 anchored in Hagushi Anchorage, berth H-137. 1355 underway and at 1430 moored port side USS *Giraffe* (1X-118); commenced taking on lube oil. 1500 all lines clear of 1X-118 and underway to take on diesel fuel from USS *Kaskaskia* (AO-27). 1802 commenced fueling. 1847 fueling completed; received 19,772 gals. of diesel oil and 1,400 gals. of lube oil. 1852 all lines clear of AO-27 and underway to take station B-27. 1903 sighted two unidentified aircraft on starboard, distance 10 miles. Went to GQ. 1909 unidentified aircraft on starboard bow, distance three miles. 1915 ships in transport area commenced firing on aircraft. 1917 this vessel commenced firing on two aircraft on starboard beam, approaching from transport area. 1919 ceased firing. Targets did not appear damaged, aircraft retiring to westward. 2010 all enemy aircraft clear of vicinity; secured from GQ.

May 13, 1945-0727 proceeding on course to patrol station C-23. 0805 relieved USS *Spectacle* (AM-305). 1125 received message to proceed to investigate submarine contact by USS *Yokes* (APD-69). 1246 commenced two ship search at 12 knots. Assisting ASP aircraft (PBM) in area. 1858 went to GQ as unidentified aircraft in vicinity, distance eight miles. 2006 enemy aircraft closed to five miles flying low. 2100 four enemy aircraft approached to within nine miles. 2103 enemy aircraft identified as *Dinah* shot down by friendly night fighter on port quarter of this vessel, distance four miles. 2118 unidentified aircraft clear of vicinity.

May 14, 1945-this vessel conducting retiring search plan in company with USS *Yokes* (APD-69); Commander C.A. Kunz, USNR, ComCortDiv-31, OTC of operation, aboard this vessel. 0726 discontinued search, results negative; proceeding to close USS *Biscayen* (AGC-18) in transport area for further orders.

0917 anchored in berth H-137. 0950 underway proceeding to relieve USS *Triumph* (AM-323) on station A-38-A. 1915 went to GQ as unidentified aircraft closed to 11.5 miles. At 1955 aircraft identified as friendly; secured from GQ.

May 15, 1945-1615 relieved on station by USS *Walter C. Mann* (DE-412); ordered to close USS *Biscayne* (AGC-18) for visual orders. 1855 anchored in berth H-175. No enemy air action.

May 16, 1945-0307 sounded GQ as enemy aircraft approaching from north and west. 0310 enemy aircraft in immediate vicinity. 0422 secured from GQ. 2025 single enemy aircraft approaching from south, sounded GQ. 2047 enemy aircraft clear of vicinity; secured from GQ. 2245 enemy aircraft approaching from north, sounded GQ. 2252 enemy aircraft passed overhead at high altitude, not observed visually. 2303 island batteries and some ships in Anchorage fired at high altitude plane. 2336 enemy aircraft clear of vicinity; secured from GQ.

May 17, 1945-anchored in berth H-175, Hagushi Anchorage. 1935 sounded GQ; enemy aircraft approaching Okinawa from the north and west, nearest 11 miles and closing. 2020 closed to within seven miles but not observed visually. 2100 enemy aircraft clear of vicinity; secured from GQ. 2130 enemy aircraft approaching Okinawa; sounded GQ. 2357 enemy aircraft clear of vicinity; closest approach this vessel-three miles; not observed visually. 2359 secured from GQ.

May 18, 1945-0538 underway to take on diesel fuel from USS *Cimarron* (AO-22). 0635 previous fueling orders cancelled and closing USS *Kiswaukee* (AOG-9) instead. 0715 moored starboard side to AOG-9 and commenced fueling. 0750 fueling completed; received 24,184 gals. diesel fuel. 0759 underway to berth H-163, anchoring at 0820. 0945 underway en route Okinawa to Guam escorting USS *Eldorado* (AGC-11). Other screening vessel is the USS *Brown* (DD-546). Captain Wallace in USS *Eldorado* is OTC; screen commander is Commander C.A. Kunz, USNR,ComCortDiv-31,in this vessel. 1055 heard very loud explosion, observed ship under fire of Japanese shore batteries off Naha. Ship apparently hit and burning. 1105 observed second ship apparently hit and burning. (NOTE: The ship under fire was the USS *Longshaw* (DD-559). She had run aground on a reef while providing gun support for our ground forces and was destroyed.)

May 22, 1945-0705 arrived off channel entrance, Apra Harbor, Guam. 0855 moored alongside USS *Tabberer* (DE-418) at mooring buoy #206, starboard side to USS *Norman* (DE-416) moored outboard of USS *Tabberer*. 0915 USS *Brown* (DD-546) moored alongside port side this vessel. Reported to CTU 94.7.1 for general availability and repairs.

May 26, 1945-0810 all hands mustered at quarters; Lieutenant Commander B.H. Bossidy, USNR, relieved Lieutenant Commander J.P. Farley, USNR, as commanding officer of the USS *Sederstrom* (DE-31).

USS *SNOWDEN* (DE-246)

Snowden sailed for New Orleans on September 3 en route to Bermuda for her shakedown cruise which lasted until October 14. She was then ordered to Charleston, South Carolina. Late in the month, she escorted *Almaack* (AK-27) to Panama and in November, *Sloat* (DE-245) to New York. The ship was assigned to convoy UGS-24 there, on November 11 and escorted it to Norfolk and Casablanca, arriving on December 1. She picked up another convoy there and returned to New York on December 24, 1943.

Snowden got underway for a short training cruise to Norfolk on January 5, 1944 and then escorted *Arkansas* (BB-33) to New York. In January, she escorted convoy UGS-31 to Gibraltar, via Norfolk, and in February returned to New York with convoy UGS-30 which arrived on March 8. The escort then moved to Norfolk and joined Task Group (TG) 21.15, a hunter-killer group, which sailed on March 24.

That evening, a sound contact was made by *Snowden,* but she was ordered out of the area so that aircraft from *Croatan* (CVE-25) could drop sonar buoys, which produced negative results.

On April 28, *Snowden*, *Frost* (DE-144), and *Barber* (DE-161) left their screening positions to make fathometer readings at the head of an oil slick. *Snowden* made a reading 560 feet. The trio dropped two depth charge patterns of 39 charges each. Two undersea explosions followed as U-488 died.

The task group was forced to return to port for resupply of depth charges on May 5 before continuing operations in June and July. On June 12 *Snowden, Frost,* and *Inch* (DE-146) made a surface radar contact. *Inch* illuminated the target with star shells, and it was identified as a submarine. *Frost* commenced firing as *Snowden* was out of range. An SOS was received by *Frost* which was followed by a loud explosion from the submarine. The three escorts picked up 60 survivors from the sunken U-490. On July 3 *Frost* and *Inch* killed U-154. *Snowden* put a boat in the water and it collected such debris as paper with German writing, German cigarettes, and human flesh. The submarine was definitely sunk.

On August 22, *Snowden* joined TG 22.5 and operated in the Caribbean until December 30, 1944 when it returned to Norfolk. On March 25, 1945 the task group sailed to the north-central Atlantic to hunt enemy submarines. No contact was made until April 15. *Snowden* left the barrier patrol to screen *Croatan* while *Stanton* (DE-247) and *Frost* attacked. Six minutes later, both ships were shaken by a violent explosion. At 0114 the next morning, there was an even larger explosion, which shook ships 12 miles away, followed by several minor ones. That was the end of U-1235.

Crew of the USS Snowden (DE-246) at Pearl Harbor, August 1945.

The hunter-killer group entered Argentia, Newfoundland on April 25 for three days and then put to sea for two more weeks of hunting. *Snowden* stopped at the Brooklyn Navy Yard on May 14 for two weeks and then moved down to Norfolk.

Snowden remained at Norfolk until July 4 when she sailed for Pearl Harbor via Guantanamo Bay, Panama and San Diego. The escort was in Pearl Harbor from August 14 until September 11 when she retraced her route to Norfolk for overhaul and inactivation, arriving on September 28, 1945. After the overhaul was completed she sailed to Green Cove Springs, FL and in March 1946 was placed in reserve, out of commission, with the Atlantic Reserve Fleet.

On June 6, 1951, *Snowden* was again placed in active service. She held refresher training at Guantanamo Bay in July and August and them conducted exercises out of Newport, Rhode Island from September 1951 to March 1952. After further refresher training at Guantanamo Bay in June and July, she sailed to the North Atlantic and participated in her first North Atlantic Treaty Organization (NATO) fleet exercise. After calling at ports in Norway and Scotland, she returned to the Caribbean and spent the remainder of the year there.

From 1953 to 1957 *Snowden* operated with the Atlantic Fleet along the east coast, ranging from Labrador to the Caribbean. She participated in her second NATO exercises from September 3 to October 21, 1957 with port calls in France. The escort resumed her normal east coast operations until February 1960 when she became a Group 1, Naval Reserve Training Ship.

Snowden was decommissioned in August and placed in service as a Group II, Naval Reserve Training Ship and berthed at Philadelphia. She was recommissioned on October 2, 1961 and assigned to Key West, Florida. She operated from there until April 1962 when she was ordered to return to Philadelphia where she was again decommissioned and resumed her former status as a Group II, Naval Reserve Training Ship. She remained in this category until August 20, 1968 when she was ordered to prepare for inactivation and striking. *Snowden* was struck from the Navy list on September 23, 1968 and sunk as a target on June 27, 1969.

Snowden received three Battle Stars for World War II service.

USS *SPANGENBERG* (DE-223)

In early 1945, orders came for the USS *Spangenberg* (DE-223) and other ships of Task Group 66 to report for duty under the British Admiralty for anti-submarine patrol and convoy escort support group work in and south of the Irish Sea, where sinkings by German submarines were numerous. During that period the ship used Londonderry as the home base.

Many times over the years, stories of those days were told and retold; a return visit was talked about wistfully. Then one day the DE sailor read of a C.I.E. tour for Ireland which included visits to all four Provinces, with stops at the Giants Causeway and Londonderry - "It's fate," the sailor said, and immediately booked the tour.

After a great week touring the South and East, on the eighth day, the tour continued traveling north on through the "Green Glens of Antrim," to the first site to be revisited - the extraordinary coastal rock phenomenon, Giants Causeway. What an experience - to be standing there again on the same ground and sites as the faded photos in his WWII album—that sailor couldn't believe it was actually happening. Hopping from one stone to another, pointing out a spot here - where one shipmate is seated in the old black and white photos; there - where another buddy is studying the formations and listening to the guide. The happiness and excitement were contagious. Not much change there. A modern Visitors Centre, Shop and Tea Room have replaced the lone cottage, however, that is the sole structure seen in the old photos and post cards.

In May of 1945, the crew of the USS *Spangenberg* enjoyed a few days of R & R at a military facility - Camp Cromore - located near the seaside town of Port Rush. The tour's itinerary, unfortunately, didn't allow for a stop in Port Rush, but several 1940s vintage quonset huts, similar to those at Camp Cromore, were spotted on farms along the road to Londonderry.

The highlight of the trip was the evening in Londonderry. It was after 6 P.M., a little late, by the time the tour arrived at the hotel. The sailor was undecided whether to try to visit the city that evening. When the hotel manager overheard the sailor's conversation with his friends at dinner, he told him that there were still four more hours of daylight, more than enough for a visit to the city. There was no way he was going to let that WWII sailor miss the opportunity of revisiting Londonderry. The manager, Kevin McFadden, actually called his brother Francis, who arrived at the hotel, with his own car, within ten minutes. Francis took the sailor on a private tour. For more than an hour, they explored the entire city; the driver urging the sailor to try to remember all the special places from 1945, then, proceeding with pleasure directly to them.

The first stop was the "Diamond" at the top of Shipquay Street, the site of the War Memorial from other wars. The view down Shipquay Street toward the clock tower in the Guild Hall was unchanged, except for the new street lights. VE Day was celebrated by the crew of the DE 223 in the square in front of the Guild Hall in Londonderry (a few days late). It was quiet there, almost deserted at that time of night; gone were the joyous, boisterous, laughing and cheering crowds.

The docks and the waterfront buildings were closed and quiet, some deserted, but standing there looking out on the River Foyle toward the Sea, the sailor could almost see the DE 223.

He wasn't able to go into the old Naval Base. In 1945, they had assisted in escorting German U-boats, which had surrendered at sea, back to that base. Now it is occupied by the R.U.C., so the base was viewed from the waterside.

Next he recognized the gray stone church he used to visit each time before the ship left port; time barely touched that ancient structure.

One place they couldn't locate. The **Old PUB**. Back in the early '40s the servicemen left their hats nailed to the wall of the pub before shipping out, to be collected on their way back home. The Londonderry natives enjoyed hearing that story although they were too young to remember much about the war years. Maybe on his next visit there, he'll have more time for research, and the sailor will find that Pub!

It's hard to say who enjoyed the tour of Londonderry more - the sailor or the driver. The hotel manager and staff had to hear, in detail, an account of each stop in the city, immediately upon the guest's return. Some hearty laughs were enjoyed by all. No one wanted the day to end. The memories are many, and will linger long. It had been an enchanting day. It was a perfect day.

The DE sailor was back on board the 223.

USS *STEWART* (DE-238)

Clarence A. Brown, PhM1/c, remembers the USS *Stewart* (DE-238) convoyed the Presidential Yacht with President Roosevelt and staff to the USS *Iowa*. They proceeded to the Atlantic in a zig zag pattern while the President headed to the Tehran/Casablanca Conference. It was at this time, November 1943, he recalls the Thanksgiving Dinner was not really appreciated by the crew. Brown and the Commissary Officer Ens. West surveyed the main dish (turkey) and found the cooks had substituted bologna in its placed.

In March 1944, the USS *Stewart* encountered sixty foot seas and bad weather off Reykjavik, Iceland. It was joked at the time that the ship rode like a bucking bronco for it was built by Texas cowboys at Brownsville. The rough seas proved a real testament to the sturdiness of the USS *Stewart*.

USS *GARFIELD THOMAS* (DE-193)

The USS *Garfield Thomas* (DE-193) was built by the Federal Shipbuilding and Drydock Corporation at Newark, New Jersey. Its construction was part of the Naval Expansion Program launched by Congress to implement the declaration of war following the Japanese attack on Pearl Harbor. It was christened and slid down the ways 11 December 1943. The ship was named in honor of Lt. (jg) William Garfield Thomas, who lost his life in action on the USS *Boise* in a surface engagement in the South Pacific in October 1942.

First Captain of the *Garfield Thomas* was Lt. Comdr. Richard G. Werner, a veteran skipper who had commanded the USS *Brennan* (DE-13), one of the first DEs commissioned by the Navy. He also received training in anti-submarine warfare aboard British corvettes operating in English waters.

The ship was manned by a nucleus crew of seasoned sailors plus a contingent of men from naval camps and schools. This land-trained crew assembled at Norfolk, VA, for special pre-commissioning training as a unit and transferred to New York City for embarkation in January 1944. The ship was commissioned at formal ceremonies at the Brooklyn Navy Yard, 24 January 1944. Representing the Navy, Rear Admiral Monroe Kelly received the ship into active service and transmitted first operations orders to the captain.

The ship put out to sea two weeks later, bound for "shakedown" cruise and exercises in waters off Bermuda. Three hours out of port she encountered the worst storm of her history. For two days the craft rocked and tossed, manned by seasick crew and officers. To men at sea for the first time, it was a memorable initiation.

The seagoing career of the *Garfield Thomas* is noted for its complete absence of combat action against the enemy. She assisted in convoying a carrier to Brazil. The equatorial crossing thus made shellbacks of the crew. She made two convoying trips to North Africa shortly after the German surrender at Bizerte. On one of these trips, a convoy ahead and within vision was attacked by German planes, but this was as close as Mediterranean action came to the *Thomas*. On the first trip, the ship lay in the harbor at Bizerte when news of D-day occurred. The ship was in Bizerte for the second time during the invasion of Southern France. A half-dozen convoying trips to the British Isles followed. Cardiff and Plymouth became familiar haunts of the *Thomas's* sailors. Frequently at sea, action reports were received of submarine activity ahead and astern, but the charmed existence of the *Thomas* persisted. On VE-Day she was tied up in Cardiff, South Wales, and most of them heard the Lord Mayer of Cardiff, resplendent in wig and red robes, officially proclaim victory over Germany.

After exercises at Guantanamo Bay, Cuba, the *Thomas* was transferred to the Pacific Fleet. With her division, she steamed through the Panama Canal, took on stores and supplies at San Diego, and headed for Pearl Harbor, Hawaii.

There the crew received briefly refresher training. Again she was in port when decisive news broke - namely, the first atomic bombing of Japan. With her division, escorting a transport, she was enroute to Eniwetok, Marshall Islands, when announcement of Russia's declaration of war against Japan was broadcast on the radio. She lay in the harbor at Eniwetok, after a convoy run to Ulithi when Japan signed the terms of surrender in Tokyo Bay.

With Eniwetok Atoll in the Marshall Islands as her home base, the *Thomas* made convoy trips to Ulithi, acted as relief for a destroyer escort at Ponape, carried provisions and fuel to mine sweepers at Rongelap Atoll, and patrolled the approaches to Eniwetok.

In December the *Thomas* received orders to proceed to Pearl Harbor for further instructions. Without regards the crew made ready and left Eniwetok with pleasant prospects of Christmas in Pearl Harbor.

After a brief period at anchor the *Thomas* was assigned a thirty-day weather patrol in the northern Pacific. This patrol set a new record for the ship in length of time of a single cruise and was comparable in weather conditions to its first unforgettable cruise to Bermuda.

During her span of Navy service, her personnel changed substantially. In April of 1945, Lt. Cmdr. Werner was transferred, and her Executive Officer, Lieut. E.D. Duryea succeeded him in command. In Pearl Harbor in August 1945, Lt. Duryea was succeeded by Lt. Cmdr. J. Ross Pilling, Jr. With the end of the war, the personnel of the *Thomas* began to change considerably. In November 1945, Lt. Cmdr. Pilling was succeeded by Lieut. Walter D. McCord, Jr. Both officers and men were regularly transferred or discharged each month. In December 1945 only forty of the original crew remained.

On 9 February 1946 the USS *Garfield Thomas* left Pearl Harbor and, after a second transit of the Panama Canal, arrived at the Brooklyn, NY Navy Yard on the first of March. Her final cruise with the U.S. Navy was to Green Cove Springs, Florida, where she was moored with the other Navy ships in the "mothballed" Atlantic Fleet Reserve. On 27 March 1947 the USS *Garfield Thomas* was decommissioned.

However, the final chapter in the history of this gallant ship is yet to be written. On 15 Jan. 1951 the *Garfield Thomas* was transferred under the Military Assistance Program to Greece, and renamed the *Panther*. She is still cruising the familiar waters of the Mediterranean with the Greek navy. A book with letters and pictures was received from her present captain, and was on display with other memorabilia at the 1989 reunion.

The USS *Garfield Thomas* cruised the equivalent of seven round-the-world trips with the U.S. Navy. In addition to crossing the Equator, her men are also Golden Dragons by virtue of having crossed the 180th Meridian, twice. In the quiet, faithful pursuit of duty, the globe-trotting *Thomas* made its contribution to the struggle against aggressor nations. With her active days over with the U.S. Navy, the "Willie G" which she was affectionately called by her crew, can proudly survey her record and feel certain that she accomplished the purpose for which she was created.

HMS *WALDEGRAVE*
Submitted by Peter Seaborn A/B

It was the film "The Enemy Below" which kindled a flame of remembrance of my seatime, the all to familiar lines of the Destroyer Escort that was involved, were a joy to behold to my fading memory of HMS *Waldegrave*.

As a countryman living in a scattered community there was little opportunity to keep alive memories of the Royal Navy. I was never destined to meet old shipmates who served with me on our particular D.E. whose crew were recruited from far and wide throughout the British Isles.

Although only a few months covered the acceptance of the all the D.E.s by the R.N., we were, as it transpired, among the last half dozen of the Buckley's transferred by the United States Navy. As a consequence our crew were not to be accorded the privilege of commissioning in the U.S. as had been the earlier procedure, but accepted the ship from the Royal Canadian Navy at Lisahally in Northern Ireland, together with the *Narbrough* and *Whittaker*. The pennant numbers of K578 (Ex 569), K579 (Ex570) and K580 (Ex 571) were already visible and I made a mental note that *Whittaker* 580 added to 13...as indeed did her previous number! Although not by nature prone to superstition, alas it was ironic that she was to be torpedoed later in the year with the tragic loss of almost half her crew.

In early 1944 it was presumed that most escort groups had already been formed, the bulk of which were usually of the same class and so it proved that we were to operate mainly "unattached."

After a few sorties into the Atlantic and a "working up period," we sailed South to where the action was continuous. April and May found us executing various duties including Mock Invasion Exercises, Patrols and Convoys. The "hushed-up" tragedy of Slapton Sands passed us by, the awful loss of many American lives should never have been! If ever proof was needed that the English Channel was not for the exclusive use of the Allied forces, perhaps this infamous incident served to drive home the fact.

The Battle of the Narrow Seas lasted for almost six years and although many thousands lost their lives, it was particularly distressing to lose Allied soldiers training to take part in the largest invasion in history. It was a sobering thought that within minutes of leaving a South Coast Port one could be confronted by the enemy above or below the waves, every sonar contact was a potential U-boat and attacks by fast enemy forces were a daily and nightly occurrence.

During this pre-invasion period two incidents remain clear in my mind. Whilst engaged in one "cloak and dagger" night operation off the French Coast the crew were closed up at Action Stations with strict instructions to maintain silence.

As a communication number on "A" gun I received a message for the Gun Captain and left the platform to confer with him. My headphone lead pulled me up having become entangled with an obstruction and I jerked my head hard several times to free it. This proving unsuccessful I retraced my steps and found to my horror that the cable was wrapped around the firing trigger!

On reflection, doubt whether the fact that I was only sixteen years old at the time would have cut much ice with the Captain had the gun fired then...thus screwing up the delicate operation!

Some days later the ship was on lone patrol in the S. Western Approaches of the Atlantic. Everyone having been engaged at one time or another on such onerous work will appreciate the seemingly endless monotony of patrolling a section of the ocean.

One particular day we attacked a possible U-boat several times, apparently without success. Only the multitude of dead fish on the surface were evidence of our countless depth charges. Having lost contact it was decided to gather some of this fruitful harvest to supplement our uninteresting diet. So it was that I found myself together with three other seamen and an officer assigned the task of hauling in as much as possible in the ship's whaler.

Our boat was tossed about considerably, and urged on by the officer, we struggled to load enough for a couple of days supply, getting soaked in the process. Having achieved this difficult task we pulled toward the ship only to see her turn away gathering speed. Stern down, to our astonished gaze she gradually receded from our view!

The next five hours seemed the longest of our lives, the sea worsened and we got colder in our sodden clothes, more truculent and hungry as time wore on. With hopes fading as darkness approached, we glimpsed the sight of a D.E. appearing over the horizon and eventually *Waldegrave* was alongside. Never was the recovery of the seaboat more swiftly executed in hazardous conditions prevailing and the ships more expertly handled by our brilliant Captain whose parentage earlier was seriously in doubt, than at that time!

Why were we left for so long? Why were minutes so valuable? Many questions were left unanswered and we were never to know the reason for such action. We did however enjoy the fish but we were never to repeat the exercise again.

D-day found us escorting a convoy of ships bound for the American beaches and thereafter our duties involved countless participation in convoys, Anti E-boat and U-boat patrols and escorting Capital Ships.

I can still "hear" voices on the American troopships calling out to us during our frequent return from the beaches to collect convoys..."What's it like over there, Limey?" Some of those lads were never to return to their homeland, as were many in other theatres of the war, may they rest in peace. They shall not grow old as we shall grow old...

In June 1945 the youngsters of HMS *Waldegrave* were drafted from their beloved ship destined for other duties abroad...but of course that is another story.

USS *WHITEHURST* (DE-634)

Henry Purefoy Whitehurst Jr. born on February 16, 1920 at New Bern, North Carolina was appointed a midshipman on July 14, 1938 and, because of the exigencies of war, graduated with the Naval Academy's Class of 1942 on December 19, 1941. He reported to the heavy cruiser *Astoria* (CA-34) on the morning of January 18, 1942 at Pearl Harbor, Hawaii.

Whitehurst served as a junior watch and division officer in *Astoria* as that ship took part in the Battles of the Coral Sea and Midway, and was in the cruiser when she participated in the landings on Guadalcanal on August 7, 1942. The next day, *Astoria* screened the vital transports as they unloaded supplies and equipment for the Marines ashore, and that evening stood out to a night retirement station off Savo Island.

A little after 0152 on the morning of August 9, a Japanese force under Vice Admiral Gunichi Mikawa—which had slipped undetected into the waters south of Savo Island—unleashed a devastating night attack on the southern and northern forces. In the former, *Chicago* (CA-29) was damaged and the Australian heavy cruiser HMAS *Canberra* crippled so badly that she later sank.

The Northern Force, unaware of the enemy's presence until too late, soon took staggering punishment. *Vincennes* (CA-44) and *Quincy* (CA-39) sank before daylight, but *Astoria* lingered on while her surviving officers and men labored to save their ship. However, the damage proved too great; and *Astoria*—like her two sister ships—eventually succumbed shortly after noon on August 9. Among the dead suffered in the Battle of Savo Island was Ensign Whitehurst.

(DE-634: dp. 1,400; l. 305'0"; b. 37"0"; dr 9'5" (mean); s. 23.5 k.; cpl. 186; a. 3 3", 4 1.1", 8 20mm., 2 dct., 8 dcp., 1 dcp (hh.), 3 21" tt.; cl. Bucklely)

Whitehurst (DE-634) was laid down on March 21, 1943 at San Francisco, California, by the Bethlehem Steel Company; launched on September 5, 1943; sponsored by Mrs. Robie S. Whitehurst, the mother of Ensign Whitehurst; and commissioned on November 19, 1943, Lieutenant Commander James R. Grey in command.

Following sea trials, calibration tests, and shakedown off the West Coast, *Whitehurst* proceeded to Hawaii, arriving at Pearl Harbor on February 4, 1944. Underway for the Solomons on the 7th, the destroyer escort sailed via Majuro and Funafuti in company with *James E. Craig* (DE-201) and Sc-520—escorting SS *George Ross*, SS *George Constantine* and SS *Robert Lucas*—and arrived on February 23 at Espiritu Santo in the New Hebrides.

After shifting to Noumean, New Caledonia, and back to Espiritu Santo, *Whitehurst* joined *Osterhaus* (DE-164) and *Acree* (DE-167) on March 22 to escort oilers *Kankakee* (AO-39), *Escambia* (AO-80), and *Atascosa* (AO-66). *Whitehurst* and *Atascosa* were detached from that task unit on March 26 to proceed independently to a rendezvous with other task forces operating in the area. While *Atascosa* refueled ships from Destroyer Squadron 47, an enemy plane appeared. All ships present, including *Whitehurst*, opened fire but scored

no hits as the plane climbed upward and out of sight. Once refueling had been completed, *Whitehurst* and the oiler returned to Espiritu Santo.

At the completion of a mission escorting *President Monroe* (AP-104) to Milne Bay, New Guinea, *Whitehurst* remained in waters off New Guinea on local escort duties until May 17. She then participated in the amphibious operation against Wake Island, screening the amphibious ships as they landed troops of General Douglas MacArthur's forces. *Whitehurst*, in company with other units of Task Unit (TU) 72.2.9, later escorted echelon S-4 of the invasion forces to Humboldt Bay. The destroyer escort subsequently joined *Wilkes* (DD-441), *Swanson* (DD-43), and *Nicholson* (DD-442) to screen echelon H-2 as it steamed toward Bosnic, Biak, in the Schouten Islands, for landings there.

Arriving off Biak on May 28, *Whitehurst* took up a patrol station off the western entrance to the channel between Owi Island and Biak. While there she received an urgent message from LCI-34 which had been taken under fire by Japanese shore batteries. *Whitehurst* arrived on the scene in time to be shelled herself; but the enemy's rounds fell harmlessly nearby and caused no damage to the ship. The destroyer escort soon was relieved by *Stockton* (DD-646) and *Swanson* in covering LCI-34, and then protected LCT-260 as that landing craft embarked casualties from the beachhead. *Whitehurst* subsequently screened echelon H-2 as it retired from Biak to Humboldt Bay.

Whitehurst performed escort duties and trained through the summer of 1944. The tempo of the war, however, was increasing. With the Japanese being driven from one island after another, American planners look toward the next rung of the ladder to Tokyo—the Philippine Islands. Accordingly, *Whitehurst*, Lieutenant Jack C. Horton, USNR, now in command, was placed in the anti-submarine and anti-aircraft screen of TU 77.7.1, a group of fleet tankers slated to supply units of the 7th Fleet on its drive into the Philippines. On October 27—a week after American troops had landed on Leyte—two enemy planes attacked *Whitehurst*, but both were driven off by anti-aircraft fire from the ship's guns.

Two days later—on October 29—*Whitehurst* received word that, on the previous day, *Eversole* (DE-404) had been torpedoed and sunk by a Japanese submarine. While *Bull* (DE-693) picked up survivors from the sunken destroyer escort, *Whitehurst*—detached from TU77.7.1 to conduct a search—soon picked up a contact. At General Quarters, the destroyer escort conducted three attacks without positive results. When *Whitehurst* pressed home a fourth depth charge attack, her efforts were crowned with success. In quick succession, five to seven explosions rumbled up from the depths. Another violent underwater burst soon followed, causing a concussion that damaged *Whitehurst's* detecting gear.

Bull continued the search after *Whitehurst*—with her damaged sound gear—requested her to do so but found nothing except a stretch of disturbed water. As the waves calmed, lookouts in both ships noticed many pieces of wood and other debris bobbing in a widening oil slick. The Japanese submarines I-45—one that had killed *Eversole*—had been destroyed. While *Bull* continued picking

Members of the crew of the USS Whitehurst (DE-634) at Puson, Korea. In the background are a POW Camp and Army mess hall. (Submitted by Allgren)

up *Eversole* survivors in the vicinity, *Whitehurst* returned to TU 77/7.1 and with that task unit headed back to Kossol Roads in the Palaus.

Nearly a month later, following another stint of local escort operations, *Whitehurst* again came to grips with the enemy. While escorting a 12-ship convoy from Leyte to New Guinea, *Whitehurst* came under attack by two Japanese "Lilly" medium bombers. One skimmed low and dropped a bomb that fell well clear of the ships. The second started a glide bombing attack, but *Whitehurst's* guns tumbled that raider into the sea.

After arriving with the convoy at New Guinea on November 25, *Whitehurst* spent the remainder of 1944 and the first few months of 1945 in escort operations between New Guinea and the Philippines. She did not again engage the enemy until the Okinawa Campaign.

When the American landings on Okinawa commenced on April 1, 1945, *Whitehurst* was among the many screening vessels protecting the valuable transports and cargo vessels. On April 6 while on patrol station off Kerama Retto, the destroyer escort drove off an enemy lane that had attacked the cargo vessel SS *Pierre*. Three days later, the escort vessel was relieved of her escort duties off Kerama Retto, and she shifted to Okinawa to operate off the southwest coast of that island.

Taking up station on the 10th, she was still steaming in that capacity early in the afternoon two days later when a low-flying enemy plane closed the ship only to be driven off by *Whitehurst's* gunfire. At 1430, four "Val" dive bombers approached the area from the south; and one detached itself from the group and headed for *Whitehurst*. It circled and soon commenced a steep dive while two of its companions also commenced an attack, one from the starboard beam and one from astern. The latter two planes spun down in flames, destroyed by anti-aircraft fire, but the original attacker continued down in spite of the 20 millimeter hits that tore at the plane. This "Val" crashed into the ship's forward superstructure on the port side of the pilot house, penetrating bulkheads and starting fires that enveloped the entire bridge, while the plane's bomb continued through the ship and exploded some 50 feet off her starboard bow.

Whitehurst circled, out of control, while *Virgilance* (AM-324), patroling a nearby sector, rang up flank speed and raced toward the burning destroyer escort to render assistance. By the time *Vigilance* finally caught up with *Whitehurst*, the destroyer escort's crew had put out the most serious fires; but the minesweeper proved invaluable in aiding the wounded. The prompt and efficient administering of first aid and the injection of plasma undoubtedly saved many lives—21 of the 23 wounded transferred to *Vigilance* were saved. With a *Vigilance* signalman on board—*Whitehurst's* signal bridge personnel had been decimated—the damaged destroyer escort limped into Kerama Retto for temporary patching. Then, seaworthy enough for a voyage to Hawaii, *Whitehurst* reached Pearl Harbor on May 10 and was docked for repairs and alterations.

Once the yard work had been completed and the ship had been converted to a floating power station, *Whitehurst* departed Pearl Harbor on July 25, 1945, bound for the Philippine Islands. Soon after she reached Luzon, Japan capitulated. Nevertheless, the ship supplied the city of Manila with power from August through October of 1945. She was scheduled to depart Manila on November 1 bound for Guam; but a typhoon in the vicinity resulted in a two-day delay. *Whitehurst* eventually reached Guam on the afternoon of November 7.

Operating as a unit of Escort Division 40, *Whitehurst* supplied electrical power to the dredge YM-25 into 1946. *Whitehurst* was decommissioned on November 27, 1946 and placed in the Atlantic Reserve Fleet at Green Cove Springs, Florida, in January 1947.

Reactivated in the summer of 1950 as a result of the outbreak of war in Korea, *Whitehurst* was recommissioned on September 1, 1950 and soon sailed for the Far East. The destroyer escort earned three Battle Stars for her activities during the Korean War between February 25 and September 19, 1951.

She remained in the Far East until 1955, when she returned to Pearl Harbor via Midway. After working locally out of Pearl Harbor for a year, the destroyer escort operated between Hawaii and Guam into 1956. Early in that year, she broadened her duties and itinerary by performing surveillance duties among the islands and atolls assigned the Trust Territories for the Pacific Islands. She also performed search and rescue missions in the Marianas and Carolines, periodically stopping at various islands to provide medical care for the natives and to record population changes.

Departing Guam on February 22, for Yokosuka, Japan, the ship sailed via the northern Marianas, the Bonins, and the Volcano Islands. She spent two weeks in Japanese waters before returning to Guam on March 17. Returning to the Central Carolines for patrol duties in early April 1956, *Whitehurst* stood by a damaged seaplane at the island of Lamotrek for two weeks before she returned to Guam on April 14, en route to Pearl Harbor.

After a period of local operations out of Pearl Harbor, *Whitehurst* headed back to the Far East and touched at Guam, Formosa, Hong Kong, and Sasebo, Japan, before representing the United States Navy at the graduation ceremonies of the Republic of Korea Naval Academy on April 10. She returned to Sasebo before shifting to Yokosuka en route to Midway and Hawaii. Arriving at Pearl Harbor on April 30, 1957, *Whitehurst* underwent four weeks of upkeep and repairs before beginning six weeks of duty with 20th Century Fox during the filming of the World War II adventure movie "The Enemy Below." During that time, she portrayed the destroyer escort USS *Haynes*.

Upon completion of the filming of the movie, *Whitehurst* operated off Oahu until late in September, when she was ordered to Seattle, Washington for duty as training ship with 13th Naval District. The veteran destroyer escort trained reservists on weekend drill cruises and, during this time, made one extended cruise to Guaymas, Mexico, in November 1957. After being overhauled at Seattle from February to April 1958, *Whitehurst* returned to active training duties, becoming a Group II ASW reserve ship in July. On December 6, 1958, *Whitehurst* was decommissioned and placed in an "in service" status as a unit of the Select Reserve ASW Force.

Thereafter, into the 1960s, *Whitehurst* cruised one weekend per month and made one two-week cruises per year. During the fiscal year 1961, the destroyer escort placed second in the national competition and the battle efficiency competition among the West Coast Group II Naval Reserve destroyer escorts.

Commissioned on October 2, 1961 for duty with the Pacific Fleet, Lieutenant Commander Donald L. MacLane, USNR, in command, *Whitehurst* operated actively with the fleet after being "called to the colors" as a result of the Berlin crisis that autumn. The destroyer escort departed Seattle on the 4th, bound for her new home port of Pearl Harbor, Hawaii.

After a period of training in the Hawaiian area, *Whitehurst* departed Pearl Harbor on February 10, 1962 for a deployment to the Western Pacific (WestPac). During the deployment she operated with the 7th Fleet out of Subic Bay, Philippines, and made a goodwill visit to Sapporo, Japan. The ship also operated in the South China Sea and the Gulf of Siam.

Returning to the United States via Hawaii, *Whitehurst* arrived at Seattle in company with *Charles E. Brannon* (DE-446) on July 17, 1962. Subsequently decommissioned on August 1, 1962 and placed in Group II in-service status as a Naval Reserve training ship, *Whitehurst* resumed operations out of Seattle. During 1963, the ship received two major changes in her configuration when her 40-millimeter mounts and ship-to-shore power reels—the latter items having enabled her to function as a floating station—were removed.

Whitehurst, in subsequent years, visited San Diego, CA; Bellingham, Port Angeles, and Everett, WA; and Esquimalt, British Columbia. On January 17, 1965, while operating in the Strait of Juan de Fuca, and steaming in dense fog off the Vancouver narrows, *Whitehurst* collided with the Norwegian freighter SS *Hoyanger*. Both ships then ran aground in shallow water. The destroyer escort suffered a five-foot gash in her stern above the waterline while the freighter got off with three feet of scraped bow plates. The following day, both ships were pulled off by tugs.

Whitehurst operated locally out of Seattle and ranged as far south as San Diego and San Francisco into 1967. One of the highlights for the destroyer escort in 1966 was the visit of astronaut Commander Richard F. Gordon Jr., in November of 1966. The ship transported Gordon and his family from Seattle to his home town of Bremerton on November 18 before she returned to her home port.

Soon *Whitehurst's* home port was shifted to Portland, Oregon from Seattle Washington. The ship she was to replace, *McGinty* (DD-365), was being deactivated as part of and economy drive. However, *Whitehurst's* days were also numbered, and she, too, was soon deactivated. On July 12, 1969, the destroyer escort was taken out of service and struck from the Navy list. She was eventually taken to sea and sunk as a target by *Trigger* (SS-564) on April 28, 1971.

Whitehurst earned six Battle Stars for her World War II service and three Battle Stars for Korean Service.

USS *WILLIE* (DE-372)

"We are sailing for Guam," with these words of news plus the very common fact of "we may run into a typhoon on our way, but nothing to worry about." So, we didn't worry, and soon after we were on our way. We were off, yes off in more ways than one. We were setting sail for a new experience, but none knew it, none had the slightest idea that a new experience lay before them, one that will live after many of us are gone, and our children telling sea stories to their children.

We left Okinawa the morning of the 28th of September 1945, and things were pretty much the same routine. Every hatch which was supposed to be closed, was tightened down, and all loose gear and equipment was secured. From all outward appearances, it was to be just another trip. Little did we know - little did any of us realize that a new chapter was about to be unfolded in our Life Book, nor did any think that for one, the final chapter was to be unfolded in his book.

Time went rather rapidly, what with the Captain holding a surprise inspection that afternoon. It wasn't an ordinary inspection by any means, for there was only a half hour allowed for Field Day. It was more to test and check our water tightness, and a final check to see that all gear was secured properly. After the Captain had been appeased, and the temper of the crew once again lowered back to its normal tempo, events happened in their natural rotation: Chow - Movies - and Sleep.

The morning of the 29th found the sea rough and stormy; the skies overcast with very threatening clouds; and the news that the Typhoon was headed our way. Our course lay directly in the path of the oncoming storm, so it was altered, partly to miss it and partly to give us greater clearance, in case it too changed course. It changed course alright, but it was too late for us to change, or do much more about it. All we could do is head for it, and hope that it changed course once again, or that all the stories we heard about Destroyer Escorts being so sea worthy were true. As for stories, you be the judge, and see if DEs are or aren't.

The ship was pitching and rolling along, tossing us to and fro in our sacks, when suddenly the world seemed to slide and dip, and throw everyone and everything to the port side. The time was shortly after 1944 (or 7:44 p.m.), the position of the ships was: Latitude 19°-50' North, Longitude 127°-0' East.

Mattresses and bedding with men, went sailing across the ship. Oil spurted and rushed from our reserve tanks, fore and aft. The ship had met its match. A wave had hit us (easily 100 feet high) and one of us had to give. It was the *Willie*. We were thrown on our port side (about a 95° roll) and then another force righted the doings of the first wave. During the brief interval of going over and coming back (which to some was a second, and others an eternity) many thoughts flashed across our minds, and fear gripped everyone. In every story there is at least one main IF, in this one there are two: IF the lights hadn't gone out, and IF the oil hadn't spurted out, it probably could have been laughed off as a joke, after the ship had regained its upright position again. But once men saw the oil rushing out and men scrambling, fighting, and pushing to get out the hatch, and up the ladder, it didn't take long before we knew that something was definitely wrong. This all took place within a minute, and I am surprised at how many impressions and unconscious impressions the mind is capable of recording in such a short time. Oil gushing forth; the ship at a 95° list; the boom of waves boating against our hull; lights slowly growing dimmer and dimmer as the circuits were shorted by the salt water and gear and life jackets scattered to the four corners of the compartments.

All emotions were pushed aside or left hanging half expressed, and fear and anxiety seized everyone. It was every man for himself. Life jackets were snatched from their storage racks, and any other gear then available and men thought would help save their lives. It was thought by many that various things had happened to us; we had hit a reef; others a ship; some thought it was a mine; and others thought our mast broke loose and had landed on top of us. It didn't seem possible that a wave could do the damage that was so obvious. In everyone's mind was the thought of us sinking, and the horrors were plainly stamped on everyone's features.

Contrary to the story I've just told about the men and the struggle and the desperate situation, let me clear it up slightly. No one was in their right mind when they suddenly found themselves thrown from their bunks, standing on the bulkhead of the ship, then up right again. But soon after righting our selves, self control came back and the rushing and pushing was stopped. Anxiety still ruled, yes, but common sense was a little stronger. We could all get through the escape hatch, one at a time, pushing only made for confusion and more injuries. Unfortunately the escape hatches were never made larger on Destroyer Escorts. Men can pass through them alright, but with a life jacket on, and oil on the ladders, it makes it difficult to say the least.

Our weather deck hatches were all sprung and pushed in. The ones on the starboard side wee actually bent in about eight inches, and water was fast gaining an entrance. The men who did the "Shoring" on the hatches, inexperienced as they were, proved their worth. It was an excellent job of "patching" and served its purpose admirably. Mention should be made also of the men who were below decks, in the engine rooms and firerooms. If their quick thinking and resourcefulness hadn't shut off all the valves and various other throttles to the boilers, we might not be here telling of it. Words cannot praise too highly valor and courage, so it would be useless for me to try, but if feelings for the acts done that night were gold, several of the men would be millionaires today.

While these men were below turning off valves, most of the other men had succeeded in getting to the torpedo deck, where they clung to anything and everything. The wind had reached an unmeasurable velocity, and the barometer had reached its lowest point (28.24). The waves and swells were monstrous in their proportion, and the men who did gain their way to the top, were risking their

lives just being up there. Each man had thoughts and reacted to them accordingly. There was born in each man a feeling if there were none before, it was stark hideous fear. He was afraid to die. He was not ready to die. He wanted to live - to live for all the reasons in the world; wanted to live because he was afraid to die; afraid of a watery tomb, and afraid to cross the eternal threshold beyond which no man knows what lay, yet all men know could never be re-crossed. He thought of the horrors of drowning; the feeling of being trapped below decks; the cries of the hurt and frightened; they could feel the wind lashing and cutting at every part of their bodies, tearing his hair, burning his eyes, and filling his mouth; he could feel the wind trying to loosen his precious hold, feel the wind trying to pull him loose, pulling, pushing, howling wind. He could feel and see the lonesomeness and vastness of the mighty ocean, as an occasional empty life jacket light rode high on a mountainous wave, then suddenly blot out as rapidly as it had risen. He could feel the crash of the wave once again, the smell of the oil, the slimy footing of the ladders, and taste of salt water and oil mixed; they could feel the confusion once more. Then the coldness, or the wind, or the reality of being topside, exposed to all of nature's hell, slowly occurred to them. One by one they crawled, hands and knees, bucking the wind, rain and sea until they had inched their way back to the hatch. Some to help with the damage repair parties, others to just move around and see what was wrong, others to help with the bailing; others to stand or sit in utter blankness. Either too stunned with reality, or too frightened to move further. They were left to face their maker and thoughts as best they could, while everyone else helped bail or with the shore-ing. A group of men had stayed topside, throwing over the ammunition from the after 40mm gun, which had broken loose, constituting a further hazard to the safety of the men and ship. Word was finally gotten around that the ship was not sinking; it was just a wave; and we were still afloat, but needed all the cooperation possible.

Volunteers were asked for (and gotten) to go below and re-light the boilers.

We were floundering around, waiting for the final wave; but a ship once more; a ship that had power and fight left in her. Although damaged beyond estimation, steam was gotten up, and we were once more fighting back, this time for our lives. The leaks from the sprung hatches were shored up, and a minimum of water was coming in. Soon everyone was engaged in bailing out the water that had shipped in from the too numerous openings.

When the first wave hit us and knocked us over, it took just about half the ship with it. It broke our port yard arm as easily as one would a toothpick. Water was taken down the stack (or thought so at the time) and all our life rafts except one which landed on the torpedo deck and all but one floater net went over. Our motor whale boat was ripped from its cradle and thrown madly to the pleasures of the wild sea. One of our lookouts was picked up from the starboard side of the bridge and thrown against the superstructure. He suffered only the shock and great amount of water which rushed over him. Our other look-out was not so fortunate. He was a boy of nineteen, well liked by all on board ship. The last anyone saw of him was when the wave was receding. He was thrown over the ship, along with the whale boat, and then disappeared into the raging infernal. Our first contact with any outside ship, was at about 1020 (1:20 a.m. on the morning of the 2nd) and the ship was sent out to search the area and to forward the message to other ships and aircraft. We had left a trail from the scene of the accident up to one day out of port. Wreckage, and life rafts, life rings, and our motor whale boat along with the floater-nets were lost in that vicinity, so if he wasn't killed from the force of the wave, he has a good chance of being found soon.

Work has been done to the ship, work that we could do with the equipment that was left. All the living compartments have been cleared up of all the oil and water, and except for the forward and after compartments where the fumes from the oil are too great, are being lived in once more. The gear and equipment has been examined and one of the earliest estimates of damage sustained was 600 thousand dollars. We still have to get a more accurate check, as they haven't had time for a thorough check, and the estimate was one of the roughest kind. It is believed that it will mount up to a million dollars when the final check is made.

Some of the more obvious losses and damages are: Port Yard Arm gone; no life lines or rails along the sides of the ship; all 20mm guns unlocked and swung helter skelter; the two 5 inch guns off centered or twisted; gun mounts on the torpedo deck tore up and twisted all out of shape; starboard 20mms midships and forward, disarranged; deck buckled in several places; three depth charges torn from their racks; and large rolls of line washed over; along with the incomparable other damages too numerous to mention. The interior is still in an inestimable status, all radar and radio communication wash out, and thousands of other pieces of equipment strewn about in various stages of ruin and rust.

The result of all this has yet to be decided upon, but I think that the question is answered, all too well, when someone asks if Destroyer Escorts are "Sea Worthy."

USS *WILLMARTH* (DE-638)

Kenneth Willmarth born on 13 February 1914 in Cleveland Township, Chippewa, Wis. Graduated from the State Teacher's College at Eau Claire, Wis., with a BS before he enlisted in the Naval Reserve at Minneapolis, Minn., on 17 June 1941. After receiving instruction as an apprentice seaman in *Prairie State*, the former battleship *Illinois* (BB-7), from 18 September to 9 October, Willmarth received an honorable discharge in 10 October to accept an appointment as midshipman in the Naval Reserve the following day. After training again in *Prairie State* (IX-15) and receiving a commission as ensign on 17 January 1942, Willmarth joined *Vincennes* (CA-44) while the cruiser lay alongside the east jetty, Navy Yard annex, South Boston, Mass., on 28 February 1942.

Initially a junior watch and division officer in the ship's "M" division, Ens. Willmarth served in *Vincennes* until the predawn darkness of 9 August 1942 in the Solomon Islands when an avalanche of steel unleased by Vice Admiral Gunichi Mikawa's cruiser force smothered *Vincennes, Astoria* (CA-34), and *Quincy* (CA-39) of the northern screening group in some 20 minutes time. Ens. Willmarth was among those killed in *Vincennes* as his ship took at least 57 known shell hits and possibly absorbed two torpedoes; the battered heavy cruiser sank within an hour of the start of the engagement.

(DE-638: dp. 1,400; 1. 306'; b. 37'; dr. 9'5" (mean); s. 23.5 k.; cpl. 205; a. 3 3", 4 1.1", 10 20 mm., 3 21" tt., 1 dcp. (hh.) 2 dct., 8 dcp.; cl. *Buckley*)

Willmarth (DE-638) was laid down on 25 June 1943 at San Francisco, Calif., by the Bethlehem Steel Company's Shipbuilding Division; launched on 21 November 1943; sponsored by Mrs. Eva Willmarth, the mother of Ens. Willmarth; and commissioned on 13 March 1944, Lt. Comdr. James G. Thorburn, Jr., USNR, in command.

Following shakedown out of San Diego and postshakedown availability to her builder's yard, *Willmarth* was assigned to Escort Division (CortDiv) 40. She stood out of San Francisco Bay on 31 May, as screen for the four-ship Convoy 2410 bound for Hawaii, and arrived at Pearl Harbor on 9 June.

On 12 June, together with *Donaldson* (DE-44) and *McCoy Reynolds* (DE-42), *Willmarth* screened the sortie of the Marshall Island-bound Convoy 4212-A. After delivering the convoy safely at Eniwetok nine days later, *Willmarth* proceeded on to the Treasury Islands, anchoring in Blanche Harbor at 1130 on the 26th.

Shifting successively to Tulagi and Purvis Bay, *Willmarth* operated on local escort and patrol missions in the Solomon and Treasury Island groups for the remainder of July. She escorted a small convoy to Dreger Harbor, New Guinea, between 1 and 5 August and then shifted to Milne Bay for repairs on her port propeller.

Underway for the Treasury Islands on 24 August, *Willmarth* made radar contact with an unidentified ship at 0200 on the 25th. *Willmarth* tracked the stranger and challenged her at 0335, when about two miles distant. The latter did not reply, but instead altered course away from the destroyer escort and increased speed. *Willmarth* in turn churned up 18 knots and went to general quarters at 0340.

Willmarth repeated the challenge at 0406 but again received no reply. On the port beam of her target, the escort vessel illuminated the stranger with her searchlight and discovered her to be a freighter of some 8,000 to 10,000 tons. Only 2,500 yards away, *Willmarth's* men could see the freighter's crew manning their guns to challenge the destroyer escort.

Willmarth opened the range to 4,000 yards as the freighter responded with two different call signs, perhaps seeking to confuse the escort vessel. Just as *Willmarth* began to flash a call for recognition signals, the freighter commenced fire with 3-inch guns. The destroyer escort rang down for 20 knots and opened the range to 8,000 yards, refraining from firing because of the stranger's appearance and location, "indicating that it was friendly." With respect to the freighter's fierce, but unfortunately ineffective—fire, *Willmarth's* war diarist noted charitably that the ship's "range was excellent, but deflection was off." No shells landed closer than 1,000 yards away.

Willmarth subsequently anchored at Blanche Harbor later on the 25th. Late the next day, she got underway on an escort assignment and convoyed *Stratford* (AP-41) to Green Island, Bougainville, arriving on the 29th to screen the transport as she unloaded. She eventually escorted the troopship to Emirau Island and Torokina, Bougainville, before proceeding independently to the Treasury Islands. She conducted training exercises over the balance of September before she performed local escort missions and the like out of her Treasury Islands's base into October.

Willmarth departed Blanche Harbor on 6 October in company with *Whitehurst* (DE-634), bound for Dutch New Guinea. She arrived three days later and sortied on the 12th with Task Unit (TU) 77.7.1 which included *Ashtabula* (AO-51), *Saranac* (AO-74), *Chepachet* (AO-78), *Salamonie* (AO-26), *Mazama* (AE-9), and merchant ship SS *Pueblo*. Other escorts were *Witter* (DE-636), *Bowers* (DE-637), and *Whitehurst*.

Willmarth operated with TU 77.7.1 until she was released late on the 13th to escort *Chepachet* and SS *Pueblo* to Kossol Passage, in the Palaus. Arriving there at 1821 on the 14th, she remained anchored for two days before beginning to patrol the harbor entrance on the 17th. Relieved of this duty by *Lovelace* (DE-198), *Willmarth* got underway the forenoon on 20 October to screen the sortie of *Ashtubula, Saranac, Chepachet, Salamonie, Mazama*, and SS *Durham Victory* for the Philippines.

Willmarth proceeded north with her convoy, while American troops splashed ashore on the beaches of Leyte to commence the liberation of the Philippines. On the 23d, three days after the main landing began, the destroyer escort anchored off Leyte midway between the northern and southern transport areas while her oilers refueled the ships from Task Group (TG) 77.2. That evening, *Willmarth* steamed eastward toward a night anchorage, and at 1825, observed antiaircraft fire over the northern transport area.

USS Willmarth (DE-638)

Underway again off Homonhon Island early the next morning, the destroyer escort received a report of enemy aircraft orbiting over the northern transport area. As she steamed along the convoy's flank, she commenced making black smoke at 0844 to lay a protective screen in anticipation of the enemy's arrival. While the radio crackled with reports of ships under attack, *Willmarth* spotted no enemy planes nearby, only many puffs of "flak" splattering the skies to the westward of her screening position in the refueling group.

With the receipt of "flash white" at 1343, the oilers resumed refueling TG 77.2. *Willmarth* shifted to Samar Island shortly before 1700 before going to general quarters at 1706 upon receipt of a "flash red." After waiting for well over an hour for the enemy to make an appearance, the convoy stopped and prepared to anchor for the night.

At 1843, however, three "Jills" roared in low from the east, torpedoes slung menacingly beneath their bellies. *Willmarth's* guns opened fire on two just before they released their "fish." One torpedo holed *Ashtabula* and forced her to halt, dead in the water. While the oiler's repair parties controlled the flooding and patched the hole, the convoy passed out of Leyte Gulf and reformed in the wake of the attack. Eventually, *Ashtabula,* repairs effected, rejoined at 2230.

Willmarth and the convoy remained underway throughout the evening, maneuvering on various courses and speeds in Leyte Gulf until the first rays of sunlight streaked the eastern skies. After going to general quarters at 0458, the destroyer escort remained at battle stations throughout the day. Less than an hour after her crew first closed up at action stations, two "Jills" attacked the convoy from the westward. *Willmarth* immediately opened fire with her 3-inch and 1.1-inch batteries. As one "Jill" roared across the stern of the convoy, it was caught by gunfire from *Willmarth* and other ships of the convoy and crashed in flames far astern.

While maneuvering and making smoke to mask the convoy, the destroyer escort spotted a floating mine which she sank with gunfire. Soon thereafter, another "Jill" passed through the area and drew fire from *Willmarth.* Unfortunately, the shells were not observed to hit; and the plane escaped.

The convoy anchored in the fueling area at 1152, three hours after the last attack. *Willmarth* and the other escorts screened the convoy and provided an anti-submarine screen patrol around the valuable auxiliaries. Later that afternoon, *Willmarth* repulsed an attack made by a lone plane which came out of the sun in a glide-bombing attack at 1420. The destroyer escort's gunfire damaged the plane and caused it to spin into the water about five miles away.

The convoy departed the fueling area at 1646. Frequent alerts and enemy planes enlivened the evening hours as the group maneuvered throughout the night in a retirement formation. *Willmarth's* war diarist noted that the Japanese planes seemed loathe to attack ships in the fueling area during day light, probably because of the heavy concentration of anti-aircraft fire that could be directed at an attacker.

The next day, 26 October, saw a repetition of the same routine that had kept the destroyer escort active since her arrival in Leyte Gulf three days earlier. After maneuvering on screening duties through the night, the warship spotted a lone "Val" dive bomber making an attack at 0550; *Willmarth* opened fire from 6,000 and her sister escorts were laying smoke screens to cover the convoy for the next hour. Thereafter, they provided anti-submarine screening protection while the oilers conducted fueling operations.

After following the same routine on the 27th, *Willmarth* departed Leyte Gulf and headed for the Palaus. At 0800 on 28 October, *Willmarth*-escorting the oilers earmarked to refuel the 7th Fleet ships, rendezvoused with the carriers of Task Group 77.4 and screened the refueling operations for the balance of the day. Detached that afternoon, *Willmarth* screened *Ashtabula* and *Chepachet* as they voyaged to Kossol Roads, in the Palaus. Arriving on 31 October, *Willmarth* refueled from *Mascoma* (AO-83) and anchored, her job done.

The respite afforded the destroyer escort was a brief one, however, for she got underway on 1 November for Hollandia and Seeadler Harbor, escorting a convoy. Entering Humboldt Bay on the 4th, *Willmarth* anchored there over the next two days before proceeding to sea to screen the sortie of TG 78.4—HMS *Ariadna*, 12 LSM's, 4 LCI's, 8 LCI (G)'s, PC-1122 and PC-1133—on the 7th.

For the next three days, *Willmarth* screened the convoy to its destination—Mapia and Asia Islands, near Morotai—before arriving in the invasion area on the 11th. As the convoy passed Morotai, *Willmarth's* lookouts observed antiaircraft fire between 0415 and 0530. Two "bogies" passed within four miles of the convoy; but, as *Willmarth's* war diarist recorded, "evidently they either did not sight us or were not interested, as they proceeded directly toward the area from which flak appeared." There was a reason why *Willmarth* did not open fire on the two planes that seemed so close—she carried only the reliable air-warning radar in the entire convoy and to open fire prematurely would have disclosed the

position of the little convoy and exposed it to possible air attacks. At 0832, the destroyer escort anchored just off the southern coast of Morotai, near *Ariadne,* while the remainder of the convoy (save the LCMs) proceeded to another part of the island to load for the impending invasion of Mapia and Asia Islands. The mission of the assault group was to establish weather station and LORAN—long range radio aid to navigation facilities.

On 13 November, with the assault ships having embarked their troops, *Willmarth* got underway in company with TG 78.14, bound for Pegun Island. At 0500, two days later—she was joined by *Shaw* (DD-373) and *Caldwell* (DD-605). *Willmarth,* the two destroyers , *PC-1122* bombarded the southern part of the island prior to the landings and provoked no return fire from the beach. After a half-hour of firing, HMS *Ariadne* signalled that "H" hour was 0630, meaning that the first wave of LVT (A)s would hit the reef at that time.

Willmarth remained at her bombardment station for the rest of the morning, ceasing fire as the first assault wave splashed toward the beachhead. The accompanying LCI (G)s laid their own barrage, thus obviating the need for the destroyer's gunfire. By noon, the island was in American hands. When surrounded, the remaining garrison—only 12 to 14 Japanese soldiers—committed suicide.

Meanwhile, since she was not needed for bombardment, *Willmarth* patrolled to the northward of the invasion beach and came across canoes full of natives to the north. One native, speaking good English, told *Willmarth* that the remainder of the Japanese garrison, about 170 men, had waded across the reef to Bras Island the previous night—thus accounting for the sparse reception given the invasion forces.

While planes were being laid to go after this remnant on Bras Island, *Willmarth* conducted anti-submarine patrol around the unloading assault craft and made abortive attempts to pull several LCIs that had been stranded by low tides off the reefs. At 1730 on the 15th, the destroyer escort succeeded in towing one off after about an hour's time and began operations to free another one of the infantry assault craft. However, the destroyer escort's efforts were frustrated by the line's parting and the near approach of darkness.

Four LCI (G)s had to be left on the reef—as was one LCI—when the task group headed for Morotai. Arriving on 17 November, *Willmarth* fueled from *Salamonie* before anchoring. Underway again on the 18th, with the Asia Island occupation force, *Willmarth* and two PCs served as escort for *Ariadne*, four LCMs, four LCIs and four LCI (G)s. Embarked in the assault craft were 400 troops.

Three-fourths of a mile off Igi Island, *Willmarth, Ariadne,* and *PC-1122* conducted shore bombardment from 0542 to 0619 on the 19th. Troops splashed ashore from landing craft eight minutes after the bombardment ceased and met no opposition. An unfortunate result of the shore bombardment was that two natives were wounded and one killed—the Japanese had evacuated the island in the face of imminent invasion of the previous evening.

Willmarth subsequently screened the movement of the convoy to the Mapia Islands, where the landing craft loaded troops and unloaded shore personnel and supplies. When the loading was completed at 1800 on the 20th, the convoy shifted to Asia Island, where the destroyer escort screened the landing craft as they embarked more troops on the 21st. *Willmarth* continued her screening duties until arriving in the southern anchorage near the naval base at Morotai Island at 1238 on 22 November. While there, the escort vessel witnessed an enemy night air raid on the airfield installations on Morotai. The Japanese boldly conducted their attack despite antiaircraft fire and searchlights. Local port restrictions forbade the use of any antiaircraft batteries larger than 40 millimeter! *Willmarth's* war diary sadly noted this restriction, recommending that 3-inch gunfire could do very little damage to shore installations in the area.

While the rest of TG 78.14 departed Morotai on the 23d, *Willmarth* remained behind as LSM-205 and LSM-314 loaded equipment for the Asia and Mapia Island forces. She then escorted those craft to Hollandia where they delivered their cargo. Over the next three days, *Willmarth* escorted the two landing craft on their appointed rounds, dropping off supplies at Asia and Mapia Islands. At one point, the arrival of the little convoy at Mapia on the 26th almost went unnoticed.

Willmarth experienced great difficulty contacting anyone on shore: "We finally succeeded in rousing someone by blowing our siren and whistle together." A jeep soon appeared on the beach, its occupants using the headlights to signal. Heavier swells than at Asia Island made unloading through the surf difficult. One of the LSMs was holed several times by scraping on the jagged coral heads of the reef. When unloading was completed at 1130, the diminutive convoy headed for Hollandia.

On 1 December 1944, *Willmarth* and the other ships from CortDiv 40 set sail for Manus, in the Admiralties, for assignment to Service Squadron (ServRon) 4. Arrived at Seeadler Harbor the following day, *Willmarth* spent the next three months operating on local escort missions between Manus, Ulithi, Hollandia, and the Palaus.

On 4 March 1945, *Willmarth* reported to the Commander, 5th Fleet, for duty. Between the 5th and 18th, she conducted antisubmarine patrols in the Palaus before being sent to Ulithi to refuel and replenish. She got underway again on the 21st to screen the sortie of TF 54—the pre-invasion bombardment group—as it got underway for Okinawa.

Assigned to screen TF 54, *Willmarth* operated with Fire Support Unit 2 (TU 54.1.2) built around *Colorado* (BB-45), in Fire Support (FS) areas 4 and 5, off Okinawa. The destroyer escort screened *Colorado* for the entire day on 26 March as the battleship delivered gunfire support for the troops ashore. Over the next two days, the warship screened fire support units and escorted them to night retirement areas. She was refuelled at Kerama Retto on the 30th before returning to screening duties with heavy units off the island.

On 1 April, she was steaming on station 16 of a circular screen around TU 54.3.2, a night retirement group built around *Idaho* (BB-42), when several enemy planes flew near the convoy. Screening destroyers fired upon the intruders who probably did not come to attack the Allied force but merely to keep it awake and permit it little rest.

Detached from this duty to provide a screen for *Arkansas* (BB-33), one of the oldest battleships on active service in the Navy, *Willmarth* operated to seaward as the battleship worked inshore to open fire on Japanese positions holding up the American advance near Naha airport. After commencing this duty at 0630, *Willmarth* had been serving on antisubmarine patrol for over six hours when Japanese shore battery guns boomed out salvoes at *Arkansas*.

Arkansas' main battery, trained round to reply and quickly commenced counterbattery fire. At the time of the initial firing. *Willmarth* was located about one mile southwestward of the battleship, maintaining her screening position to seaward. At 1323, a Japanese shell hurtled over *Willmarth's* bridge "plainly heard" by all men there. It splashed beyond the ship, 150 yards away. With only one boiler operating (the other had been secured to repair a leaking gasket) the destroyer escort was hampered in getting away, but she headed seaward at her best speed. Soon another shell landed only 15 yards beyond the destroyer escort's starboard and quarter. While increasing the range, *Willmarth* turned toward each splash, thus avoiding getting hit by the Japanese guns. *Arkansas,* by this time beyond gun range of the Nipponese guns, did not conduct any further counterbattery fire; *Willmarth* soon emerged from the enemy battery's zone of fire and proceeded to sea unscathed.

After retiring to Kerama Retto soon thereafter for fueling, *Willmarth* operated on screening station A-27 until 6 April, when she returned for Kerama Retto with an appendicitis patient on board for medical treatment. Several bogies flew near the ship while she steamed to the fleet anchorage, and one was drowned by a nearby ship at 0200.

At 1525, while still three miles north of Kerama Retto, *Willmarth* spotted three "Val" dive bombers. One peeled off and maneuvered to make an attack. Ten minutes later, it attempted to crash into the ship. Bracketed by flak, the "Val" bore in, apparently intent on crashing into the destroyer escort. Heavy 3-inch and 1.1-inch fire bracketed the plane when she became visible, dodging in and out of the broken clouds overhead. Seven 3-inch bursts rocked the plane as she made her deadly approach. Lookouts on the destroyer escort noted a thin line of smoke tracking from the suicider's port wing as he went into his dive. The 20-millimeter battery on *Willmarth* opened fire when the plane's range lessened to 2,000 yards; and, at 800 yards, the Oerlikons seemed to have their effect. Pieces of the "Val's" wing began flying off in the slipstream, indicating that the shells were beginning to hit. Six feet of the port wing soon broke away, shot off by the flak, and the "Val" spun into the sea 20 yards off the ship's port side, slightly abaft her beam.

Willmarth entered Kerama Retto at 1610; and, while preparing to anchor, saw LST-447 hit by a suicide plane south of the harbor entrance. Flames had engulfed the entire amidships section of the stricken landing ship, and explosions tore holes in the stricken ship's side. The jagged edges in turn ripped gashes in *Willmarth's* hull at the waterline. One hole, unfortunately opened up one of the destroyer escort's fuel tanks and the oil leaking out made further close operations hazardous.

Willmarth stood clear while dense smoke from the burning LST further complicated firefighting. Eventually, the destroyer escort picked up the ship's survivors and later transferred them to *Crescent City* (APA-21). While steaming to the ship's anchorage in the harbor, she took an enemy plane under fire as it approached from the south; and multiple gunfire from all ships present in the harbor knocked it down.

Willmarth anchored, transferred her appendicitis patient ashore, and patched the hole in her side caused by the damaged *LST-447* before proceeding on the 7th to screening station "Able-60" near the transport area off the west coast of Okinawa. Following her shift to another screening station on the morning of the 8th, *Willmarth* escorted *Saranac* (AO-74) to Kerama Retto on the 9th. On 10 April, the destroyer escort departed the Okinawa area, bound for Guam in the screen for 12 transports.

Arriving at Guam on the 14th, *Willmarth* developed boiler trouble while there and spent the entire month of May and most of June undergoing repairs. On 28 June, the destroyer escort got underway for Ulithi. En route, she picked up a sonar contact, and in company with *Trippe* (DD-403), over the ensuing two days, conducted an unsuccessful hunt. *Willmarth* then proceeded on to Ulithi where she arrived on the last day of June.

Underway again on 3 July, *Willmarth* stood out of the Ulithi lagoon screening the logistics force of the 3d Fleet which would provide the needed supplies for Admiral William F. Halsey's fast carrier task forces as it pounded the Japanese Homeland. During the passage north, the destroyer escort plane guarded for *Steamer Bay* (CVE-87) and conducted anti-submarine screening operations. She picked up the crew of a downed TBF Avenger on 20 July. On that occasion, two swimmers from *Willmarth* helped to get the downed airmen on board. However, one of the crewmen died. The two survivors and the body of the dead man were transferred to *Steamer Bay* later that day.

Willmarth subsequently planeguarded for *Gilbert Island* (CVE-107) in early August, continuing her screening and escort duties with TG-30, the replenishment group for the 3rd Fleet. She was at sea when the atomic bombs were dropped upon Hiroshima and Nagasaki on 6 and 9 August, respectively, and when Japan surrendered on the 15th.

Willmarth remained on escort duty off the coast of Japan in September. In mid-September, the ship underwent an availability in Tokyo Bay and rode out a storm there on 18 September. Departing Tokyo By on 24 September to return to the United States. *Willmarth* touched at Pearl Harbor, San Diego, and the Panama Canal before undergoing an overhaul at Norfolk which lasted until late in October.

Shifting to the St. John's River, Fla., soon thereafter, *Willmarth* prepared for inactivation with the Florida group of the 16th (Reserve) Fleet. Berthed in the Green Cove Springs facility, *Willmarth* was decommissioned on 26 April 1946 and placed in reserve. She remained there until struck from the Navy list on 1 December 1966. Sold on 1 July 1968 to the North American Smelting Co., of Wilmington, Del., the ship was broken up for scrap soon thereafter.

Willmarth received four Battle Stars for her participation in World War II.

USS *LERAY WILSON* (DE-414)
Submitted by George J. Chaisson

The "Lucky Leray" she was nicknamed, perhaps in a moment when some member of her crew wanted to play the sardonic soothsayer. Actually, most men who have served aboard her during the last and most intense year of the Pacific War considers themselves fortunate in retrospect.

The *LeRay Wilson* was present with an escort carrier unit at the Battle of Samar Island and escaped gunfire from enemy cruisers and battleships 14 odd miles away only because of the presence and partial sacrifice of another small unit of CVE's, DD's, and DE's immediately to northward.

Later, in the invasion of Lingayen Gulf Luzon, the *Leray Wilson* helped escort a large group troop of transports safely through a gauntlet of attacking Japanese planes. While on screening duty inside the gulf after landing day, the *Wilson* was hit by an enemy bomber, but although her torpedo tubes were sliced off at the end and a spectacular gasoline fire was started on the superstructure deck, the torpedoes did not explode and the fire was quickly extinguished before damage could be done to any enclosed compartment.

Back in action in time to take part in the invasion of Okinawa, the *Leray Wilson* did patrol duty protecting the invasion fleet around that island, not only on D-Day but also later for a period of 50 consecutive days, during which the American ships were subject to airplane attacks more frequently and more violently desperate than at any other time in the whole war. Of the more than 400 enemy "raids" taking place in that time, several came within attacking distance of the *Leray Wilson,* but the ship was not hit, and her crew had the satisfaction of seeing a number of Japanese planes blow up in midair. One enemy fighter making a surprise low attack over the crowded Hagushi Beach anchorage had a wing disintegrated by gunfire from the *Wilson,* and fell into the water some 1500 yards away.

The ship was placed in commission the afternoon of May 10, 1944 at the Tennessee Coal and Iron Company dock, Houston, Texas. One of the new 5-inch gun turret type of DE, propelled by two 6,000 horsepower steam turbines, the *Leray Wilson* was built at an approximate cost of $3,000,000 by the Brown Ship Building Company of Houston, Texas.

She was named after a Metalsmith Second Class, USN, who was killed in action during a surprise Japanese bombing attack at Darwin, Australia, on February 19, 1942. Despite the rapidity with which the attack developed and the very obvious danger of being trapped by an explosion, Wilson, a member of the after repair party of an American warship, went immediately below decks and had just completed closing all doors and hatches when a bomb hitting the ship within a few feet of him caused his death. Because of his courage and efficiency in the performance of his hazardous task, the flooding of the ship following the explosion was confined to two compartments. Wilson was posthumously awarded the Silver Star.

The new ship's Commanding Officer was Lieutenant Commander Matthew V. Carson. The Executive Officer was Lieutenant Felix L. Englander, USN, a member of the Annapolis Class of 1940 and a former anti-aircraft control officer on the USS *Philadelphia*. Four of the eight other officers and more than two-thirds of the crew of 184 men had never been to sea.

After a readiness for sea period at Galveston, Texas, the ship set sail for shakedown training at Bermuda on May 28, 1944, with two other new DEs. She arrived on June 3, and began four weeks of what many of her crew consider their most intensive period of activity, trying out all the new equipment, taking kinks out of the personnel organization and getting used to their jobs and life at sea.

On July 2 the *Leray Wilson* left Bermuda and two days later was in Charlestown, Massachusetts, Navy Yard, where a number of alterations were made and the ship's battle information center and plotting room modernized.

The ship arrived at the Panama Canal Zone on July 25. From there she went to San Diego, and, after a pause, to Pearl Harbor, which she entered on August 19. There she took part in further training exercises in preparation of action against submarines, planes, and surface targets.

On September 22, she was in Eniwetok, Marshall Islands. And on October 1, she was ordered to proceed to Seeadler Harbor, Manus, Admiralty Islands, where she was to stage for the invasion of Leyte, the largest undertaking of its kind in the Pacific was up to that time.

The *Wilson's* officers and men, not knowing what was in store for them, and many never having heard of Manus before, were amazed at the mass of ships they saw upon entering Seeadler Harbor. The large anchorage contained virtually the entire 7th Fleet, consisting of most of the old battleships that had been "sunk" at Pearl Harbor, several cruisers, 13 escort carriers, and all the transports, cargo ships, minesweepers, destroyers, destroyer escorts, landing craft, and supporting ships necessary for a tremendous landing operation. The *Leray Wilson* had to thread its way through the ships to the berth assigned it like a man hunting a partner on a crowded dance floor.

On October 12, Task Force 77, the striking power of the 7th fleet, got underway for the objective. Among the approximately 65 ships in the formation was the *Leray Wilson*, which with a unit of CVEs later separated from the cruisers and battleships. The ship encountered her worst storm on the 17th of October, when a typhoon harried severely the invasion fleet.

It was at 0725 on October 25, an overcast day, when the ship's tactical voice radio brought forth the astounding news that large enemy warships were sighted only 15 miles away. The three destroyers in the *Wilson's* task unit placed themselves in a protecting line between the vulnerable escort carriers and the enemy force, while the *Wilson* and four other DEs formed and anti-submarine screen on the other side of the carriers, which were launching planes as fast as they could and at the same time making maximum speed to get away from the faster Japanese ships.

At 0848 the enemy commenced firing, and 50 minutes later, several

splashes from their shells were seen near the three screening destroyers, which had been making a show of return fire at extreme range. But the Japanese were prevented from closing by constant attacks from our planes and by accurate fire from another group of CVEs, DDs and DEs which were taking the brunt of the enemy's onslaught. A sister ship of the *Leray Wilson*, the *Samuel B. Roberts*, was one of three American ships of this nearby task unit sunk after having successfully made a heroic torpedo attack against the vastly more powerful Japanese battleship and cruiser force. But the Japanese decided to turn back, and in so doing lost for all time the initiative in the Pacific naval war.

About two hours after the battle had begun, an American torpedo bomber, which had been hit by enemy gunfire crashed off the *Leray Wilson's* starboard bow. Its three-man crew was rescued by the *Wilson*.

The carriers with which the *Leray Wilson* was operating provided local air support over Leyte for about two weeks and on November 3 were back in Manus. Later that month the *Leray Wilson* was with them again in the Philippine Sea, protecting shipping lanes from possible enemy air and submarine attacks.

On December 10 the *Leray Wilson* left Manus for the third time and proceeded to Cape Torokina, Bougainville, Solomon Islands, where transports and landing craft of the 7th Fleet were taking aboard troops for the coming invasion of Luzon. The *Leray Wilson* helped escort these back to Manus and in early January went with them to Lingayen Gulf.

At 0710 on Jan. 10, 1945, while the *Wilson* was patrolling an anti-submarine sector inside Lingayen Gulf, an enemy twin-engine bomber identified as a Nell was seen approaching from seaward. It had made a dive from a covering cloud close by and was only about 1,000 yards away and 25 feet above the water when the ships commenced firing with its port 20 mm and forward 40 mm guns. Many hits were observed and the aircraft took fire, flames coming from the port engine and wing. But it could not be stopped and struck the ship's superstructure deck amidships. The fuselage did a somersault and crashed into the water about 100 feet on the other side. Fire that broke out on the ship was extinguished in less than eight minutes as repair parties speedily brought hoses to bear from fire plugs forward and aft. Eleven men of the crew were lost in action. Another, carried over the side by the concussion, was rescued with comparatively minor injuries by a DE standing by to assist.

The *Leray Wilson* left the gulf that night and proceeded as an escort for a convoy returning to Leyte. She was back in Manus on January 23 for repairs and availability.

On March 5, the *Wilson* arrived in Saipan, Marianas Islands, to prepare for the invasion of Okinawa. She helped escort one of the amphibious groups which arrived at Okinawa on D-day. She was again in the Ryukyus on May 1 after a trip to Saipan and back. Her former Executive Officer, Lieutenant Commander Englander, was now in command. This time the *Leray Wilson* remained in he waters around Okinawa as part of an anti-submarine and anti-aircraft screen until June 19, while the Japanese air forces did its utmost to destroy our invasion shipping. The *Wilson's* men became all to accustomed to being aroused at midnight for general quarters.

The ship on the 19th proceeded with a merchant convoy to Ulithi Atoll, Caroline Islands. There she was assigned to a fueling and replenishment group for the fast carrier task groups, now putting finishing touches on the destruction of the Japanese military machine. For most of the next two months of the *Leray Wilson* was steaming in waters east of Honshu, protecting the oilers and provision ships which were making possible the Third Fleet's continuous operations against Japan.

Finally the war was won. And for the *Leray Wilson*, after steaming more than 80,000 miles, it was trail's end when on September 4, almost surrounded by some of the world's mightiest battleships and cruisers which had preceded the Allied occupation forces, she lay at anchor in Tokyo Bay.

The USS Borum (DE-790).

SEA STORIES

"TRIM BUT DEADLY"
VOLUME III

TYPHOON: THE ORDEAL OF A SHIP

*A first-hand account of a battle against an
implacable enemy.*
Submitted by N.W. Tashman, Jr., BM 1/C USNR

Somewhere in this country walk our saviours. They are the creators of our hull, a hull whose perfect construction defied destruction by a force more formidable than any mortal enemy - a raging sea that slugged, hammered and lashed at our ship for thirty-eight hours, and howling angry solid sheets of wind that tried to tear us apart.

What man builds, man can destroy. That power is in the hands of the enemy. But power to resist and to protect is built into our ships - tough steel to withstand gunfire, good engines, the finest equipment for detecting the enemy, "metal tested" and proved guns. Add to these, cool, calculating officers and a well-trained crew.

Our men had shown fearlessness in action against the enemy, against magazine fires, burning oil, and torpedo attacks. But against this new enemy they admitted fear. All were on edge, some were numb, others prayed. They came through and for this they give full thanks to the men who built our ship. Had these men put the hull together carelessly, had they not thought of the tests the ship would meet, all the fight and strategy put up by skipper and engineers, and all the prayers of the crew would have been in vain. That we know. And for that we will be ever grateful to the ununiformed, undecorated and often unfairly belittled shipyard workers. Other ships foundered and sank. Of three, with hundreds of men aboard, only ninety-six survived. Certainly they fought and prayed as we did. Perhaps somebody let them down.

After the captain's inspection of personnel topside in perfect weather one Saturday morning, we relaxed. Those who rested were lucky for that was the last rest for the next forty-eight hours. Sunday morning the sea was choppy. Nothing was thought of that. We had ridden the outer edge of a typhoon last trip out. We'd rolled 52 degrees and it would take something more to cause comment.

Up to about 11 A.M. ships in our task force refueled. It took good seamanship to perform in the heavy sea. About noon all further refueling operations were cancelled. By 1400 (2 P.M.) scout planes returning to flat tops were having a tough time landing. Two planes still aloft at 1500 (3 P.M.) were flagged off — impossible to land on the rolling, pitching deck of the aircraft carrier.

The pilots, asking for instructions, got this, as heard on our own TBS (talk between ships):

"Turn your plane loose and bail out. Destroyer will be standing by to pick you up."

Back came the word from one of the pilots, "Repeat!"

The order was repeated word for word and the pilot was heard to say, "That's what I thought you said the first time."

They bailed out as ordered and were picked up shortly after "hitting the silk" and landing in the frothy sea.

Then ships by units were formed up, to ride out what was figured to be just another slight interruption in the progress of the campaign against the enemy. The barometer continued to fall. The sea continued to fall. The sea continued to rise and the wind to gain in intensity. Now reports began to come in: "Man over board. Keep a sharp lookout."

The first such report, struck a fearful note. It also created a great respect for the sea and invited extra precautions.

Visibility was zero — that means you couldn't see fifty yards. Blasts from whistles were practically useless. The wind prevented the whistles carrying any place but to leeward.

The barometer was down to 28.15 (29.90 is normal). Men below in the engine room were just about walking on the bulkheads as the ship heeled over from 45 degrees to the high of 67 degrees. Men on watch topside anxiously asked whether we were taking any water through the seams, each time we'd fall off the top of a forty-foot wave and hit the bottom with a resounding woomph that seemed to shake every inch of the hull from stem to stern. Reports were heartening. The only water below decks was coming in through ventilators.

Some men on off-watch sections remained in the gun shields. They seemed to feel that watching the sea they'd be able to know what was coming or at least be the first to know. Others were frightened and worried. They lay below in their sacks, lashing themselves in so as not to be thrown out. The more they saw of the typhoon, the more fearful they were we wouldn't pull through. Men who had never been seasick were feeling badly. Chow was out of the question.

For hours we had proceeded unharmed through the storm. Now our life lines and stanchions were being knocked down — some carried away. Number 3 life raft was gone. Number 1 gun shield, bearing the brunt of each thwack of solid sea that covered our fo'c'sle, was the worse for wear. The motor whaleboat was beginning to strain at her gripes as wind and sea took alternate turns at her.

A depth charge broke loose on the fantail. Our charges had been set on safe - no fear of it going off, but 300 pounds of TNT rolling around on the loose was dangerous. A few men detailed to it soon had the charge secured. It was not so easy. The fantail was under water and the men had to work with safety lines.

The sea at last dealt a Sunday punch to the motor whaleboat. It followed through, again and again, methodically, just seeming to take time enough to draw back and put everything behind it.

And each time the wind seemed to say, "You can't do it by yourself, let's work together." And the sea didn't even take time to answer until it forced the gripes to part and dropped the boat between the davit and the deck housing.

That done, the sea started back on the stubborn gun shield, attacking with confidence. Smack, thwack, crack, whoomph! The center shield was stove in six inches. Another hour of pounding and one of the braces that held the shield to the deck held no more. And as it gave way, it peeled up the deck with her like the cover on a tin of sardines.

Water filled the passageways below. A pillow-flat board and 5x5 shoring were placed below the gap to strengthen the deck and bulkheading surrounding the gash. We still shipped water and the water-tight doors were secured for safety.

Out on gun No. 2 the war cruising watch was still trying to stand, keeping an eye out for men who might be washed over the side.

Our skipper had the wheel now and there he stayed for the next five hours. Orders had come through from SOPAC, "Every man for himself." A rendezvous was designated and from then until we

passed two seagoing tugs laboring along forty-eight hours later, we saw no ships.

Wind was rushing along at a steady blow of eighty knots and gusts reached 115 knots. Floater nets with the help of the sea were picked up out of their racks and draped over men and guns as if they were silk fish nets, and considering the fact that they were made of two and a half inch line and carried some fifty pounds of rations and gear to be used in case of abandon ship, the gun crew breathed easy when they checked and found no one hurt.

Then one of her loaded magazines jumped her rack. A gunner's mate and a boatswain's mate juggled it as the ship lurched and bounced crazily.

The gunner was scared. The boatswain's mate was not so well versed in the ingredients he was juggling. Jokingly he remarked to the gunner, "Hang on, Ain't you got not guts?" Meekly but fast came the answer, "I got guts, but I don't want to see 'em."

"Boats' scurried up a scuttle after getting the loose magazine back in its rack and returned with some line cut off a life ring. Records were made in knot tying as the men turned to secure the ammunition. That done they returned to their gun station as happily as if they were entering a cafe.

Injuries were slight among the men on watch, though the quartermaster was thrown across the wheelhouse and his back cut wide open. How he made it to sick bay or how "Pills" ever was able to work on him no one was able to figure out. One and a half hours later he had eighteen stitches in his back.

It seemed as if the storm would never blow over. At 1400 (2 P.M.) of the second day, all topside watches were secured. Men hung together in groups down below awaiting word to man their stations. No one believed the enemy would be around to call in that weather. Yet this was a Navy ship. She must be ready to fight, even in a typhoon. Old salts were asked their opinion over and over again. Most of them had confidence in the ship. A few said they had seen worse. Assuringly they said we were in no danger. "The ol' pig iron bastard will ride it out O.K."

About 1600 (4 P.M.) of the second day the captain reported that the barometer had hit low and was beginning to rise slightly. He said the worst was over, but when he said it would be at least another twenty-four hours before we could look for any rest from the beating, the men actually groaned. They were glad to know the worst was over, but they still feared that what they had taken was all she could take and that another 24 hours would sound her death knell.

By 0400 (4 A.M.) of the third day, we were back on the watch. By noon there was sun. The sea was still running high. The wind was fresh and moderate. We were alone. Nothing was in sight but sky and water. We headed for our rendezvous.

After hours of steaming we were still alone. Our TBS was out. Our sound was out. Our radar was out and our radio couldn't transmit. Soon "Sparks was reporting what little he could pick up. A station was calling us, "Report your position."

We couldn't. We heard them call the three ill-fated ships. No answer. Hours later reports were heard to task force commanders, "Four ships unheard from." We were one of them.

The sea was just about normal now. Outside of the visible damage aboard ship, life was beginning to take on some of the old routines.

One thing began to concern most everyone — the injured man was running a high fever. The sulfa shot into his veins and sprinkled in the wound had not prevented infection and Doc advised transfer to a ship with better medical facilities. Hour after hour we searched our horizons.

A plane came out of nowhere, blinked his challenge at us. We blinked back and he proceeded on his way before we could say any more.

Sparks finally got radio going. We reported to the rendezvous. A new one had been ordered. We headed that way and it was good to sea ships again. Christmas was just ahead. It would be a Merry Christmas after all.

We were ordered to return to port for repairs. We transferred our quartermaster to a flat top that had all the facilities of the modern hospital. We were sorry to see him leave us as he was placed in the stretcher and trollied between ships. He was a good shipmate and he even did us a good turn as he left. That flat top sent back 300 pounds of turkey for our Christmas dinner!

Nobody said anything, but the crew would gladly have eaten beans that Christmas Day. They had enough to be thankful for.

EULOGY TO A DE

Submitted by: George L. Clark

As we live and die, so do our ships. Christening and commissionings are the gentle highlights of a ship's history- and what greater glory than to be victorious over the enemy at sea. Most DEs did not experience the glory attained by the USS *Samuel B. Roberts* (DE-413), the USS *England* (DE-635) and certain others; there were those that were sunk or extensively damaged after valiant battle; and there were those that performed seemingly routine duty in perilous seas keeping the supply lines open. Most Destroyer Escorts survived World War II; some to serve in the Naval Reserve; some to be recommissioned to participate in the sea war off Korea or to patrol the South China Seas off Vietnam in the sixties; some to be sold to foreign governments; some to be scrapped for whatever their metal value might be and some to be used for test purposes. Rare, indeed, is the sight of a combatant vessel selected to remain a timeless memorial (at this writing, the USS *Stewart* (DE-238) is the only DE to be so honored). In time all ships become obsolete and wait to be cast aside, indifferently, by memo, signed or initialed by some higher authority in the naval hierarchy.

On May 5, 1969, a message from the Chief of Naval Operations to the Chief of Navy Material authorized the CNM to make available the ex-USS *Alvin C. Cockrell* (DE-366) for venerability tests which were to be performed by the Naval Weapons Center (NAVWPSNCEN), China Lake, California. At that time the *Cockrell* was berthed at the Inactive Ship Maintenance Facility, Mare Island Naval Shipyard, Vallejo, California. Here, according to the NAVWPSCEN/*Cockrell* file, "the dehumidification equipment was removed and limited stripping of items requested by Fleet units was accomplished. Fuel tanks had been emptied, and combustibles were removed in preparation for the tests. The 5"/38 caliber guns and handling equipment were left on the target by special request". The *Cockrell* was then towed to southern California waters. Again, the NAVYWPSNCEN/COCKRELL file: "The Naval Weapons Center is engaged in a series of warhead effectiveness tests in steel ships. The general purpose is to screen candidate warheads for the Harpoon missile and to study the effectiveness of warhead

Damage to the after-bow section as viewed from the port side. Note that the Chiefs' Quarters and the forward mess deck are obliterated. (USN Photo, Courtesy of Leroy Doig, III, Command Historian, Naval Weapons Center, China Lake, CA.)

Damage to the bow section as viewed from the starboard side. Here, the 5-inch turret has remained intact. Also note that the ships' number has been painted out. (USN Photograph, Courtesy of Leroy Doig III, Command Historian, Naval Weapons Center, China Lake, CA)

Damage to the stern of the ship as viewed from the starboard side. It appears that the after 5-inch gun turret has been blown over the side. (USN Photo, Courtesy of Leroy Doig, III, Command Historian, Naval Weapons Center, China Lake, CA.)

mechanisms and tradeoffs of explosive weight in the context of ship vulnerability.

One series has taken place in DEs and DDs during exercises at sea off both the Atlantic and Pacific coasts. The ex-*Cockrell* is the fourth in a series to undergo testing in a mooring at Northwest Harbor of San Clemente Island (SCI). Experimental warheads were built in a blast-fragmenting design that represented the maximum available warhead weight for the proposed missile configuration. Two were detonated in the primary test locations in the ship and one over the deck. Warheads were placed in the centerline locations inside the ship to best contain the damage for assessment. All hatches, doors and scuttles in the area of detonation were dogged before each detonation, and damage control procedures were followed as necessary through the tests series. Upon completion of the tests at SCI, the target hull was towed to a designated sinking area where a Walleye warhead was detonated on the keel. The ship sank immediately. A subsequent message reveals that the remains of the *Cockrell* now rests in four hundred and thirty five fathoms of water some twenty five miles off the coast of Oceanside, California.

On September 20, 1969, a routine message originated by NAVWPNSCEN to the Chief of Naval Operations reads:

"Ex-*Alvin C. Cockrell* (DE-366) sunk as planned after utilization as test bed for project harpoon wart. *Hull* was sunk 190827 Tango at Lat 33-13N Long 117-45W."

Thus was documented the *Cockrell's* obituary on September 19, 1969, twenty-seven years less five days after the demise of First Lieutenant Alvin C. Cockrell, Jr., USMCR, who lost his life in action against Japanese forces on Guadalcanal on September 24, 1942 for which he was awarded the Navy Cross.

For a naval ship that served so well in wartime and in peacetime, and for the men who served aboard, this may seem an inglorious conclusion. Undoubtedly it had been written, "Better to go down in the service of your country than to be consigned to the cutter's torch." I like to believe this ship performed a noble service to our Navy in those sheltered waters off San Clemente Island and that her demolition furthered the study of naval force to the benefit of all Americans.

The foregoing was prepared by George L. Clark, QM3/c, USS *Alvin C. Cockrell* (DE-366) who served aboard the *Cockrell* during World War II and again aboard the *Cockrell* in Vietnam, 1961-1962, and who expresses his gratitude to Leroy Doig, III, Command Historian, Naval Weapons Center, China Lake, California, for researching his files and making available photographs and documents relative to the *Cockrell's* last moments.

TO THE BRAVE
By D. Cartmell

I.
Not a hint but a story bold
On this shell is proudly told
Of the men who died at sea
That our nation might be free

II.
To the enemy they gave fight
Fought until the black of night
The decks ran water and blood
Many fell but still we stood

III.
We won the battle and victory
And added a chapter to history
Say a prayer for these our men
Who helped bring peace again.

(3) LITTLE D.E.s PLUS (1) EQUALS (6) JAP SUBS SINK
By R.B. Hillyer

USS *George* (DE-697) Flagship Of Operations C.O.M.C.O.R.T Div. 39 & 40:
19 May 1944 - 31 May 1944
USS *George* DE-697, USS *Raby* DE-698, USS *England* DE-635, and USS *Spangler* DE-698.

USS *George* (DE-697) Thursday, 18 May 1944

OPERATIONAL AND ADMINISTRATIVE REMARKS ZONE DESCRIPTION -11
Beginning of Operations C.O.M.C.O.R.T. Div. 39 and 40.

1600-1800
Moored as before. 1653 Underway from fueling station; maneuvering on various courses and at various speeds clearing berth. 1659 Standing out of Port Purvis in company with USS *England* and USS *Raby*. SOPA is Commander Hamilton Hains, USN, in USS *George*. Ships formed in column with USS *George* as guide. Standard distance is 500 yards. 1714 Set course 265° T. & P.G.C., speed 16 knots.
H. R. Anderson,
Lieut., USNR

USS *George* (DE-697) Friday, 19 May, 1944

0000-0400
Steaming in company with USS *Raby* (DE-698) and USS *England* (DE-635) en route from Purvis Bay on course 336° T. & P.G.C., 334° P.S.C., at speed of 16 knots. Ships are in column, USS *George* (DE-697) as guide, USS *England* in No. 2 position, USS *Raby* in No. 3 position. Standard distance is 500 yards. Engines are in split plant operations with Boilers No. 1 and No. 2 lit off on main steam line. Port steering motor in use. 0030 Formed scouting line with USS *Raby* bearing 270° relative at 4000 yards, and USS *England* bearing 090° relative at 4000 yards.
H. Parkman, III,
Ensign, USNR.

1200-1600
Steaming as before. 1200 Position: Lat. 05 28's.; Long. 158 52' E. 1343 Submarine contact established by USS *England* (DE-635). 1351 Maneuvering on various courses and at various speeds conducting submarines search plan as USS *England* made attack runs on submarine. 1515 Lowered motor whaleboat into water to pick up floating objects and debris in water. 1536 Motor whaleboat hoisted aboard. Maneuvering on various courses and at various speeds as before.
John H. Butts
Lieut. (jg), USNR.

1800-2000
Steaming as before. 1832 Ceased retiring search; steaming to USS *England* (DE-635) to check oil slick. 1847 Made test of oil on surface; sub believed definitely sunk. 1900 Maneuvering on various courses and at various speeds to form scouting line.
Julius Rappaport,
Ensign, USNR.

USS *George* (DE-697) Saturday, 20 May, 1944

0000-0400
Steaming in company with USS *England* (DE-635) and USS *Raby* (DE-698) on base course 202° T. & P.G.C. 201° P.S.C. at 15 knots. Formed scouting lines with USS *George* as guide; USS *Raby* bearing 270° relative; and USS *England* 090° relative, distance 4,000 yards from guide ship. Commander Escort Division THIRTY-NINE aboard USS *George*. Boilers No. 1 and No. 2 are lit off. Starboard steering motor in use. 0155 Changed speed to 112° T. & P.G.C., 110° P.S.C.; changed speed to 5 knots, 076 R.P.M. 0229 Stopped port engine. 0245 Changed speed to 6 knots. 0330 Changed course to 202° T. & P.G.C., 188° P.S.C.
John H. Butts,
Lieut. (jg), USNR.

1600-1800
Steaming as before. 1632 Changed course to 312° T. & P.G.C., 312° P.S.C. 1647 Changed speed to 17 knots, 265 R.P.M. 1655 Left station to investigate underwater sound contact. 1702 Contact negative; maneuvering on various courses and at various speeds to regain station. 1738 Resumed station on course 312° T. at speed 17 knots; USS *England* bearing 090° relative, USS *Raby* bearing 270° relative, distance 4,000 yards.
John H. Butts,
Lieut. (jg), USNR.

USS *George* (DE-697) Saturday, 21 May, 1944

0000-0400
Steaming in company with USS *Raby* (DE-698) and USS *England* (DE-635) on course 312° T. & P.G.C. 312° P.S.C. at 17 knots. USS *George* is guide in scouting line with USS *England* on starboard beam, 4,000 yards, and USS *Raby* on port beam, 4,000 yards; SOPA is Commander Escort Division THIRTY-NINE in USS *George*. Engines are in split plant operation. Starboard steering motor in use.
A.H. Parker, Jr.
Lieut. (jg), USNR

0800-1200
Steaming as before. 0800 Position: Lat. 02° 11.5' S; Long. 154° 49' E. 800 Mustered crew on stations; no absentees. 0930 Made daily inspection of magazines and smokeless powder samples; conditions normal. 1050 USS *England* left screen to investigate sound contact. 1056 Contact negative; *England* resumed her station is screen.
H. Parkman, III,
Ensign, USNR.

1200 - 1600
Steaming as before. 1200 Position: Lat. 01° 27' S.; 153° 59' E. 1309 Sighted unidentified aircraft bearing 330 at distance of 13.5 miles. 1410 Aircraft disappeared.
Julius Rappaport,
Ensign, USNR.

1600 - 1800

Steaming as before. 1616 Commenced test firing of all guns. 1628 Ceased test firing, having expended the following ammunition: three (3) rounds of 3"/50 SPDN 3510; nineteen (19) rounds of 1.10; and forty (40) rounds of 20mm. 1640 Tested hydraulic depth charge release by dropping one (1) Mk 9 depth charge off port rack.

A.H. Parker, Jr.,
Lieut. (jg), USNR.

USS *George* (DE-697) Monday, 22 May, 1944

0000-0400

Steaming in company with USS *England* (DE-635) and USS *Raby* (DE-698) on course 312° T. & P.G.C., 319° P.S.C., at speed of 15 knots. USS *George* is guide in scouting line, with *England* bearing 090° relative, distance 4,000 yards, and *Raby* bearing 270° relative, distance 4,000 yards. Commander Escort Division THIRTY-NINE is in *George*. Engines are in split plant operations with Boilers No. 1 and No. 2 lit off on main steam line. 0235 USS *England* reports sub contact. 0240 Contact negative. 0348 Sugar love radar reports unidentified surface target bearing 303° T., distance 8.5 miles.

Julius Rappaport,
Ensign, USNR.

0400 - 0800

Steaming as before. Maneuvering on various courses and at various speeds conducting anti-submarine attack. 0411 Fired hedgehogs. 0412 Heard underwater explosion. 0413 Maneuvering on various courses and at various speeds circling point of last contact with submarine, attempting to regain contact.

A.H. Parker, Jr.
Lieut. (jg), USNR

1200 - 1600

Steaming as before. 1200 Position: Lat. 01° 39' N.; Long. 153° 40' E. 1217 Changed course to 325° T. & P.G.C., 321° P.S.C. 1232 Maneuvering on various courses and at various speeds conducting search for submarine. 1400 Changed course to 048° T. & P.G.C., 044° P.S.C.,; changed speed to 15 knots. Resumed scouting line with USS *George* as guide, USS *England* bearing 090° relative, distance 4,000 yards, and USS *Raby* bearing 270° relative, distance 4,000 yards. 1420 Changed speed to 291° T. & P.G.C., 290° P.S.C. USS *England* assumed position of USS *Raby* assumed position of USS *England*.

H. Parkman, III,
Ensign, USNR.

1600 - 1800

Steaming as before. 1609 *Ventura* (PV-1) passed close aboard; refused to take message. 1711 Changed course to 216° T. & P.G.C., 200° P.S.C.

Julius Rappaport,
Ensign, USNR.

USS *George* (DE-697) Tuesday, 23 May, 1944

0000 - 0400

Steaming in company with USS *England* (DE-635) and USS *Raby* (DE-698) on course 216° T. & P.G.C., 200° P.S.C., at speed of 15 knots. USS *George* (DE-697) is guide in scouting line with USS *England* bearing 090° relative, distance

5 miles, and USS *Raby* bearing 270° relative, distance 5 miles. ComCortDiv 39 is aboard USS *George*. Engines are in split plant operation with Boilers No. 1 and No. 2 lit off. Port steering motor is in use. 0017 Changed course to 126°T. & P.G.C., 121° P.S.C. 0120 Changed course to 036° T. & P.G.C., 043° P.S.C. 0150 Increased distance between ships to 7.5 miles. 0155 USS *England* reports sound contact. 0158 Changed speed to 10 knots. 0202 Contact reported negative. 0225 Changed speed to 15 knots.

H. Parkman, III,
Ensign, USNR.

0400 - 0800

Steaming as before. 0610 USS *Raby* reports surface contact, identified as submarine. 0620 USS *Raby* commenced Hedge-hog attack. 0730 USS *George* commenced runs on submarine. 0731 Fired Hedge-hogs. 0742 Fired Hedge-hogs. 0746 Fired Hedge-hogs.

Julius Rappaport
Ensign, USNR

0800 - 1200

Steaming as before. 0800 Position: Lat. 01° 27' N.: Long. 149° 21' E. 0800 Mustered crew on stations; no absentees. 0801 Fired Hedge-hogs. 0813 Fired Hedge-hogs. 0820 USS *England* commenced making runs on contact. 0834 USS *England* fired Hedge-hogs. 0837 USS *England* fired Hedge-hogs and made three hits. 0841 USS *England* dropped 13-charge pattern of depth charges. 0850 Maneuvering on various courses and at various speeds conducting retiring search plan. 1036 Shifted from port to starboard steering motor. 1108 Made daily inspection of all magazines and smokeless powder samples; conditions normal. Gunnery Department reports one hundred seventeen (117) Hedge-hogs fired. 1156 Maneuvering on various courses and at various speeds investigating oil slick for wreckage.

A.H. Parker, Jr.
Lieut. (jg), USNR.

1200 - 1600

Steaming as before. 1200 Position: Lat. 01° 24' N.; Long. 149° 21'E. 1219 Changed course to 275° T. & P.G.C. 1221 Changed course to 281° T. & P.G.C. 1234 Maneuvering on various courses and at various speeds to examine box in water. 1258 Regained station as guide in center of line of bearing of ships; changed speed to 15 knots, and changed course to 320° T. & P.G.C., 326° P.S.C. 1343 Changed course to 036° T. & P.G.C. 1410 Changed course to 090° T. & P.G.C., 092° P.S.C.

John H. Butts,
Lieut. (jg), USNR.

1800 - 2000

Steaming as before. 1845 Sound contact reported by USS *England*.
1855 Contact negative.

Julius Rappaport,
Ensign, USNR.

USS *George* (DE-697) Wednesday, 24 May, 1944

0000 - 0400

Steaming in company with USS *Raby* (DE-698) and USS *England* (DE-635) on course 216° T. & P.G.C., 202° P.S.C., at speed 15 knots. Formed in

scouting line, USS *George* (DE-697) is guide, USS *Raby* bearing 090° relative, and USS *England* bearing 270° relative, distance 8 miles apart. Engines are in split plant operation. Boilers No. 1 and No. 2 on main steam line lit off. Port steering motor in use. 0122 Radar contact surface target bearing 217° T. & P.G.C., range 7 1/2 miles. 0130 Maneuvering on various courses and at various speeds conducting submarine attack. 0140 Surface contact disappeared. 0141 USS *England* reports sound contact; USS *George* secured sound search. 0215 Commenced maneuvering on sound search; no attacks runs were made.

John H. Butts,
Lieut. (jg), USNR.

0400 - 0800

Steaming as before. 0408 Change course to 210° T. & P.G.C., 194° P.S.C. 0452 Changed course to 300° T. & P.G.C., 294° P.S.C. 0508 Changed course to 030° T. & P.G.C., 032° P.S.C. 0616 Changed course to 300° T. & P.G.C., 294° P.S.C. 0643 Changed course to 210° T. & P.G.C., 194° P.S.C. 0720 Maneuvering on various courses and at various speeds investigating point of contact. 0754 Changed course to 180° T. & P.G.C., 166° P.S.C.

H. Parkman, III,
Ensign, USNR.

0800 - 1200

Steaming as before. 0800 Position: Lat. 00° 55' N.; Long. 149° 16' E 0800 Mustered crew on stations; no absentees. 0927 Changed course to 270° T. & P.G.C. 0946 USS *England* reports sound contact; makes run on target. 1021 USS *Raby* takes over from USS *England* and makes runs—loses contact. 1040 USS *England* regained contact; passed over submarine. Fathometer showed two flashes at 35 fathoms. 1046 Made daily inspection of all magazines and smokeless powder samples; conditions normal. 1107 USS *England* fires Hedgehogs—not hits. 1120 USS *England* commences conning USS *George* on to target—a creeping barrage attack. 1152 USS *George* fired a 32-depth charge pattern. 1156 Changed course to 230° T. & P.G.C. 1159 Changed course to 250° T. & P.G.C.

Julius Rappaport,
Ensign, USNR.

1200 - 1600

Steaming as before. 1200 Position: Lat. 00° 31' N.; Long. 149° 12'E. 1202 USS *England* fired depth charges. 1203 Maneuvering on various courses and at various speeds awaiting results of the depth charges dropped by USS *England*. Results negative; maneuvering on various courses and at various speeds crossing through area of last contact. 1300 Commenced retiring search plan with USS *England* on our port beam, 4,000 yards distance, and USS *Raby* on our starboard beam, 4,000 yards.

A.H. Parker, Jr.,
Lieut. (jg), USNR.

1600 - 1800

Steaming on course 040° T. & P.G.C. in line of bearing with USS *Raby* on our starboard beam and USS *England* on our port beam, conducting a retiring search plan at 15 knots. 1701 Changed course to 310° T. & P.G.C., 312° P.S.C.; changed scouting position with USS *England* as guide, USS *George* bearing 090° relative, distance 4,000 yards, and USS *Raby*

639

bearing 270°relative, distance 4,000 yards. 1730 Changed course to 265° T. & P.G.C., 263° P.S.C. 1740 Maneuvering on various courses and at various speeds to form scouting line. 1759 Formed on new scouting line, course 220°T. & P.G.C., speed 15 knots, USS *Raby* is the guide, USS *George* bearing 090° relative, distance, 4,000 yards, and USS *England* bearing 270°relative, distance 4,000 yards.

John H. Butts,
Lieut. (jg), USNR.

USS *George* (DE-697) Thursday 25 May, 1944

0000 - 0400

Steaming in company with USS *England* (DE-635) and USS *Raby* (DE-698) on course 036° T. & P.G.C., 042° P.S.C., speed 12 knots. USS *Raby* is guide with USS *England* on *Raby's* port beam, 8 miles, and USS *George* on *Raby's* starboard beam, 8 miles. Engines are in split plant operation. Port steering motor in operation. 0205 USS *Raby* reports possible sound contact. 0216 Contact reported negative.

A.H. Parker, Jr.,
Lieut. (jg), USNR

0800 - 1200

Steaming as before. 0800 Position: Lat. 01° 44' N.; Long. 149° 49.5' E. 0800 Mustered crew on stations; no absentees. 0813 Changed course to 216° T. & P.G.C., 201° P.S.C. 0914 Maneuvering on various courses and at various speeds investigating sound contact. 0939 Contact negative. 0958 Resumed scouting line course 216° T. 1030 Made daily inspection of magazines and smokeless powder samples; conditions normal. 1127 Changed course to 126° T & P.G.C., 122° P.S.C.

H. Parkman, III,
Ensign, USNR.

1200 - 1600

Steaming as before. 1200 Position: Lat. 00° 55' N.; Long. 148° 59' E. 1300 Changed course to 216° T. & P.G.C. 1306 Changed course to 230° T. & P.G.C., 223° P.S.C. 1342 Maneuvering on various courses and at various speeds while investigating possible submarine wreckage. 1540 Changed course to 126° T. & P.G.C., 122° P.S.C.; resumed former scouting formation with USS *Raby* as guide

Julius Rappaport,
Ensign, USNR.

USS *George* (DE-697) Friday, 26 May, 1944

0000 - 0400

Steaming in company with USS *Raby* (DE-698) and USS *England* (DE-635) on course 040° T. & P.G.C., 042° P.S.C., at speed of 15 knots. Formed in scouting line with *Raby* as guide. We are stationed on starboard beam of *Raby* at distance of 8 miles. USS *England* on port beam of *Raby* at 8 miles. Engines are in split plant operation. Boilers No. 1 and No. 2 are lit off. Starboard steering motor in operation. 0052 Changed course to 080° T. & P.G.C., investigating sound contact. 0055 Contact negative; returned to station. 0200 USS *England* departed to proceed to appointed rendezvous. 0210 Changed course to 343° T. & P.G.C., investigating sound contact. 0215 Contact negative; resumed station. 0330 Changed course to 210° T. & P.G.C., 205° P.S.C.

Julius Rappaport,
Ensign, USNR.

0400 - 0800

Steaming as before. 0619 Maneuvering on various courses and at various speeds investigating sound contact. 0634 Contact negative; returned to station. 0700 Changed course to 120° T. & P.G.C., 122° P.S.C. 0740 Changed course to 210° T. & P.G.C., 197° P.S.C.

A.H. Parker, Jr.,
Lieut. (jg), USNR.

0800 - 1200

Steaming as before. 0800 Positions: Lat. 01° 02' N. ; Long. 149° 53' E. 0800 Mustered crew on stations; no absentees. 0930 Made daily inspection of magazines and smokeless powder samples; conditions normal. 1144 Maneuvering on various courses and at various speeds investigating oil in water. 1152 Regained station, course 210° T. & P.G.C., speed 15 knots.

John H. Butts,
Lieut. (jg), USNR.

1600 - 1800

Steaming as before. 1624 Changed course to 125° T. & P.G.C., 123° P.S.C.; position now off port beam of USS *Raby*. 1629 Changed course to 185° T. 1730 Sighted ship bearing 180° T., distance 15 miles, identified as USS *England*.

Julius Rappaport,
Ensign, USNR.

1800 - 1200

Steaming as before. 1824 USS *England* joined formation and took station on port beam of USS *Raby*, distance 4,000 yards. 1830 Changed course to 220° T. & P.G.C., 206° P.S.C. 1930 Changed course to 249° T. & P.G.C., speed 17 knots, in order to open out to night range of eight (8) miles from guide, USS *Raby*.

A.H. Parker, Jr.,
Lieut. (jg), USNR.

2000 - 2400

Steaming as before. 2000 Position: Lat. 00° 02' N.; Long. 149° 04' E. 2304 Maneuvering on various courses and at various speeds investigating contact reported by USS *Raby*. 2323 USS *England* fire hedge-hog attack on submarine.

John H. Butts,
Lieut. (jg), USNR

USS *George* (DE-697) Saturday, 27 May 1944

0000 - 0400

Maneuvering on various courses and at various speeds searching area of hedgehogs hit on submarine in company with USS *England* (DE-635) and USS *Raby* (DE-698). Engines are in split plant operation; Boilers No. 1 and No. 2 lit off on main steam line. Starboard steering motor in use. 0033 Commenced retiring search on submarine in company with USS *Raby*, on course 000° T. & P.G.C., at 15 knots, leaving USS *England* at the scene of attack. 0050 changed course to 09° T. & P.G.C., 092° P.S.C. 0056 Changed course to 180° T. & P.G.C., 167° P.S.C. 0142 Changed course to 270° T. & P.G.C., 258° 0208 Changed course to 000° T. & P.G.C., 010° P.S.C. 0302 Changed course to 090° T. P.G.C., 092° P.S.C.

H. Parkman, III,
Ensign, USNR.

0400 - 0800

Steaming as before. 0402 Changed course to 180° T. & P.G.C., 167° P.S.C. 0508 Changed course to 270° T. & P.G.C., 258° P.S.C. 0540 Changed course to 000° T. & P.G.C., 346° P.S.C. 0600 Radar reports three ships bearing 055° T., distance 14.5 miles. 0641 Ships identified as friendly. 0645 Maneuvering on various courses and at various speeds searching contact area for debris.

Julius Rapport,
Ensign, USNR.

1200 - 1600

Steaming as before. 1200 Position: Lat. 01° 28.5' S.; Long. 147° 56'E. 1317 Changed course to 200° T. & P.G.C., 182° P.S.C. 1320 Changed speed to 18 knots, 285 RPM 1409 Changed course to 190° T. & P.G.C., 174° P.S.C. 1424 Changed course to 180° T. & P.G.C., 166° P.S.C. 1513 Changed course to 175° T. & P.G.C. 1518 Maneuvering on various courses and at various speeds entering Seeadler Harbor. 1555 Lying to, awaiting orders from Port Director to fuel and obtain ammunition.

John H. Butts,
Lieut. (jg), USNR.

END OF FIRST PART OF OPERATION
COMCORT DIV 39 & 40

1600 - 2000

Lying to in Seeadler Harbor awaiting permission to fuel and obtain ammunition. 1617 Maneuvering on various courses and at various speeds approaching starboard side of USS *Raby*. 1648 Moored port side to USS *Raby* with standard destroyer moor. 1703 Draft of ship: fwd., 10' 1" aft., 9' 00". 1715 Commenced taking fuel from USS *Bankhead*. 1911 Completed fueling, having received 75,192 gallons fuel oil at 60° temperature. Draft of ship: fwd., 10' 10"; aft. 10' 6". 1923 Underway from fueling station, maneuvering on various courses and at various speeds clearing berth. 1940 maneuvering on various courses and at various speeds approaching anchorage. 1944 anchored in Seeadler Harbor, Manus Island, in 11 fathoms of water with 60 fathoms of chain to the port anchor on the following bearings: Beacon.

J.L. Cleveland,
Lieut. (jg), USNR.

USS *George* (DE-697) Sunday, May 28, 1944

0000 - 0400

Anchored to Seeadler Harbor, Manus Island, in 11 fathoms of water with 60 fathoms of chain out to the port anchor on the following bearings: Beacon "How," 182° T.; Beacon "George," 142° T.; and Beacon "Easy," 256° T. Steaming on Boiler No. 1 for auxiliary purposes.

A.H. Parker, Jr.,
Lieut. (jg), USNR.

0800 - 1200

Anchored as before. 0800 Mustered crew on stations; no absentees. 0910 Made daily inspection of magazines and smokeless powder samples; conditions normal. 1030 USS *Spangler* (DE-696) moored alongside to port with standard destroyer moor.

J.L. Cleaveland,
Lieut. (jg), USNR.

1600 - 1800

Anchored as before. 1759 USS *Spangler* underway from our port side.

> H. Parkman, III,
> Ensign, USNR.

1800 - 2000

Anchored as before. 1823 Underway from anchorage, maneuvering on various courses and at various speeds standing out of Seeadler Harbor, Manus Island. 1856 Set course 065° T. & P.G.C., 067° P.S.C., speed 18 knots. USS *George* is guide in a column formation, standard distance between ships 500 yards. The column is formed as follows: USS *George;* USS *England:* USS *Raby;* and USS *Spangler.*

> Julius Rappaport
> Ensign, USNR.

BEGINNING OF SECOND PART OF
OPERATION COMCORT DIV. 39 & 40

2000 - 2400

Steaming as before. 2000 Position: Lat. 01° 57' S.; Long. 147° 26' E. 2232 Changed speed to 12 knots while USS *England* and USS *Spangler* took night stations of eight miles between ships on our port beam, and USS *Raby* took station on our starboard, distance 8 miles. 2234 Changed speed to 18 knots and commenced Zig-zag Plan No. 8. 2354 USS *Spangler* reports surface contact bearing 208° T., distance 7 1/2 miles from them. 2359 Changed course to 235° T. & P.G.C. in order to close USS *Spangler.*

> A.H. Parker, Jr.
> Lieut. (jg), USNR.

USS *George* (DE-697) Monday, 29 May 1944

0000 - 0400

Steaming on various courses and at various speeds in company with USS *Spangler* (DE-696), USS *Raby* (DE-698), and USS *England* (DE-635), investigating surface contact. Commander Escort Division THIRTY-NINE is aboard USS *George.* Engines are in split plant operation. Boilers No. 1 and No. 2 are lit of. Port steering motor in use. 0125 Commenced retiring search plan on course 220° T. & P.G.C., at 15 knots. Ships are in line; USS *Raby* bears 270° relative, USS *Spangler* and USS *England* bear 090° relative, distance between ships, 4,000 yards. 0200 Changed course to 310° T. & P.G.C. 0214 Changed course to 040° T. & P.G.C. 0304 Changed course to 130° T. & P.G.C. 0334 Changed course to 220° T. & P.G.C.

> John H. Butts
> Lieut. (jg), USNR.

1200 - 1600

Approaching USS *McCord* in order to transfer personnel. 1346 Lieutenant Albert Stevens, I-V(S), USNR, transferred to USS *McCord.*

Lt. Albert Stevens, Special Intelligence Officer aboard for decoding messages from the Japanese submarines.

> A.H. Parker, Jr.
> Lieut. (jg), USNR.

USS *George* (DE-697) Tuesday, 30 May 1944

0000 - 0400

Steaming on scouting line in company with USS *England* (DE-635), USS *Raby,* (DE-698) and USS *Spangler* (DE-696) on course 210° T. & P.G.C.,

201° P.S.C., speed 12 knots, with USS *Raby* 15,000 yards on our port beam and USS *Spangler* and USS *England* 15,000 and 30,000 yards, respectively, on our starboard beam. Commander Escort Division THIRTY-NINE in USS *George* in charge of group. USS *George* is guide. Engines in split plant operation. Starboard steering motor in use. 0100 Commenced zig-zag Plan No. 8 and increased speed to 13 knots. 0230 Maneuvering on various courses and at various speeds, in company with USS *Raby,* proceeding to vicinity of USS *Heerman* to investigate contact picked up by her. 0334 Relieved USS *Heerman.* 0340 Maneuvering on various courses and at various speeds investigating contact, in company with USS *Raby.*

> A.H. Parker, Jr.,
> Lieut., (jg), USNR.

0400 - 0800

Steaming as before. 0600 Changed course to 160° T. & P.G.C.; speed 10 knots. 0605 Picked up sound contact. Maneuvering on various courses and at various speeds attacking submarine. 0618 Fired hedgehog; small underwater explosion. 0622 Fired hedgehog; small underwater explosion. 0631 Fired hedgehog; three hits on submarine, depth of submarine 26 fathoms. 0640 Fired hedgehog. 0655 Maneuvering on various courses and at various speeds while USS *Raby* makes submarine attack.

> John H. Butts
> Lieut. (jg), USNR

0800 - 1200

Maneuvering on various courses and at various speeds making runs on submarine. 0800 Position: 01° 37' N.; Long. 149° 30' E. 0800 Mustered crew on station; no absentees. 0810 USS *Raby* commenced making runs on submarine. 0845 Commenced making runs on submarine. 0941 Fired 13-charge depth charge pattern. Maneuvering on various courses and at various speeds investigating contacts. 1030 Made daily inspection of magazines and smokeless powder samples; conditions normal.

> H. Parkman, III,
> Ensign, USNR.

1200 - 1600

Steaming as before in company with USS *Raby* on course 250° T. & P.G.C., 241° P.S.C., continuing investigation of sound contact. 1200 Position: Lat. 00° 30' S.; Long. 145° 49' E. 1330 Maneuvering on various courses and at various speeds running on submarine contact. 1348 Fired hedgehogs.

> Julius Rappaport,
> Ensign, USNR.

1800 - 2000

Maneuvering on various courses and at various speeds while USS *Raby* maintains sound contact with submarine. 1922 Radar reports surface attack 120° T., distance 7 1/2 miles. Maneuvering on various courses and at various speeds to investigate contact.

> John H. Butts,
> Lieut. (jg), USNR.

2000 - 2400

Steaming as before. 2000 Position: Lat. 00° 30' S.; Long. 149° 45' E. 2004 Contact negative; maneu-

vering on various courses at 10 knots maintaining sound contact with underwater object.

> H. Parkman, III,
> Ensign, USNR.

USS *George* (DE-697) Wednesday, 31 May, 1944

0000 - 0400

Steaming in company with USS *Raby* (DE-698) investigating sound contact. Maneuvering on various courses and at various speeds in search of submarine contact. Engines are in split plant operation. Boilers No. 1 and No. 2 are lit off. 0300 USS *Raby* reports radar contact. 0304 USS *George* picks up radar contact bearing 320° T., distance 1,700 yards. Changed course to 140° T.; maneuvering on various courses and at various speeds to close submarine. 0311 Submarine submerged. Maneuvering on various courses and at various speeds to pick up sound contact.

> Julius Rappaport,
> Ensign, USNR.

0000 - 0800

Steaming as before. 0411 USS *Raby* fired Hedge-hogs. 0446 USS *George* took over contact and started run. 0651 USS *George* fired hedgehogs. 0705 USS *Raby* took over contact. 0714 USS *Spangler* took over contact and started run. 0716 USS *Spangler* fired hedge-hogs. 0720 USS *England* took over contact and started run. 0735 USS *England* fired Hedge-hogs and made a hit. 0740 Heard underwater explosion. 0741 Continued maneuvering on various courses and at various speeds investigating area of explosion.

> A.H. Parker, Jr.,
> Lieut. (jg), USNR.

0800 - 1200

Steaming as before. 0800 Position: Lat. 00° 51' N; Long. 149° 59' E. 0800 Mustered crew on stations; no absentees. 0901 Maneuvering on various courses and at various speeds investigating oil slick on water, distance 11 miles. 1030 Made daily inspection of magazines and smokeless powder samples; conditions normal. 1032 Maneuvering on various courses and at various speeds obtaining oil samples and wreckage from surface of water.

> John H. Butts
> Lieut. (jg), USNR

2000 - 2400

Steaming as before. 2000 Position: Lat. 02° 00' N.; Long. 150° 22' E. 2000 Changed course to 300° T. & P.G.C. 2015 Changed course to 210° T. & P.G.C., 199° P.S.C.; changed speed to 12 knots. USS *England* 7 1/2 miles on our port beam. 2124 Maneuvering on various courses and at various speeds investigating sound contact. 2135 Contact negative; resumed course 210° T. & P.G.C., speed 12 knots.

> John H. Butts,
> Lieut., (jg), USNR.

USS *George* (DE-697) Thursday 1 June, 1944

Daily Log Missing

USS *George* (DE-697) Friday 2 June, 1944

0000 - 0400

Steaming in company with USS *Raby* (DE-698), USS *Sprangler* (DE-696), and USS *England*

(DE-635) on course 090° T. & P.G.C, 086° P.S.C., at speed 15 knots, acting as anti-submarine screen for USS *Hogatt Bay*. Using a Anti-submarine Screen Plan No. 54. USS *George* is in No. 1 position, USS *England* in No. 2 position, USS *Spangler* in No. 3 position, and USS *Raby* in No. 4 position in screen. ComCortDiv 39 in USS *George*. Zig-zag Plan No. 6 is in use. USS *Fletcher*, USS *Jenkins*, USS *Radford*, and USS *Lavallette* also with this formation, 5,000 yards ahead as attack screen. Engines are in split plant operation, with Boilers No. 1 and No. 2 lit off main steam line. Port steering motor in use.

John H. Butts,
Lieut, (jg), USNR

USS *George* (DE-697) Saturday, 3 June 1944

0000 - 0400

Steaming in scouting line on course 040° T. & P.G.C., 044° P.S.C., speed 12 knots, with USS *George* as guide, USS *Spangler* on our starboard beam 8 miles, and USS *England* and USS *Raby* on port beams, distance between ships 8 miles. Engines in split plant operation. Starboard steering motor in use.

A.H. Parker, Jr.
Lieut. (jg), USNR.

USS *George* (DE-697) Sunday, 4 June 1944

0000 - 0400

Steaming in company with USS *England*, USS *Raby*, and USS *Spangler* on course 229° T. & P.G.C., 219° P.S.C., at 13 knots. Zig-zag Plan No. 31 in use. Formed in scouting line, USS *George* as guide, USS *Spangler* bears 270° relative, distance 4,000 yards, USS *England* bears 090° relative distance 4,000 yards and USS *Raby* bears 090° relative, distance 8,000 yards. ComCortDiv. 39 in USS *George*. Engines are in split plant operation, No. 1 and No. 2 boilers lit off on main steam line. Starboard steering motor in use. 0107 Ceased zig-zag Plan No. 31. 0125 Took station in column, USS *George* guide, USS *England* in No. 2 position, USS *Raby* in No. 3 position, and USS *Sprangler*, in No. 4 position, distance between ships 500 yards. 0126 Commenced zig-zag Plan No. 31.

H. Parkman, III
Ensign, USNR.

0400 - 0800

Steaming as before. 0500 Ceased zig-zagging. 0505 Changed course to 180° T. & P.G.C., 191° P.S.C. 0530 Changed course to 000° T. & P.G.C., 009° P.S.C. 0658 Changed course to 180° T. & P.G.C. 0710 Maneuvering on various courses and at various speeds preparing to enter Seeadler Harbour, Manus Island. 0730 Anchored 725 yards from Berth No. 2, Seeadler Harbor, in 16 fathoms of water with 63 fathoms of chain to the port anchor on the following bearings: Beacons "Dog," 068° T.; "Fox," 155° T.; and "Cast," 194° T.

J. Rappaport,
Ensign, USNR.

END OF SECOND PART OF OPERATIONS
C.O.M.C.O.R.T. DIV. 39 & 40

0800 - 1200

Anchored as before. 0800 Mustered crew on stations: no absentees. 0900 Lieutenant S. Scott Beck, I-V(S), USNR, was detached in accordance with second endorsement to basic orders CMTB/P16-4/00, WWS/0116, of 17 May 1944. 1025 Went to Fire Quarters; fire above the forward magazines. 1027 Fire extinguished, no casualties; secured from Fire Quarters. 1050 Made daily inspection of magazines and smokeless powder samples; conditions normal. 1139 Underway to refuel.

B.A. Carstens,
Lieut. (jg), USNR.

1200 - 1600

Underway as before, maneuvering on various courses and at various speeds to go alongside tanker. 1234 Moored starboard side to USS *Leopard* with standard destroyer moor. 1240 Commenced taking on fuel. Draft of ship: fwd., 10'00"; aft., 10'00". 1420 Completed taking on fuel, having received aboard 59,989 gallons fuel oil. Draft of ship: fwd., 10'10"; aft., 10'7".

J. Rappaport,
Ensign, USNR.

1600 - 1800

Moored as before. 1628 Underway from USS *Leopard*, maneuvering on various courses and at various speeds en route to anchorage. 1605 Anchored in Berth No. 2, Seeadler Harbour, in 12 fathoms of water with 45 fathoms of chain to the port anchor on the following bearings: Beacons "Easy," 157°; "Charlie," 199°; "Able," 312°; and "Baker," 346°.

J.L. Cleaveland
Lieut. (jg), USNR.

START OF THIRD PART OPERATIONS
C.O.M.C.O.R.T. DIV. 39 & 40

1800 - 2000

Anchored as before. 1830 Underway, maneuvering on various courses and at various speeds standing out of Seeadler Harbour in company with USS *Spangler*, USS *Raby*, and USS *England*, our station bearing 065° relative from USS *Hoggatt*, distance 4,000 yards, on base course T. & P.G.C., 063° P.S.C., speed 16 1/2 knots. 1950 Commenced zig-zag Plan No. 6.

A.H. Parker, Jr.
Lieut. (jg), USNR.

APPROVED:
FRED W. JUST
Lieut., USNR
Commanding

EXAMINED:
W.T. Good,
Lieut., USNR,
Navigator

TWO MINUTE WAR
By Robert W. Carter RdM 2/c.

It occurred on Mother's Day 1945 at "the point" where 50 years of life expectancy suddenly became 2 minutes. Like those DE's that had proceeded us, it became our squad's job to take up the watch, Okinawa. We were 5 DE's and a CVE (small aircraft carrier), the DE 747 USS *Bright*. Our assignment was to pick-up the Japanese aircraft by radar: track, determine their course, speed, altitude, make-up and report to the Command Combat Unit.

About 4 p.m. (1600 hours) we picked up a Betty at 26 miles west, circling at 5,000 ft. By 5 p.m. (1700 hours) there were 80 Zero's beneath it. We came to General Quarters (when I use "we" it refers to the ships crew) and soon they were coming at us, down each side, single file, the attack lasted for about an hour, we were shooting them down like ducks. The tougher the attack the cooler the crew.

Then at about 5:50 p.m. (1755) a Zero topped a small island 14 miles to the south of us. We had it immediately, clocked at 360 knots (7 miles a minute), 12 ft. off the water. It targeted us amidship. All port guns came into action, shot off the wings and part of the tail assembly, but it kept coming. The ship made a 90 degree port tun to reduce the target angle, we were about one second late.

The Zero's port wing stub caught the smoke machine, flipped it (the Zero) into the fantail, the bomb went off between the screws and the armed head of the bomb, stopped in the main magazine. The water tender had flooded it and saved the ship. The stern of the ship was raised so high the flying bridge was nearly inundated, the order, "abandon ship" was given, but the ship just stood on it's end for a few minutes (an eternity) and slowly began to settle back; came to a stop with the main deck clearing water by less than a foot. We didn't sink.

That's the longest war in history, written in the shortest story. It has been told over and over, a million times, by other sailors on other ships at other times. My congratulations to those who can relate to this two minutes.

HEROIC ACTION SAVES TANKER AFTER COLLISION OFF EAST COAST
By A.W. McCanless

The tanker SS *St. Mihiel* is afloat today, ready once again to carry her vital gasoline supply to distant battle zones, because of the recent heroic effort of two destroyer escorts of the Atlantic Fleet, the USS *Stewart* and the USS *Edsall*.

Rammed by another tanker, the SS *Nashbuck*, with whom she was in convoy, a few hundred miles off the East Coast, on the afternoon of last April 19, the *St. Mihiel* was damaged amidships and instantly set aflame from bow to stern. Six million gallons of high octane gasoline provided fuel for the raging inferno.

Deadly fumes swept beneath the heat of the flames and drove the crew to the rail. Thirty-two of these men died before reaching the safety of liferafts and boats. Others, too badly burned and exhausted to swim, were kept alive only by the life jackets which had been thrown over the side.

Four other destroyer escorts, the USS *Rhodes*, USS *Brister*, USS *Sellstrom* and the USS *Richey*, helped to rescue survivors from the St. Mihiel.

The tanker was unmanned and ablaze from stem to stern when the first destroyer escort to reach the scene, the USS *Stewart*, came alongside. She was under the command of Lieutenant Commander Alvin Chesley Wilson, Jr., USNR, whose father lives at 306 Emariland Boulevard, Knoxville, Tennessee. Firefighting crews on the *Stewart* poured streams of water on the blazing ship. From the port side they beat down the flames so men could board her with chemical foam apparatus and every piece of firefighting equipment that was portable aboard.

By cooling the decks and forcing the flames back over the open hatches and eventually killing the fire at the source, the Navy crew from the *Stewart* stood in constant danger of becoming surrounded and trapped.

Canvas hose lines smoldered as they lay on the

hot decks. Constantly present in the minds of the men who had volunteered to come aboard the abandoned tanker was the thought than an explosion might occur. The *Stewart* did not stay alongside because she could not submit her own explosive-filled magazines to the consuming heat for long.

The fire had been brought under control when the USS *Edsall*, the destroyer escort which had come as a relief for the *Stewart*, arrived. They relieved the begrimed, exhausted men from the *Stewart*, and with the remainder of the *St. Mihiel's* crew safely brought the battered, slow moving ship through the fogshrouded, crowded channel leading to a safe anchorage in New York, while the USS *Stewart* escorted the SS *Nashbuck* into the harbor.

PEARL HARBOR ATTACK REMEMBRANCE OF THE AFTERNOON OF DEC. 7, 1941
By Bernt C. Johnson

(Greenwich, Conn.) Dad and I were at local boatyard putting winter cover on the family pleasure boat. The owner of the boat next to ours called over. He had heard of the Pearl Harbor attack, on his portable radio. Dad said, "We'd better go right home." Mother and younger brother were home alone.

My older brother Arthur (18) was aboard USS *Nevada* (BB-36), during the attack *Nevada* was the only battleship to get underway and head for the channel to the sea, damaged but moving. A group of Jap planes took notice. Hit again and in danger of sinking and blocking the one channel to the sea, *Nevada* was run aground in the shallow waters, clear of the channel.

Family didn't hear anything for some time, finally received word, Arthur was not hurt. Younger brother Wilton and I received Christmas cards, from Arthur, in March 1942. I have in my World War II album, this card, postmarked USS *Nevada*, Dec. 7 AM 1941, waterstained.

Second contact with Pearl Harbor, August 1945. I was aboard a Destroyer-Escort, USS *Douglas L. Howard*, DE-138, when our group of DEs put into Pearl. We had been a Hunter-Killer Group (ASW), running down German U-Boats in Atlantic, until German surrender May 1945. I was in Pearl Harbor when Japanese surrendered.

Over the years since, all three brothers, have been in Pearl Harbor, plus my son (career Navy), two uncles, a cousin, and some high school classmates— all Navy. Mother was there also.

1984 Discovered Destroyer-Escort-Sailors-Assoc. Now nationwide, with thirty chapters. 1987-DESA had a Destroyer-Escort history book published. Histories of 560 World War II DEs, told who these ships were named after. Usually some Naval person, many of whom were killed earlier in WWII...Imagine the surprise to find one Destroyer-Escort in our group, Hill DE-141, was named after Chief Boatswain Edward Hill, who was blown off the bow section of USS *Nevada,* and killed, during Jap attack Dec. 7, 1941.

Dec. 7, 1941. During the attack on the *Nevada,* the catapult plane was destroyed. The pilot, Ensign Frederick Davis, was not in the plane, was running toward one of the ship's anti-aircraft guns when cut down. Destroyer-Escort USS *Fred Davis*, DE-136, was launched in summer of 1943.

January 1944 Anzio Beachhead, Italy. *Davis*

DE-136 and *Jones* DE-137 were using special radio jamming equipment, to confuse radio controlled flying bombs directed by German bombers. This would cause the flying bombs to fly away from the landing forces.

Fall 1944. *Jones* DE-137 joined with my DE in the Atlantic. *Davis* DE-136 had joined another group.

April 24, 1945. *Davis* DE-136 with its Hunter-Killer Group, was U-Boat hunting in North Atlantic, not far from our group, when it was torpedoed, split in two and sank with large loss of lives. Germany surrendered about two weeks later!

When USS *Douglas L. Howard* DE-138 (my ship) entered Pearl Harbor in August 1944, USS *Hill* DE-141 followed us in.

My brother, Arthur, Pearl Harbor Survivor, died just before I learned of the namesakes of the two Destroyer-Escorts.

DON'T FRUSTRATE- JUST SIMULATE
By Ensign Carroll F. Sweet, Jr.

I have a friend way back home,
Who cannot figure out,
How while at peace we shell and bomb
And put the foe to rout.

So I pause to narrate
Our Navy's wondrous scheme.
How when in doubt we simulate;
Things aren't as they seem.

In battle order row on row
We sally forth from port,
To meet a hypothetic foe
And to have a little sport.

And with the vivid golden dawn
His fleet's reported near.
Now the battle lines is drawn.
Our men they know no fear.

Torpedoes hit us everywhere.
They fail to irritate.
It takes but moments to repair
Of course, we simulate.

Shells and bombs upon us rain;
They sting no more than flies.
Our foe strikes every blow in vain
He who simulates never dies.

Yes, even when the battle's done
Simulation sees us through;
For even though we may not win
We can pretend we do.

When the galley serves some bits,
That we mayhap do hate,
Presto, we're dining at the Ritz.
Of course, we simulate.

Sometimes sweetheart never bothers
To mail the weekly letter,
But we always hear from Ginger Rogers;
We simulate it better.

Should our liberty be delayed,
So we cannot get our brew,
We will never be dismayed;
Simulation sees us through.

When, though rare, Pay Call is late,
We never worry much,
'Cause we can always simulate
We're Henry Ford or such.

But just one pain spare us pray,
The most unhappy fate,
Homeward bound do not delay.
Home we cannot simulate.

TASK GROUP 21.16—DE'S FIRST U- BOAT KILL
By R. Byxbee TM2/c

As the year 1944 approached, the battle of the Atlantic had already started to turn in favor of the Allies. The so called "Happy Times" for the German U-boat captains and their crews were rapidly coming to an end. Soon many of them would be entombed in their iron coffins.

By the end of June 1943 there were 35 Destroyer Escorts available for sea duty. Not all of these ships could be used in the Atlantic; as the Navy had to meet the pressures of a two ocean war. But by December of that year DE's were beginning to appear on the flanks of Trans-Atlantic convoys, and as screens for baby flat tops; leading hunter killer groups on offensive anti-submarine missions.

March 1944 was the month in which the DE's made their first U-boat kill. Sharing the honors were the USS *Thomas* (DE-102) (Lieutenant Commander D.M. Kellogg USNR) USS *Bostwick* (DE-103) (Lieutenant Commander J.H. Church Jr., USNR), and USS *Bronstein* (DE-189) (Lieutenant S.H. Kinney USN). These ships were units of Task Group 21.16, built around the new escort carrier USS *Block Island* (CVE-21) under the able command of Captain Logan C. Ramsey. The baby flat top's screen included the destroyer USS *Corry* (DD-463) (Lieutenant Commander G.D. Hoffman) and USS *Breeman* (DE-104) (Lieutenant Commander E.N.W. Hunter), but these two did not get into the action that was soon to follow.

On the night of February 29th the group were steaming in the vicinity of lat. 49-00N., long 26-00 W., where at least 18 Nazi submarines were reported to be holding rendezvous. At 2208 *Bronstein* reported a radar contact at 6,000 yards, and was ordered to move in on the target. The flare of a depth charge marker lit up the dark sea scape. Both *Bostwick* and *Thomas,* developing their own contacts, were silhouetted as they bore in on a coordinated attack. At 2213 *Bronstein* fired a star shell that revealed a surfaced U-boat. Apparently the Nazi submariners were concentrating a torpedo attack on *Bostwick* and *Thomas,* and did not detect *Bronstein* closing in on them, until Kinney ordered his gunners to open fire. After several 40 millimeter shell hits on its bridge, the U-boat dived. *Bronstein* made two hedgehog attacks pelting the sea with pattern after pattern. Then *Bostwick* and *Thomas* followed through with five hours of thundering depth charge and hedgehog bombardments. At about 0324 that March morning the surface heaved with a blast that left a malestrom in the DE's wake. U-709 (identified by post war German records) had been sunk while *Bostwick* and *Thomas* had been concentrating on U-709 *Bronstein* had made sound contact with a target of her own. After numerous depth charge runs, a pattern of 18 charges were set to go deep. The barrage was still on its way down, when a large explosion erupted from the sea. Post war German records revealed U-603 had been sunk. There were no survivors.

After a brief rest in Casablanca, Task Group 21.16 was again underway, ordered to the area northwest of the Cape Verd Islands; where the Nazi "Milk Cows", were known to be operating. Early morning of St. Patrick's Day was a busy one for the group *Block Island's* aircraft had spotted a U-boat on the surface in the vicinity of the refueling grounds. Several sonar contacts had been made and tracking with depth charge runs went on well into the daylight hours. Finally at 0705 a large oil slick was visible on the surface. *Corry* and *Bronstein* were ordered in to attack. After several tracking and depth charge runs on the target, at 1318 U-801 came plunging to the surface. For about five minutes of firing and many 5 inch and 3 inch hits on the submarine, the crew had only time enough to abandon ship. At 1326 as *Corry* closed in to ram, the battered U-Boat sank stern first. Forty-seven of the crew were picked up.

That afternoon of March 17, 1944 was a jubilant one on board all the ships of Task Group 21.16. In only 17 days they had made three U-Boat kills; a record to be envied by any group of A/S vessels.

A SAILOR'S PRAYER
By Ensign Carroll F. Sweet, Jr.

Oh Lord our constant guiding light,
Be with us yet through this long night.
And give us grace Thy path to see,
That we may tread it after Thee.

We the people of this fair land,
Know we at a chasm stand,
Know that we are at a loss,
Without Thy help to guide us 'cross'.

Please, Oh Lord, show us the way
To lead the world to better day.
Grant us the strength this charge to bear;
Grant us the wisdom to get us there.

Grant us the courage to meet the test.
Grant us the ability to do our best.
And, oh father, grant us the sense
To see the need for reverence.

In Jesus name we ask it. Amen.

PROUDLY WE SERVED:
THE USS *MASON* (DE-529)
By Martin Davis, Ph.D., DESA Director of Historic Projects

As we are aware, destroyer escorts and the men who served aboard them have made major contributions during World War II, the Korean War and Vietnam War. In each of these conflicts, there was a single, identifiable enemy.

In the case of the USS *Mason*, the crew had to face enemies on two fronts during World War II: the uniformed enemy aboard and prejudice at home!

In early 1944, as part of a dual experiment concerning desegregation and efforts to improve manpower utilization and efficiency, the Bureau of Naval Personnel assigned 160 black enlisted men and 44 white officers and petty officers to the USS *Mason*, a newly-commissioned destroyer escort.

The black enlisted men who reported aboard

USS Brister (DER-327) dropping depth charges.

USS Brister (DER-327) dropping depth charges.

Securing the rack after discharging depth charges. (USS Brister (DER-327)).

Signalmen Buchanan, DuFau, Jones and Dunn, USS Mason (DE-529).

C Division, Polk, Garrison, Hill, Ticeson and McMillan, USS Mason (DE-529).

Gunnery drill. (Quad 1.1") USS Mason (DE-529).

were volunteers who were identified as having high potential. A number of them had received post-boot camp naval specialty training recently opened to them. Until 1942, most of these sailors would have been destined to serve as messmen. Because of the composition of her crew, a black photojournalist was aboard for a period of time in order to record this "experiment."

The *Mason* operated as a convoy escort with destinations in Britain, Northern Ireland and North Africa. In addition, she served as part of a "hunter-killer" anti-submarine patrol. The *Mason*, in company with four other destroyer escorts accompanied an ill-planned trans-Atlantic convoy composed of tugboats, barges and other small vessels. Almost a half of the convoy was lost due to a storm; this has been recorded in a book, *Ordeal of Convoy N.Y. 119.*

Eventually, all of the white petty officers and some of the officers were replaced with black personnel. One of the black officers, Lt. James E. Hair, had a double distinction because he was a member of the "Golden Thirteen," the first group of black men to receive Navy Commissions.

In analyzing the results of the *Mason* event, the Navy confirmed what it believed to be true even before the test began: black sailors did not respond well when assigned to an all-black organization under totally white officers. On the other hand, it was strongly demonstrated that they could perform well at any technical job or assignment level if provided with proper training and the opportunity to obtain experience.

The lessons of the manning of the *Mason* proved to be far more meaningful than was realized at the time. In addition to this ship, the Special Programs Unit of the Navy Department of Personnel conducted other experiments and advances. This Unit made it possible for black women to serve in the Navy Nurse Corps and the Waves. Also, blacks became eligible for commissions starting with the Golden Thirteen and, importantly, *Patrol Craft* 1264 was manned in a similar manner to the *Mason*, with the same results. The Navy's first black admiral, Vice-Admiral Samuel L. Gravely Jr. served as an ensign aboard PC 1264.

All of these Navy men and women were engaged in the double war against the enemy overseas and prejudice at home. They and their black-skinned brothers in the World War II Army, Army Air Force and Marine Corps were the victors. Their efforts became major steppingstones leading to President Harry S. Truman's landmark 1948 Desegregation Order of the Armed Forces. This Order, in turn, dramatically helped in paving the way for future desegregation in the civilian sector.

It is in this context that the men of the *Mason* are truly to be regarded among the "Black Pioneers of World War II." The USS *Mason* Association meets every other year. Their motto is "Proudly We Served." They certainly did!

USS *PETERSON* (DE-152)

By Bob Miller GM3/c

The Bosn' Mate - the Gunner's Mate - The
    Quartermaster too
Went to sea in a Wee DE the old one fifty-two
They sailed the sea in their DE this wild and
    salty crew
They drank their rum until they were numb like
    all good sailors do.

The Bosn's Mate - The Gunner's Mate - The
Quartermaster too

Went to mess-ate SOS and guessed what's in
the stew

Ate meat called horse and of course strong
coffee was their brew

They searched for subs as well as pubs like all
DE men do

The Bosn's Mate - The Gunner's Mate - The
Quartermaster too

Could drink their grog and sail through fog to
where the Shamrock grew

In weather foul when winds would howl and the
salty spray it flew

On deck they stood like sailors should this wild
and salty crew

The Bosn's Mate - The Gunner's Mate - The
Quartermaster too

Were hearty gobs who did their jobs on old one
fifty two

They told tall tales of mighty gales upon the
ocean blue

How they sank the subs and drank their suds
like all DE men do

The Bosn's Mate - The Gunner's Mate - The
Quartermaster too.

DE LEADERS AT THE WHITE HOUSE NAVY MEMORIAL . . .

DESA leaders made the most of the Veterans Day dedication of the plaque to the Coast Guard Yard in Baltimore beginning the busy weekend schedule in our Nation's Capital.

Shortly after arriving at BWI Airport on November 8, President Sam Saylor and Executive Administrator Don Glaser were driven to Washington by Vice President Ottis Clingerman for a meeting at the Navy Memorial to discuss the bas-relief with Admiral "Bill" Thompson.

Result of this session with the Navy Memorial officials, Executive Director Captain Howard Loving, art director Leo Irrera and bas-relief project director Captain Bob Jones, was an agreement to recast the DE bas-relief because it did not meet fully the specifications in design and/or production. All hands, including Admiral Thompson, agreed the need for a more complete representation in keeping with the high standards already established for this striking memorial at Market Square on historic Pennsylvania Avenue—Main Street USA.

Presidents Thompson and Saylor have set "no later than the end of June 1991" as the time for the new bronze sculpture to be completed and attached to a granite base in the shadow of the Lone Sailor statue.

John Cosgrove also had scheduled a meeting at The White House for 4:30 the afternoon of November 8, 1991 to present the two-volume *Trim but Deadly* history of DE Ship and Sailor. However, because President Bush unexpectedly called a news conference with Defense Secretary Cheney about the same time, our presentation was made to aide Don Rhodes. Photos were taken in front of Tom Freeman's painting of the USS *Wyman* (DE-38), at the entrance to the Navy Mess, witnessed by a small statue of the Lone Sailor (originally presented to President Reagan at the time of the Navy Memorial dedication in October 1987).

"We watched the President's news conference on TV while waiting in the old Executive Office Building and it was really exciting," said Ottis Clingerman, "to look out the window directly into the White House where the action was.

"Mr. Rhodes and an assistant, Ms. Anne Mency, took the four of us on an exciting tour of the White House, including the press room where the photo-TV media were packing up and the print media in their respective cubbyholes writing their stories," said Don Glaser describing that part of the extraordinary visit.

By the time President Saylor stood at the podium, the briefing room was virtually empty, except for a *DE News* reporter and a few staffers. Sam took advantage of those historic minutes to note that our mission was accomplished, that we delivered the two-volume embossed set which carries presidential pictures and messages."

But there was more.

"While the President was preparing to leave for Camp David the unexpected tour of the Commander-in-Chief's residence continued," according to Ottis Clingerman, "right to meeting President Bush as he was leaving the Oval Office. He welcomed us, the ex-DE sailors, thanked us for the books, directed an aide to put them wit other items he wanted to go over. I can hardly wait to tell Mary how he introduced us to his daughter Doro, and grandchild, Ellie, as he moved towards the waiting chopper," concluded DESA's impressed vice-president.

President Saylor told President Bush of the Baltimore Convention resolution, supporting the Desert Shield action, and that he had our full confidence in resolving the Persian Gulf problems.

"The four of us left the White House, walking by the Oval Office, the Cabinet Room, then up to the Pennsylvania Avenue gate, returned our necklace pass, took a long look back at the White House, now bathed in bright flood lights, our Flag proudly waving, and taking a minute to reflect on our little more than an hour visit at the home and office of our Commander-in-Chief. It's always a moving experience to visit that mansion," said John Cosgrove, "and this was one of the most impressive ever. We have a thoughtful President, and the staffers we met reflected their Boss."

COMMEMORATIVE STAMP

Friday morning host VP Clingerman returned President Sam and Executive Administrator Don to Washington this time to meet officials at the U.S. Postal Service at the L'Enfant Plaza headquarters. The meeting was set up at the request of Jim Boren (USS *William C. Cole* DE-641) to learn "just what is the status of DESA's appeal for a DE Commemorative Stamp?" DESA National Representative also attended this hour-long session with Associate Postmaster General Edward E. Horgan Jr., Dickey Rustin, Manager of Stamp Information Branch, and John Hagarty, USPS Congressional liaison officer.

We were told that the Destroyer Escort would be included in the World War II commemorative series, but nothing specific about how the DE would be identified. The impression received was that the DE could be included or bunched with service and accomplishments of destroyers and similar ships operating in various duties assigned these vessels during the World War II period.

Dr. James H. Boren, better known as "Jim" to most of his international friends, and appointed by President Saylor as Chairman of the Ad Hoc Committee for a DE Commemorative, was not satisfied with the response, nor the status so described at the meeting. His experience as an administrative assistant to an outstanding senator, coupled with his bureaucratic experience in Washington, came to bear. He said he was committed to dedicate a year if necessary to get a commemorative for DE Ship and Sailor. Then he described briefly a simple, but effective way to get the needed attention to accomplish this goal.

"We came away from this meeting not totally satisfied, but wiser and more determined to concentrate and consolidate the vast power and resources of DESA and friends to see that those shipmates who made the supreme sacrifice in the name of freedom and justice are remembered and appreciated. The role of these men and their valiant ships will not go unnoticed," concluded spokesman Boren.

(Reprinted with permission *DESA News*, January-February 1991 issue.)

PRESIDENT TRUMAN SEES USS *WILKE* (DE-800) HEDGEHOG EXERCISE WITH GERMAN U-BOAT

On Thursday morning, November 21, 1946, President Harry S. Truman, wearing slacks, a vividly pink shirt with his familiar cap, and his party left their quarters at Key West, Florida, for the pier on the submarine base, for the purpose of boarding the former German submarine U-2531 and to participate in exercises involving the USS *Jack W. Wilke* (DE-800).

According to former skipper of the *Wilke*, John F. "Jack" Maloney, Key West area was the test area for all new experimental anti-submarine warfare. The U-2513, one of the German subs which surrendered to the British, was a high speed type boat, capable of making 16 knots while submerged, and with its secret "Schnorkel" breathing device, it would remain submerged much longer than any of our submarines at that time.

The President stood in the control room during the U-boat dive to 450 feet, where she leveled off and cruised at this depth for about a minute. At 0954, the order to surface was given and by 1000 the submarine had risen to a depth of 50 feet, or periscope depth. The President manned the periscope and became an interested spectator as to what was going on above the surface. During the surfacing to this level, the port engine became flooded, which caused smoke to escape into the after battery room. This was soon corrected and the ship surfaced at 1015.

The Destroyer-Escort USS *Jack W. Wilke* (DE-800), Lieutenant Commander R.J. Dressling, USN, commanding, accompanied the U-2513 and simulated an anti-submarine attack as the President's U-boat came back to port. The *Wilke* fired a full pattern of hedgehogs 2,000 yards from the U-2513 and then regular depth charges. Two blimps flew over the brilliant green waters bordering the Gulf stream during the submarine trip which lasted from eight o'clock until noon.

Later that evening, President Truman accompanied by members of his party, walked to the tennis courts on the base, where an enlisted sailors dance was in full swing. At the President's approach, the music stopped playing, and "Attention" was sounded. The jubilant gathering soon crowded around him. He made a few impromptu remarks, stressing that our

great country belonged to them, the young men and women who helped make our country great, and pleaded to them to keep it great. He urged them "to read the Constitution—because the Constitution was the Government of the United States—and to abide by the Constitution." He told the gathering that we are living in the greatest age in history. The visit concluded and the President returned to his quarters.

Source: Log of the President's vacation trip to Key West, Florida November 17-23, 1946, Harry S. Truman Library, Independence, Missouri.

In his stirring address to the nation following the signing of the Japanese surrender in 1945, President Truman saw in the victory of war a lesson of liberty: It was the spirit of liberty which gave us our armed strength and which made our men invincible in battle. We now know that the spirit of liberty, the freedom of the individual, and the personal dignity of man are the strongest and toughest and most enduring forces in all the world.

President Truman and his party await commencement of exercises while on board the USS Wilke (DE-800).

"Trim But Deadly" volumes now in the President's Library at The White House. Don Rhodes accepts the publications from DESA President Sam Saylor (r) and DESA National Representative John P. Cosgrove (l) on Nov. 8, 1990 in the White House. Tom Freeman's excellent painting of the USS Wyman (DE-38) makes an appropriate backdrop.

March-December 1941

Mar.	11	U.S. Lend-Lease Act signed
Apr.	13	USSR and Japan sign Neutrality Pact
	17	Yugoslavia capitulates
June	22	Germany invades USSR
July	1	U.S. forces begin occupying Iceland
Aug.	9	Roosevelt and Churchill meet in Atlantic Conference (to August 12); Atlantic Charter proclaimed
Oct.	31	U.S. destroyer *Reuben James* sunk by U-boat
Dec.	7	Pacific war begins with Japanese attacks on U.S. and British posts (Pearl Harbor and Malaya) (8 Dec. west of International Date Line)
	8	United States declares war on Japan
	10	Japanese take Guam, make first landings on Luzon
	11	Germany and Italy declare war on United States, which takes reciprocal action
	20	King is appointed C-in-C of U.S. Fleet
	23	Wake Island falls/U.S. Army troops arrive in Australia

January-December 1942

Jan.	1	United Nations Declaration signed
	7	Siege of Bataan begins
	31	U.S. Army troops arrive in Ireland
Feb.	9	First meeting of the Organization of the Joint Chiefs of Staff
	12	USS *ANDRES* (DE-45) keel laid, Phila. Navy Yard. USS *DRURY* (DE-46) keel laid, Phila. Navy Yard
	15	Singapore surrenders to Japanese
	22	Roosevelt orders MacArthur to leave Philippines
	28	USS *BRENNAN* (DE-13) keel laid, Mare Is. Navy Yard. USS *DOHERTY* (DE-14) keel laid, Mare Is. Navy Yard
Mar.	14	USS *AUSTIN* (DE-15) keel laid, Mare Is. Navy Yard. USS *EDGAR G. CHASE* (DE-16) Keel laid, Mare Is. Navy Yard
	30	MacArthur appointed Supreme Commander SWPA, Nimitz Cincpac
Apr.	1	USS *EDWARD C. DALY* (DE-17) keel laid, Mare Is. Navy Yard. USS *GILMORE* (DE-18) keel laid, Mare Is. Navy Yard. USS *DECKER* (DE-47) keel

Apr. (Con't)

		laid, Phila. Navy Yard. USS *DOBLER* (DE-48) keel laid, Phila. Navy Yard. USS *DONEFF* (DE-49) keel laid, Phila. Navy Yard. USS *ENGSTROM* (DE-50) keel laid, Phila. Navy Yard
	5	USS *BAYNTUN* (DE-1) keel laid, Boston Navy Yard. USS *BAZELY* (DE-2) keel laid, Boston Navy Yard
	15	USS *BURDEN R. HASTINGS* (DE-19) keel laid, Mare Is. Navy Yard. USS *LeHARDY* (DE-20) keel laid, Mare Is. Navy Yard
	18	U.S. (Doolittle) B-25 raid on Japanese
	30	USS *HAROLD C. THOMAS* (DE-21) keel laid, Mare Is. Navy Yard. USS *WILEMAN* (DE-22) keel laid, Mare Is. Navy Yard
May	4	Battle of the Coral Sea (to May 8)
	6	Corregidor surrenders
	8	Germans begin preliminary offensives in USSR
June	3	Battle of Midway (to June 6)
	7	Japanese invade western Aleutian Islands
	9	Japanese conquest of Philippines completed
	26	USS *JACOB JONES* (DE-130) keel laid, Consolidated, Orange, TX
	29	USS *BENTINCK* (DE-52) keel laid, Bethlehem Steel, Hingham, MA
	30	USS *ROBERT E. PEARY* (DE-132) keel laid, Consolidated, Orange, TX
July	2	USS *EDSALL* (DE-129) keel laid, Consolidated Steel, Orange, TX
	10	USS *HAMMANN* (DE-131) keel laid, Consolidated Steel, Orange, TX
	14	USS *POPE* (DE-134) keel laid, Consolidated Steel, Orange, TX
	15	USS *STEWART* (DE-238) keel laid, Brown Shipbuilding, Houston, TX. USS *STURTEVANT* (DE-239) keel laid, Brown Shipbldg. Houston, TX
	18	USS *PILLSBURY* (DE-133) keel laid, Consolidated Steel, Orange, TX
	20	USS *MOORE* (DE-240) keel laid, Brown Shipbuilding, Houston, TX
	21	USS *BUCKLEY* (DE-51) keel laid, Bethlehem Steel, Hingham, MA
Aug.	1	USS *CHARLES LAWRENCE* (DE-53) keel laid, Bethlehem

Aug. (Con't)

		Steel, Hingham, MA
	4	USS *KEITH* (DE-241) keel laid, Brown Shipbuilding, Houston, TX
	7	U.S. Marines and Army land on Guadalcanal
	17	U.S. first attack on European target (Rouen-Sotteville). U.S. Marines conduct raid on Makin Island (to Aug. 18)
	19	Canadian and British force raids Dieppe
	24	Battle of the Eastern Solomons (to Aug. 25)
Sept.	7	USS *CHARLES R. GREER* (DE-23) keel laid Mare Island Navy Yard, Vallejo, CA. USS *WHITMAN* (DE-24) keel laid Mare Island Navy Yard, Vallejo, CA. USS *RUEBEN JAMES* (DE-153) keel laid Norfolk Navy Yard. USS *SIMS* (DE 154/APD-50) keel laid Norfolk Navy Yard. USS *GREINER* (DE-37) keel laid Puget Sound Navy Yard, Bremerton, WA. USS *WYMAN* (DE-38) keel laid Puget Sound Navy Yard, Bremerton, WA. USS *LOVERING* (DE-39) keel laid Puget Sound Navy Yard, Bremerton, WA. USS *SANDERS* (DE-40) keel laid Puget Sound Navy Yard, Bremerton, WA. USS *DANIEL T. GRIFFIN* (DE-54) keel laid Bethlehem Steel, Hingham, MA
	12	Eisenhower assumes post as C-in-C Allied Expeditionary Force (for Northwest Africa). Fighting on Bloody Ridge, Guadalcanal (to September 14)
	15	U.S. Army lands in New Guinea. USS *TOMICH* (DE-242) keel laid Brown Shipbuilding Co., Houston, TX
	22	USS *BERRY* (to G.B. 15Mar43) (DE-3) keel laid Boston Navy Yard. USS *BLACKWOOD* (DE-4) TO G.B. 27Mar43) keel laid Boston Navy Yard
	30	USS *J. RICHARD WARD* (DE-243) keel laid Brown Shipbldg. Co.
Oct.	1	USS *WINTLE* (DE-25) keel laid Mare Island Navy Yard, Vallejo, CA. USS *DEMPSEY* (DE-26) keel laid Mare Island Navy Yard, Vallejo, CA
	15	USS *BYARD* (to G.B. 18June 43) (DE-55) keel laid Bethlehem Steel, Hingham, MA (Ex-USS *DONALDSON*)

Oct. 17 USS *EVARTS* (DE-5) keel laid Boston Navy Yard
USS *WYFFELS* (DE-6) keel laid Boston Navy Yard

19 USS *LEVY* (DE-162) keel laid Federal Shipbuilding Co., Newark, NJ
USS *McCONNELL* (DE-163) keel laid Federal Shipbuilding Co., Newark, NJ

29 USS *DUFFY* (DE-27) keel laid Mare Island Navy Yard, Vallejo, CA

Nov. 7 USS *FLAHERTY* (DE-135) keel laid Consolidated Steel Corp, Orange, TX

9 USS *FREDERICK C. DAVIS* (DE-136) keel laid Consolidated Steel Corp.
USS *OTTERSTETTER* (DE-244) keel laid Brown Shipbuilding Co.

11 USS *OSTERHAUS* (DE-164) keel laid Federal Shipbuilding Co., Newark, NJ
USS *PARKS* (DE-165) keel laid Federal Shipbuilding Co., Newark, NJ

12 Naval Battle of Guadalcanal (to Nov. 15)

14 USS *CANNON* (DE-99) keel laid at Dravo, Wilmington, DE

21 USS *SLOAT* (DE-245) keel laid Brown Shipbuilding Co., Houston, TX

26 USS *STADTFELD* (DE-29) keel laid Mare Island Navy Yard, Vallejo, CA
USS *MARTIN* (DE-30) keel laid Mare Island Navy Yard, Vallejo, CA

27 USS *GRISWOLD* (DE-7) keel laid Boston Navy Yard
USS *STEELE* (DE-8) keel laid

Boston Navy Yard
USS *CARLSON* (DE-9) keel laid Boston Navy Yard
USS *BEBAS* (DE-10) keel laid Boston Navy Yard
USS *DONNELL* (DE-56) keel laid Bethlehem Steel, Hingham, MA

29 USS *EMERY* (Ex-Br. EISNER) DE-28) keel laid Mare Island Navy Yard

30 USS *HERERT C. JONES* (DE-137) keel laid Consolidated Steel Corp.
USS *BARON* (DE-166) keel laid Federal Shipbuilding Co., Newark, NJ
USS *ACREE* (DE-167) keel laid Federal Shipbuilding Co., Newark, NJ
USS *AMICK* (DE-168) keel laid Federal Shipbuilding Co., Newark, NJ

Dec. 4 USS *FOGG* (DE-57) keel laid Bethlehem Steel, Hingham, MA

7 USS *SNOWDEN* (DE-246) keel laid Brown Shipbuilding Co., Houston, TX
USS *STANTON* (DE-247) keel laid Brown Shipbuilding Co., Houston, TX
USS *CHRISTOPHER* (DE-100) keel laid at Dravo, Wilmington, DE

8 USS *CROUTER* (DE-11) keel laid Boston Navy Yard
USS *BURGES* (to G.B. 2June43) (DE-12) keel laid Boston Navy Yard
USS *DOUGLAS L. HOWARD* (DE-138) keel laid Consolidated Steel Corp.

11 USS *CALDER* (to G.B. 15July43) (DE-58) keel laid

Bethlehem Steel, Hingham, MA (Ex-USS *FORMOE*)

14 USS *FARQUHAR* (DE-139) keel laid Consolidated Steel Corp., Orange, TX

15 USS *HOPPING* (DE-155/APD-51) keel laid Norfolk Navy Yard
USS *BULL* (DE-693) keel laid Defoe Shipbuilding Co., Bay City, MI

16 *J.R.Y. BLAKELY* (DE-140) keel laid Consolidatd Steel Corp., Orange, TX

21 USS *HILL* (DE-141) keel laid Consolidated Steel Corp., Orange, TX

24 USS *SEDERSTROM* (ex-Br. *GILLETTE*) (DE-31) keel laid Mare Is. Navy Yd.
USS *FLEMING* (DE-32) keel laid Mare Island Navy Yard, Vallejo, CA

30 USS *SWASEY* (DE-248) keel laid Brown Shipbuilding Co., Houston, TX
USS *MARCHAND* (DE-249) keel laid Brown Shipbuilding Co., Houston, TX

31 USS *FOSS* (DE-59) keel laid Bethlehem Steel, Hingham, MA
USS *GANTNER* (DE-60) keel laid Bethlehem Steel, Hingham, MA Editor's Note: According to *The Dictionary of American Naval Fighting Ships* (Volume 1, 1959), in 1942, the keels for 88 DEs were laid. BDEs 1-50 were originally intended for transfer to Great Britain, but only nine of the 1942 DEs were transferred.

JANUARY-DECEMBER 1943

Month and Day	Ship	Number	Keel Laid At	Disposition
January 1	*Scott*	DE-214	Philadelphia Navy Yard	APD-64
1	*Burke*	DE-215	Philadelphia Navy Yard	APD-65, 1/45
2	*Alger*	DE-101	Dravo Corp, Wilmington,	DE to Brazil 3/45; renamed *Babitonga*
4	*Fessenden*	DE-142	Consolidated Steel, Orange, TX	DER-142
4	*Fiske*	DE-143	Consolidated Steel, Orange, TX	
10	*Seid*	DE-256	Boston Navy Yard	
10	*Smartt*	DE-257	Boston Navy Yard	
10	*Walter S. Brown*	DE-258	Boston Navy Yard	
10	*William C. Miller*	DE-259	Boston Navy Yard	
11	*Huse*	DE-145	Consolidated Steel, Orange, TX	
12	*Brackett*	DE-41	Puget Sound Navy Yard	ex BDE
12	*Reynolds*	DE-42	Puget Sound Navy Yard	ex BDE
12	*Mitchell*	DE-43	Puget Sound Navy Yard	ex BDE
12	*Donaldson*	DE-44	Puget Sound Navy Yard	ex BDE
13	*Frost*	DE-144	Consolidated Steel, Orange, TX	
14	Allied Casablanca Conference begins (to January 23)			
14	*Atherton*	DE-169	Norfolk Navy Yard	
16	*Duckworth*	DE-61	Bethlehem-Hingham Shipyard	ex USS *Gary*; to G.B. 8/4/43
16	*Thomas*	DE-102	Norfolk Navy Yard	
19	*Inch*	DE-146	Consolidated Steel, Orange, TX	
19	*Blair*	DE-147	Consolidated Steel, Orange, TX	
22	Papua, New Guinea ends (first decisive defeat of Japanese on land)			

Date	Name	Hull No.	Builder	Notes
22	Brough	DE-148	Consolidated Steel, Orange, TX	
22	Durik	DE-666	Dravo Corp., Pittsburgh, PA	APD-68
23	Tisdale	DE-33	Mare Island Navy Yard	ex BDE
23	Eisele	DE-34	Mare Island Navy Yard	ex BDE
25	Chatelain	DE-149	Consolidated Steel, Orange, TX	
27	Hurst	DE-250	Brown Shipbuilding, Houston, TX	
27	Camp	DE-251	Brown Shipbuilding, Houston, TX	
27	Cabana	DE-260	Boston Navy Yard	
27	Dionne	DE-261	Boston Navy Yard	
29	Neunzer	DE-150	Consolidatd Steel, Orange, TX	
30	Booth	DE-170	Norfolk Navy Yard	
30	Carroll	DE-171	Norfolk Navy Yard	
February 6	George W. Ingram	DE-62	Bethlehem-Hingham Shipyard	APD-43
6	Bostwick	DE-103	Dravo Corp., Wilmington, DE	
6	Howard D. Crow	DE-252	Brown Shipbuilding, Houston, TX	
6	Pettit	DE-253	Brown Shipbuilding, Houston, TX	
7	Reeves	DE-156	Norfolk Navy Yard	APD-52, 9/44
7	Fechteler	DE-157	Norfolk Navy Yard	
9	U.S. Forces complete Guadalcanal Campaign			
11	Banquist	DE-739	Western Pipe & Steel, San Pedro	
13	Ira Jeffery	DE-63	Bethlehem-Hingham Shipyard	APD-44
13	Poole	DE-151	Consolidated Steel, Orange, TX	
15	Manning	DE-199	Charleston Navy Yard	
15	Neuendorf	DE-200	Charleston Navy Yard	
21	U.S. Forces seize the Russell Islands			
22	Duff	DE-64	Bethlehem-Hingham Shipyard	ex USS Lamons; to G.B. 8/23/43
22	Cooner	DE-172	Federal Shipbuilding, Newark, NJ	
22	Eldridge	DE-173	Federal Shipbuilding, Newark, NJ	
22	Enright	DE-216	Philadelphia Navy Yard	APD-66
22	Coolbaugh	DE-217	Philadelphia Navy Yard	
22	Darby	DE-218	Philadelphia Navy Yard	
22	J. Douglas Blackwood	DE-219	Philadelphia Navy Yard	
22	Francis M. Robinson	DE-220	Philadelphia Navy Yard	
22	Solar	DE-221	Philadelphia Navy Yard	
22	Weber	DE-675	Bethlehem Steel, Quincy, MA	APD-75, 1/45
22	Schmidt	DE-676	Bethlehem Steel, Quincy, MA	APD-76, 1/45
22	Bunch	DE-694	Defoe Shipbuilding, Bay City, MI	APD-79, 7/44
23	Canfield	DE-262	Boston Navy Yard	
23	Deede	DE-263	Boston Navy Yard	
23	Elden	DE-264	Boston Navy Yard	
23	Cloues	DE-265	Boston Navy Yard	
24	Fair	DE-35	Mare Island Navy Yard	ex BDE
24	Manlove	DE-36	Mare Island Navy Yard	ex BDE
24	Waterman	DE-740	Western Pipe & Steel, San Pedro	
28	Peterson	DE-152	Consolidated Steel, Orange, TX	
March 1	Lee Fox	DE-65	Bethlehem-Hingham Shipyard	APD-45
1	Cates	DE-763	Tampa Shipbuilding	
1	Gandy	DE-764	Tampa Shipbuilding	
8	Amesbury	DE-66	Bethlehem-Hingham Shipyard	APD-46
8	Joyce	DE-317	Consolidated Steel, Orange, TX	
9	Harveson	DE-316	Consolidated Steel, Orange, TX	
9	Foreman	DE-633	Bethlehem Steel, San Francisco	
9	Earl K. Olsen	DE-765	Tampa Shipbuilding	
9	Slater	DE-766	Tampa Shipbuilding	
11	Capel ex USS Wintle	DE-266	Boston Navy Yard	to G.B. 8/16/43
11	Cooke	DE-267	Boston Navy Yard	ex USS Demsey; to G.B. 8/16/43
13	Weaver	DE-741	Western Pipe & Steel, San Pedro	
15	Essington	DE-67	Bethlehem-Hingham Shipyard	G.B. 9/7/45
15	Kirkpatrick	DE-318	Consolidated Steel, Orange, TX	
16	Convoy Battle is climax of Battle of the Atlantic (to March 20)			
16	Chase	DE-158	Norfolk Navy Yard	APD-54, 11/44
16	Ricketts	DE-254	Brown Shipbuilding, Houston, TX	
16	Sellstrom	DE-255	Brown Shipbuilding, Houston, TX	
19	Fieberling	DE-640	Bethlehem Steel, San Francisco	
20	Breeman	DE-104	Began at Dravo, Wilmington,	DE; finished at Norfolk Navy Yard
21	Whitehurst	DE-634	Bethlehem Steel, San Francisco	
22	Blessman	DE-69	Bethlehem-Hingham Shipyard	APD-48
22	Menges	DE-320	Consolidated Steel, Orange, TX	

23	*Hilbert*	DE-742	Western Pipe & Steel, San Pedro	
24	*Burrows*	DE-105	Dravo Corp., Wilmington, DE	
24	*Leopold*	DE-319	Consolidated Steel, Orange, TX	
26	*Ramsden*	DE-382	Brown Shipbuilding, Houston, TX	
26	*Mills*	DE-383	Brown Shipbuilding, Houston, TX	
27	*Rich*	DE-695	Defoe Shipbuilding, Bay City, MI	
29	*Bates*	DE-68	Bethlehem-Hingham Shipyard	APD-47
29	*Joseph E. Campbell*	DE-70	Bethlehem-Hingham Shipyard	APD-49
April 1	*Oswald*	DE-767	Tampa Shipbuilding	
1	*Ebert*	DE-768	Tampa Shipbuilding	
4	*England*	DE-635	Bethlehem Steel, San Francisco	
5	*Affleck*	DE-71	Bethlehem-Hingham Shipyard	ex USS Oswald; to G.B. 9/29/43
5	*Fowler*	DE-222	Philadelphia Navy Yard	
5	*Spangenberg*	DE-223	Philadelphia Navy Yard	
5	*Newell*	DE-322	Consolidated Steel, Orange, TX	
6	*Mosley*	DE-321	Consolidated Steel, Orange, TX	
7	*Dacres*	DE-268	Boston Navy Yard	ex USS Duffy; to G.B. 8/28/43
7	*Domett*	DE-269	Boston Navy Yard	ex USS Eisner; to G.B. 9/3/43
7	*Foley*	DE-270	Boston Navy Yard	ex USS Gillette; to G.B. 9/8/43
7	*Garlies*	DE-271	Boston Navy Yard	ex USS Fleming; to G.B. 9/13/43
10	*Lamons*	DE-743	Western Pipe & Steel, San Pedro	
12	*Aylmer*	DE-72	Bethlehem-Hingham Shipyard	ex USS Harmon; to G.B. 9/30/43
12	*Pride*	DE-323	Consolidated Steel, Orange, TX	
15	*James E. Craig*	DE-201	Charleston Navy Yard	
15	*Eichenberger*	DE-202	Charleston Navy Yard	
16	*Kyne*	DE-744	Western Pipe & Steel, San Pedro	
19	*Balfour*	DE-73	Bethlehem-Hingham Shipyard	ex USS McAnn; to G.B. 10/7/43
19	*Rhodes*	DE-384	Brown Shipbuilding, Houston, TX	
19	*Richey*	DE-385	Brown Shipbuilding, Houston, TX	
22	*Lake*	DE-301	Mare Island Navy Yard	
22	*Lyman*	DE-302	Mare Island Navy Yard	
22	*Tatum*	DE-789	Consolidated Steel, Orange, TX	APD-81, 12/44
23	*Laning*	DE-159	Norfolk Navy Yard	APD-55, 11/44
23	*Loy*	DE-160	Norfolk Navy Yard	APD-56, 11/44
23	*Gould* ex USS *Lovering*	DE-272	Boston Navy Yard	to G.B. 9/18/43
23	*Grindall*	DE-273	Boston Navy Yard	ex USS Sanders; to G.B. 9/23/43
24	*Senegalais*	DE-106	Dravo Corp., Wilmington, DE	ex USS Corbesier; to France 1/2/44
26	*Bentley*	DE-74	Bethlehem-Hingham Shipyard	ex USS Ebert; to G.B. 10/13/43
26	*Marts*	DE-174	Federal Shipbuilding, Newark, NJ	to Brazil 3/45; renamed BOCAINA
26	*Pennewill*	DE-175	Federal Shipbuilding, NJ	to Brazil 8/44; renamed Bertioga
27	*Barber*	DE-161	Norfolk Navy Yard	APD-57, 11/44
28	*Witter*	DE-636	Bethlehem Steel, San Francisco	APD-58
28	*Spangler*	DE-696	Defoe Shipbuilding, Bay City, MI	
28	*Snyder*	DE-745	Western Pipe & Steel, San Pedro	
28	*Borum*	DE-790	Consolidated Steel, Orange, TX	APD-82
30	*Savage*	DE-386	Brown Shipbuilding, Houston, TX	
30	*Vance*	DE-387	Brown Shipbuilding, Houston, TX	
May 1	*Frament*	DE-677	Bethlehem Steel, Quincy, MA	APD-77, 1/45
3	*Bickerton*	DE-75	Bethlehem-Hingham Shipyard	ex USS Eisele; to G.B. 10/17/43
3	*Micka*	DE-176	Federal Shipbuilding, Newark, NJ	
3	*Reybold*	DE-177	Federal Shipbuilding, Newark, NJ	to Brazil 8/44; renamed Bauru
7	Allied 18th Army Group captures Tunis and Bizerte			
8	*Hemminger*	DE-746	Western Pipe & Steel, San Pedro	
10	*Bligh*	DE-76	Bethlehem-Hingham Shipyard	ex USS Liddle; to G.B. 10/22/43
10	*Braithwaite*	DE-77	Bethlehem-Hingham Shipyard	ex USS Straub; to G.B. 11/13/43
10	*Maloy*	DE-791	Consolidated Steel, Orange, TX	APD-83
11	U.S. Army lands on Attu			
12	*Kephart*	DE-207	Charleston Navy Yard	APD-61
12	*Cofer*	DE-208	Charleston Navy Yard	APD-62, 7/44
12	*Jenks*	DE-665	Dravo Corp., Pittsburgh, PA	APD-67
13	*Algerien*	DE-107	Dravo Corp., Wilmington, DE	ex USS Cronin; to France 1/23/44
15	*Lansing*	DE-388	Brown Shipbuilding, Houston, TX	
15	*Durant*	DE-389	Brown Shipbuilding, Houston, TX	
17	*Bullen*	DE-78	Bethlehem-Hingham Shipyard	to G.B. 10/25/43
17	*Herzog*	DE-178	Federal Shipbuilding, Newark, NJ	to Brazil 8/44; renamed Beberibe
17	*McAnn*	DE-179	Federal Shipbuilding, Newark, NJ	to Brazil 8/44; renamed Bracui
17	*Haines*	DE-792	Consolidated Steel, Orange, TX	APD-84, 12/44
20	*Gardiner*	DE-274	Boston Navy Yard	ex USS O'Toole; to G.B. 9/28/43
20	*Goodall* ex USS *Reynold*	DE-275	Boston Navy Yard	to G.B. 10/4/43; sunk 4/29/45

20	Goodson			
	ex USS George	DE-276	Boston Navy Yard	to G.B. 10/9/43
20	Gore	DE-277	Boston Navy Yard	ex USS Herzog; to G.B. 10/14/43
22	Lovelace	DE-198	Norfolk Navy Yard	
22	George	DE-697	Defoe Shipbuilding, Bay City, MI	
24	Byron	DE-79	Bethlehem-Hingham Shipyard	to G.B. 10/30/43
24	Crowley	DE-303	Mare Island Navy Yard	
24	Rall	DE-304	Mare Island Navy Yard	
24	Lowe	DE-325	Consolidated Steel, Orange, TX	
26	Falgout	DE-324	Consolidated Steel, Orange, TX	
28	Calcaterra	DE-390	Brown Shipbuilding, Houston, TX	
28	Chambers	DE-391	Brown Shipbuilding, Houston, TX	
28	Bowers	DE-637	Bethlehem Steel, San Francisco	APD-40
30	Japanese resistance on Attu ends			
31	Harmon	DE-678	Bethlehem Steel, Quincy, MA	
June 1	Neal A. Scott	DE-769	Tampa Shipbuilding	
1	Muir	DE-770	Tampa Shipbuilding	
2	Conn	DE-80	Bethlehem-Hingham Shipyard	to G.B. 10/31/43
2	Cotton	DE-81	Bethlehem-Hingham Shipyard	to G.B. 11/8/43
5	Thomason	DE-203	Charleston Navy Yard	
5	Jordan	DE-204	Charleston Navy Yard	
5	Keats	DE-278	Boston Navy Yard	ex USS Tisdale; to G.B. 10/19/43
5	Kempthorne	DE-279	Boston Navy Yard	ex USS Trumpeter; to G.B. 10/23/43
7	Trumpeter	DE-180	Federal Shipbuilding, Newark, NJ	
7	Straub	DE-181	Federal Shipbuilding, Newark, NJ	
7	Raby	DE-698	Defoe Shipbuilding, Bay City, MI	
7	Runels	DE-793	Consolidated Steel, Orange, TX	APD-85, 12/45
8	Newman	DE-205	Charleston Navy Yard	APD-59
8	Liddle	DE-206	Charleston Navy Yard	APD-60, 7/44
9	Cranstoun	DE-82	Bethlehem-Hingham Shipyard	to G.B. 11/13/43
9	Cubitt	DE-83	Bethlehem-Hingham Shipyard	to G.B. 11/17/43
9	Bright	DE-747	Western Pipe & Steel, San Pedro	
14	Brister	DE-327	Consolidated Steel, Orange, TX	
15	(Thomas J.) Gary	DE-326	Consolidated Steel, Orange, TX	
21	U.S. Forces land on New Georgia			
21	Halloran	DE-305	Mare Island Navy Yard	
21	Connolly	DE-306	Mare Island Navy Yard	
23	Curzon	DE-84	Bethlehem-Hingham Shipyard	to G.B. 11/20/43
23	Dakins	DE-85	Bethlehem-Hingham Shipyard	to G.B. 11/23/43
23	Tunisien	DE-108	Dravo Corp., Wilmington, DE	ex USS Crosley; to France 2/11/44
23	Marsh	DE-699	Defoe Shipbuilding, Bay City, MI	
23	Tills	DE-748	Western Pipe & Steel, San Pedro	
25	Willmarth	DE-638	Bethlehem Steel, San Francisco	
28	Kretchmer	DE-329	Consolidated Steel, Orange, TX	
29	Finch	DE-328	Consolidated Steel, Orange, TX	
29	Greenwood	DE-679	Bethlehem Steel, Quincy, MA	
30	Operation Cartwheel (Rabaul) launched in Southwest Pacific			
30	Deane	DE-86	Bethelehem-Hingham Shipyard	to G.B. 11/26/43
July 1	Merrill	DE-392	Brown Shipbuilding, Houston, TX	
1	Haverfield	DE-393	Brown Shipbuilding, Houston, TX	
5	Ekins	DE-87	Bethlehem-Hingham Shipyard	to G.B. 11/29/43; lost
5	Gustafson	DE-182	Federal Shipbuilding, Newark, NJ	
5	Samuel S. Miles	DE-183	Federal Shipbuilding, Newark, NJ	
5	Finnegan	DE-307	Mare Island Navy Yard	
5	Creamer	DE-308	Mare Island Navy	canceled 9/5/44
5	Hollis	DE-794	Consolidated Steel, Orange, TX	APD-86, 12/44
7	Roberts	DE-749	Western Pipe & Steel, San Pedro	
9	Kingsmill	DE-280	Boston Navy Yard	to G.B. 10/29/43
9	Lawford	DE-516	Boston Navy Yard	to G.B. 11/3/43
9	Louis	DE-517	Boston Navy Yard	to G.B. 11/9/43
9	Lawson	DE-518	Boston Navy Yard	to G.B. 11/15/43
10	Allies invade Sicily			
14	Redmill	DE-89	Bethlehem-Hingham Shipyard	to G.B. 11/30/43
15	Rudderow	DE-224	Philadelphia Navy Yard	
15	Day	DE-225	Philadelphia Navy Yard	
17	Swenning	DE-394	Brown Shipbuilding, Houston, TX	
17	Willis	DE-395	Brown Shipbuilding, Houston, TX	
18	Paisley	DE-519	Boston Navy Yard	to G.B. 11/20/43
18	Loring	DE-520	Boston Navy Yard	to G.B. 11/27/43
21	Retalick	DE-90	Bethlehem-Hingham Shipyard	to G.B. 12/8/43
21	Currier	DE-700	Defoe Shipbuilding, Bay City, MI	

21	McClelland	DE-750	Western Pipe & Steel, San Pedro	
22	Palermo falls to U.S. Seventh Army			
24	Allied bombers incinerate Hamburg (to August 3)			
26	Lloyd	DE-209	Charleston Navy Yard	APD-63
26	Otter	DE-210	Charleston Navy Yard	
26	Koiner	DE-331	Consolidated Steel, Orange, TX	
26	Wiseman	DE-667	Dravo Corp., Pittsburgh, PA	
27	Loeser	DE-680	Bethlehem Steel, Quincy, MA	
29	Wesson	DE-184	Federal Shipbuilding, Newark, NJ	
29	Riddle	DE-185	Federal Shipbuilding, Newark, NJ	
29	O'Reilly	DE-330	Consolidated Steel, Orange, TX	
August 1	U.S. B-24s bomb Ploesti, Romania (Operation Tidal Wave)			
1	Gendreau	DE-639	Bethlehem Steel, San Francisco	
1	Vammen	DE-644	Bethelehem Steel, San Francisco	
2	Ely	DE-309	Mare Island Navy Yard	
2	Delbert W. Halsey	DE-310	Mare Island Navy Yard	
4	Riou	DE-92	Bethelehem-Hingham Shipyard	to G.B. 12/14/43
4	Rutherford	DE-93	Bethelehem-Hingham Shipyard	to G.B. 12/16/43
4	Janssen	DE-396	Brown Shipbuilding, Houston, TX	
4	Wilhoite	DE-397	Brown Shipbuilding, Houston, TX	
4	Gaynier	DE-751	Western Pipe & Steel, San Pedro	
9	Gunason	DE-795	Consolidated Steel, Orange, TX	
11	Cosby	DE-94	Bethlehem-Hingham Shipyard	to G.B. 12/20/43
11	(Joseph C.) Hubbard	DE-211	Charleston Navy Yard	APD-53, 6/45
11	Hayter	DE-212	Charleston Navy Yard	APD-80, 6/45
12	Swearer	DE-186	Federal Shipbuilding, Newark, NJ	
12	Stern	DE-187	Federal Shipbuilding, Newark, NJ	
14	Hoste	DE-521	Boston Navy Yard	to G.B. 12/3/43
14	Moorsom	DE-522	Boston Navy Yard	to G.B. 12/16/43
14	Manners	DE-523	Boston Navy Yard	to G.B. Dec. 6, 1943; damaged by U-boat
14	Mounsey	DE-524	Boston Navy Yard	to G.B. 12/23/43
16	Major	DE-796	Consolidated Steel, Orange, TX	
17	U.S. B-17s raid Schweinfurt and Regensburg			
17	Osmus	DE-701	Defoe Shipbuilding, Bay City, MI	
18	Rowley	DE-95	Bethlehem-Hingham Shipyard	to G.B. 12/22/43
18	Richard S. Bull	DE-402	Brown Shipbuilding, Houston, TX	
18	Richard M. Rowell	DE-403	Brown Shipbuilding, Houston, TX	
18	Curtis W. Howard	DE-752	Western Pipe & Steel, San Pedro	
18	Weeden	DE-797	Consolidated Steel, Orange, TX	
22	Yokes	DE-668	Consolidated Steel, Orange, TX	completed as APD-69
23	Keppler	DE-311	Mare Island Navy Yard	
23	Lloyd Thomas	DE-312	Mare Island Navy Yard	
23	Strickland	DE-333	Consolidated Steel, Orange, TX	
23	Sutton	DE-771	Tampa Shipbuilding	
23	Milton Lewis	DE-772	Tampa Shipbuilding	
24	Mountbatten appointed Supreme Allied Commander in Southeast Asia			
24	Fitzroy	DE-88	Bethlehem-Hingham Shipyard	to G.B. 10/16/43
24	Price	DE-332	Consolidated Steel, Orange, TX	
24	Gillette	DE-681	Bethlehem Steel, Quincy, MA	
25	Rupert	DE-96	Bethlehem-Hingham Shipyard	to G.B. 12/24/43
25	Stockham	DE-97	Bethlehem-Hingham Shipyard	to G.B. 12/28/43
26	O'Neill	DE-188	Federal Shipbuilding, Newark, NJ	
26	Bronstein	DE-189	Federal Shipbuilding, Newark, NJ	
26	William T. Powell	DE-213	Charleston Navy Yard	DER 1945
26	Chaffee	DE-230	Charleston Navy Yard	
27	Varian	DE-798	Consolidated Steel, Orange, TX	
30	Daniel	DE-335	Consolidated Steel, Orange, TX	
31	Forster	DE-334	Consolidated Steel, Orange, TX	
31	Cockrill	DE-398	Brown Shipbuilding, Houston, TX	
31	Stockdale	DE-399	Brown Shipbuilding, Houston, TX	
31	Edward H. Allen	DE-531	Boston Navy Yard	
31	Tweedy	DE-532	Boston Navy Yard	
31	John J. Vanburen	DE-753	Western Pipe & Steel, San Pedro	
September 1	Seymour	DE-98	Bethlehem-Hingham Shipyard	to G.B. 12/23/43
4	Scroggins	DE-799	Consolidated Steel, Orange, TX	
5	William C. Cole	DE-641	Bethlehem Steel, San Francisco	
7	Marocain	DE-109	Dravo Corp., Wilmington, DE	to France 2/29/44
7	Earl V. Johnson	DE-702	Defoe Shipbuilding, Bay City, MI	
8	Eisenhower announces Italian surrender			
9	Allies land at Salerno			
9	Baker	DE-190	Federal Shipbuilding, Newark, NJ	

9	Coffman	DE-191	Federal Shipbuilding, Newark, NJ	
9	Hodges	DE-231	Charleston Navy Yard	
9	Kinzer	DE-232	Charleston Navy Yard	completed as APD-91
13	Roy O. Hale	DE-336	Consolidated Steel, Orange, TX	
14	Unnamed, canceled 10/2/43			
		DE-754	Western Pipe & Steel, San Pedro	
15	Eversole	DE-404	Brown Shipbuilding, Houston, TX	
15	Dennis	DE-405	Brown Shipbuilding, Houston, TX	
15	Spragge	DE-563	Bethlehem-Hingham Shipyard	to G.B. 1/14/44
16	Underhill	DE-682	Bethlehem Steel, Quincy, MA	
21	Pavlic	DE-669	Consolidated Steel, Orange, TX	completed as APD-70
22	Stayner	DE-564	Bethlehem-Hingham Shipyard	to G.B.12/30/43
22	Thornborough	DE-565	Bethlehem-Hingham Shipyard	to G.B. 12/31/43
22	Torrington	DE-568	Bethlehem-Hingham Shipyard	to G.B. 1/18/44
23	Eisner	DE-192	Federal Shipbuilding, Newark, NJ	
23	Garfield Thomas	DE-193	Federal Shipbuilding, Newark, NJ	
25	Hova	DE-110	Dravo Corp., Wilmington, DE	to France 3/18/44
25	Inglis	DE-525	Boston Navy Yard	to G.B. 12/29/43
25	Inman	DE-526	Boston Navy Yard	to G.B. 1/13/44
25	O'Toole	DE-527	Boston Navy Yard	
25	John J. Powers	DE-528	Boston Navy Yard	
26	Paul G. Baker	DE-642	Bethlehem Steel, San Francisco	
27	Unnamed, canceled 10/2/43			
		DE-755	Western Pipe & Steel, San Pedro	
28	Holton	DE-703	Defoe Shipbuilding, Bay City, MI	
29	Trollope	DE-566	Bethlehem-Hingham Shipyard	to G.B. 1/10/44
29	Henry R. Kenyon	DE-683	Bethlehem Steel, Quincy, MA	
October 4	O'Flaherty	DE-340	Consolidated Steel, Orange, TX	
5	John C. Butler	DE-339	Consolidated Steel, Orange, TX	
6	Hissem	DE-400	Brown Shipbuilding, Houston, TX	
6	Holder	DE-401	Brown Shipbuilding, Houston, TX	
6	Tyler	DE-567	Bethlehem-Hingham Shipyard	to G.B. 1/14/44
6	Narbrough	DE-569	Bethlehem-Hingham Shipyard	to G.B. 1/21/44
7	Wingfield	DE-194	Federal Shipbuilding, Newark, NJ	
7	Thornhill	DE-195	Federal Shipbuilding, Newark, NJ	
8	Howard F. Clark	DE-533	Boston Navy Yard	
8	Silverstein	DE-534	Boston Navy Yard	
10	Halsted	DE-91	Bethlehem-Hingham Shipyard	to G.B. 11/3/43
14	U.S. B-17s suffer heavy losses in raid on Schweinfurt			
14	Mason	DE-529	Boston Navy Yard	
14	John M. Bermingham	DE-530	Boston Navy Yard	
14	George M. Campbell	DE-773	Tampa Shipbuilding	
15	Odum	DE-670	Consolidated Steel, Orange, TX	completed as APD-71
16	Crosley	DE-226	Philadelphia Navy Yard	completed as APD-87
16	Cread	DE-227	Philadelphia Navy Yard	completed as APD-88
16	Waldegrave	DE-570	Bethlehem-Hingham Shipyard	to G.B. 1/25/44
17	Damon M. Cummins	DE-643	Bethlehem Steel, San Francisco	
18	Jack W. Wilke	DE-800	Consolidated Steel, Orange, TX	
19	Delong	DE-684	Bethlehem Steel, Quincy, MA	
19	Cronin	DE-704	Defoe Shipbuilding, Bay City, MI	
20	Whitaker	DE-571	Bethlehem-Hingham Shipyard	to G.B. 1/28/44
20	Riley	DE-579	Bethlehem-Hingham Shipyard	
21	Rinehart	DE-196	Federal Shipbuilding, Newark, NJ	
21	Roche	DE-197	Federal Shipbuilding, Newark, NJ	
23	Somali	DE-111	Dravo Corp., Wilmington, DE	to France 4/9/44; named Arago '68
25	Dale W. Peterson	DE-337	Consolidated Steel, Orange, TX	
27	Register	DE-233	Charleston Navy Yard	completed as APD-92
27	Brock	DE-234	Charleston Navy Yard	completed as APD-93
27	Martin H. Ray	DE-338	Consolidated Steel, Orange, TX	
27	Holmes	DE-572	Bethlehem-Hingham Shipyard	to G.B. 1/31/44
27	Hargood	DE-573	Bethlehem-Hingham Shipyard	to G.B. 2/7/44
28	U.S. Marines conduct diversionary raid on Choiseui Island			
31	U.S. Marines land on Bougainville; Battle of Empress Augusta Bay			
November 1	U.S. Marines land on Bouganville			
1	Richard W. Suesens	DE-342	Consolidated Steel, Orange, TX	
1	Edmonds	DE-406	Brown Shipbuilding, Houston, TX	
1	Shelton	DE-407	Brown Shipbuilding, Houston, TX	
3	Raymond	DE-341	Consolidated Steel, Orange, TX	
3	Lewis	DE-535	Boston Navy Yard	
3	Bivin	DE-536	Boston Navy Yard	
3	Rizzi	DE-537	Boston Navy Yard	

3	*Osberg*	DE-538	Boston Navy Yard	
4	*Corbesier*	DE-438	Federal Shipbuilding, Newark, NJ	
4	*Conklin*	DE-439	Federal Shipbuilding, Newark, NJ	
5	*Hotham*	DE-574	Bethlehem-Hingham Shipyard	to G.B. 2/8/44
5	*Ahrens*	DE-575	Bethlehem-Hingham Shipyard	
5	*Barr*	DE-576	Bethlehem-Hingham Shipyard	
5	*Alexander J. Luke*	DE-577	Bethlehem-Hingham Shipyard	DER 1945
5	*Robert I. Paine*	DE-578	Bethlehem-Hingham Shipyard	DER 1945
7	*Leslie L.B. Knox*	DE-580	Bethlehem-Hingham Shipyard	
8	*Abercrombie*	DE-343	Consolidated Steel, Orange, TX	
8	*Oberrender*	DE-344	Consolidated Steel, Orange, TX	
8	*Wagner*	DE-539	Boston Navy Yard	completed as DER-539 1955
8	*Vandiver*	DE-540	Boston Navy Yard	completed as DER-540 1955
8	*Sheehan*	DE-541	Boston Navy Yard	
8	*Joseph M. Auman*	DE-674	Consolidated Steel, Orange, TX	completed as APD-117
8	*Coates*	DE-685	Bethlehem Steel, Quincy, MA	
8	*Frybarger*	DE-705	Defoe Shipbuilding, Bay City, MI	
10	*Jack C. Robinson*	DE-671	Consolidated Steel, Orange, TX	completed as APD-72
15	*John Q. Roberts*	DE-235	Charlestown Navy Yard	completed as APD-94
15	*William M. Hobby*	DE-236	Charlestown Navy Yard	completed as APD-95
15	*Edwin A. Howard*	DE-346	Consolidated Steel, Orange, TX	
16	*Robert Brazier*	DE-345	Consolidated Steel, Orange, TX	
17	*McNulty*	DE-581	Bethlehem-Hingham Shipyard	
18	*Straus*	DE-408	Brown Shipbuilding, Houston, TX	
18	*La Prade*	DE-409	Brown Shipbuilding, Houston, TX	
18	*McCoy Reynolds*	DE-440	Federal Shipbuilding, Newark, NJ	
18	*Gilligan*	DE-508	Federal Shipbuilding, Newark, NJ	ex Donaldson
18	*Oswald A. Powers*	DE-542	Boston Navy Yard	
19	*Carter*	DE-112	Dravo Corp., Wilmington, DE	
20	U.S. 2nd Marine Division lands in assault on Tarawa			
22	Allied Cairo Conference (to November 26)			
22	*Jesse Rutherford*	DE-347	Consolidated Steel, Orange, TX	
24	*Metivier*	DE-582	Bethlehem-Hingham Shipyard	
24	*George A. Johnson*	DE-583	Bethlehem-Hingham Shipyard	
27	*Eugene E. Elmore*	DE-686	Bethlehem Steel, Quincy, MA	
28	Allied Big Three begin Teheran Conference (to November 30)			
28	*Bassett*	DE-672	Consolidated Steel, Orange, TX	completed as APD-73
28	*Holt*	DE-706	Defoe Shipbuilding, Bay City, MI	
29	*Jack Miller*	DE-410	Brown Shipbuilding, Houston, TX	
29	*Stafford*	DE-411	Brown Shipbuilding, Houston, TX	
December 1	*Ray K. Edwards*	DE-237	Charleston Navy Yard	completed as APD-96
1	*Arthur L. Bristol*	DE-281	Charleston Navy Yard	completed as APD-97
1	*Charles J. Kimmel*	DE-584	Bethlehem-Hingham Shipyard	
1	*Daniel A. Joy*	DE-585	Bethlehem-Hingham Shipyard	
1	*Don O. Woods*	DE-721	Consolidated Steel, Orange, TX	completed as APD-118
2	*William Seiverling*	DE-441	Federal Shipbuilding, Newark, NJ	
2	*Ulvert M. Moore*	DE-442	Federal Shipbuilding, Newark, NJ	
3	Allied meetings resume at Cairo (to December 7)			
6	*Walter C. Wann*	DE-412	Brown Shipbuilding, Houston, TX	
6	*Samuel B. Roberts*	DE-413	Brown Shipbuilding, Houston, TX	
8	*Lough*	DE-586	Bethlehem-Hingham Shipyard	
9	*Groves*	DE-543	Boston Navy Yard	
9	*Alfred Wolf*	DE-544	Boston Navy Yard	
13	*Truxton*	DE-282	Charleston Navy Yard	completed as APD-98
13	*Upham*	DE-283	Charleston Navy Yard	completed as APD-99
13	*Gentry*	DE-349	Consolidated Steel, Orange, TX	
14	*Key*	DE-348	Consolidated Steel, Orange, TX	
14	*Russell M. Cox*	DE-774	Tampa Shipbuilding	
15	*Thomas F. Nickel*	DE-587	Bethlehem-Hingham Shipyard	
16	*Kendall C. Campbell*	DE-443	Federal Shipbuilding, Newark, NJ	
16	*Goss*	DE-444	Federal Shipbuilding, Newark, NJ	
18	*John B. Gray*	DE-673	Consolidated Steel, Orange, TX	completed as APD-74
19	*Traw*	DE-350	Consolidated Steel, Orange, TX	
20	*Leray Wilson*	DE-414	Brown Shipbuilding, Houston, TX	
20	*Lawrence C. Taylor*	DE-415	Brown Shipbuilding, Houston, TX	
20	*Jobb*	DE-707	Defoe Shipbuilding, Bay City, MI	
21	*Peiffer*	DE-588	Bethlehem-Hingham Shipyard	
21	*Tinsman*	DE-589	Bethlehem-Hingham Shipyard	
22	*Maurice J. Manuel*	DE-351	Consolidated Steel, Orange, TX	
23	*Clarence L. Evans*	DE-113	Dravo Corp., Wilmington, DE	
23	*Ringness*	DE-590	Bethlehem-Hingham Shipyard	completed as APD-100

	23	*Knudson*	DE-591	Bethlehem-Hingham Shipyard	completed as APD-101
	26	U.S. 1st Marine Division lands on Cape Gloucester, New Britain			
	29	*Naifeh*	DE-352	Consolidated Steel, Orange, TX	
	30	*Rednour*	DE-592	Bethlehem-Hingham Shipyard	completed as APD-102
	30	*Tollberg*	DE-593	Bethlehem-Hingham Shipyard	completed as APD-103

NOTE: *Of these 418 vessels, 300 went to U.S.N. as DEs, six later going to Brazil, 70 went to Great Britain, 23 were completed as APDs, 6 went to France, 2 were completed as DERs (1955).*

Jan.-Dec. 1944	January 3, 1944	*Melvin R. Nawman*	DE-416	Brown Shipbuilding, Houston, TX	
	3	*Oliver Mitchell*	DE-417	Brown Shipbuilding, Houston, TX	
	3	*Grady*	DE-445	Federal Shipbuilding, Newark, NJ	
	3	*Formoe*	DE-509	Federal Shipbuilding, Newark, NJ	
	4	*William J. Pattison*	DE-594	Bethlehem-Hingham Shipyard, MA	completed as APD-104
	5	*Beverly W. Reid*	DE-722	Consolidated Steel, Orange, TX	completed as APD-119
	8	*Parle*	DE-708	Defoe Shipbuilding, Bay City, MI	
	10	*Kenneth M. Willett*	DE-354	Consolidated Steel, Orange, TX	
	11	*Doyle C. Barnes*	DE-353	Consolidated Steel, Orange, TX	
	12	*Tabberer*	DE-418	Brown Shipbuilding, Houston, TX	
	12	*Robert F. Keller*	DE-419	Brown Shipbuilding, Houston, TX	
	13	*Charles E. Brannon*	DE-446	Federal Shipbuilding, Newark, NJ	
	13	*Albert T. Harris*	DE-447	Federal Shipbuilding, Newark, NJ	
	15	*Myers*	DE-595	Bethlehem-Hingham Shipyard, MA	completed as APD-105
	15	*Walter B. Cobb*	DE-596	Bethlehem-Hingham Shipyard, MA	completed as APD-106
	16	Eisenhower assumes duties as Supreme Commander, Allied Expeditionary Force			
	19	*Earle B. Hall*	DE-597	Bethlehem-Hingham Shipyard, MA	completed as APD-107
	19	*Harry L. Corl*	DE-598	Bethlehem-Hingham Shipyard, MA	completed as APD-108
	21	*Leland E. Thomas*	DE-420	Brown Shipbuilding, Houston, TX	
	21	*Chester T. O'Brien*	DE-421	Brown Shipbuilding, Houston, TX	
	22	U.S. Army lands at Anzio			
	22	*William C. Lawe*	DE-313	Mare Island Navy Yard	
	22	*Willard Keith*	DE-314	Mare Island Navy Yard	
	24	*Lloyd E. Acree*	DE-356	Consolidated Steel, Orange, TX	
	25	*Jaccard*	DE-355	Consolidated Steel, Orange, TX	
	26	*Belet*	DE-599	Bethlehem-Hingham Shipyard, MA	completed as APD-109
	26	*Julius A. Raven*	DE-600	Bethlehem-Hingham Shipyard, MA	completed as APD-110
	27	*Bray*	DE-709	Defoe Shipbuilding, Bay City, MI	completed as APD-139
	31	*Douglas A. Munro*	DE-422	Brown Shipbuilding, Houston, TX	
	31	*Dufilho*	DE-423	Brown Shipbuilding, Houston, TX	
	31	U.S. Forces land on Kwajalein (secured February 7)			
	13	Combined Chiefs of Staff order intensive bomber offensive against Germany			
	14	*Ruchamrin*	DE-228	Philadelphia Navy Yard	completed as APD-89
	14	*Kirwin*	DE-229	Philadelphia Navy Yard	completed as APD-90
	14	*Mack*	DE-358	Consolidated Steel, Orange, TX	
	15	*George E. Davis*	DE-357	Consolicated Steel, Orange, TX	
	17	U.S. Forces land on Eniwetok Atoll			
	17	*Gosselin*	DE-710	Defoe Shipbuilding, Bay City, MI	completed as APD-126
	20	"Big Week" of air attacks on Germany opens			
	23	*Haas*	DE-424	Brown Shipbuiilding, Houston, TX	
	29	U.S. Army force lands in Admiralty Islands			
	1	Unnamed	DE-135	Mare Island Navy Yard	
	6	*Johnnie Hutchins*	DE-360	Consolidated Steel, Orange, TX	
	6	*Begor*	DE-711	Defoe Shipbuilding, Bay City, MI	completed as APD-127
	7	*Woodson*	DE-359	Consolidated Steel, Orange, TX	
	19	*Cross*	DE-448	Federal Shipbuilding, Newark, NJ	
	20	*Rolf*	DE-362	Consolidated Steel, Orange, TX	
	21	*Walton*	DE-361	Consolidated Steel, Orange, TX	
	22	*Hanna*	DE-449	Federal Shipbuilding, Newark, NJ	
	28	*Cavallaro*	DE-712	Defoe Shipbuilding, Bay City, MI	completed as APD-128
	April 5	U.S. Air Force bombers raid Ploesti, Rumania			
	6	*Joseph E. Connolly*	DE-450	Federal Shipbuilding, Newark, NJ	
	10	*Rombach*	DE-364	Consolidated Steel, Orange, TX	
	11	*Pratt*	DE-363	Consolidated Steel, Orange, TX	
	17	*Donald W. Wolf*	DE-713	Defoe Shipbuilding, Bay City, MI	completed as APD-129
	22	U.S. forces land in Hollandia area, New Guinea			
	27	*Heyliger*	DE-510	Federal Shipbuilding, Newark, NJ	
	May 1	*Alvin C. Cockrell*	DE-366	Consolidated Steel, Orange, TX	
	1	*French*	DE-367	Consolidated Steel, Orange, TX	
	3	*McGinty*	DE-365	Consolidated Steel, Orange, TX	
	7	*Cook*	DE-714	Defoe Shipbuilding, Bay City, MI	completed as APD-130
	12	*Cecil J. Doyle*	DE-368	Consolidated Steel, Orange, TX	
	22	*John L. Williamson*	DE-370	Consolidated Steel, Orange, TX	
	23	*Thaddeus Parker*	DE-369	Consolidated Steel, Orange, TX	

23	U.S. Army breaks out at Anzio beachhead			
27	*Kline*	DE-687	Bethlehem Steel, Quincy, MA	completed as APD-120
27	*Walter X. Young*	DE-715	Defoe Shipbuilding, Bay City, MI	completed as APD-131
June 4	U.S. Army enters Rome			
5	*Williams*	DE-372	Consolidated Steel, Orange, TX	
6	Allies land at Normandy (Operation Overlord)			
6	*Presley*	DE-371	Consolidated Steel, Orange, TX	
12	*Raymon Herndon*	DE-688	Bethlehem Steel, Quincy, MA	completed as APD-121
15	U.S. Marines and Army invade Saipan			
17	*Balduck*	DE-716	Defoe Shipbuilding, Bay City, MI	completed as APD-132
19	Battle of the Philippine Sea			
29	*Scribner*	DE-689	Bethlehem Steel, Quincy, MA	completed as APD-122
18	*Diachenko*	DE-690	Bethlehem Steel, Quincy, MA	completed as APD-123
21	U.S. Marines and Army land on Guam			
24	U.S. Marines land on Tinian			
25	U.S. Third Army breaks out at Saint-Lo (Operation Cobra)			
26	*Burdo*	DE-717	Defoe Shipbuilding, Bay City, MI	completed as APD-133
August 1	U.S. 12th Army Group becomes operational in France			
3	*Horace A. Bass*	DE-691	Bethlehem Steel, Quincy, MA	completed as APD-124
9	Eisenhower establishes HQ in France			
15	Allies land in southern France (Operation Anvil-Dragoon)			
17	*Wantuck*	DE-692	Bethlehem Steel, Quincy, MA	completed as APD-125
25	*Paris liberated*			
30	*Kleinsmith*	DE-718	Defoe Shipbuilding, Bay City, MI	completed as APD-134
September 15	U.S. Marines land on Peleliu			
17	First Allied Airborne Army units dropped in Holland Operation			
October 4	*Weiss*	DE-719	Defoe Shipbuilding, Bay City, MI	completed as APD-135
20	U.S. Sixth Army lands on Leyte			
23	Battle for Leyte Gulf (to October 26)			
31	*Carpellotti*	DE-720	Defoe Shipbuilding, Bay City, MI	completed as APD-136
November 7	Roosevelt elected to fourth term as U.S. President			
24	United States begins B-29 raids on Japan			
December 13	U.S. Army completes capture of Metz			
15	U.S. Army lands Mindoro			
16	Germans attack in Ardennes (Battle of the Bulge)			

NOTE: Of these 69 keels laid in 1944, 28 were completed as APDs.

Jan.-Sept. 1945	January 9, 1945	U.S. Army land on Luzon		
	20	Hungary signs armistice with Allies		
	30	Anglo-American talks prior to Yalta Conference began at Malata		
	February 3	U.S. Army reaches Manila		
	4	Yalta Conference begis (to February 12)		
	19	U.S. Marines land on Iwo Jima		
	25	B-29 raid on Tokyo demonstrates effectiveness of incendiary bombs		
	27	*Walsh*	DE-601	Bethlehem-Hingham Shipyard, MA	completed as APD-111
	March 3	Japanese resistance in Manila ends		
	7	U.S. Army crosses Rhine on bridge at Remagen		
	9	*Hunter Marshall*	DE-602	Bethlehem-Hingham Shipyard, MA	completed as APD-112
	11	U.S. Eighth units land on Mindanao		
	20	*Earhart*	DE-603	Bethlehem-Hingham Shipyard, MA	completed as APD-113
	April 1	U.S. forces land on Okinawa		
	3	*Walter S. Gorka*	DE-604	Bethlehem-Hingham Shipyard, MA	completed as APD-114
	7	U.S. Navy planes sink Japanese battleship Yamato in East China Sea		
	9	Allies begin major attack on Gothic Line (Italy)		
	12	Roosevelt dies; Truman succeeds as U.S. President		
	12	*Rogers Blood*	DE-605	Bethlehem-Hingham Shipyard, MA	completed as APD-115
	19	*Francovitch*	DE-606	Bethlehem-Hingham Shipyard, MA	completed as APD-116
	25	United Nations conference opens in San Francisco		
	28	Mussolini is executed by partisans		
	30	Hitler dies in bunker; Donitz is chosen as head of state		
	May 5	German forces in Netherlands, northwestern Germany and Denmark surrender		
	7	All German forces surrender unconditionally (2:41 a.m. at Rheims)		
	8	Proclaimed V-E Day		
	July 16	Big Three begin Potsdam Conference (to August 2)		
	16	Atomic bomb successfully tested at Los Alamos		
	26	Potsdam Declaration issued		
	August 6	Atomic bomb dropped on Hiroshima		
	9	Atomic bomb dropped on Nagasaki		
	14	Japan surrenders, ending World War II		
	30	U.S. forces begin landing in Japan		
	September 2	Japan signs Instrument of Surrender on USS *Missouri*—Proclaimed V-J Day		**source**: Anne E. McCarthy, DE

Historian, and Department of Defense Commemorative Events of National Significance, edited by John P. Cosgrove.

THE "CAPTAIN" CLASS—U.S. BUILT DEs FOR GREAT BRITAIN

During the early stages of the Battle of the Atlantic, British shipyards were unable to keep up a rate of production to even maintain numbers to compensate for the tragic rate of attrition amongst destroyers during the first two years of war, according to an article by D.J. Collingwood which appeared in *DESA News* issue of September-October, 1991.

The transfer of the 50 old 4-stackers in exchange for leases on British overseas bases was a welcome stop gap, but by 1941 there was a desperate need for new construction escort vessels for defense convoys against the increasing German U-boat action.

Under Lend-lease agreements the USA made arrangement to build and deliver some 150 Destroyer-Escorts designed to meet British Admiralty requirements. This design had been under consideration by the U.S. Navy for some time, but the first keels were not laid down until April, 1942.

Here is a listing of those 78 Gallant Captains officially classified by the British Admiralty as Frigates:

CAPTAIN (TURBO-ELECTRIC) CLASS

Ship	Builder	Laid Down	Launched	Commissioned	Fate
K-314 *Bentinck* (ex-DE-52)	Bethlehem (Hingham)	29 June 42	22 Aug 42	19 May 43	Ret USN 5 Jan 46
K-315 *Byard* (ex-DE-55)	Bethlehem (Hingham)	15 Oct 42	13 Mar 43	18 June 43	Ret USN 12 Dec 46
K-349 *Calder* (ex-DE-58)	Bethlehem (Hingham)	11 Dec 42	27 Mar 43	15 July 43	Ret USN 19 Oct 45
K-351 *Duckworth* (ex-DE-61)	Bethlehem (Hingham)	16 Jan 43	1 May 43	4 Aug 43	Ret USN 17 Dec 45
*K-352 *Duff* (ex-DE-64)	Bethlehem (Hingham)	22 Feb 43	29 May 43	23 Aug 43	CTL 30 Nov 44
K-353 *Essington* (ex-DE-67)	Bethlehem (Hingham)	15 Mar 43	19 June 43	7 Sept 43	Ret USN 19 Oct 45
*K-462 *Affleck* (ex-DE-71)	Bethlehem (Hingham)	5 April 43	30 June 43	29 Sept 43	CTL 26 Dec 44
K-463 *Aylmer* (ex-DE-72)	Bethlehem (Hingham)	12 April 43	10 July 43	20 Sept 43	Ret USN 5 Nov 45
K-464 *Balfour* (ex-DE-73)	Bethlehem (Hingham)	19 April 43	10 July 43	7 Oct 43	Ret USN 25 Oct 45
K-465 *Bentley* (ex-DE-74)	Bethlehem (Hingham)	26 April 43	17 July 43	13 Oct 43	Ret USN 5 Nov 45
*K-466 *Bickerton* (ex-DE-75)	Bethlehem (Hingham)	3 May 43	24 July 43	17 Oct 43	Lost 22 Aug 44
K-467 *Bligh* (ex-DE76)	Bethlehem (Hingham)	10 May 43	31 July 43	22 Oct 43	Ret USN 12 Nov 45
K-468 *Braithwaite* (ex-DE-77)	Bethlehem (Hingham)	10 May 43	31 July 43	13 Nov 43	Ret USN 13 Nov 45
*K-460 *Bullen* (ex-DE-78)	Bethlehem (Hingham)	17 May 43	7 Aug 43	25 Oct 43	Lost 6 Dec 44
K-508 *Byron* (ex-DE-79)	Bethlehem (Hingham)	24 May 43	14 Aug 43	30 Oct 43	Ret USN 24 Nov 45
K-509 *Conn* (ex-DE-80)	Bethlehem (Hingham)	2 June 43	21 Aug 43	31 Oct 43	Ret USN 26 Nov 45
K-510 *Cotton* (ex-DE-81)	Bethlehem (Hingham)	2 June 43	21 Aug 43	8 Nov 43	Ret USN 5 Nov 45
K-511 *Cranstoun* (ex-DE-82)	Bethlehem (Hingham)	9 June 43	28 Aug 43	13 Nov 43	Ret USN 3 Dec 45
K-512 *Cubitt* (ex-DE-83)	Bethlehem (Hingham)	9 June 43	11 Sept 43	17 Nov 43	Ret USN 4 Mar 46
K-513 *Curzon* (ex-DE-85)	Bethlehem (Hingham)	23 June 43	18 Sept 43	20 Nov 43	Ret USN 27 Mar 46
*K-550 *Dakins* (ex-DE-85)	Bethlehem (Hingham)	23 June 43	18 Sept 43	23 Nov 43	CTL 25 Dec 44
K-551 *Deane* (ex-DE-86)	Bethlehem (Hingham)	30 June 43	29 Sept 43	26 Nov 43	Ret USN 4 Mar 46
*K-552 *Ekins* (ex-DE-87)	Bethlehem (Hingham)	5 July 43	2 Oct 43	29 Nov 43	CTL 16 April 45
K-553 *Fitzroy* (ex-DE-88)	Bethlehem (Hingham)	24 Aug 43	1 Sept 43	16 Oct 43	Ret USN 5 Jan 46
*K-554 *Redmill* (ex-DE-89)	Bethlehem (Hingham)	14 July 43	2 Oct 43	30 Nov 43	CTL 27 April 45
K-555 *Retalick* (ex-DE-90)	Bethlehem (Hingham)	21 July 43	9 Oct 43	8 Dec 43	Ret USN 25 Oct 45
*K-556 *Halsted* (ex-*Reynolds*, ex-DE-91)	Bethlehem (Hingham)	10 July 43	14 Oct 43	3 Nov 43	CTL 10 June 44
K-557 *Riou* (ex-DE92)	Bethlehem (Hingham)	4 Aug 43	23 Oct 43	14 Dec 43	Ret USN 25 Feb 46

K-358 *Rutherford* (ex-DE-93)	Bethlehem (Hingham)	4 Aug 43	23 Oct 43	16 Dec 43	Ret USN 25 Oct 45
K-559 *Cosby* (ex-Reeves, ex-DE-94)	Bethlehem (Hingham)	11 Aug 43	30 Oct 43	20 Dec 43	Ret USN 4 Mar 46
K-560 *Rowley* (ex-DE-95)	Bethlehem (Hingham)	18 Aug 43	30 Oct 43	22 Dec 43	Ret USN 12 Nov 45
K-561 *Rupert* (ex-DE-96)	Bethlehem (Hingham)	25 Aug 43	31 Oct 43	24 Dec 43	Ret USN 20 Mar 46
K-562 *Stockham* (ex-DE-97)	Bethlehem (Hingham)	25 Aug 43	31 Oct 43	28 Dec 43	Ret USN 15 Feb 46
K-563 *Seymour* (ex-DE-98)	Bethlehem (Hingham)	1 Sept 43	1 Nov 43	23 Dec 43	Ret USN 5 Jan 46
K-572 *Spragge* (ex-DE-563)	Bethlehem (Hingham)	15 Sept 43	16 Oct 43	14 Jan 44	Ret USN 28 Feb 46
K-573 *Stayner* (ex-DE-564)	Bethlehem (Hingham)	22 Sept 43	6 Nov 43	30 Dec 43	Ret USN 24 Nov 45
K-574 *Thornbrough* (ex-DE-565)	Bethlehem (Hingham)	22 Sept 43	13 Nov 43	31 Dec 43	Ret USN 29 Jan 47
*K-575 *Trollope* (ex-DE-566)	Bethlehem (Hingham)	29 Sept 43	20 Nov 43	10 Jan 44	CTL 6 July 44
K-576 *Tyler* (ex-DE-567)	Bethlehem (Hingham)	6 Oct 43	20 Nov 43	14 Jan 44	Ret USN 12 Nov 45
K-577 *Torrington* (ex-DE-568)	Bethlehem (Hingham)	22 Sept 43	27 Nov 43	18 Jan 44	Ret USN 11 June 46
K-578 *Narbrough* (ex-DE-569)	Bethlehem. (Hingham)	6 Oct 43	27 Nov 43	21 Jan 44	Ret USN 4 Feb 46
K-579 *Waldegrave* (ex-DE-570)	Bethlehem (Hingham)	16 Oct 43	4 Dec 43	25 Jan 44	Ret USN 3 Dec 45
*K-580 *Whittaker* (ex-DE-571)	Bethlehem (Hingham)	20 Oct 43	12 Dec 43	28 Jan 44	CTL 1 Nov 44
K-581 *Holmes* (ex-DE-572)	Bethlehem (Hingham)	27 Oct 43	18 Dec 43	31 Jan 44	Ret USN 3 Dec 45
K-582 *Hargood* (ex-DE-573)	Bethlehem (Hingham)	27 Oct 43	18 Dec 43	7 Feb 44	Ret USN 4 Mar 46
K-583 *Hotham* (ex-DE-574)	Bethlehem (Hingham)	5 Nov 43	21 Dec 43	8 Feb 44	Ret USN 13 Mar 56

Displacement: 1,430 tons/1,452 tonnes (standard); 1,823 tons/1,852 tonnes (full load).
Length: 306 ft/93.27m (oa); 300 ft/91.44m (wl).
Beam: 37 ft/11.28m
Draught: 11 ft 3 in/3.43m (mean).
Machinery: two boilers; 2-shaft GEC turbines with electric drive.

Performance: 12,000shp; 23 kts.
Bunkerage: 359 tons/364 tonnes
Range: 6,000nm at 12kts
Guns: three 3 in (3x1); two 40mm (2x1); eight 20mm (8x1) (some ten 20mm, nil 40mm).
Complement: 200

CAPTAIN (DIESEL-ELECTRIC) CLASS

Ship	Builder	Laid Down	Launched	Commissioned	Fate
K-310 *Bayntun* (ex-DE1)	Boston NYd.	5 April 42	27 June 42	20 Jan 43	Ret USN 22 Aug 45
K-311 *Bazely* (ex-DE-2)	Boston NYd.	5 April 42	27 June 42	18 Feb 43	Ret USN 20 Aug 45
K-312 *Berry* (ex-DE-3)	Boston NYd.	22 Sept 42	23 Nov 42	15 Mar 43	Ret USN 15 Feb 46
*K-313 *Blackwood* (ex-DE-4)	Boston NYd.	22 Sept 42	23 Nov 42	27 Mar 43	Lost 15 June 44
K-347 *Burges* (ex-DE-12)	Boston NYd.	8 Dec 42	26 Jan 43	2 June 43	Ret USN 27 Feb 46
K-316 *Drury* (ex-DE-46)	Philadelphia NYd.	12 Feb 42	24 July 42	4 April 43	Ret USN 20 Aug 45
*K-470 *Capel* (ex-DE-266)	Boston NYd.	11 Mar 43	22 April 43	16 Aug 43	Lost 26 Dec 44
K-471 *Cooke* (ex-DE-267)	Boston NYd.	11 Mar 43	22 April 43	16 Aug 43	Ret USN 5 Mar 46
K-472 *Dacres* (ex-DE-268)	Boston NYd.	7 April 43	14 May 43	28 Aug 43	Ret USN 26 Jan 46
K-473 *Domnett* (ex-DE-269)	Boston NYd.	7 April 43	14 May 43	3 Sept 43	Ret USN 5 Mar 46
K-474 *Foley* (ex-DE-270)	Boston NYd.	7 April 43	19 May 43	8 Sept 43	Ret USN 22 Aug 45
K-475 *Garlies*	Boston NYd.	7 April 43	19 May 43	13 Sept 43	Ret USN 20 Aug 45

(ex-DE-271)

*K-476 *Gould* (ex-DE-272)	Boston NYd.	23 April 43	4 June 43	18 Sept 43	Lost 1 Mar 44
K-477 *Grindall* (ex-DE-273)	Boston NYd.	23 April 43	4 June 43	23 Sept 43	Ret USN 20 Aug 45
K-478 *Gardiner* (ex-DE-274)	Boston NYd.	20 May 43	8 July 43	28 Sept 43	Ret USN 12 Feb 46
*K-479 *Goodall* (ex-DE-275)	Boston NYd.	20 May 43	8 July 43	4 Oct 43	Lost 29 April 45
*K-480 *Goodson* (ex-DE-276)	Boston NYd.	20 May 43	8 July 43	9 Oct 43	CTL 25 June 44
K-481 *Gore* (ex-DE-277)	Boston NYd.	20 May 43	8 July 43	14 Oct 43	Ret USN 2 May 46
K-482 *Keats* (ex-DE-278)	Boston NYd.	5 June 43	17 July 43	19 Oct 43	Ret USN 27 Feb 46
K-483 *Kempthorne* (ex-DE-279)	Boston NYd.	5 June 43	17 July 43	23 Oct 43	Ret USN 20 Aug 45
K-484 *Kingsmill* (ex-DE-280)	Boston NYd.	9 July 43	13 Aug 43	29 Oct 43	Ret USN 22 Aug 45
*K-514 *Lawford* (ex-DE-516)	Boston NYd.	9 July 43	13 Aug 43	3 Nov 43	Lost 8 June 44
K-515 *Luis* (ex-DE-517)	Boston NYd.	9 July 43	13 Aug 43	9 Nov 43	Ret USN 20 Mar 46
K-516 *Lawson* (ex-DE-518)	Boston NYd.	9 July 43	13 Aug 43	15 Nov 43	Ret USN 20 Mar 46
K-564 *Pasley* (ex-Linsay, ex-DE-519)	Boston NYd.	18 July 43	30 Aug 43	20 Nov 43	Ret USN 20 Aug 45
K-565 *Loring* (ex-DE-520)	Boston NYd.	18 July 43	30 Aug 43	27 Nov 43	Ret USN 7 Jan 47
K-566 *Hoste* (ex-Mitchell, ex-DE-521)	Boston NYd.	14 Aug 43	24 Sept 43	3 Dec 43	Ret USN 22 Aug 45
K-567 *Moorsom* (ex-DE-522)	Boston NYd.	14 Aug 43	24 Sept 43	16 Dec 43	Ret USN 25 Oct 45
*K-568 *Manners* (ex-DE-523)	Boston NYd.	14 Aug 43	24 Sept 43	6 Dec 43	CTL 26 Jan 45
K-569 *Mounsey* (ex-DE-524)	Boston NYd.	14 Aug 43	24 Sept 43	23 Dec 43	Ret USN 25 Feb 46
K-570 *Inglis* (ex-DE-525)	Boston NYd.	25 Sept 43	2 Nov 43	29 Dec 43	Ret USN 20 Mar 46
K-571 *Inman* (ex-DE-526)	Boston NYd.	25 Sept 43	2 Nov 43	13 Jan 44 Ret	USN 1 Mar 46

CTL Declared Constructive total loss after heavy damage and not repaired.

BROTHERS OF THE CRUEL SEA

by Jimmy Green
HMS *Grindall* (K-477, ex DE-273)

I joined the Royal Navy in 1940 and served as an Electrical Artificer for ten and a half years, serving during that time in many ships and many places, including Bermuda, the Persian Gulf and Freetown.

My story, which may interest readers, is about the time I served on *H.M.S. Grindall* (K-477, ex DE-273), a small frigate built in Charlestown, Boston Navy Yard, U.S.A., where we commissioned her in September, 1943. She was often referred to by other ships crews as "The Cockney Ship" because most of our men were from London and the home counties. We affectionately named her "The White Lady."

One of our important trips was to spend six weeks in the Bay of Biscay, sending in three hourly weather forecasts for D-day. We left Londonderry in April and returned about 9 June 1944. We then joined the 5th Escort Group based in Belfast, a support group to assist large convoys. We sailed ahead of them and then joined them to assist the escort in the dangerous water for the final run into harbour. Our group had many U-boat encounters and three boats were sunk by the group.

H.M.S. Grindall and *H.M.S. Keats* destroyed U-285 off Southern Ireland near the end of the war. There were no survivors.

On one trip we met a very large convoy just off Northern Ireland when suddenly two merchant ships were torpedoed and we had the very sorry sight of sailing through the survivors in the sea. It was just like the film "Cruel Sea" shown on television, but I am pleased to say that usually two rescue trawlers were at the rear of these convoys to rescue the men.

At the end of the war we sailed from Belfast to Lochalsh where we finally had to escort U-532 to Liverpool. We sent an armed guard on to the U-532. During the trip down, one of the German crew was washed overboard during rough weather. We searched round the area but failed to find him. It saddened our crew to think he was killed when the war was finished. On arrival Admiral Max Horton put us on show to the public with this U-boat.

Well, the story began again in 1977 when a small advert was put in *The Sunday People*, by Werner Middendorf, a former crew member of the U-532 who lives in Dortmund, to contact any *H.M.S. Grindall* crew. We answered it and after lots of searching and letter-writing, we traced many of our former comrades. We have had several happy reunions in Germany and England with the captain and crew of the U-532.

We visited the U-boat memorial at Kiel in Germany, where a memorial garden contains bronze plaques with the names of the captains and crews of every U-boat sunk. Fifty-five thousand men were lost altogether.

On another occasion we held a reunion at Southsea and took the German crew on a trip to the *H.M.S. Dolphin* museum at Gosport, the British submarine base. We also visited Nelson's flagship, *H.M.S. Victory*, which the Germans were very interested to see. The captain of the U-boat, Herr Kapitan Junker, is still alive, aged about 82, and *Grindall's* ship engineer, Leslie Blacker lives in Cornwall.

Jimmy Green RN, Author of "Cruel Sea"

Captured German Submarine, U-532. The photograph was taken on U-532s arrival in the Mersey, May 17, 1945

WHY THE BRITISH CALLED DEs FRIGATES

by D.J. Collingwood, B.A.
HMS Cubitt (DE-83)

It is probably puzzling to Americans that the DEs were rated only as "Frigates" by the Royal Navy. The main reason for this was that none of the BDEs were fitted out with the triple torpedo tubes which the U.S. Navy DEs had. (They were in short supply and not really necessary for escort work which is what we needed them for.)

British Admiralty classifications demanded that any ship of "destroyer" status MUST have torpedo tubes... hence the "downgrading of the DEs" to frigate status. Another reason was probably the small calibre of the DE's main armament. No Royal Navy ship above minesweeper size had ever mounted guns as small as 3" (which all BDEs had) and even our "Hunt" class escort destroyers had the far more effective twin 4" Mk XIX mountings... so there was yet another reason for the "downgrading!"

HMS Grindall in the North Atlantic 1944. Captain W. Cole Cdr. R.D.R.N.R., Engineer Officer L. H. Blacker, R.N.

1945 WW II Crew Members (L to R): S. Dick Boress, EM2c Don Somers, Ensign (Engineer) Kenneth A. Williams, GM2c

The USS Snowden (DE-246) at Pearl Harbor in August, 1945.

DESA REPORT

by Don Glaser, Executive Administrator

The executive administrator is expected to run the business of the Destroyer-Escort Sailors Association from the bridge while directing a steady supply of energy from the engine room. In fulfilling great responsibilities of this job one could easily grow into a two-headed monster. They say two heads are better than one, but I am sure the members would not want this to happen.

The job offers the best of good news/bad news syndrome. Every day the mail is loaded with new memberships applications, new stories of experiences in DEs by those who sailed them through World War II, Korea and Vietnam—plus exciting activities of the Ten-hundred class, now called FF and FFGs.

The bad (or actually sad) news part of the job is removing names from the active list and adding them to the Taps columns. However, it is gratifying to see an increasing number of widows and families who ask to be continued as Associate Members. They want to continue to receive issues of *DESA News*, to keep informed of the DE activities.

During my 15 years as a member of DESA, I have seen many interesting changes: the growth and increased concern by members in chapter organizations, locating shipmates unseen for decades, the recording and disseminating remarkable history made by DEs. Oddly enough, some of those DEs are still making history under flags of foreign nations. And, so many of them are still affectionately called by their American names and numbers in the story-telling.

My years after moving from elected chairman in 1985 to the newly-created position of executive administrator in 1987 have been especially rewarding. I have seen the establishing and the expansion of DE museums in various parts of the country; the dedication of the bronze sculpture honoring DEs at the Navy Memorial in Washington, our unbelievable history recorded in the three volumes aptly titled *Trim but Deadly*. Each issue of *DESA News* contin-

The USS Crowley (DE-303) anchored in Tokyo Bay, preparing to depart for return to the United States after the signing of the Japanese surrender, Sept. 2, 1945.

ues to report the saga, the odyssey of naval history, wherever DEs sailed and are still sailing.

Personally, I would like to thank some very special people who have been of special service to DESA and to me in so many ways. First, my wife Eleanor who has put up with the long hours, lost weekends in travel, planned as well as unplanned. Second, my secretary and daughter-in-law Dori who is always there when needed, even after long hours of proofing *DESA News*; and third, our receptionist Rhea Lane with her pleasant voice and ability to stay on an even keel during the peaks and valleys of the usual working day. Also, thanks to old friends, Bill Bouton and Pauline Kundis, who are always able to make that extra effort when needed.

Then there are the Chapters always supplying the extra hands when there is extra heavy work loads, specifically the Suncoast and Orlando Chapters, always ready for the stuffing parties for convention mailings and other membership mailings.

Last, but not least, museum curators Jeff Presnell and R.L. Norris; Bob Scott and the Carolinas Chapter for the many dedicated hours at Patriots Point.

All my years with DESA have been enjoyable and I am grateful to all who have helped me make our association successful in so many ways. We have accomplished much and there is much yet to do. We will continue our successes because of so many helping hands.

NATIONAL CONVENTIONS & KEYNOTE SPEAKERS

Aug. 26-28, 1976, Orlando, FL—Delbert D. Black, Master Chief Gunners Mate, USN (Ret.). Ship: *Doyle C. Barnes (DE-353)*.

Aug. 18-20, 1977, St. Louis, MO—Rear Admiral, Bruce Keener, III, USN, Chief of Naval Operations Staff Member and former Executive Officer of *USS Savage (DER-386)*. (Stan Musial attended the reception.)

Aug. 16-19, 1978, Baltimore, MD—Captain Richard C. Ustick, USN, Director Division of Professional Development, U.S. Naval Academy, Annapolis, MD.

Aug. 15-18, 1979, Charlotte, NC—The Honorable Robert T. Conner, Asst. Secretary of the Navy. (The Honorable Ken Harris, Mayor of Charlotte, NC, gave a welcoming address and read the Governor's Proclamation.)

Aug. 13-16, 1980, New Orleans, LA—Vice Admiral William Rowden, USN, Deputy Chief Naval Operations for Surface Warfare. (Master of Ceremonies was Dr. James H. Boren, *USS William C. Cole (DE-641)*, President of "International Association of Professional Bureaucrats.")

Aug. 5-8, 1981, Buffalo, NY—Vice Admiral Samuel L. Gravely, Jr., USN, (Ret.), Former Commanding Officer of *USS Falgout (DE-324)*, Director Defense Communications Agency (DCA).

Aug. 17-21, 1982, Norfolk, VA—Admiral Harry D. Train, II, USN, Commander-in-Chief, Atlantic Fleet.

Aug. 2-6, 1983 Long Beach, CA RMS *Queen Mary*—Vice Admiral Harry C. Schrader, Jr., USN, Commander Naval Surface Force, Pacific Fleet.

Aug. 6-10, 1984, Houston, TX—Vice Admiral Samuel L. Gravely, Jr., USN, (Ret.), Director Defense Communications Agency (DCA).

Aug. 5-9, 1985, Orlando, FL—Captain John A. Williamson. USNR, (Ret.), former Executive Officer, *USS England (DE-635)*.

Aug. 3-8, 1986, Philadelphia, PA—Speaker at Early Bird Party: W. Graham Claytor, Jr., former Secretary of the Navy who served as Commanding Officer of the *USS Lee Fox (DE-65)* and the *USS Cecil J. Doyle (DE-368)*, Chairman of the Board of Directors and President of National Railroad Passenger Corp. (AMTRAK). Speaker at Banquet: Rear Admiral Richard K. Chambers, USNR, Special Assistant to the Chief of Naval Personnel for Naval Reserve & Director of Naval Reserve Personnel Management.

Sept. 7-11, 1987, Seattle, WA—Keynote Speaker: Rear Admiral Joseph P. Reason, Commander, Seattle Naval Base. Special Speaker: Vice Admiral David E. Jeremiah, Director, Navy Program Planning.

Sept. 2-6, 1988, St. Louis, MO—H. Lawrence Garrett, III, Under Secretary of the Navy.

Sept. 11-15, 1989, Charleston, SC—Vice Admiral John W. Nyquist, Assistant Chief of Naval Operations (Surface Warfare).

Aug. 26-Sept. 1, 1990, Baltimore, MD—Vice Admiral John A. Baldwin, Jr., President of the National Defense University.

Aug. 25-29, 1991, Las Vegas, NV—Rear Admiral William M. Fogarty, Commander Joint Task Force Middle East

Aug. 10-14, 1992, Buffalo, NY—Rear Admiral George A. Huchting, Manager, Direct Reporting Program for AEGIS

Sept. 6-10, 1993, Nashville, TN—Admiral Frank B. Kelso, II, Chief of Naval Operations, U.S. Navy

DE SCULPTURE—FIRST OF 22 AT MEMORIAL

by John P. Cosgrove

For nearly two centuries, historians describe how Pennsylvania Avenue has served as the Nation's ceremonial route, symbolizing the moments of triumph and of tragedy that have shaped our country.

On September 1, 1990 this tradition continued in a somewhat different form. It was a celebration at the Navy Memorial unveiling a bronze sculpture honoring a very special Navy vessel—the *Destroyer Escort*.

In an impressive ceremony made up largely of 2,000 DE sailors, spouses and friends, Admiral David E. Jeremiah, Vice Chairman of the Joint Chiefs of Staff, and Vice Admiral Samuel L. Gravely, Jr., USN Retired, unveiled the 33" x 36" bronze bas-relief. This is the first of 22 sculptures depicting highlights of naval history, mounted on granite blocks surrounding The Lone Sailor, centerpiece of the Memorial at 8th and Pennsylvania Avenue, N.W.

Captain John A. Williamson, USNR Retired, delivered the main address. He described outstanding feats of the DE Ship and Sailor in all oceans during World War II, Korea, and Vietnam. "New men in new ships," he emphasized, "is what set the DE sailor apart, a new breed in the naval service," performing beyond greatest expectations.

The highlight of the hour long program was a message from a World War II Navy flyer, President George Bush, which said in part:

"Those who served aboard Destroyer-Escorts during World War II were part of a generation that was called to defend our way of life against the forces of tyranny and Nazi aggression. DE crews fought courageously to protect the life line of ships that supplied the arsenal of freedom. Sinking enemy submarines, battling kamikazes, and rescuing downed aviators and sailors in distress, they played a pivotal role in the war at sea and contributed greatly to the Allied victory."

Deacon Melvin Baranoski, one time MM2/c in USS *Booth* DE-170 asked God's blessing in the invocation for "this bronze sculpture, which may be the only marker for those shipmates lost at sea and for those who have only a watery grave."

Admiral David E. Jeremiah, Vice Chairman of the Joint Chiefs, the Nation's second highest ranking military officer, who began his career in DEs, recalled his experiences in "these proud ships, from a proud tradition, and the fighting spirit of DEs."

DESA President Sam Saylor reminded all that "the Destroyer-Escort was a unique vessel. It played a brief, but major role in wars and skirmishes in U.S. Naval history. As such it is truly fitting that a permanent sculpture be placed here."

Representing spouses, mothers, and sisters was DESA Auxiliary Chairlady, Mary E. Clingerman. She placed a six foot Hawaiian lei over the broad shoulders of the Lone Sailor, and said "We see the Lone Sailor as a member of our family. He could be anyone who served his country. He is near and dear to our hearts, and so representative of the DE sailor honored here today."

Dr. James H. Boren (USS *William C. Cole* DE-641) was the master of ceremonies. The Navy Band, directed by Chief Mark Cockran, provided a musical salute.

In his concluding remarks, John Williamson summed it up: "This is a very special occasion for all of us who had the honor to sail and serve in the DE Navy."

Above: *Dedication ceremony begins at Navy Memorial. Destroyer-Escorts were famed as convoy defenders and multi-purpose ships in World War II, Korea and Vietnam. They sank submarines, battled kamikazies, supported amphibious operations and rescued aviators and sailors. The bronze sculpture commemorating these ships and their crews was the **first** dedicated at the Navy Memorial, Sept. 1, 1990.*

Right: *Colors are posted in program honoring DE Ship and Sailor. The majestic National Archives building, home of the Declaration of Independence and the Constitution, makes an impressive backdrop as Admiral David E. Jeremiah leads salute.*

THE LONE SAILOR WATCHES OVER THE DE MEMORIAL

"The DE sailor was a young American with limited service and limited seagoing experience who, when called upon to serve, fought and worked with such calmness, courage and efficiency, as to exceed all reasonable expectations. New men in new ships. That is what set the DE sailor apart, a new breed in the naval service."

LtCdr R. W. Copeland, USNR
USS Samuel B. Roberts

Destroyer-Escort aka DER, BDE, WDE and APD. Trim but deadly convoy defenders, multi-purpose vessel of WW II, Korea and Vietnam; sank submarines, battled kamikazes, fought like battleships.

The US Navy Memorial is a tribute to those who served and are serving in the Navy. Depicting highlights in naval service, the twenty-two bronze sculptures celebrate that heritage and history time-honored traditions of the sea. The Destroyer-Escort enjoys the singular distinction of being the only vessel so honored. Two DE sailors are members of the Memorial Foundation Board, W. Graham Claytor, Jr. and John P. Cosgrove. (Photos by Stan Jennings)

The USS Ahrens (DE-575) steaming in the Pacific Ocean.

VETERAN'S BIOGRAPHIES

DESTROYER ESCORT · SAILORS ASSOCIATION ·

"TRIM BUT DEADLY"
VOLUME III

Publisher's Note: *All members of the Destroyer Escort Sailors Association were invited to write and submit biographies for inclusion in this publication. All material was printed as received, with a minimum of editing. The Publisher is not responsible for errors or omissions contained herein.*

ROBERT I. ADAIR, TM 2/c, was born May 26, 1923, Cleveland, OH, USS *Calcaterra* (DE-390). Enlisted in the Coast Guard July 1942. Boot camp and captain of the port training at Manhattan Beach, NY.

Receiving Station, Coastal Patrol, Miami, FL, Fowey Rock Light House Coastal Lookout. Torpedo School, Norfolk, VA. Plank owner, DE-390, escort duty North Atlantic and Mediterranean (European Theater).

Applied for, assigned to the Navy Academic Refresher Unit at the College of Wooster, OH (played college football) preparatory for Navy Pre-flight School at the Naval Air Training Station, IA at the end of the war. Discharged March 1946.

Police officer Parma, OH 27 years. Retired as patrol captain. United Parcel Service Safety Training manufacturer 13 years. Married to Eleanore (police woman). They have three daughters, Shane Marie, Cheance Denise, and Holiday Eve. Fully retired, a freemason living in Richfield Township, OH.

JOHN S. AKERS, was born Aug. 18, 1950 in Haleyville, AL. He joined the service Jan. 13, 1970.
Served with the U.S. Navy on the USS *Lester,* (DE-1022). Stationed at the Naval Hospital in Millington, TN. He achieved the rank of hospitalman (HN).

His memorable experiences include: ORI, Guantanamo Bay, Cuba 1970; Mediterannean Cruise, October 1970 to July 1971.

He was awarded the National Defense Ribbon.

His family includes his mother, father, one brother, sister-in-law and one niece.

Akers is presently a technical sergeant 117 TAC Hospital, Birmingham, APRT (ANB), AL.

MALCOLM C. AKEY, SOM 3/c, USS *Crowley,* (DE-303), was born June 27, 1924 Wray, CO. After one year of college, volunteered for and was accepted into U.S. Navy Sept. 13, 1943. Boot camp NTS Farragut, ID. Attended West Coast Sound School. January 15, 1944 was assigned to pre-com detail and became a plank owner of the USS *Crowley* (DE-303) which was commissioned on March 25, 1944.

The *Crowley* trained for a short time off Pearl Harbor before escorting ships to Tulagi, Solomons and Russels to pick up troop ships for invasion of Palaus. After Peleiu Islands was secured was assigned to 3rd and 5th Fleet, most escorting the fast fuel tankers and CVEs as the logistic support group 30.8 and 50.8.

Rode the *Crowley* within ten miles of the "eye" of the worst recorded typhoon on Dec. 17, and 18, 1944, in which three DDs rolled over and sank.

Earned five ribbons: Asiatic-Pacific, four stars on for Palau, Iwo Jima, Okinawa and action off Japan, Philippine Liberation, one star of Leyte, American Area, European Area, and Victory. Spent nine days in Tokyo Bay off Yokasuka, made first Liberty party to Yokasuka. Left Tokyo Bay Sept. 16, 1945 for decommissioning in San Francisco Bay.

Sent to Re. Sta. T.I. California was discharged Shoemaker March 23, 1946.

Returned to Wray, CO. Attended Colorado Agriculture College. Married to Doris Briggs and they have two children, a son Ronnald, who's wife is Carolyn. They also have grandchildren Brian, Cynthia, and Jason. Their daughter is Phyllis. Since 1946 they have owned and operated a combination grain and cattle ranch.

JAMES E. ALLEN, BM2/c, USS *Abercrombie* (DE-343). Born in French Link, IN March 30, 1926. Enlisted USN Jan. 3, 1942, at the age of 15. After boot camp at Norfolk, VA, he was assigned to the Naval Air Station Norfolk for training in Air Group Nine. After training, he was assigned to Fighting Sqd. 9 Air Group Sqd. 41 aboard the USS *Ranger* (CVE-4) where he saw action during the invasion of Africa. He then transferred to a destroyer, the USS *Murphy* (DD-603). This ship was assigned to anti-submarine patrol in the Atlantic and later to the invasion of Sicily. After serving on the *Murphy*, he was transferred to Orange, TX in early 1944.

In May 1944, he became a plank owner of the *Abercrombie*. After the shakedown cruise, the ship headed for the Pacific. There, he saw action at sea and was involved in the invasions of the Philippines and spent many hours on the ping line during the invasion of Okinawa. He was discharged Dec. 3, 1945. He enlisted in the Naval Reserves and was recalled to active duty in 1950 for the Korean Conflict. He served as part of a skeleton crew who took the USS *Navarro* (APD-204) out of mothballs and recommissioned her. He stayed on at Stockton, CA and recommissioned the USS *Sanborn* (APD-193), upon which he served until his discharge in 1952.

He was honored with the following medals: American Campaign, Asiatic-Pacific Campaign with four Bronze Stars, European-African Middle Eastern Campaign with two Bronze Stars, World War II Victory, Navy Occupation Service with Asia clasp, National Defense Service, Philippine Liberation Ribbon with two Bronze Stars, Philippine Presidential Unit Citation, Korean Service.

He is now a retired electrical contractor, living in Dayton, OH with his wife Phyl, whom he married Jan. 11, 1946. They have three children and six grandchildren: daughter Linda and husband Irven Retherford and their two daughters Emily and Kate, son Michael and wife Cindy and their two children Jonathan and Kelley, and daughter Teri Cromer and her two daughters Shannon and Krista. His son and daughter-in-law Michael and Cindy Allen blessed them with a new granddaughter, Caroline Elizabeth, born March 11, 1992.

MAHLON ALLGREN, (BUD), GM2/c, USS

Whitehurst (DE-634), joined the Naval Reserve January 1950 in Youngstown, OH. Discharged September 1950 to enlist in the Navy. Attended boot camp at Great Lakes, IL. Aboard the USS *Whitehurst* January 1951. Served in Puson, and Mokpo, Korea; Pearl Harbor, Guam, and San Diego, CA.

Discharged T.I. July 1954. Worked as a heavy industrial machine erector and field serviceman. Joined DESA in 1990. Married for 37 years and has three sons, Joe, Jered and Jim.

JAMES T. ALLISON, WT1/c, USS *Johnnie Hutchings* (DE-360). Enlisted November 1942. Attended boot camp San Diego. Diesel School - Hemphill Institute of Technology, Los Angeles. Assigned to USS *Kern* via New Caledonia. Reassigned to USS *Pyro* in the New Hebrides and transported ammunition from Brisbane, Samoa, and Port Chicago, CA to New Guinea 1943. Rated fireman second class. Drew straws for Oil Burning School at Philadelphia Navy Yard and won. After school rated fireman first class and transferred to Norfolk, VA. Reassigned to USS *Johnnie Hutchings* (DE-360) then under construction at Orange, TX. Commissioned ship there and after shakedown at Bermuda returned to the Pacific via Panama Canal to the Philippines and anti-submarine patrol. August 1945 encountered enemy subs and sank two and one probable in Ryukya sea lanes. Wars end they were in Okinawa and censorship ended but could think of nothing to write home about except their locations.

Later liberty in Shanghai and patrol duty to Tsingtao and later to USA. Discharged February 1946 from New Orleans, LA.

Following years, auto body repair at Ford dealership and later for self. After a burnout worked at Brooklyn AFB, Mobile, AL from 1951 to 1967. Base closure to Teledyne Continental (Aircraft) which moved onto the base.

Retired February 1985.

Attended the first reunion of DE-360 in 1975 after 25 years in Washington, DC and several others since along with DESA conventions.

Married 43 years, four children and eight grandchildren and expect more later.

MILTON LYMAN AMSDEN, GM2/c, was born May 29, 1926, enlisted in Navy January 1945. Boot camp San Diego, Gunnery School at Bainbridge, MD. Served one year at Manicani, Philippine Islands, ship repair base 3864. Back to Alemeda, CA to decommission USS *Barataria* AVP-33. Discharged Bremerton, WA.

Reenlisted January 1951. Served on USS *Chowanoc* at Adak, AK. Transferred to USS *Formoe*

(DE-509) at San Diego. Home port Newport, RI and Key West, FL. Operated in the Caribbean and out of New Port for three years.

Member of VFW, American Legion, Disabled American Veterans, Destroyer Escort Sailors Association.

Married Anne Earley September 1958, has three children, a son John, and daughters Mary, Jaquline and Julie. They also have four grandchildren. Self-employed as an electrical contractor now residing in Broadus, MT.

JOHN B. ANDERSEN,

was born Oct. 13, 1922 in Green, CT. He joined the service November 1942. Serving with the U.S. Navy on USS *Baron* (DE-166). He was stationed in the Pacific. He achieved the rank of MOMM2/c and was discharged January 1946.

His memorable experiences include being plank owner, USS *Baron,* typhoon, Pacific, camps, Tinian, Saipan.

Married and has three sons. Retired after 45 years in the auto business.

RICHARD EARL ANDREWS,

GM2/c, USS *Lloyd* (DE-209), USS *Allen* (DE-531). Enlisted July 4, 1942. Boot camp Newport, RI three weeks; Norfolk three weeks, Gunnery School. Assigned Armed Guard, Brooklyn. First ship merchant tanker MS *Florida.* Duty Caribbean and South Atlantic until March 1943. New tanker SS *St. Antonio.* One trip Casablanca, one Algiers.

Later 1943 transferred Norfolk, make-up crew for DE-209. Commissioned Feb. 11, 1944. After shakedown the *Lloyd* and 13 other DEs escorted large convoy to Mediterranean. Relieved by British escorts. Proceeded to Bizerte, Tunisia. Nine days later, escorted convoy to States. *Lloyd* proceeded to Philadelphia to be converted to APD. Was transferred to Gunnery School in Washington, DC. After school was transferred to Seattle, WA and assigned USS *St. Croix* (APA-231), commissioned Dec. 1, 1944. Worked South Pacific until war ended. Discharged Oct. 31, 1945.

January 1951 recalled to service and assigned USS *Allen* (DE-531) in mothballs. Recommissioned Feb. 26, 1951. Assigned Third Naval District as a reserve training ship. Cruised the North Atlantic and Caribbean until discharged April 1952.

At present retired from city of Richmond, VA as fleet superintendent. Married over 47 years.

EDMOND JOSEPH ANUSZCZYK,

was born Sept. 6, 1924 in Brenham, TX and baptized in St. Mary's Church on Sept. 8, 1924. At 18 months, Wanda and Edmond left by car for Massachusetts they arrived at the home of Leon's parents, 182 Church St.,

New Bedford and stayed for about two months. They then moved to 40 Garfield St. Acushnet, MA where Edmond lived until he was called into the Armed Services. He served in the U.S. Navy as a signalman aboard the USS *Holder* (DE-401).

Edmond's ship left with a large convoy from Norfolk, VA headed for the Mediterranean Sea. As they got nearer to the Algerian coast, a German torpedo plane struck the *Holder.* The ship was towed to Algiers and on to Oran. After the ship received some patchwork, it was towed to Brooklyn, NY.

He received a 30 day survivor leave and that is when he first met Viola Westling at Lincoln Park, Dartmouth, MA.

Edward then went back overseas aboard the USS *Panamint* (AGC-13) but this time going to the Pacific side, crisscrossing the Pacific Ocean many times including crossing the Equator and the International Date Line.

The USS *Panamint* was one of the command ships used in the invasions and Okinawa was one of the islands invaded on April 1, 1945. This was a success and the next stop was Ie Shima, a little island of the coast of Okinawa. It was here that GI war correspondent, Ernie Pyle was killed.

Shortly after the war ended, the ship moved into Ominato Guard District, Northern Honshu for the Japanese surrender ceremonies. Col. Devereau, a prisoner on Hokkaido was released and came aboard the *Panamint.*

Edmond was honorably discharged from the U.S. Navy and married Viola Westling on May 24, 1947 in Sacred Heart Church, Middleboro, MA.

Of all the Anuszcyzyks found so far, dating back to the early 1800s, Edmond has to be noted as the most active and diversified person.

His hobbies include, stamp collecting, photography, baseball, basketball and football.

Member of American Legion, Acushnet, MA; Bourne Chamber of Commerce, Buzzards Bay, MA; Cape Cod Chamber of Commerce, Hyannis, MA; Canal Sportsman Club, Bourne, MA; Fall River Rod and Gun Club, Westport, MA; Fraternal Order of Police, Rhode Island; Harbor Beach Club, Mattapoisett, MA; Knights of Columbus; St. Isidore, The Farmer, Council No. 4373, Westport, MA, 1st, 2nd and 3rd degree.

He was awarded the American Campaign, European African Campaign with Bronze Star, Asiatic-Pacific Campaign with Bronze Star, Navy Occupation-Japan, World War II, National Defense, Korean Service.

Married to Viola who was born May 24, 1928 in Middleboro, MA. In her younger years, she lived on West St. and went to the public schools there. Viola graduated from high school in 1946. She is not one to join organizations. She does like parties, bingo and shopping.

Edmond J. and Viola had two children.

Viola's parents were - Earle Lawrence Westling (Wallace) and Anna Edith Jardullo (Giardullo).

RAY WILLIAM ARENSMAN,

was born Oct. 14, 1921 in Huntingburg, IN. January 1942 joined the U.S. Naval Reserve V-7 Program. August 1943 entered USNR Midshipman School at Columbia University, New York City. November 1943 commissioned ensign, USNR.

January-April 1944 served aboard USS *Austin* (DE-15), convoying in the Aleutians, Adak-Attu; April - July 1944 Submarine Chaser School, Miami, FL; July-August 1944 Aircraft Recognition School, Columbus, OH; September 1944-June 1945 served as gunnery officer aboard USS *Janssen* (DE-396), convoying the USS *Bogue,* a CVE, on anti-submarine duty in Atlantic. This group captured the German submarine now on display at Chicago's Museum of Science Industry. June 1945-October 1945. Served on USS *Janssen* (DE-396), through Panama Canal to Hawaii; October 1945-May 1946, returned through Panama Canal and long decommissioning of USS *Janssen* (DE-396), in Green Cove Springs, FL; May 1946, discharged from active duty, but stayed active in U.S. Navy Reserve for several years. He achieved the rank of Lt(jg) USNR.

1946 to date: completed doctorate in business education and economics at Indiana University under GI Bill.

Taught business and Social Studies in high school for three years, then taught business administration and economics at six universities for 30 years.

Retired in 1987 from University of Evansville as Emeritus Professor of Economics.

Married to Helen Mae Lukemeyer, who served in Air Evacuation with Army Nursing Corps.

They have two children, Ann and Fred and four grandchildren.

"Had I to do it over again, I'd again choose the DDs and DEs of the "Donald Duck Navy"! stated Arensman.

WILLIE H. ARMSTRONG,

CS2/c, USS *Coates,* (DE-685), born in Chicago, IL, Feb. 29, 1928. Wisconsin resident since 1931. Enlisted in Navy Feb. 15, 1946. Boot training at San Diego, CA. Reported aboard the USS *LSM 437* bound for Pearl Harbor, HI. At Pearl Harbor he served on the USS *ATR-81.* The Navy sold the tug and he was transferred to the USS *Los Angeles* (CA-135) and spent Christmas, 1946, in China.

Willie served on the Atlantic coast aboard the USS *Coates* (DE-685). In February 1951 the ship was in mothballs at Green Cove Springs, FL and because of the Korean Conflict was recommissioned and Willie was a member of that crew. He served on the USS *Coates* for three years, three months; assigned shore duty at the Great Lakes Naval Training Center in Illinois; honorably discharged in 1957 rated CS 2nd class.

CHARLIE R. ARNOLD,

SSML3/c, USS *Eldrige* (DE-173), USS *Otterstetter* (DE-244), USS *Arcadia* (AD-23), selective volunteer (drafted) April 21, 1943. Born July 22, 1924 in Kossuth, MS. Went to boot camp Bainbridge, MD and gunner school at Norfolk, VA.

Served in the North Pacific and South Pacific. Medals received while serving are - American Area Campaign Medal, European African Middle Eastern Area Campaign Medal, World War II Victory Medal. Honorably discharged Dec. 17, 1946.

Married Inez Fennel, March 18, 1950 in Corinth, MS. Raised three daughters: Dora Jean, Sue and Patricia, and one son Tony. They have four grandsons: Phil, Josh, Zack and Jeremy. For the past 41 years he has been a barber hair stylist in Memphis, TN.

EDWARD JULIAN AUSTIN, TM2/c, USS *Chatelain* (DE-149) and USS *Alecto* (AGP-14). Enlisted June 1943. Boot camp Bainbridge, MD. Assigned to USS *Chatelain* (DE-149); on board at commissioning Sept. 22, 1943. Shakedown to Bermuda. Convoy to Londonderry, Ireland and return to New York. Convoy to Gibraltar and return to New York. Assigned to Task Force 22.3; USS *Guadalcanal* (CVE-60); USS *Chatelain* (DE-149); USS *Flaherty* (DE-135); USS *Pope* (DE-134); USS *Pillsbury* (DE-133) and USS *Jenks* (DE-665).

Actions: April 9, 1944 - sunk U-515, April 11, 1944 planes off Guadalcanal sunk U-68, June 4, 1944 surfaced and captured U-505, April 24, 1945; USS *Davis* (DE-136) torpedoed off Argentia, Newfoundland; Task Group sank U-546 the attacker.

Awarded the Presidential Unit Citation for capture of U-505; American Theatre (one Battle Star and European African Theatre with two Battle Stars.

Discharged December 1945.

Married Evelyn Rowland on Aug. 14, 1945. They have children Stephen Edward born Nov. 9, 1947. He has two daughters; Karen Lynn born Oct. 28, 1951, has one son and one daughter, Kevin Roland born May 6, 1957 has one daughter.

Retired independent oil marketer with gas retail outlets in Georgia, North Carolina and Virginia.

OMER E. BAILEY, was born Nov. 30, 1918 in Dexter, MO. He joined the service April 24, 1942, serving in the Navy. Stationed at USNTS, Great Lakes, IL; NTSCH (Radio Oxford, OH USSPC 1193, SCTC, Miami, FL; NTS, NOB, Norfolk, VA; USS *Neunzer* (DE-150), USS *McGinty* (DE-365). Achieved the rank of RM1c.

He was awarded the American Area Ribbon, World War II Victory Ribbon, European African Middle Eastern Area Ribbon and the Asiatic-Pacific Area Ribbon.

His wife died May 11, 1987. They have two daughters, and two grandsons. Bailey is now retired from General Motors, Pontiac Div.

CLAYTON D. BAIRD, Lt. (jg), USS *Edwin A. Howard* (DE-346). Entered NROTC in September 1941 at University of Texas at age 17. Because of acceleration of training due to the outbreak of war, graduated from school of Naval Science and commissioned as ensign at age 19. After a short tour of duty aboard USS *Cronin* (DE-704) assigned to Subchaser Training Center in Miami. After graduation assigned to USS *E.A. Howard* (DE-346). Saw service in the Atlantic Theatre, Mediterranean Theatre and Pacific Theatre of operations and the Philippine Liberation. Received the Navy Occupation and Victory Medal, plus two major Battle Stars for action in the Philippines and Borneo.

Returned to inactive duty in April 1946. Entered University of Houston in June 1946 and received BBA degree in August 1947. Employed August 1946 by Baird's Bakeries and is currently chairman of the board. Mrs. Baird's Bakeries is a regional wholesale baking operation with some 3,200 employees and twelve plants.

He has been married over 45 years and has two children, Clayton Jr. and Dorothy Elizabeth.

JACK L. BAKER, RM3/c, USS *Johnnie Hutchins* (DE-360), born Sep. 3, 1926, San Francisco, CA. Enlisted Sept. 18, 1943. Boot camp Farragut, ID. Naval training school (radio) at University of Idaho, Moscow, ID, June 1944 to Norfolk, VA to a DD DE Pool. Assigned to DE-360 being built in Orange, TX. In August 1945 to Orange, TX to board ship as a plank owner. Ship commissioned Aug. 28, 1945. En route to Bermuda on shakedown. Picked up survivors of USS *Warrington,* sunk in the Gulf by hurricane. Took survivors to Norfolk, then continued on shakedown. After shakedown, short time in Atlantic, went to Charleston Navy Yard, Boston, MA, then back to NOB Norfolk, for ship's orders through Panama Canal and to Pacific for remainder of war. Most memorable: sinking of Japanese submarines between Okinawa and the Philippines Aug. 9, 1945. At end of war, ship sent to Korea, then to Shanghai, China. In November they were sent to Tsingtao, China. December 1945 ship ordered to return to USA via Pearl Harbor, then to San Pedro, CA, for transfer of crew and mothballing of ship. Honorably discharged April 19, 1946.

He spent 38 years as an outside salesman, selling auto parts, paint, etc. to the automotive aftermarket. Retired 1989. Now living in (Boulder Hill) Montgomery, IL. *(See photos, page 743.)*

CHARLES BALL JR., F1/c, *Chester T. O'Brien,* (DE-421). Enlisted U.S. Navy, Nov. 19, 1943. Boot camp - Farragut, ID. Entered basic engineering school, Great Lakes, IL. After schooling sent to Philadelphia, PA, then to Norfolk, VA for D-Pre-commissioning. Assigned to *Chester T. O'Brien,* (DE-421), Houston, TX. Onto Bermuda for shakedown cruise. Returned Boston Navy yards and assigned to escort fleet of aircraft carriers to Naples, Italy. Back to drydocks in New York, then to Panama Canal and Pacific. During WWII they performed escort duties to Philippines and China. War ended and they came back to California. Honorably discharged April 20, 1946.

Campaign Ribbons, Asiatic-Pacific Area, American Area, Philippine Liberation, Victory Medal, World War II.

Married Louise M. DeLima in 1946. They have six children, 15 grandchildren. Spent his working career in material handling equipment. Retired in 1988.

Charter member of Massachusetts. DESA and active in DESA. Residing in Feeding Hills, MA.

JOHN P. BANNON, was born Sept. 10, 1924 in North Bellmore, Long Island, NY. Enlisted in Coast Guard June 1942. Served until February 1946. Served on CGC 75007 and 1943 until 1945 served on USS *Camp* (DE-251), as seaman and then as fireman. Got off the camp July 1945 in San Diego station at Terminal Island, bouy deport, worked machine shop, then discharged February 1946.

August 25, 1945 tied knot to the best. Worked as a carpenter as civilian until 1966. Went to work for the New York City Transit Authority. Worked as iron worker until he retired July 1987. Moved to Pennsylvania. He occasionally thinks back on the past, ship and shipmates come to mind.

HERMAN WADDELL BARBER, CEM, USS *Blackwood* (DE-219), enlisted in the U.S. Navy May 1940 with boot camp at Norfolk, VA. Upon completion was assigned to USS *Schley* (DD-103). Travelled to Hawaii and was assigned to Kaneohe NAS from January 1941 to November 1942, including the attack on Pearl Harbor on Dec. 7, 1941. Transferred to Johnson Island from November 1942 until May 1943 after which was assigned to *J. Douglas Blackood* (DE-219) until May 1946. Next assigned to USS *Pine Island* (AV-12) and participated in Operation High Jump at the South Pole. Next assigned to USS *Kearsarge* (CV-33) and USS *Midway* (CVA-41). Spent two years in the Reserve Fleet in Newport News, VA and then assigned to the USS *Block Island* (CVE-106) where he made warrant officer (electrician). Next assigned to USS *George Clymer* (APA-27) and participated in the Korean War, after which assigned to ships repair unit, Charleston, SC during 1954 and 1955. Then served on USS *Essex* (CV-10) until September 1956 after which went to the Reserve Fleet in San Diego, CA until June 1957. Then served on the USS *Kearsarge* (CV-33) until February 1960. He was then assigned to the USS *Delta* (AR-9) until retirement in 1961 as CWO-3.

During the following years, he worked for the cities of Torrance and Beverly Hills, CA and the State of California, retiring in December 1977 after 13 years of service.

He is married and is now living in retirement as a full time RVer.

CURTIS L. BARRETT, was born Aug. 21, 1923 in Athens, GA. He joined the U.S. Navy Reserve April 13, 1943. Stationed at Bainbridge, MD; Norfolk, VA; Marc Island, CA; Philadelphia, PA. He was discharged Nov. 10, 1945. Achieved the rank of SSML 2/c.

Barrett is married and has two sons and one grandson. Retired from drycleaning and in cattle farming now.

CHARLES VERLIS BARTIMUS, was born

April 4, 1925 in Mattoon, IL. Left high school and enlisted in the U.S. Navy on April 3, 1943. Took boot camp training at the Great Lakes Naval Training Station, Great Lakes, IL.

Attended Radio Operators Training School at the University of Chicago, SCTC in Miami, FL and the Naval Training Center at Norfolk, VA.

Became a plank owner of the USS *Charles J. Kimmel*, (DE-584), when it was christened at Bethlehem Shipyard, Bingham, MA on Jan. 15, 1944, by Mrs. Charles G. Kimmel, mother of Lt. Charles Jack Kimmel, USMC for whom the ship was named.

Served in the North Atlantic, Mediterranean and Southwest Pacific Theaters. Earned the Victory Medal, Asiatic-Pacific Area Campaign Medal with one star, Philippine Liberation Ribbon (one star) and the American Area Campaign Medal. Honorably discharged on March 10, 1946 with a radioman second class rating.

Received a BS and MS in education degrees from Eastern Illinois University of Charleston, IL. Was an educator in the states of Illinois and Arizona for 35 years, in the capacity of teacher, principal and for 25 years, as a public school superintendent.

Charles and his wife, Thelma Tutt Bartimus, has one son, Ted Alan Bartimus, who is married to Michelle Dilree Bartimus. The granddaughters are Nicole Dilree, Ashley Helen Bartimus and Paige Kathleen Bartimus.

BART BASCHE, was born Nov. 21, 1925 in Iona,

MN. He joined the U.S. Navy Jan. 6, 1944. Released May 6, 1946. Served also with the U.S. Naval Reserve. Stationed at NTS, Great Lakes, IL; Service School at Great Lakes, IL. USS *Waterman* (DE-740) served in Pacific. Torpedo School, Great Lakes, IL; USS *Howze* (AP-134).

He achieved the rank of gunners mate third class, SV-6 U.S. Naval Reserve.

His memorable experiences includes the two typhoons.

He was awarded the Asiatic-Pacific with one Silver, and one Bronze Star, World War II Victory, Navy Occupation Service, Asia Clasp, National Defense, Philippine Liberation, with two Bronze Stars, Philippine Presidential Unit Citation, Philippine Independence.

Married Betty Diederich, Feb. 25, 1952. They have two children, Debby and Richard and two grandchildren, Eric and Beth. Retired from manufacturing business in 1988. Now living in Las Vegas, NV and loving it. Volunteer-church, AARP, SBA-SCORE, hospital.

W. RUSSELL BAUM, TM2/c, USS *Willis* (DE-395). Helped to commission USS *Willis* at Brown

Shipbuilding Company, Houston, TX. Lt. Comdr. G.R. Atterbury was their first captain.

Served aboard in the Atlantic fleet until June 1945. During this time the *Willis* was assigned to a hunter-killer group formed around the carrier *Bogue* (CVE-9). The *Bogue* task force was given credit for the sinking of 12 subs.

They were awarded the following: Presidential Unit Citation with Blue Star, American Campaign Medal, European African Middle Eastern Campaign Medal with one Battle Star, Asiatic-Pacific Campaign Medal, World War II Victory Medal, Navy Occupation Service Medal (Asia Clasp).

He left the *Willis* June 1945 because of removal of the torpedo tubing before going to the Pacific Fleet.

Was discharged in February 1946, came back to Reading, PA. Learned the plumbing trade from which he retired in 1987. Married in 1953 and has one son Kevin.

Last two years he attended reunions held by *Willis* crew members. Both reunions were a big success. They managed to get a roster list of 108 men and a taps list of 40 men. They are still looking for more crew members.

ROY E. BAYLESS, (JOE), EM3/c, USS

Neuendorf, (DE-200). Entered Navy June 10, 1943 at Huntington, WV and went to boot camp at Great Lakes. Member of commissioning crew USS *Neuendorf* Oct. 18, 1943 at Charleston, SC.

After shakedown cruise to Bermuda the *Neuendorf* was assigned to escort duty in the Pacific escorting tankers, resupply echelons and anti-sub patrols in the Solomons, New Guinea, Wadke, the Philippines, etc.

In early January 1945 they participated in a massive convoy on the Lingayen operation encountering numerous air strikes for several days. Following this they handled several escort assignments then spent an extended period in Iloilo, Panay Island.

The *Neuendorf* returned to San Diego in October 1945 and he was discharged at San Pedro, CA in April 1946.

Married and has two children and three grandchildren. Attended Cleary College, San Bernardino Valley College and University of California.

Worked at Detroit Willow Run Airport in various positions including assistant airport manager 1946-1959; airport director, city of Riverside, CA, 1959-1974; director of Aviation City of Austin, TX, 1974-1985; airport consultant, 1985-1991; president California Association of Airport Executives 1967; California Airport Manager of Year 1972; Chairman Airport Administrators Council, Southern California Association of Governments 1970-1974; President American Association of Airport Executives 1976; Chairman Aviation Advisory Panel Texas A&M 1980-1985;

Board of Directors Airport Operators Council International 1980-1983. Now fully retired and lives in Cape Coral, FL, winters and Mercer, WI, summers.

WALLACE R. BEAMER, RDM 3/c, born May

18, 1921 at Vienna, VA. Enlisted in USN June 10, 1942 at Washington, DC Boot Camp NTS Norfolk, VA. Attended Aviation Radio School, Jacksonville, NAS 1942. Transferred to Norfolk for sea duty and commissioned USS *Reuben James* (DE-153) on April 1, 1943 (first DE built for the United States Navy), second ship to bear that name, after USS *Reuben James* (DD-245) was sunk by a German sub in North Atlantic October 1941. Training ship at SCTC Miami, FL. Two convoy trips to North Africa as ASW ship, shot down Junkers-88 in night torpedo attack, sank U-879 on April 19, 1945 in North Atlantic with USS *Buckley* (DE-51), while operating as a killer group, that included USS *Wilke* (DE-800) and USS *Scroggins* (DE-799).

After the war, served on the USS *Philadelphia* (CL-41) making two trips to Le Havre, France to bring home troops to New York. Made two midshipmen cruises to Mediterranean, one on carrier USS *Randolph* (CV-15) in 1947 and another on carrier USS *Midway* (CVB-41) in 1948.

Honorably discharged at Norfolk NAS April 16, 1948. He was awarded the American Theater, European Theater, German occupation, World War II Victory and Good Conduct.

Retired June 1, 1986, lives in Waldorf, MD with wife Maryjane. They have two sons, one daughter and four grandchildren. Die hard Redskin fan since 1938 and a season ticket holder.

Note: A third USS *Reuben James* (FFG-57) is now serving proudly in the Pacific Fleet, **the spirit still lives on!**

HENRY C. BEATTIE, QM2/c, USS *Abercrombie*

(DE-343), born Aug. 24, 1924, in Philadelphia, PA. Enlisted in the Navy July 27, 1943. Great Lakes Nav Gra Sta., IL. August 21, 1943, Quartermaster School, Newport, RI, Feb. 12, 1944. USS *Abercrombie* commissioned, Orange, TX, May 1, 1944.

To Pearl Harbor, Manus, AI; Philippines; Okinawa, Japan. Discharged March 11, 1946. Employed as an independent grocer 1946-1947; U.S. Post Office 1967-present. Lives in Manlius, NY with wife Marilyn. They have one son, two daughters, and six grandchildren.

C. HENRY BEAZLEY, TE3/C, USS *Greenwood*

(DE-679), was born on April 7, 1925 in Lancaster, PA, and graduated from J.P. McCaskey High School in June of 1943. Immediately upon graduation he entered the Navy for a six year hitch.

His boot training was at Sampson, NY after which he attended Class "A" torpedo school at Newport, RI.

Next, he received P.T. schooling at Melville, RI and was assigned to Ron 15 in the Mediterranean to participate in the invasion of Southern France. October 1944, he was released from P.T. Sqdn. 15 at Karouba Docks and transferred stateside.

After a short leave at home, he arrived at Treasure Island, CA on his way to the Pacific. He was assigned to P.T. Ron 10 in the Philippines and moved south on July 1, 1945 to participate in the invasion of Borneo at Balikpapan.

At wars end, he was reassigned to the Naval Supply Depot on Calicoan in the Philippines to complete his overseas obligation where he received his mailman third class rating.

His final three years of enlistment were spent aboard the *Greenwood* as the designated mailman, a petty officer of the watch, and petty officer of a C.I.C. radar watch.

He was married in 1950, has three grown sons and one grandson, and is now retired from the U.S. Postal Service as a letter carrier.

LOVELIN ALFRED BELL, MM1/c, USS *Joseph E. Campbell* (DE-70 APD-49). Enlisted in the Navy July 3, 1942. Had boot training and 16 weeks machinist mate school in San Diego, CA. Reported aboard the USS *McLanahan* (DD-615) in San Pedro, CA November 1942. Went to the East Coast on shakedown. Made one trip to Oran, Algeria, North Africa on convoy duty. Was transferred to SCTC Miami, FL June 11, 1943. Went to Norfolk, VA from SCTC.

In September 1943 went to Hingham, MA with a draft to put the USS *Joseph E. Campbell* (DE-70) in commission on Sept. 22, 1943. Went to Bermuda on shake down. Was on convoy escort duty in North Atlantic and Dutch West Indies to Algeria and Tunisia North Africa. The (DE-70) was the flag ship for the division. During December 1944 and January 1945 the (DE-70) was converted to the (APD-49) Staton Island, NY Navy Yard.

After Staton Island went to Hawaii, Marshall Islands, New Guinea, Philippines, Okinawa and Japan. After the war it was back to the east coast. Left (APD-49) Dec. 30, 1945 in Philadelphia. Discharged Jan. 5, 1946 in New Orleans.

Was self-employed as co-owner of Bell Lumber yard in July 1946. Later that year enlisted in the Reserves. Ordered to active duty Oct. 21, 1950. The lumber yard business was closed.

Served aboard USS *Weeden* (DE-797) a reserve training ship on the West Coast and was discharged Jan. 25, 1952.

Returned to lumber business as sole owner of Bell Lumber Yard. Forced into retirement Oct. 30, 1976 due to cancer.

Presently still retired. Married to Lula 44 years and have two children, Scott and Martha.

RUDOLPH GEORGE BENZ, was born July 16, 1924 in Treves Rhineland, Germany. He joined the service Dec. 8, 1943. Served with the U.S. Navy. He was stationed at NTS Sampson, NY and on board the USS *Taylor* (DE-415). He achieved the rank of B2/c. His memorable experiences include the typhoon in the Pacific, sub sunk in last days of war.

He was awarded the Pacific Theater Ribbon, seven stars, Victory Medal, Philippine Liberation Medal.

Benz is married and has two sons. Retired. Previously boiler inspector for insurance company.

ROBERT EDWARD BERRYMAN, RM2c, United States Naval Reserve at time of honorable discharge on Dec. 7, 1945 at Great Lakes Naval Station, Great Lakes, IL.

His enlistment began with swearing in at the Federal Building in Detroit, MI on Jan. 12, 1942. His boot training was conducted at Great Lakes Naval Training Station in Great Lakes, IL. He qualified for Naval Radio School training and was transferred to U.S. Naval Reserve Radio School training and was transferred to U.S. Naval Reserve Radio Operators School at Indianapolis, IN. Upon graduation from the radio school, as a RM3c (radioman third class, petty officer) he was sent to Pier 92 in New York City for further transfer to the Sub Chaser Training Center in Miami, FL in August of 1942. He completed the training program and became a member of the ship's company.

He applied for destroyer escort assignment and was ordered to report for assignment as radioman third class to the USS *Donnell* (DE-56), being built at the Bethlehem-Hingham Shipyard at Hingham, MA. He was sent to the Hingham Shipyard in April 1943, as a "plank owner" member of the original crew of the USS *Donnell,* (DE-56). He was aboard the USS *Donnell* (DE-56) when it was commissioned in July 1943. They completed their shakedown cruise at Bermuda Island and received assignment to Destroyer Div. #11 of the Atlantic Fleet, assuming convoy duty in the Atlantic Ocean from Aruba and Curacao to Londonderry, North Ireland, convoying oil tankers. He was advanced in rating to radioman second class during their shakedown cruise. He was asked to take the test for V-12 Officers Training and was selected from their division to be assigned to the V-12 program at Western Michigan University in Kalamazoo, MI.

Following treatment for leg and back problems, he was assigned an instructor for Camp Robert Small (the first black sailors radio operators school in the U.S. Navy) in November 1944 and served in the capacity of Code-Procedure Instructor at Camp Robert Small until his honorable discharge from the U.S. Naval Reserve as RM2c (Radioman second class) petty officer on Dec. 7, 1945.

Since his separation from the U.S. Naval Reserve he has been active in the radio-television field as an active sportscaster, newscaster and music show personality (a job that he is now doing as a semi-retired, free lance actor-writer-music show host for a local radio station). He and his wife Marge, have been married 41 years and are justly proud of their three daughters and a son and five grandchildren.

They currently reside in Grand Blanc, MI (their home since February 1962).

ROBERT JAMES BILLIGMEIER, S1/c, USS *Griswold* (DE-7), born June 20, 1945, Oakes, ND. Enlisted in Navy May 26, 1943. Boot camp Great Lakes, IL; placed in OGU at Great Lakes, sent to San Diego, then New Orleans and became passenger on LST 267; went through Panama Canal. Boarded USS *Griswold* at Eniwetok, Marshall Islands. Routine con-

voy work in Pacific from November 1943 to Feb. 26, 1944, then had 12 days R&R in Sidney, Australia. Back to high rough seas, then ordered to Pearl Harbor and further ordered to Mare Island, CA for overhaul. Ten days leave ended on May 26 with message that ship was ready to depart for Pearl Harbor. Four months tour kept *Griswold* near Pearl Harbor working with U.S. submarines in training operations; then spent five months escorting oil tankers between Eniwetok and Ulithi Atoll, Caroline Islands, carrying fuel to the fleet in Philippine Sea. In March-April 1945 *Griswold* sat in one space eight weeks (long swing around the hook), shifting berths only once. In late May 1945 was at Okinawa and saw heavy action until late June. Left for Leyte Gulf with stop at Samar where someone acquired a macaque monkey for a mascot which they kept on ship until their return. Long periods spent at sea, off Japan, which finally ended when Hirohito capitulated. Returned to the States through Golden Gate Bridge September 1945. Spent remainder of time in Great Lakes Navy Hospital until discharge Feb. 2, 1946.

In fall of 1946 went to Washington, DC and attended Chamberlain Vocational High School; graduated June 1948. Had several employers until 1951 when hired by C&P Telephone Company in installation, repair and prewire. Disability retirement April 1970; moved to Montana for 10 years; returned to Virginia 1981 when he remarried. Has one son, three daughters and five grandchildren.

DAVID P. BILLINGS, Lt (jg), was born Sept. 19, 1922, Portland, OR. Enlisted in the Navy, December 1942, while a student at UC Berkeley.

Called to active duty on July 1, 1943. V-12 Navy program at U.C. Berkeley. Graduated from U.C. Berkeley February 1944. Degree in mechanical engineering. Sent to premidshipmans training school at Asbury Park, NJ.

Sent to U.S. Naval Academy May 1944. August 1944 received his ensign commission. Sent to Naval Training Center in Miami, FL. Went to DE Training School, steam-electric. Received orders to report to the USS *Micka*, (DE-176) operating out of Recife, Brazil. Flew via NATS to Recife. Reported aboard the USS *Micka* on Nov. 6, 1944 - assistant engineering officer (a diesel-electric powered ship).

Ports of call: Recife, Bahia, Rio de Janero.

Escort duty: USS *Marblehead,* various baby aircraft carriers. Sailed to New York and Casco Bay, ME March 1945 doing duty in the North Atlantic, anti-submarine patrol.

May 1945, convoy duty. Went to Oran, Algeria French Africa, then to Charleston, SC Navy Shipyard to be outfitted for Pacific duty.

July 1945 sailed to Guantanamo Bay, Cuba and then through the Panama Canal headed to San Diego and Hawaii.

Japanese surrendered on Aug. 14, 1945, one day before the USS *Micka* arrived at Pearl Harbor. The USS *Micka* stayed at Pearl Harbor. (Was going to the Mariannas).

October 1945, returned to San Francisco, CA. Assigned to the shore patrol. Placed on inactive duty on Dec. 23, 1945. Promoted to Lt(jg) while on inactive duty. Discharged from the U.S. Naval Reserve, under honorable conditions, effective Sept. 1, 1955. Was never involved in combat.

Married Janet Grimes on Jan. 19, 1957. They had children: Christopher J. (adopted) born Dec. 13, 1946, Brian D. born Feb. 9, 1959 and Catherine A. born Jan. 24, 1961. He was widowed on Aug. 31, 1989. Worked as mechanical engineer in industry. Retired in July 1985. Now doing consulting work in the field of mechanical engineering.

EDSON BIRCHARD, (NED), was from Randolph, VT. He enlisted in the USN United Nations duty aka Korean War Nov. 7, 1950 when he was 19. Boot camp completed February 1951 Newport, RI. Graduate Personnelman School to USS *Darby* (DE-218) April 1951, Norfolk, VA. Gitmo refresher and Sonar School duty Key West and Mainbrace Fall 1952 to Scotland and Norway. Transfered to USS *Ault* (DD-698) October 1953 affords a round the world cruise and Korea War zone duty. Petty officer in charge, ship's office and legal recorder May 1953 to honorable discharge August 1954 PN1, U.S. Navy.

He was awarded the Good Conduct, National Defense, U.N. Service, Korean Service, and Commanding Officer Commendation.

Miami University, BS education 1957 and MS Bus. SUNY Albany 1963. After 17 years as Vermont High School teacher and summer II, he entered U.S. Immigration and Natz. Service as a full time immigration inspector, 1976.

NCUJHS, Derby, VT 1990 and USINS Derby Line 1991 recognized Birchard for public service as chairman Building Committee. He lives in Derby, VT with wife as proud grandparents.

ELZIE H. BLAIR, was born Nov. 2, 1930 in Grayson County, KY. He joined the U.S. Navy Oct. 27, 1948. Stationed at NTC Great Lakes, USS *Marsh* (DE-699), February 1949 to October 1952. He achieved the rank of boilerman first class.

His memorable experiences include a collision with USS *Taussig* while still a seasick "boot."

He was awarded the Good Conduct Medal and various ribbons during the Korean campaign.

Married for 38 years to wife Vi and they have two children Jonette and David and nine grandchildren.

Retired after various jobs, mostly construction related woodworking.

JOHN WADE BLANKENSHIP, JR., was born July 28, 1933 in Black Mountain Buncombe County, NC. Enlisted in the U.S. Navy Aug. 10, 1950. Recruit Training Command, San Diego, CA - Service School Command, (MM Class A School) Great Lakes, IL - USS *Chester T. O'Brien* (DE-421). He achieved the rank of machinist mate third class.

His memorable experience includes recommissioning ship in San Diego April 1951; after sea trials, assigned to Atlantic Fleet. Conducted ASW operations in Atlantic and Caribbean Sea. Made midshipman cruise out of Norfolk, VA to Europe in summer of 1953.

He was awarded the National Defense Sevice Medal, Navy Occupation Service Medal and the European Clasp.

He was married 30 years, and is now divorced. He has two sons and three daughters.

Retired from the USNR after 31 years. Retired from U.S. Postal Service after 30 years. Commander of VFW Post 9152 Black Mountain, NC CWO4 in North Carolina State Defense Militia.

ALTON R. BLANKS, F1/c, USS *Schmitt* (DE-676-APD-76), born in Columbia, SC, on April 23, 1927. Enlisted in the Navy April 3, 1945. Boot camp: Bainbridge, MD. Served aboard USS *Canberra* (CA-70) prior to reporting for duty aboard USS *Schmitt*, Feb. 1, 1946, Norfolk, VA. Served aboard until discharged July 25, 1946, Charleston, SC. Remained active in Naval Reserve until July 25, 1954, as a TEM3/c. Enjoyed the yearly two weeks active duty.

Retired from the U.S. Postal Service Dec. 8, 1978 with more than 34 years as a letter carrier. Was co-chairman for another successful Schmitt reunion May 1989 in Charleston, SC. It is a pleasure to renew the friendship at each Schmitt reunion.

PETER L. BOCKIUS, JR., was born Nov. 24, 1916 in Wilmington, DE. He joined the U.S. Coast Guard Sept. 24, 1941 in Philadelphia. He achieved the rank of boatswains mate first class at the time of discharge Nov. 27, 1945.

USCGC *Naugatuck*, Philadelphia captain of the port, U.S. Coast Guard Academy, USCG "Danmark." USCG 83 417 Cape May, SCTC Miami. USCGS, Norfolk, VA; NOB, Houston, TX, DE-388; plank owner, Casablanca invasion; Ellis Island, NY wire splicing cargo loading, USS *Gen. M.C. Mergs*.

Met Jane Virginia Claney from Point Pleasant Beach and Maplewood, NJ in Rio de Janero. Married June 21, 1949. They have a son.

Graduated University of Delaware. Retired E.I. Dupont DeNemoors & Co., sales and transportation. Former councilman, Mountainside, NJ and Bay Head, NJ; Board of Adjustment and Planning Board, Bay Head, NJ.

ROBERT M. BOHAM, was born Jan. 16, 1926 in Stamford, CT. He was drafted into service September 1944 and served until July 1946 with the U.S. Navy. He served on many different ships through November 1967 at which time he retired as FTMC (E7) fire control tech. (missiles).

His memorable experiences include: Persian Gulf/Red Sea circa 1958; South America, East Coast 1957 (work with S.A. navies); seven tours-6th Fleet (Mediterranean) Flag ship USS *Newport News* (CA-148) 1955.

He was awarded the Good Conduct (five awards), American Theatre, European Occupation.

He now lives in Lyons, CO with wife Grace. They have one son.

Retired after 20 years in the Navy. Employed ten years as bank vault teller, seven years as a security guard.

GROVER F. BOTKIN, RDM 2/c, GM2/c, USS *Emery* (DE-28). Enlisted December 1942, boot camp, gunnery school and radar training in Virginia. Plankowner USS *Emery* April 1943. Spent 27 months on *Emery*, convoy and invasion support in all areas of South Pacific combat zones. Received four Bronze Stars. After World War II, August 1945 sent to inland sea of Japan serving on the USS *Prime* (AM-279) cutting and exploding Japanese mines.

After seven months in Japan, transferred to Tsingtao, China and assigned to Chinese Naval Training Command training Chinese naval personnel to fire air to air and surface to air machine guns. The Communist army closed in and caused them to move to Shanghai headquarters. Shortly thereafter they were disbanded and he returned to California serving on the cruiser USS *Tuscon*, destroyers *Maddox* and *Agerholm* as instructor for helm, gunnery and radar. After six years of sea duty, left the Navy. During Korea conflict joined the Air Force remaining for nearly 18 years, retiring as first sergeant of a 327-man supply squadron. Then worked as a professional federal, state and city police officer. Retired again in 1982, married, has four children, residing in Billings, MT.

PAUL REYNOLD BOUCHER, enlisted at Portland, ME, Oct. 28, 1942. Boot camp in Newport, RI. Attended Metalsmith School, Norfolk, VA G'tmo Bay from April 1943 to May 1944. Assigned to *Silverstein* (DE-534) until February 1946. Served aboard *Gunston Hall*, LSD-5, in atomic bomb tests at Bikini. Patient at Naval Hospital, Long Beach, CA from October 1946 to October 1947. Four years in Reserve Fleet in San Diego. Served on the *Cassin Young*, (DD-793), 1951-1954, *Cascade* (AD-16), until spring of 1956, Argentia, Newfoundland until February 1959. Shore duty in Green Cove Springs, FL until June 1961. Assigned to *Rigel* (AF-58), until retirement in July 1962.

In business for himself in California for the next four years. Worked at Holston Army Ammunition Plant in Kingsport, TN for 20 years, retiring in 1986. He and wife, Hilde, live in Tennessee. They have one son, one daughter, two granddaughters and they became great-grandparents in January 1991.

JOHN B. BOY, Lt. Cmdr., USNR, C.O., USS *Holton* (DE-703), graduated Georgia Tech 1938, (NROTC). Called active duty February 1941. Attended LDF School then assigned Officer-in-Charge SC-330 (non-commissioned sub-chaser). Inshore Patrol, Little Creek, VA.

Ordered SCTC, Miami, FL March 1942. Remained as gunnery shakedown officer. Ordered as CO to PC-613 March 1943, under construction Jacksonville, FL. After commissioning assigned Caribbean escorting convoys between Cuba and Trinidad.

Ordered as C.O. to USS *Holton* (DE-703) December 1943, under construction Bay City, MI. After commissioning May 1, assigned escort duty with Norfolk to Mediterranean convoys. *Holton* ordered to Pacific for duty with Philippine Sea Frontier December 1944. Primarily escorted convoys to and from Philippine Sea Frontier boundaries. In September *Holton* assigned to Amphibious Group Seven, Okinawa. Escort with convoy carrying occupation forces to Korea. Made several trips to various China ports carrying military personnel to arrange occupation. November 1945 *Holton* ordered back to States. Left *Holton* at San Diego, CA December 1945, released from active duty following month.

In January 1946 started with United States Sugar Corp. at Clewiston, FL. Elected president and CEO in June 1970. Retired in June 1987. Divide time between homes at Boca Grande, FL and Clewiston. They have three children and five grandchildren.

CHARLES B. BOYER, was born in Urbana, OH June 29, 1924. Joined the service March 10, 1943 in the Navy.

Went to boot camp at Great Lakes Naval Training Station, Great Lakes, IL and to Sonar School at SCTC, Miami, FL. Assigned to USS *Manning* (DE-199) crew while the ship was under construction, in Charleston, SC. The *Manning* was commissioned and christened on Oct. 1, 1943. Steamed in the Atlantic and Pacific Theatres of War. Credited with one enemy aircraft shot down and two assists. Became part of the Pacific inactive fleet in San Diego, CA on Jan. 1, 1946. Left the *Manning* as part of the original crew of 78 and was discharged on Feb. 9, 1946 as a SOM3/c USNR.

After one year as postmaster in Milford Center, OH, attended Tri-State University, Angola, IN and graduated with a BS in mechanical engineering. Retired after 33 years at Battelle Memorial Institute, as a research scientist in the field of high pressure with seven patents, on Dec. 31, 1988. Lives in Columbus, OH with wife Marty. They have one son and one daughter, with two granddaughters each.

CARL BRAGDON, JR., DC2, USS *Tabberer* (DE-418), born May 5, 1932 Bar Harbor, ME. Graduated from high school class of 1950. Enlisted in Navy in June 1951. Took boot camp training at Newport, was in the last company (278) to go through Newport. Was assigned to the USS *Tabberer* (DE-418) from September 1951 to March 1954, then transferred to the USS

Compton (DD-705) until June 1955 when discharged. Attended Fire Fighting School at Newport, RI and Damage Control School at the Philadelphia Naval Yard. He is married and has two children, and two granddaughters. He owns his own business selling and servicing major home appliances. He is a member of DESA and Tin Can Sailors Association.

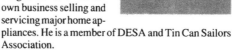

VERNON J. BRAHAM, was born Sept. 23, 1934 in Belleville, WV. He joined the Navy October 1951, serving to September 1955. He was stationed in Newport, RI; Key West, FL. Served aboard USS *Melvin R. Nawman* (DE-416), 1952-1955.

He achieved the rank of GMSN.

Married and has one son and one granddaughter. He has been a furnace operator at Corning Glass for the past 34 years.

LUKE M. BRIDGES, Cox, BM3, was born June 18, 1925 in Beanscove, PA. Joined Nov. 19, 1942. Attended boot camp NTS, NOB, Norfolk, VA. Plank over USS *Weber* (DE-675); A.P. 75 June 30, 1943 - Jan. 16, 1946. Discharged Jan. 19, 1946. Reenlisted Oct. 2, 1946. Commissioned USS *Manchester* (CL-83) Oct. 29, 1946. Served on board until February 1950. Discharged at San Diego, CA same month. Made all the trips on the *Weber* and the *Manchester*.

In battle of Okinawa. Going through a mine field in the China Sea. They got eight mines in one day.

Worked 35 1/2 years at the Kelly Tire Company. He is now retired. Married Elizabeth J. Turner. Has four daughters and 22 grandchildren. Member of VFW Post 1411, American Legion Post 13 Cumberland, MD.

He was awarded the American Theatre Medal, European Theatre Medal, Pacific Theater Medal with one Star, Philippine Liberation Medal, Victory Medal, Navy Occupation Medal, China Service Medal and Good Conduct Medal.

WALTER E. BROMLEY, F1-WT, enlisted USN August 1945 at Paducah, KY. Boot camp Sampson, NY. Assigned USS *Fieberling* (DE-640) December 1945.

Went to China 1946 and Hawaiian Islands in 1947.

Decommissioned *Fieberling* at Long Beach, CA

1948 then assigned Long Beach Group, Pacific Reserve Fleet until discharged in 1949.

He was awarded the Good Conduct, China Service and World War II Victory.

Retired 1987 after 42 years with Illinois Central Gulf Railroad Signal Department.

Married Gwen Lundgren in 1948. They have three children, two sons, one daughter and three grandchildren. Now resides in Gilbertsville, KY.

RICHARD GEORGE BRONS, was born March 21, 1925 in Floral Park, NY. He joined the service Feb. 27, 1943. Inducted March 4, 1943 and was discharged March 8, 1946.

Served with the USNR. NRS New York, NY; NTS Great Lakes, IL; NTS School (RM) Chicago, IL; SCTC, Miami, FL; NOB Norfolk, VA; RS Boston, MA; USS *Daniel A. Joy* (DE-585); USNH St. Albans, NY; RS Brooklyn, NY; PSC Lido Beach, LI, NY. He achieved the rank of RM1/c.

Screening of reinforcements for landing on Leyte, PI, Nov. 21, 1944; landings at Lingayen Gulf, Mangarin Bay and Mindoro, Philippines; convoy/escort duty of major task-force to Okinawa through typhoon and high seas in which the cruiser *Pittsburgh* had its bow torn off and the USS *Joy* clocked a 48 degree roll.

He was awarded the American Theatre Medal, European-African-Middle Eastern Theatre Medal, Asiatic-Pacific Theatre Medal with two stars, Philippine Liberation Theatre Medal with one star, Presidential Philippine Unit Citation Medal, Victory Medal, and the Good Conduct Medal.

Married over 45 years. They have three children, Richard Jr., Suzanne and Russell, and six grandchildren.

Retired since March 30, 1990. Traveling and getting re-acquainted with old shipmates!

CLAUDE E. BRIDGES (See page 743)

CHARLES E. BROWN, FT2, USS *Naifeh* (DE-352) and USS *Ingersoll* (DD-652), was born in Lakeview Plantation, ME on Sept. 4, 1936. He enlisted in the Navy in January 1955. Boot camp and FTA School at NTC Bainbridge, MD. Joined USS *Naifeh* (DE-352) in San Diego in February 1956. Two WestPac cruises including a summer of island surveillance out of Guam. Transferred to USS *Ingersoll* (DD-652) in April 1958 with another WestPac cruise. Discharged in San Diego in January 1959.

After separation in 1959 he settled in the Boston area where he started an apprenticeship for machinist in the Boston Navy Yard in 1962. In 1964, half way through his training he was laid off there and transferred to the Hunter's Point Naval apprenticeship there in 1966.

That shipyard closed in 1974 and he went to various jobs both in the private sector and Mare Island Naval Shipyard and eventually settling into a position at the University of California at Berkeley in 1980 where he supervises a small machine shop that builds specialized scientific apparatus for researchers in the Materials Science and Mineral Engineering Department. He hoped to retire from there in five or six years. Toward that end he and his spouse, Susan Forsythe, are building their dream home on the north coast of California.

CHARLES R. BROWN, was born in Lawton, MI, July 31, 1923. After two years, ten months and seventeen days in the Navy during WWII, discharged as gunner's mate second class. He enlisted in the Army as a staff sergeant on Jan. 13, 1948. He was discharged Jan. 16, 1956, eight years and three days after enlisting. He was first sent to Ft. Knox, KY where he went through an NCO leadership course, and from there he was shipped to Germany where he was assigned to Headquarters and Headquarters and Service Company of the 63rd Tank Bn., 1st Inf. Div. in Grafenhwor, Germany. That was in May 1948. He served a little over a year there and was returned to the United States for reassignment.

He was assigned to Co. C of the 72nd Tank Bn., 2nd Inf. Div., Ft. Lewis, WA. That was October of 1949. When the Korean War broke out in June of 1950, they all prepared for a tour in Korea. He left Seattle, WA on Aug. 3, 1950 and arrived Pusan, South Korea about Aug. 16, 1950.

Their next stop was the Naktong River. While he was on the Naktong River, he took a fragment wound from a North Korean mortar that landed in front of the tank and he was awarded the Purple Heart.

They finally got back down below the 38th Parallel and that was about the time that Gen. MacArthur was relieved of his command and Gen. Ridgway took over, and they, the 72nd Tank Bn., especially C Co., were designated as General Ridgway's fire brigade. They were at one time assigned to the Turkish Brigade. He remained with Co. C and they did various assignments. He was also assigned to the 187th Airborne Div., a regiment out of the 187th.

He came back to the States on Aug. 3, 1951. He was out of the States exactly one year to the day. He got married in Chicago and after his 30 day leave he reported to the 11th Armd. Cav. Regt. in Ft. Carson, CO. He was assigned to the 10th Mountain Inf. Div. in Ft. Riley, KS. He was sent back to Germany where he was assigned to the 443rd Ordnance Co., ammunition.

He spent about three years in that outfit. It was about 15 months getting his quarters to get his wife over there. She arrived, they adopted two girls, and his wife delivered their son in the 16th Field Hospital in Nuremberg, Germany, in November of 1955.

They got home to Lawton, MI on the day before Christmas 1955. He then reported to Ft. Carson, CO. They told him not to get too comfortable because he would be going right back to Germany. Brown got mad and told the sergeant major that he had over six years service on an indefinite enlistment and he could type up his resignation. Brown took his discharge and came home Jan. 16, 1956.

Retired from Clark Equipment Co., Battle Creek, MI March 1, 1985. Employed part time by Gilmore Department Store, in Kalamazoo, MI.

CLARENCE ARLEIGH BROWN, PhM1/c, USNR; USS *Stewart* (DE-238), USS *LCI* (M) 805, USS *New Orleans*. Enlisted in USNR Sept. 23, 1942. Boot camp (all petty officer company #1106) at Great Lakes, IL. Assigned to McIntyre Dispensary, Great Lakes until October 1943 for learning and working in different areas of the hospital. October 1943, boarded the USS *Stewart* at NOB, Norfolk, VA. Made several convoys including: Aruba, Canal Zone, Cuba, Bermuda, Azores, Newfoundland, and Iceland.

July 1944, transferred to Amphibious Group for training and independent duty, Solomon Islands, MD. Joined Order of the Alligators. October 1944, got new construction; LCI (M) 805, Pier 42, North River, NY LCI (M)'s 802-807 proceeded to the Asiatic-Pacific Theatre, participating in the Philippine Liberation, Okinawa Campaign, and the Occupation of China. December 1945, assigned as senior PhM, working passenger, aboard the USS *New Orleans*, leaving China for San Francisco, CA. Discharged Dec. 19, 1945, Great Lakes, IL.

On Aug. 28, 1943, married Betty Mae Johnson. Furthered his education by earning a PhB at Milton College, WI (1947) and MS at the University of Wisconsin (1955). Retired in 1984 at age 62, after 38 years in secondary education and counseling at Mukwonago, WI.

Active in VFW Post #5470, American Legion Post #375, DESA National and DESA - N. IL. Served on the Emergency Medical Services Committee for the Metro Area in 1970, and was awarded the Presidential Commendation by President Nixon for life saving actions.

They have three sons: David (pharmacist), James (teacher), Bruce (ophthamologist). Presently living in Mukwonago, WI.

JASPER M. BROWN, was born in Upper Darby, PA Jan. 24, 1923. MM3/c USS *Robert F. Keller* (DE-419). Worked two years Westinghouse building low pressure turbines for Navy. Enlisted Sept. 6, 1943. Boot camp Sampson, NY; MM School Wentworth, Boston, MA.

In May assigned to USS *Keller* crew trained in Norfolk, VA. Commissioned *Keller* at Brown Shipyard, TX June 1944. After shakedown in Bermuda, went to Pacific. Campaign ribbons were American Campaign Medal, Pacific Campaign Medal (six Stars), World War II Victory Medal, Navy Occupation Medal with Asia Clasp, China Service Medal (Extended), China War Memorial Medal, National Defense Service Medal, Philippine Republic Presidential Unit Citation Badge, Philippine Liberation with two stars. Discharged Jan. 25, 1946.

May 17, 1944 married Isobel F. Rodger at Norfolk Naval Chapel. Worked five years erecting steel rolling doors, then went into builders hardware manufacturing for 38 years. Sold business and retired in 1989. They have two sons and four grandsons.

RICHARD OWEN BROWN, FN1/c, USS *Coolbaugh* (DE-217), enlisted in Navy March 7, 1944. Boot camp Farrigut, ID Camp Hill Co. 329. Great Lakes, IL for Basic Engineer School in June 1944. August 19, 1944 to Shoemaker, CA transported to New Hebrides October 1944 then to Purvis Bay, Tulagi. Boarded USS *Coolbaugh* October 1944 duty in New Guinea, Manus and Philippines. January 1945 escorted from New Guinea to Lingayen Gulf. February 28, 1945 the ship left for Caroline Islands for Iwo Jima. After the island was secured the ship departed for Pearl Harbor arrived the day President Roosevelt died. July 1945 ship came back to the States for dry dock. After repairs ship went to Long Beach then through Panama Canal to East Coast, duty from Key West, FL to Newfoundland. Departed ship August 1947. Discharged and returned to Oregon.

Married Oct. 15, 1947. Went to work on railroad May 26, 1948. Retired age 60, September 1986 as locomotive engineer.

While working on railroad joined Navy Reserve and retired October 1976 with over 25 years of service as chief enginemen.

H.N. BRUCE, (BUCK), GM2/c, USS *Stanton* (DE-247), USS *Burleigh* (PA-95). Enlisted in Navy on Nov. 16, 1942. Attended boot camp, Bainbridge, MD - Co. 45. Gunnery School, Newport, RI. After school assigned to USS *Stanton* under construction in Houston, TX. After commissioning and shakedown to Bermuda and Caribbean Sea had convoy duty in Atlantic and Mediterranean. Was in convoy with *Holder* in Mediterranean when USS *Holder* (DE-401) was torpedoed in night air attack by German JU88s and Donniers. He received one Battle Star. Transferred to USS *Burleigh* (PA-95) under construction in Brooklyn, NY. After commissioning, loaded 500 Marines and left for Pearl Harbor. Returned to San Francisco and took on troops and equipment and went to South Pacific for maneuvers and divers training for salvage crew. Participated in landing at Okinawa from April 1, 1945 to April 11, 1945. He received one Battle Star. Went to Wakayama, Japan and joined magic carpet fleet and returned troops back to USA.

Discharged on January 28, 1946 from Sampson, NY. Married Lois Lowry on June 15, 1946. They have two sons, Ron and Rob. Both served in the Navy from 1966-1972 and they have four granddaughters.

G. LOGAN BRUSH, USS *Neuendorf* (DE-200). Enlisted in the Navy at Detroit, MI. March 1, 1943 at the age of 17, and sworn in that date. Served boot camp Green Bay then went to Purdue University for Naval Electrical Training, receiving a third class rating.

Sent to Norfolk for assignment to the USS *Neuendorf* (DE-200) prior to commissioning on Oct. 18, 1943. Serving in the Pacific after shake down in the Atlantic. Was discharged in San Pedro March 8, 1946 serving only on the *Neuendorf.*

JOHN BULL, Y1c, staff of commander Escort Division 16. Enlisted in the Navy on Oct. 9, 1942, age 20. Discharged April 6, 1946. Boot training Newport, RI. Then transferred to Bureau of Naval Personnel, Washington, DC.

Requested sea duty and assigned to USS *Deede* (DE-263) crew training in Norfolk, VA. Ship commissioned in Boston. Transferred to staff of ComCortDiv 16, serving aboard DEs 259 through 264 whenever commander transferred his flag.

Joined Pacific Fleet and participated in island campaigns, as well as extensive convoy service in Central and Western Pacific Ocean.

While aboard USS *Dionne* (DE-261) ship rescued a tiny Japanese girl adrift in ocean off Saipan. Also during assault on Marianas, they captured seven Japanese prisoners attempting to escape from Saipan.

Served in USS *PC 809* crew, which rescued several B-29 airmen crashed between Iwo Jima and Saipan after bombing runs.

Retired and he and his wife live in Wilmington, DE.

GLENN E. BURGDORFF, was born June 26, 1921. He joined the Navy in Quincy, IL, Nov. 5, 1942. Passed the test in St. Louis, MO. Left St. Louis on Nov. 11, 1942. Got to Great Lakes Training Station at 8:00 p.m. on Nov. 11, 1942. He got boot camp training at Camp Green Bay, Chicago, IL, Co. #1667. Only a few barracks had hot water at the time they had boot training.

Went to New Orleans on Jan. 17, 1943. Went to Seamen's School. The *Edsall* crew left New Orleans on April 7, 1943 for Orange, TX. Stayed in barracks until April 10, 1943, then went aboard the DE USS *Edsall* 129 at 2:30 p.m. was commissioned. Went to Galveston, TX on April 23, 1943. Went to Bermuda for shakedown, on May 11, 1943. Left June 4, 1943 headed for Boston arrived there June 6, 1943. Left Boston June 18, 1943 got to Norfolk, VA on June 20, 1943. Were doing a lot of convoying, left Norfolk on Aug. 6, 1943 and arrived at Miami, FL on Aug. 8, 1943. Stayed until Aug. 16, 1943. Went to Cuba got there the August 18. Only stayed one day then back to Miami, FL on Aug. 21, 1943. They were then a school ship for new officers coming out of school.

On Sept. 23, 1943 they were searching for German subs off the coast of Florida, they put the USS *Edsall* in dry dock. After leaving dry dock went back to Florida and more school ship.

In January 1944 they went to Charleston, SC left January 20, 1944 and went back to Florida. Picked up a convoy and escorted it to Glaveston, TX, then convoy to Portland, ME then to New York. Left on April 9, 1944 for Port Arthur, TX. Took tankers to New York on April 27, 1944. From there convoy to Argentina, Newfoundland got there on May 1, 1944 then back to Portsmouth, VA and went to dry dock. On May 8 back to Norfolk, VA, then to Bermuda, then back to Boston. Left Boston on June 17, 1944 for Casco Bay, ME.

On June 25, 1944 left for Norfolk, VA. On July 1, 1943 convoy tanks and troops to Tranton, Italy. Left on July 20 and went to Brooklyn Navy Yard. On August 15 back to Casco Bay then to Norfolk, VA on Aug. 24, 1944 convoy to Tarant, Italy then back to Earl City, NJ.

On Oct. 6, 1944 was transferred to go to Fire Control School at Norfolk, VA. He graduated from F.C. School made third class F.C. in December 1944. Was transferred to Bayonne, NJ to meet the *Edsall.* Then went to Boston on Jan. 26, 1945. Left Boston arrived South Hampton, England then took the convoy across the channel to La Hay, France on Feb. 6, 1945. Left England and got to Brooklyn, NJ February 25. On March 27 left with convoy arrived at Liverpool, England on March 27, 1945.

Came back to Brooklyn, NJ on April 12, 1945 with a tanker that got hit.

On April 15, 1945 was sent to Norfolk, VA for school, then back to the ship. On April 21, 1945 had orders to go to school at Washington, DC Fire Control School. On June 6, 1945 was sent back to the USS *Edsall* (made fire control man second class) in Brooklyn, NJ.

Left there stopped in port at Norfolk, VA, then to Guantanamo Bay, Cuba. Then to Puerto Rico, left from there to enter the Panama Canal for the West Coast. On July 23, 1945 entered port at San Diego. On August 4, they arrived at Pearl Harbor. He was going to school when war ended.

On September 21, arrived at Balboa Canal Zone then through the canal to Philadelphia. Left there October 26 for Florida, got to the St. John's River on Oct. 27, 1945 to put in moth balls.

In December 1945 was sent to Chicago for discharge FC2/c. He married Marilyn Danhaus on May 1, 1947. She works at a florist shop and cooks for the "Golf Pro" at Arrowhead Golf Club house. He lost his father in 1952 and his mother in 1968. He was in the dairy business for 48 years. He moved from Quincy, IL to Camp Point, IL in August 1962. They have a daughter Cindy 38 with a 15 year old and husband Gary Viar; a daughter Kay 30 with a ten year, eight year and six year and a husband Brad Erke.

RALPH EARL BUTLER, was born Dec. 8, 1919 in Adhall, TX. He joined the service April 1942 in the U.S. Coast Guard assigned to the USS *Moseley.* He was also stationed in Duluth, MN; New York City, Miami, FL. He achieved the rank of boatsman first class.

Married to Freda Mae. They had a son David Alan, and two grandchildren Erin 11, and Chris 13. Retired transportation director for Caddo Parish School Board. Member of Gideons. Very active Sunday school teacher of adults.

FRANK ARTHUR BUY, QM3, USS *Ahrens,* (DE-575), was born May 10, 1925 in Newark, NJ. Enlisted in the U.S. Navy April 5, 1943.

Went to boot camp USNTC, Great Lakes, IL in Co. 501 and later transferred to Choir Co. 515. Graduated from boot June 17, 1943 to retained choir. August 19, 1943 was assigned to Signal School USNTS, Urbana, IL then to Norfolk, Dec. 14, 1943 to precommissioning crew, USS *Ahrens* (DE-575). After all of the unusual training, commissioned the "Mighty A" on Feb. 12, 1944, at Hingham, MA. After all of their well-known heroics, brought the ship into Green Cove Springs, FL, Jan. 21, 1946 for decommissioning.

Discharged from Navy on March 19, 1946 at Jax, FL.

Returned to work at ADT Security Systems. On Feb. 17, 1947, reenlisted in USNR (inactive) until Dec. 13, 1950, when recalled to active duty. Served in the USS *Tarawa* (CV-40) and USS *Wright* (CVL-49), until discharge Feb. 7, 1952. Returned to ADT and completed 38 years in Jersey City and Newark, NJ.

Retired Aug. 1, 1980 to reside in St. Lucie County, FL, with his wife Jane and newly acquired, Irish Setter pup enjoying life to the fullest.

JOHN D. BYRD, JR., CEM, USS *Frost* (DE-144), entered the Naval Reserve in Birmingham, AL on Sept. 11, 1942 as EM3/c. Boot camp was at the Corpus Christi Naval Air Station, Corpus Christi, TX with assignment as electrician in airplane interim overhaul.

Transferred to the Norfolk Receiving Station for ship assignment. He became a plank owner of the USS *Frost* at Orange, TX. After shakedown the *Frost* was part of a convoy and then assigned to anti-submarine duty in a hunter/killer group with carrier USS *Croatan.* He attended Gyro Compass School at the Norfolk Fleet Training Center returning to the *Frost.* He was married on July 14, 1945. His replacement arrived at the New London Shipyard and he went to Boston awaiting discharge. Discharged in October 1945 returning to Birmingham.

He returned to employment with Western Electric

Company as a telephone equipment installer. This work was in Alabama, Florida, Georgia, Kentucky, Tennessee and Louisiana. In December 1971 he changed employment to South Central Bell as an equipment engineer. Retired on June 30, 1984 remaining in Birmingham. He has one daughter and one granddaughter.

JOHN R. CALL, BKR3/c, USS *Earl V. Johnson* (DE-702), USS ARD-19, was born Feb. 21, 1926 in Homer, NY. Enlisted Navy Jan. 12, 1944. Boot camp at Sampson Naval Base. Sent to Boston Receiving Station (Fargo Building) to escort assignment. Went aboard USS *Earl V. Johnson* in April. Convoy duty three times to Mediterranean parts at Bizerte and Sicily.

December 1944 to Pacific through the canal. Convoy duty to Philippines, New Guinea, Okinawa and other islands.

Transferred to the floating dry dock ARD-19 after a short stay in the medical department on the USS *Markab* (tender) in October 1945.

Left the ARD in January aboard troop transport for discharge in Boston on March 6, 1946.

Married Barbara Miner in North Reading, MA on Sept. 16, 1944.

Raised one son Robert and one daughter Patricia.

Spent seven years as a Baker and retired after 31 years with Carrier Air Conditioning as a foreman.

FRANK D. CAMP, was born July 25, 1944 in Kingsville, OH. He joined the U.S. Navy on board the USS *Peterson*, (DE-152), July 27, 1961. He was stationed in Homestead, Key West, FL. He achieved the rank of SFM2.

His memorable experience includes Cuban Missile Crisis October 1962 "Pete" was part of the famous blockade around Cuba. The morning they left they thought they were just shifting berths. Instead they sailed out into open water and didn't return to Key West for about three months. The Brown Baggers had the hardest time as most had all their clothes at home.

Married June 27, 1970 to Diann McKinney in Key West. They have two children, Roberts Camp, 17 and Kelly L. Camp, 12.

Frank runs a small used car lot H&G Auto Sales in Sierra Vista, AZ.

THOMAS ROBERT CAMPBELL, S1/c, USS *Fredrick C. Davis,* (DE-136) was born in Columbia, SC on Nov. 2, 1926. He enlisted in the Navy on Dec. 9, 1942. He was a plank owner of the *F.C. Davis,* it being commissioned July 14, 1943, Orange, TX. The *F.C. Davis* participated in convoy duty in the North Atlantic and Mediterranean Sea. On April 24, 1945 the *F.C. Davis* was

torpedoed and sunk by German submarine U-546 in the North Atlantic. Thomas Robert Campbell was among the loss of 119 crew members. He was awarded the Purple Heart posthumously. *Submitted by his brother, Howard R. Campbell*

JOHN R. CANN, CMOMM, enlisted March 1937, boot camp Newport; USS *Case* (DD-370) for three years; USS *Farragut* (DD-348) one year. Re-enlisted March 1941 instead of being drafted in the Army (Navy was not military training then). Served on the USS *John Penn;* Diesel Schools; USS *Jacob Jones* (DE-130) pre-commissioning detail and sailing on it for a year; U.S. Naval Training Base Gulfport, MI for one year. Discharged September 1945.

Went to USMS Merchant Marine Officers Training School graduating second engineer and commissioned ensign USMS. Left sea in 1948 as chief Marine engineer and lieutenant commander USMS.

Civilian career. Engineering inspector for Hartford Insurance Company, stationary engineer, founder and CEO Apex Technical Schools for 30 years.

Married 49 years to Helen Lily and have five children. John, Dorothy, William, Lily Ann, Thomas and seven grandchildren.

It was an honor and privilege to serve in the U.S. Navy. The satisfaction of helping your country in the time of need is a great reward in itself plus the lifetime use of the training and experience gained in the area of good humanistic and professional living and career traits.

JAMES W. CANNON, was born Jan. 15, 1926 in Halifax County, NC. He joined the U.S. Navy July 31, 1943. Stationed at NTS Bainbridge, USS *Underhill* (DE-682), FPO, San Francisco, CA; Tadcent, CA. He achieved the rank of MAMC3/c.

His memorable experience includes six roundtrips Gitmo to Trinidad, one trip to England, two trips to North Africa.

He was awarded the Asiatic-Pacific, American Area, ETO, Philippine Liberation, Victory, Purple Heart.

Divorced, has three daughters, and one granddaughter. He was a medical technologist until retirement 1989.

EDWARD CAPRAUN, SF3/c, USS *Bangust* (DE-739), was born Feb. 6, 1919 in Trenton, NJ. Enlisted U.S. Navy, May 1944. Boot training Sampson, NY. Shipped by rail to Shoemaker, CA spent one night on Treasure Island. Shipped out of Oakland, CA; USS *Yarmouth* for Pearl Harbor arrived Aug. 2, 1944 assigned USS *Bangust* Aug. 21, 1944. Became a shellback

on Aug. 30, 1944. During their tour as SOPA Escort Div. their ship rolled 62% + in a typhoon.

They encountered several sub and air skirmishes. They traveled into the South China Sea to escort empty tankers out. They did escort with CVE and refueling the 3rd and 7th Fleet. They intercepted a surrending Jap sub replaced crew with Americans and took Japs aboard their ship.

On Aug. 30, 1945 received his SF/3c rating in excess of compliment. Left Japan Oct. 2, 1945 left Pearl October 13. Left Long Beach for Panama November 6. Arrived Panama November 15 went through canal arrived Philippines November 22.

After his time in Navy he was a home builder and remodeler and was manager of home center for some 27 years. He is now retired. Celebrated his 50th anniversary on Nov. 10, 1990.

LLEWELLYN F. CARPENTER, JR., EM2/c, USS *Damon M. Cummings* (DE-643), USS *Mansfield* (DD-728), USS *Barton,* born in Long Beach, CA April 27, 1927. Enlisted on his 17th birthday. Went through his boot training in San Diego, CA and was assigned to the *Cummings* on July 22, 1944 as a seaman in the deck force. His first tour of duty was in the South Pacific where the *Cummings* was on convoy duty from Guadalcanal to Tokyo Bay. The highlights from this include; riding out the Great Typhoon Cobra, the invasion of Okinawa, the Japanese surrender, and the biggest thrill was meeting his cousin D.E. Smith in Saipan after 1 1/2 years at sea.

In August 1946 Llewellyn was transferred to the *Mansfield* where he served as an EM2/c, until February 1948 when at that time he was transferred to the *Barton.* He was discharged in Norfolk, VA on Jan. 11, 1950.

Llewellyn (Bob) is employed as a national accounts manager for a large corporation. He and his wife Louise reside in Manhattan Beach, CA. They have four children, Larry, Dianne, Kenneth and Kareen.

RICHARD W. CARROLL, MOMM3/c, USS *Wesson* (DE-184), enlisted June 21, 1943. Boot camp at Great Lakes, IL. Ship training at Norfolk, VA. Assigned to USS *Wesson* November 1943, shakedown was in the Atlantic, but served in Pacific outstandings operations was in the Marshall Islands, Roi, Kwajalein, Majuro and Eniwetok. Captured a Japanese sloop sailing vessel then on to Marianas, Guam, Saipan and Tinian, Palau Islands. The Mighty *Wesson* seem to never hit ports or have leave. Captain and men stayed on the go until in Okinawa and kamikaze attack hit the torpedo tubes and almost sank the Mighty *Wesson.* Seven great guys died in the fight. The *Wesson* returned on her own powers with one screw all the way to good old USA. Repaired and sent back to duty the ship was awarded seven Battle Stars.

Carroll was released from the *Wesson* in August 1945. Discharged November 1945. He was commended by the captain for outstanding duties during attacks. His wife is Valiera and he has a son Richard, Jr. He was a contractor and building material yard owner for 35 years in Mendota, IL. A realtor from 1978-1980. Retired in Tucson, AZ. A member of DESA and NI DESA and most Vet service organizations.

MARCUS W. CARTER, S1/c, USS *Snowden* (DE-246), was born May 9, 1921 the fourth of four sons and five daughter's to Cyrus and Betty Carter of Fayetteville, NC. Entered the Navy Nov. 11, 1942. Boot camp two months provost guard six months; DE school one month; all at NTS (NOB) Norfolk, VA. Proceeded to Houston, TX as a member of the USS *Snowden* (DE-246) and commissioned her on Aug. 23, 1943 after several convoys, escort missions in the Atlantic. In March 1944 the *Snowden* was assigned to (DER-13) and served with the USS *Croatan* (CVE-25). The *Snowden* earned three Battle Stars for her action in the North Atlantic. The war ended in the Europe. The *Snowden* stayed in Norfolk Navy yard the month of June and on July 4 she sailed for Pearl Harbor, via Panama Canal arriving on Aug. 14, 1945. On September 11, she returned to Norfolk by same route arriving on Sept. 28, 1945.

Discharged Oct. 8, 1945 NTC Great Lakes, IL. Life member of DESA and member of VFW Post 670 Marcus went to Barber School in August 1946 and still in the same business in Fayetteville, NC. Married the former Naomi Faircloth on Nov. 24, 1946. They have one daughter, Barbara.

MAURICE P. CARTIER *(See page 743)*

DERWENT DALE CARTMELL, MoMM2/c, USS *Earl K. Olsen* (DE-705), USS *Booth* (DE-170), born May 16, 1924, oldest of three brothers. Enlisted in December 1942, took boot training at Great Lakes Naval Station. Sent to diesel school at Chicago Navy Pier and received rating of MoMM 2/c.

Original crew of YMS-160 transferred to USS *Alcor* R10, then USS *Booth* (DE-170) and then to USS *Earl K. Olsen* (DE-765). Did convoy duty to North Africa and England.

After VE Day, sent to Pacific for picket duty until end of war, saw action three times. The *Olsen* entered Tokyo Bay with guns blazing to clear mines. While on *Olsen* served as chaplain, and as section chief at discharge in February 1947.

Was often seasick but enjoyed serving in the Navy. Visited 71 cities in 17 countries and took part in sea rescue.

Attended Lehigh University and Newark College of Engineering. Married Nov. 27, 1947 to Beneth and had two daughters.

Is active in the Masonic Fraternity, and an avid hunter and fisherman.

SALVATORE JOHN CAVALLARO, was born Sept. 6, 1920 in New York City. Enlisted in the Naval Reserve Jan. 6, 1942 and was commissioned ensign Jan. 28, 1942 after training in landing craft he joined USS *Lyon* (AP-71) for the invasion of Sicily he was assigned to guide the landing of the waves of assault boats and with his skill and courage under repeated strafing and bombing attacks carried on throughout the night and early daylight hours of July 10, 1943 he was killed in action when his LCT was struck by shellfire he was posthumously awarded the Navy Cross for his gallant service at Sicily. *Submitted by Leonard R. Homan* (USS *Cavallaro* APD-128).

DARRELL VICTOR CAVOLT, S1c, USS *Emery* (DE-28), was born May 24, 1925 in Terre Haute, IN. Enlisted in USNR Jan. 11, 1943 at Indianapolis, IN.

Stations: boot camp at Great Lakes, NTS Camp Moffatt, Co. 72, graduated March 11, 1943. Transferred to NTS NOB Norfolk, VA. Attended DE Training School. Assigned to the USS *Emery* (DE-28) as part of the original crew. Was in the 1st Div. deck force most of his time aboard the *Emery*, later was a striker in the Sonar Div. Battle Station was gunner on forward 20mm.

There were several memorable experiences he remembers aboard the *Emery* but two experiences that stand out were #1 the time their Skipper got them lost and they finally found that they were in sight of the Island of Truk. The Skipper at the time was Lt. Cmdr. Coburn. The other, #2 was the terrible storm they were in at Peleliu. The flying bridge was secured except for one man, Cavolt. He was standing watch in the sonar shack. The sonar unit was out of the water more than it was in.

They earned, Asiatic-Pacific, American Area and the Victory Medal. They also earned four Battle Stars on the Asiatic-Pacific Medal for the following operations; Gilbert Island - Nov. 13, to Dec. 8, 1943. Marshall Islands, occupation of Kwajalein and Majuro Atolls - Jan. 29 to February 1944. Western Caroline Islands, capture and occupation of Southern Palau Islands - Sept. 6 to Oct. 14, 1944. Iwo Jima, assault and occupation of Iwo Jima Feb. 15, to March 16, 1945.

R/S San Francisco, CA and San Francisco Navy Ship Yard in the Disbursing Office until discharged at Shoemaker, CA Feb. 2, 1946.

Cavolt and his wife Mary Frances were married Oct. 22, 1945 in San Francisco, CA. They were both born in Terre Haute, IN.

After his discharge he worked at Commercial Solvents Corp. as a pump operator. He then worked at Moore's Auto Exchange as credit manager and before leaving Moore's, Bob Moore and Cavolt operated a used car lot. He was a sales manager for Miller Motors for a short time and then worked on the New York City Railroad as a flagman. He was also the credit manager for the Corner and Ideal Furniture Store.

They left Indiana in 1952 to come to Southern California. He worked at the Morris Plan Company as collection manager and was a loan officer when he joined Citizens National Bank, in 1955. They merged

with Crocker National Bank and retired at 59 years after 30 years as a vice president and senior loan officer. They are presently living in the Hemet, CA area, where they built their home in October of 1985.

They presently have a 34' Southwind motorhome that they use to make their trips in so they don't have to worry about lodging for their two Shih Tzu dogs.

They have three children, five grandchildren and seven great-grandchildren.

GIL CEFARATT, was born in Los Angeles, CA. He enlisted in the U.S. Navy and went to boot camp in San Diego, CA, attending Navy Radar School at Point Loma. He served in the Radar section on an LSM, AKA, APA, DD and two DE's plus being attached to FASRON 120 at Sangley Point, Philippines, where he worked in the Radio/Radar repair shop, and flew as a Radar Operator on PBMs on Barrier Patrol flights over the China Sea, and flew on training flights on PB4Y-2s. He went to Pearl Harbor on the *USS Marsh (DE-699)* in 1947. He remembers "borrowing" the mascot for the Sub Base, and there being a search on the ship until the mascot was turned over. (Sorry about that submariners.) He was transferred to the *USS Raby (DE-698)* doing patrol duty at Perry Island off Eniwetok Atoll in the Marshall Islands. He also remembers being on radio duty one night and receiving a message from the Senior Officer in Charge requesting the ship's boat the following day. He neglected his duty and asked his relief to deliver the message to the captain who never received it. The Senior Officer never got his boat, so it was very embarrassing. If the Captain reads this, I would like to say again, "I am sorry, Captain."

While at Pearl Harbor, four DEs used a cruiser for target practice. It was a cruiser used during one of the A-bomb tests. The DEs and a hundred plus airplanes strafed and bombed the cruiser for 36 hours before a torpedo from a submarine sunk her. He left the *Raby* in January, 1948, due to an emergency leave and was assigned to the destroyer *USS Rupertus* before being discharged.

He is member of the P-47 Western Regional Pilots Society, F-117A Assn., B-26 Marauder Assn., PB4Y Assn., DESA, and a number of P-38 Associations. He is Vice Chairman on the Amelia Earhart Education and Historical Committee in North Hollywood, CA.

GODFREY CHESHIRE, JR., was born July 18, 1918 in New Orleans, LA. He joined the service Sept. 5, 1940. Served with the USNR. Stationed with Patrol Wing 8, USS PC-1077, USS *Harold C. Thomas* (DE-21).

He achieved the rank of lieutenant commander and was the commanding officer of USS *Harold C. Thomas* (DE-21).

Married and has three children. He is now retired.

JAMES BENTON CHILDERS, JR., was born Nov. 24, 1926 in Johnson City, TN. Spent his early years in Merchantville, NJ; Big Stone Gap, VA. Family moved to Miami, FL in 1938.

Joined the USNR V-6 Nov. 8, 1944 and went to boot camp at Bainbridge, MD for 10 weeks. Sent to Basic Engineering School at Gulfport, MS which he finished. Assigned to the USS *Tweedy* (DE-532) which he picked up in Charleston, SC. Served in the Atlantic until the end of the war when they went to Green Cove Springs, FL for de-commissioning. Stayed in the active reserve until Aug. 28, 1950 at which time he was recalled to active duty, during the time in the Reserve he had changed his rating from fireman to personalman interviewer, and sent to San Diego Naval Training Center where his job was to check the in-coming recruit to see if they had any potential athletes coming in. Late 1951 his job was evaluated by a board and found to be useless so he was discharged as PNI 3 Feb. 28, 1952.

Lived in Miami, FL from 1955 to 1972 when he moved to the Florida Keys. He also maintained a house in Ocean City, MD and Fenwick Island, DE where he has been active in the souvenir and novelty industry.

Married to Helen Lucinda (Gaskin) born 1946, Waco, TX. They have two daughters Virginia Bolton and Jackie Kaiser, both living in or near Fenwick Island and operating the family business known as Sea Shell City, Fenwick Island, DE.

As of December 1991 he is retiring from active business.

WILLIAM E. CHRISTIAN, JR.,

was born March 31, 1923, at Highland Park, NJ. He entered the Naval Reserve in November 1942, at New York, NY; attended boot camp at Great Lakes, IL January-April 1943, Radio School at Northwestern University, Evanston, IL, April-August 1943 and Amphibious Radio School, Camp Bradford, VA, October 1943. Christian served on the USS LST 131 from commissioning at Evansville, IN in November 1943, through the Marianas and Palau campaigns in the Pacific until transferred at Agana, Guam, to the USS LST 902 (later named Luzerne County) for returned to the States on points. He was discharged at Long Beach, NY in March 1946.

After reenlisting in November 1946, Christian served in a reserve battalion at the USNR Armory, Perth Amboy, NJ. At this time, the USS PC-1186 (later named Ipswich). Being the only radioman on the roster, every time the PC-1186 went on a cruise, Christian was on board, standing a one-operator watch. He was, at this time, enrolled in a degree program at Seton Hall College (later to become Seton Hall University) at South Orange, NJ.

The PC-1186 made three cruises from 1947 to 1950. The first one was a cruise to Miami, FL and Havana, Cuba where the ship docked at the United Fruit Company Pier. This was the first U.S. Naval Vessel to visit Cuba after WWII.

In August 1950, Christian was recalled to active duty as an RMN1 and served as leading radioman on the USS Robert L. Wilson (DDE-847) from September 1950 until November 1951. At this time, he received his second honorable discharge from the U.S. Naval Reserve.

Christian married Barbara Nelson in June 1955 and they raised two sons and two daughters. He was admitted to practice before the Interstate Commerce Commission in 1973 and now lives in New Jersey.

EDWARD W. CLARK,

SC1/c, enlisted Oct. 7, 1942. Boot camp San Diego, CA. Went to DE School, Norfolk, VA. Was assigned to USS Flaherty (DE-135). Was aboard DE-135 when it was put in commission at Orange, TX. After a couple convoys, in the North Atlantic, they were assigned to an anti-submarine task force. This assignment resulted in earning four Battle Stars, and Presidential Unit Citation, for the capture of German U-Boat 505 in June of 1944. Left Flaherty in July of 1945 volunteering for underwater demolition, was accepted. On his way to Ft. Pierce, FL for training, when the war ended. Discharged five weeks later.

After several self-employed business adventures, retired in 1979 as general contractor. Bought home on one of Washington's better fishing lakes. This is where he currently spends much of his time, fishing and growing a wide variety of flowers. He has one son and one granddaughter.

ELMER O. CLARKE,

was born in Calais, ME in 1923. Joined the service Oct. 26, 1942. Served in the Navy stationed in many locations. He achieved the rank of RMC.

His memorable experience includes the sinking of U-1062. He was awarded two Battle Stars.

Clarke has a brother in Brisbane, Australia and a niece, nephew, and stepson.

Retired but works 25 hours a week as a bookkeeper.

WILLIAM P. CLARK,

Lt., was ordered to active duty in July 1943 and was assigned to Midshipman's School at Columbia University, NY. Upon graduating as an ensign in October, he was immediately ordered to

the USS Fleming (DE-32) operating in the Pacific. They participated in the Gilbert and Marshall Island campaigns.

For advanced training he was sent to Submarine Chaser Training Center (SCTC) Miami, FL and then to Radar School, Hollywood Beach, FL.

Upon completion of training he was directed in October 1944 to the USS Stern (DE-187). While serving as Combat Information Center officer (C.I.C) on the DE-187, they took part in the following campaigns - Saipan, Philippines (Leyte and Luzon), Iwo Jima and Okinawa. No submarines sunk but shot down eight enemy aircraft, one U.S. Navy F4U (they rescued the pilot unharmed) and two Baca bombs (pilot driven aerial torpedo).

As executive officer, he assisted in mothballing the DE-187 at Green Cove Springs, FL.

Discharged January 1946. Joined the Wall Colmonoy Corporation, an international special alloy and aircraft parts manufacturer. Still working for same company as chairman and chief executive officer. Resides in Michigan.

ROBERT L. COATES,

S1/c, USS Engstrom (DE-50), joined March 17, 1944. He took boot camp in Faragut, ID. He went aboard DE-50 in June 1944 at Adak in the Aleutian Islands. After a period there, he went to San Francisco where the ship was overhauled. Once the overhaul was complete, he went to the South Pacific on the Engstrom. The last island he was at was Iwo Jima.

Coates was pulled off the 50 for being too young and was sent to Navy Pier Chicago for a full honorable discharge.

He married Bona J. Poe in 1948 in Topeka, KS. They moved to Portland, OR in 1952 and, except for a brief stint in northwest Montana, have made their home in Oregon ever since. They have two children and two grandchildren. While raising their children, they became involved in raising and showing Appaloosa ponies all across the United States. They spent some 30 years in the retail grocery business in Oregon, where they owned several of their own stores.

Now you will find them retired on the Oregon Coast where they enjoy salmon fishing, or in their travel trailer seeing the sites in the Sun Belt states.

JOHN E. COIE, JR.,

Cmdr., commissioned USS Straub (DE-181) as X.O. October 1943. Served as C.O. 1944-1945. Operated in North Atlantic convoys and in South Atlantic "Hunter Killer" groups.

Commissioned Ens. USNR Northwestern University Midshipmen's School March 1941. Served on USS Salt Lake City (CA-25) in South Pacific 1941-

1942. Saw action at Marshall Islands, Wake Island, Coral Sea and Guadalcanal. Commissioned USS *Baltimore* (CA-68) as #1 turret officer 1943. Trained at SCTC Miami, FL June-September 1943. Recalled for active duty 1950 (Korea). Served as chief staff officer ComDesRon One and as X.O. USS *Henderson* (DD-785). Retired as commander USNR May 15, 1983.

Married Ruth A. Bartels of Chicago, IL Oct. 27, 1941 in Long Beach, CA; one son, John and two daughters Valeria and Caroline. Retired from Pacific Telephone Company as district manager 1979. Retired from real estate sales 1982.

PAUL RAYMOND COLE, fire controlman first class, enlisted in the Navy in Lansing, MI in 1942. Was in boot camp at Great Lakes, IL in November 1942 after schooling in 1943. He was assigned to the USS *Huse* (DE-145) as fire controlman first class. Their ship sank five subs in the North Atlantic. Also in the North Atlantic for days at a time they couldn't go outside on ship as the waves were higher than the mast. They were like a cork in a bathtub.

Was discharged from the Navy in Nashville, TN Jan. 9, 1946. Married in Washington State in 1947, August 13 a Friday. Has one daughter, four grandchildren, and five great-grandsons. Retired from United Can Co. in California. They moved to Oregon in 1990 to Grants Pass. Now selling real estate and recuperating from open heart surgery.

BERNARD F. COLVIN, was born Feb. 14, 1924 in Pittsfield, MA. He was inducted into the U.S. Coast Guard Nov. 25, 1942. His memorable experiences include the Atlantic Ocean and Mediterranean Sea; hunter-killer duty in North and South Atlantic.

He was awarded the Navy Commendation and two Battle Stars.

Married to Rosemary Cornwell in September 1948 and they have two children, one son, one daughter, and two grandchildren.

Retired from the General Electric Company after 42 years.

MARTIN B. CONSERVA, RDM 3/c, USS *John M. Bermingham* (DE-530) and USS *Fargo* (CL-106). Enlisted in the Navy Oct. 27, 1943 (Navy Day). Born in Boston, MA, Dec. 29, 1925. Boot camp in Sampson, NY then assigned to Naval Section Base and Radar School in Florida. In 1944 joined crew USS *Bermingham* at Norfolk, VA. Convoy duty in North Atlantic and North Africa. Late in 1945 decommissioned ship in Charleston, SC. Early 1946 went aboard USS *Fargo* on shakedown in Atlantic and West Indies.

Discharged May 17, 1946. Married to a lovely

lady, Louise Anderson, Sept. 26, 1947. Raised eight children (six girls - two boys), now enjoying 14 grandchildren - the fifteenth expected the summer of 1991.

Six months after discharge started a piano rebuilding and refinishing shop with father, Martin, Sr. It grew into an excellent business over the years due to family participation and is still in operation in Medford, MA. Proud to say he was elected president of Piano Technicians Guild (1970), Medford Kiwanis (1976), Medford Chamber of Commerce (1986), and Humarock Civic Association (1988).

LAWRENCE F. COSTANTINE, GMC, USS *SC 507,* USS *LCI (R) 73.* Enlisted in the Navy July 2, 1942, Pittsburgh, PA. Born Jan. 29, 1923 in Aliquippa, PA. Went to boot camp at Newport, RI, Co. 913. After boot camp went to Pier 92, New York, NY. Assigned to USC SC 507 in Miami, FL, in October 1942.

Sent overseas to Casablanca, North Africa in November 1942. Was in air raid while in dry dock which was featured in *Look* magazine. Ran patrol duties off of the coast of Africa.

Returned to the States in 1944, went on 30 day leave. Sent to Norfolk, VA. Joined J2 outfit, sent to Lido Beach, NY for training, then on to Shoemaker, CA for further training. Requested sea duty and shipped to Taclobin, Philippines. Picked up USS LCI (R) 73 - made invasion of Balakapan, Borneo. Was in typhoon at Buckner Bay, Okinawa, in 1945. Ran high and dry on the beach, was shipped back to the States for discharge. Was discharged as second class gunner's mate. Reenlisted just prior to Korean War. Served on DE DER's 2100 can, 2200 cans. Served during time of Vietnam War also.

Retired as chief gunner's mate in August 1968 from USS *Hubbard* (DD-748). Has 13 Campaign Bars, six Battle Stars, received Secretary of the Navy Achievement Medal for Sea Dragon.

Retired from Rapid Transit Company as diesel mechanic. Went to two colleges in Southern California, received two degrees. Now resides in La Verne, CA.

VERDIS O. COOK, was born April 18, 1918 in Elba, AL, moved to Florida in 1940. Joined the Navy shortly after Pearl Harbor, (January 1942). After several months of schooling, he went aboard the USS *Wyffels* which was being built in Boston, MA, he made the shakedown cruise to Bermuda, then one trip across the pond to Casablanca, then transferred to another (DE-186), USS *Swearer* which was being built in Newark, NJ for duration of the war with rating of CRM.

Married and has one son, and one grandson.

JOHN W. CORBETT, was born March 29, 1924 in Concord, NH. Joined the U.S. Navy December 1942,

(DE) USS *Duffy* #27, APC-17. Boot camp at Great Lakes, Navy Pier, Chicago Training School. Achieved the rank of motor machinist first class.

His memorable experience includes the typhoon in the Pacific Dec. 17-18, 1944 near Philippines.

He was awarded two Asiatic-Pacific Stars, one for the Philippine campaign, Leyte Gulf.

Married Irene Valliere July 19, 1947 and two children.

Retired April 1, 1990 as president of insurance brokerage company.

FRANCIS J. CORLISS, was born in Boston, MA Oct. 3, 1925. He joined the U.S. Navy Oct. 1, 1943, serving as QM 2/c. Stationed at NTS Newport, RI October 1943-November 1943; NOB Norfolk, VA December 1943 to March 1944. Stationed on USS *Gendreau* March 1944 to Jan. 25, 1946.

He achieved the rank of QM 2/c. His memorable experiences include the explosion and loss of the ammo ship USS *Serpens* on Jan. 29, 1945, Lunga Point, Guadalcanal; battle of Okinawa, radar picket duty and destroying six Jap planes.

He was awarded the American Theatre of War, Asiatic-Pacific, two Battle Stars, and the World War II Victory Medal.

Married Marie September 1948, has seven children (five boys and two girls). Past Commander, VFW Post 2626, Foxboro, MA, P.G.K. K of C Council 6063, Foxboro, MA; Past President Letter Carriers Union, Honorary Kentucky Colonel.

Retired from U.S. Postal Service May 1, 1986.

EDWARD T. COULTER, SF3/c, USS *Hanna* (DE-449), was born May 29, 1927 at Weaverton, Washington County, MD. Enlisted in the U.S. Navy May 29, 1944. Entered in boot training at Great Lakes Naval Training Station Camp Green Bay, IL. After training, was assigned to Destroyer and Gunnery School at Naval Operation Base, Norfolk, VA. Transferred to Brooklyn Navy Yard, Brooklyn, NY. Assigned to USS *Hanna* (DE-449), became a "plank owner" on commissioning ceremonies Jan. 27, 1945. The ship was named in honor of William T. Hanna USMC, killed October 1942 at Battle of Guadalcanal and sponsored by his mother, Mrs. William P. Hanna. Lt. Commander Means Johnston, Jr. Commanding Officer.

After shakedown cruise out of Bermuda and Guantanamo Bay and Cuba, they were transferred to COM DES PAC Pacific, escorting supply ship to Panama Canal and assigned to escort supply and troop ships out of Eniwetok, Marshall Islands, sailing to Carolines, Gilberts, Philippines, Mariana and Wake Islands, then sailing to Tokyo Bay, Japan. Received

...lers to return to U.S. by way of Hawaiian Islands to ... Diego Naval Base, CA. *Hanna* was decommis... ...ned May 31, 1946.

... Reassigned to USS *Nevada* (BB-36) for tempo-... ...ry duty, attaching equipment to deck preparing for ... atomic bomb test in the Marshall Islands. Reas-... ...ed to LST 570 with a skeleton crew sailing her ... ...ugh Panama Canal to Charleston Naval Yard, Charleston, SC for decommissioning.

Discharged June 2, 1946 from U.S. Naval Service ... Naval Training Center, Bainbridge, MD.

Married to Raphael Mary Morrison, May 1948. Raised five children in Maryland suburbs of Washing-...on, DC. Retired from U.S. Department of Commerce, Coast and Goedtic Survey. Living in Pinellas Park, FL. Member of DESA National Chapter of Florida Suncoast Chapter DESA. Ed and Rae devote as much time as possible helping sick and handicapped veterans in VA Hospitals.

S. STUART CRAFT, DKIC, USS *Daniel T. Griffin*
(DE-54), born in Lexington, VA, March 9, 1918. Entered Navy 1943; had boot training at Bainbridge, MD and was assigned to Storekeepers School there. After graduation, was ordered to Pier 92 in New York and duty aboard the USS *Daniel T. Griffin* (DE-54). Made five trans-Atlantic voyages.

In 1944 the "Danny T" was converted to High Speed Transport (APD-38) at New York Navy Yard. They were then ordered to duty in the Pacific, and participated in the invasion of Okinawa. After Japan's surrender, they had occupational duties in Kure, Japan. Discharged Dec. 9, 1945 at Bainbridge, MD as DKIC.

Retired from sales department of Continental Baking Company in Washington, DC. Craft and his wife Marion and living in Southern Maryland in Tompkinsville on the Wicomico River, and spend the winters in Punta Gorda, FL. Every two years, they have a "Danny T" reunion, which they enjoy very much. Renewing friendships and swapping ship stories is really great.

CHESTER B. CRAIL, was born Nov. 9, 1921 in Covington, KY. Joined the USNR July 6, 1942. Stationed in Great Lakes, IL; San Diego, Miami, Mare Island, CA and three quarters of the South Pacific Ocean.

He achieved the rank of FC 2/c. His memorable experiences include boarding the USS *Wilemann* for the first time at Mare Island, CA and seeing two seaman painting over something on the forward side of the ship. The letters and numbers were BDE-22. They were in the process of painting over the B leaving only DE-22, the number on their ship as it was then commissioned on June 6, 1943.

Received word that the war had ended while they were at sea and recalling that, although they were not supposed to have cameras, he was one of the few saps who had none and therefore could take no pictures of his shipmates.

GEORGE W. CRANE, FCR2/c, USS *Fessenden* (DE-142), joined the U.S. Navy in Napa, CA on March 12, 1943, spent boot camp in Farragut, ID and attended Fire Control School in San Diego, CA. Boarded DE-142 in Orange, TX on Aug. 24, 1943.

On their third run from Norfolk, VA to Bizerte, Tunisia, their convoy was attacked by German bombers and torpedo planes. He was at his battle station on the flying bridge and witnessed ships blowing up all around. What is not generally known is that a few hours before this attack, their ship had a sailor with acute appendicitis and they changed their point position with a destroyer in order to transfer the sick man to a ship with an MD aboard. That destroyer was sunk during the attack.

In September 1944, they were attached to the Mission Bay Hunter-Killer Group chasing German U-boats in the southern Atlantic and on the last day of that month they made contact with an underwater submarine and fired a full hedge hog pattern. He'll never forget the shout that went up as they made a direct hit and there was a tremendous underwater explosion. They sank U-boat 1062 that day.

He left the ship in June 1945 to attend the Advanced Fire Control School at Anacostia Naval Base in Washington, DC. On Aug. 15, 1945, one day after VJ Day, he married his bride of 45 years. Now retired from the electrical business, they live in Napa Valley, CA.

GEORGE CRISCIONE, Ships Cook 3/c, DE-250 USS *Hurst*, enlisted in the U.S. Coast Guard Aug. 10, 1943. Born in Paterson, NJ July 5, 1926. He served on 83 foot Coast Guard Cutters. *Wm. Weigel* AP-119, troop ship Coast Guard Cutter *Papaw*. Trained at Manhatten Beach, NY for boot camp. Went to U.S. Coast Guard Academy Sonar School in Key West and Gunnery School at Navy base in Newport, RI.

Was in European-Asian Theatre. Got Good Conduct Medals and honorable discharge. Went to Bizerte, Casablanca, Liverpool, Weymouth, South Hampton and Le Havre. Did convoy duty to Europe in North Atlantic. In May of 1945, the war was over with Germany. They went through the Panama Canal to Hawaii. He waited for the invasion of Japan, then searched the South Pacific. Tahiti, Bora Bora, America Samoa, Fifi etc. for survivors of plane crashes and ship wrecks. The war was over.

Member of DESA. Received discharge April 22,

1946. Married Gina Barone of Sicily, Italy. Has three girls and a boy, nine grandchildren and one grandson presently in West Point. Has has photo studio for past 45 years.

CARL A. CRITTENDEN, FC2/c, USS *Sloat* (DE-245), inducted in the USNR Sept. 14, 1943. Born in Flint, MI Dec. 7, 1920. Attended boot camp in Farragut, ID. Sent to Lake Union, Seattle, WA for Advance Fire-Control Training School. Boarded USS *Sloat* DE-245 in Portland, ME for convoy duty in the Atlantic and the Mediterranean. Then sent to Flt. Serv. School in San Diego, CA.

Returned to USS *Sloat* (DE-245) for more convoy duty in the North and South Atlantic. Sent to Norfolk, VA for advanced Fire-Control training. Returned to USS *Sloat* (DE-245) at Boston Navy Yards. Proceeded to the Pacific Theater until the war ended.

Debarked from USS *Sloat* (DE-245) in Guam for return to the United States. Discharged from U.S. Naval Separation Center in Great Lakes, IL on Jan. 5, 1946. His rank at discharge was fire-controlman second class, USNR.

Married Ruth Brazeau Feb. 3, 1947. They have four daughters, one son, six grandchildren, three girls and three boys. Retired from the Knights of Columbus, New Haven, CT as a field director April 30, 1986. Enjoying retirement in Swartz Creek, MI. Keeps busy playing golf, gardening and traveling.

He was awarded the American Campaign, Asiatic-Pacific Campaign, European African Middle Eastern Campaign, Navy Occupation Service, and China Service Extended.

EDMUND PHILIP CRIVELLO, SOM1/c, USS *Hopping* (DE-155). Entered U.S. Regular Navy Oct. 31, 1942 and sent to Norfolk Training Station for boot camp.

After boot camp, he was trained for sonar, for anti-submarine warfare. Promoted to SOM3/c and was assigned to USS *Hopping* (DE-155). They were assigned to the 6th Div., 2nd Atlantic Fleet for convoy duty.

On Nov. 8, 1943, during one Atlantic crossing he was wounded in action, shrapnel wounds of the legs. After 48 years later he was notified by the Awards Department of the Chief of Naval Operations, that he was due to receive the Purple Heart, as a result of his correspondence to them which included the record of the war diary for that day. Six months later he received the award.

Other awards include the American Theatre, European Ribbon, Victory Ribbon, Good Conduct Ribbon.

Fleet Sonar School for Maintenance, Fleet Sonar (Key West), FL served as instructor; Great Lakes

Training Station for radar; Great Lakes Naval Hospital for skin rashes from duty.

Discharged June 15, 1946 as CSOM.

Married since Dec. 28, 1946 to present wife Virginia. They have four children and eight grandchildren. His son Edmund Jr. served in the Gulf War as a first sergeant - Infantry. He received the Bronze Star for which he is very happy.

He has been married 45 years and has retired from First National Bank of Maryland. As a lead data base analyst.

WALTER FRED CROSKEY, MM1/c,
(8592404), USS *Otter* (DE-210). Volunteered for Navy Air Force December 1942. Failed physical due to color-blindness at Wold Chamberlain Field, Minneapolis, MN. Enlisted USNR April 1943. Boot camp, Camp Waldon Co. 302, Farragut NTS, ID. Attended Machinist Mate School, Kansas University, Lawrence, KS until November 1943. NTS Norfolk, VA. Assigned to USS *Otter* (DE-210), Charleston, SC. Commissioned to USS *Otter* escort duty. Convoys to North Africa, Sicily, sub-chasing in North Atlantic. Sent to Galveston, TX for conversion. V-J Day arrived. *Otter* sent to Jacksonville, FL. Worked out of Mayport, FL until discharge in April 1946.

Attended University of Northern Iowa and Iowa State University, graduating from there in architectural engineering in 1951.

In 1952 started own construction company in Waterloo, IA. Twenty years later entered the real estate business which still continues.

Celebrated 44 years of marriage. Three children, Dr. Kent Croskey, TV Engr. Tim Croskey and nurse Holly Ann Yue, and seven grandchildren.

GORDON W. CURTIS, S1/c, USCG (R), was
born Jan. 9, 1926. Stationed on board the USS *Rhodes* (DE-384), USCGC *Dione* (WPC-107), USS *Dearborn* (PF-33). Enlisted in the Coast Guard July 1943. Went to boot camp Manhatten Beach, Brooklyn NY.

On horse patrol out of Ft. Macon, LBS, Beaufort, NC; USS *Rhodes*, Chambers St Rec Sta, Radio School Atlantic City, Rec Sta Manhatten Beach, USCGC *Dione* WPC-107, USS *Dearborn* (PF-33). Convoy duty to Oran, Bizerte, North Atlantic, Londonderry Ireland. Weather ship in the South Atlantic and North Atlantic.

Spent a month in hospital in Iceland. Returned to U.S. discharge April 1946. Married Jean Runyarn April 1948. Lived in Grand Rapid. Raised three daughters, Kathy, Kaven, Karla and two sons, Ken and Kevin. Retired after 39 years as conductor CSX Railway. Member of DESA, American Legion Post 459 and VFW Post 8664.

CHARLES J. CZECH, SR., Y1c, USS *Joseph E. Campbell*, (DE-70) (APD-49). Born May 16, 1916 in Cohoes, NY. Inducted U.S. Navy Sept. 13, 1943. Went to boot camp at USNTS Sampson, NY. Received Y3c in boot camp.

Assignments: Temp. Ships Co. at Sampson; ship repair unit E6-305; USS *Joseph E. Campbell* - brief duty in Atlantic then to Florida, San Diego, Hawaii, Ulithi, Eniwetok, New Guinea, Philippines, Okinawa. Participated in landing of units of U.S. Army of Occupation at Yokohama and at Otaru, Hokkaido, Japan.

Back to States Christmas 1945. Honorably discharged from U.S. Navy on Feb. 7, 1946 as Y1/c.

While doing "picket" duty off Okinawa on June 8, 1945, Japanese torpedo plane (Jill) dropped torpedo at their ship, but missed them; their ship shot down Japanese plane.

Married Frances T. Wrzochalski June 28, 1942. Raised two sons: Charles Jr. and Richard. Retired from Norton Company 46 years service. Member of Watervliet, Cohoes and Troy Seniors. DESA, Norton Retirees and NEAT.

STANLEY J. CZWALGA, was born Jan. 6, 1924
in Lucesboro, PA. He joined the Navy April 1, 1943. Stationed on board the USS *Bowers* (DE-637). He achieved the rank of gunners mate second class. His memorable experience includes being straffed at Okinawa and suicide attack.

Married Freda Hamelik July 20, 1946. They have a daughter Peggy and son David who died in 1972. He is now a retired quality control manager.

JAMES WILLIAM DAVIS, was born April 14,
1924 in Williamsport, IN. He joined the service Dec. 17, 1942. Served with the USNR as MOMM1c. Stationed in the Pacific Theatre.

All of his experiences in the Pacific campaigns were memorable.

He was awarded three campaign ribbons, for Marshall Islands, Marianas and Carolinas.

Married to Eva and has two step-children, Chuck and Patty Jo. They also have five grandchildren, and five great-grandchildren. Davis is a retired carpenter. He participates in square and round dancing.

RAYMOND B. DAVIS, was born Aug. 29, 1925 in
Providence, RI. He joined the service April 30, 1942. Served with the USNR. Stationed at Newport Naval Training Station, RI; Wentworth Institute, Boston; and USS *Bowers* (DE-637).

Discharged June 14, 1946 as machinist mate first

class. His memorable experiences include sea trials and comm. of USS *Bowers* (DE-637) in California. Survived kamikaze attack on the ship on April 16, 1945 which had over 100 casualties at Okinawa. On way back to States, met his brother Al at Pearl Harbor.

He was awarded the World War II Victory Medal, American Theater Medal, Asiatic-Pacific Theatre Medal, Philippine Liberation Medal, and the Good Conduct Medal.

Married for 40 years to Josephine. They have one child Raymond Jr., (also married with three children).

Retired oil heating service and installation contractor. His hobbies include: pistol and rifle competition, fishing, boating, attending the launching and commissioning of U.S. Navies newest AEG-15 missile destroyers (DDG-51) and 53. Also cruisers *C.G. Allen* the east coast.

ROBERT EVERETT DAY, ET2/c, USS *Thaddeus Parker* (DE-369), graduated from high school in June 1963. Boot camp March 1964 at the Great Lakes. Stationed at Great Lakes while waiting for Electronics Technician School, graduated ET School and assigned to the USS *Mitscher* (DL-2) until she went into the yards for update. Transferred to the USS *Albany* (CG-10) in March 1966 then to the USS *Thaddeus Parker* (DE-369) in the Reserve Fleet in January 1967. When the *Parker* was sent to the yards he was assigned to the USS *Cascade* (AD-16) in September 1967 and discharged in March 1968. While on active duty he made several Mediterranean cruises. He attended Canton College of Technology and graduated in June 1970 with an associated degree in Electrical Technology. He is the owner of Day's Farm Equipment business and resides in Madrid, NY.

FREDERICK D. DE CAIN, was born July 1, 1921
in Chelsea, MA. He enlisted in the U.S. Navy Nov. 3, 1942, and was discharged Nov. 4, 1945. Stationed at Treasure Island and Mare Island, CA; Aleutian Islands; V-12 Program Harvard University.

He achieved the rank of sonarman second class at the time of his discharge. His memorable experiences include the Aleutian campaign, being selected for officer training.

He was awarded the Good Conduct, American Area, World War II Victory, and Asiatic-Pacific Medal.

Married in 1945. Has one son, also a Navy man. He has been married to Edna for 50 years.

Retired and traveling.

FRANK P. DeNARDO, SM3/c, USS *Chatelain*
(DE-149), ATA-211. Enlisted in Navy Jan. 1, 1943. Attended boot camp and Signal School, Newport, RI. After school assigned to DE-149 for commissioning at Orange, TX. Made one convoy run 1943 to Ireland, England and Mediterranean, with six DEs and an old four stacker.

After returning to the States, they formed a killer group with the USS *Guadalcanal*, to hunt German submarines. They sunk the U68, U515, picked up most of the crew of U515.

June 4, 1944 boarded U505 prior to regular boarding party. With the help of Pillsbury signalman, removed decoding machine and all charts to the carrier. U505 was towed to Bermuda.

Next assigned to Miami, FL to shore patrol duty.

Followed by transfer to Port Arthur, TX and ATA-211, ending up in Japan August 1945. Returned to Pearl Harbor, boarded USS *Nevada* and returned to U.S. and discharged at Boston, MA Dec. 11, 1945.

He was awarded campaign ribbons for American Campaign with foreign service, European African with three stars, Asiatic-Pacific, Victory Medal, Presidential Unit Citation with one star.

Married to Violetta Clement June 29, 1944.

In 1949 joined the Civil Air Patrol as pilot. Spending 20 plus years as squadron commander, receiving Bronze Medal of Valor. Resigned 1970.

Worked for Firestone Rubber and Latex Company, 15 years. Worked for General Dynamics Corp., as experimental mechanic for 20 years, retired 1988 at age 65.

Is a member of the VFW, Destroyer Escort Association, USS Guadalcanal Task Force Association. Now living in San Diego, CA and is retired.

WILLIAM J. DENNY, MM2/c, USS (DE-698), USS *Bennington* (CV-20), enlisted in the Navy, Jan. 19, 1943. Attended boot camp and Machinist School at Great Lakes, IL. After school they were assigned to new USS *Raby* ((DE-698). After shakedown to Bermuda, went to South Pacific for next 23 months. They did a lot of convoy and ping-line duty at several islands. In May 1944 they did some steaming with USS *Spangler* (DE-696), USS *George* (DE-697) and USS *England* (DE-635), together they sank six Jap subs in seven day. USS *England* sank the most. After the typhoon on Okinawa (July 1945) they returned to Guam and was there at the end of war in August 1945. While there the USS *Indianapolis* came in harbor, few days later it was sunk, with a great loss of over 800 men.

After a month at home in November 1945 they were assigned to USS *Bennington* (CV-20) and was on it with duty around Pearl Harbor, until discharged on April 6, 1946.

After discharge, went back to Indianapolis, IN and to work at the Penn RR where he was previously employed. Worked there until June 1947, then went to Indianapolis Power and Light Company and retired after 34 years.

On July 27, 1946 he married Ruth Salter, had two sons and two daughters and now has nine grandchildren.

ROY E. DeVORE, JR., was born Feb. 25, 1926. Joined U.S. Navy in Athens, GA 1943 while a student at University of Georgia. Attended boot camp at Great Lakes; Radio School, University of Chicago, then to sea. Assigned to destroyers in the Pacific Theatre.

Rendezvouzed with newly commissioned USS

Elden (DE-264) (Boston) at Pearl Harbor and assigned escort duty Pacific fleets - 3rd, 5th and 7th, where they escorted everything moving in enemy waters, plus island invasions of Marshall-Gilberts, Kwajalein, Carolinas, Admiralties, Saipan, Tinian, Guam, Iwo Jima, Okinawa, Philippines and was with the fleet that was waiting off the coast off Japan when bomb was dropped and then entered Tokyo Bay for the surrender.

Memorable experiences: Battle of Leyte Gulf, Iwo Jima, Okinawa, Tinian Island, the night the Japanese tried to float past the destroyer screen during the early morning hours, and the 13 days typhoon that almost claimed them all, and the loss of 19 shipmates in Tokyo Bay.

In 1990 received WWII medals and stars for forementioned action from Sen. Sam Nunn and the Navy department. Also, in 1990, he received from Philippine Government the Philippine Liberation Medal and the Philippine Government Presidential Unit Citation.

Retired in 1985 after 40 years as president and founder of DeVore-Knight & Co., a food brokerage firm. He has since gone back into business again as a food broker.

Married for 38 years, has two children, Don and Diane, both married and he also has two grandsons, Ryan and Nicholas DeVore.

SALVATORE DI MILLA, SOM2/c, USS *Fogg* (DE-57), enlisted in the Navy (USN) October 1944. Boot camp, Sampson, NY Sonar School, Key West, FL. Radar School, Fargo building, Boston, MA. Boarded the USS *Fogg* on April 1, 1945. The ship was a sad sight, fantail was missing (ship was torpedoed December 1944). Served as sonar operator, radar instructor (radar training ship) and leading division petty officer. Transferred to Sonar School, Key West, FL on July 4, 1946. Was a sonar instructor until discharged on Oct. 27, 1947. Had planned to make the Navy a career, but a middle ear problem put an end to that.

Received BA degree from Northeastern University. Worked at Raytheon Company 38 years in various engineering and management positions. Retired in 1988 at the age of 62. He and his wife, Rose, live in N. Andover, MA. They have one daughter and one son.

ALLAN G. DOLK, was born Jan. 6, 1921 in Warren, OH. He enlisted in the Coast Guard Dec. 8, 1941. Stationed on board the USS *Mills* 383, Baltimore Coast Guard Base, Carpenters Mate School NYC, Naval Training Station, Norfolk, VA (DE); Houston, TX, USS *Mills*, Northern Ireland, England, France, North Africa, Attu. He achieved the rank of CM3c.

His memorable experiences include the storms at sea, German torpedo bombers.

He was awarded the American, European African and Asiatic-Pacific and Good Conduct.

Married Aini Violet Rinta Feb. 14, 1948 in Baltimore, MD. Raised two daughters: Janice and Nancy.

Retired from Bethlehem Steel Company, Sparrows Point, MD as turn supervisor in 1982. He is a member of American Legion Post 38, VFW Post 6694 and DESA.

CHARLES A. DOMENICO, was born June 25, 1926 in Hammonton, NY. He joined the service June 1944 serving with the Navy as seaman first class on the USS *Hayter* (DE-212). Attended boot camp at Bainbridge, MD. Sent to Pier 92 New York and boarded USS *Hayter* (DE-212). He was also stationed at Algiers, Bizerte, Sicily, Nova Scotia same, *Hayter* converted to (APD-80).

Was in the Atlantic when USS *Davis* (DE-136) was sunk by U-546 German, *Hayter* crew assisted in rescuing survivors and hit the German U-546. Germans were rescued and taken as prisoners of war. Half of crew rescued. November 6, 1945 discharged from Philadelphia Naval Hospital.

Married Josephine M. Mento June 6, 1945. They raised four sons and have five grandchildren. He is a retired parts manager.

Member of VFW, American Legion and Disabled American Veterans in Hammonton, NJ. Domenico retired in 1991.

RAYMOND DOOLAN, educated at St. John's and New York Universities where he majored in Management and Business Administration. Mr. Doolan has been employed in this capacity for U.S. Commercial companies in Europe, Saudi Arabia, Pakistan and the Far East.

Naval military service includes University of Chicago training as a Communication Specialist (signals and radio) and combat with the Navy Atlantic and South Pacific Destroyer Escort Task Forces. During

WWII he served on the USS *Charles J. Kimmel* (DE-584) and the USS *Mississippi* (BB-41). He was honorably discharged in 1946. Mr. Doolan is a 1962 graduate of the U.S. Air Force Air University, and is a qualified Airman serving as a captain with the U.S. Air Force Auxiliary since 1962. He supported Flight Training Activities for pilots and reserve crews in 1982 at Andersen Air Force Base Guam for B-52 bomber and KC-135 Tanker Crews on Refuel Training Missions in the Western Pacific for the Strategic Air Command (SAC).

Mr. Doolan additionally has been employed in a covert capacity by the Central Intelligence Agency (CIA) in various overseas countries of Europe the Sub Continent and the Far East. He has also provided assistance to other Law Enforcement Agencies of the United States Government including Immigration and Naturalization Service (INS) and the Federal Bureau of Investigation (FBI) and Guam and Honolulu, HI.

During a five year residency in Japan he taught business and cultural subjects at the University level in Kyoto at Doshisha College. He has previously worked as an advisor to Japanese private industry and in 1988 completed a study of Asian Industrial Systems at Sophia University in Tokyo. Pacific Western University of Los Angeles, CA also awarded him a bachelor of science degree for a major field of study of Government Administrations in 1987.

Mr. Doolan is a 1984 graduate of the Federal Mediation and Conciliation Service School, office of Technical and Arbitration Service Washington, D.C. He retired in 1988 as the Executive Administrator Wage and Hour Division Department, Department of Labor, for the U.S. Territorial Government of Guam.

Mr. Doolan continues to travel extensively to foreign and Western Pacific countries in his capacity as consultant for research projects, that require commercial and government expertise in his various fields of specialization.

JAMES W. DOWNS, RM2/c, USS *Gilligan*, (DE-508). Enlisted June 7, 1943. Boot camp and Radio School, Sampson, NY. Assigned to USS *Gilligan* then under construction. Commissioned *Gilligan* May 12, 1944. Shakedowns to Bermuda. Escort duty in South Pacific. Invaded Philippine Islands at Lingayen Gulf Jan. 9, 1945. Struck by kamikaze Jan. 12, 1945. Repairs in Pearl. Returned to duty arrived in Okinawa April 17, 1945. Struck by aerial torpedo May 27, 1945; repaired and returned to duty and after 63 days on "Ping Line" left area. Discharged March 6, 1946.

Married Regina C. Serfass Oct. 18, 1947. Raised two sons, and five grandchildren. Became a licensed Pennsylvania funeral director and operates own business today. Active in American Legion Post #88 and DESA.

CLARENCE DUBOIS, MMM3/c, DE *Grenier* 37 and USS *Charles Carrol* (APA-28) enlisted in Navy Feb. 10, 1943. Attended boot camp and machinist school in San Diego. After school he was assigned to USS *Grenier* (DE-37). Sailed out of California on battleship and met DE *Grenier* in Honolulu and stayed at sea for 24 months without going to foreign ports or United States. Their duty was to bring supplies to other ships. He received three Battle Stars and three ribbons

before being discharged on March 20, 1944.

Worked at many jobs before going in the oilfield drilling for 15 years then he was a self-employed grocer for 18 years. He retired June 1990 to enjoy life with his wife of 44 years (Nita Babineaux) one daughter, son-in-law and three grandchildren. His hobby is cooking for friends and in his outside kitchen.

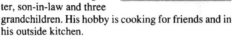

WILSON C. DUBOIS, RMSN, entered this world on Dec. 12, 1938 in St. Albans, VT. Attended public schools in Vermont, Philippine Islands, and Massachusetts. A 1967 and 1970 graduate of the chemistry and plastics engineering curriculums at the University of Lowell (MA) received an advanced degree from the same institution in 1975. Has published one textbook in the field, hold two patents, and published 12 papers including seven with the U.S. Navy.

Worked in urethane synthesis, wire and cable, environmental research, materials engineering, and the defense industry. Industrial activities include membership in the Society of Plastic Engineers, American Chemical Society and American Association of Textile Chemists and Colorists. Currently employed as a senior industrial engineer with Raytheon Missile Systems Div. in Lowell, MA.

Married to Donna F. Bell, a Johnson State College graduate (Vermont), of St. Albans, VT. Two children: Kristen Lynn and Karen Lindsey DuBois.

Enlisted in the naval reserve community in December 1955 and assigned to SURDIV 1-19 with boot training at Bainbridge, MD. Served aboard the USS *Johnnie Hutchins* (DE-360) home ported in Boston with Atlantic seaboard and Caribbean ASW training responsibilities.

Enlisted in the U.S. Air Force and assigned to Texas, Mississippi, Florida, Morocco, Japan, Korea, and Montana. Responsibilities were Military Police Security Forces. In Korea volunteered for the K-9 Corps, a subordinate section of the military police's security forces. Released from USAF active duty to pursue engineering curriculum.

Enlisted in the Naval Reserve Community after 20 year respite and assigned to SIMA Newport. With plastics engineering background, billeted in the molder's rate as E-4. Developed Foundry (SHOP 81-A) proposal for SIMA NPT for presentation to management. Assigned to training section HQ DET-101 and presented lectures ranging from hygiene to DC, MIL courtesy, tooling, missile systems and naval history. ACDUTRA assignments were SIMA NPT, Rhode Island.

Transferred to USS Orion (AS-18) DET-202 in Brooklyn, NY. Assigned to training department in the same capacity as SIMA NPT. ACDUTRA assignments were USS *Orion* (A-'8), La Madellena, Italy. Received REDCOMTWO Letter of Commendation.

Transferred to NSSNLONDET-301 drilling at SSF New London, CT. Assigned as unit's public affairs officer with USN/USNR/DET-301 publicity responsibilities. Several articles written regarding naval history, DET-301 activties and personal experiences. Articles published in local, regional and national USN and USNR publications. ACDUTRA assignments were SSF New London. Received NSSFNLONDET-301 Letter of Appreciation.

During this interim, promotion was secured for

ML-2, ML-1 and later to MLC. Several NAVEDTRA courses completed with selection focused on LDO requirements. Awarded decorations for American Defense, Meritorious Service (two awards), Short Overseas Tour, Long Overseas Tour, and Distinguished Unit Citation.

Transferred to USS *Fulton* (AS-11) DET-10 New London, CT. Assigned to training department assistant training officer with responsibility of optimizing unit's shop qualification readiness.

An active member of several masonic bodies enjoying family, numismatics, and writing historical narratives in spare time.

NORMAN E. DUCHARME, RDM3/c, USS *Block Island* (CVE-21), and USS *Williams* (DE-372). Enlisted July 1943. Basic NTS Sampson, NY. Radar School, Virginia Beach, VA. Special Projects School (Radar Counter Measures) RMS Naval Research Lab, Washington, DC. Assigned to AFAF Flag Unit NAS Norfolk, VA. Special assignment for radar intercept duty aboard the USS *Block Island* (CVE-21). On May 29, 1944 CVE-21 struck by three torpedoes from the U-549 and sunk off the coast of Africa. Survived and rescued by DE-578. Returned to Norfolk from Casablanca aboard the USS *Kasaan Bay* (CVE-69).

Various assignments and schooling by the Flag Unit AFAF until December 1944. Transferred to COMDESPAC Oahu, HI and assigned to the USS *Williams* (DE-372) in February 1945.

Carried out escort and anti-submarine duty in the south and west Pacific, crossing the Equator 12 times.

The most frightening experience came following the war on Sept. 29, 1945. Leaving Okinawa for Guam the DE-372 was caught in the center of a typhoon and suffered severe damage.

Quoting ships log: "Without warning the ship was struck by a huge coamber wave which broke over the ship rolling her to port an estimated 85 degrees. Damage was heavy, radar antenna and port yardarm torn off, flooding from air vents and bent hatch's throughout ship, oil from vent outlets covered crews compartments to a depth of 6". A list of other damages too lengthy to mention. One forward lookout washed overboard and never found."

DEs are not only trim and deadly, they are sturdy and a credit to the people that made them.

Worked 28 years for Simonds Saw & Steel Co. retiring on disability in 1975. Lifelong residents of Fitchburg, MA. Married and has four children and ten grandchildren.

He was awarded the American Theater, European African Middle Eastern with one Battle Star, Pacific Theater, Asian Occupation Medal, Philippine Liberation, World War II Victory Medal, and the National Defense (1947-1951).

JULIUS J. EBERL, was born in New Washington, OH Dec. 28, 1923. Enlisted in April 15, 1943. He was discharged with the rank of SF3/c. Attended boot camp at Great Lakes, IL.

Spent four months at the Great Lakes Naval Hospital with rheumatic fever, then after completing training went SCTC at Norfolk, VA - then at Philadelphia Navy base commissioned the USS *Blackwood* (DE-219). Went on shakedown cruise to Hamilton, Bermuda. Did some duty on the Atlantic Coast. Went through the Panama Canal to the South Pacific. Was transferred while in the Solomons to the west Rec Sta. in Los Angeles where they commissioned the USS *Burlson* (APA-67). Went back to the South Pacific. After island hopping in the Pacific made the invasion of O̶ ̶nawa.

When the war ended they took military government to Korea, then operated with the Chinese Nationalists - moving their troops up the Chinese Coast. Went back to the States, where the ship was prepared for the Bikini Operation. Was discharged at the Naval Armory in Toledo, OH Feb. 28, 1946.

He was awarded the Asiatic-Pacfic Medal with one star, and the African European Middle Eastern American Medal.

He is now retired, after having worked 35 years as a construction boilermaker, out of Union Local #744, Cleveland, OH. He's been married to Helen for 36 years. They have a son Randall and a daughter, Jayne. He also has two grandchildren Matthew and Megan.

LEROY EDMONDS,

was born May 19, 1925 in East Providence, RI. Inducted into the USNR Oct. 14, 1943. Stationed at Quonset Point, NAS; USS *Waterman* (DE-740). He achieved the rank of steward third class.

He was awarded the World War II Victory Medal, American Area Ribbon, Philippine Liberation Ribbon with one star, Asiatic-Pacific Area Ribbon with seven stars.

Married to Helen Laughlin and has two sons, Jerry and Bobby and two daughters Jeanne and Linda. They also have seven grandchildren.

He is now a retired truck driver. Spends time now working in his garden.

GEORGE R. EISENHART, (IKE),

CEM, USS *Monrovia* (APA-31); USS *French* (DE-367).

Enlisted in the Navy March 1942. Attended boot camp and Electrician's Mate School in Newport, RI. Upon completion of school sent to USS *Monrovia* (APA-31) flagship of Atlantic amphibious force (Atlantic fleet) in the invasion of North Africa and Sicily.

Transferred to Turbine School, Syracuse, NY; then to SCTC Miami, FL then to Orange, TX to put USS *French* (DE-367) in commission (plank owner).

Many escort and bombardment tours during duty in South Pacific. Last assignment was to search and find, pick up survivors from USS *Indianapolis*, then into Tokyo Japan at wars end.

Back to USA in November 1945 for discharge at Bainbridge, MD and then home to Philadelphia. Went back to work at Philadelphia Naval Shipyard for 35 years. Retired in 1983.

Still living in Philadelphia, but not for long. Actively involved in Masonic bodies, DESA, Philadelphia Chapter, Navy League.

JOHN ELBERSON,

USS *Bowers* (DE-637), entered the Navy March 16, 1943. He went to boot camp at Sampson, NY, torpedo school at Newport, RI, DE training school at Norfolk, VA, and then on to San Francisco, CA and Mare Island where he was assigned on the USS *Bowers* (DE-637). After a January shakedown cruise the USS *Bowers* left for the South Pacific where she did escort duty. At Okinawa she was the victim of a suicide plane. The USS *Bowers* lost 105 of her crew of 200 in dead and wounded. After a repair

ship made her sea worthy, she sailed to Philadelphia where she was converted to an APD-40. John was discharged at Long Beach, CA. He achieved the rank of TM3/c.

In civilian life he worked as an auto mechanic. He married Marion Hartke in 1948 and they have three children. Retirement in 1988 is next.

DONALD A. ELCHERT,

RD-3, Fostoria, OH, joined the Navy October 1945, went to boot camp at Camp Peary, VA, Radar School at Pointe Loma, CA, assigned to the USS *Dayton* (CL-105), transferred to the USS *Coolbaugh* (DE-217) from June 1946 to October 1947, discharged at Norfolk Naval Air Station in October 1948.

Retired as a lieutenant from the Fostoria City Fire Department in 1982 after 27 years. Married November 1958 and has two sons and one grandson.

EDWARD E. ELLIOTT,

WT2/c, was born at Ft. Amador, Ancon, Panama Canal Zone on May 15, 1924. His father was in the U.S. Army and his mother was from Columbia, South America. His parents both died by the time he was seven years old and he was raised by his grandmother in Scottsburg, IN. He had a brother and a sister who were both younger than him.

On March 15, 1943 he joined the Navy and went to boot camp at Great Lakes Naval Training Station. After boot camp he went to Norfolk, VA and became a plank owner of the USS *Fechteler* (DE-157) which was commissioned on July 1, 1943. On May 5, 1944 the *Fechteler* was torpedoed and sunk in the Mediterranean Sea with the loss of 29 of his beloved shipmates. He was the oil king on the *Fechteler*. After his survivors leave he was assigned to Oil Burning School at the Philadelphia Naval Base and on Feb. 2, 1945 he was assigned to the USS *Jack C. Robinson* (APD-72) which was commissioned on that date also. He was the oil king on that ship also. He served on the *Jack C. Robinson* until the war was over. They were in the Pacific and had several exciting experiences. When the war was over he became eligible for discharge while they were at Manila in the Philippines and was transferred to a dutch freighter and sent back to the States where he was discharged from the Baltimore, MD Naval Base on Dec. 11, 1945.

STANTON F. ELLISON,

was born Oct. 19, 1918 in Bon Jellico, KY (Whitley County). He joined the service Aug. 27, 1941. (Called to active duty Sept. 9, 1941.)

Served with U.S. Naval Reserve, for duration of emergency during WWII plus six months. He was stationed: Navy recruiting station, Louisville, KY;

Commander Service Force, 7th Fleet, Pacific; Navy Receiving Station, Milne Bay, New Guinea; Navy Base 3205, Manus Island, Pacific; Navy Advanced Base Unit #4, Pacific; Navy Base 3964, Leyte Island, Philippines; Navy Base 3142, Luzon Island, Philippines; Discharged Great Lakes, IL Feb. 12, 1946; Recalled to active duty November 1951, Navy Receiving Station, Anacostia, VA; Naval Radio Station, Cheltenham, MD; U.S. Navy and Marine Corps Reserve Training Center, Lexington, KY; USS *Roberts* (DE-749) Atlantic Fleet; Naval Intelligence School (German) Washington, DC; Commander-in-Chief, U.S. Naval Forces Europe Representative Frankfurt, Germany; Naval Support Activity, London, G.B.; Commander, Carrier Air Group One, Cecil Field, FL; USS *Roosevelt* (CVA-42), Naval Station, Mayport, FL; Navy Recruit Station, Louisville, KY; transferred to Fleet Reserve, Nov. 4, 1966 as YNC, USN. Retired May 1973.

His memorable experiences: witnessing and participating in the joy and jubilation with other service personnel in the Pacific area when the Japanese ask for a cease fire. Touring the Berlin Wall in 1962. Visiting the American cemetery in the Luxembourg (Europe) where Gen. George S. Patton and 5,000 GIs are interred.

He was awarded the Good Conduct with one Silver and one Bronze Star, Naval Reserve Medal, American Defense Medal, American Campaign Medal, Asiatic-Pacific Medal with one Bronze Star, World War II Victory Medal, National Defense Medal, Philippine Liberation Ribbon (one Bronze Star), American Expeditionary Force Ribbon.

After transferring to the Fleet Reserve, he worked 10 1/2 years for various government agencies and retired from the Bureau of Prisons on April 9, 1977.

He works in and around his home, tends a small garden and travels; mostly to Florida. He enjoys visiting friends, splicing the main brace at times. He belongs to several military organizations and re-hashes military experiences with shipmates. Sometimes he can smell the cordite from shell fire and see the kamikaze planes come in. Fortunately no one gets injured.

HENRY GLEEN ELROD,

USS *Menges* (DE-320) was born Dec. 9, 1920 at Sandy Springs, SC in Anderson County. Attended school at Pendleton, SC. Graduated May 28, 1937. In 1938 he worked at Clemson College, Clemson, SC. In 1939 he worked in photography. Early in 1940 he went to work in New Port News, VA. They worked in ship building and dry docking. In 1942 he worked at Bethlehem Steel Company at Curtiss Bay Fabricating Shop. They built liberty ships and electric welding. Left in 1943 to get a doctors statement to acquire a release from defense work. He then joined the U.S. Coast Guard. He was inducted at Camp Croft, SC on Nov. 29, 1943 and sent to Curtiss Bay Training Center for boot camp training. He was assigned to USS *Menges* (DE-320) at Brooklyn Navy Yard in New York on Sept. 8, 1944. He served from Sept. 8, 1944 until Oct. 22, 1945. He was ship photographer and Jack of Dust. They were on convoy duty in the Atlantic to ports in Plymouth England, Liverpool, England and convoy to North Africa, Oran, Algeria.

They trained at New London, CT for Hunter/Killer Group: Then on to North Atlantic for submarine patrol duty. They sank a U-Boat 866 on the coast of Nova

Scotia. While waiting to be reassigned they helped train the Coast Guard Academy Cadets in the Carribean. They were at the Virgin Islands on VJ night. Got off the ship in Boston Navy Yard and went by train to separation center at Cocks Spur Island, Savannah, GA.

Returned home on Oct. 25, 1945. He opened a commercial and portrait photography studio. He and his wife operated the studio for 40 years. They retired July 9, 1983 and keep busy traveling, doing church and community work. He married Jane Bryant from Asheville, NC on June 22, 1942. They have recently celebrated their 50th anniversary.

KENNETH ROY EMERICK, EM1/c, USS *Waterman* (DE-740), enlisted in the Navy Feb. 26, 1943. Born Dec. 29, 1923 in Detroit, MI. Went to boot camp at Great Lakes, IL. Graduated April 13, 1943. Attended the Navy Training School for Electricians at Purdue University. Graduated July 3, 1943.

Sent to Norfolk, VA then to the West Coast. Assigned to the USS *Waterman* (DE-740) which was commissioned Nov. 30, 1943 in Long Beach, CA. Had a six weeks shakedown cruise before leaving for Pearl Harbor and the South Pacific. After a bad typhoon in June 1945, had to escort the bowless *Pittsburg* and the damaged *Deluth* to Guam. Participated in the initial occupation of the Japanese empire. Returned by the Panama Canal to Green Cove Springs, FL where the *Waterman* was mothballed, Discharged March 6, 1946.

Married Joyce Storick in 1947. Raised two daughters and one son. Graduated from the University of Detroit in 1951 and worked as an electrical engineer for Fisher Body until January 1984. Retired to Stuart, FL.

MANUEL ENOS, was born Nov. 1, 1926 in Massachusetts. He joined the Navy Dec. 20, 1943. Stationed with the Navy on board the USS *Lawrence C. Taylor.* Attended boot training in Sampson, NY. He achieved the rank of GM2/c.

His memorable experiences include being in seven

major battles in the Pacific through Okinawa and sank the last Jap submarine of the war.

He was awarded the Asiatic-Pacific Ribbons with seven stars, Philippine Liberation Medal, Presidential Unit Citation, and the China Expeditionary Medal.

Married for 41 years, has six grown children (three boys and three girls) all married. Also has ten grandchildren. He has retired from the U.S. Postal Service. Does volunteer work, helps the city's needy and elderly. His hobbies are fishing and camping.

EDWARD L. ESSO, MOMM2/c, was born May 6, 1924 Paterson, NJ. Enlisted in Navy Feb. 27, 1943 boot camp at Newport, RI. Went to Hospital Corp School, Portsmouth, VA, then went to N.O.B. Norfolk, VA assigned to USS *Lovering* (DE-39) in Bremerton, WA Puget Sound Navy Yard. Their captain was lieutenant commander A.H. Donaldson. Went on shakedown cruise then to Gilbert Islands operated from Tarawa. Went to Marshall Island operated from Kwajalein and Majuro and Eniwetok, then did escort missions to Saipan and Guam in the Marianas Islands then to Ulithi, then to Okinawa doing Ping duty around the island. From there Iwo Jima the Ryukyus Island invasion. The USS *Lovering* (DE-39) received three Battle Stars. Went back to States and decommissioned Oct. 16, 1945. Assigned to USS *Sardonyx* (PYC-12). Discharged Nov. 6, 1945. Lido Beach, Long Island, NY.

Married 29 years, has three children, Joseph, Edward, Jr. and Denise. Retired machinist 51 years Aug. 1, 1989.

WILFRID G. ESSWEIN, was born Feb. 15, 1927. Enlisted U.S. Coast Guard Feb. 13, 1945. Went to boot camp at Manhattan Beach, Brooklyn, NY.

May 14, 1945 assigned to receiving station in San Francisco, CA then to Seattle, WA; June 1945, assigned to U.S. Coast Guard operating base in Ketchikan, AK; September 1945 assigned to USS *Sellstrom* (DE-255) for duty in Bering Sea, South Pacific and China. Returned to States in June 1946 for discharge.

Enlisted in U.S. Navy Reserve in March 1947.

Called to active duty during the Korean War on Dec. 4, 1950.

Assigned to USS *President Jackson* (APA-8), transporting troops to and from Japan, Korean and Alaska.

Discharged in March 1952. Has been married for 36 years. Has three children and six grandchildren.

Employed at A.G. Edwards and Sons assistant to the art curator.

THOMAS J. FABRIZIO, WTC/c, USS *Hopping* (DE-155), born in Hartshorne, OK, Oct. 22, 1923. Enlisted in the U.S. Navy Jan. 13, 1943. Boot training at Great Lakes, IL. After boot training went to Norfolk, VA.

Commissioned the USS *Hopping* (DE-155) May 21, 1943. Went to Bermuda for a shakedown cruise.

They were assigned to convoy duty in the Atlantic. Made nine trips across the Atlantic which included Casablanca, Ireland, England and France.

The USS *Hopping* (DE-155) was converted to an APD-51 at Staten Island, NY, Sept. 23, 1944 to Dec. 1, 1944. Entered the Pacific by the way of Panama Canal Dec. 26, 1944. Took part in the invasion of Okinawa April 1, 1945. Was hit six times by shore batteries from Tsuken Jima April 9, 1945.

After the war was over, went to the Philippines. Left the USS *Hopping* (APD-51) Oct. 19, 1945. Returned to San Francisco Nov. 17, 1945. Discharged from Great Lakes, IL Nov. 26, 1945.

Married to former Catarina Fuccy. They have two children, Norma Jean and Russell James Fabrizio and two grandchildren, Bryce Thomas and Mark Thomas.

They will celebrate their 47th wedding anniversary Feb. 23, 1993.

Retired from General Electric Company, Warren, MI, Nov. 1, 1983.

They celebated their sixth ship reunion in October 1992 in San Diego, CA.

NAT J. FARAGASSO, was born March 16, 1909. Inducted USN Jan. 22, 1944. Sent to Great Lakes boot camp. Assigned to Cooks & Bakers Schools, Norfolk, VA. Assigned to USS *Gosselin* (APD-126). Reported for duty Saturday December 1944 in New Orleans. Shakedown cruise off Bermuda then via Panama Canal to the Pacific, Eniwetok, Ulithi, etc.

Arrived on April 6 in the Okinawa area on a convoy assignment.

From April 27 the *Gosselin* was part of the Okinawa screen - shooting down one Japanese plane.

In August joined the third fleet of Honshu. He was one of the first group to enter Sagamiwan and Tokyo Bay and began official occupation of Japan.

Assigned to liberate and evacuate prisoners of war from Omord Camp. First to reach and evacuate prisoners. Left his ship in Yokosuka in November 1945. Discharged at Lido Beach, Lond Island, November 29.

Married Mary D. Dwyer May 15, 1937 Jersey City, NJ. Now both retired living in Florida. They have two sons and two grandchildren.

DANIEL P. FARLEY, was born May 22, 1922 in Methuen, MA. He joined the service October 1942 with the U.S. Coast Guard. Stationed with U.S. Coast Guard as RM1/c on board USS *Savage* (DE-386). Attended boot camp at Manhattan Beach; Radio School at Atlantic City, NJ; and U.S. Coast Guard Radio Station WSL, Long Island, NY.

Farley's memorable experience's include convoy

duty, submarine attacks in the Atlantic, air attacks in the Mediterranean.

Married Margaret Daniel, whom he met while attending Radio School in Atlantic City. He has six grandchildren and eight grandchildren.

Retired from United Technology. Now a violinist with the Manchester Symphony Orchestra, also a 16 piece dance band.

JOHN D. FERGUSON, was born Oct. 18, 1924 in Jefferson Valley, NY. He joined the service March 23, 1943 serving until Feb. 11, 1946. Served with the U.S. Navy APD-81 on board the USS *Tatum*. Also stationed at Sampson Naval Training Station, NY. He achieved the rank of RDM3/c.

His memorable experiences include the kamikaze attacks, Okinawa.

He was awarded the Asiatic Pacific with one star and the European African Middle Eastern with one star.

Married 42 years and has four children. Retired after 40 years with Con Edison Co. in New York.

JOHN HOWARD FERGUSON, Yeoman 1/c, USS *Garfield Thomas* (DE-193) was born at home in the Central New Jersey village of East Millstone on Feb. 16, 1924. Upon graduation from high school in 1941 he worked as a business machine operator before joining the U.S. Navy in April 1943. After completing boat training at Newport, RI he attended Yeoman School also at Newport. Upon graduation Ferguson reported to Norfolk, VA where the crew for the USS *Garfield Thomas* (DE-193), then under construction in Newark, NJ, was being assembled. After commissioning at the Brooklyn Navy Yard and completion of a "shakedown" cruise to Bermuda, the *Garfield Thomas* began service with the Atlantic Fleet Escort Division 6. Convoy trips were made to Brazil, through the Mediterranean to Bizerte, to England, Wales and Scotland including two runs toward Murmansk, Russia. After VE Day the *Garfield Thomas* along with Escort Div. 6 was transferred in June 1945 to the Pacific Fleet, where she performed escort duty in the Marshall and Gilbert Islands including a weather patrol in the North Pacific Aleutian Islands area. Return trips to Pearl Harbor were the highlight of their Pacific Fleet duty. Ferguson left the *Garfield Thomas* in Hawaii and returned to San Francisco on an Army transport. He was discharged as yeoman first class at Lido Beach, Long Island, NY on Feb. 14, 1946.

Ferguson was married to his high school sweetheart, Lillian Robertson, on May 27, 1945, while on a brief leave. They have three children, John Jr., Gary, and Ellen, and six grandchildren.

Immediately after discharge from the Navy, Ferguson matriculated at Rutgers University where he earned a BS in business administration. He was employed as a personnel manager with American Cyanomid County, Wayne, NJ, and retired after 42 years with the company on Feb. 28, 1987. Ferguson and his wife Lillian retired to a new home on Long Beach Island, NJ where they enjoy swimming, boating, traveling, church activities and volunteer work.

DAVID S. FERON, SOG2 USS *Woodson* (DE-359), joined Naval Reserve 1951 - applied for active duty May 1952 - attended boot camp at Bainbridge, MD; assigned to Fleet Sonar School, Key West, FL - graduated March 1952; assigned to USS *Woodsen* (DE-359) until discharge June 1954. Graduated Adelphia University BBA, CMA - employed Price Waterhouse 1958-1961. Controller of Farrand Optical Company, Inc.

1965-1969, transferred to Farrand Industries, Inc. 1970 as controller - treasurer. Appointed executive vice president 1981; 1986 appointed chief executive officer of Farrand Optical Company, Inc. Currently senior vice president of Ruhle Companies, Inc., Valhalla, NY. Member of Board of Directors of six companies and member of antique auto clubs, Land Trusts, Community Land Owner Association, also Who's Who in American Universities and colleges 1957-1958, Who's Who in American 1990 and Who's Who World Wide 1991.

Married and has five daughters, Carrie, Nancy, Kathleen, Kerri and Kelly, and one son Kenneth.

LEONARD LEE FERRELL JR., S1/c, USS *Martin H. Ray* (DE-338), inducted Oct. 22, 1943 born July 1, 1925. Went to boot camp, Great Lakes, IL and went to Norfolk, VA for training and then assigned to USS *Ray* (DE-338) being built at Orange, TX. Commissioned Feb. 28, 1944. Made two trips across Mediterranean and did escort duty North Atlantic.

Discharged Dec. 17, 1945. Worked 40 1/2 years as a surface coal miner and retired July 6, 1987 live in Providence, KY with wife Jean and have two children, a son, Greg and a daughter, Jennifer. They also have four grandchildren and one great-grandson.

He was awarded four Battle Ribbons, American European African and Middle Eastern.

They lost their power in middle and north Atlantic.

PAUL E. FIELDS, attended boot camp at Owensboro, KY. Sgt. Puckett, a tough drill sergeant and very strict. He got a broken rib when playing black mans bluff. He trained them well, St. Louis, MO for week or two.

St. Charles, MO rifle range. Rained nine days out of eleven days that they trained in the mud. They were taken out by river boat, St. Louis, MO to Wolf Lake, IL schooling and drilling Norfork, VA schooling.

Orange, TX to board ship. Back to Norfork, VA, for their shakedown and battle practice. They then went on convoy duty. They were in Casablanca where they lost one of their ship mates he was thrown out an upstairs window from the sixth floor of a hotel.

In the Mediterranean Sea they were attacked by German night fighters. Several ships were sank. The planes were black and all they could see were bombs, guns flashing, sometimes the exhaust could be seen from the planes. The USS *Langsdale* DD that President Roosevelt's son was on was sank, and several of their merchant ships were sank and damaged. Some were ran up on the beaches to save them. Just a few a minutes, that he will never forget.

He was oil king on board and he had an experience that was almost fatal, he dropped the oil check stick in the bilge when he was checking the oil level of a generator and his belt got fastened on a bolt between the deck plate and the generator, he was fast every time the ship would roll from side to side the bilge water and oil would come up in his face and head he could not breath, until the ship would roll to the opposite side.

One of his buddys heard him yelling and kicking, and came and helped him to get loose. He thinks of him often. He is proud to have served his country with these special guys that God put heart to do a job, they did it well.

WILLIAM E. FIESEL, USS *Borum* (DE-790). Enlisted in Chicago, IL December 1942. Reported Great Lakes, NTS, January 1943, Camp Lawrence Co. 88, Hammocks first seven weeks, quite an experience. Attended Machinist Service School at Great Lakes. Shipped to Norfolk, VA, then to Orange, TX. Commissioned USS *Borum* (DE-790) November 1943. Shakedown Bermuda - Marine troop - ship convoy to Panama Canal, and Pacific F.P.O. at Coco Sola, C.Z. ordered to escort 'Jeep' carriers to Norfolk, VA and reassigned Atlantic, F.P.O.

Early March convoy to North Ireland via Azores-Plymouth, England, homeport.

Convoys and patrols until June 4. Left Weymouth, England with LSTs convoy for Normandy invasion June 5. Recalled for next day GO - USS *Borum* (DE-790) one of six DE's in invasion. 790 there H-Hour, D-Day. 790 also operated with PTs in Channel Islands Operation - taking shore battery hit Sept. 9, 1944. Continuous service, 16 months in ETO - New York, June 15, 1945 to Philly Navy Yard refit for PAC.

He left 790 Jan. 24, 1946 for discharge.

A salute to all his shipmates, especially those who served in the 'Black Gang.'

Married and has eight children, youngest boy, sergeant, 82nd Airborne Div.

Retired after 43 years, Libby Owens-Ford Glass Company, Ottawa, IL.

JOSEPH FILIPIAK, WT1/c USS *Grady* (DE-445), was born March 6, 1918 in Maspeth, NY. Enlisted in the Navy Nov. 20, 1939. Boot camp in Newport, RI. Assigned to USS *Reuben James,* USS *Hamilton,* USS *Greer,* Naval Training School, Miami, FL, Pre-Com. Dept. Pt. Newark, NJ, USS *Grady,* (DE-445).

USS *Grady* was built and commissioned in Brooklyn Navy Yard, September 1944. Shakedown was in Bermuda. Left for San Francisco, then to Pearl Harbor. Operated with USS *Saratoga.* Went to Eniwetok, Marshall Islands, Ulithi, Atoll, Caroline Islands.

Participated in the invasion and capture of Iwo Jima. Went to Solomon Islands, New Hebrides Islands.

Participated in invasion of Okinawa. Shot down kamikaze plane. Without receiving a scratch, the USS *Grady* (DE-445) logged 58 days of combat duty at Okinawa.

The *Grady* had many close misses. Traveled 68,903 miles, fired 28,882 rounds of ammunition, escorted 16 convoys over 25,760 miles of ocean without losing a ship.

Awarded the American Area Ribbon, Asiatic-Pacific Ribbon with two stars, Philippine Liberation Ribbon.

Honorably discharged Dec. 7, 1945. Married DoLores Kunreuther. They have four children, Barbara, Joseph, Paul, DoLores and also has four grandchildren.

Retired from Exxon Corp. as motor tank salesman after 30 years. Likes to whittle with woodcarving in spare time.

JOHN H. FINNELL, was born Oct. 2, 1920, Bridgeport, CT. Enlisted Nov. 19, 1942. Stationed at U.S. Navy. Achieved the rank of radioman third class.

Received the following awards: the Good Conduct, Victory Ribbon, Philippine Republic, Presidential Unit Citation Badge, Philippine Liberation, Asiatic-Pacific Area Service Medal, four Battle Stars.

Married to Cecelia, and they have three sons, Thomas, James and Michael and five grandchildren.

He is now retired from Bridgeport, CT, fire department. Retired from Nabisco brands as manager of safety and security. He now plays golf and fish and enjoys his grandchildren.

On Oct. 4, 1944 the USS *Bowers* joined a group of fleet oilers off Humboldt Bay, New Guinea for escort

to Leyte Gulf, Phillipine Islands. The *Bowers* entered Surigao Straits on October 23 and continued to protect the fleet oilers throughout the Leyte campaign. On October 24 two Japanese torpedo bombers came in at dusk and dropped two torpedoes. He was topside with Ralph Bagley RM3/c (later killed in the invasion of Okinawa when the USS *Bowers* was hit by a suicide plane and more than half their crew were killed or missing.) It was an eerie feeling to watch the wake of the torpedo as it headed directly for the ship, later it was determined that the torpedo passed under the *Bowers,* and into the fleet oiler USS *Ashtabula* (AO-51) off their starboard side. There were no personnel casualties, and the fleet oiler completed her mission before effecting repairs.

BERNARD FISGAER, was born June 1, 1925 in Philadelphia, PA. Inducted into service Sept. 1, 1943. Served with the U.S. Navy stationed at Bainbridge, MD. Attended boot camp at Sampson, NY Mai Man School; FPO New York, USS *Cross* (DE-448).

He achieved the rank of mailman third class.

His memorable experiences include the battle of Okinawa, and ships attacked by kamikazes.

He was awarded the Victory Medal, American and Pacific Theaters of War.

Married to Ruth and has daughter Eileen, son Alan and granddaughter Valarie. He is now an accountant.

RAYMOND E. FITCH, was born April 24, 1926 in Woburn, MA. He joined the service March 2, 1944. Joined the USNR. Stationed at NTS, Sampson, NY - USS *Loy* (DE-160/APD-56) staff Florida, Group 16th Fleet.

He achieved the rank of EM 3/c at the time of discharge.

His most memorable experience includes the ship being hit by a kamikaze May 27, 1945.

Fitch was awarded the World War II Victory Medal, American Area Medal, Asiatic Pacific Area Medal with one star, Philippine Liberation Area Medal with one star and one Unit Commendation.

Married for 43 years to Myra. They have five children and nine grandchildren. Now retired plant engineering manager.

ARTHUR CHARLES FLEISCHMANN, SM2/ c, USS *Gantner* (DE-60), USS ATR-59, enlisted November 1942. Boots Newport, RI. Attended Signal School University of Chicago, February 1943 through May 1943. Transferred to Miami for further training. Transferred to Boston for assignment and commissioning USS *Gantner,* Bethlehem Shipyard, Hingham, MA, July 29, 1943.

After shakedown in Bermuda, USS *Gantner* assigned North Atlantic convoy duty. Made seven trans-Atlantic convoy voyages. October 1944 transferred to Philadelphia. Commissioned USS ATR-59, Dec. 1, 1944. After shakedown, proceeded to Norfolk, picked a crane and towed to San Diego. At Treasure Island picked up barge, towed to Pearl Harbor.

USS ATR-59 assigned temporarily at Pearl Harbor for ready duty. Went aground at Pearl Harbor, ship was dry docked for repairs.

Discharged November 1945. Married July 1944. Has son and daughter and four grandchildren. Semi-retired May 1989.

Member DESA and AARP.

JOHN P. FLEMING, EM1/c, USS *Hopping* (DE-155), USS *K.M. Willett* (DE-354), enlisted in Navy Nov. 5, 1942. Born in Boston, MA Aug. 15, 1922.

Trained at Great Lakes, Company 1609. Attended University of Minnesota Electrical School, Company 8. Commissioned USS *Hopping* at Norfolk, served on convoy duty in North Atlantic; transferred to SCTC, Miami, March 1944.

Joined nucleus crew and commissioned *K.M. Willett* (DE-354) in Texas. Went to Pacific, served with Cort. Div. 82 from New Guinea to the Philippines, Japan and China on patrol, convoy and ASW duties. Left. K.M. Willett at Samar, returned to San Diego. Discharged on Feb. 10, 1946 in Boston.

Married Marjorie F. Keane, June 1947. They have a daughter Janet and son John. Worked as electrical contractor. Joined Boston Fire Department served as firefighter and arson investigator. Retired. Later employed by Northeastern University Boston as fire marshal; retiring in 1989. Resides in West Roxbury, MA.

JAMES W. (JACK) FLINCHEM, JR., was born April 3, 1925 Winston Salem, NC. Inducted into the Navy June 17, 1943, re-enlisted into the Air Force April 12, 1948. As a plank owner of the USS *Fair* (DE-35) served aboard from the Tarawa through Okinawa. Served in the Air Force from Japan to Germany and many places off to numinous to list.

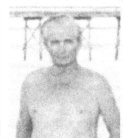

He considers himself to be a jack of all trades. Spending his time now as a retired DAV enjoying life between North Wilkesboro, NC and Calabash, NC and is still a sailor at heart, Girls, he's still single.

DICK FLOCKENZIER, was born Aug. 29, 1925 in Mansfield, OH. Joined the Navy August 1943. Served with the U.S. Navy on board the USS *Richard M. Rowell* (DE-403). Discharged Dec. 15, 1945, FC3/ c.

Graduated from Ohio University - BS degree. Majored in accounting. He is now a manufactures agent.

Memorable experiences: typhoons off Okinawa, sinking of Japs subs, sinking of aircraft carrier Bismark, sea right in front of them off Iwo Jima. They picked up survivors.; picking up a downed Jap pilot; USS Shelton (DE-407) hit by torpedo. They went alongside to get crew off; night battle of Manila - Jap destroyer sunk. Seeing his first kamikaze plane. Married and has four children, Nancy, Rick, Steve and Mark.

WALTER B. FLYNN, was born Oct. 8, 1920 in New York, NY. Inducted into the service Oct. 28, 1942, serving in the U.S. Navy.

Stationed at NRS, New York, NY; NTS, Sampson, NY; NTS, Moorehead, KY; NTS, Norfolk, VA; USS *Dobler,* (DE-48); RS Brooklyn, NY; USN Disc Barracks; Hart Island, NY; PSC, Lido Beach, NY.

Flynn achieved the rank of EM1/c.

His memorable experiences include Gibraltar, Mediterranean, Palermo, and Sicily.

Has son, Roger who is presently in the Air Force. Retired Borough superintendent Dept. G.S. Bureau of Gas and Electricity, Queens, NYC.

CAPTAIN H.R. FORCE, USCGR (ret), served aboard the USS *DE Long* (DE-684) as a watertender from time of commissioning in December 1943, until September 1944. Later he was transferred for duty aboard the USS *Elkhart* (APA-80) until discharge in May 1946. He was recalled to active duty as a boilerman first class for service for the duration of the Korean Conflict. Later he received a direct commission in the U.S. Coast Guard Reserve, retiring with the rank of captain after completing 30 years total Navy and Coast Guard time. He retired as corporate security manager for Chevron Corporation with world wide responsibilities. At the present time he is vice president of Coast Watch, a maritime consulting firm, and president of California Peace Officers' Association Foundation.

FRANK J. FORMICHELLA, was born Oct. 15, 1925 in P.O.B. Summit, NJ. Joined the U.S. Navy Oct. 23, 1942 on his 17th birthday. Attended boot camp at Newport, RI. Armed guard, served on USS *Beckham* (APA-133), USS *J.E. Campbell* (APD-49), USS *Wilkes Barre* (CL-103). His highest rank achieved was that of GM2/c, and he was discharged as GM3/c.

His memorable experiences include Iwo Jima, Okinawa, Korea and most of Navy life was most memorable.

He was awarded the World War II Medal, European African, with one star, Asiatic-Pacific with two stars, American Area.

Married the beautiful Faye Langley. They have two lovely daughters, Diana and Jacquelyn, five grandchildren and two great-grandchildren.

Discharged December 1946. Professional welterweight boxer and heavy equipment operator until joining Summit Police Department Jan. 1, 1952. Served the department through the ranks until September 1986 at which time after 35 years retired as chief of Summit Police Department. Worked as assistant director of Police Academy. Retiring in 1990. Couldn't stay out of uniform.

JAMES B. FORTENBERRY, was born Dec. 6, 1923 in Lowesville, NC. He joined the service Jan. 12, 1943 (selected Vol.). Served with the Navy on board the USS *Borum* (DE-790). Radioman, ETO, Norfolk, Charleston, Bainbridge, Boston. He achieved the rank of RM3/c.

His memorable experiences include their ship

being escorted, first assault wave on Omaha Beach June 6, 1944.

He was awarded the ETO Medal, American Theater, Victory Medal, and Good Conduct.

Married to Sue, has daughter Buffy Rowe, two grandchildren, William and Mary Rowe.

Retired, self-employed accountant.

FRED PERSHING FOSTER, Momm1/c, joined the Navy Reserve November 1942, completing boot camp at Great Lakes and Diesel School at Navy Pier, Chicago. He was assigned to the USS *Carlson* (DE-9) (Plankowner) in Boston with shake down cruise to Bermuda, then through the Panama Canal for escort duty in the South Pacific, including Guadalcanal. He was transferred to the USS *Logan* (APA-196) (Plankowner) commissioned as Astoria, OR October 1944 and continued South Pacific duty until discharged Nov. 11, 1945.

A mass memorable experience was watching the flag raised on Mount Huribachi, Iwo Jima.

Born March 4, 1919 in Wayne County, KY he graduated from Dundee High School, Ohio County, KY in 1937. He worked at Maloney Electric, St. Louis, MO until joining the Navy. He married his childhood sweetheart Feb. 6, 1943.

After the war, he farmed and worked in construction serving as recording secretary for his labor union several years. He is active in Dundee United Methodist Church, a past master of Dundee Lodge 733 F&AM, Member of Rizpah and Scottish Rite Temples, Madisonville, KY; Royal Arch and Knight Temples, Owensboro, KY.

In retirement, he continues a relaxed country life in Hartford, KY, with his wife, family friends and travel.

WALTER F. FOURNIER, DE *Marsh* (699), entered Navy service March 15, 1944, after cancelling pension from Army Dec. 10, 1941, and going through his draft board. Six weeks at Sampson and having passed third class electrical exam. Assigned to Pier 91 New York on old *Seattle*, while waiting for his ship the DE *Marsh* (699).

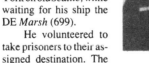

He volunteered to take prisoners to their assigned destination. The last trip was to Newport, RI, so he returned via Northampton, MA, his hometown for a couple of days. On checking back at Pier 91, was placed for Capts, MA, but the following morning looking at bulletin board his assignment to the DE *Marsh* had come through, to report to Newport for training and ship. First trip was to escort two baby flattops to Mediterranean Sea, because of damage being done by German subs. Drop anchor at Malta, left there for Naples to prepare for invasion of

Southern France, the *Marsh* placed smoke screen for invasion, left for escort duty to Marseille but was recalled before reaching port to drop anchor at Algiers, Africa, to escort two Amonian ships to the South Pacific, can only recall name of one the ships *Mt. Baker*. One boiler failed going through Panama Canal, so ship sailed to San Diego and was given a four day pass, left for L.A. and four days later returning to his hotel; had an extension of another four days. Being broke with other second class from Boston went to see IBEW business agent for a job. Both having a union journeyman card, dispatched to race track where they were assigned to the starting gate, which has two bells and they had trouble with one bell not operating, this effects the horses being so high strung, and there was another project that they completed, installing a hot heater for the horse stable, their clothes were dress blues.

Left San Diego stopping at Hawaii, then on to Guam, assigned to sea and air rescue. Left ship Jan. 2, 1945 for ICC School in Washington, DC.

JIM FOUST, was born in Marshalltown, IA April 22, 1923. Went to the service in Jan. 5, 1942.

He was assigned to the USS *Hopping* as fireman third class.

Served on her until February 1943 then was assigned to the *John C. Butler* (DE-339), first one to have five inch guns.

Her record is as follows Morotai Sept. 15, 1944; Leyte Oct. 20, 1944; Battle of Leyte Gulf, Oct. 25, 1944; Luzon Jan. 9, 1945, Iwo Jima; Feb. 19, 1945, Okinawa April 1, 1945, Kamikaze attack April 20, 1945 picked of five of them suckers. No casualties on their side. Score: us five-them zip.

They received the President Unit with Battle Star Navy Unit Citation and the Philippine Liberation Citation.

He left the B*utler* on points, discharged in Minneapolis Dec. 20, 1945.

Returned home to finish raising his family two boys and one daughter. Now has two grandsons, one granddaughter and two great-grandchildren.

That is it for the history; he and his wife are looking forward to the good life.

JOHN WILL FOWLER, was born Oct. 3, 1923, in Doles, GA. Enlisted Aug. 2, 1943. Served with USNR, USS *MacDonough* and USS *Harold C. Thomas* (DE-21). He was awarded the Asiatic-Pacific, and World War II.

He achieved the rank of S1/c.

His memorable experience includes being active in most of island action on to Japan patrol duty at Alaska. Decommissioned DE-21, and discharged Nov. 29, 1945.

He was awarded the Victory Medal, World War II, American Theatre, Asiatic-Pacific with one star.

Wed Rosemary Young, Oct. 31, 1945 in Los Angeles. They have two sons, John Jr. and Robert E., also has one daughter Rosemary and eight grandchildren.

Took early retirement because of health, as supervisor, Dolese Bros. to small acreage. Past Commander VFW Post #10841.

FRANK "FRIZIE" FRAZITTA, EM2/c, USS *Wiseman* (DE-677). Born Nov. 20, 1924. Lived in Pittsfield, MA. Entered Navy in May 25, 1943. Boot camp at Sampson, NY. Electrical Training School at Naval Armory, Detroit, MI, then to Norfolk until ship was ready for commissioning in New Orleans on April 4, 1944. Made three convoys-North Atlantic, Bizerte, Africa and Sicily protecting ships and fighting off enemy submarines. December 1944, ships torpedoes were removed and refitted with transformers. Sailed through the Panama Canal to the South Pacific on more convoy duty ending up in Manila to supply electrical power to Manila and military installations.

He was awarded American Area, Asiatic-Pacific

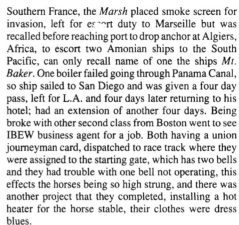
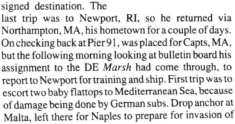

Area, European-African Area, Philippine Liberation and World War II Victory Medal.

Discharged December 1945. College graduate-BSEE degree in 1949. Worked 36 years as engineer for various Aerospace companies, on missiles and space satellites. Retired, but active in the hypnosis field. Presently regional VP for the NW/Rocky Mountain Regt. for the Association to Advance Ethical Hypnosis.

Married to Gwen Hislop, September 1973. No children.

LEE R. FUSON, entered service March 12, 1943 at Cincinnati, OH. Went through boots at Great Lakes and training at Norfolk Training Station as A.S., came out CM3/c. Assigned to *Charles R. Greer* (DE-23), and put her in commission at Mare Island, CA.

Pearl Harbor was their home port. First assignment convoy duty to Ellice Islands. On the way crossed the equator Oct. 14, 1943. Participated in capture and defense of Tarawa and Marshall Islands. Convoy duty to Eniwetok and Ulithi Islands. Came through the typhoon December 17 and 18, 1944 and anchored at Majuro Islands for minor repairs with most of our fleet, wagons, carriers, cruisers, and destroyers, etc.

Promoted to CM2/c 1944 and transferred to submarine tender USS *Proteus* (AS-19) at Guam early 1945. They were in the first group of ships to enter Yokosuka Naval Base, Japan. They accepted surrender of three large Japanese submarines, with snorkels and catapult planes, on the way from Guam to Japan.

They were anchored alongside the USS *Missouri* and witnessed the signing of the surrender documents. Admiral Nimitz pulled dress inspection on them.

He was in charge of crating and recording all Japanese small war equipment on base before being discharged in the first group of sailors, because all his time was served at sea after training.

On the way home they took northern route to Seattle, WA on a converted troop ship, and ran into a storm almost as bad as the Philippine typhoon. They went backward for two days. Gun shields were folded over and some compartments were flooded.

BERNARD F. GALLAGHER, enlisted on Jan. 2, 1941 in the 7th Div. USNR. Discharged July 17, 1941. Reenlisted Oct. 23, 1942. Discharged Nov. 18, 1945, during his enlistment he served at the receiving station, Fargo Building, Boston, MA, then the U.S. Naval Magazine, Prudence Island, RI. From there assigned to the USS *Forster* (DE-334) from the time of commissioning, at Orange, TX, on Jan. 24, 1944. While aboard the *Forster* they did convoy duty in the Atlantic, visited many ports in Africa, England, Bermuda, Cuba-after they served in the Pacific area.

They ended the war at Pearl Harbor. One of the most memorable experiences was the German air attack on the convoy on April 11, 1944, a sister ship, the USS *Holder* (DE-401) was hit by a torpedo, they were ordered to assist and remove the wounded.

Qualified for the American Area, European African Middle Eastern Area with one Bronze Star, Asiatic-Pacific Area ribbons. He's been married for 47 years. Has four children, five grandchildren. He stayed in the Reserves and is now retired as a YNC. In civilian life he served for 20 years as a New Bedford firefighter, now retired.

GILBERT DALE GALLEA, CMM enlisted 1936-1945. Boot camp San Diego, assigned to USS *Vestal* R-4. Made many ports in peace time, also all the islands in the South Pacific during World War II. *Vestal* was along side of USS *Arizona* Dec. 7, 1941.

Commended by the commanding officer at Meritorious Mast for remaining at station when ship was going down. Captain ran this ship aground and received the Congressional Medal of Honor.

Left *Vestal* for new construction first part of 1944. Assigned to small craft training center in Miami, FL. Put *Robert F. Keller* in commission at Glaviston, TX; Bermuda for shake down, then to Boston and Norfolk, then back to the South Pacific. (Hunter Killer Group). Sank many mines and subs and sank the last sub of the war. Was in Iwo Jima and Okinawa conflict. *Keller* was with *Spencer, Monahan* and *Hull* when they were sunk in typhoon in December 1944.

He was awarded the Good Conduct with one star, American Defense, Asiatic-Pacific five stars, Philippine Liberation.

Left *Keller* at Guam for discharge on an L.S.T. for Honolulu, then San Francisco and paid off in Bremerton, WA. Member of PHSA.

As a civilian, building contractor, owned laundromat and spent 20 years in real estate. Retired at 62, is now 75. Lives in Centralia, WA with wife Betty. They have two daughters, four grandchildren and a great-grandchildren on the way.

LAWRENCE E. GAMBLE, RM2/c, enlisted in the Navy Oct. 28, 1942. Boot camp spent at Great Lakes, IL and 16 weeks Radio School at Madison, WI. Served first on USS *Osterhaus* (DE-164), then became flag radioman for commander of Escort Div. II, serving aboard the USS *Levy* (DE-162). Spent time all over the Pacific from Pearl Harbor to Tokyo.

Campaign ribbons were points, Philippine Liberation, American Area, Asiatic-Pacific three stars, Good Conduct and Victory Ribbon. Was aboard the USS *Levy* (DE-162) when on Aug. 22, 1945, Capt. H.D. Grow

negotiated and accepted the surrender of Mille Atoll, the first surrender of Japanese held territory. This was a feature story in *Life Magazine* in fall of 1945.

Discharged Dec. 24, 1945. Married Jean Goode in 1947 and they have lived in rural Lafayette, IN for 40 years. They have two children and two grandchildren. They have always loved traveling and have been to Europe three times and have been to all the States except Alaska. Retired in 1986 after 40 years of farming. Has attended three DESA conventions and annually attends the reunion of the USS *Osterhaus.*

ROBERT D. GAMMON, SOM1/c, joined the Navy Aug. 1, 1942. Attended boot camp at Newport, RI. Subchaser training center, Miami, FL. Fleet Sound School, Key West, FL.

December 1942 commissioned crew SC1004, San Pedro, CA. 1943 anti-sub patrol Pacific N.W. sea frontier. 1944 commissioned crew USS *Paul G. Baker* (DE-642) San Francisco, CA. 1944-1945 Southwest Pacific sea frontier (*Baker*); convoy duty; anti-sub patrol; screening troop landings; picket line Okinawa; transferred from *Baker* Aug. 8, 1945; Fleet Radar School, San Diego, CA.

Honorably discharged Dec. 18, 1945 as sonarman first class.

He was awarded the American Theater Medal, Asiatic-Pacific Medal (two stars), Philippine Liberation Medal.

Retired from NE Power Company. Married and has one son, living in Newberry, MA.

WILLIAM J. GARDNER, was born Oct. 22, 1920 in Jeffersonville, IN. He was inducted into the service Nov. 10, 1943. Discharged April 15, 1946. Served on the USS *Gendreau* (DE-639). Stationed at Great Lakes, IL-NTS NOB Norfolk, VA. He achieved the rank of machinist mate second class.

His memorable experiences are the same as the other crew members of the *Gendreau.*

He was awarded the American Area Ribbon, Asiatic-Pacific Area with two stars, World War II Victory Ribbon and the Navy Occupation Ribbon.

William is married and has one stepdaughter.

Retired as a power dispatcher, city of Murray, UT.

ROGER P. GARNER, enlisted in the U.S. Navy on Nov. 15, 1961. He took recruit training in Great Lakes, IL. After a short term as mail orderly at the Radarman School at Great Lakes he entered Class A Radar School. Upon completion of school he reported aboard his first ship, the USS *Rhodes* (DER-384) attached to Escort Sqdn. 16 in Newport, RI. From Sept. 30, 1962 to Jan.

23, 1963 he served as a radar man manning an Airborne early warning station, conducting Sonar School exercises in the Caribbean. When the Cuban Missile Crisis came about the "*Ramblin Rhodes*" was there.

On May 1, 1963 he reported to the USS *Mills* (DER-383) after a short TDY tour on two destroyers tenders in Newport, RI. After a few radar picket runs to the Caribbean and a couple of sonar school exercises in Key West, FL the *Mills* received orders to Operation Deepfreeze. Deepfreeze was quite a cruise, they circumnavigated the Globe, crossed the equator, the International Date Line and both the Antarctic and Arctic Circles and went through the Panama and Suez Canals. Upon return to the United States Escort Sqdn. 16 was broken up and the *Mills* was assigned to DESRON 601 in Key West, FL. Roger served the remainder of his active duty here.

The things he remembers most are all the icebergs in Antarctica, going through a hurricane off Cape Hatteras, being on the bridge of the *Mills* when the bow plowed into a wave and the water level was slightly below the bridge windows, transiting the Panama Canal and returning from Operation Deepfreeze with only one main engine fully functional while trying to approach the pier in a fog so thick they could not see more than ten feet. The radarman really did a good job getting them in there.

Roger was awarded the Antarctic Service Medal, Good Conduct, Navy Expeditionary Medal, Armed Forces Expeditionary, and the National Defense Service.

Roger is married to his lovely wife of 17 years Jane. Roger and Jane enjoy the company of all the DESA people at the State and National Liberty weekends and the national conventions. He is trying to find any of his old shipmates. He has found one so far.

Roger is interested in any history of either one of the two ships he was on. He enjoys reading about the Navy and the Coast Guard and their histories. He is presently employed at GTE as a craft level test engineer and network construction employee.

EMIL J. GAUDET, S1/c, USS *Tatum* (DE-789) enlisted USN on July 20, 1942 and was honorably discharged on Nov. 6, 1945 as S1/c. He was assigned to Staten Island, NY on Navy tug and from there he was assigned to USS *Tatum* (DE-789) until his discharge on Nov. 6, 1945.

He was engaged in the Asiatic-Pacific Area, the Okinawa Gunta Operation and the liberation of the Philippines. Had a tour of Nagasaki after the dropping of the A-bomb.

Married Marjorie Larkin on July 27, 1947 and had three children. Became a printer under the G.I. Bill, retired at age 65 from General Electric Company in Lynn, MA but continued to work at a local printing company.

BILL GAYLORD, SOM 1/c, USS *Tourmaline* (PY-20), USS *Albert T. Harris* (DE-477), USS *Borie* (DD-704), USS *The Sullivans* (DD-537). Enlisted at age 17 in San Francisco, June 1942, West Sound School in San Diego. Assigned to USS *Tourmaline,* (PY-20) in 1943. Spent year convoying New York to Key West. Ship became a school ship for Harvard Communication School in Boston in November 1944. Shake down cruise to Bermuda then escorted captured Italian sub

through Panama Canal. Arrived in Western Pacific early 1945. In Philippines on V.J. Day. Spent next four months at Shanghai, Hong Kong, Hainan and Hai Phong. Discharged in 1946.

Graduated University of California, Berkeley in 1950. Recalled to active duty September 1950. Served aboard USS *Borie* (DD-704) in Korea. Returned to recommission USS *The Sullivans* (DD-537), in 1951. Released to inactive duty November 1951.

Married in 1947 and has four children and eight grandchildren. Retired in 1982 after 30 years as a probation officer in California.

MICHAEL GELFAT, was born in Paris, France on June 6, 1911. He enlisted in the U.S. Navy March 6, 1944. He became a plank owner of the USS *Pratt* (DE-363) in September 1944. He served as SoM3/c until the end of the war.

They left the States in late November 1944 and performed convoy duty in the Philippine Sea frontier from late December 1944 until the end of the Pacific conflict in September 1945. They were then assigned occupation duty until the end of 1945.

The most significant and memorable experience is the day in mid-August 1945 when they heard that the Japanese had requested surrender terms.

He is now retired from the Federal Civil Service and he spent most of his time in Veteran Affairs.

GORDON D. GILLETTE, S/1c, USS *Chambers* (DE-391) entered U.S. Coast Guard Reserve at Cleveland, OH serving on following stations and vessels: Cleveland Mobile R.O. Oct. 2, 1942-Oct. 21, 1942; Manhattan Beach Training Station Oct. 22, 1942-Dec. 18, 1942; Northport Station Dec. 18, 1942-Dec. 26, 1942; Georgia Lifeboat Station Dec. 26, 1942-Dec. 10, 1943; East Hampton Station Dec. 10, 1943-June 1, 1944; Long Beach Receiving Station June 1, 1944-June 2, 1944; Coast Guard Receiving Unit, Manhattan Beach, Brooklyn, NY June 2, 1944-June 9, 1944; USS *Chambers* (DE-391) June 9, 1944-Oct. 19, 1944; ODCGO 3rd ND Oct. 19, 1944-Dec. 8, 1944; Coast

Guard Barracks, New Chambers St., New York City (hospitalized one month and over nine months recuperating from a hernia operation and scarlet fever). December 8, 1944-Sept. 25, 1945; Coast Guard Separation Center, Detroit, MI (Sept. 26, 1945-Oct. 2, 1945). Discharged as seaman first class

He was entitled to the American Area Campaign Medal and European African Middle Eastern Medal, Honorable Discharge Button, Honorable Service Button and Honorable Service Emblems.

During the years following separation from service, he was employed by General Motors as a welder, resigning from GM in 1956. The rest of his employment years were spent with the Norfolk & Western Railway from 1956/1985. Retired as a conductor in December 1985.

He has been married to Jeanette over 14 years and has three children, Linda, Robert and Kim. They also have five grandchildren.

WALTER E. GILLIAM, JR., MM2/c, USS *William Seiverling* (DE-441). Graduated from high school in 1951 and enlisted in the Navy Feb. 25, 1952. Completed boot training at San Diego, CA and was assigned to the *Wm. Seiverling* in June of 1952. First cruise went to Wonsan Harbor, Korea and returned to the Far East two more cruises. Spent entire enlistment assigned to the *Wm. Seiverling*, being discharged in February 1956.

Returned to Springfield, OH and resumed employment at International Harvester (Navistar) working as a repairman the last 20 years of his 39 years there, retiring in June 1990. Married the former Joan Fullerton in September 1953 and has twin daughters Debra and Denise and two grandchildren.

CHARLES L. GILLILAND, enlisted USNR Oct. 10, 1942, reported for active duty July 1, 1943 with the V-12 program. Commissioned ensign May 10, 1944. Attended various schools then reported to USS *Connolly* (DE-306) on Sept. 6, 1944. Detached USS *Connolly* (DE-306) Nov. 28, 1946. Reported on board USS *Muir* (DE-770) Jan. 7, 1946. Released to inactive duty July 30, 1946.

He was associated with drilling units of the Naval Reserve until 1967, at which time he transferred to the Retired Reserve in the rank of commander.

He has lived in Hutchinson, KS most of the time since leaving active duty. He spent 42 years in the highway paving business as treasurer of the largest paving contractor in Kansas. He retired from business Jan. 1, 1989. He has been doing some traveling since that time. Trips to Russia, Switzerland, Germany and France as well as around the U.S.

MAX J. GILPATRICK, Y1/c, USS *Hollis* (DE-794-APD-86) enlisted in the Naval Reserve October 1942. Upon completing boot camp at Great Lakes attended Yeoman School at Bryant-Stratton Commercial College Boston. First assignment was Bureau Supplies and Accounts, Washington, DC for four months then to Norfolk, VA for assignment to the USS *Hollis* (DE-794). On board when ship commissioned in January 1944 at Orange, TX. While on board saw escort duty in the Atlantic, participated in the invasion of Southern France in the Mediterranean and after ship was converted to an APD as flagship for the Underwater Demolition Teams, spent rest of shipboard time in

the Pacific. Was in Tokyo Bay when Japanese surrender was signed on board the *Missouri*, Sept. 2, 1945.

In October 1945 discharged at Great Lakes and returned to civilian life in Bloomington, IN. Spent six years with Coca-Cola and in 1951 was employed by the Naval Weapons Support Center Crane, IN in the Quality Evaluation Laboratory. Work centered around maintaining the quality of Navy and Marine Corps Pyrotechnic items used by the Fleet.

He and his wife Barbara have two sons, Stephen and Michael and one granddaughter, Erin.

DONALD M. GLADSON, CMoMM, USS *Gustafson* (DE-182). Born Bridgeport, IN, 1920. Enlisted in U.S. Navy October 1942. Boot training Camp Green Bay, Great Lakes, IL. Diesel School Navy Pier, Chicago, and General Motors School, Brooklyn Village, OH. After a short training period at SCTC Miami, assigned to 182 August 1943. Was a "plank owner" and served 27 months aboard the *Gus.* Saw duty in South Atlantic, Caribbean, Eastern U.S., Mediterranean and Hawaii. Honorably discharged December 1945.

Married to former Mary E. Millet in 1949. They have two daughters and two grandchildren. Retired from Indianapolis Union Railway Company in 1981 after 32 1/2 years clerical service. Now living in Clearwater, FL. Charter member of DESA and Suncoast Chapter DESA.

GENE W. GLANTON, was born Oct. 12, 1925 in Russelville, AL. He was inducted into the USN October 1942. Stationed in the South Pacific. He achieved the rank of QM1/c.

His memorable experiences include Saipan and Poi Poi.

Married and has one son and one daughter.

He is employed as an engineer (mechanical MSU 1952). Consultant in environmental service compounds.

CHARLES RICHARD GLEASON, F1/c, USS *Kline* (APD-120) (DE-687). Was working for the Glen L. Martin Company in Baltimore when he was inducted in the service, September 1944, 23 years of age no children. After boot training at Great Lakes, NTC, he reported to fleet-replacement Norfolk, VA. Assigned to the *Kline* #1 fire-room, after a few days they were underway for Panama, cleared the canal and stopped at San Diego (destroyer) base from there to Pearl Harbor, there they exchanged their four boats for LCVPRs. They went to Maui from Pearl picked up Under Water Demolition Team Eleven and was under way for Leyte, PI. There they joined a very large task force, after getting under way they were told the invasion was to be Okinawa, a place none of them had ever

heard of located in the Ryukyu Islands, there he learned the meaning of war, from the Ryukyu's to Guam for repairs. After completion of repairs they went back to Leyte and another task force to invade Bruni Bay Borneo, they left there for Morotai to join another invasion fleet to hit Balikpapan Borneo. Upon leaving there to Manila, RI, then to San Diego, unknown to the crew they were going to work their way up the west coast for the purpose of getting their swimmers accustomed to the cold water they would have to deal with for the fall invasion of the main land of Japan (something else the crew didn't know). While in San Diego the atomic bomb was dropped so that changed everything forever. They got underway for Nagasaki, Japan. There they took a tour of what was once a city now reduced to total destruction by only one bomb, he hopes it was the last.

He was discharged in Jacksonville, FL February 1946, went home to West Virginia for a short time then to Baltimore, MD where he worked for a few years. From there to Florida where he worked for Pan Am and retired as a crew chief in the maintenance department. In 1973 his wife passed away whom he had married in 1942.

He now lives on Lake Okeechobee, FL alone.

JOE GONZALES, was born March 16, 1922 in Galveston, TX. He entered the service Sept. 22, 1942 and was discharged Jan. 14, 1946. Served with the U.S. Navy. Stationed at NAS, Norfolk, VA; USS *Keith* 241. He achieved the rank of CM2c.

Sinking enemy sub and picking 21 survivors. Crossed the equator 1944. Dec. 2, 1943 went to Iwo-Jima.

He has been married 43 years to Marion. They have three children Gloria, Linda and Joe Davis. Retired carpenter, member of USS *Keith* 241 Vets Association and DESA.

CHARLES I. GOODWIN, (BUD), was born in Shamokin, PA Feb. 6, 1926. Moved to Milltown, NJ, 1941; still living there in 1992. Graduated from New Brunswick High School, New Brunswick, NJ. Member of New Brunswick High School State Championship Basketball team, 1944.

Enlisted in U.S. Navy, June 1944; served until June 1946. Received boot training at Great Lakes and amphibious training at Camp

Bradford, VA. Served aboard USS *Hissem* (DE-400), October 1944 to June 1946 as S1/c. Convoyed to England, France, Wales. Survived major storm in North Atlantic (see "Trim but Deadly," Volume 1, page 34). In 1945, after VE Day, sailed through Panama Canal to Pacific. War in Asia ended while en route to Hawaii. Continued to several islands, then to Tokyo Bay. Returned to U.S. in spring of 1946. Put *Hissem* in mothballs at Green Cove Springs, FL. Received honorable discharge from Lido Beach, Long Island, NY, June 4, 1946.

Employed by Public Service, New Brunswick, NJ for 40 years, 20 years electric meter technician (12 of those years as shop steward). International Brotherhood Electrical Workers; 20 years supervisor wire inspectors and meter technicians. Retired 1987.

Elected to DESA Board of Directors at annual convention in Charleston, SC, 1989. Presently (1992) serving as vice president of DESA, with a current membership in the U.S. of 12,000. Organized Garden State Chapter, DESA, in 1981. Current membership (1992) over 400.

Active in local government for 20 years, serving as municipal chairman.

Married to Roberta Matlack, August 1950. They have three children, Barbara, Daniel and Kyle. They also have two grandchildren, Kim and Kelly Goodwin.

ROY E. GRAHAM, WT 3/c, USS *Whitehurst* (DE-643) was born Aug. 1, 1924 graduated from high school Morgantown, WV. June 11, 1943 joined the Navy June 14, 1943. Boot camp at Great Lakes, attended DE training school, Norfolk, VA. Assigned to nucleus crew of the *Whitehurst* under construction in San Francisco. She was commissioned Nov. 19, 1943. After a shakedown they headed for the Pacific for Jan. 29, 1944. Stopping in Pearl Harbor then on to the South Pacific. Participating in a number of invasions through out the islands. Hit by an enemy plane while patrolling at Okinawa on April 12, 1945, losing 42 crew members and injuring 22. Left the *Whitehurst* while she was being repaired in Pearl Harbor. The ship was credited with sinking one submarine and a number of planes.

Earned four ribbons and five stars during the tour in the Pacific. Served a short time on the USS *Alegan* (AK-225) and the USS *McDougal* (AG-126) before being discharged in April 1946. Retired in 1986 after 30 years as a boiler inspector for Hartford Steam Boiler Inspection and Insurance Co. Married and has one son.

JAMES J. GRANDJEAN, joined the U.S. Naval Reserve in November 1942. Went to boot camp in Newport, RI, thence to U.S. Naval Training School on Fischers Island, NY for harbor defense anti-submarine training as a sonarman.

Was assigned to Norfolk Training Station as part of a Navy Infantry Training unit called Gavu. After training was shipped to Oran, North Africa with full field packs and rifle and bayonet in May 1943. This unit participated in the invasion of Sicily. Ultimately working up the coast to Palermo, Sicily where a naval operating base was established. After several months he was reassigned to a submarine detection base at the harbor entrance of Mers-El-Kabir, North Africa. For several months. He was then rotated back to the U.S. and assigned to a submarines detection station Network on Sandy Hook, NJ. Including Staten Island, NY and Brooklyn, NY.

He was sent to Fleet Sonar School, Key West, FL and found to be tone deaf. He was then sent to training at Quartermaster School, Gulfport, MS. On graduation he was assigned to USS *Jack W. Wilkes* (DE-800) as a quartermaster. The *Jack W. Wilkes* did patrol duty in the North Atlantic and participated in the sinking of a sub in company with USS *Buckley, Reuben James* and *Scroggins* in April 1945.

The *Wilkes* was assigned to a convoy to Europe which proved to be the last. Two days out of New York the European War was ended and the convoy dispersed. *Wilkes* returned to Philadelphia Navy Yard for refitting and ultimate deployment to Japan. While undergoing repairs Japan surrendered and a wild time was had by all in the city of Philadelphia.

He was discharged in January 1946 as quartermaster second class.

He was married in October 1947 to Lorretta Bracczyk and they had one first class Nancy in August 1949.

He rejoined the inactive naval reserve in January 1950. In October 1950 he was ordered to Brooklyn Receiving Station for active duty. He was ultimately assigned to USS *Shields* (DD-596) in San Francisco, CA. *Shields* was a deployed Task Force 78 in Korea until January 1952 when she returned to San Diego, CA. He was again discharged.

He was awarded the American Defense, European Mediterranean, American Theater, Victory, Korean Serive, Korean Presidential Citation and the Good Conduct.

He worked for the state of New Jersey Division of Motor Vehicles as an examiner starting in 1949. He received promotions and ultimately was appointed as chief of vehicle inspection for the entire state services and he retired in 1985 with 38 years of service.

He and his wife are the parents of five children, one deceased, who are grown. His wife died in 1978 at age 52.

HOWARD R. GREEN, SR., QM1/c, USNR,
served on USS *Weeden* (DE-797) and on the YTB-545.

He entered the Navy the day after his high school graduation in 1943. Entered boot camp at Sampson, NY and stayed at Sampson to attend Quartermaster School. Really enjoyed the boot camp training, the Service School and the various activities, including playing football on the Sampson Team.

Transferred to Norfolk Naval Base for a few weeks and then on to Orange, TX to join the newly launched USS *Weeden* (DE-797). After outfitting and commissioning - on to Bermuda for their shakedown. They found out fast that a DE sailor is half "Bucking Bronco Cowboy" and 1/2 sailor.

They ran convoys out of Norfolk to Bizerte - Oran and other North Africa ports. Most of the cities were badly destroyed. Made one trip also to Plymouth, England and before returning to Boston for refitting and on to the Pacific via Panama Canal, New Guinea Philippines (ran several convoys in the Philippine area.) Also to such as Eniwetok, Okinawa (picket duty), and on to Nagasaki, Japan after the war to ferry prisoners of war back to Manila. After this duty returned to the States and to Pier #92 New York City then to YTB-545 Staten Island until discharge in mid-1946.

He became involved in sales work and also mar-

ried in 1947. Has had a great family, two boys and two girls and a great wife. Now has also four grandchildren.

He retired after 32 years with Gibson Greeting Cards (as a regional sales manager) in early 1989. In 1989 they also became involved with DESA and really enjoy both the local and national meetings.

As he looks back, the Navy was really a great experience and he recommends it to any young man.

BERNARD J. GREENOUGH, Cox., USS
Connolly (DE-306), entered the Navy April 6, 1944 from Burlington, VT. After boot camp at Sampson, NY was sent to San Francisco, CA. Mare Island Navy Yard to commission the USS *Connolly* (DE-306) on July 8, 1944. After shakedown cruise to Pearl Harbor, Dahu Hawaiian Islands. Then cross International Date Line, on the Eniwetok Atoll, Marshall Islands, Saipan and Marianas Island; on to Iwo Jima Volcano Island for their first engagement acting as anti-submarine screen. After leaving Iwo Jima they crossed the Equator, Tulagi, Florida Islands, farthest south, Ulithi Atoll, Western Carolines. Then on to their engagement; Okinawa Gunta Nasei Shoto as submarine and amid aircraft screen. On April 17, 1945 assigned to hunter killer mission into East China Sea. After discharge on Feb. 8, 1946, returned to Winooski, VT and attended school. After finishing school took a job as office manager in a construction firm.

Married Julia P. Marietta. They have one daughter, Donna Marie, and live in Burlington, VT.

BUDDY JOE GRESHAM, Coxswain, USS *South
Dakota* (BB-57), USS *McCawley* (APA-4), USS *George Clymer* (APA-27), USS *Doyle C. Barnes* (DE-353), enlisted in Navy on Aug. 17, 1942.

After boot camp at San Diego, CA was assigned to USS *South Dakota* at Pearl Harbor. Took part in the battle of Santa Cruz Island, Oct. 26, 1942 and the battle of Savo Island (Guadalcanal) Nov. 15, 1942. Transferred to USS *McCawley* Dec. 25, 1942 at Wellington, New Zealand. Participated in the invasion of Rendova Island. During this invasion the USS *McCawley* was torpedoed and sunk by the Japs June 30, 1943. Transferred July 10, 1943 to USS *George Clymer* and participated in the invasion of Bougainville Nov. 1, 1943.

Received orders to return to USA Feb. 12, 1944 for new construction of USS *Doyle C. Barnes* built in Orange, TX. Commissioned July 13, 1944. After shakedown in Bermuda, went to the Pacific, and participated in the liberalization of the Philippines, and surrender of the Japanese at Kuching Borneo Sept. 10, 1945.

Campaign ribbons were Victory Medal, American Theatre, Asiatic-Pacific with four stars, Philippine Campaign with one star and Good Conduct. Discharged Dec. 14, 1945 at Camp Wallace, TX.

Attended wo years of college and worked for General Tire and Rubber Company, Waco, TX, 35 years. Retired in 1986. Lives in Waco, TX with wife Helen. Raised a set of twins (boy and girl). Enjoys fishing, playing golf, and playing with their three grandchildren.

DONALD C. GRIBBLE, was born Nov. 3, 1909 in
Kansas. Joined the Navy February 1942. Stationed in U.S. on board SC-674, USS *Connolly*.

He achieved the rank of CMOMM and was discharged October 1945.

Married and has two children and six grandchildren. Employed with Ford Lincoln Mercery dealer from 1951 to 1991. Retired in October 1991.

EUGENE GROSS, Y3/c, USS *Waterman* (DE-
740) graduated from high school in June 1942. Enlisted in the Navy Dec. 12, 1942. Discharged Dec. 12, 1945.

Stationed at boot camps at Great Lakes, IL. Went to Radio School, University of Chicago. Sent to Philadelphia Navy Yard 1943 August. After two weeks there, sent to Norfolk, VA Navy Yard, assigned to DE-740 USS *Waterman*. December 1942 went to Mare Island Navy Yard, then sent to San Diego, CA to ship. Spent the next 20 month in the Pacific from Guam, Tarawa, Philippines, Eniwetok, Ulithi, and then into Japan. The first DE division in Japan Aug. 25, 1945. Finally took the ship back to the U.S. stopping in Hawaii, Panama and the canal to Philadelphia and was sent to Long Beach, NY for discharge.

The first DE to return to U.S. after war from Japan.

Gene Gross went into the maintenance business right after discharge from the Navy. After 40 years in business. Sold out and moved to Florida and retired. They have four children one boy and three girls and three grandchildren.

RAY D. GROSS, was born Sept. 29, 1919. Inducted
into the service June 1, 1944, Baltimore, MD, and Bainbridge, MD. Served with Navy on board the USS *Bunch* (APD-79). Stationed in the Pacific area. He achieved the rank of S1/c (storekeeper striker).

His memorable experiences include the Panama Canal, Okinawa invasion on Hawaii. Training with the frogmen and also going to Shanghai, China, and Formosa. Lost man over board. Rescued personnel from USS DE *Dickerson* (old four stack can hit by kamikaze plane).

Widowed in 1980, married 30 years. Has one daughter, and five grandchildren. He turned 72 years old on Sept. 29, 1991. His mother is still living at 91 years of age December 1991. Belongs to VFW since February 1946 when discharged at Bainbridge Naval Station, MD. Made big mistake coming out.

Retired after 21 years as milkman Green Spring Dairy, Baltimore, MD.

EUGENE M. GROSSMAN, Lt. (Jg) USNR, USS

O'Neill (DE-188), USS Grady (DE-445). Graduated Columbia Midshipman's School Nov. 24, 1943. Assigned to USS O'Neill while ship was still being built at Port Newark, NJ. On board during shakedown cruise in Bermuda and while on convoy duty to Londonderry, North Ireland March 1944. Detached, attended Subchaser Training Center, Miami, FL where qualified as communications officer. To Norfolk, VA July 1944 to assemble crew for USS Grady (DE-445), also then under construction in New Jersey. Finally through the canal to Pearl Harbor and saw action at Iwo Jima and and radar picket line at Okinawa. While patrolling entrance to Kerama Retto attacked by kamikaze but not hit after Japanese surrender.

Attended Downstate Medical Center in Brooklyn, NY, MD degree June 1950. After internship and residency training setup practice in Tarrytown, NY (1954-1976). Since 1976 has been working in nutrition research for General Foods in Tarrytown. Married to Cissy and they have three children and two grandchild.

DAVID T. GRUBBS, SM1/c, MM3/c, USS Reybold (DE-177), USS Riverside (APA-102). Enlisted in the Navy April 11, 1943. Born Feb. 12, 1925 in Hilda, SC. Attended boot camp at Bainbridge, MD and DE training in Norfolk, VA. Commissioned Sept. 29, 1943.

Bermuda for shakedown, operated under COM-SUB-LANT. Completed escort run from Rhode Island to Canal Zone, with ammo ship Nitro.

Joined 4th Atlantic Fleet 24th Escort Sqdn. Jan. 15, 1944. Escorted ships back and forth Recife Brazil to Trinidad. Air and Sea Rescue, guarded sea lanes between Brazil and Gibraltar. Reybold was transferred to Brazil Aug. 9, 1944.

He was transferred to USS Riverside (APA-102). Trained at Newport, RI and Philadelphia, PA. Riverside was commissioned Dec. ·18, 1944 in New York.

Assigned to Pacific Theatre moving troops, Pearl Harbor, HI. Caroline and Marshall Islands, Philippines, Okinawa and Korea. Memorable experience: Kamikaze attacks in Okinawa. We stayed in Okinawa until the A-bomb dropped August 1945. Medals: European African Theatre, Asiatic-Pacific Theatre, Philippine Liberation, American Campaign and World War ll. Discharged President Field, San Pedro, CA Dec. 5, 1945.

Married Rebecca Bennett Sept. 16, 1946. Raised three sons and lives in Sunnyvale, CA. Retired from United Airlines SFO March 1, 1985 as a aircraft maintenance foreman with 34 years of service.

GEORGE JULIUS GUEMPEL, MOMM3/c, (USS Fair DE-35). Entered service on Jan. 21, 1943. Completed Naval Training School (Diesel) in Richmond, VA on May 27, 1943. Spent the rest of the war on the USS Fair in the Pacific on anti-submarine patrol and escorting convoys of oilers and LST's. Fair with

Charrette (DD-581) sank Japanese sub I-21 on Feb. 5, 1944. Fair engaged attacking aircraft and suicide boats off Saipan and Okinawa. Fair received five Battle Stars for World War II service.

Guempel was honorably discharged on Feb. 18, 1946. He worked as a machinist with the Bristol-Myers Corp. in Hillside, NJ for 31 years before retiring in 1986. He died Oct. 3, 1990 and is survived by wife Helen C., two sons, Eric and Mark and a brother Edward.

JAMES PATRICK GUNN, GM3/C, was born April 14, 1924 in Boston, MA. Enlisted February 1942 in the U.S. Navy. Attended boot camp at Newport, RI. First sea duty in Armed Guard on board M.S. Challenger, 1942.

1942 next sea duty aboard tanker SS Chilbar. Commissioned DE-239, USS Sturtevant, Galveston, 1943. Ran Atlantic convoy duty. Commissioned gun boat USS LCS-L-3 #1 Boston in 1944.

Shore duty, fall of 1944 at ammo depot, Earle, NJ until November 1945 when discharged. Married Francis Farrell. They have three sons and one daughter. Member of Boston Fire Department 1949 to 1968. Retired with disability from injuries. Public Service Specialist, FCC 1977 to 1986 early retirement.

Senior Security, Boston Stock Exchange, since 1987. May 1942, M.S. Challenger sunk off Trinidad. December 1942 S.S. Chilbar discharge, fuel/gas in Algiers for three days. Only ship in port. High security, air raids, little sleep.

HOWARD GWYNNE, was born June 30, 1925 in Philadelphia, PA. He was inducted into the Navy June 28, 1943. Stationed at Sampson NTC, USS Wyoming and USS Bowers (DE-637). He achieved the rank of gunners mate second class.

He was awarded four Battle Stars, Philippine Presidential Unit Citation including all awards given to ship.

Married to Anne and has two children and two grandchildren.

Semi-retired. Recreation director for township.

JOE C. HALEY, was born April 26, 1925 in Denver, CO. He was inducted into service April 20, 1943, serving in the Navy. Stationed at Farragut, ID. Attended Diesel School in Ames, IA. Also served on board the USS Haverfirld, 393. He achieved the rank of MOMM3/c.

He was awarded the Presidential Unit Citation

with one star, Asiatic-Pacific Area, European African Area, one star, and the American Area.

He is married. Retired after spending 43 years in construction running cranes.

ARTHUR A. HALL, JR., was born June 15, 1917 in Nashville, (Davidson), TN. Joined the Navy Aug. 28, 1943. Stationed at Great Lakes, IL; USS Bowers (DE-687), Norfolk, VA, Mare Island, CA.

He achieved the rank of F1/c. His memorable experiences include learning to live with other people and seeing Australia.

He was awarded one star, consolidation of Solomon Islands; one star, Western New Guinea operation, Toem-Wakde-Sarmi area operations; one star, Leyte Operation; Leyte landings October 1944; one star Okinawa, Gunto Operation April 1945; Philippine Republic Presidential Unit Citation Badge October 1944.

His father and mother are deceased. Married to Louise C. Hall and also has two sisters, Frances Newsom and Mary Berry. Retired after 31 years with the U.S. Postal Service.

About the USS Bowers (DE-637).

They got hit on April 16, 1945 at Ie Jima, just off Okinawa by a kamikaze plane. They had 105 casualties out of 200, 49 killed, 56 wounded, many of whom died later from their wounds. There is no mention of these facts, either in Volume One or Volume Two of "Trim But Deadly." It only mentioned the ship by name, but gave no account of the invasions they were in. It would be a pity that there would be no history of the ship and sacrifices made by the officers and crew. Their DE division was six ships, DE-633, DE-634, DE-635, DE-636, DE-637, and DE-638. Only DE-638 escaped attack. They were attached to the 7th Fleet, 54th Div. All five of the others were damaged by kamikaze planes while on duty on advanced radar positions, on the outer picket line. Their division probably lost more ships than the other DE Divisions in World War II.

Thirteen was a big number of men attending the convention in Las Vegas. Many survivors were also disabled in many ways. All 13 at the convention were under the same impression. If they didn't get their history into "Volume Three," no one would know of the sacrifices made by the USS Bowers and other ships in their division.

The repair ship USS Nestor made repairs to make them seaworthy. They lived in very depressive conditions, at the scene of the tragedy for two months. They arrived in Philadelphia on June 16, 1945. Many have flashbacks today. Some after 30 days leave at home go to the hospital for psychiatric help. The account gives their war record, Solomon Islands, New Guinea, Leyte, Philippines, and Okinawa. They did a great deal of escort service.

EUGENE S. HALL, (GENE), PN2, USS Coates (DE-685), entered the Naval Reserve on March 30, 1951 at the Atlanta Naval Air Station, Chamblee, GA. After completing a Reserve Class "A" PN School in Dallas, TX in June 1953 he was ordered to active duty in August of that year. He reported aboard the Coates on Aug. 15, 1951 as a PN3. He was discharged a PN2 on March 29, 1955. Hall remained in the Naval Reserve, cross trained to CTA, and retired in 1976.

During his "Reserve years" Hall was in law en-

forcement. He retired as the assistant chief investigator for the Fulton County District Attorney's Office in 1987 after 30 years service.

He now lives in Conyers, GA just outside Atlanta. He still works in law enforcement and is employed as an investigator in the Rockdale County Sheriff's Office.

CURTIS A. HALLMAN, was born Jan. 11, 1925 in Aiken, SC. Inducted into service Jan. 27, 1944, in the Navy. Stationed at NTS Bainbridge, MD; PCO USS *Samuel B. Roberts;* USS *YOG-79,* USS APL-42. He achieved the rank of seaman first class.

His memorable experience includes being shipwrecked on USS *Samuel B. Roberts,* at sea for over 50 hours and survived.

He was awarded the American Area Camp Medal, Asiatic-Pacific Camp Medal, Point System, and the World War II Victory Medal.

Married to Frances A. Hallman. Married 44 years. They have three children: Curtis Wyman, Fabian Lamar, and Kathy Sue. He is now retired.

THOMAS L. HAMILTON, was born Dec. 8, 1931. Married and has seven children and 14 grandchildren. Joined Navy Jan. 5, 1951. Attended boot camp, Great Lakes, IL.

Attained rank of QM3 was more of a signalman.

After boot leave arrived Green Cove Springs, FL. Was the first group assigned to recommission the USS *Howard D. Crow* (DE-252).

He served his entire enlistment aboard the same ship.

Was discharged in December 1954 when his father died while at sea coming from an exercise in the North Atlantic.

Currently a self-employed carpet layer.

ROBERT EARL HAMMERMEISTER, was born May 18, 1936. He joined the U.S. Navy Aug. 19, 1954.

He was stationed at the Naval Training Center, Great Lakes, IL; VF-94 Moffett Field, CA; USS *Yorktown* (CVA-10); Fasron 120, Iwakuni, Japan; Mare Island Naval Shipyard, Vallejo, CA. Naval and Marine Corps Reserve Training Center, Treasure Island, San Francisco, CA; Navy 570, U.S. Navy Housing Activity, Yokohama, Japan; USN Construction Battalion Center, Port Hueneme, CA; COMSTPAC, Ft. Mason, San Francisco, CA; USNS *General Hugh J. Gaffey* (TAP-121); USS *Marsh* (DE-699); USS *Lang* (FF-1060).

He achieved the rank of PN2-personnel man second class.

His memorable experiences include putting Army and Marine troops ashore in Da Nang, Vietnam. Ushering in the HMS *Queen Mary,* into Long Beach Harbor while on board the USS *Marsh* (DE-699).

He was awarded the National Defense Service Medal, Vietnam Service Medal with two Bronze Stars, Expert Pistol Shot Medal (Navy), National Defense Service Medal, Good Conduct Medal (3rd) Award, Presidential Unit Citation Medal (for service on *Yorktown* (CVA-10).

Married Linda C. Wagner in Honolulu, HI Sept. 19, 1989. He is now working for Santee Dairies, Los Angeles, CA.

RAYMOND E. HANSCOM, (RAY), was born Feb. 14, 1926 in Marshfield, ME. He joined the service Aug. 22, 1943 and was discharged Oct. 10, 1950. Served with the U.S. Naval Reserve. Stationed at NTS Newport, RI; Massachusetts Radio School, Boston, MA; USS *Howard F. Clark* (DE-533); USS *Oliver Mitchell* (DE-417); USS *Marquette* (AKA-95); Atlantic, Pacific, Caribbean and Mediterranean.

He achieved the rank of radioman second class.

His memorable experiences include Iwo Jima, Okinawa, Philippines, Yellow Sea, Sub and Mine Hunting, December 1944 typhoon and the kamikazes.

He was awarded five combat stars.

Married and has four sons and one daughter. He has a new passive solar home in Sunrise County, ME.

He is now involved with creative writing, and short fiction.

CLIFFORD F. HARP, S1/c, (USCG), USS *Lansing* (DE-388). Graduated from high school in 1939. In 1940 went to Columbus, OH and worked at Curtiss Wright Airplane Factory. Enlisted in Coast Guard in October 1942 at Toledo, OH.

Boot camp at Manhattan Beach, Brooklyn, NY, then to C.O.T.P. Chelsea Barracks. Finally got assigned to USS *Lansing* (DE-388) at Brooklyn, Navy Yard, convoyed to Africa, returned to U.S. then to Cuba, Panama, and Pearl Harbor. Returned to New York by Panama Canal, then went to Green Cove Springs, FL for preservation with mothball fleet.

Campaign ribbons are American Area, European African Middle Eastern Area, Asiatic-Pacific, Coast Guard, Good Conduct, and the World War II Medal.

Worked as architectural draftsman for Smith Lumber Company in Barnesville, OH for about 27 years. Now retired. He and his wife, Helen, live in Barnesville. They have two sons, and one daughter.

THOMAS WATSON HARRELL, was born Oct. 12, 1921 in Cuthbert, GA. He was inducted Nov. 18, 1942. Served with the Navy as QM2/c, USS *Crouter* (DE-11) was Norfolk, VA.

He was discharged QM2/c Oct. 15, 1945. His memorable experiences include reporting to the Leyte Gulf in the Philippines in April 1945. The day after their arrival in Leyte Gulf, their ship got underway with 26 other ships and headed north for the invasion of Okinawa. They arrived at Okinawa on Easter Sunday morning at went to GQ at 2:30 a.m. and remained at GQ until 10:30 a.m. Then they saw some of the results of Japanese kamikaze planes that hit some of their ships.

Married to Jimmie Carolyn for 43 years. Has four children, two daughters and two sons. Retired Baptist minister. Retired school teacher; currently working as a sales associate for Belk-Matthews, Warner Robins, GA.

JOHN J. HARRIGAN, was born Feb. 4, 1925 in Coal Valley, PA. Enlisted May 12, 1943. Served in the Navy as MOMM2/c, USS *Lake* (DE-301), Sampson, NY (DE-301); YW-119. He achieved the rank of motor machinist second class.

His memorable experiences include typhoon's encountered; battles-Iwo Jima, Palau, Wake, South Pacific Commendation and three Battle Stars.

Went to Diesel School, Richmond, VA. Married to Marjorie Heckard Harrigan and has three sons, three grandsons. He is a retired machinist.

CAREY HARRIS, was born March 18, 1924. Inducted into service May 21, 1943. Inducted into service with the U.S. Navy on board the USS *Greiner* (DE-37). Stationed USNTS, Bainbridge, MD/NTS NOB Norfolk, VA, USS *Greiner* (DE-37).

He achieved the rank of cox. His memorable experiences include a three day typhoon in the South Pacific in 1945.

He was awarded the American Campaign Ribbon, and the Asiatic-Pacific Ribbon with three stars.

He has a wife, three sons, two daughters, and nine grandchildren. He is now a retired forester.

CARLTON S. HASELGARD, was born Oct. 9, 1922. Enlisted March 15, 1943 Newport boot camp, Norfolk, DE Training. Assigned DE-137 Orange, TX. Commissioned, shakedown Bermuda, Charlestown, SC, Washington Navy ? Glider bomb mission to the Mediterranean, Gibraltar, Algiers, Bizerte, Naples, Anzio, Capri, Tranto, St. Raphael, New York, Hunter

Killer Group, MA, Pearl Harbor VJ-Day, Eniwetok, Wake Island, Kwajalein, San Diego and discharged Feb. 3, 1945.

Received three Battle Stars, November 6, 15 plane raid November 26, 40 plane Anzio invasion, Southern France, shot down four, hell, jammed numerous glider bombs.

Awarded Navy Unit Commendation for duty at Anzio.

His memorable experience includes shooting down ? as it winged over to miss their mast, undergoing incessant air attack at Anzio, dive bombed under flares, near misses lift ship out of water, survived shelling railroad gun on harbor enemy mine laying aircraft DE boats.

Married Mary Mickelson Sept. 9, 1945. They have three boys and two girls, four grandchildren. Retired carpenter of 37 years. He is now living in Gloucester, TX and is a member of DESA.

ADRIAN HAY, was born March 1, 1924 in Mazie, KY. He was inducted into the service Dec. 27, 1943, serving with the USNR, stationed at Great Lakes, USS *Haas* (DE-424). He achieved the rank of water tender second class.

His memorable experiences include sinking of sub off coast of Philippines, picket duty for suicide planes at Okinawa; typhoon, Okinawa, Shanghai, China 1945; September 1945 Hong Kong China 1945-Haiphong Indo China.

He received one star (Pacific Theater), one star, (Philippine Liberation) American Theater and Victory Medal.

Married 37 years and has five children, Leona, Myra, Greg, Anthony, and Steve.

He is retired from Elliott Co after 40 years. Shares his time at Kentucky, Ohio and Florida.

WAYNE HAYES, (WOODY), Lt. Cmdr., was born Feb. 14, 1913, in Clifton, OH. He graduated from Newcomerstown High School, OH in 1931 and from Denison University (Ohio) in 1935. He earned a Master of Education Administration degree from the Ohio State University in 1939.

His Navy duty extended from 1941-1946: P.T. officer at the Norfolk Naval Base; P.C. boat skipper; executive officer of DE 196, captain, USS *Rinehart* (DE-196). During the Vietnam Conflict, a Navy boot camp company carried his name; the Navy awarded him its Public Service Medal for his speaking tours in Vietnam.

In 1942, he married Ms. Ann Gross. Their son is now Franklin County (OH) Municipal Court Judge Steven B. Hayes.

Woody coached football at Mingo Junction, OH (1937), New Philadelphia, OH (1939), Denison University (OH) (1946), Miami University (Ohio) (1949) and The Ohio State University (1951-1979).

He was elected to the National College Football Hall of Fame in 1983 and was awarded the coveted Amos Alonzo Stagg award in 1986.

Lt. Commander Hayes died March 12, 1987. "He Loved the Battle; He Lived to Win!" Excellence was his password!

In Memoriam Lt. Commander Wayne Woodrow (Woody) Hayes 1913-1987. Presented by Max R. Swigert* (DE 177); DESA member, Columbus, OH. *With permission from Judge Steven B. Hayes (son).

CLAUDE C. HAZLETT, (LUCKY), was born Jan. 10, 1928 in Columbus, OH. Inducted into the service Jan. 12, 1945, serving with the U.S. Navy, Great Lakes IL. Stationed on USS *Tabberer* (DE-418), USS *Otterstetter* (DE-244), USS *Carson* (AVP-52). Also stationed in Okinawa. Served with the Pacific Fleet, WWII China, Japan, Invasion, Korean War, Korea, Yellow River, Panama and with the Atlantic Fleet.

He achieved the rank of MOMM2.

He remembers mostly the commeraderie of the two ships he was on during WWII. But ship's distinguished themselves with saving many lives during the seven or more typhoons that they went throught. Just before the dropping of the atom bomb, he remembers waking up one morning and seeing the Japanese invasion fleet surrounding their task force. Hundreds of ships - horizon to horizon.

He was awarded the American Defense, Pacific with three stars, Japan-Korean Occupation, World War II Victory, Philippine Liberation, Good Conduct and China Service.

He was born in the ghettos of Ohio. Joined the Navy at 17 years. After WWII moved to Racine, WI. Has four children by first wife. Married Virginia Peterson Struli after his first wife's death. Drove a city bus for five years. Joined the Racine, WI Police Department where he became a sergeant. Later became the chief of police of the town of Mt. Pleasant.

"Lucky" retired in 1983. Spends time hunting and fishing in Wisconsin and Wyoming. Spends the summer in Wisconsin and winters in the home he built in Auburndale, FL. Still works part time, process serving, private investigation and security.

JOSEPH E. HECHT, SMC USNR-Ret. 40 years. Was born July 20, 1923 in Upper Darby, PA. Joined Naval Reserve on July 18, 1941 (Phila). Went to boot camp in Newport, RI. Went to Signal School in Toledo, OH and Chicago Armory, to Norton Heights, CT. Assigned to Armed Guard. Served in all theaters, including Murmansk. Released 1945 on points. Remained in reserve until 1981. Became a plank owner (NERA) along with Charlie Grier (1946) in Philadelphia (life member). Recalled for Korean War.

Became a crew member of the USS *J. Douglas Blackwood* (DE-219) out of Philadelphia (1958). Again, recalled on *Blackwood* for Berlin crisis, spent over 10 years on *Blackwood,* then to USS *Douglas H. Fox* (DD-779). Finished his service career, Wilmington, DE.

Other activities include Folsom, West Trenton, Gtmo. Owner of Bronze Star, Citation, International

Date Line, Equator awards. Retired letter carrier (Upper Darby), now living Pocono Mountains, PA. Also a plank owner in Naval Memorial.

ODE TO SIGNALMEN

Here's to the SIGNALMEN of the ARMED GUARD. They were a sturdy lot. They were on a 24-hour watch, while at sea. Sometimes, they were awakened in the middle of the night, to answer a flashing buoy. Other times, to answer a sun reflection.

Sometimes, it was rather slow going, when they had to tie signal flags together. Some ships had two (2) signalmen, while most had only one (1). It was rather tough to remember a message, before putting it down on paper.

Here's to the SIGNALMEN of the ARMED GUARD, may they rest in peace for a job WELL DONE.

I was very proud to be a SIGNALMAN of the ARMED GUARD. But even PROUDER, to have been an ARMED GUARDSMAN.

SMC J.E. Hecht USNR-Ret.

NORMAN EARL HENDERSON, EM2/c, USS *Eldridge* (DE-173). Entered Naval Reserve in 1943. After boot camp at Great Lakes, IL was assigned to electrical school at Detroit, MI. After electrical training was assigned to USS *Eldridge* (DE-173) and boarded her at Brooklyn Navy Yard, New York. He served as an electrician and on a 20mm gun crew while escorting convoys across the Atlantic and Mediterranean until the war ended in Europe. USS *Eldridge* was then assigned to the Pacific area and was on duty as anti-submarine and anti-aircraft patrol out of Saipan and Okinawa until the war ended.

He helped mothball the *Eldridge* at Green Cove Springs, FL and in May 1946 received his discharge at Great Lakes, IL.

He continued his electrical career and became an electrical engineer for the Babcock and Wilcox Co. a major manufacturer of fossil fuel and nuclear powered steam generators. He retired from B&W in 1973 and went to work for a high tech. aluminum ceramic company, Diamonlite Products. Retired from that company as manufacturing engineering manager after ten years

Enjoying retirement as an artist, antique dealer, and antique small engine restoration and show.

He and Marjorie have been married 45 years, have two daughters, Beth and Greta and two granddaughters.

PERCY A. HENDRICKSON, was born July 2, 1924. Inducted into the service Aug. 6, 1943. Served in the Navy on board the USS *Newman* (DE-205)-APD-59. He achieved the rank of BM2/c.

His memorable experiences includes sinking Jap sub off Cebu; liberation of Philippines; escort convoys to Europe.

He was awarded the Philippine Medal, one star, American Theatre Medal, Victory Medal, Asiatic-Pacific Medal, three stars, and the European Theatre Medal.

Married to Eleanor and they have three sons. Retired in 1980 from federal government as a aircraft electrician. Employed part-time as gas station attendant.

J.C. HENRY, GM2/c, USS *Dobler* (DE-48) and USS *Hampton* (APA-115).

Attended boot camp at Norfolk, VA, #557 September 1942. Went to Gunners Mate School in Newport, RI, assigned as plank owner of USS *Dobler*, Philadelphia Navy Yard, commissioned in May 1943 - 18 months and six trips of convoy duty from Norfolk to the Mediterranean area including one convoy with the *Block Island* who was sunk the next day after dropping off from their convoy. Several engagements with subs and aircraft in and around the Mediterranean. Transferred to new construction the USS *Hampton* (APA-115) and spent one year in the Pacific before the war was over. Uncle Harry did not hesitate, he dropped the big one thus saving hundred of thousands of lives including his own. Troops they had for the invasion were the first to disembark on Japanese soil at Amori in Northern Honshu - and thus for them, they went back to the farm.

Worked at Aberdeen Proving Ground, MD as a security specialist and retired after 37 years. Married to Elizabeth M. Henry and resides in Charlestown, MD.

HAROLD EUGENE HENSLER, MM2/c, USS *Abercrombie* (DE-343),

eldest of three sons born to Victor W. and Emma (Pepperman) Hensler, born Sept. 3, 1925 in Pine Run near Linden, PA. Joined U.S. Navy October 1943. Attended boot camp Sampson, NY. Basic Engineering School Great Lakes, IL. Was part of the commissioning crew of USS *Abercrombie* (DE-343), also served on USS *McCaffery* (DD-860), ex-*Rupert* (DE-96) and USS ATR-57. Was discharged at Bainbridge, MD June 1946.

Earned Pacific Theater Ribbon (three stars), Philippine Liberation Ribbon (two stars), American Theater and World War II Victory Ribbons.

In civilian life was employed by Bethlehem Steel Co., Williamsport, PA as machine shop foreman until 1958, moving to Tempe, AZ. Now employed by Garrett Turbine Engine Co., Phoenix, AZ.

Harold and Phyllis (Bay) Hensler married June 1946 in Baltimore, MD. They have one daughter and two sons; Cynthia, Ernest and Scott, five granddaughters and one grandson.

They have a machine shop on the old homestead on Pine Run near Linden, PA where they hope to retire in a few years.

CHARLES L. HERR, RM2/c, USS *Finch* (DE-328) and USS *Dufilho* (DE-423).

Enlisted in Navy Feb. 13, 1943. Boot camp at Great Lakes, IL. Assigned NTSCH (Radio) at Bedford Springs, PA and NTSCH (DF) Casco Bay, ME.

Commissioned *Finch* Dec. 20, 1943. Shakedown cruise to Bermuda then convoy duty to North Africa, Naples, and England. En route to Philippines the war ended.

Finch was involved in the rescue of prisoners of war from Formosa following the war, and received the Admiral's highest award for valor.

Transferred to USS *Dufilho* at Hong Kong for return trip to States.

He was awarded the American Area, European-African Middle East, Asiatic-Pacific, China and Victory.

Married Lucille C. born Dec. 31, 1949. Lives in Muncie, IN. They have two sons, three daughters, and eight granddaughters.

Financial secretary of Muncie Knights of Columbus, Member Post 19 American Legion, TCS, and DESA.

Retired from Ball Corporation as systems analyst on Aug. 28, 1985.

RAYMOND H. HERR,

was born Feb. 24, 1918 in Lanc. Co., PA. Inducted into the Navy April 11, 1944. Stationed on the USS *Lewis* (DE-535), Great Lakes Boot Camp, Norfolk, VA, Boston Navy Yard, MA. He achieved the rank of WT3/c, (T).

His memorable experience includes the invasions of Iwo Jima and Okinawa; typhoon May 5, 1945.

He was awarded the American Theatre, Victory Medal, and Asiatic-Pacific with two stars.

Married for 53 years and has three children, eight grandchildren, and three great-grandchildren.

He is now retired.

LUTHER JAY HESS

(See Bio, page 743.)

NORMAN W. HICKEY, GM2/c, USS *George W. Ingram* (DE-62/APD-43)

was born Feb. 1, 1926, Cranford, NJ. Enlisted November 1943. Attended boot camp at Sampson, NY. Joined USS *Ingram* January 1944. Remained until discharge to Naval Reserve April 1946. Ten years in Reserve.

Memorable experiences include 18 North Atlantic convoy crossings with 10th Fleet. Prior to Normandy invasion escorted largest troop convoy ever assembled in any war. Last Atlantic crossing resulting in a daylight U-boat battle near the Azores which resulted in the sinking of LST-359 and the torpedoing of USS *Fogg*. They were 30 days crossing having zigzagged more than 10,000 miles. A month later they were towing a captured Italian submarine through the icy Cape Cod canal. Following the final European invasion of Southern France they were converted to an APD and next to the Pacific joining the 7th Fleet and Task Force 78. At wars end they left Okinawa for Inchon, Korea escorting the 3rd Marines. They also occupied Tientsin, Chefou and Tsingtao Northern China. They believe they were first crew to touch mainland of China following wars end. (August 1945).

Following discharge returned to work at Royal Insurance, New York and enrolled at Rutgers University under GI Bill. Retired from Royal Insurance Co. 1986 as corporate secretary and director of litigation. Now resides in Short Hills, NJ with wife Marie of 41 years and they have two daughters, three granddaughters. His hobbies include golf and traveling.

JOHN N. HINES, YNC, USS *Dennis* (DE-405),

was born July 10, 1920 Hartford City, IN. Enlisted as apprentice seaman, USNR, July 17, 1942. Served 18 months at Naval Air Station, Bunker Hill, IN. Assigned to USS *Dennis* March 20, 1944 at commissioning in Houston, TX as yeoman second class.

After shakedown in Bermuda, *Dennis* was assigned to the Pacific Fleet, operating with CVEs, DDs, and other DEs of the 3rd, 5th and 7th Fleets, participating in four invasions; Morotai, Iwo-Jima, Philippines and Okinawa.

Received the Presidential Unit Citation, Asiatic-Pacific Medal with four Bronze Stars and Philippine Liberation Ribbon with two Bronze Stars.

Most memorable experience was the Battle of Leyte Gulf on Oct. 25, 1944, where Taffy 3 was attacked by the main Japanese Fleet. *Dennis* was one of 13 ships in Taffy 3, sunk were two CVEs, 2 DDs and one DE, not to mention heavy damage to the other eight ships. This battle later proclaimed to be the greatest sea battle in naval history.

He was discharged Nov. 22, 1945 as chief yeoman. Reenlisted September 1946 and assigned duty with the Reserve Training (TAR) Program then retired with 20 years active service Oct. 4, 1963. Later retired from a rubber company in 1982 and residing summers in Cadillac, MI and winters in Sarasota, FL.

Married 50 years in January 1992, has three children, four grandchildren. *Submitted by John M. Hines.*

WILLIAM H. HINES, (WOODIE), was born April 3, 1922 in St. Flo, NJ. He was inducted into the service June of 1943. Attended five weeks of boot camp and 16 weeks of GM School. Received Navy U.S. 1st after school - GM 3rd on ship.

Stationed in Bainbridge, MD; boot and GM School. After OGU, stationed on USS *Neal A. Scott* (DE-769). In charge of small arms on ship. GQ gun 21, 20mm-single.

He achieved the rank of GM 3rd, (passed second class, no openings).

His memorable experiences include encountering wolf pack at straight of Gibraltar; sinking two subs, but getting credit for one; Europe and North Africa.

He was awarded ribbons with Bronze Star.

Married to "Dodie" and they have two children Sandra and Bill and now have one daughter and four sons. All great.

Today he fishes with a 1972 Grady White 21' long off shore of Jersey two to three times a week. Under 20 miles-weather permitting. Still loves the water.

EARL S. HOCK, was born May 4, 1920 in Bloomsburg, PA. Joined the service June 1944. Served with the Navy Ordnance Div., boarded ship for boot camp. He achieved the seaman first class. Trained in Brainbridge, MD. Discharged from Great Lakes.

His memorable experiences includes the sinking of two subs and height of the sea in 1945 from a hurricane in the Atlantic. He received Service Stars.

Divorced with six grown children. Retired after 32 years with Mirck and Co. His hobbies are hunting, fishing, and playing golf.

RAYMOND HOELZLE, S1/c, USS *Conklin* (DE-439), born May 20, 1927 in Pittsburg, PA. Enlisted Sept. 8, 1944 and trained at Great Lakes, IL, Co. 1782. Transferred to USS *Stansbury* (DMS-8). Transferred to USS *Conklin* (DE-439) at Ulithi. The *Conklin* (DE-439) suffered typhoon damage in the invasion of Okinawa, returned to Mare Island for repairs and overhaul then to San Diego to be mothballed. Attended Material Preservation School in San Diego then went to the *Pine Island* (AV-12) spring of 1946.

Made three cruises to China, Japan, Hong Kong, and the Philippines. May 20, 1948 extended for another year. Discharged May 20, 1949 with rating fire control

2. Visited Utah on way home and met present wife (Carmella) and married Aug. 8, 1949. Farmed with mechanic work as a by-line until 1978 until sons graduated from college, having done farming ever since. Had two sons, one is a mechanical engineer and the other is a veterinarian in Cave Junction, OR. His clinic is called Dr. Joe's Pet Hospital. He will retire in five years when his wife retires as a bus driver. He resides near Delta, UT in a place called Abraham.

ED HOFELLER, EM2c, USS *Frost* (DE-144). Joined the Navy right out high school went through boots at Newport, RI. Sent to Corpus Christi, worked for Chaplins Dept. as radio announcer, stage manager, ran bowling alley and motion pictures. Went to motion picture in New York watched S/S *Normandy* burn and capsize.

Went to sea in 1943 as a EM3c on the *Frost* out of Orange, TX. They sank four German subs. They picked up survivors of the destroyer *Warrington* which capsized in a hurricane and buried the dead.

Discharged in 1945 went to college to become an electrical engineer but didn't work in that field.

He was awarded the Bronze Star and the Presidential Citation.

Married Denise Marie Bovar in 1948. Moved to Houston, TX. Had four children, three boys and a girl and now have five grandchildren. Has spent 50 years working with Boy Scouts and have a Silver Beaver Award.

Spent 40 years in the restaurant equipment business selling, designing, repairing, food service equipment. Sold his business in 1987 and retired to Lesiure World, CA.

HERBERT R. HOLBERT, Y2/c, USS *Jobb* (DE-707). Entered the Naval Reserves Aug. 22, 1942. He had six weeks training at Great Lakes. While on nine day leave he married Carol Corley and the next day shipped out to Pearl Harbor. He was assigned to E&R at the sub base 128 P.H. T.H. After working his way up from A/S to F/2, installing new radar and other repairs he was asked to become a yeoman taking care of all sub repair orders coming in to Pearl. After 18 months he wanted to see some action plus see his wife. He put in for new construction. He returned to the States on CV-11 and after 30 days leave was sent to Norfolk for training and assignment to USS *Jobb* (DE-707). They were commissioned on July 4, 1944 and after shakedown etc., was sent to South Pacific. The remaining time was spent in New Guinea, Borneo, and Philippine area. They were awarded five Battle Stars for action there.

He retired from Safeway Stores Inc. in 1983 and now lives on a farm where he was born. They have three daughters, one son, nine grandchildren and two great-grandchildren. Their son is in the Navy serving on the USS *Robert G. Bradley* (FFG-49) and is now in preparation for their second tour in the Persian Gulf. He's so proud to be a part of DESA.

He was awarded the Good Conduct, World War II, Occupation Service, Asiatic-Pacific Campaign.

HORACE W. HOLLIDAY, was born April 17, 1923 in Roanoke, AL. He joined the Navy Jan. 3, 1943. Served in the Navy as EM2/c, on board the USS *Snyder* &45. Stationed in San Diego, CA, Pearl Harbor, Midway Island.

Discharged as EM2/c.

His memorable experience includes being able to see WWII to the end.

Married to Irma P. Holliday. They have sons, Sandy Sanford Holliday, Phillip Horace Holliday. Now retired and enjoying life.

DOUGLAS V. HOLMBERG, was born Sept. 15, 1921 in Trammel, Dickson County, VA. Joined the service June 16, 1943.

Served with the U.S. Navy, Signalman, Communication Div.

Served at Washington, D.C. (NRS), Bainbridge, MD (NTS), Norfolk, VA (NTS/NOB), Mare Island, CA; Treasure Island, CA; Pearl Harbor, HI; Pacific Theater, Panama Canal Zone; Plank owner USS *Foreman* (DE-633).

His rank at the time of discharge was signalman third class.

His memorable experience includes the initiation of crossing the International Date Line; being hit in battle by a Japanese kamikaze; being bombed by another group while on picket line duty in Okinawa. Their ship was involved in the pre-invasion shelling of various Pacific Islands, i.e., Leyte, Philippines, Okinawa, Ryukyu Islands, Solomons, Caroline, the Marianas and the Marshall Islands Chain. Their R&R in Sydney, Australia. Their return to the U.S. and their trip through the Panama Canal. All in all it was a very worthwhile yet trying experience. The DE Navy proved its merit and courage throughout the war both in the Atlantic and Pacific theaters.

Married to Norma Jean Holmberg. They have three grown children, namely, Wayne Douglas, Martha Claire, and Glenn Stuart and two grandsons, Joshua and Nathan Holmberg.

In 1984 he retired from the U.S. Government as a real estate appraiser.

His hobbies include photography, woodworking and traveling.

FORREST A. HOLSTROM, was born in Geneseo, IL Nov. 5, 1924. Entered the service (USNR) Jan. 6, 1944. Stationed at Farragut, ID, Detroit Armory. Served on the USS *Blessman* (APD-48) DE-69.

He achieved the rank of EM2/c.

His memorable experiences include New York City, Panama Canal, San Diego, Los Angeles, San Francisco, Philippines, Iwo Jima, Japan, Pearl Harbor, and many Pacific Islands.

He received the usual medals.

Married to Lylah and they have children Ed and Laura. He is now retired and in city politics.

FRED H. HOLTHE, was born Oct. 26, 1924 in Chicago, IL. He was inducted into the U.S. Navy

March 1, 1943. Stationed at USNTS Great Lakes, IL; NTS-NOB; Norfolk, VA; USS *Bronstein* (DE-89). December 1943 to March 1946 nucleus crew.

He achieved the rank of EM2/c.

His memorable experiences include being first DE to sink German sub (U-603) also participated in sinking U-801.

He was awarded the American Area Ribbon, European Theatre with three stars, World War II Victory Ribbon, and the USS *Bronstein* (DE-189) was awarded the Presidential Unit Citation.

Married Sara Oct. 11, 1952, and they have four children and five grandchildren.

He is now retired.

HARRY H. HOLTON, SR., Capt., was born

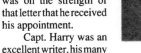

November 1914. Married Millie after graduation from U.S. Naval Academy 1938.

At the age of 17 he wrote his congressman asking to be appointed to the Naval Academy, it was on the strength of that letter that he received his appointment.

Capt. Harry was an excellent writer, his many letters to various officers and crew will remain lasting memories.

Millie was a hair dresser for 22 years, which later turned out to cause part of her years of illness. Harry Jr. and a daughter live nearby in the Sacramento area.

After the war and until his retirement he served as public relations officer for Admiral "Bull" Halsey.

When the *Scott* crew was in training Harry was part of the group in Key West. At commissioning in Philadelphia Naval Yard he was their executive officer.

In the fall of 1943 at the age of 28 became their skipper, he guided the USS *Scott* and her crew safely across the the Atlantic Ocean many times. He was as Regular Navy as any officer could be and rated an excellent navigator.

Underneath that stern, serious face was a compassionate man. The safety of the convoy, ship and men under his command was always first and foremost, to which each and everyone of them owe him their deepest gratitude. (Thank you Capt. Harry), from the bottom of their hearts.

December 1944 Holton was transferred to the USS *Brock* (DE-236) (APD-93) at Charleston, SC. Heading to the Pacific Theatre of the war.

In his later life, Harry Holton became a deeply religious man, his feelings towards his family friends, and shipmates was always on his mind. It became necessary for him to stay close to home to care for "Millie". He lived for the Navy.

How sad and fitting it was that he died while attending the Naval Reunion of the USS *Scott* (DE-214), Staunton, VA with his officers and crew nearby, at the railings of the second deck of the Holiday Inn Friday, October, 1985. *Submitted by Glenn A. Anderson.*

LEONARD R. HOMAN, GM2/c, USS *O"Neill*

(DE-188), was born in Buffalo, NY April 1, 1924. Entered Navy March 5, 1943, sent to Sampson for boot training then sent to gunnery school at Newport, RI May 4, 1943. After GM School sent to Norfolk, VA for crew of USS *O"Neill* sent to Brooklyn Navy Yard for commissioning and shakedown cruise to Bermuda assigned to Atlantic convoy duty from Dec. 12, 1943 to Dec. 16, 1944 at which time he was transferred to New Orleans for assignment aboard USS *Cavallaro* APD-128 commissioned March 13, 1945, shakedown then sent through Panama Canal to Pacific operations for convoy and amphibious duty in the Pacific during June, July, August 1945 as escort for USS *Auburn* (AGC-10) OM 5th Amphibious flagship during occupation of Japan Sep-

tember, October November 1945 left Task Group, headed to Oakland, CA January 1946 to put ship into mothball fleet he was then discharged Feb. 22, 1946.

Married Carol Engelhardt Aug. 7, 1947 (deceased) and has three wonderful daughters and five grandchildren. He is presently working for the Lancaster Central School District at Lancaster, NY.

ALBERT HOMER, JR., MM2/c, USS *Naifeh*

(DE-352). Was born Sept. 21, 1923, Memphis, TN. Entered the Navy in March 1943 he took boot camp in Bainbridge, MD. After boot camp he was sent to Machinist Mate School in Boston, MA. Completed Class "A" School and sent to Boston's Fargo Building for transportation to Naval Escort Repair Unit in Argentia, Newfoundland after one winter there he was transferred to Norfolk, VA for assignment aboard USS *Naifeh* (DE-352). In Orange, TX. The ship was commissioned July 4, 1944. There was shakedown in training at Bermuda. Then convoy duty to Europe and North Africa. The USS *Naifeh* (DE-352) received orders in December to report to the Pacific Fleet, assigned to the Philippine Sea Frontier at Leyte Gulf.

He was on the *Naifeh* on various operations. The ship did convoy duty to other Island, Palau, Guam and Okinawa also others. Once she displayed the three star flag of Vice Admiral on his inspection tour of the islands after the war ended the *Naifeh* (DE-352) was detached from the Philippine Sea Frontier and sent home to San Diego, CA. He was discharged in March 1946, and the ship DE commissioned in June 1946 to the Pacific Reserve Fleet at San Diego. After leaving Navy he worked many years for the U.S. Government in the Defense Department he and wife Maxine have three daughters. Real smart young ladies.

He and his wife have now retired and living in Jacksonville, FL.

ORLANDO R. HORNUNG, was born Aug. 17,

1920, Sciotoville, OH. Joined Jan. 9, 1940, Regular Navy for six years. Trained in N.T.S. Great Lakes, IL.

Fought battles on the USS *Colorada* which left Pearl Harbor about three weeks before the attack on Pearl Harbor. The ship went to Bremerton, WA Naval Yard for an overhaul. Left the ship to help commission the USS *Massachusett*. Went to the ship to help commission the USS *Massachusett*. Went to the European Theater as the *Massachusett* was the Flag Ship of the North African invasion of Casablanca, Nov. 8, 1942. The ship sank the French battleship, "Jean Bart", which was commanded by German and French personnel. The *Massachusett* was credited for sinking a battleship and two destroyers. The *Massachusett* took two hits and was bracked shell fired from Casablanca. February

6, 1943 left for the Pacific. Fought in the battle of the Coral Seas, #2 Munda, Solomon Islands, New Hebrides, Tarawa, Gilbert Islands, Makin and on to Nauru. There were other battles such as the Marshall Islands, Taroa, Maleolap Tolls, and Kwajalein. February 1944 Truk was struck to revenge Pearl Harbor. Total of 209 planes were destroyed and 41 ships were sunk or damaged. The *Massachusett* was under several air attacks while in the Pacific. Left the ship to help commission the USS *Walton* (DE-361) in Orange, TX, September 1944.

Convoyed from the States to Guam, Iwo Jima, Philippines, Hong Kong, Korea, and Formosa Straits. Mostly convoy and submarine operations.

The *Massachusett* passed through a pattern of three torpedoes in the battle of Casablanca. Another one was with the *Walton,* shooting their way through a mine field in the Yellow Sea. Was escorting a hospital ship, USS *Mercy,* Sept. 7, 1945 after the war was declared over. The ship was going to Jensen-Ko, Korea. Discharged Jan. 21, 1946. He achieved the rank of MM1/c.

He worked as a pipefitter, retired after 35 years from General Motors.

Married and has two daughters, three sons and three granddaughters.

He was awarded the Victory Medal, American Area, Asiatic-Pacific with two stars, Philippines Liberation, American Defense, Good Conduct and European Theater of Operation of with one star.

BASIL ROBERT HOSBROOK, joined Navy on

Oct. 23, 1943. He attended boot camp at Great Lakes Naval Training Center, Chicago. Assigned to USS *Haines* (DE-792) as S1/c in Atlantic Ocean and Mediterranean Sea.

Was transferred to USS *Goodrich* (DD-831). Was hospitalized at U.S. Naval Hospital, Chelsea, MA. Met Theresa Powell while in Navy at Boston and were married on Aug. 4, 1945. They were blessed with four daughters and now have 12 children and one great-granddaughter.

Discharged from Navy at Toledo, OH on Jan. 7, 1946. Worked at General Motors, Dayton, OH for 11 years, then worked as special inspector for Corning Inc. Greenville, OH for 30 years, taking early retirement due to ill health in 1987.

Joined National DESA and Ohio Chapter of DESA in 1982.

JAMES HOWERTON, SF2/c, USS *Lovelace* (DE-198), enlisted in Navy July 4, 1943. Attended boot camp at Sampson, NY, assigned September 1943 to USS *Lovelace* (DE-198), Norfolk, VA. Shakedown in Bermuda, to the Pacific Theater in January 1944,

operated with "The New Guinea Express" to Philippines to Okinawa in 1944/1945. October 1945 returned to stateside via "Pearl" to San Diego. Decommissioned USS *Lovelace* (DE-198) May 1946, transferred to USS *Manning* (DE-199).

Discharged July 1946. Was awarded the American Theatre, Asiatic-Pacific four stars, Philippine Liberation, Good Conduct and letter of commendation in service record.

Attended Coyne Electrical School, Chicago, IL in 1948-1949 October 1950 joined Consolidated Vultee Aircraft Company, San Diego, later known as General Dynamics, Convair Division.

Married Virginia Calder June 1946. They have five children, six grandchildren and presently reside in La Mesa, CA.

GENE RAYMOND HUBLER, was born Feb. 22, 1935 in Muncie, IN. Served March 1955 through 1959 and was discharged in 1963.

Served with the U.S. Navy, on board the USS *Bache* (DDE-470). Attended boot camp in Bainbridge, MD, Norfolk, VA and Bayonne, NY.

Achieved the rank of commessaryman (E4) third class petty officer. His memorable experiences includes mission to free trapped U.S. destroyer in Suez. (Commissary Research Div.); six month cruise, 27,851 miles in 131 days in 1957; first U.S. ships to pass through the Suez Canal since its closing.

He was awarded the Good Conduct Medal.

Widowed and has six children all of who are married and living in the south.

He owns and teaches a California Licensed Security Firearm Training School, and is an NRA training counselor and has 25 years with the California Hunter Safety Program. He's taught 1,500 firearm classes over 20,000 students.

JAMES FREDERICK HUIET, SR., (FRITZ), was born June 24, 1925 in Trenton, SC at Edgefield County. Inducted into service March 3, 1943 in Columbia, SC. He was discharged Feb. 11, 1946 in Charleston, SC. Served with the U.S. Navy Reserves V-6. Stationed at Bainbridge, MD for 13 weeks.

Stationed on USS LST-212, 1943-1945 two Battle Stars, Mediterranean Sea, and Normandy invasion on June 6, 1944 Omaha Beach; USS *Straub* (DE-181)

1945-1946 convoy to Oran North Africa, then to Pacific until war ended.

Discharged as gunners mate second class.

His memorable experiences includes being on board LST-212 passed through Straits of Gibraltar on Easter Sunday, attacked by dive bombers and submarines at same time-shut down one plane, third LST to land on Omaha Beach on June 6, 1944, made 33 round trips across English Channel with fresh troops returns with casualties and war prisoners.

He was awarded the European African Eastern with two Battle Stars, Asiatic-Pacific, American Campaign, and the World War II Victory.

Married Jean Beel and has five children, Fred Jr., Sandra, Connie, Beverly and Lt. George Wallace, USN F-14 Tom Cat Jet Pilot and eight grandchildren.

Retired from U.S. Post Office as postmaster for 27 years.

QURLIE HUMBLE, was born Jan. 31, 1923 in Gonzalez County, TX. Joined Jan. 6, 1942 in San Antonio, TX. Served with the U.S. Coast Guard. Attended boot camp at Ft. Lauderdale, FL. Camp LeJune, NC; USCG Academy; New London, CT. He achieved the rank of GM3/c. His memorable experience includes the Normandy Invasion as the 83 footer was loaded with 20 depth charges.

Aboard A 83358 patrol boat in Connecticut and took patrol boat to the invasion of Normandy Beach. June 6, 1944, there nine months. Was once aboard troop transport *William Weigle*, six months. When he returned from Normandy he was stationed at Ellis Island, NY. He was at Manhatten Beach, also gunnery school, Curtis Bay, MD. Went aboard DE-323 USS *Pride* made North Atlantic Convoy and several convoy trips to Europe. In June aboard the DE they left for Panama and Japan. War had ended when they reached Panama. He was discharged Nov. 13, 1945 in New Orleans.

He was awarded the Bronze Star, Letter of Commendation, from Adm. Halsey.

Cora and he married Dec. 10, 1945. They have been married 46 years. Retired and cutting wood in the Ozark Mountains.

JOHN E. HUME, FC1/c, enlisted in the Navy Jan. 17, 1942. Attended boot camp, Company 140 and Fire Control School, Great Lakes. Advanced Fire Control School, Washington, D.C. Subchaser Training Center, Miami. In March 1943 was transferred to Houston, TX as part of precommissioning crew USS *Sturtevant*, (DE-239), commissioned June 16, 1943. Assigned to Division 3 Atlantic Fleet which served as escorts to convoys.

Two trips to Casablanca, two to Gibraltar, five to Londonderry, Ireland, two to Liverpool, England, two to Cardiff, Wales, one to Southhampton, England. After V-E Day, their division transferred to the Pacific. After VJ Day, transferred back to Atlantic Fleet. They were the first division of DEs to enter Green Cove Springs, FL to be decommissioned.

BILL S. HUMIENNY, USS *Edward H. Allen* (DE-531), YN2, was born Jan. 21, 1936 in Brooklyn, NY. Attended parochial school in Brooklyn, NY and high school at St. John Kanty Prep in Erie, PA. Enlisted in the Navy May 1954 and attended recruit training in Bainbridge, MD.

Also served aboard USS *Iowa* (BB-61) and shore duty in London, England CINCUSNAVEUR. Discharged honorably June 1960 at U.S. Naval Station Brooklyn.

While aboard USS *Allen*, they took Navy Reservists on two week training exercises with other DEs from the Brooklyn Navy yard COMTHREE.

While stationed in London, England married Ellen Mulligan in April 1958. Has one son Gary married June 30, 1991 to Diana Curia.

After six years in the Navy went to automotive school, worked for Pepsi Cola 10 years as a auto mechanic. Just recently retired from New York Telephone Co. after 20 years service as a SET. He is a member of DESA, SOLDESA, Iowa Veterans Association, ABA, Navy League and American Legion.

FAY LEROY HUTSON, SC1/c, USS *England* (DE-635), enlisted in the Navy on Aug. 11, 1943 in Muskigan, MI. Boot camp at Great Lakes, IL. After school went to Norfolk, VA where he was assigned to USS *England*. Ship was commissioned and was headed for South Pacific, where he spent the next 12 months before being hit, May 9, 1945 at Okinawa. USS *England* established an unmatched record during World War II by sinking six Japanese subs in 12 days. It was awarded a Presidential Unit Citation for it's action which contributed so important to the Allied victory in the Pacific.

Fay was seriously wounded and spent the next 14 months in different hospitals. He was discharged with 100% disability. Fay was honored on June 12, 1982 aboard USS *England* (CG-22) which was docked at Portland, OR during the Rose Festival. There Fay was treated with royalty and spent the entire day with Capt. H.H. Mauz, Jr., the ship's commander, Capt. Webb, Fay's commanding officer was also present. Fay was also honored at a ship reunion in Seattle, WA in 1987 in which he had the privilege to visit with the servicing Ship Mates, including his skipper, Capt. John A. Williamson. This was the highlight of his life. Fay has resided in Sweet Home, OR the past 27 years. He passed away Feb. 16, 1990.

WILLIAM G. JAMES, JR., TSgt., USAF (Ret.) Ex-Navy RMSN, USS *Spangler* (DE- 696) Enlisted U.S. Navy April 7, 1948, born Aug. 9, 1928 in Damon, TX. Went to boot camp at NTC San Diego after brief assignment to USS *Spangler* at Pearl Harbor returned to San Diego for Radio School, 1949. Assigned back to USS *Spangler* at Pearl Harbor after school. Remained on the *Spangler* when it returned to San Diego as a support ship for Fleet Sonar School.

Married Martha Schneider Nov. 15, 1951 in El Cajon, CA. Was transferred from USS *Spangler* in

February 1952 to U.S. Naval Hospital Balboa San Diego, for back surgery, while assigned to hospital his wife passed away in naval hospital on April 2, 1952. Discharged from U.S. Navy May 1, 1952 at naval station, San Diego. Returned to Washington, TX working with father running a dairy and farming. Enlisted in U.S. Air Force and remarried in November 1953 and was assigned as basic training instructor at Lackland AFB, San Antonio and Parks AFB, CA transferred to Keesler AFB in 1957 for Air Traffic Control Radar Repair School. Upon completion in 1958 he was assigned to the air training command's ATC Radar Repair School instructor staff continuing in that status until November 1963. He was then assigned to 2876th GEEIA Sqdn. Clark Air Force Base, Philippines with duty at numerous sites in Vietnam. Returning for over shoulder training at Bunker Hill Air Force Base (changed to Grissom AFB, IN) in 1964. Upon return to Philippines he installed new ATC radar in Vietnam. Returned to States in November 1965 assigned to Brookley Air Force Base, AL becoming NCO/C of Comm. Sqdn. radar section after Brookley closed. He was transferred to Keesler Air Force Base, MS in 1969 pending retirement in November 1969. His marriage to Doris Steenken of Burton, TX in 1953 which produced five sons includes set of twins.

He received awards and decorations as follows: Navy Good Conduct Medal, Good Conduct Medal with three Bronze Loops, Air Force Good Conduct Medal with one Bronze Oak Leaf Cluster, Air Force Outstanding Unit Award, National Defense Service Medal with one Bronze Service Star, Vietnam Service Medal with one Bronze Service Star, Air Force Longevity Service Award with four Bronze Oak Leaf Clusters, Small Arms Expert Markmanship Ribbon, Republic of Vietnam Campaign Medal.

He was a truck driver until an accident caused his second retirement in 1984. He is a charter life member of DESA, life member of Air Force Sergeants Association, life member Disabled American Veterans, life member Veterans of Foreign Wars, PUFL member American Legion, member first Texas DESA, member retired member Enlisted Association, member NRA, life member Texas State Rifle Association. He lives in Houston, TX with his wife.

JOSEPH F. JENNINGS, SR., was born Dec. 10, 1910 in Agusta, GA. Joined the service April 4, 1944. Stationed with the U.S. Navy on USS *Forester* (DE-334) serving on the Atlantic and Pacific Oceans. Achieved the rank of fireman first class at the time of discharge.

Now single with one son, one daughter, six grandchildren and two great-grandsons. He is a property manager, and resides in Decatur, GA.

ARMAND LUVERNE JOHNSON, EM1/c was born Oct. 12, 1920 in Kandiyohi County, MN. Enlisted Lansing, IL Aug. 10, 1942 with boot camp in Great Lakes, IL; October 10, 1942 Purdue University Electrical School, West Lafayette, IN; February 1943 USS *Hogan* a minesweeper, with duty in the Caribbean area; April 1943 SCTC School, Everglade Barracks, Miami, FL; June 21, 1943 USS *Engstrom* (DE 50) commissioned at the Navy yard, Philadelphia, PA. After the shakedown cruise to Bermuda, they went to North-Pacific, eighteen months convoy duty in Aleutian Islands; January 1945 South-Pacific convoy duty Marshall Islands to and from Iwo Jima. One memorable occasion, two Japanese officers came on board at Truk, Atoll Islands after the Japanese surrender. They received the Asiatic-Pacific Victory Medal, American Theatre and Good Conduct Ribbons. A barber since 1956, now retired and doing odd jobs. A member of American Legion and Northern Illinois DESA Chapter.

Married Leatha White Dec. 3, 1941 son Armand Lee (Sept. 13, 1943) children Kevin, Kelly, Eric; daughter Doris Banta (Jan. 5, 1947) children Steven J. Banta (Oct. 26, 1969) who is a Naval air traffic controller at Glenview Naval Air Station in Illinois and Carol Severson and her son Timothy Severson. Now living in Lansing, IL and looking forward to his 50th wedding anniversary in 1991.

AUGUSTUS P. JOHNSON, JR., was born Oct. 15, 1922 in Bailey Island, ME Joined Merchant Marine 1942 and enlisted in the Navy M2 Reserve June 23, 1942, Portland, ME received the rate of S1/c assigned to the USS *Y.P.* (375) Boston, MA. Cruised to Mayport, FL for nine months on special experimental projects.

Transferred to new construction June 1943. Assigned to USS *Dionne* July 1943 after shakedown to Bermuda. Got underway for Pacific, took part in the invasion of the Gilbert Islands. Served in the Marshall Islands operation invasion of Mariana Islands. Transferred to new construction, assigned to USS *Sherbourne*, (APA 205), Richmond, CA. Loaded troops and ammunition for the forward areas. Left San Francisco for Pearl Harbor. Eniwetok was reached on March 28. Discharged cargo, proceeded to Kwajalein. Arriving March 31, proceeded to Ulithi April 6. Discharged cargo and troops at both ports. Embarked Marine Corp troops, proceeded to Guam. Landed troops, continued to Saipan, took troops aboard in convoy to Okinawa, weather poor. Plenty of action, unloaded troops under fire. Cruiser hit nearby by suicide plane. Fast trip from Ulithi back to Frisco non-stop for 15 days. Left with a full complement of troops for Manila, PI.

They unloaded troops and supplies on the 4th of July, arrived at Cebu on the sixth, off to Leyte, P.I. They

then proceeded to New Guinea, Mindanao and Samar, PI. Landed troops for occupation of Japan. Kure, Honsho, Japan. Assigned to Magic Carpet. Assigned to Bureau of Naval Personnel, Washington D.C.

Discharged January 1948 in Washington D.C. achieving the rating of BM2/c.

Awards include eight Battle Stars, American Theatre, Asiatic-Pacific, Philippine Liberation Medal, World War II Victory Medal, Japanese Occupation, Philippine Independence Medal, Philippine Presidential Unit Citation, and Good Conduct Medal.

Living in New Jersey and has two sons, two grandchildren. Worked with P. Ballantine & Sons for 24 years, went to Anheuser Busch for 15 years. Retired in 1986.

EARL F. JOHNSON, FP2/C USS *Alvin C. Cockrell,* (DE-366). Joined the Naval Reserve in St. Louis, MO in 1947 and was called to active duty in May of 1953. Served on the *Cockrell* from June of 1953 to May of 1955. Their ship did carrier plane guard duty, ASW patrol, and spent three months as station ship in Hong Kong. Upon being assigned to the *Cockrell* in 1953, pipefitter Johnson found most every pipe from the gallery to the heads stopped up. After four solid months of work, (and no watches) every pipe on the ship was open, including the heads. He was awarded the Silver Wrench, and the T.P. accommodation.

After discharge in 1955 he returned to California and graduated from California State University, Long Beach as a finance major. He has been in the securities investment business for 30 years, and married 40 years. He has five children and two grandchildren. Earl is active with the U.S. Navy League, and is on the board with the Long Beach Council. He also serves with the Los Angeles Chapter of DESA.

GEORGE LEROY JOHNSON, RM1/c, was born in Red Oak, IA and reared on a farm. Graduated from Red Oak High School, was employed in a flour mill and entered the Coast Guard in Omaha, NE on April 14, 1942.

Took boot training at Manhattan Beach, NY to Boston and assigned to the USS *Spencer*, a Coast Guard Cutter. After four trips to Londonderry, Ireland he was transferred to Radio School in Atlantic City, NJ. From there he was assigned to the USS *Howard D. Crow* (DE-252). Commissioned in Houston, TX with a shakedown cruise to Bermuda. Back to Norfolk, VA and assigned to convoy duty in North Atlantic, with trips to Londonderry, South Hampton, Liverpool, Gibraltar and Casablanca, Africa. After VE day they were fitted for the Pacific and to Guantanamo Bay for drills, and through Panama Canal to San Diego and on to the Hawaiian Islands. Was transferred to the District Radio Station there after VJ Day and returned to U.S. via Seattle, WA on to St. Louis, MO for discharge on Nov. 21, 1945.

Married to Helen Mae Carlson one year before entering the service. They have three children, Robert, James, and Patricia. Purchased a portable milling service in Emerson, IA after discharge, was employed in Emerson State Bank and then appointed Postmaster of the Emerson Post Office. Retired in 1981 and still live in Emerson. They love to travel and visit their eight grandchildren and spend the winters in Texas or Arizona.

WAYNE WESLEY JOHNSON, was born Aug. 19, 1925 in Decature County, GA in the Sylvania community. Entered the Navy (830-66-31) Sept. 9, 1943 in Jacksonville, FL. Boot camp at Bainbridge, MO, later on to Norfolk, VA and Mare Island, CA. He served as a seaman first class. He was killed in Okinawa April 16, 1945. Remembered the new friends he had made in Sydney, Australia. He received the

Purple Heart, Consolidation of Solomon Islands, Western New Guinea Operation, Leyte Operation, Okinawa Unit Citation Badge.

His father and mother are both deceased. He has two brothers still living, Lealand and Alvin John, and one sister, Mrs. Irma J. Barber.

WILLIAM ISSAC JOHNSON, JR., EM2/c was born Dec. 26, 1922 in Tasewell, VA. Sworn in the Navy Jan. 18, 1943 at Baltimore, MD. Spent two months in boot camp at Great Lakes, IL. Went to electrical school in St. Louis, MO and from there to Charleston, SC and went aboard the USS *Neuendorf*, (DE-200). After commissioning Oct. 18, 1943 and a shakedown cruise to Bermuda the *Neuendorf* went through Panama Canal and on to New Caledonia. After 27 months in the South Pacific the ship came back to San Diego. Received five medals including the American Theatre, Good Conduct, Victory Medal, Philippine Liberation with one star, and the Asiatic-Pacific Theatre with four stars. Discharged with the rank of EM2/c. Remembers being bombed and strafed in San Bernadino Straits in Philippines, and chasing Japanese submarine off Luzon.

Bill was the only child of William I. Johnson, Sr. and Linda E. Johnson who originally came to Maryland from Virginia in 1929. He has two children, William I. Johnson, III and Lynn Vaughn. He now lives in northeast Maryland and has been a real estate salesman for 25 years, now employed by Century 21 in Elkton, MD.

CARROLL L. JONES *(See page 744)*

CARROLL L. JONES *(See page 744)*

ROBERT H. JONES, SM1/c USS *Carroll* (DE-171), was born Dec. 17, 1924 in Elizabeth, NJ. Enlisted in Navy Dec. 16, 1942. Attended boot camp at Bainbridge, MD. He then went to Signalman School at University of Chicago. After training, assigned to USS *Carroll*, (then under construction). USS *Carroll* was commissioned Oct. 24, 1943 in Norfolk Navy Yard. After shakedown, assigned to convoy escort duty in

Atlantic. Between Jan. 1, 1944 and May 9, 1945 made eight voyages between Norfolk and Gibraltar, Casablanca, Bizerte, Oran and Algeria. After war ended in Europe, was one of first DEs transferred from Atlantic to Pacific. (Passed through the Panama Canal June 10, 1945). Sailed for Eniwetok, Saipan and Ulithia.

Until Nov. 3, 1945 patrolled smaller islands of Palau Group. On Oct. 6, 1945 surrender of Sonsorol, Fanna, Meir and Tobi Islands took place on the ship. Then supervised evacuation of Japanese troops from these islands. November 3, 1945 left for East Coast-arrived Jacksonville, FL Dec. 14, 1945. (decommissioned June 19, 1946).

He was discharged in 1946. Married Aug. 21, 1948 to Ruth Parsons, Cranford, NJ. Teacher of instrumental music for 38 years, retiring 1989. Lives in Florham Park, NJ with wife. They have two daughters, one son and four grandchildren.

EDWARD M. JORDAN, Seaman first class was born March 28, 1926 in English Consul, MD. He enlisted in Navy February 1944. Boot camp at Bainbridge, MD. Commissioned (DE-643) (*Damon C. Cummings*) June 29, 1944 at San Francisco made all of the *Cummings* cruises, including convoy duty to many Pacific Islands, invaded Okinawa Sunday, April 1, 1945 and was part of the occupational forces of Japan. Medals include the Asiatic-Pacific Campaign with star, American Campaign, World War II and Occupational Service. Discharged May 1946.

Married Lillian May Cook in June 1948. They raised two beautiful children (Eddie and Donna) and they have four grandchildren. After 43 years working for Koppers Company and Environmental Elements Corporation, he retired as a methods engineer. He is now widowed, residing in Pasadena, MD and a happy member of DESA.

RICHARD H. JORDAN, MOMM 2/c, USCGR. Joined Navy on Jan. 22, 1942 at Boston 1st Naval District. He was stationed there for a short time, transferred to Southwest Harbor, ME. He was there for

about six to eight months, then to Provincetown, MA, and on to Orange, TX, Brown Shipbuilding where he went aboard (DE-252) USS *Howard D. Crow*.

They did their shakedown Cuba, Bermuda, and off to convoy duty in the North Atlantic, 11 round trips and then to the Pacific, Solomons and many of the small islands there. They took the largest convoy to cross the Atlantic up until that time. He states that he believes it was 104 ship. They never lost a ton of shipping to enemy action.

He was discharged December 1945. Has since held several jobs, mostly in sales, now retired.

His wife passed away Friday Dec. 13, 1985.

ROBERT KENNETH JORDAN, was born Nov. 18, 1928 in Dodson, TX. Joined the U.S. Navy April 3, 1948. Served on USS *Marsh* (DE-699). He was on duty in CIC when the USS *Marsh* had a collision at sea Feb. 22, 1949 at 10:20 p.m. He was later transferred to air control/GCA. He had achieved the rank of AC 2/c (GCA-control operator operator) at the time of discharge.

Married 40 years to Thelma, they had two children, one boy and one girl. Robert retired (disabled) from Civil Service in 1986 and resides in Somerville, AL.

FREDERICK E. JOYCE, was born May 24, 1930 in Lynn, MA. He was inducted into the U.S. Navy June 1947. Served on the USS *Greenwood* (DE-679). Attended boot camp at USNTC Great Lakes, IL; Class "A" Electric School, Great Lakes, IL; Key West, FL.

Discharged May 1952 as EM3/c.

He believes his entire five years of enlistment was memorable.

Married the former Patrica A. Cronin June 16, 1950. They have four children, two boys and two girls. They also have nine grandchildren and one great-grandchild.

He retired from Massachusetts Electric as crew leader after 32 years.

HARRY E. KAHLER, CGM, USS *Neuendorf* (DE-200), was born May 25, 1918 in Grundy Center, IA. Enlisted in the Navy October 1937 and was honorably discharged in December 1945 at Long Beach, CA.

Reported aboard the USS *Neuendorf* December 1943 from the USS *Idaho* (BB-42) with a short stop at the U.S. Navy Gun Factory School. Served aboard the *Neuendorf* until honorably discharged in December 1945, with the rank of CGM. He received the American Defense Ribbon with one Bronze "A", European Afri-

can and Middle Eastern Theatre Ribbon, American Theatre, Asiatic Pacific and one Bronze Star for each of the operations in which he served. He also received the Good Conduct Medal. After World War II attended college at Long Beach State for several years and enlisted in the U.S. Army April 1950 for duty at Ft. Bliss, TX and White Sands Missile Range, NM. Retired as a U.S. Army CWO-3 November 1961.

In civilian life he worked as an aerospace engineer for 21 years at Vandenberg AFB, CA for the ITT Federal Electric Corporation and retired again in 1984.

FRANK F. KAMINSKI,

was born Nov. 21, 1917 in Westfield, MA. Enlisted in the Navy June 1936, upon graduation from high school. Assigned to USS *Case* (DD 370) precommissioning detail. Make shakedown to the Mediterranean and joined the Pacific Fleet. In September 1939 he was transferred to (DD 351) USS *Macdonough*, and sailed to Pearl Harbor as part of Hawaiian detachment on neutrality patrol. He left  Pearl Harbor in 1940 and was discharged in San Diego in June as fire controller first class. He was out long enough to get married (six months to be exact) and re-enlisted Dec. 15, 1942.

Assigned to Pier No. 92 Master at Arms detail for working parties on the Normandy which was gutted by fire.

After one month he went to Algiers, LA for precommissioning detail USS *Stewart* (DE 238) at Brown Shipyard Houston turning basin. He had the pleasure of serving under Comdr. Turner one of the best skippers to work for. Left the *Stewart* nine months later, but before that he escorted the F.D.R. *Yacht Potomac* up the river of the same name. This was when he returned from Yalta on the *Iowa*. He then attended Fire Control School and assigned to commission USS *Xanthus* AR-19

They were in a DAK Aleutians when the war ended. He was discharged on Oct. 1, 1945, to pick up where he left off with his family. He received the Victory Medal, American Campaign, American Defense, Asiatic-Pacific Campaign and two Good Conduct Medals.

He has two sons and is now retired and enjoys his woodworking hobby.

WALTER B. KANTOR, SK2/c, USS *Martin* (DE-30), enlisted in the Navy on Jan. 27, 1943, boot camp at Great Lakes, IL. Then to Sub-Tracer Training School

at Miami, FL. Assigned to USS *Martin* (DE-30) at Mare Islands, CA as part of nucleus crew.

Participated in several campaigns in the Gilbert, Marshall, Marianas Islands and lots of escort duty with different task forces.

His final campaign was the liberation of the Philippine Islands and Battle of Leyte Gulf. He received the Liberation Medal from the Philippine government. He also received campaign ribbons for Asiatic-Pacific with one Bronze Star, World War II Victory Medal, Good Conduct and American Theatre Medals.

Discharged Jan. 14, 1946. Went back to work with Sears and after 43 years, he retired July 31, 1984. He and his wife Kathleen have been married for 41 years, with one son, Michael and daughter-in-law, Terry. The have lived in Decatur, GA, for 38 years.

JOSEPH KEARNEY, GM 2/c, graduated Bloomfield Senior High, Bloomfield, NJ, D-Day, 1944, and enlisted in the Navy in July, 1944. He had boot camp with the 4th Regiment, Bainbridge, MD, and Gunners Mate School, being assigned to the *USS Hanna (DE-449)* doing picket duty in the Philippines and other South Pacific Islands. He was discharged in June, 1946, and recalled to service in September, 1950, on the *USS Brownson (DD-868)* which arrived in Reykjavik, Iceland in May, 1951, with the *USS McCard (DD-868)* to help secure the Icelandic government from communist takeover. He was discharged in June, 1952. His decorations include the Victory Medal, Asiatic Pacific, American Defense, Korean and Philippine Liberation Medal.

He is currently the sales engineer for MAZAK Corporation. He married Mary G. on October 22, 1955, residing in Caldwell, NJ. They have a son, Joseph W., Jr., and a daughter, Nancy M.

WILBERT KEEFER (BOOTS), was born Aug. 25, 1925 at Beaver Falls, PA. Volunteered for service Nov. 1, 1943. Boot camp at Great Lakes Naval Training Center. Attended Torpedo School at Great Lakes also. Joined the crew of the USS *Wilhoite* (DE 397) about March 1944. The *Wilhoite* became a part of the killer squadron of six DEs escorting the (CVE 9) USS *Bogue* and sailed the North Atlantic killing German submarines for which they received a Presidential Citation.

He remembers late one night when he was on deck on watch when radar reported a blimp which looked like at least a cruiser on the scope. After they could not get a response from the signals that they sent over, the skipper ordered them to go in with the idea of shelling the ship if it proved to be the enemy. He states that it goes without saying that they were scared because they were no match for any enemy cruiser or battleship.

They were relieved when after putting a light on the sighting they found that it was only an iceberg.

Discharged at Bainbridge with a TM3/c rating on May 15, 1946.

He retired in August 1988 after 35 years in the banking business as an assistant vice-president for Peoples Bank of West Pennsylvania in Monaca, PA and moved to Orlando, FL. He has a wife (Edith) and two girls who have families also living in Orlando.

CLIFF KELLEY, was born Jan. 24, 1922 in Shelton, WI. Joined the U.S. Navy September 1942. (DE-17) *Edward C. Daly*. Stationed at NAS Pasco WV, Bremerton, WV, and on to California. Served in Kwajalein, Guam, Tinian, Saipan and Iwo Jima. He remembers Okinawa, Mare Island and returning home.

Married with five children. Retired and now leading a band which plays the sounds of the 40s.

WENDALL S. KELLEY, S2/c, USS *Burdo*, APD 133 (DE-717), one of four sons of Richard and Ruth A. (Morrill) Kelley. All four sons served in the U.S. Navy. Wendall was born March 29, 1928 in Franklin, NH. He attended schools in Greenfield, MA and the Detroit, MI area.

He joined the Navy on June 1, 1945. Served as seaman second class. USNR- USS *Burdo* APD-133.

Wendall worked, after the war, as a seaman aboard ships on the Great Lakes, and later on ships trading at several South American countries.

After several years he gave up the seafarers life, and retired in 1990 as a maintenance supervisor at the Northfield Schools, Northfield, MA.

He and his wife, Muriel (Fournier) Kelley live on Manning Hill, in Winchester, NH.

ROBERT ARON KEMPE, was born March 6, 1922 in Minneapolis, MN. Joined the U.S. Navy in 1944. Stationed in Pacific Theatre Operations. At the time of his discharge he had achieved the rank of lieutenant (jg.)

He married Virginia Lou Wiseman in 1946. They have two children and two grandchildren. Worked as president for Kempe Everest Company, Venture management consultant director  and officer at Chagrin Valley Enterprises, Inc., executive officer and past chairman for Northern Ohio section, American Nuclear Society and an author of nine patents in field. He now resides in Hudson, OH.

JOHN R. KENNEDY, QM1/c USS *Burke* (DE-215), was born Dec. 29, 1922 in Washington, DC. Enlisted in the Navy in October 1942. Boot camp at Norfolk, VA. QM School Newport, RI. De Pool Norfolk. Stationed on the USS *Burke* from August 1943 until May 1945. Went on convoys to Europe and Africa, transferred to USS *Lake Champion* (CV-39) in May 1945 as plank owner. He was awarded the Atlantic Blue Ribbon Medallion for CV-39s record breaking speed run from Straits of Gibraltar to Hampton Roads, VA on Nov. 21-26 1945, at 32.048 knots breaking the Queen Mary's 1938 record. He was discharged in

January 1946. Received AB in journalism from University of Notre Dame in 1949. Special Agent FBI from 1950-1976. He worked as a staff advisor for Airport Security Council from 1976-1988.

He is now retired and residing in Long Island, NY. He married the former Charlotte M. Mahoney of Washington, DC, they have nine children, including two USN and one U.S.A. commissioned officer.

PHILLIP L. KENNEY, was born in Hopkinton, RI. He served as a World War II gunners mate with 23 months combat overseas on the USS *Pettit* (DE-253) Mediterranean, No. Atlantic and on the USS *Elba* on the Pacific. Also served with US Army (FS-267).

He attended Roger Williams College, graduating as accounting major. Received certificates in RISD Blue Print Reading and Estimating, HUD Basic Residential Apartment Management, and various other areas.

Married to wife Barbara with one son, Wayne (40 yrs.) and one daughter, Leslie (36 yrs.)

He is very involved in many civic organizations, serving on the Cranston City Council for two terms, Cranston Civil Service Revue Board for one term, Treasurer Cranston Bicentennial Commission, YMCA Board Camp Fuller, worked as fund raising chairman for Cranston East Accepella Choir tour of USSR, and several others.

He is a member of the Disabled American Veterans, D.E. Sailors Association, Coast Guard Combat Veterans. He serves as a volunteer driver of DAV van at Veterans Hospital. Phillip is a 32 degree F&AM-Palestine Temple Prov. Shrine and Overseas Lodge of Masons.

He states that his main objective in life is to give his best, to be and accept himself and others as humans.

RALPH KERN, was born April 4, 1925 in Toledo, OH. Joined the service July 1943. Stationed on the USS *Koiner* (DE-331). Attended Great Lakes NTS in September 1943, Navy Pier Chicago Diesel School and Oil Burning School in Philadelphia, PA. He was discharged from the Navy Dec. 19, 1945 with the rank of WT2/c. Total service time July 1943-Dec. 19, 1945. He remembers making nine round trips across the Atlantic to Mediterranean and England, and coming back from England picking up Wendel Wilkes son in mid-Atlantic for his fathers funeral. He qualified as a second class swimmer.

He married Jeanne Eakins Sept. 1, 1951. They have seven children and 13 grandchildren. He is a retired tool and diemaker from Toth Industries 5901 Enterprise since April 6, 1990.

GLEN THEODORE KETTLEHUT, MMO3/c

H.C. Jones (DE-137), Enlisted in 1945. Boot camp in Great Lakes, IL. Service in Guam, Eniwetok, Marshalls-Gilberts area. With the *H.C. Jones* when she returned to the U.S. and via the Panama Canal to New York for repairs at the Brooklyn Navy Yard and on to Green Cove Springs, FL for decommissioning and into the moth ball fleet.

Discharged and returned to Rochester, MN. Attended Jr. College and joined the Western Electric Company as a field installer for 18 years. He worked 10 more years in engineering and 12 years in engineering quality assurance. Retired with AT & T Co. after 40 years service.

He presently lives in Littleton, CO and has a lovely wife Bonnie who he has been married to for 39 years. They have three children and two grandchildren. He is enjoying every moment of his retirement.

CHARLES H. KEYS, EMP1/c USS *Coolbaugh* (DE-217), entered the Navy in December 1942 and went to boot camp at Bainbridge, MD. Then, Electrician Mates School in Newport, RI and then Sound Motion Picture Technicians School in the Brooklyn Navy Yards. From there was assigned to Ships Company U.S. Training School SK Indiana University, Bloomington, IN. In October 1944 reported aboard the USS *Trenton* (CL-11). They were assigned to the 9th Fleet with the USS *Richmond* (CL-10) and the USS *Concord* (CL-12) in the North Pacific. They bombarded the northern Japanese Islands to keep the enemy off balance.

In 1945 he was transferred to the NROTC V6 program at Bucknell University and then the University of Pennsylvania. Discharged from active duty in June 1946 and enlisted in the Active Reserve. In August 1950 was recalled to active duty and assigned to the USS *Coolbaugh* (DE-217). In April 1952 was released to inactive duty and discharged in June 1954.

Married Betty Derk of Sunbury, PA in July 1946. They have two children, Penny Lee and Ronald. They live in Glendale, AZ.

Was employed by the Western Electric Co. in Baltimore, MD on July 3, 1940. Worked in the maintenance department as an electrician's helper and then as an electrician. In June 1955 became an electrical supervisor. In August 1969, he became maintenance manager at the Atlanta Works and later at the Phoenix Works. Retired Nov. 1, 1988 and is now actively promoting DESA and the Arizona Chapter.

RICHARD T. KING, was born April 14, 1925 in Cook County, IL. With six weeks to go to finish his senior year of high school, he was drafted into the service in April 1944. With the remainder of his class

making plans for graduation, he reported to the Great Lakes Naval Training Center. After training and a short leave, they were transported by train to the west coast and soon sailed beneath the Golden Gate Bridge in a troop transport. At Kwajalein he came aboard the USS *McConnell* (DE-163) and remained aboard this ship through the war years until his discharge in January of 1946. As a fireman and mostly below deck, he well remembers the sounds of the guns and exploding depth charges. Also the refueling at sea and the many stormy days as they escorted oil tankers, troop ships and aircraft carriers through the typhoon season. Days later when the storm subsided, one could see palm fronds, coconuts, pieces of wood and other litter floating on the surface, even though no land could be seen. Often, after they had been to sea for many days, they would enter some island port only to re-fuel, pick up mail, food supplies and be on their way again. If they were lucky, they got some mail and saw a movie on the fantail.

He received the American Theatre Medal, Asiatic Pacific, Philippines Liberation Medal and the Victory Medal.

He has now been retired for seven years and loving it. He resides in Manton, MI.

ALLEN T. KIRKLEY, born in Buffalo, NY on Feb. 23, 1932. He was the son of Elbert A. and Marjorie (Allen) Kirkley.

Enlisted May 3, 1950 at Springfield, MA. Boot camp at Great Lakes. Fleet Sonar School Key West.

Recommissioned USS *Delong* (DE-684) at Green Cove Springs in February 1951. Three years aboard were highlighted by many and varied trips including Scotland, Norway, Nova Scotia, the Bahamas, Cuba and crossing the equator to Curacao and Brazil.

Also attended West Point, Annapolis, and St. Petersburgh, FL for Armed Forces Day of 1952. He was discharged March 1954. Served four more years in the reserves, mostly inactive.

Married wife Dolly, August 1954, they have three daughters and five grandchildren.

He spent ten years as a letter carrier, and part-time police officer. Spent last 27 years in industrial sales. Belongs to the American Legion, AmVets. and active in Western Massachusetts Chapter of DESA. He enjoys vacations in Florida and seeing old friends at Delong reunions.

WILLIAM R. KISIL, SR., EM3/c, entered the Navy Aug. 13, 1943. Took boot training at Sampson, NY; Electricians School at Bainbridge, MD; then to Norfolk, VA for D.E. training and instruction to be a motion picture operator. Then reported to the USS *Carter* (DE-112) before commissioning at Philadelphia. After formalities was put to sea for a shakedown in Bermuda. The *Carter* did convoy duty to Oran and Bizerte until their squadron was formed and became a killer group and flagship of Div. 79.

The most impressive moment was standing on deck while going through the Straits of Gilbraltar. Looking at two continents from one spot. They received credit for one sinking.

After Germany surrendered the squadron engaged in the sub round up and the ship retired to Florida. He was drafted to a ferry group to bring back a lend lease ship from England, the USS *Foley* (DE-270). The USS *Tonawanda* (AN-89) was his next nautical home. He traveled the Caribbean until discharge March 31, 1946.

He received the Victory Medal, American Theatre with one star, and the European Theatre.

He worked 23 years at G.E. engineering support work and as professional photographer at the same time. Also worked 20 years as a construction electrician with IBEW. He is happily married to an Irish girl, they have six daughters, one son and 14 grandchildren. He retired July 1, 1990.

EARL R. KNIGHT, was born June 27, 1923 in Pittsburgh, PA, and enlisted in the USNR in February, 1943. After Boot Camp in Sampson, NY, and Group III Service School in Norfolk, VA, he was assigned to the *USS McAnn (DE-179)* with convoy duty from Charleston to the Panama Canal and Trinidad to Brazil. On February 23, 1945, he was assigned to the *USS Bassett (DE-672)*. He went to Pearl Harbor, the Philippines, Manila, Guam, Borneo, New Guinea, Okinawa, and Japan. His most memorable experience was picking up and tending survivors in the Philippine Islands in 1945 when the awesome gruesome reality of war came home to him as he had to jump into the shark infested waters during the rescue. He was a metalsmith, 1/c.

That night the awesome, gruesome reality of the war came home to him. The had to jump into the shark infested waters and cut the belts loose where buddies were belted together.

Clinging to the nets many did not believe they were being rescucd and they had to yell in their ears and pull them to make them let go. Many had burns, shark bites, sun burn and salt water sores and would cry out in agony when you touched them.

He and his wife, Jane Hart, reside in McMurray, PA, and have a son, David, a daughter, Nancy, and two grandchildren. He is a salesman.

JUNIUS A. KOCH, MOM1/c, enlisted in the Navy Sept. 5, 1942 at Omaha, NE. After completing boot

training at Great Lakes Naval Training Center he had diesel training at Richmond, VA.

In January 1943 he was assigned to the USS *Rhind* (DD-404) and went aboard in Norfolk. After doing convoy escort duty several months in the Atlantic the *Rhind* was assigned to patrol duty in the Mediterranean when on July 26, 1943 it took a near hit from German bombers off the coast of Sicily. The USS *Rhind* was the only one of the five sister ships to come out of the Mediterranean in one piece.

After returning to the States for repairs, Junius was transferred to the USS *Rall* (DE-304) and went aboard in San Francisco naval yards.

After the *Rall* was hit by a Japanese kamikaze in April 1945 it returned to the U.S. for repairs, Junius went home on leave and married Norma J. Rattman.

After discharge in October he took over the farming from his father and farmed for 16 years. In 1961 Junius went into building construction and retired in 1987.

Junius and Norma have been married for over 46 years and have six children, 15 grandchildren and one great-grandchild. They still live in Nebraska where they both grew up.

DONALD W. KORTH, JR., LT. (jg), USS *Mack* (DE-358), was born April 21, 1922 in Clarion, PA. He enlisted in the V-7 Program while at Princeton and earned his Ensign's commission at Annapolis in August 1943.

He trained at SCTC in Miami, FL and joined the *Mack* in Orange, TX for commissioning, subsequently shaking down in Bermuda, proceeding to Boston and thence to Hollandia, New Guinea, the Philippines and Tsing Tao, China. He served as chief engineering officer and senior deck watch officer.

Discharged in July 1946, he spent 40 years in construction and property management on the U.S. mainland, in Hawaii and Saudia Arabia.

He is currently a construction consultant, is selecting California LOTTO numbers with his computer, is serving in various volunteer capacities and is a member of several organizations including DESA.

Married in 1947 and divorced in 1980, he has two successful children-his daughter, Ingrid, is a FIRST VP of Dean Witter Reynolds and his son, Ted, is a partner of his own architectural firm in San Francisco. He married Joye Jacopetti Waters in 1990 and is living in Alameda, CA. He has four grandchildren, three boys and one girl.

PETER KOVACH, S1/c, USS *Riddle* (DE-185), was born April 5, 1924 in St. Clair, PA. He entered the Navy on July 24, 1943. He was sent to boot camp at

Bainbridge, MD and then to DE training school in Norfolk, VA. He boarded the USS *Riddle* on Nov. 17, 1943 and spent the next 21 months as a radioman apprentice in the Pacific. The *Riddle* was in the Marshall Islands, Hollandia, Marianas (Saipan and Tinian), Palau, Ulithi, Leyte, Luzon, Formosa, Iowa Jima and Okinawa operations. The *Riddle* was credited with sinking a Japanese submarine on July 4, 1944. One April 12, 1945 the *Riddle* was hit by a kamikaze. The plane struck Kovach's battle station, the after three inch gun, port berth charge rack and the main deck on the port quarter. Part of the plane pierced the main deck, passed through the carpenter shop and the side of the ship. The *Riddle* returned to the U.S. by way of the Guam and Pearl Harbor to San Pedro, CA. Kovach was discharged on March 2, 1946.

After discharge, Kovach attended various colleges and universities. He received his B.S. degree from Millersville State and went into teaching in New York and Pennsylvania. He then moved to Maryland and continued teaching and worked on his graduate studies. He received several graduate degrees in education. Kovach taught at the elementary, junior, and senior high school levels. Kovach worked as a teacher, counselor, resource teacher, recreation supervisor, football and baseball coach. He worked with students, faculty, parents, community and other agencies.

He was married to Julie Kosct for 35 years until she died on Jan. 31, 1989. He is now retired from teaching and is living in Rockville, MD. Kovach is enjoying life by traveling, reading and attending horse racing and other sports events.

JOHN A. KOWALESKI, MOMM1/c, USS *Elder* (AN-20), was born November 1915 in Stamford, CT. Boot camp at Sampson, NY (MM) and (MOMM) school at Dearborn, MI. Later assigned to *Baranoff* which was a cargo ship in Tiburon, CA. Transferred to Floating Drydock as a crane operator at San Diego, CA. Reassigned to USS *Elder* (AN-20). Left the U.S. for Pearl Harbor then on to New Guinea. Joined convoy to the Philippines. After the Armistice he was assigned to salvage operations Manila Bay, recovering Philippine silver pesos. Transferred to Separation Center and home. Discharged February 1946. Signed for inactive reserve. Recalled June 1951 and recalled to Brooklyn Navy Center. Assigned to USS *Sturtevant* (DE 239) in moth balls Green Cove Springs, FL. Recommissioned and trained in sub chasing along Atlantic Coast.

Discharged at Boston Navy Yard October 1952. Retired 1980 after 33 years as a firefighter. He is a widower with one son.

BOB KRONEMYER, CDR, USNR (Ret.), USS

Osmus (DE-701), quit his desk job in Washington and began second career right after Pearl Harbor. Boarded ship in New Orleans as commissioning gunnery officer February 1944, and debarked San Pedro as navigator November 1945. In between, chased German subs in North Atlantic and Japanese subs in South Pacific. He earned Atlantic and Pacific Theatre Ribbons with two Battle Stars.

Through the G.I. Bill he began his third career as a lawyer after completing Harvard Law School in 1949, and rejoined the human race 35 years later in 1984. In between, chased paper in Illinois and California for 35 years. Life began when he married Nancy Davis in 1952, they have had three children and two grandchildren during the past 38 years. Now in fourth career as full-time LaJolla real estate investor and part-time novelist and playwright. Has found going around the world in cruise ships more fun than the USS *Osmus*.

DONALD J. KRUSE, MM2/c, USS *Underhill* (DE-682), was born June 7, 1924 in Saugerties, NY. Enlisted Nov. 16, 1942. Boot camp at Sampson, NY, then to Great Lakes for Machinist School. Was then sent to Norfolk, VA for ship assignment. Was there for the big explosion at Air Field September 1943. He drove Packard ambulance five trips to Portsmouth Hospital by orders of some lieutenant.

Assigned to *Underhill*, went to Quincy, MA for commissioning; plank owner. After shakedown, convoys and escort duties in Atlantic and Mediterranean. Had tubes removed and AA guns installed, went to Pacific duty. Crossed equator, shellback, convoy and escort duties to Okinawa. While on command escort of 96th Combat Engineers in LST's back to Philippines for R&R duty, they ran into Japanese mother sub and four small suicide subs. They got the mother sub first and then went to ram one small sub and one hit them. Their ship cut in between bridge and stack, with the front half down, the other half stayed afloat until they got them off some time later. There were 112 killed with 116 alive but injured. He was in the forward engine room, while the forward fireroom and everything forward was gone. He received the Purple Heart in the Philippine Hospital 3149. Discharged March 16, 1946.

He was called back in for the Korean War, Dec. 4, 1950 until March 27, 1952. Total Navy time served was eight years and one month. Was aboard the USS *Siboney* (CVE-112) during Korean War for Atlantic and Mediterranean duty.

Retired the end of 1980 from Bendix Corporation as a test driver. Married Mary Alice, with three sons, Don, John and Mike. They have one granddaughter, Rachael. Now residing in Troy, NY.

EDWARD GEORGE KULESA, SC 2/c, USS *Weeden* (DE-797), enlisted June 28, 1943, attached to the USS *Weeden* Feb. 19, 1944 after boot camp in Orange, TX. He saw action in the American, European, African, Asiatic Pacific and the Philippine Theatres to include Subic Bay, Manila, Okinawa and Nagasaki. He received medals for these theatres to include: the American Theatre, European African Middle Eastern Theatre, Asiatic Pacific, Philippine Campaign Liberation and the World War Victory Medal. He was honorably discharged April 10, 1946.

Married in 1947, went to work for the Delco Battery Company, then to Flako Company, where he worked in food preparation. He later did assembly work, his last job being with Resistoflex, where he worked as an assembler of planes and aero space, including work on several shuttle flights.

He retired at the age of 60, passed on Nov. 21, 1990, cremated and buried at sea, a lasting love of his. He is survived by wife Mary and twin daughters, Alice and Marie.

NIVO D. LATORRACCA, was born Sept. 30, 1919 in Los Banos, CA. Joined the U.S Navy Feb. 9, 1942. Attended U.S. NTS at San Diego; RS San Pedro; SCTC Miami, FL; SCOLS Training Comp; USNTA DC, Wim., VA. Served on the USS *California*, USS *Lee* (DE-65). He had achieved the rank of EM1/c at the time of his discharge.

He remembers the torpedo of USS *Fogg* on Dec. 20, 1944. He received the Good Conduct Medal.

Married Aug. 4, 1945. He and his wife have two daughters and three grandchildren. They are all in good health. Owned his own food distributing company, which he sold in 1989 and is now retired.

BERNARD A. LATTERELL, was born May 31, 1924 in Foley, MN. Joined the U.S. Navy Jan. 13, 1943. Attended boot camp at Great Lakes, IL, NTS Norfolk, VA on board the USS *Pope* (DE-134).

The *Pope* was with the USS *Guadacanal* during

the capture of U-505. Two other submarines were taken by task units of which the *Pope* was a member, the U-515 sank Easter Sunday April 9, 1944, they took aboard the survivors, only 15 or so. Also when the USS *Frederick C. Davis* (DE-136) was sunk on April 24, 1945. The U-546 was sent to the bottom. In October 1944 near the coast of Ireland the *Pope* weathered a four day storm, a single wave estimated at more than 50 feet ripped a large searchlight from the signal bridge, smashed into the port lookout station as if it had been made of cardboard deposited a flag bag on the torpedo tubes, tore gun shields loose from the deck, leaving holes which the water poured into.

Discharged Jan. 8, 1946 with the rank of GM3/c. He received the American Area Victory Medal, European African Middle Eastern with two stars, and the Presidential Unit Citation with one star.

DONN W. LAVOIE, EM 2/C, USS *Howard F. Clark* (DE-533), assigned to the *Clark* by the U.S. Navy Jan. 13, 1944, serving on the ship until the end of WWII. While on the *Clark*, he kept a personal ship's diary which was later printed and available for public enjoyment. Donn married MaryAnn and fathered three sons, Donn Jr., Tom, and John. As a member of the Naval Reserve, Donn served aboard the aircraft carrier *Princeton* (CV-37) during the Korean conflict.

Following his honorable discharge in 1953 Donn returned to Minneapolis, MN to live the remainder of his life. Using the knowledge he learned in his service, Donn pursued a career in electrical high voltage equipment rehabilitation. This profession eventually took him to the presidency of the Twin Cities Chapter of the American Society of Appraisers as a machinery and equipment evaluation engineer. Within the final, year of Donn's life, he attended one reunion of the *Clark* crew, after joining the DESA organization. Donn passed away Jan. 9, 1991. He was laid to rest exactly 47 years to the date after his assignment to the USS *Howard F. Clark*. Donn was survived by his wife of 40 years MaryAnn, his sons and two grandchildren Jay and Davis. Donn always spoke of his Navy memories with a smile on his face and a gleam in his eyes.

FRANK A. LAWLER, S1/c, GM, USS *Stewart* (DE-238), Coxswain, USS *Endicott* (DMS-35), was born Oct. 2, 1926 in Kearney, NJ. Enlisted June 1944. Attended boot camp at Sampson, NY with Dewey Unit Co. 229, Gunners Mate School Bainbridge, MD (Class 4E-45). Assigned to the USS *Stewart* (DE-238) January 1945. Two convoys to Liverpool, England. After surrender of Germany through Panama Canal to San Diego, thence to Des Pac at Pearl Harbor.

After Japanese surrender in September 1945 he

was reassigned to fleet recreation Oahu T.H. until January 1946. In January 1946 reassigned to USS *Endicott* (DMS-35) until discharge at San Diego in October 1947. He received the American Theatre, European Theatre, Asiatic-Pacific Theatre and Victory Medals.

Married former Lillian Erickson in March 1951. They have five daughters and 14 grandchildren.

Joined Operating Engineer Union Local 68 in 1952 worked in various power plants, retired as chief operating engineer in May 1985.

Upon retirement moved to West Bath, ME and enjoys woodworking, sailing, gardening and travel.

RICHARD C. LAWRENCE, FCSN, *William C. Cole* (DE-641),

was born July 4, 1927 at Richland Center. Enlisted at age 17 in April 1945. Graduated from Richland High School June 1945. Reported at Milwaukee for induction, June 6, 1945. Attended boot camp at Great Lakes, IL. In August Richard took a troop train to San Pedro, CA. Boarded ship after 22 days and ended up in Saipan.

October 1945 assigned duty to USS *William C. Cole* (DE-641). First day aboard, out to sea, had port lookout watch, little rough, never so sick in all his life. Spent 26 months on her, never sick again.

He was in luck, same month they headed back to Puget Sound Navy Yard, Bremerton, WA.

Spring of 1946 underway for China. Returned in July 1946 to San Diego. Again returning to Far East March 1947-August 1947 operating out of Pusan, Korea. Returning to Long Beach, CA the (DE-641) was decommissioned and placed in reserve, March 1948.

He finished his Navy days at Long Beach attached to Destroyer Moth Ball Fleet. Discharged July 8, 1948.

After returning home fell in love and married Katherine Haas on Aug. 23, 1949. Blessed with two sons, three daughters, seven grandchildren and one great-grandson. Moved in November 1957. He had worked in chemical plants for 35 years. Retired Dec. 31, 1991.

GEORGE ELLWOOD LAYMAN, enlisted Oct.

29, 1942 and took boot camp at Norfolk, VA. Sent to Sonar School at Key West, FL, graduating in February 1943, with third class rating. Assigned to USS *Austin* (DE-15), new construction at Mare Island, CA. Spent entire war in Pacific, including 13 months in Aleutians on convoy and weather patrol. Participated in air-sea rescue on B-29 flight routes. Last assignment was to accompany small task force to search out enemy isolated on Marianas Islands. Returned to San Pedro November 1945, for decommissioning. Discharged at Camp Shelton, VA, on Jan. 1, 1946, and returned to work at DuPont textile factory.

Retired as laboratory supervisor in 1982. Married, with two sons. Hobbies include gardening, stamp collecting, auto racing (spectator) and establishing contact with former crew members. Holds membership in National Association of Sonormen and Destroyer Escort Sailors Association. Resides in Stuarts Draft, VA.

P.J. LEE, (TOM),

was born Dec. 20, 1926 in Marquette, MI. Enlisted in U.S. Navy May 1943 as AS to serve for a period of two years. Reported to active duty April 18, 1944 USNRS, Milwaukee, WI, transferred USNTS, Great Lakes, IL. May 24, 1944 rating changed to F2/c. Transferred to NTS (Electrical) St. Louis, MO June 15, 1944. Later on to USS *Wesson* (DE-184) Dec. 9, 1944 for service in the South Pacific, USS *Audrain* (APA-59) April 7, 1945. Wounded in action while in the service of his country and sent to USN Hospital in Pearl Harbor April 25, 1945. Back on the USS *Wesson* for further transfer December 10 and on the USS *Petrof Bay* (CVE-80). Received USN personnel Separation Center in Boston, MA and he was discharged with an honorable discharge on June 2, 1946. He re-enlisted USNR, V-6, at USN PSC, Boston, MA as F1/c to serve for a period of four years. Released from active duty.

Most memorable experience for him was the day the *Wesson* was hit by a suicide plane at Okinawa. He regained partial consciousness on the main deck, their ships cook Bob Fletcher was kneeling by him and praying. He encouraged him to pray also, and assured him that he would be okay. Bob was right, for Tom is still going strong, and visits Bob every chance he gets.

Tom is married with four children and ten grandchildren. Now retired.

ROBERT EDWARD LEE, JR.,

was born July 23, 1925 in Henderson, NC. Inducted Oct. 2, 1943 in U.S Naval Reserve. Boot camp at Naval Training Center, Bainbridge, MD. Served on USS *Moale* (DD-693) Feb. 28, 1944-May 9, 1946 in Organized Reserves, USS *Sturtevant* (DE-239) from August 1951 until March 3, 1953.

He was in the battles of Ormac Bay in Philippines Dec. 2, 1944, shore bombardment in Leyte Gulf, Lingayan Gulf, Mindora Philippines, Okinawa and Iwo Jima.

Memorable experience for him was serving on USS *Sturtevant* (DE-239) in the Atlantic during Korean conflict and especially being helmsman at GQ, and the first reunion with shipmates of the *Sturtevant* after 37 years of separation.

He was discharged from Naval Reserve in May 1954, with the rank of yeoman stenographer second class.

Received American Area Campaign Ribbon, Philippine Liberation Medal with one Bronze Star, and Asiatic-Pacific Ribbon with four Bronze Stars.

He is now retired from the postal service, involved in locating missing shipmates for reunion of USS *Sturtevant* (DE-239), serving as secretary/treasurer *Sturtevant* Reunion Association. Edits and publishes a monthly newsletter for retired postal employees in Columbia, SC. He is divorced with no children.

HARRY MARTIN LEIPPE, SoM2/c, USS *Joseph E. Connally* (DE-450),

entered the USNR April 1944. After boot camp at Farragut, ID and sonar operator training at West Coast Sonar School in San Diego, CA, he was assigned as plank owner to the USS *Joseph E. Connally* (DE-450), which sailed from Boston in February 1945. VJ Day found his ship steaming with the Halsey's Third Fleet near Japan. His most hazardous duty entailed securing and projecting movies for the crew of (DE-450). He also designed cartoons for the ship's weekly bulletin. Interesting ports of call in the Pacific included Manila, Mog Mog, Jinsen, Shanghai, Yokosuka Naval Base, and on Dec. 8, 1945 the city of Tokyo.

After his discharge in June 1946 the GI Bill enabled him to attend college. After first completing high school in Watsonville, CA he enrolled in the Norfolk, VA branch of the College of William and Mary. Received a B.A. degree in Greek and English Literature from Calvin College 1951, in Grand Rapids, MI. After some years in Southern Baptist seminaries, he enrolled in the University of California at Berkeley where he received an MA in sculpture June 1969. A Fulbright Scholarship in Italy, 1960-61, provided further training in sculpture. After 28 years at New Mexico Highlands University in Las Vegas, New Mexico, he retired in January 1990. His assignments there included teaching, administration and metal arts program director. He and his wife, Nancy Uitti-Leippe are presently constructing a bronze foundry at home in Las Vegas, NM.

JOHN C. LEMM, (JACK),

MM3/c, was born June 24, 1927 in Lawrenceburg, IN. Enlisted in the U.S. Navy June 2, 1945 and inducted at Indianapolis, IN. Attended boot camp at Great Lakes Training Center. Served on the USS *Marsh* (DE-699), September 1945-April 1948, USS *Endicott* (DMS-31) April 1948. He was discharged in April 1948 as MM3/c.

Memorable experiences include when the USS *Marsh*, turbine electric power, was converted to a power supply ship and supplied power to Guam in 1945, and supplied power to Kwajalein Atoll where B-29s flew to Bikini Island for the A-bomb test in 1946.

He received the World War II Victory Medal, American Area Campaign Medal, Asiatic Pacific Campaign Medal, and Bikini A-Bomb Test Campaign Medal.

Married to Celeste T. Hill, Oct. 7, 9150 in Lawrenceburg, IN. Raised two daughters, Pam and Terri and two sons, Denny and Tom. He also has three grandchildren, Holly, Brandon and Erica. He retired in February 1990 after 39 years in public utility with American Electric Power. Today he is touring the U.S., Canada and Alaska with his motorhome. He is a member of Knights of Columbus #934, VFW Post #1969, Madison Regatta Inc., and DESA.

RICHARD J. LERNER, was born June 20, 1919 in Armstrong Co., PA. Joined the U.S. Navy Nov. 18, 1942 in Pittsburgh, PA. Served with the USN Advanced Amphibious Force on the LSM-220 and DE-252. Stationed in Norfolk, VA; Key West, FL; Saltash, England; Samar and Okinawa.

Recalls the barracks being bombed their first night in England, and the typhoon in Okinawa in 1945.

He received the World War II Victory Medal, American Campaign, European African Middle Eastern Campaign, Asiatic-Pacific, Korean Service, and Good Conduct Medal.

Married to Dorothy Crytzer, with two daughters Rita and Linda by a previous marriage. Worked as civilian employee for U.S. Air Force as foreman in guided missile facility. Attended Air Force University and Hughes Aircraft Training Facility, Air Force Management School. He is now retired. Family Historian, traveling when able, had both knees replaced due to arthritis. Enjoys tinkering with electronics and doing some light wood work; mostly toys and trinkets.

JOSEPH E. LETTERMAN, S1/c, USS *Tatum* (DE-789) (APD-81), was born Sept. 3, 1922 in Candler, NC. Inducted into service May 1943, Camp Croft, SC. Went to boot camp at NATTC Jacksonville, FL. Transferred from NATTC Jacksonville to NOB Norfolk, VA. In USS *Tatum* crew one year Atlantic and Mediterranean, and one year in Pacific. Shakedown Bermuda; convoy to Panama; Casablanca; Plymouth, England; Belfast, Ireland; Oran, Africa; Flagship in Pacific via Panama Canal; Hawaiian Island; Marshall; Carolina; Okinawa; Philippine Island, Japan. Scrubbed; one German submarine in English Channel, and four Japanese planes at Okinawa.

In 12-14 typhoons during two years aboard the USS *Tatum*. No two men will give the same description of a typhoon on a DE.

Discharged Dec. 6, 1945, Shelton, VA as S1/c. Medals include the American Area, World War II Victory, Asiatic-Pacific, European African, Philippine Liberation and two Battle Stars.

Retired from Asheville Police Department after 28 years service, last 20 were spent as detective sergeant. Married Esther McCall. They have with two sons Stephen (43) and Henry (42), and one grandson Matthew Clark Letterman (5).

FRANCIS J. LEVITZKI, CM2/c, USS *Savage* (DE-386) Hackensack, NJ, was born Nov. 1, 1925. Enlisted in U.S. Coast Guard June 1943. Trained at MBTS New York. Assigned to CGND, 3rd 5th ND, Little Creek Barracks in Virginia. USS *Savage* (DE-

386), made all USS *Savage* convoy trips to Mediterranean Ports, England, Ireland, Coast of France, English Channel. Nine road trip crossings without any losses, repelled air and underwater attacks in Mediterranean Sea.

War ended in Europe, USS *Savage* was sent to Adak, Aleutian Islands, ran sorties to Russia, coast off Japan, Alaska, Okinawa, China, Korea, Yellow Sea duty. Returned to U.S. via Pearl Harbor, San Diego, Panama Canal to Charleston, SC. Decommissioned at Green Cove Springs, FL. Was detached and sent to New York. Discharged May 1946.
Member of VFW #876, River Edge, NJ and DESA.

Married to Carol. They have one daughter, Susan, and one son, Ray. They also have a granddaughter, Jessica and grandson, Justin. Now retired after being self-employed for 40 years in New Jersey, building-construction. Now living in Mechanicsville, VA.

HOWARD EARL LEVY, FC3/c, USS *Jaccard* (DE-355), was born Dec. 6, 1925 in Slidell, LA. After graduating from high school in 1942 he worked for the local electric utility until he was inducted into the USNR on Feb. 11, 1944. He was sent to Farragut, ID for six weeks of boot camp. From there he went to San Diego for Rangefinder School. After graduation he was sent to Norfolk Naval Base in Virginia and later to Boston to catch his ship USS *Jaccard* (DE-355).

Leaving the East Coast and going through the Panama Canal he headed to the Philippines for convoy duty in that area until the end of the war. After the war the *Jaccard* went to China, Japan and Okinawa using the Manila area as home base.

Returning to the States by way of Guam and Honolulu he arrived in San Pedro, CA on May 17, 1946. He left the *Jaccard* and went to New Orleans, LA, where he was discharged on May 27, 1946.

He immediately went back to work for the same electric utility until his retirement on Jan. 1, 1991.

He and his wife of 40 years, Dorothy have two daughters, Lennell and Debbie, and five grandchildren.

VICTOR ALAN LEWIS, Ensign, U.S. Naval Reserve, was born in Sommerville, MA, son of Mr. and Mrs. Murray Lewis of 245 Allen Street, Randolph, MA Aug. 2, 1919. He graduated from Stetson High School in Randolph and attended Springfield College, where he was active in athletics, including varsity track and gymnastics. He also coached track, swimming, tennis and gymnastics.

He enlisted in the United States Naval Reserve as a Seaman second class at Squantum Naval Reserve Aviation Base, Boston, MA, and on Feb. 17, 1941 reported there for elimination flight training and re-

leased the following April 10. Recalled to active duty two weeks later, he was transferred to Naval Air Station, Jacksonville, FL. One month later he accepted appointment as Aviation Cadet and had advanced flight training at Jacksonville and Miami, and on Dec. 1, 1941 was designated Naval Aviator. He was then commissioned Ensign to rank from Oct. 14, 1941.

Transferred to Naval Air Station, Norfolk, VA still under training with Advanced Carrier Training Group, Atlantic Fleet, from there he went to the West Coast in February 1942. He reported fro duty with Torpedo Squadron 8 aboard the USS *Hornet*, and on May 21st was ordered out to the Pacific war area. he first saw combat action in the Battle of Midway and was reported Missing in Action on June 4, 1942. He was officially Presumed Dead one year later.

He was awarded the Navy Cross posthumously, and also a ribbon for and facsimile of the Presidential Unit Citation awarded to the officers and men of Torpedo Squadron 8. The citations follow:

NAVY CROSS: "For extraordinary heroism and meritorious devotion to duty as a pilot of a Navy torpedo plane in action against enemy Japanese forces in the Battle of Midway, June 4 and 5, 1942. In the first attack against an enemy carrier of the Japanese invasion fleet, Ensign Lewis pressed home his attack in the face of withering fire from enemy Japanese fighters and anti-aircraft batteries, thereby contributing to the success of our forces...There can be no doubt that he gallantly gave up his life in the service of his country..."

FIRST PRESIDENTIAL UNIT CITATION TO TORPEDO SQUADRON EIGHT: "For extremely heroic and courageous performance in combat during the Air Battle of Midway, June 4, 1942. Flying low without fighter support, Torpedo Squadron Eight began the perilous mission "Intercept and Attack!"...against crushing enemy opposition, scoring torpedo hits on Japanese forces. Realizing to a man that insufficient fuel would prevent a return to the carrier, the pilots held doggedly to the target, dropping torpedoes at point-blank range in the face of blasting anti-aircraft fire that sent the planes, one by one, hurtling aflame into the sea. The loss of 29 lives, typifying valor, loyalty and determination, was the price paid for Torpedo Squadron Eight's vital contribution to the eventual success of our forces in this epic battle of the air."

In addition to the Navy Cross and the Presidential Unit Citation Ribbon, Ensign Lewis was posthumously awarded the Purple Heart Medal.

EVERT LINDSTROM, (SWEDE), was born Jan. 4, 1926 in Chicago, IL. Joined the USNR Dec. 1, 1943. Stationed at Great Lakes, IL, Norfolk, VA and San Diego, CA. Served on the USS *Johnnie Hutchins* (DE-360). He had achieved the rank of SOM3/c at the time of his discharge.

He recalls riding out typhoon, and sinking three midget subs. He received the Philippine Liberation, American Campaign, Asiatic-Pacific, World War II Victory Medal, Navy Occupation, China Service, National Defense, and the Navy Unit Commendation.

He is now widowed since 1979, with one son. Retired from Illinois Bell Telephone Company after 39 years.

BONAVENTURE JOE LINKUS, QM3/c, USS *Seid* (DE-256), was born in Elizabeth, NY. Enlisted in the U.S. Navy on March 5, 1943. Sent to boot camp (Co. 468) Newport, RI. QM School (Class 1576) Newport, RI. Sent to receiving stations in Pleasanton, CA, and Noumea, New Caledonia.

Was assigned to USS *Seid* in the South Pacific until decommissioning at Long Beach, CA.

Discharged at Lido Beach, LI, NY February 1946. He received the Asiatic-Pacific Ribbon with two stars, Philippine Liberation, American Theatre Ribbon and the Victory Ribbon.

He was a designer at various engineering companies. He is now retired.

Married to Emily (Malinowsky) Linkus and have three daughters and two grandchildren.

ROBERT W. LISLE, enlisting in the V-7 program enabled graduation from Penn State December 1942. After attending Notre Dame Midsipman's School and SCTC in Miami assigned to USS *Manning* (DE-199) being completed in Charleston. The ship was commissioned Oct. 1, 1943 and after usual shakedown in Bermuda, passed through the Panama Canal direct to Pearl Harbor. Spending most of its time in the 7th Fleet, the ship participated in the New Guinea and Philippine campaigns. Served in torpedo and gunnery departments.

After return ordered to BUPERS for a short stay followed by duty as classification officer at Camp Peary and Norfolk. Became civilian May 17, 1946.

Employed at International Harvester Farm Equipment dealer in Kittanning, PA and in 1947 bought out retiring dealer in Gasport, NY in partnership with college roommate. Also had Gulf Oil heating oil business. After 37 years sold out and retired.

Married in 1948, two daughters. Now spending winters in Sun City, AZ.

JOHN O. LIVESAY, SC2/c, was born Jan. 7, 1924 in Stone, KY. Family moved to Pennsylvania in 1931. Attended South Fayette Township Public Schools (Class of 42). Enlisted in USCGR on Dec. 7, 1942. Attended boot camp Manhattan Beach Jan. 10, 1943 to April 7, 1943. Hotel Galvez in Galveston, TX April 1943-to June

1943. Attended Cooks and Bakers School Curtis Bay, MD from June 1943 until September 1943. Transferred to receiving station in New Orleans, LA in October 1943, and boarded the USS *Mills* Nov. 1, 1943.

He was discharged Oct. 13, 1945 in Detroit, MI. First sailor discharged from 8th Naval District who saw Japan. He received the American Theatre, European African Battle Ribbon with one star, Asiatic Pacific, and Good Conduct Medal.

Married to Mary E. Dams May 12, 1945. Mary passed away Nov. 25, 1981 and he married Shirley J. Galicic May 27, 1983. He has one son, John Livesay, Jr., and one step-daughter, Robin R. Mehok. Retired from Union Electric Steel in 1987. Member of American Legion Post #485, Syria Shrine in Philadelphia and past Master of Lodge # 759, F&AM of Pennsylvania.

MARVIN S. LOEWITH, was born March 10, 1919 in Bridgeport, CT. Joined the UNSR in August 1940. Served on the USS *Carlson* (DE-9). He had achieved the rank of lieutenant commander at the time of his discharge. He served in the Okinawa campaign and this was a memorable experience for him. Received a Bronze Star for his service in Okinawa.

He is now a widower with three children and five grandchildren. Involved in a variety of community and consulting activities. Retired Sr. vice-president of Connecticut General Life Insurance Co. Served 7 1/2 years as Connecticut Public Utilities Commissioner.

PERRY C. LOGAN SR., born Jan. 12, 1924 in Fort Wayne, IN, to Leslie R. and Lois (Snyder) Logan Sr. Inducted into U.S. Navy Feb. 15, 1943, entered into active service March 1943 in Toledo, OH. Stationed at NTS Great Lakes, IL for EM Recruit Training, USS *Waterman* (DE-740), Purdue NTCW Layfayette, IN and NOB Norfolk, VA, also for EM training.

Received Philippine Liberation with one star, American Theatre, Asiatic-Pacific with seven stars, Point System. He had achieved the rank of electrician's mate first class at the time of his discharge in November 1945.

Married to Margaret A. Rimmel Oct. 3, 1942 in Brimfield, IN. They had two daughters, Kay and Annette and three sons, Perry, Jr., Kent and Lee. Also six grandchildren. He retired as an electrician at Philips Industrial Components in Albion. He was a member of American Legion and VFW Posts, was an Orange Township Precinct Committeeman, a member of National Campers and Hikers Association, and Noble Chain Links. He is now deceased, survived by his wife and children.

RANSFORD EMERY LOVELY, was born July 30, 1925 in St. Albans, ME. Joined the U.S. Navy Dec.

14, 1943 as an apprentice seaman. Attended boot camp at Sampson, NY, then on to Norfolk, VA and Orange, TX. Served on the USS *Edwin A. Howard* (DE-346). He had achieved the rank of fireman first class at the time of his discharge.

Received the Asiatic-Pacific Area Ribbon with one star, Philippine Liberation Ribbon with one star, European African Middle Eastern Ribbon, World War II Victory Medal and the American Area Ribbon.

Married three times, and has ten children and four step-children. Retired truckdriver and mechanic. Now living in Hartland, ME with third wife, Leona.

JACK LEON LOY, was born Oct. 2, 1922 in Springfield, OH. Joined the U.S. Navy Jan. 7, 1941. Served on the USS *California* March 16, 1941 to Dec. 12, 1941. The USS *California* sank Dec. 7, 1941 in Pearl Harbor. He was then assigned to USS *Astoria* (CA-32) from Dec. 13, 1941 to Aug. 8, 1942 for Battle of Coral Sea, Battle of Midway, Guadacanal invasion, Battle of Sano Island, and surface battle with Japanese fleet. The *Astoria* along with the cruisers *Quincy* and *Vincennes* were sank. Later served on to the USS *England* from Dec. 10, 1943 to Aug. 24, 1945.

He received the Presidential Unit Citation for sinking six Japanese submarines in 12 days. He had achieved the rank of boatswain's mate first class at the time of his discharge.

Married to Joanne for 45 years and they have four children, Gayla, Donna, Jay and Michael.

ANDREW LUPTAK, EM3/c, USS *Manlove* (DE-36), enlisted in the U.S. Navy Feb. 12, 1943. Boot camp and Electrical School at Sampson Naval Base, Sampson, NY. Served aboard the USS *Manlove* (DE-36) from August 1943 to February 1945, escorting ships (troop and ammunition) bound for Kwajalein, Eniwetok, and Saipan. The *Manlove* was credited with the sinking of a Japanese submarine off the Marshall Islands. Left the *Manlove* for reassignment, spent 16 weeks at Camp Perry, VA for Electrical School. Ended up in Samar in the Philippine Islands. Discharged from the Navy, at U.S. Naval Personnel Separation Center in Bainbridge, MA Feb. 18, 1946.

Married to Florence Houba of Cleveland, OH on July 17, 1948. They have four sons, Robert, David, Andy Jr., and Joseph, and ten grandchildren. Worked at G.E. from 1946 until 1963. Left G.E. to start a quartz business venture with a friend. Retired Dec. 31, 1990, and is planning on doing a little traveling with Florence, God willing.

WALTER F. LYNCH *(See page 744)*

HIRAM PEARSON MACINTOSH, IV, CDR USNR (Ret.), USS *Thomas* (DE-102), entered the

Naval Reserve June 3, 1942 as an ensign. First tour of duty as personnel officer, VCNO. Assigned to USS *Aquamarine* based at Anacostia, MD as first lieutenant and gunnery officer. Later promoted to executive officer. Transferred to Sub Chaser School, Miami, FL for training. From there he attended Gunnery School, Naval Gun Factory, in Washington, DC. Assigned to USS *Thomas* (DE-102) and put her in commission November 1943. Assigned to Hunter Killer Group with USS *Block Island*. On first cruise in Atlantic Ocean made contact with Wolf Pack resulting in two kills. Returned to the U.S. and was sent out with large convoy headed for Africa. *Block Island* sent out with another group and was sunk. Only carrier lost in Atlantic. Operated with USS *Carp* and had more action on subsequent cruises. Returned to inactive duty September 1945. Joined MSTS Reserve Unit at Philadelphia Navy Yard. Became XO, then made commanding officer NCSO Unit. Retired MTH 26 years in Naval Reserve July 1, 1969. Became sales representative for Goodall Rubber Company for the next 22 years. Left Goodall for Bevco Industries where he worked for 14 years before retiring. As a retiree he is a volunteer guide, Morris Arboretum, University of Philadelphia, volunteer worker for Chestnut Hill Hospital, treasurer Wissahickon Ski Club, active fisherman, hunter and gardener.

Married on June 3, 1944 to lieutenant (jg) Rita Gilbert USNR. (only out ranked her by two months and it has remained for 47 years.) They have one daughter Laurie who married Rich Mickle, with three children-Ian (five yrs), Scott (three years), and Bonnie (three months).

HOMER E. MADDOX, USS *Jack Miller* (DE-410), enlisted U.S. Navy Jan. 3, 1942 at Ashland, KY. Boot training at Navy Pier, Chicago, IL. Next assignment was Naval Air Station, Corpus Christi, TX. At completion of Link Trainer School was link trainer instructor for two years at NAS Corpus Christi.

Next assigned to (DE-410) crew in training at Norfolk, VA in Sonar School. In April 1944 he went aboard the *Jack Miller* as a plank owner at the Brown Shipyard in Houston, TX. After shakedown cruise in Bermuda headed for the Pacific via the Panama Canal. For the next 19 months the *Jack Miller* operated throughout the Pacific on anti-submarine patrols, convoy screening, escort duty and picket line duty around Okinawa during and after the invasion of the island. The *Jack Miller* received two Battle Stars for WWII Service. She returned to the States Nov. 5, 1945.

He was discharged from the Navy Dec. 18, 1945 and returned to his home and his job at Armco Steel Inc. at Ashland, KY and retired from there in 1983.

He states that he is proud to have served in the U.S. Navy and to have served on the USS *Jack Miller*.

DENIS F. MALONEY, was born May 11, 1926 in Green Bay, WI. He joined the U.S. Navy Sept. 17, 1943. NTS at Great Lakes, IL and NTS NOB at Norfolk, VA. He served on the USS *Bowers* (DE-637), the USS *Murrelet* (AM-372) and USS *Plarmigan* (AM-376). He had achieved the rank of coxswain at the time of his discharge.

Remembers the night in the Lady Gulf when the torpedo bomber came in and dropped its torpedoes at them. He was on #6-20mm gun and he saw the sparks as it was launched at them. He states that they were very lucky, for they were out for five to ten days suppling fuel and ammo to all the big ships which they were patroling. The torpedo was set for 15 feet and they were carrying about 10 to 12 feet of water, which missed them and hit a tanker next to them, which wasn't sunk because its tanks were empty. Then the next day Tokyo Rose reported them sunk. He also remembers when they were hit in Okinawa. He could of hit that plane with a broom, it came right over him on the fantail on his gun mount then banked to the left and hit the bridge. He helped get the ship in control by getting a phone from the anchor room to the deck which was connected to the after sterring room to get the ship under control.

He received the American Area Campaign Medal, Asiatic Pacific Area Campaign Medal, three Bronze Stars, Philippine Liberation Ribbon with one star, Victory Medal.

He has been married to his wife for 43 years, they have five children and five grandchildren. He is retired, enjoying life, and busier than ever. He wouldn't change his life for anything or what the kids have now days. They were taught to be self reliant and men

ANTHONY V. MARINO, RM1/c, was born Sept. 1, 1922 in Chelsea, MA. Joined the Navy Dec. 1, 1942. Attended boot camp at Great Lakes, Northwestern Un. Radio School, and Anti-submarine Radio School, Casco Bay, ME. He was assigned to the USS *Manlove* (DE-36), commissioned Nov. 8, 1943 Mare Island Navy Yard, his duty consisted of anti-submarine and escorting convoys.

In joint attack with PC-1135 on April 1, 1944 they sank a Japanese transport submarine I-32. Patrolling off Okinawa assault, the *Manlove* was damaged by a Japanese kamikaze.

He received five Battle Stars for WWII services. Transferred to new construction and assigned to APD-109. Commissioned Hingham Shipyard, MA. Assigned to Pacific. Last duty was in Wakayama, Japan as port

director. He returned to the the States and decommissioned in Green Cove, FL.

JOHN A. MARKS, was born May 31, 1925 in Cambridge, MA. He joined the Navy July 7, 1942. Attended boot camp in Newport, RI for six weeks. Schooling August 1942-December 1942 at Cooks & Bakers in Philadelphia, PA. January 1943 on to Norfolk, VA for further training. He was commissioned USS *Flaherty* (DE-135) Atlantic task group Guadalcanal, convoy duty, submarine hunter killer duty until May 1944. Assigned to training May 1944 to commission USS *Johnnie Hutchins* (DE-360) August 1944 for duty in the Atlantic. Panama Canal to Pacific enroute to Philippine Liberation. At the time of his discharge he had achieved the rank of SC1/c. While in the Navy he served on many different ships. He was stationed in Korea and China.

He remembers the sinking of Nazi U515 on surface which was the last naval engagement of WWII; the shore patrol of Shanghai, China in 1945.

He received many medals for his service which include nine medals and six stars for WWII, with a total of 14 medals throughout service.

He is the father of two sons, two daughters, and four grandchildren. Retired after 21 years as chief commissary man and resides in Chula Vista, CA.

NED J. MARROW, CM3/c, USS *Barr* (DE-576), was born on March 14, 1923 in Galeton, PA. He was the son of Mary and Carmin Marrow. Attended Sampson NTS from October 1-Dec. 30, 1943. From there to Norfolk, VA for Seaman School. He served aboard the USS *Barr* (DE-576) from February 15, to Oct. 23, 1944. USS *Barr* joined Killer Group TU21-11, made up of one CUE-21 USS *Block Island*, USS *Buckley* (DE-51), USS *Ahrens* (DE-575), USS *Paine* (DE-578) and DE *Elmore* (DE-686), which departed Norfolk April 22, 1944 for duty in the South Atlantic.

The USS *Barr* was torpedoed May 29, 1944 while carrying out search operation in the Azores Gibraltar area. *Barr* had four dead, 12 missing, and 14 injured. The *Barr* was towed by *Dewilhoite* (DE-397) and Netherlands tug *Antis* to Casablanca from June 5-June 26. The ship was temporarily repaired and towed back to Boston by the USS *Cherokee* (AFT-66) at the same time CU-21 was torpedoed and sunk. It was the only carrier to be sunk in the Atlantic.

In civilian life Ned was employed by NYCRR and worked as a conductor on PC and Conrail Railroad. Ned married Evelyn married in Chicago in 1948 and they have one daughter Christine and one granddaughter Kathryn. They have resided in Horseads, NY since 1948.

Ned has taken retirement after 40 years of railroad service and enjoying all his Navy conventions and reunions.

WALTER H. MARSCHLOWITZ, CMM, USN,

enlisted July 1936. Attended boot camp and Machinist Mate School in Norfolk, VA. Transferred USS *Rigel* Des. Base San Diego, CA; ships crew and repair force aboard USS *Whitney*; USS *Dobbin*, USS *Altatr*, aboard USS *Whitney* Dec. 7, 1941 Japanese attack at Pearl Harbor. He serviced destroyers at Noumea, New Caledonia, during Solomons invasion in May 1943. Transferred to General Electric School Turbo Electric Drive Syracuse, NY. He graduated and was sent to Submarine Chaser Training School in Miami, FL. February 1944 put USS *Gunason* (DE-795) in commission at Orange, TX. Convoyed Trinidad to Cuba, three convoys Hampton Roads to Bizerte, Plymouth, Oran. Transferred to Pacific convoys Hollandia to Manila, Subic Bay to Okinawa, Leyte to Tokyo Bay.

He was discharged in 1945 with an honorable discharge. Became stationary engineer for the City of Philadelphia. Retired chief engineer Philadelphia National Bank Building. He received the Good Conduct Medal with Clasp, National Defense with Fleet Clasp, Pacific Theatre with one star, American Theatre, European African Theatre, Victory Medal, Philippine Liberation Medal, Philippine Presidential Unit Citation, and Occupation Medal with Asiatic Clasp.

He is married with two children and four grandchildren. Past president of Institute of Engineers, member Pearl Harbor Survivors Association, DESA, and the American Legion.

DONALD WILBUR MARTIN, was born April

23, 1925 in Libertyville, IA. Joined the U.S. Navy April 2, 1943. Attended USNTS in Great Lakes, IL, NTS (diesel) at the University of Illinois in Urbana, IL and NTS NOB at Norfolk, VA. Served on the USS *Swearer* (DE-186) as plank owner. Active duty South Pacific until the end of the war. Green Cove Springs, FL. Discharged April 25, 1946 in Jacksonville, FL with the rank of MOMM second class.

Remembers going through the Philippines, pitch black with an unidentified vessel closing on the bow, all hands at battle stations waiting for the vessel to come within range of their searchlights. This vessel turned out to be friendly. He received nine Battle Stars for his service.

Married to his wife Ruthie E., for 46 years. They have one daughter, Donna (45), grandson, Oscar A. Johnson (24), two great granddaughters and one son, Frederick (44), no children. Donald farmed and worked as a service station operator, trucking, aerospace and

back to trucking. He retired in 1983 and is now helping his son-in-law with his coin operated business by working on and testing pin ball machines. His hobbies are fishing and more fishing.

VINCENT MARTINEZ, was born Nov. 14, 1934

in Glen Cove, NY. He joined the service in November 1953. In 1953 after boot camp he went to Little Creek, VA, from there to the USS *Zellars* (DD-777) for about 18 months then on to the USS *D.J. Buckley* (DDR-808) for the rest of his term. He received his training at Bainbridge, MD and was a barber, laundryman then deck hand (which he liked the best) on the ship. He passed his test for third class boatsmate, but by the time it came through he was on his way out.

He saw many places while in the Navy some of which are France, Italy, Spain, Ireland, Iran, Portugal, Norway, Gibraltar, England, New Foundland, and Wales just to name a few. He recalls a football game in Lisbon, Portugal, and looking for downed pilots off the *Formosa*.

He received National Defense, Navy Occupation, and Good Conduct Medal.

He married Sophie, they have one daughter and one son. He works as a part-time court officer and volunteer fireman. He also is a part-time postal worker and an avid gardener.

WADE MAUPIN, RM2/c, USS *Stewart* (DE-238),

The USS *Stewart* had escorted convoys and served on submarine patrols in the North Atlantic, Mediterranean and Caribbean Seas during the WWII European conflict. After VE Day the ship received orders to proceed to Pearl Harbor and the Pacific area of operations via the Panama Canal.

Fortunately the ship was in the Panama Canal Zone long enough for them to go ashore in Colon, Panama, and celebrate the successful conclusion of the European conflict, and to drink a few rounds of rum and celebrate joining with the Pacific Fleet.

The USS *Stewart* (DE-238) was built by the Brown Shipbuilding Company in Houston, TX November 1942. It was commissioned May 1943, served in the Atlantic, Mediterranean and Caribbean Seas until July 1945. It operated in the Pacific Ocean August 1946 until the end of the war, and sailed to the St. Johns River at Green Cove Springs, FL where it was decommissioned. It now proudly rests at Sea Wolf Park at Galveston, TX.

VICTOR KEITH MAY, F1/c, USS *Gandy* (DE-

764), was inducted into Navy Oct. 21, 1943. Attended boot camp at Great Lakes, IL, and Gunnery School at Norfolk, VA. Assigned to USS *Gandy* (DE-764) and in February 1944 the USS *Gandy* was commissioned. Shakedown cruise and submarine practice in Bermuda March 1-April 1, 1944. Made nine convoy trips to England, Ireland, Scotland and Wales. On first escort duty out of New York they helped sink German U-Boat #50 on April 16, 1944 when the *Gandy* rammed submarine and sank. There were 13 German survivors which were picked up by USS *Joyce*. After D-Day made way to Pacific via Cuba, Virgin Islands, Panama Canal, California, Hawaii, Marshall and Caroline Islands, Leyte, Philippines and Okinawa. Escorted 8th Occupation Army into Tokyo, Japan. Escort trips off Japan, patrol duty off Philippines. Departed ship Norfolk, VA April 1946 for Bainbridge, MD and discharged.

He worked as an auto mechanic from 1947 until 1990. Now retired and living in Manassas, VA with his wife Charlene. He is active in Fraternal Order of the Independent Order of the Odd Fellows, and a member of DESA.

EDWARD M. MAZIARKA, FC3/c, USS

Willmarth (DE-638), was born Sept. 24, 1924 in Chicago, IL. Enlisted in the Navy March 1943, boot camp training at Great Lakes, IL. Then served aboard the USS *Texas* (BB-35) in the "O" Division. He was sent to Fire Control School, Norfolk, VA then to DE Training School in Miami, FL. He was assigned to the USS *Willmarth* (DE-638) in San Francisco, CA for commissioning in March 1944. His battle and watch station was on the Flying Bridge as the gunnery talker for the gunnery officer.

The USS *Willmarth* was assigned to the 40th DE Div., consisting of DE-633 through DE-638. Participated in numerous invasions, such as Pegan and Igi Islands, Leyte and Okinawa Campaigns. The USS *Willmarth* received four Battle Stars in the Pacific Theatre of war.

After Okinawa, he was transferred to Advance Fire Control School in San Diego, CA. Completing the course, he was then assigned to the USS *Benham* (DD-796). He was discharged March 12, 1946 at Great Lakes, IL and earned the following ribbons: American Area Ribbon, Asiatic-Pacific Area Ribbon with two stars, Philippine Liberation with one star, World War II Victory Ribbon.

Returned to civilian life March 1946. Married to the former Margaret Frederick in June 1947. Worked for Otis Elevator Co. as an elevator constructor doing service, repair, and maintenance. He worked there for 38 years and retired in the Las Vegas, NV area. He is the father of daughter Nancy, son James and two grandsons Gregory Miller and James Emil.

FRED MELDON MCAULEY, WT1/c, USS

Chase (DE-158), was born May 24, 1919 in Savannah, GA. He enlisted in the U.S. Navy, Oct. 19, 1942. Served seven months at USN Inshore Patrol Base, Cockspur Island, GA. Transferred to NOB Norfolk, VA at Little Creek for the USS *Chase* (DE-158), commissioned July 18, 1943, which following shakedown cruise in the *Chase* was assigned as a screening vessel in a large merchant ship convoy UGS-18 to Gibraltar, crossing in 19 days. Detached from convoy USG-18, the *Chase* was ordered to Algiers to join CTG-21.4 to relieve the USS *Schenck*, leaving North Africa to escort Tanker Convoy TO-9 to Aruba, Netherland Antilles, and then to New York. During this first crossing to North Africa, Fred was promoted to rate WT2/c, dated Sept. 1, 1943.

Developing sonar problems, the *Chase* was detached for repairs to NOB Trinidad for three days before proceeding to Aruba and rejoining CTG-21.4 to New York, where it was relieved from escort duty (October 30). In early November, the *Chase* was assigned to escort duty with Convoy OT-1 to Aruba in the Caribbean, and from there to Gibraltar and the Mediterranean ports of Algiers, Bizerte, and Tunis in North Africa. Returning with CTG-21.4 to Aruba, arriving December 26, then for a brief stop at Curacao before putting in port at Guantanamo Bay, Cuba (December 29).

In January 1944, the *Chase* rejoined CTG-21.4 in a third convoy to North Africa, escorting Convoy OT-12, arriving in Algiers on Feb. 1, 1944. Departed the following day to escort Convoy OT-12 on its return to Aruba, then arriving back at Guantanamo Bay on February 22. After CTG-21.4 was dissolved, the *Chase* returned to Brooklyn Navy Yard, New York. After arriving in New York, Fred transferred to Philadelphia Navy Yard, PA for Oil Burning School. In July 1944, he reported to Miami, SCTC, where he was assigned to the nucleus crew for DE-368.

Transferred to Orange, TX in August 1944, and commissioned Oct. 16, 1944 with USS *Cecil J. Doyle* (DE-368). The *Doyle* ran aground during shakedown cruise, and was sent to Boston Navy Yard for overhaul and repairs. Returned to Bermuda to complete shakedown cruise; rendezvous with HMS *Crane* (CVE) through the Panama Canal to San Diego, CA.

Departed San Diego to Pearl Harbor for training and gunnery practice, concurrently with CVE-64. Departed Pearl Harbor to points west, eg Marshall's, Caroline's, with assignment to Palau Islands. In August 1945, the *Doyle* was the first surface ship to respond in the rescue operations of survivors of the USS *Indianapolis* (CA-35) sinking, rescuing 93 of her crew. A month later the *Doyle* arrived in mainland Japan, Sept. 11, 1945, for POW evacuation of southern Honshu, Osaka and Wakayama. Fred returned to the States aboard the USS *John C. Hancock* (CV) arriving at San Pedro for discharge Oct. 26, 1945.

He married October 1944, to Yvonne Johnson, in Port Arthur, TX. They have three sons, two grandson and two granddaughters. Retired from Union Camp Corporation's Paper Mill in Savannah, GA, after 41 years of service.

Awards include: American Campaign Service Medal, European African Middle Eastern Campaign Medal, Asiatic Pacific Campaign Medal, and World War II Victory Medal.

ALDEN W. MCCANLESS, (MAC), was born May 17, 1926, enlisted Washington, DC May 22, 1944. Boot camp at Camp Peary, VA, Radio School at Bainbridge, MD. Boarded the USS *Stewart* (DE-238)

at New York in February 1945, shortly after marrying Carolyn Kreitlow of Buffalo, MN.

Served on the *Stewart* in both the Atlantic and Pacific theatres until reassigned to a Military Government unit on Yap Islands in the Western Carolines. Discharged at Bainbridge, MD Feb. 19, 1946 with the rank of RM3/c.

Most memorable experience aboard the *Stewart* occurred April 10, 1945 when the *Stewart's* crew extinguished a fire on the S.S. *St. Mihiel* which was carrying millions of gallons of flaming aviation fuel.

Following discharge, returned to clerk's job at the Internal Revenue Service in Washington, DC. Earned a bachelor's degree in night school and after assignments in Minnesota, Illinois and Missouri, became district director of Internal Revenue in Phoenix. Later served in that same capacity in St. Louis, MO and Dallas, TX, retiring back in Arizona in 1981.

Currently involved in motorhome travel, the old car hobby and part-time tax accounting.

JAMES R. MCCONKEY, was born May 8, 1925 in Guernsey County. Inducted into service November 1943. Attended Radio School at Auburn, AL and ATB at Coronada, CA. He served on the USS *Harmon* (DE-678). He had achieved the rank of sergeant first class (radioman) at the time of discharge.

He is divorced with two granddaughters and one grandson. He is a retired trucker for Roadway Express, and resides in Cambridge, OH.

JOHN E. MCCULLOUGH, RM3/c USN, USS *Levy* (DE-162), was born May 20, 1925 in Philadelphia, PA. Joined the Navy Nov. 5, 1942. Boot camp at Bainbridge, MD from November 1942 until February 1943. Fleet Radio School, Bedford Springs, PA February 1943 until May 1943. Reported to USS *Levy* at Boston Navy Yard June 1943, proceeded to Canal with convoy for Noumea, Espiritu and Tulagi/Guadalcanal. Arrived Bora Bora August 1943...first landfill since sighting Galapagos.

First major operation, Bougainville, Nov. 1, 1943 (for some reason BuNavships does not list them as being there). Sent south November 2 when heavy Japanese units sent to contest landings. Took part in Hollandia, Lae, Finschafen operations. Manus and Los Negros on D plus one. Eniwetok on D plus one. Sent to search for submarine which sank Liscombe Bay at Tarawa. Guam and Saipan landings. Took part in Leyte/Samar assaults, refueling Halsey's BB's and fast carriers.

On the way to Pearl their convoy was joined by a Betty flying 50 feet of water. He looks at them, they look at him, before anyone in convoy can get to a gun

he was gone. On to San Diego in December 1944 where their torpedoes were replaced by a Quad 40mm mount. 30 day leave for all hands, then back to Pacific for Okinawa operation. Great typhoon survivor. Admitted to Naval Hospital Majuro, then to Kwajelein, flew in MacArthur's Bataan to Aiea Hospital at Pearl. Back to the States aboard *Enterprise*. To hospital St. Albans, NY then to control tower Mustin Field, PA. Honorably discharged in August 1946.

He received the Good Conduct Medal, Philippine Liberation Medal with two stars, Pacific Theatre with five stars, American Theatre, and Victory Medal.

He is married with four children the youngest of which is 14. He is in film and videotape production. Owner of Film Factory, Inc. producing commercials and corporate video.

ALFRED F. MCDONALD, JR., GM2/c, was born March 20, 1927 in Buffalo, NY. Served on board USS *Hampton* (APA-115), USS *Toledo* (CA-133), USS *Houston* (CL-81), USS *Silverstein* (DE-534). Enlisted in the Navy July 26, 1944. Attended boot camp at Sampson, NY. Amphibious Training at Ft. Pierce, FL November 1944 through January 1945. Commissioned USS *Hampton* (APA-115) in February 1945. South Pacific duty, invasion of Japan, September 1945, Magic Carpet duty October 1945-January 1946. Decommission USS *Hampton* March 1946. Naval Gun Factory March 1946. Commission Toledo October 1946 USS *Houston* April 1946-European Good Will Tour, decommissioned *Houston* November 1947, discharged and recalled to duty January 1951. Recommissioned USS *Silverstein* (DE-534) for Korean War, Formosa Patrol, plane guard for all air strikes. Shore bombardment, east coast of Korea, from Sonjin, Humgnam, Wonsan Harbor and the bomb line while assigned to the Task Force 95.2 from November 1951-March 1952.

He retired after 30 years service as a lieutenant in the Buffalo, NY Police Department.

ROBERT MCKNIGHT, MOMM2/c, served aboard the USS *Engstrom* (DE-50) between 1943 and 1946. He received the American Theatre, European Theatre with two stars, and Asiatic Theatre with three stars.

After service Robert worked for the Pennsylvania Railroad as an electrician for 29 years. He lived alongside the Chesapeake Bay and was a boat lover. He had his own dock and nice home  which he enjoyed very much. He passed away with cancer April 28, 1975 at the age of 52. *Submitted by wife Martha McKnight*

ARTHUR D. MCNAMARA, served aboard the USS *Richey* (DE-385) (USCG) from time of commissioning October 1943 to date put in mothballs May 1946.

CHARLES M. MCRAE, USNR, USS *Grady* (DE-445), was born Oct. 29, 1924 in Jordon, MT. Joined the service Oct. 25, 1943. Attended RT School at Delmonte, CA, Torpedo School San Diego, CA. He had achieved the rank of torpedoman's mate third class at the time of his discharge. He remembers being on the picket line in Okinawa for 58 days. He received the Asiatic-Pacific Campaign Medal with two stars.

He married Mabel Koger July 25, 1953, they have two sons. He is a retired teacher and counselor. Belongs to DESA and Disabled American Veterans.

KENNETH L. MCRAE, (KEN),
was transferred from Army Reserve (Ninth Coast Artillery), to Naval Reserve. Commissioned as an ensign, assigned to Armed Guard Service in 1942. Served with Navy gun crews on USS *S.B. Hunt* and USS *Walter E. Ranger* 1942-1943.

After Armed Guard Service he was assigned to Sub Chaser Training School, Miami, FL, with additional study at Fleet Sound School Key West, FL.

On completion of schools was assigned to USS *Thomas* (DE-102), as ASW officer in 1944. They made one convoy trip to the Mediterranean and then were assigned as Killer Group escort to small carriers in the Atlantic.

In December 1945, he was released from Naval Reserve and returned to Joseph Dixon Crucible Co. (now Dixon Ticonderoga) until retirement in 1975. Married to Louise Carter in July 1950. They now live in Florida.

GEORGE J. MENTGEN,
Plankowner, USS *Willmarth* (DE-638), was born in the small town of Peru, IL on May 5, 1926. He attended L.P. High School and worked until enlisting in the Navy at the age of 17 in August 1943. He took boot training at Farragut Naval Training Station in Farragut, ID. After boot camp he was sent to Norfolk, VA for fireman school. After completing school he was then sent to Mari Island, CA to be assigned to the USS *Willmurth* (DE-638). He was a plank owner as he was one of the original crew to commission and decommission the ship at Green Cove Springs, FL.

He was assigned to the forward fireroom. The *Willmurth* was assigned to the 40th DE Div. DEs 633-638. It traveled through all the Islands from Hawaii through bombardment of Japanese homeland. Was in Tokyo Bay when Treaty was signed. Participated in many invasions and battles of the Pacific. Earned five Battle Stars in these operations.

After decommissioning (DE-638), George was discharged at Great Lakes Naval Station in April 1946 with the rank of WT third class.

In civilian life he worked at various factories, did construction work, and went to college. Received BA from WIU of Macomb, IL and MIA from N.I.U.

Dekalb, IL with major in PE, geography and social science. He taught at various schools from 1954 until 1958, he then started a career with the Illinois Department of Corrections, Juvenile Div. at Joliet in August 1959. Worked later as a recreation, PE and health instructor in 1968, moved up to a vocational and career counselor and supervisor.

He is married and has five children, three boys, two girls, six granddaughters and two grandsons. He is now retired after 32 years with the Illinois Department of Corrections and school district. He was 65 years old as of Aug. 1, 1992. His hobbies include hunting, fishing, bowling, horseshoes, and various other sports. He also serves on their ships reunion committee.

Involved in various civic and civilian activities. He served as the Grand Knight of the Knights of Columbus from 1983-1984, charter president of FSCME to name a few. Union 1756, Member of Veteran of Foreign Wars, Catholic W.V., American Legion and Veterans Alumni Association.

VICTOR MEREDITH,
worked for Illinois Central Gulf Railroad on Kentucky Div. as telegraph operator until drafted into the Navy in 1942 at Louisville, KY. Boot camp at Great Lakes, Co. 839. After August 1943 he was sent to Virginia Beach to Radar School. Went on board USS *Straub* (DE-181), commissioned at Brooklyn, NY October 1943. Convoy and A.S.W. in North Atlantic, South Atlantic and Mediterranean Sea until June 21, 1945. Returned to Boston Navy Yard for re-armament ready for Pacific. Ship was last returned from convoy duty. Transferred off DE-181 to Norfolk, VA to attend Radar Material School. After school DE-181 was in Pacific, so he was transferred to PF-1 USS *Asheville* and was decommissioned Jan. 8, 1946 as RD 2.

Discharged at Great Lakes Feb. 4, 1946. Returned to ICRR and worked as telegraph operator and train dispatcher over Kentucky, Tennessee and Mississippi division until retirement. Joined the USNR in 1956. Discharged in 1978 as OSC. Saw duty on DE DD-DDg Aux. ships. LST LPH and FF on East and West Coasts. Best reserve duty was a trip to Nice, France on Mediterannean and flight back to Greece. Operated with the 6th Fleet.

WILLIAM MICHAEL MERTES, (MIKE),
EM2/c, USS *Charles Lawrence* (DE-53/APD-37) was born Feb. 26, 1925 in Grand Rapids, MI. Enlisted July 30, 1942 at Chicago, IL. Went to boot camp at Great Lakes, IL. Norfolk, NOB DE Training School. Assigned May 31, 1943 to USS *Charles Lawrence* (DE-53) in Hingham, MA.

Assignments: Shakedown cruise to Bermuda, convoy duty to Casablanca and Londonderry, convoys

to Guadalcanal, Manila, Leyte, and invasion of Okinawa.

Discharged Jan. 12, 1946. Married Carol Dehn on Sept. 17, 1955 in New York. He has two sons and one daughter. Now retired after 37 years as broadcast engineer.

RALPH L. MESICK,
RDM 2/c, *USS Fiske (DE-143)*, joined the U.S. Navy on April 7, 1943, in Seattle, WA. Boot camp in Athol, ID and was assigned to Company 245-43 at Camp Scott, Farragut, ID. He was sent to Radar Operators School at Point Loma, CA, and assigned as a plank owner on the *USS Fiske (DE-143)* commissioned on August 25, 1943. He had convoy duty across the Atlantic to Casablanca or Bizerte 1943-44. In May, 1944, the *Fiske* became part of a hunter-killer group including the baby flat top carrier *Wake Island*. On August 2, 1944, the *Fiske* took a torpedo amid-ship which broke her in half. He was picked up by the *USS Farquhar (DE-139)*. He went to Chelsea Naval Hospital, Springfield, MA; Fargo Barracks, Boston; Norfolk, VA, for Radio Maintenance School; Detroit, MI, for Electronics School; and Treasure Island, CA, being assigned to the *USS President Jackson (APA-18)* which made several trips across the Pacific including crossing the equator. He was discharged on May 8, 1946, at USNB, Bremerton, WA.

He joined the Navy Reserve in February, 1948, and was called for Korea serving on the *USS Chandler (DD-717)*. After a trip to Korea and Japan, he was assigned to the re-commissioning of the *USS Rolette (AKA-19)* at Mare Island, CA, and sailed through the Panama Canal to the East Coast. In December, 1952, he retired from the U.S. Navy. In May of 1955, he joined the Air Force Reserve, 403rd Troop Carrier Wing, Portland, OR. He joined the Oregon Air National Guard until 1977, completing his tour as Chief Master Sergeant. He returned to the Air Force Reserve until retirement in 1983 as Chief Master Sergeant. He joined the Oregon National Guard Reserve which later became the Oregon State Defense Force and serves as Battalion Commander.

His awards include: Purple Heart, Air Force Outstanding Unit, Navy Good Conduct, American Campaign, European-African Mideast Campaign- 1 device, Asiatic Pacific Campaign, WWII Victory, National Defense, Korean Defense- 1 device, Air Force Longevity Service- 4 OLC, Armed Forces Reserve- 1 device, Air Reserve Forces Meritorious Service Award- 4 OLC, Small Arms Expert Marksmanship Ribbon, United Nations Service, Oregon Meritorious Service, Oregon National Guard Commendation, Oregon 30 Year Faithful Service, Oregon Faithful Service- 5 OLC, Oregon Perfect Attendance- 1 Silver OLC, State Defense Force Association of the U.S. Medal, and various Letters of Commendation.

He spent some time in college, married, was blessed with 4 children (2 red-headed girls and 2 tow-headed boys), went to work for the U.S. Government DOE Bonneville Power Administration as an electrician. He retired in 1988 with 38 years of service including his military time.

LESTER F. MEYER,
CM1/c, USS *Mills* (DE-383), Entered the Coast Guard March 1942. Boot camp at Manhattan Beach T.S. Brooklyn, NY; Buffalo Base, NY; CGTS Curtis Bay, MD, SCTC/DCGO Miami, FL,

USNRS, Houston, TX; USS *Mills* (DE-383); USS *Wakefield*; DCGO Long Beach, CA; PSC #9 St. Louis, MO. Made shakedown and all convoys in the European African Middle East area: England, Ireland, Wales, Oran, Algiers, Bizerte, Casablanca, Gibraltar, Azores; the Asian Pacific area, Aluetians with Adm. J. Fletchers 9th Fleet Patrol. After VJ Day occupation of Northern Honshu, Matsu Bay, (Sept. 8, 1945). Returned to U.S. on USS *Wakefield* from Singtau, China and was discharged Feb. 14, 1946.

Worked as self employed cabinet maker from 1946 until 1991. Semi-retired. Married Priscila Carmody, April 19, 1947, they have one daughter Jan Resler, and one grandson, Dirk Resler. Member of VFW, DESA, NI DESA and DAV.

CLARENCE MIERKOWSKI, USNR, F1/c, USS *Edmonds* (DE-406), was born in Dubois, IL. Joined the service Oct. 11, 1943. Served with the U.S. Navy Escort Div. 63. Attended boot camp at Great Lakes, IL.

He remembers the night of Feb. 21, 1945 when USS *Bismarck* (CVE-957) was sunk by a Japanese suicide plane attack and the USS *Edmonds* succeeded in rescuing 378 survivors including the commanding officer and the executive officer of Iwo Jima.

He received the American Theatre Ribbon, Asiatic-Pacific Theatre Ribbon with one Silver Star, representing five Bronze Stars earned for participation in Morotai, Leyte, Luzon, Iwo Jima, and Okinawa campaigns; and Philippine Liberation Ribbon with two Bronze Stars, for serving in the Philippine area for at least 30 days, for participating in the initial landing operations at Leyte, and for being under direct enemy attack during the Luzon campaign.

He is married to Marvella and now retired from Roller Derby Skate Corp. where he worked as a tool and die machinist. Resides in Litchfield, IL.

ROBERT W. MILLER, RDM1/c, USS *Wesson* (DE-184), was born Sept. 20, 1924. Boot camp at Sampson, NY, July 1943, Radar School, then assigned to nucleus crew of *Wesson*.

Ship assigned to Pacific Theatre January 1944 and involved in many major invasions from Marshall Islands through Philippines and finally Okinawa where ship received suicide plane with loss of 15 crew. After repairs in Mare Island, *Wesson* returned to participate in occupation duty of mine destruction in Japan's Harbors until November 1945. Discharged January 1946. Received eight Battle Stars and four medals.

USS *Wesson* was caught in a typhoon in fall 1944 while refueling off the Philippines with loss of three other destroyer screen ships which capsized due to low fuel.

He married Grace M. Bodine in Brooklyn, NY while on repair leave in May 1945 and have three sons and six grandchildren.

Recalled to active duty for Korean Conflict. Served additional 16 months aboard USS *Beale* (DD-481).

Retired from Therm Incorporated, Ithaca, NY aerospace manufacturer in 1989 after 40 years, serving the last nine as vice-president of quality.

R.W. MILLER (Bob) *(See photo, page 744.)*

ROBERT E. MILLS, USS *Lovering* (DE-39), was born July 2, 1925 in Norway, ME. Inducted into service March 11, 1943. Boot camp at NTS Newport, RI. Commissioned (DE-39) Bremerton, WA as sergeant first class.

Memorable experience for him was being at preshelling of Eniwetok (Marshall Islands) escorted ship with emergency ammunition to the wrong side of the Island. DE-39 had stern lifted out of the water, disabled port screw was dry docked for repairs. He received three Battle Stars for his service in the South Pacific.

Married with eight children, seventeen grandchildren, and one great-grandchild. He retired from Boise Cascade after 37 years. Now resides in Bethel, ME with his wife Elizabeth.

JOHN MITCHELL *(See photo, page 744.)*

ARMIN F. MOHR, RM2/c, USS *Vance* (DE-387) and USS *Durant* (DE-389), was born Aug. 13, 1925. Enlisted in the Coast Guard June 30, 1943 and reported to Manhattan Beach, NY. Boot camp served on the USS *Vance* from commissioning to decommissioning (September 1943-February 1946). Made nine TransAtlantic convoy trips to Casablanca, Bizerte, Sicily and Oran. Observed the first German Submarine surrender (U-873) off the Azores. The *Vance* escorted the sub back to the U.S. after the end of the European War, proceeded to the Pa- cific (Pearl Harbor).

Awarded the World War II, American Campaign, European African Middle Eastern Campaign and Asiatic-Pacific Campaign Medals.

Served in the U.S. Navy during the Korean War.

Married Lucille Dubinsky Sept. 12, 1954. Completed college, Johns Hopkins University in 1971 with a BSE. Has worked for Westinghouse for 39 years in the space department. Presently working as a senior engineer.

Raised two daughters and one son and has three grandchildren.

ALBERT E. MONAHAN, GM2/c, enlisted in the U.S. Navy in February 1943. Went to boot camp for eight weeks in Bainbridge, MD. Also attended Gunnery School there for six weeks. Went aboard the USS *Pope* (DE-134) in June 1943. Was discharged in November 1945 from Lido Beach, NY.

Brothers Serving Together

A million to one shot brought Al and Monahan together. Albert went aboard the USS *Pope* (DE-134) in June 1943. Bill joined the Navy the same month and year after attending Diesel Training School, was the one man out of a graduating class of 200, that was assigned to the USS *Pope* (DE-134). They served together for two years with only a few sailors knowing that they were brothers. Al was transferred off the ship to Advanced Gunnery School after the Red Cross notified the ship's captain that their father had passed away. The ship was tied up in New Foundland at the time and the airport was closed due to a storm. The brothers could not make it home for the funeral.

Al went aboard the USS *Pope* (DE-134) and took part in the ships shakedown to Bermuda. Then went on to convoy duty after one trip to Africa. Bill joined him on the *Pope* after two more trips of convoy duty.

Their ship was assigned to submarine hunting. The *Pope* was very successful, taking part in two sub sinkings and the capture of the first German submarine, the U505 off the West Coast of Africa, in June 1944. The U515 was sunk on Easter Sunday, April 9, 1944. One April 24, 1945, their sister ship, the USS *Davis* (DE-136) was torpedoed and sunk by the German Sub U546. The *Pope* took part in the chase and the sinking of the U546 eleven hours later. One of the last operations of the *Pope* was escorting to Cape May, NJ, the first German submarine U858 to surrender in the North Atlantic after VE Day.

The USS *Pope* (DE-134) and all personnel that served aboard during the capture of the U505 were awarded the Presidential Unit Citation.

After the war the brothers crossed paths again. Bill joined Al as a member of the East Orange Fire Department. They both served 34 years and retired as captains.

WILLIAM C. MONAHAN, MOMM2/c, enlisted in the U.S. Navy in June 1943. Went to boot camp for eight weeks in Newport, RI, then to Diesel Training School at Richmond, VA.

William C. Monahan   *Albert E. Monahan*

Went aboard the USS *Pope* (DE-134) October 1943 at its home port in New York. Was discharged in February 1946 at lido Beach, NY.

Al and Bill Monahan

MONTY E. MONTAGNE, SOM1/c, USS *Chambers* (DE-391), was born in Sioux City, IA on Feb. 26, 1923. Joined the U.S. Coast Guard on July 28, 1942 at Omaha, NE. Discharged Sept. 13, 1945 in San Pedro, CA.

Served aboard the U.S. Coast Guard Cutter *Haida*

from Oct. 19, 1942 until March 16, 1945, in the Aleutian Islands and the North Pacific. Transferred to the USS *Chambers* (DE-391) and served aboard from May 5, 1945 to Sept. 9, 1945.

Their Flotilla of six Coast Guard DEs included the USS *Vance* (DE-387), USS *Lansing* (DE-388), USS *Durant* (DE-389), USS *Calcaterra* (DE-390), USS *Chambers* (DE-391) and the USS *Merrill* (DE-392). Made one convoy run to Oran, North Africa, then returned to the States and outfitted in New York with increased AA ordnances, proceeded to Guantanamo Bay, Cuba, shakedown AA and Anti-Submarine Training. More of the same at San Diego and then to Pearl Harbor.

They planned an ETD from Pearl Harbor for Eniwetok, but because of VJ Day the tour was cancelled.

He recalls one experience when the USS *Caboom* (the name of the ship has been changed to protect the innocent) had a possible sonar contact in the North Pacific and made several depth charge runs on same. They relieved this ship on station the next day and observed more dead fish in one mile square then the Fulton Fish Market had processed in 20 years. He states that rumor was that it was a Navy ship, but that he's not one to spread rumors.

He received the American Theatre of Operations, European Theatre of Operation, Asiatic Pacific Theatre of Operation, Good Conduct Medal and World War II Ribbons.

He has been married for over 47 years, though he says it only seems like 80. He was a Work Unit Conservationist (USDA) with the Soil Conservation Service for five years after receiving a B.S. degree in Wildlife Management, from South Dakota State College. He then spent 20 years as a Wildlife Management Biologist with the Forest Service (USDA) on three National Forests in the California Region.

He retired from federal service in 1978. His three children (two boys and one girl) and his two granddaughters, Sarah and Sunshine are receiving the benefit of his wisdom and experience but seem to be on another wavelength and are not receiving most of his transmissions.

JOSEPH SCOTT MOORE, GM 2/c, USS *Burrows* (DE-105), was born Aug. 20, 1926 in Clarence, NY. Lived in Rochester, NY from age three. Enlisted in September 1943. Sampson Naval Training Station at Norfolk, VA, Philadelphia, PA and then on to the USS *Burrows* (DE-105) for commissioning. He stayed with the 105 for eight convoys across the Atlantic one of which, went to Bizerte, Tunisia, then on to the Pacific until wars end.

After discharge in May 1946, returned to Roches-

ter, then joined the Active Reserve. Called back in September 1950. Went aboard the USS *Diphda* (AKA-59) at Port Chicago, CA with five holds of ammo, left for Japan where they shuttled ammo back and forth to Korea, bases, ships at sea etc.

Returned to the States and went back to Rochester and then returned to California with wife and son whom he got to see for the first time. Discharged in March 1952, stayed in California until 1954 and moved to Nevada, had three more children. He is now retired and living in Sparks, NV. Member of DAV and VFW Post 10053, Verde, NV.

WILLIAM J. MORGAN, enlisted in the Navy in 1943, reporting to Great Lakes Naval Training Station in January 1944. Upon completion of boot camp and a short tour of duty at NATTC, Memphis, TN, he was assigned to USS *Holt* (DE-706) and remained aboard throughout the succeeding 20 months in both the Atlantic and combat duty with the Seventh Fleet in the Philippines, Borneo and Okinawa campaigns. He was discharged in January 1946 and re-enlisted in the Naval Reserve as a QM2/c. Recalled to active duty at the outbreak of the Korean War, he served on board USS *LSM* (R) 257 and USS *LSM* (R) 404, the latter in offensive operations off both coasts of Korea. He retired from the Naval Reserve in 1965 as a lieutenant.

In civilian life, Morgan was active in many transportation organizations, having served as national president of the Private Truck Council of America. He retired as vice-president of transportation from Frito-Lay, Inc. Married for over 43 years, he has two sons, David and Jeffrey, and two grandsons.

SIDNEY R. MORROW, was born Oct. 4, 1922 in Lawson, MO. He joined the U.S. Naval Reserve in September 1942. Attended Iowa State College, Northwestern University, Asbery Park and later on the USS *O'Flaherty* (DE-340). At the time of his discharge he had attained the rank of lieutenant (jg).

He remembers the screening operation, typhoons, limping back to Guam with only one rudder, and the all out kamakazi attack on Kerama Retto area during the Okinawa invasion. He received awards for the Battles of Luzon, Saipan, and Okinawa.

He married Shirley Rasmussen, they have two children, Thomas Reid Morrow and Lindsay Ann Pastirik. He is now retired and resides in Bedford, VA.

EDWIN J. MOSCINSKI, GM3/c, USS *Baron* (DE-166), entered Naval Reserve on April 13, 1943. Upon completion of boot camp at Great Lakes Naval Station, he advanced to Gunners Mate School.

In October 1943 he left the United States aboard

the USS *Rochambeau*. On Dec. 19, 1943 he boarded the USS *Baron* at sea, just off the coast of Guadalcanal. He assisted in the invasion of the Marshall Islands, Saipan, Tinian and Guam.

In was by the toss of a coin that he parted from the USS *Baron* on May 14, 1945, to return to the U.S. He then entered the Electro-Hydraulic School in San Diego, CA. One Nov. 30, 1945 he left the Navy with an honorable discharge.

The medals he earned include: The American Theatre of War, Asiatic-Pacific Theatre of War with two Battle Stars and the World War II Victory Medal.

He retired from Preway Inc., located in Wisconsin Rapids, WI after 33 years. He is an active member in the Greater Polonia Past 185, Polish Legion of American Veterans, and is presently adjutant for the post.

He and his wonderful wife, Genevieve, recently celebrated their 40th wedding anniversary. They have four beautiful children and eight grandchildren. Their home is located in Stevens Point, WI where he met his wife and raised his family.

ELIOT S. MOVER, was born April 18, 1923 in Newark, NJ. Inducted into service July 1, 1943. Service in the Atlantic, South Pacific and Okinawa with the Navy Reserves, Destroyer Escort, USS *Charles S. Kimmel* (DE-584), 7th Fleet. Discharged from the Reserves in February 1950 with the rank of lieutenant (jg).

He remembers the explosion of the USS *Mt. Hood* in 1945, the invasion of Lingayen Gulf, the typhoon in the South Pacific in 1945, kamikaze attacks, and the rescue of 22 aviators from desert island. There was only one casualty from *Kimmel* during the war, when one of their shipmates drowned in the Panama Canal.

He received the awards for the Atlantic Theatre, Pacific Theatre (two stars), Victory Medal and Philippine Liberation.

Married in 1946 to Helen Raphael with two children, Heidi (1950), Richard (1954). Lived in Newton, MA almost all of his life and was president of Bunny Bear, Inc. for 27 years. Also served as president of National Trade Association and auxiliary police captain. Now semi-retired and member of Ancient and Honorable Artillery Company of Massachusetts (militia group).

MARSHALL E. MULLINGS, was born in Washington, DC in 1918. He served in the USCG from 1938 until 1940 and had boot camp aboard the cutter *Chelan* and was stationed at the Coast Guard Academy when the hurricane of 1938 wreaked havoc on New London.

He re-enlisted in the Coast Guard in 1942 and served at the Coast Guard Academy and reported aboard the Cutter 83377, he then graduated from Motor Machinist Mate School and was assigned to New Smyrna Beach. He is a plank owner of the USS *Falgout* where he spent the next two years as oil king. His most memorable experiences were when his ship plucked four German fliers from the Mediterranean Sea, and when they were attacked by German bombers off of Gibraltar. He graduated from fire school at Ft. McHenry in Baltimore and remained there in charge of a small search and rescue boat until his release in the latter part of 1945.

He is married to Josephine Dawes and is the father of Mary, Georgia, Joyce, Wayne, Janis, Lawrence, and Harvey (deceased). After becoming a great-grandfather and having three major operations in six months he has now retired and is recuperating at home.

JAMES S. MUNROE, was born Jan. 9, 1917 in Cambridge, MA. Joined the USNR in June 1938 and commissioned ensign at that time. Entered active duty in July 1941 and served as line officer in the Reserves. At the time of discharge he had achieved the rank of lieutenant commander.

Married Nancy Baldwin July 11, 1941, they had one son. He is now retired and lives in San Marino, CA.

JOE E. MYATT, MM3/c, attended boot training in Camp Peary, VA in Old Williamsburg. To Norfolk No. B, then on to Boston for commissioning of USS *Lewis* (DE-535) Sept. 5, 1944. He then went to Bermuda for shakedown. Escorted "Big MO" to Pacific via Panama Canal chipped concrete on both sides. Remembers the invasion of Okinawa and Iwo Jima and the Luzon operation.

Received the Pacific Theatre Ribbon with three Bronze Stars, American Theatre, Good Conduct Medal, Victory Medal, and Philippine Liberation.

He recalls several frightening times with the war and big typhoon named "Vieper". Returned to California after the war, mothballed the *Lewis* and transferred to USS *Silverstein* (DE-534), then to Millington, TN near Memphis for discharge.

Married to Frances Edwards, they had one son Larry Joe Myatt. Went into the farm tractor business for 32 years, later liquor store for seven years. Life member of VFW Post 4862, American Legion is a Kentucky Colonel commissioned in 1970 by Governor Louie B. Nunn. He retired in 1981.

ROBERT NAPIERALA, MoMM1/c, USS *Lake* (DE-310) was born in Toledo OH Feb. 15, 1925. He joined the Navy in 1943. Attended boot camp and Basic Engineering School in Great Lakes, IL. Went to Mare Island and was assigned to USS *Lake* (DE-301) which they put in commission. He did duty in the Pacific to the end of the war, then went to Korea for a brief stay before returning to the States in November 1945, and decommissioned (DE-301). He was then assigned to LST 475 and later transferred to LST 560 which they took from San Francisco to Charleston, SC to decommission. Was discharged from Great Lakes in 1946 and returned to Toledo.

He married Kathleen Linenkugel in 1949. They have two daughters and five grandchildren. He attended the University of Toledo. He worked at Baker Brothers as a proposal engineer, then went to work for Jeep and retired in 1987 as a process engineer.

ANTHONY R. NATALE, was born April 14, 1925 in Philadelphia, PA. Joined the U.S. Navy Aug. 9, 1943. Boot camp at Bainbridge, MD, further training at Norfolk, VA DE School. Then to Mare Island to board the USS *Bowers* (DE-637) which was being commissioned. From there they had shakedown cruise then on to South Pacific. Stopped at Pearl Harbor and went to sea from there. He was injured April 16, 1945 while in service aboard destroyer escort off Okinawa, when ship was hit by a Japanese suicide plane. He was treated at several Navy hospitals for his injuries including the U.S. Navy Hospital in Pearl Harbor, Oakland, CA, and Bainbridge, MD. He was hospitalized from time he was

injured until he was discharged. Achieved the rank of sergeant first class at the time of his discharge. He received the Purple Heart for the wounds he received as a result of enemy action in the Asiatic-Pacific area.

He married June 1956. They had one son, one daughter, and four grandchildren. He is now retired.

ALBERT F. NELSON, entered Naval service in 1943. Boot training in "Dago" FC School, Destroyer Base, "Dago", DE training in Norfolk, assigned to USS *Slater* (DE-766) in Tampa, FL, commissioned the same, "plank owner" shakedown to Bermuda, made five convoy trips to Europe. Went to Liverpool twice; Glascow, Scotland; Cardiff, Wales twice. Stationed in Pacific, Philippines, occupation force in Japan. He returned to the States in Green Cove Springs, FL. Decommissioned to mothball fleet, reentered service, posted to USS *Purdy* (DD-734). Made several trips to Mediterranean, also a Northern European Patrol, then to New Orleans for duty as a Reserve Training ship.

Discharged in 1951 and married Charlotte Brunes in 1953. They have five children. Worked in first commercial taconite plant as an electrician. Retired from IBEW trade.

He enjoys fishing, hunting, and his five grandchildren. Earned European African Middle Eastern, Asiatic-Pacific, World War II Victory Medals and National Defense Ribbon.

JESSE ELMO NELSON, F1/c, USS *Edmonds* (DE-406), enlisted into active service March 28, 1944. Place of entry into active service was Livingston, TN. Stationed at Williamsburg, VA for boot camp. He served aboard the USS *Edmonds* (DE-406) for one year, eight months and 16 days. He boarded the ship at Boston, MA. Entered Norfolk, VA Naval Base, then went to New Hebrides Islands, on to New Guinea. In and out of Eniwetok Navy Base several times. Escorted Gen. Douglas MacArthur back to Leyte Island, then on to Manila. They were in a big battle off Leyte, where a lot of the Japanese fleet were sunk. From there they

went to Iwo Jima. Their next mission was in Okinawa, where they spent 81 of the 82 days. He was discharged Dec. 13, 1945 in Nashville, TN.

He received the American Theatre Medal, Asiatic-Pacific Medal with one star, Philippine Liberation Medal with two stars, and Victory Medal. The *Edmonds* received five Battle Stars for WWII service, and never lost a man.

The most interesting things that he recalls are being in Pearl Harbor and seeing President Roosevelt, being in Leyte Gulf and seeing their P-38s and Jap zeros in dog fights. He remembers escorting Gen. MacArthur back to the Philippines and picking up 378 survivors from the Bismark Sea at Iwo Jima.

He married Claudean Eckel Nelson. They have one son Jesse Carlos Nelson, one grandson, Darryl Nelson, one granddaughter Amy Nelson Webb and one great-granddaughter Autumn Webb. They celebrated their 50th wedding anniversary Oct. 20, 1991. He retired from the U.S. Army Corp of Engineers in 1976, and live in Rickman, TN.

JOSEPH B. NELSON, JR., MoMM1/c, USS *Richey* (DE-385), enlisted in the Coast Guard Feb. 18, 1943. He was born Feb. 25, 1925 in Worcester, NY. Boot camp at Manhattan Beach, NY and Motor Machinists Mate School at Brooklyn, NY and Wolf Creek, IL.

Assignments included: 9th ND St. Louis, COTP Cincinnati, CGRB Huntington, and USS *Richey*. North Atlantic convoy duty until Germany surrendered, then *Richey* was sent to the North Pacific operating from the Aleutians. Participated in the Japanese surrender and occupation and duty in the China Theatre.

Married Angelina Hren, Dec. 29, 1946. They had two daughters, Geraldine and JoAnn and a son, Joseph III. Had 45 years service with family automobile business. Member and past commander Worcester American Post 1584 and member VFW Post 2752 in Schenevus, NY.

RICHARD A. NOLBERT, was born June 13, 1947 in Elizabeth, NJ. Joined the U.S. Navy Aug. 19, 1965. Boot camp at Great Lakes, IL. NAS at Key West and Mayport, FL. Attended Sonar School in Key West, FL. Later on to the USS *Perry* (DD-844). He had achieved the rank of sergeant third class at the time of his discharge.

He recalls the North Atlantic Cruise and Westpac Cruise including Vietnam and Korea. Awards include the Armed Forces Expeditionary, National Defense, Vietnam Expeditionary.

He married his wife Chris October 1969 in St. Louis, MO. They have two daughters, Dawn (19 yrs.) and Tanya (16 yrs.). He has worked as an industrial engineer for United Parcel Service since September 1969.

ALBERT J. NOORT, SM 1/C, USS *Doherty* (DE-14), enlisted in the Navy February 1943. Attended boot camp at Great Lakes, IL. Assigned to Shore Patrol April 1943, Great Lakes Treasure Island July 1943. Assigned to USS *Doherty* (DE-14) September 1943. Aleutian Islands November 1944 as School Shop for U.S. submarines. January 1945 convoy duty in South Pacific, Eniwetok, Truk Island, Guam, Saipan, and Okinawa. He had many memorable experiences. Most rewarding when they rescued 10 men from B29 crew about 150 miles northwest of Saipan on May 13, 1945. He was discharged February 1946.

He worked 33 years driving redi-mix concrete truck for Ozinga Brothers. Retired in 1988. Lives in Lansing, IL with wife Betty, four daughters, four sons and 15 grandchildren.

WILLIAM JOSEPH O'DONNELL, QM3/c, USS *YP307*, USS *Barr* (DE-576) (ADD-39), enlisted at San Francisco in the USNR as sergeant second class (no boot camp) at age 17 on Jan. 22, 1942. Shipped on *YP307* for Panama sea duty March 5, 1942, received inoculations and complete uniforms. Early 1944 he was rotated out to Lido Beach, NY, thence assigned to USS *Barr* (DE-576) then being converted to (APD-39) at the South Boston Navy Yard. Just prior, Barr had been torpedoed by the German submarine U-549. As an APD *Barr* worked with UDT-13. Participated fully in the Iowa Jima and Okinawa actions unscathed on Sept. 19, 1945 departed the *Barr* in Japan on emergency leave. Was subsequently discharged at Treasure Island, CA on Nov. 5, 1945.

He resumed his education at which place he met and married Ossie Rhodes. Raised four children and now have three grandchildren. Retired as an administration advisor staff for Pacific Bell after 36 years. They have nine grandchildren and one great-grandchild. Life member DESA and Golden Chapter of DESA.

TED O'GORMAN, Capt., was born on July 13, 1908 in Philadelphia, PA. In WWII he was executive officer on the USS *Fechteler* (DE-157), which was engaged in escort for ships en route to the war zone. Returning from one escort trip, the *Fechteler* was struck by a torpedos apparently aimed at the troop ships. He was delighted to observe from the bridge that the well trained crew manned their stations at the motor boat and the rigs to release the floating rafts. He then proceeded to the DE *Lanning*, which was waiting for them.

Effective Aug. 1, 1968, he was transferred to the Navy Reserve retired list as a captain with over 26 years of service with a total of 2492 points on which to compute retirement pay. Captain O'Gorman is married to Mary Elizabeth Cronin. Their daughter, Molly, has presented them with two grandchildren.

Today he is enjoying the life of a retiree, supported by Nynex and Navy pensions, and conducting programs he designed for New York City Probation and Family Court Agencies.

WALTER V. O'GRADY, SR., was born April 4, 1918 in Malden, MA. He entered the Naval service from Newark, NY on June 28, 1943 and, after a six month assignment to a repair facility in Argentia, Newfoundland, served aboard the USS *Ulvert M. Moore* (DE-442) as a fireman first class.

The USS *Moore*, under the command of Franklin D. Roosevelt, Jr., departed Pearl Harbor on Oct. 31, 1944 to join a hunter-killer group which included the USS *O'Flaharty*, USS *Stafford*, USS *Sieverling*, and a small carrier, the USS *Corregidor*. On November 24 the *Moore*, *Stafford*, and *Sieverling*, accompanied the hunter-killer group of the DEs *Goss*, and *Campbell* and the small carrier USS *Tulagi*. This group was involved in the battles of Luzon, Iwo Jima, and Okinawa. The ship was credited with the sinking of a Japanese submarine on Feb. 1, 1945. The USS *Moore* was later assigned to occupation duties in Tokyo Bay.

Walt was discharged on Dec. 5, 1945. He married Lucy E. Nanstiel on June 18, 1944 and has four children. In civilian life, he operated as a heating contractor. Walter and his wife now live in a retirement community in New Jersey.

ROBERT A. OHNEMUS, was born Sept. 18, 1916 in Geddes, SD. Enlisted in the Navy at Sioux Falls, SD, he was sworn in at Omaha, NE Sept. 20, 1939. Received recruit training at USNTS Great Lakes, IL, was in Co. 28. Served aboard the USS *Grebe*; USS *Pasig*; SCTC Miami, FL; R/S Brooklyn, NY; and USS *McCoy Reynolds*. He was chief machinist for the last two years of regular service. Naval service East and

West Coast of U.S. from Hawaii to New Caledonia, from Palau to Okinawa.

He was discharge from regular Navy in October 1945. Joined the Naval Reserve in 1946 and spent over 20 years in Reserves before retiring. Came to Pullman, WA and started working for a Chevrolet dealer and worked for 30 years as body shop manager before retiring.

Medals include the American Defense, American Theatre, and Asiatic Pacific with five Bronze Stars.

He is a member of Pearl Harbor Survivors Lilac City Chapter #1, Spokane, WA.

DONALD F. OLSEN, QM2/c, USS *Carroll* (DE-171), joined the Navy at an early age. Went to boot camp at Bainbridge, MD. Was sent to QM School at Newport, RI. Sent to join USS *Carroll* at Norfolk, VA after school at Newport. Ship was brand new and christened her and put to sea for a shakedown at Bermuda. They had to return to Brooklyn Navy Yard as they hit a reef and lost their sonar. They joined their first convoy and escorted it to North Africa. They made many trips across the Atlantic and helped in attacks on subs trying to strike at the convoys. Most subs were in wolfpacks. They helped in the sinking of the submarine five miles off Block Island, RI.

He still remembers the night that their chief cook found a horse and brought it up the gangway to the quarter deck. He states that they had one hell of a job getting it turned around and off the ship. Overnight the horse was tied to the life lines on the deck. When the tide went out, they almost pulled him into the drink.

In March of 1946 Don returned home, joined an insurance firm, got into politics, became mayor of his hometown and then was elected surrogate judge of the county. He now lives with his wife, Ellie, in Perth Amboy, NJ. They are the parents of three children, Kathy, Don Jr., Peter, and they also have two grandchildren.

GERARD OLSEN, (GERRY), FC2/c, was born Dec. 13, 1919 in Brooklyn, NY. He was inducted onto the Navy April 12, 1944. He attended Recruit Training School at Sampson, NY for five weeks, and Fire Control School in Newport, RI for 15 weeks. Served on the USS *Jos. E. Campbell* (DE-70) in Atlantic convoy, and (APD-49) in the Pacific Theatre, Okinawa and the Philippines. Served as fire controlman second class.

He remembers the days and nights at Okinawa, preinvasion, UDT at night and picket duty after invasion and shooting down Japanese kamikaze planes.

He received the American Theatre, Asiatic-Pacific Theatre with one star, Philippine Liberation Theatre, and Victory Medal.

He married Irene Schwartz Sept. 22, 1946, they raised two sons Gary and Glenn and one daughter Sharon Sandra. All three children are engineers in defense and married. Retired from Sperry in 1984, after 46 years of service as a production engineering supervisor. Now active in the American Legion Mineola Memorial Post 349. Enjoys carving carousel horses and spending time with his two grandchildren Diana and Susan. Member of DESA.

JAMES SOLLERS ONETO,

QM3/c, USS *Biven* (DE-536), entered the Navy in December 1943. After completion of boot camp at Sampson, NY, he was sent to QM School in Newport, RI, finishing training in Gulfport, MS, where school was relocated. Assigned to DEs upon completion of course. Further training at Norfolk, VA, before being sent to Boston, MA, to the *Biven*. Shakedown in Bermuda, then through the canal to the Southwest Pacific via Galapagos, Bora Bora and Manus. Various escort, patrol and picket duties ranging from New Guinea and the Philippines to Okinawa and China.

After separation finished college and then law school. Six years in private practice with law firms specializing in Admiralty Law. Then appointed to the Federal Maritime Commission, Washington, DC, serving first in the office of the General Council, then in the trial division, and presently in the office of Administrative Law Judges.

Married and has no children. Currently working on a photographic study (outboard, inboard and interior views) of the John C. Butler Class Destroyer Escorts for possible publication as a memorial to the epic defense of the Escort Carriers off Samar.

HARRY E. PAHEL,

was born Jan. 15, 1916 in Pitcairn, PA. Joined the Navy on Feb. 16, 1944 at Los Angeles, CA and was sent to Farragut, ID for basic training in Co. 441-44, Bn. 2.

Achieved the rank of MoMM3/c and assigned to the USS *Lyman* (DE-302) at Manus Island in November of 1944. This ships crew earned ribbons for World War II Victory, Asiatic-Pacific with four Bronze Stars, Philippine Liberation with one Bronze Star plus were the first DE to enter Tokyo Bay and remain there until the peace treaty was signed aboard the USS *Missouri*.

Discharged on Dec. 16, 1945 at San Pedro, CA and returned home to wife and two daughters. Joined by a third daughter the following year. They have five grandchildren and two great-grandchildren.

Most of his working years were spent as a machine shop foreman and second operation supervisor for engineering firms dealing in automatic screw machine products. Retired and moved 60 miles from their home town of South Gate, CA to Canyon Lake. Involved with the local Volunteer Fire Department and Emergency Preparedness Program. Teaches CPR and First Aid for the American Red Cross. Travels with their Recreational Vehicle Club once a month and take short jaunts with their travel trailer in tow.

Joined DESA in 1990, attended the Las Vegas Convention in 1991 and they are planning to attend the Buffalo Convention in 1992. They coordinate former crew members news in a periodic newsletter and are in the process of locating other shipmates.

AUBREY L. PAINTER,

was born July 7, 1923 at Clifton Forge, VA. He was sworn into the Navy in 1943 after graduating from high school in June of the same year. After boot camp at Great Lakes, IL. He was sent to Cleveland, OH where he was made SK3/c and was sent to Norfolk, VA. While at Norfolk, VA, he was assigned to the DE training program and the USS *Finch* which was being constructed at Orange, TX at the time. He was sent to Orange, TX and the *Finch* was commissioned on Dec. 13, 1943. They went to Bermuda for their shakedown cruise. They made a convoy trip from New York to Algiers, North Africa and made convoy from Boston, MA to Plymouth, England. They made several more convoys from Curacao to various ports of North Africa. Convoys were made to Naples, Italy, Cardiff, Wales and Liverpool, England.

He was transferred from the *Finch* to Little Creek, VA on Feb. 19, 1945. Sent to Pier 92 New York form Little Creek and assigned to the SS *Cape Mohican* and sailed from New Jersey through the Panama Canal to Honolulu, HI and back to San Francisco, CA. Later to T.I. in Oakland, CA and assigned to the SS *Contest* a refrigerator ship and sailed to Seattle, WA and loaded with cargo which we supplied various ships, and various posts in the Pacific. Also sailed to Auckland, New Zealand and received a cargo. Their cargo contained potatoes, apples, various meats, celery and etc.

Because he was a storekeeper he was frozen after the end of the war. He came back to T.I. in Oakland and was sent by troop train to Camp Perry, VA and discharged from the Navy March 25, 1946. He enrolled in Lincoln Memorial University at Harrogate, TN Sept. 10, 1946. He married Kathleen Hipes Dec. 24, 1946. Graduated from LMU in June 1950 with BA degree. They have three children and three grandchildren.

He taught school for 38 years of which 34 years was teaching deaf students at Virginia School for Deaf and Blind in Staunton, VA. He retired from teaching July 1, 1988, but still enjoys sub-teaching with deaf students.

NICHOLAS DOMINIC PALERMO,

RM2/c, USS *O'Brien* (DE-421), was born in New Haven, CT, Feb. 6, 1932. Enlisted in Navy May 26, 1951. Boot camp and Shallow Water Diving, Damage Control, Radsafe and Radioman School at Newport, RI. Gunnery and Firefighting School Norfolk, VA. Service minesweeper Div. II, USS *Magpie*, sunk offshore battery Korea, Naval Hospital Key West, FL, Naval Hospital Newport, RI. TAD on USS *Sarsfield* (DDR-837). USS *O'Brien* (DE-421) assigned to convoy duty and task groups and ASW assignments all over Atlantic, on operation Springboard through Intex, Caribbean Sea, Midshipmen cruise with fleet to Northern Europe, Denmark, Norway and France. Assigned WWII occupation forces in Europe. Discharged May 1955.

Married Anniette Alberino June 4, 1955 and has two sons, one grandson. Attended college under the GI Bill, formerly employed with Olin Corp. Last position plant engineer, presently employed State of Connecticut as OSHA safety consultant. Active in American Legion Post 83 in Branford. Also belongs to Tin Can Sailors. Now living in North Branford, CT.

ALBERT E. PAPPANO,

was born Feb. 20, 1922 in Akron, OH. Completed 12 years of his education and graduated from East High School January 1940. Enlisted in the U.S. Navy May 23, 1940. Boot camp in Newport, RI.

His first ship was the USS *Tillman* (DD-135). They recommissioned the old four stack destroyer which was laying in the back bay in Philadelphia Navy Yard. His next ship was the USS *Wyoming* battleship; then was transferred to the battleship, USS *Arkansas*. A two year tour of shore duty at the Naval Training Station at Newport, RI. He went to Syracuse, NY for Turbo Electric School of Ship Propulsion for six weeks. He was sent to Miami, FL for destroyer escort training and then to the West Coast to be assigned to the nucleus crew of the USS *Bowers* (DE-637) a destroyer escort for the rest of his tour of duty spent in the pacific Theatre.

While aboard the USS *Bowers* (DE-637), they were in the invasion of Okinawa and on April 16, 1945 they were hit by a Japanese suicide plane. He was at his battle station, chief in charge of Main Engine Room. There was a tremendous explosion top side, which rocked the ship and knocked out the main breaders to port side motor. Consequently, they were making flank speed on their starboard screw, creating quite a hazard for the rest of the ships in the area. They were going around in circles, uncontrolled with nobody steering the ship. The task force commander was going to torpedo them and sink them to get rid of the threat to the rest of the ships, when someone yelled down the hatch in the engine room to stop all engines.

The explosion topside was the Japanese plane hitting their ships superstructure and dislodging a 500 pound anti-personnel bomb which he carried on the belly of his plane. The bomb went through one of the portholes in the wheelhouse through the port light lock through the 24" search light and then exploded about 20 feet off their port side spewing shrapnel fore and aft the ships deck. The gas tank on the plane exploded, causing fire to the whole superstructure. When the heroic effort of putting the fire out and the smoke and confusion cleared, they had lost half of their crew, dead, wounded or missing. The dead lay where they were killed overnight. The men that were assigned to take the dead off the ships that were hit, were so busy they had to keep their dead where they lay for about 24 hours.

The senior officer alive was Lt. T.A. Hinkle, their first lieutenant gathered the crew and told them they would positively identify the dead and move them to the quarter deck. The crew responded gallantly, although the task was a gruesome one. When the dead were all gathered, the burial party came along side to take them to the beach for burial.

They then pulled into Kerama Retta Atoll to await battle damage assessment and obtain some emergency navigating equipment. Lt. Meager, their gunnery officer was designated to carry the battle damage report and photographs back to Philadelphia Navy Yard.

They then steamed for Pearl Harbor with a very limited crew and navigating gear. Men were standing watch, four hours on and four hours off. They stayed in Pearl Harbor for two days to give port and starboard liberty. They still hadn't taken anyone aboard for duty as yet. They were still operating with a skeleton crew. They left Pearl Harbor and steamed for the West Coast arriving in San Diego, CA for their first stateside liberty and pick up an additional personnel for their trip through the Panama Canal and to the Philadelphia Navy Yard for repairs.

They were ultimately converted to an APD (Attack Personnel Destroyer) and went to sea for a shakedown cruise to Guantanamo Bay, Cuba and consequently put her out of commission in Green Cove Springs, FL.

He was discharged May 23, 1946 and went home to Akron, OH. He was married to Anne Palazzo on Oct. 19, 1946. They now have five children, three daughters and two sons and 12 grandchildren.

His civilian life comprised of being in the maintenance department as a pipefitter at Goodyear Aerospace and General Tire and Rubber Co., and spent the last four years as a maintenance foreman before his retirement in December 1980.

JEWEL K. PARKER, RDM3/c, USS *Poole* (DE-151), inducted into the United States Coast Guard on July 26, 1942. Reported for boot training at Curtis Bay, MD, USCG Training Station. After boot training he was assigned to USCG Life Boat Station near Portland, ME from Sept. 2, 1942 to April 5, 1943. Next assigned to Mounted Beach Patrol training on Hilton Head Island off the coast of South Carolina from April 7, 1943 to May 18, 1943. From there assigned to Warsaw Island, 30 miles southeast of Savannah, GA for patrol duty and radio operation, May 18, 1943 to March 30, 1944.

He next attended Radar School at Virginia Beach, VA from April 1, 1944 to April 22, 1944. Further training at the Naval Operation Base, Norfolk, VA; and on Feb. 20, 1945 was assigned to board the USS *Poole* (DE-151) as radar operator. The *Poole* was moored at the 33rd Street Pier, Brooklyn; and was designated as the flagship of Escort Div. 22. It made several missions from New York to England. He was aboard on trips to Liverpool, LeHavre, France and Southampton.

After hostilities had ceased in the Atlantic the Escort Div. 22 was one of the divisions picked for the hot spot of the war in the Pacific. On June 4, 1945 Escort Div. 22 left New York for Culebra Island in the West Indies to conduct shore bombardment training, then on to Guantanamo Bay, Cuba for nine more days training. Finally, on June 20, they set sail for the Panama Canal. Arrived there on the 22nd and traversed the canal on the 23rd, heading for San Diego. On July

1st, the division tied up at the Old Destroyer Barr in San Diego.

The *Poole* left the West Coast the evening of July 8 and laid track for Pearl Harbor. Berth Dog Eight Middle Loch, Pearl Harbor became the familiar spot for the *Poole*. The sudden ending of the war with Japan necessitated a change of plans for ships enroute to the combat zones. On September 4, the *Poole* left Pearl for occupational duty in Japan. After a month of patrol duty off Wakayama, Japan, he had enough points for discharge, Nov. 9, 1945.

From January 1946 until August 1981, he was in the electrical distribution business. For 25 of these years he was a district manager for the San Marcos district of the Lower Colorado River Authority in San Marcos, TX.

He is now retired and living in Bells, TX with his wife Earline.

GARLAND PARKS PARLIER, SF2/c, USS *Breeman* (DE-104), was born May 30, 1925 in Chase City, VA. Joined the service Aug. 2, 1943. He served in the Navy on the USS *Breeman* (DE-104) in the Atlantic and Mediterranean. He had achieved the rank of SF second class at the time of his discharge Dec. 12, 1945.

Married Marie Weaver and they have one son Lyn Parlier, daughter-in-law Lynn, grandson Chris (12) and granddaughter Sarah (5). He is a retired pipefitter and resides in Orlando, FL.

CHARLES R. PASTOR, IC3, USS *Otterstetter* DER 244, enlisted in the Organized Naval Reserves soon after graduating from Northeast High School in Philadelphia, PA January 1947. He attended weekly drills at the Philadelphia Naval Base in Submarine Repair Division 4-61 and took four 2 week training periods aboard the submarine tender USS *Howard W. Gilmore*, AS 16 in Key West, FL.

He extended his original four year enlistment two more years when the Korean Conflict broke out, in hopes of seeing service in the Pacific. Instead, he was sent down to Charleston Naval Base, SC and reported on-board a soon to be recommissioned "DER", this being the USS *Otterstetter* DER 244, a Radar Picket Type Escort Vessel.

On June 1, 1951 Charleston, SC Naval Shipyard commenced the dual procedure of reactivating USS *Otterstetter* and converting the ship from a DE to a DER, reclassified DER 244 in December 1951, *Otterstetter* was recommissioned at Charleston Naval Shipyard on June 6, 1952 and Lt. Commander John P. Sullivan assumed command.

After a shakedown cruise to Guantanamo Bay, Cuba they reported on Dec. 4, 1952 to Commander Destroyer Force, US Atlantic Fleet, as a unit of Escort Squadron 16, better known as "Com. Cort Ron 16" based at Newport, RI their home port. Their mission on Picket Duty was for continuous radar coverage of the Atlantic Coast, searching for and reporting aircraft in their sectors of responsibility. They shared these duties with 6 other DERs as well.

This North Atlantic duty was spent in all kind of weather conditions including the Hurricane of 1953, rough seas were not new to the Otterstetter and Crew as she rode out many a storm including the famous "Okinawa Typhoon" in 1945 as DE 244. They made two Springboard Operations in 1953 and 1954 in Car-

ibbean Waters on fleet exercises with Carriers, Subs, other DEs and DERs and the Cruiser *Albany*. They made ports of call in San Juan, St. Thomas, Martinique, St. John and St. Croix.

He made 3rd Class IC electrician after their first Caribbean Cruise, and passed 2nd Class exam after the second trip south, but he was discharged from active duty before the rates came through.

He was hired by "The Bell Telephone Company of Pennsylvania" in 1954 and later married co-worker Patricia Francis in 1956. They had two daughters, three sons and now have seven grandchildren all living in the Philadelphia area.

He is presently retired from Bell as of Dec. 15, 1989, after 35-1/2 years service at age 60-1/2.

He is active in the Keystone Philadelphia Chapter of DESA and member of the following naval groups: National DESA (Destroyer Escort Sailors Association), The US Navy League (Philadelphia Chapter), Tin Can Sailors and The Louisiana Naval War Memorial (DD 661). It would give him great pleasure to hear from any of his "Old Shipmates" from DER 244, June 1952 through April 1954, contact him through National Headquarters of DESA Orlando, FL.

LOUIS PAYNE, S1/c, USS *Brennan* (DE-13), was born Oct. 1, 1916 in Lofty, PA. He enlisted in the U.S. Navy April 21, 1944. Went to boot camp at Bainbridge, MD. Went to Submarine Training Center, Miami, FL and boarded the USS *Brennan* for patrol duty to protect ships from enemy subs prowling the waters around Cuba and Miami, FL.

A memorable experience for him was being 800 miles at sea in chilling, ice cold waters January 1944, when sonar picked up enemy sub. They fired their hedgehogs and depth charges. The fate of the sub was unknown.

He married Irene Fedorekin, they have one son Louis T. Payne and three grandsons. Worked 42 years for Dresser Industries, retiring in 1981. He lost his wife of 45 years on Dec. 27, 1989. Now residing in Milford, CT.

CHARLES H. PENNINGTON, was born May 12, 1923 in White Plains, NY. He enlisted in the USCG on July 3, 1942. Went to Manhattan Beach, Brooklyn, NY for boot training on July 23, 1942. Later on to Platoon Leaders School and became a platoon leader at Manhattan Beach Training Center.

Assignments: Coast Guard Station, Fort Hancock, NJ; Merchant Marine School of Navigation, NYC; Coast Guard Patrol Base, Staten Island, NY; Coast Guard Patrol Base (small boats-38496) Pier 9, East River, NY; USS *Sellstrom* (DE-255) North Atlantic convoy to England, thru Panama Canal, San Francisco, CA; Alaska; Aleutian Islands; Kuril Islands. He was discharged Nov. 20, 1945, he had achieved the rank of coxwain.

Married Veronica Verboys Dec. 12, 1944 in Stamford, CT. Raised two sons, Craig and Darryl. Retired from Burroughs Wellcome Co., after 36 years service as customer service manager. Member of DESA, residing in Greenville, NC.

MARTIN C. PFEFFER, was born Jan. 22, 1925 in Linderhurst, NY. Enlisted in the USNR July 1943. Attended United States Naval Training Station at Sampson, NY July 21, 1943. Fleet Sonar School at Key West, FL. Naval Air Base Quonset Point, RI. Assigned to the USS *Sylph* for further sonar training. Norfolk Virginia Naval Base he was assigned to the commissioning of the crew of the USS *Cockrill* (DE-398) commissioned Dec. 24, 1943.

Various assignments included convoys to Casablanca and Bizerte after a refit the *Cockrill* was assigned to the CVE USS *Bogue* Hunter Killer Group. On April 24 *Cockrill* participated in the attack on the U546, which was forced to surface and scuttled by its crew. A number of German prisoners were rescued and later transferred to the USS *Bogue*. After Germany surrendered he sailed through the Panama Canal to San Diego and on to Pearl Harbor. He was then transferred back to San Diego Sound School. The war ended and he was discharged from Lido Beach, NY Nov. 28, 1945.

He states that every day that he spent in the Navy was a memorable experience for him. The experience of riding on World War I Eagle boat built by Henry Ford. Tons of cement was poured into their hulls. They were so top heavy that when they made a turn, it seemed they were never going to right themselves. Another experience was becoming a plank owner of the USS *Cockrill* (DE-398) and associating with the officers and crew. They were the greatest. On the negative side, he was not aboard for the decommissioning.

He received the American Theatre Campaign Ribbon, World War II Victory Medal, European African Middle Eastern Campaign Ribbon, Plank Owner Certificate. He had achieved the rank of sonarman second class P.O. at the time of his discharge.

Married to Doris Green Pfeffer. They had two sons William married to Kathi with daughters Kerri, Dawn and Erin; and Wayne married to Alica with daughters Amanda and Gretchen.

Since leaving the Navy he has served as the president of D&M Glassware, Inc., worked for North Fork Auto Supply and Repair, Inc., and the New York Telephone Company for 36 years. He is now retired and he and his wife travel as much as possible. They never miss a ships reunion.

WALLACE H. PIERSON, JR., S1/c, USS *Breeman* (DE-104), enlisted in USNR in Birmingham, AL on his 17th birthday, Sept. 21, 1926. He served his boot camp at Pensacola, N.A.S., Florida, Co. 28. He was assigned to the Photo School and Squadron with a short trip to Pensacola Naval Hospital, July 6, 1944 to Pier 92 receiving station in New York, January 1945 with a week in Casco Bay, ME. He returned to New York and boarded the *Breeman* (DE-104), left for Norfolk, VA to escort the carrier USS *Card* back to New York. They refueled in Maine onto the North

Atlantic on sub patrol. On Feb. 23, 1945 at 1728 at Latitude 59 North, Longitude 24 West headed northeast the *Breeman* rolled 74 degrees in 40 to 60 feet waves with winds up to 75 mph hurricane intensity.

They arrived in Iceland with the ship and crew "shaken up" after some repairs they returned to New York for more repairs flying SAFU all of the way. After repairs they returned to sub-hunting in the Atlantic. War ending in Europe, they started running plane guard with baby carriers out of Rhode Island and Miami, FL. They hid behind Cuba in the fall of 1945 when hurricane hit Miami and the Miami NAS hard.

They returned to New York in December 1945 and returned to Green Cove Springs, FL in January 1946 to start decommissioning their ship. He was discharged on April 25, 1945 and the *Breeman* was decommissioned on April 26, 1946.

He returned to Birmingham, AL to school and construction. In April 1951 he joined the Birmingham Fire Department and in May 1956 they moved to Orlando, FL and went to work for the Sanford NAS as a firefighter. In late 1961 he returned to heavy construction and started in concrete pumping in 1964. In 1965 he went to work for Challenge Cook Brothers training and selling concrete pumps. He traveled half of the world, and in 1973 he started his own business and retired in 1991. He pumped the first concrete at Cape Kennedy in 1965 and also the first at Walt Disney World in 1969.

He has been married for 44 years to Joy Hopkins Pierson, they have three children, Sandra, Russell, Scott and four grandchildren.

VINCENT A. PIZZACAR, RDM2/c, enlisted June 9, 1943. Attended boot training at Sampson, NY. Radar School Cavalier Hotel, Virginia Beach. After schooling was assigned to USS *Spangler* (DE-696) Bay City, MI as part of the crew to ready her for commissioning. At New Orleans they loaded her with supplies, parts, etc., awaiting balance of crew and commissioned her Oct. 31, 1943. They had shakedown off Bermuda, then up to Boston for minor repairs and painting. They left Boston Christmas Eve, New Orleans on New Years Eve, then through the Panama Canal. They became flagship of CCD 39 under the command of Commander Haines. He was all over the Pacific, Northern Solomons, Truk, Ponape, Satawan, Iwo Jima, and with killer group with George, Raby, Escort Carrier *Hoggat Bay*, and four destroyers when the *England* scored six hits on Jap subs.

He earned the American Theatre Ribbon, Pacific Theatre Ribbon with four Battle Stars, and Victory Medal. Served aboard the *Spangler* from August 1943 until October 1945. While awaiting discharge, pulled

shore patrol at Sands St. Brooklyn, Earl, NJ Ammunition Depot at entrance gate and was discharged Lido Beach, LI March 16, 1946, after achieving the rank of RDM2/c.

He became a musician and married the former Mary Ann Onorato, was also a printer until letter press went under. He finally retired from New City Sanitation. They have three children, Peggy Ann, Carol and Anthony and three grandchildren. He still stays in touch with his closest shipmate Joseph E. Norris SOM3/c. God bless Joe, Frankie, and Family. He states that is very proud to have served his country.

HAROLD L. POLAND, FC3/c, USS *Deede* (DE-263) and USS *Texas* (BB-35), was born Dec. 5, 1923 in Carey, OH and enlisted in the Navy Oct. 24, 1941. Went to boot camp at Great Lakes, IL, then was stationed on USS *Texas* (BB-35) for 18 months. He was then transferred to DE School in Miami, FL and to E.E. School in Norfolk, VA.

He served on the USS *Texas* as SM1/c 20mm Midway Island and Morocco, USS *Deede* as FC3/c helm watch and three-inch gun. Fought at Eniwetok, Marshall Island, Guam, Saipan, Tarawa, Palau, Iwo Jima, Philippine Sea, and Okinawa. The DE group was part of the 3rd Fleet and 58th Task Force. Some of his memorable experiences include seeing several Japanese battleships sank by his ship, and being responsible for downing several Japanese Zeros. His groups received a Navy Commendation and four Bronze Stars. He was discharged Nov. 3, 1945 as an FC3/c. Afterwards he joined the telephone industry and retired Nov. 30, 1984. Harold has a wife Martha of 42 years, three children and five grandchildren.

CECIL EDWARD POPE, SR., was born Feb. 20, 1925 in Damascus, AL. He joined the U.S. Navy May 8, 1944. Basic training at Camp Peary, VA to Norfolk Training Station then on to New Orleans to pickup the USS *Cook* (APD-130).

He remembers the day the USS *Cook* steamed into the harbor of Hakodate and accepted the surrender of that city. He was discharged Feb. 22, 1946 with the rank of SN1/c.

Married to Sara Nell Gaines on Dec. 20, 1947. They raised four sons and two daughters; Cecil, Jr. (Ed), Mike, Don, Phil, Kathy and Angela and eight grandchildren. He retired from the construction business and now farms.

JOSEPH N.R. POULIN, was born Feb. 2, 1933 in Lewiston, ME. He joined the U.S. Coast Guard Dec. 27, 1951. He served on the USS *Conifer*, *Richey* (WDE-485), and *Duane* (WPG-33). Stationed Ports-

...uth, VA; Honolulu, HI and Boston, MA. He remem-...ts the two years that he served on the USS *Richey.*

He received the Korean Theatre of War Medal, National Defense Medal, U.N. Medal, and Good Conduct Medal. Discharged with the rank of radarman second class.

Married to Adele with six children from a previous marriage and three grandchildren. Worked as district sales manager for Dime Savings Bank of New York in Massapeque, NY. Now lives in Flushing, NY.

JAMES A. PRATHER, Coxswain, USS *Breeman* (DE-104), was born Jan. 12, 1926 in Gastonia, NC. Enlisted into the U.S. Navy September 1943, boot camp at Bainbridge, MD. Then on to Norfolk, VA as part of the crew of the USS *Breeman,* until its decommissioning. Discharged from the Navy 1947 and enlisted into the Army 1947. Retired Jan. 1, 1970 with over 26 years of military service, and the rank of first sergeant E8. From M.P. Corp. Duties in the Navy included convoy duty in the North and South Atlantic also hunter killer duty in the same area. Served in the Army from 1947 to 1950 then to the M.P. Corp. 1951 and 1970. Served two tours in Germany, one tour in Hawaii and two tours in Korea.

Married to Joan K. Prather, November 1953 in Hawaii. Raised four children two daughters and two sons. They are both retired and living in Florida.

MARION R. PRESTON, RM3/c, USS *Fowler* (DE-222), was born May 9, 1926 in Washington, DC and enlisted in the Navy May 8, 1944. Went to boot camp at Camp Perry, VA, then assigned to USS *Fowler.* Made four convoy trips to Oran, North Africa, from Norfolk, New York and Boston. The *Fowler* sank German U-869 off Morocco Feb. 28, 1945. Received one Battle Star.

On May 25, 1945 he was transferred to Fleet Radio School, Great Diamond Island, ME. Played baseball for Portland Naval Training Station.

Returned aboard *Fowler* Sept. 22, 1945 in Miami, FL, serving as school ship for Naval Training Center.

In November *Fowler* served as plane guard for Charger (CVE-30) in the Chesapeake Bay. In May 1946, he left *Fowler* in Green Cove Springs, FL for discharge in Bainbridge, MD May 18, 1946.

Retired Dec. 17, 1990 after 35 years as insurance salesman for Bankers Life Casualty Co. He has one son, and is a member of VFW Post 8189 Crystal River, FL, where he now resides.

HERMAN NICK PRILLAMAN, GM2/c, USS *Strickland* (DE-333), was inducted in the Navy Sept. 3, 1943. Born May 25, 1925 in Martinsville, VA. Went to boot camp at Bainbridge, MD, and Gunnery School at Naval Training Station at Norfolk, VA.

Commissioned USS *Strickland,* January 1943 at Orange, TX. Shakedown cruise to Bermuda and Guantanamo Bay. Convoy duty in the Atlantic Ocean, the Mediterranean Sea and Pacific Ocean. Awarded a Battle Star. Discharged Jan. 3. 1946.

He had International Harvester dealership until 1968. Semi-retired to Plantation, FL, where he owned and operated a Texaco Service Station until he fully retired in 1986.

Lives in Plantation, FL with his wife, Frances. They have four children, H. Nick Prillaman, Jr., Thomas, Diana (Adams), Paula (Kennedy) and seven grandchildren.

WILLIAM PSOMIADES, was born June 2, 1927 in Astoria, NY. Joined the U.S. Navy Oct. 10, 1944. Attended Naval Training Station in Sampson, NY, then served on several ships including the USS *Roxane* (AKA-37), USS *Alvin C. Cockrell* (DE-366), USS *Burias* (AG-69), and the USS *Richard M. Rowell.* He had achieved the rank of coxswain at the time of his discharge. He states that he is proud to have served in the finest Navy. He received the American Theatre Ribbon, and the Asiatic-Pacific Theatre Ribbon for his service.

He is married with three sons and grandchildren. Now a retired furrier and living in Astoria, NY.

WALTER "POP" QUIMBY, CMoMM, USS *Coffman* (DE-191), was born in Powell, MA. Entered Naval Service just prior to the end of WWI. Spent some time in the Naval Reserves. During World War II attended Diesel Schools at NOB, Norfolk, VA and Cleveland, OH. Then attended Sub Chaser Training School at Miami, FL. In

January 1944 he was assigned to USS *Coffman* (DE-191), being built in Newark, NJ. While serving on the *Coffman* he attained the rank of CMoMM. Upon discharge at the end of WWII, he re-joined the Naval Reserves and was recalled for the Korean Conflict. "Pop" and his wife Nina (both deceased) are survived by two sons. *Submitted by Kenneth Roberge*

HENRY RACETTE *(See Bio, page 744.)*

ROBERT F. RADER, JR., was born April 7, 1933. He joined the service May 26, 1953. Boot camp at Bainbridge, MD. I.C. CL "A" at Great Lakes from 1953 until 1954. Served with the Unites States Navy on the USS *Delong* (DE-684). He had achieved the rank of I.C. electrician third class at the time of his discharge.

He remembers Hurricane Hazel in Chesapeake Bay in 1954, the midshipman cruise in 1954 and the ship reunions of 1989 and 1990.

Married to Margaret they had two children, one daughter who is 34 and son who is deceased since 1972. They also have two grandchildren. He retired from the oil and gas industry after 35 years of service. Moved from West Virginia to Florida in 1987 and still reside there.

HOWARD EARL RALSTON, was born Jan. 21, 1925 in Hardyville, KY. Joined Coast Guard Oct. 8, 1943. Basic training at St. Augustine, FL. Attended Signal School at Manhattan Beach, NY. Receiving station at Ft. Lauderdale and Miami, FL. Transferred to Davis Island, Tampa, FL again to St. Augustine, then to Rahway, NJ. Went aboard the USS *Sellstrom* (DE-255), October 1944. On convoy duty to England and France. After V.E. Day sailed for Pacific. Duty in Aleutian, Alaska, Okinawa, Korea, China and Japan. Ship arrived back in Florida April 1946. Discharged in St. Louis, MO May 6, 1946.

He and Katie have been married for over 45 years and has four children, twelve grandchildren and two great-grandchildren. They have spent their years on a dairy and tobacco farm in South Central, KY.

LESLIE WAYNE RALSTON, was born July 1, 1926 in Ellis County, TX. Joined the service March 1944 in Dallas, TX. Served with the United States Naval Reserve. V-12 Program from 1944-1945, then on the USS *Foss* (DE-59) 1950-1951 as division medical officer during Korean duty. Had attained the rank of lieutenant, MC, at the time of discharge.

Married Dona L. Sprinke, they have four sons. He recently retired after 36 years service in radiology practice.

MANUEL RAPOZA, was born Jan. 15, 1924 in

New Bedford, MA. Inducted into U.S. Navy Aug. 23, 1943. Served on the USS *Maloy*. Received training at Newport, RI, Lido Beach, NY and Boston, MA. He had achieved the rank of RM third class at the time of his discharge.

He remembers the Normandy invasion and patrolling the English Channel. Received medals for the European and American Theatre.

He is now widowed with one son, Brian, one daughter, Nancy and five grandchildren. He is retired after 32 years of teaching high school and enjoys traveling. Resides in Fairhaven, MA.

LOUIS RAYMOND, (TEX), SOM2/c, USS *Johnnie Hutchins* (DE-360), was born Nov. 26, 1923. Enlisted in Navy July 1942, attended boot camp at Great Lakes. Underwater Sound School at Key West, and plank owner of USS *Johnnie Hutchins* (DE-360). Picked up at Orange, TX and stayed with the (DE-360) until discharged in January 1946. Went to college on GI Bill and graduated as petroleum engineer in 1950 from Kansas State. Worked in oil business from Canada to Gulf Coast in Midcontinent States until retirement in 1988.

Remembers the Okinawa hurricane in 1945, sinking three subs north of the Philippines in 1945 and getting discharged. Received the Navy Unit Commendation and three Battle Stars.

Married in 1944 to Lois Hull. They had two daughters, two sons and seven grandchildren. Also farmed in Norman, OK as a pastime. Involved with Thoroughbred and Arabian horses for the last 25 years. Lived in Norman, OK since 1957.

JOHN REDLER, SC1/c, USS *Lowe* (DE-325), was born in New Orleans, LA on May 9, 1918, and enlisted in the U.S. Coast Guard on March 22, 1942. Boot camp at U.S. Naval Station, Algiers, L.A. Assigned to USCG *Camille*, a buoy tender, as ships cook third class, earned promotion to SC1/c. He grew tired of this type of duty and put in a request for transfer to DE. Request granted, and was assigned to USS *Lowe* (DE-325) as SC1/c. First voyage from Norfolk, VA to Casablanca, N.A. He made several other crossings. One convoy in particular, Escort Div. 48 commanded by Capt. R.E. Wood and Commander R.H. French, skipper of USS *Lowe* (DE-325). The convoy left Norfolk, and the USS *Lowe* was in the straggler position, until they reached Gibraltar. They changed positions with the USS *Menges* (DE-320). On May 3, 1944 the *Menges* was torpedoed near or past Gibraltar. With 35 ft. of her stern destroyed, the *Menges* was towed to Algiers, N.A. and then across the Atlantic to the Brooklyn Navy Yards to be fitted to a stern from the USS *Holder* (DE-401) and to be sent back into action.

The convoy continued, and off Algiers N.A. was attacked by German J.U. 88 and H.E. 3 planes. A Munition ship in the middle of the convoy, carrying 500 Army Air Corps specialists was hit and exploded. The sky lit up like the "Fourth of July." Another DE was hit and the USS *Lowe* stood by to pick up survivors.

In November of 1945, he was discharged from the U.S. Coast Guard, and settled in Brooklyn, NY.

During the following years, he worked in the Motion Picture Industry, as a laboratory technician, doing such duties as negative worker, film developer and expediter. He worked for Warner Brothers, Pathe Films and News, and Technicolor Films Inc. In 1985 he retired after 38 years.

In 1946 he married a beautiful girl from Brooklyn, Esther DiCapua and became a father of two, one girl, Rosemary, now 43 and a son, John, now 34. One daughter, Susan, died at 17 months. He is the grandfather of three, David (23), Deborah (20) and Douglas (16). He is now a great-grandfather to Jonathan.

To this day, he is still happily married to the same beautiful Brooklyn girl.

CROWELL LEE REDWINE, was born Cabarrus County, NC. Joined the U.S. Navy in June 1943. Boot camp at Bainbridge, MD, worked as instructor teaching new recruits to row boats. DE Training School at Norfolk, VA. Commissioned USS *Bostwick* (DE-103) on Dec. 1, 1943. Received the European Theatre of Operations and American Theatre Ribbons, and three Bronze Stars.

Married Sarah Maxine Tucker from Cabarrus County on Feb. 1, 1947, they raised four sons and have five grandchildren. He retired from Ryder Truck Lines after 35 years service in August 1982. Now enjoys fishing, playing golf, and traveling in a motorhome with his wife. Enjoying his retirement and living in St. James, FL.

HERBERT W. REITH, was born in Long Island, NY in 1924. Entered United States Coast Guard in November 1942. Attended boot camp at Manhattan Beach, NY and Gunners Mate School at Quonset Point, Newport, RI. He served as seaman, gunners mate and signalman. Assigned to the USS *Leopold* (DE-319) for shakedown only, USS *Merrill* (DE-392) Atlantic and Mediterranean Theatres, and the USCG cutters *Bibb*, *Tany* and *Pontchartrain* after WWII.

In civilian life he worked for Bell System as a maintenance and design engineer. Retired in 1976 to Enka, NC. Presently serves on the Board of Directors of the Destroyer Escort Sailors Association. Also serves as National Secretary of the Coast Guard Combat Veterans Association. Other military and Veteran affiliations include: National Service officer for the Fleet

Reserve Association with an office at the VA Medical Center in Asheville, NC. Past president (2 terms) of the Buncombe County Veterans Council. Serves as a member of the JROTC Scholarship Committee. Past QM of VFW Post 3040 and past secretary/treasurer of Fleet Reserve Association Branch 361. Commander of Rev. Ralph F. Neagle Post 1914, Catholic War Veterans. Life member of the Veterans of Foreign Wars, Disabled American Veterans, Fleet Reserve Association, American Legion (all USCG Pos on Governors Island, NY), Catholic War Veterans, Tin Can Sailors, Destroyer Escort Sailors Association, Non-Commissioned Officers Association, United States Naval Institute and Armed Forces Communications and Electronics Association. Annual memberships include AMVETS, Navy League, Military Order of the Cootie and National Order of Trench Rats.

Other: In 1960 he received the Silver Beaver Award from the Nassau County Council, Boy Scouts of America; 1986, received 50 year award from Daniel Boone Council, Boy Scouts of America. 1991, honored by VA Medical Center, Asheville for 6,250 hours of volunteer service.

Married to the former Mae Elsie Schuebel. Father of Herbert W. III, Richard W., Hollie J., Paul A., and the late Ronald J.

WILLIAM JOHN REY, JR., USS *Pennsylvania* (BB-38), was born March 11, 1922 in New Orleans, LA. Enlisted April 8, 1940. Discharged April 12, 1946.

On Dec. 7, 1941, while in dry dock in Pearl Harbor, a Japanese bomb hit ship, resulting in 38 casualties. During the attack, he was a gunner on a 14" gun, after the attack he was assigned to go into the dry dock to retrieve bodies from destroyers *Casen* and *Downs*.

Transferred to USS *Baldwin* for the invasion of Africa at Casablanca. The Italian Navy surrendered to destroyer squadron. Transferred to Washington, DC Gunnery School, then to Miami to teach the Russians how to use guns. Transferred to U.S.S. *Grady* (DE) to Pacific Ocean for the Philippines Liberation and invasion of Okinawa and Iwo Jima. At Okinawa, Japanese kamikaze tried to hit ship, they shot down a few planes.

Bill achieved the rank of chief gunners mate. Seven medals: Philippines Liberation, American Defense, Asiatic-Pacific, American Area, African Defense, African European Area, Good Conduct and Victory.

Bill is married to Jacqueline D. Rey. He has six children and six grandchildren. Retired from Pacific Telephone Company after 40 years.

NORMAN LIONEL RICHARDSON, was born in Mobile, AL Oct. 15, 1921. He enlisted in the U.S. Navy in June 1942 in Houston, TX. After boot camp at

Great Lakes Naval Center, he studied electrical courses at Perdue University. From Miami Subchasing Training Center, he went to Cleveland, OH to learn diesel electric propulsion Shipboard Equipment. Arriving in Miami, he was assigned to the USS *Acree* (DE-167), built in Kearney, NJ and commissioned in Brooklyn Navy Yard.

After the shakedown cruise to Bermuda, he joined convoy, escorting them to Panama Canal Zone. They sailed to the South Pacific where they participated in the Hollandia Operation, authorized to wear Bronze Stars for the capture and occupation of Saipan, Guam, Tinian, and Philippine Islands. Served aboard the *Acree* until its return to the States in 1945. He was discharged from service in Camp Wallace, TX as EM second class.

He retired from Monsanto Chemical Company as an electrical foreman, moved to Florida upon his retirement in 1982. He will celebrate his 50th wedding anniversary in November 1992. He is the father of two daughters. They will host their third reunion for the *Acree* in October 1992 in Sarasota, FL.

WILFRED J. RIESTER,

was born Oct. 15, 1925 in Buffalo, NY. He entered the Navy on April 4, 1943, went to Sampson, NY for Basic Fire Control School in Bainbridge, MD. Assigned to the USS *Paul G. Baker* (DE-642) which was newly commissioned in San Francisco. After shakedown, took a convoy to Pearl Harbor, escorted carrier force to Guadalcanal, to Purvis Bay on Florida Island.

The *Baker* was assigned to Hunter Killer and air-sea rescue. On one run they accidentally rammed a whale on Nov. 27, 1944. On March 27, 1945 went to Okinawa with invading forces and laid smoke screen for landing forces, they spent 80 days on the suicide row. On April 22, 1945 bogey planes headed toward them, but turned and crashed into USS *Swallow* (CAM-65), the ship sank in four minutes, picked up 78 survivors. On May 4, 1945, planes dropped a torpedo on them, it missed and was splashed.

On Aug. 31, 1945 (VJ Day) there was a big celebration, On Sept. 17, 1945 at Tokyo Bay they checked ships in harbor and on Nov. 4, 1945 he was in the U.S. on leave. Back to West Coast and assigned to USS *General H.W. Butner* (APA), went to China to bring back troops. Disharged May 15, 1946.

He is married to Mary, they have two daughters and seven grandchildren. Father of son who was the late Kevin W. Riester. Retired as heating specialist and belongs to Boy Scouts of America, American Legion Post 1451 and DESA.

JOEL A. RIGTER,

was born in Kamrar, IA on March 28, 1934. Joined the United Sates Navy July, 13,

---

1953. Took boot camp at San Diego, CA and MM School at Great Lakes Naval Training Center from 1953 to 1954. Served on the USS *Wm. Seiverling* (DE-441) from 1954 until 1957. He had attained the rank of MM2/c at the time of his discharge.

He remembers the typhoon in 1954, while on the cruise from Japan to Midway Island.

Married to Joan with two children, Joseph and Jill and two grandchildren. He is now semi-retired from waterbed business. He spends as much time as possible seeing North America by motorhome.

WILLIAM RILEY,

GM2/c, USS *Brackett* (DE-41), enlisted Sept. 20, 1942. Attended boot camp and Gunners Mate School at Great Lakes Naval Training Station. Advanced to GM School, Treasure Island, San Francisco. USS *Brackett* was his next assignment as third class GM. Their ship did convoy duty in Central, South and Western Pacific. They took part in battles at Marshall Islands and the Marianas. They operated escort duty from the Marshall Islands.

He earned the Asiatic-Pacific with two stars, Good Conduct Medal, American Theatre and Victory Medal.

In January 1945, he was sent back to Stateside to GM and Electrical Hydraulic School in Washington, DC. Newport, RI was next for precommissioning training and new construction. The war ended, all training stopped and he was discharged at Bainbridge, MD Jan. 19, 1946.

He then married and had three sons. Worked as a millwright mechanic and finished his working years with Nabisco as a packing machine mechanic. He retired at the age of 65 with 28 years of service. He is now a member of DESA, Navy League, American Legion, and a Plank Owner Navy Memorial.

LEONARD J. ROBERTS,

GM2/c, USS *Arkansas* (BB-33) and USS *Haverfield* (DE-393), enlisted in the United Sates Navy on Feb. 18, 1941. Went to boot camp at Naval Training Station at Great Lakes, IL for a period of six weeks. Upon completion of boot camp, assigned to the USS *Arkansas* (BB-33), on Neutrality Patrol, escorting convoys to Iceland, Grenock, Scotland, Casablanca, French Morocco and Bangor, Ireland.

Assigned to the USS *Haverfield* (DE-393) in November 1943. Sailed for Bermuda for training and shakedown. On Feb. 14, 1944 he reported to Norfolk, VA and assigned to Hunter Killer Group 21.11 comprised of the USS *Bogue* (CVE-9) and five Destroyer Escorts.

After Hunter Killer duty in the North and South Atlantic and credit for sinking two German U-boats

---

and two Japanese I Boats, reported to the Boston Naval Yard on May 19, 1945 for a complete overhaul to be readied for Pacific duty.

After 48 continuous months of sea duty, was assigned to the Ammunition Depot in Hingham, MA, and from there sent back to Great lakes Separation Center for discharge on Sept. 19, 1945.

Married to Margaret and they have two sons, James and Michael Roberts and one daughter, Kathryn (Roberts) Dalen.

GEORGE H. ROMME,

was born Oct. 1, 1920. Enlisted in the U.S. Navy October 1942. Boot camp at Naval Training Station in Great Lakes, IL, QM School at Newport, RI. He had attained the rank of quartermaster second class at the time of his discharge.

He recalls the convoy duty to England, France and Mediterranean. The capture of U-505 of Dakar, East Africa, and Hunter Killer duty with USS *Guadalcanal* (CVE-60). He recieved the Presidential Unit Citation.

Married with four children and eight grandchildren. Retired from ITT Labs. Active with Fire and Rescue in local town and residing in Brewster, MA.

ROBERT W. ROOT,

was born Dec. 12, 1914 in Woodbridge, CT. Joined the U.S. Navy May 24, 1943. Attended NRS New Haven, NTS in Sampson, NY. Assigned to the USS *Blessman* APD-48 in Norfolk, VA. He had achieved the rank of MM2/c at the time of his discharge.

A memorable experience for him was at Ewo when they took a 500 lb. bomb and the ending of the war in Japan.

He is now a retired private chauffeur and resides in Shelton, CT.

RUDY ROSSI,

Plankowner, S1/c, USS *Liddle* (DE-206), born June 23, 1925 into the family of Grazino and Guiseppina Rossi, one of eight children and the youngest of five brothers, of which, two were in the Army and one was in the Navy at Guadalcanal.

He enlisted in the Navy on Sept. 1, 1943. Reported to NTS Bainbridge, MD, then NTS Norfolk, VA.

Assigned to the commissioning of the USS *Liddle* (DE-206) at Charleston, SC Navy Yard Dec. 6, 1943. Three convoy round trips across the North Atlantic and Mediterranean in 1944. Enter Sullivan shipyard at Brooklyn. Converted to (APD-60), went to the Pacific and down to Hollandia, New Guinea. Escorted LST Landings at Finchaven and Palau. Dec. 7, 1944, landed troops at Ormoc Bay. Attacked by kamikaze zero, in bridge superstructure with the loss of 38 officers and men. During the battle of Ormoc Bay, *Liddle* shot down five Japanese zeros. He will always remember the officers and the shipmates who fought so gallantly after the kamikaze hit. It was an honor for him to serve with the greatest fighting men in the world.

Rudy, returned to San Francisco for repairs of Legaspi, Mindanao and Borneo campaign June 1945, landing Australian troops. Occupation of Korea, duty in Dairen, Manchuria and Tientsin, China.

He was awarded the European African Theatre Ribbon, Asiatic-Pacific Ribbon with two stars, American Theatre, Philippine Liberation with one star, China Service, Navy Occupation Service Korea, Philippine Republic Presidential Unit Citation Badge and Victory Medal.

He returned to the States, New York, Jan. 1, 1946, then to Green Cove Springs, FL, where she was placed out of commission.

He was discharged March 10, 1946 at Lido Beach, NY. Retired 1989 from the ceramic tile business, after 30 years. He is married to the former Alice Di Luzio of 42 years. Has two children, Patricia and Rudy, Jr., and two grandsons Rudy III, and Kevin. Rudy enjoys DESA reunions, traveling and golf.

JAMES R. ROWLEY, (RAY), USS *Sierra* (AD-18), USS *Marsh* (DE-699), USS *Major* (DE-796), was born and raised in Canton, IL. Boot camp at San Diego in 1946. Schumacker, CA, he boarded the *Sierra* and was sent to Tsingtao, China. Boarded the *Marsh* in November 1946 for duty in China seas, Korea, Hong Kong, and Japan. Encountered typhoon en route to Marshall Islands. In Pearl Harbor for six weeks, San Diego, Mare Island. Duty on major hospital in San Diego, later on to the S.D. Training Center. He was then discharged and attended college in Peoria, IL, taught school for one year. Worked as an accountant for Pabst Brewery for five years.

In November 1953, he married Rosemary Dehority they have six children, four boys, two girls and seven grandchildren. Joined Chevrolet Motor Division in 1956 working in Illinois, Iowa, Missouri, and in 1962 moved to Iowa as district manager. Joined General Motors Corporation staff in Detroit in 1968. He retired in March 1989 and moved to Orlando, FL in July 1989. Presently living in Orlando. He attended the 1989 and 1990 reunions. He states that the reunions are interesting, and lots of fun. Interested in hearing from and seeing the rest of his *Marsha* and *Sierra* shipmates write them and join them at the reunions.

DARREL DEAN RUEBSAMEN, Captain, USN, was born in Hamilton Co., NE June 1, 1926. One June 1, 1943 he entered the Navy V-12 program and was commissioned ensign, USNR on March 6, 1945.

He served at sea on the USS *Otter* (DE-210), USS

Raby (DE-698), Staff Comdesron 2, and USS *Delong* (DE-684), and as commanding officer of USS *Grouse* (AMS-15), MINDIV 45, USS *Aeolus* (ARC-3) and USS *Neches* (AO-47). He served in several shore billets in the United States, and overseas in the Federal German Re-

public, Republic of the Philippines and Japan. In 1961 he was awarded the degree of Master of Science in Navy Management by the U.S. Navy Postgraduate School.

During the period 1971 to 1975 he was assigned as commander, Military Sealift Command, Far East with responsibilities that included the ocean movement of Department of Defense cargo in the ocean area from Guam west to the African coast, and the coastal and river resupply of Cambodia and Republic of Vietnam until these two countries were overrun by the communists in early 1975. During evacuation of refugees from the Republic of Vietnam in April 1975, his command provided ocean transportation for over 110,000 refugees, first for those fleeing south and later for those fleeing from the country.

Among other service medals and decorations, he was awarded the Navy Commendation Medal and the Legion of Merit. On July 1, 1975 he was retired from the Navy. He and his wife, Margaret, have been married for over 45 years. They have three children and four grandchildren.

MARTIN RICHARD RUNALDUE, Coxswain, USS *Johnnie Hutchins* (DE-360), was born May 13, 1926, in Alexandria, VA. On Jan. 2, 1944, when he was 17 he enlisted in the Navy. His training was at boot camp for six weeks at Bainbridge, MD and eight weeks at Norfolk, VA. On Aug. 28, 1944, at Orange, TX, he boarded the USS *Johnnie Hutchins*. He remained on board until May 2, 1946. Their duty was in the Pacific when on August 9, at 12:07 p.m. they sank two enemy subs and one probable at latitude 20 degree 22' 00" East.

This action was probably the last surface naval engagement of WWII. The *Johnnie Hutchins* was awarded the Navy Unit Commendation for her battle with the submarines.

On May 10, 1948 in Alexandria, VA, June Dakon and Martin were married. They now have four sons, three granddaughters, and one grandson.

He went to work for the Norfolk Southern Railroad in 1946. He worked 42 years, and retired December 1986.

They are now living in Manassas, VA.

JACK RUSSELL, EM3/c, USS *Durik* (DE-666), enlisted January 1944 and entered active duty July 1944. Jack completed boot camp at Great Lakes Electricians School at Gulfport and Gyro School at Miami. He reported for duty aboard the USS *Durik* at Boston in June of 1945, shortly after she completed the last of four Atlantic convoy crossings.

During his service aboard the *Durik* she served as a training ship for student officers, and a plane rescue ship for qualifying carrier pilots. The *Durik* also carried

out a Guantanamo Bay based general training in the Caribbean. The *Durik* participated in the massive air-sea search of the infamous "Bermuda Triangle" for the 14 men and five Navy TBM-3 Avenger torpedo bombers of ill-fated Flight 19. Jack maintained electrical gear aboard ship and his watch station was that of throttle operator in the main engine room.

On July 21, 1945 the USS *Durik* put in at the Brooklyn Navy Yard for overhaul and prepared to set sail for an extensive mission in the Pacific (probable participation in the invasion of Japan). While the crew was on a final eight day "pre-Pacific leave", the first atom bomb was dropped and VJ Day closely followed. The crew breathed a collective sigh of relief.

In April of 1946, the *Durik* sailed into Green Cove Springs, FL and they commenced decommissioning procedures. The USS *Durik*, more affectionately referred to by her hardy crew of young adventurers as the "Dirty D." and the "Triple Six," was placed in reserve on June 15, 1946.

Jack was awarded the American Area Ribbon, the World War II Victory Ribbon, and the European African Middle Eastern Theatre Ribbon.

He has since earned a doctorate in psychology at USC and completed a career at California State University at Fullerton. He has two daughters, three grandchildren and three great-grandchildren. Jack and Kathy are currently residing in Fullerton, CA, where he maintains a private counseling practice.

ERNEST RUSSO, was born Feb. 5, 1922 in Brooklyn, NY. Enlisted April 23, 1942 called to active duty Nov. 4, 1942 until April 30, 1945. He served with the United States Coast Guard in the first Naval and 3rd Naval Districts. The last ship that he served on was the USS *Chambers* (DE-391). He had attained the rank of radioman third class at the time of discharge.

Remembers the Coast Guard intelligence at the USCG Experimental Station, the North Atlantic in 1943 and the Atlantic and Mediterranean in 1945.

He received ribbons for American Theatre, and European African Theatre.

Married 1943 to Mary, sons Ernest S. and Peter M., one daughter Angela S. Retired executive for Shell Oil Co. after 39 years.

JOHN RYAN, was born April 25, 1918 in Waltham, MA. Joined the service March 22, 1943, with boot camp at Newport, RI and QM School also at Newport, RI. Plankowner with USS *Breeman* (DE-104). Served Hunter-Killer duty in North and South Atlantic. He had achieved the rank of quartermaster first class at the time of his discharge.

Remembers the time served with the Hunter-

Killer group and the action they had, and returning Polish gold to U.S. from Daka, Africa. He received one Battle Star for his service.

He was discharged Oct. 26, 1945 and entered Boston University where he received masters degree in 1948.

He is widowed with one son and two grandchildren. Retired after 42 years with Fishery Service as a chemist and food technologist.

...MES SACKELLARES, (JIM), was born Dec. 24, 1924 in Newman, GA. Joined the U.S. Navy in March 1944. Boot camp at Camp Perry, VA, Fire Control School at Seattle, WA. He was shipped out of Treasure Island, CA January 1945 and assigned to the USS *Grady* (DE-445) in Carolina Island, Iwo Jima, Okinawa, Philippines and back to the States in the fall of 1945. He was discharged May 24, 1945 with the rank of fire controlman third class.

After his discharge, he completed college at Georgia Tech and married Evelyn Parks. They have three sons, Chris, Robert and John. James retired after 40 years with paper industry in Savannah, GA.

ELMER SAILER

HERBERT MAX SCHILLER, JR., MM3/c, USS *Otterstetter* (DE-244), USS PGM-25, inducted into the Navy on March 16, 1943 in Philadelphia, PA at the age of 18. Boot camp at UTNTS in Sampson, NY. Left for Diesel School in Norfolk, VA on May 30, 1943. After school they arrived in Houston, TX on July 20, 1943 and took part in putting the USS *Otterstetter* in commission of Aug. 6, 1943. After shakedown in Bermuda, they made two convoy runs from Norfolk to Gibraltar. The first convoy was in November 1943 and the second was made in January 1944. In March 1944, they left New York and started operating along the Atlantic Coast against enemy submarines and then made one run to the South Atlantic crossing the equator on April 3, 1944 and arrived in Recife Brazil on April 6, 1944. They left Brazil for New York and on May 24, 1944, the USS *Otterstetter* was assigned to a Hunter-Killer CVE Task Group. Their group made three voyages to Argentia, Newfoundland escorting convoys enroute to the United Kingdom. The *Otterstetters* worst enemy during these voyages was the rough North Atlantic weather in which one man was lost overboard and ripped the #1 3'/50 gun shield from the deck.

On Sept. 13, 1944, he transferred from the USS *Otterstetter* to Argentia, Newfoundland and then to Boston, MA on Sept. 19, 1944 and then to Cleveland, OH for Diesel School. Finished school on Nov. 11, 1944 and on Dec. 4, 1944 started school in Miami, FL to Jan. 20, 1945.

On Feb. 3, 1945, he took part in putting the PGM-25 in commission at the Brooklyn Navy Yard, NY. Went to Miami, FL for shakedown and drills and then to the Pacific. They arrived in Panama March 29, in Santiago, Mexico near Santa Cruz April 6, in San Diego April 8, in Pearl Harbor April 18, and in Eniwetok Atoll May 4, 1945. They worked with mine sweeps for invasion of Iheya Island off Okinawa on June 25. Took part in a scouting party in mop up operations on Okinawa on June 25. Started preparing for invasion of Japan. After bombs were dropped and surrender, they were assigned to mine cleanup in the China Seas and around Korea. Left for and arrived in Nagasaki, Japan on Sept. 9, 1945 and also later in Sasebo on October 1. After mine sweeping detail, they left Dec. 18, 1945 and arrived in San Francisco on Jan. 30, 1946 by way of Eniwetok and Pearl Harbor. Left ship on January 31 and was put in mothball fleet. Campaign ribbons were American Theatre, European Theatre, Pacific Theatre with one star and Victory Medal, discharged on Feb. 8, 1946.

Finished high school and machine design course. On June 25, 1949 he married Jemma, worked in civil engineering since 1949. Retired from Civil Service in 1987 at the age of 63. He is now working part-time in Civil Engineering. They live in New Jersey, with one son , three daughters and 10 grandchildren.

JACK SCHLEMMER, RM1/c, USS *George W. Ingram* (DE-62), enlisted in Navy Dec. 13, 1942. Boot camp at Great Lakes, IL. Attended Radio School at Miami University, Oxford, OH. HF/DF School at Casco Bay, Portland, ME. Boarded the USS *George W. Ingram* Oct. 4, 1943 at Boston, MA. Made several convoys from Boston to Algiers, by way of Aruba and Curacao, Brooklyn Navy Yard to Cardiff, Wales, Londonderry, Northern Ireland many times. Left ship early 1945 for V-12 officers training school at Asbury Park, NJ. The war was winding down in Atlantic, he was transferred back to fleet at Noroton Heights, CT. From there to San Bruno, CA; Pearl Harbor, HI; Samar, Philippine Islands, and finally a base at Balikpapan, Borneo. Left Borneo Feb. 12, 1946 to pick up bases all over the area including Sydney, Australia.

Discharged March 12, 1946. On July 26, 1950, he married Lois McClellan. They have one daughter, one son and one grandson. Working as industrial supply salesman since 1950 with the same company. Still residing in Dayton, OH.

SYLVESTER J. SCHNIEDER, EM2/c, USS *Swearer* (DE-186), entered the Navy in December 1943, was processed in January 1944 and then went to Camp Farrigut, ID for boot training. Then he was sent to the North Dakota State School of Science for electri-

cal training, and from there to OGU at Treasure Island. He went to troop ship at the Admiralities (Manis) from there on to the USS *Swearer*. (DE-186). They followed the war all the way to Okinawa.

Most memorable experience for him was the battle at Okinawa and Iwo Jima, and especially the typhoon where the three destroyers turned over and they picked up nine survivors. He received the Presidential Unit Citation, and nine Battle Stars.

From Okinawa they went back to the U.S. via Pearl Harbor. He was discharged from Green Cove Springs, FL at Great Lakes, IL in July 1946. Married Aug. 21, 1948. He was owner-operator long haul truck driver where he drove cross country for 40 plus years. The last ten years was spent as a husband and wife team. They have six children and 13 grandchildren. He retired in 1990, and still drives part-time. They also travel quite a bit, golfs some and is enjoying retired life.

ALFRED EDWARD SCHREIBER, MOMM1/c, was born Sept. 23, 1925 in Weehawken, NJ. Joined the service Nov. 2, 1942 at Milwaukee, WI. Boot camp at Curtis Bay, MD to patrol boat USCGR. MM School in New London. Served with the USCG on the USS *Ricketts* (DE-254) from Oct. 3, 1943 until March 21, 1946.

A memorable experience for him was the occupation of Kusale Island in Pacific with 5,000 Japanese Marines on the Island in 1945. He did not receive an Occupation Medal for this.

Married July 13, 1950 to Betty Jane Mattick of Milwaukee, WI. They have two children, Arlene and Alan. Retired from civilian Marine job in February 1983, and the USCG on Feb. 1, 1975 (CWO4).

HARVEY H. SCHULTZ, SF1/c, enlisted in the U.S. Navy in 1941. Boot camp and welding school in San Diego, CA. Made SF third class. Stayed at San Diego base working on submarines. After six months he was sent to Perth, Australia, worked on sub tender in Pelius at Fremantle, Australia. One year later got new construction in Philadelphia. Served on the USS *Spangenberg* (DE-223). After shakedown in Bermuda had convoy duty for one year. New construction in Richmond, VA on USS *Cone* (DD-866) at Staten Island Ship Yards. Later on to Bermuda for shakedown. Ship was ordered to Pacific but the war ended due to the "H" bomb, so he was discharged.

He returned to St. Paul, MN. Went back to Refrigeration School. Worked in the engineering lab at Whirlpool Corporation for 37 years. Retired in 1987 and moved to Sauk Centre, MN. He is married with five children, nine grandchildren and one great-grandchild.

JOHN SEDORY, RDM3/c, USS *Crouter* (DE-11), born March 29, 1923 at Streator, IL. Inducted into Navy in October 1942, but not called to active duty until Jan. 13, 1943. He served his entire ship duty on the USS *Crouter* (DE-11), becoming a part of a nucleus crew at the Submarine Chaser Training Center, Miami, FL, and then being sent to Boston to board the *Crouter*. He remembers that it must have been May by the time they headed for their shakedown cruise at Bermuda, completing it in 23 days (a record at that time). After further repairs and adjustments they finally headed for the Panama Canal, reaching the docks on Aug. 1, 1943.

Their first stop outside the U.S. was Bora Bora (part of the Tahitian Islands), and from there they headed to Noumea, New Caledonia, where they received their orders from the commander of the Pacific Fleet on Sept. 3, 1943. From there until the end of the war they served screening duties for convoys of all sorts and sizes all over the Pacific. They also trained subs out of Hawaii for a time. There they were kamikaze targets for many attacks. They were also targets of a torpedo, a bomb drop off their fantail, and off shore batteries. Out of seven of the screening vessels at Okinawa at that time it is believed that they were the only vessel not hit or damaged in any way, suffering no loss of life at all.

He had been set up to attend a Radio Technician School before the war ended, so he was advised that he could either go ashore and wait for transportation back to the States, of he could stay with the ship until it returned. He decided to wait for his ship to return. When he reached the States via Hawaii, he was sent to a school which would not be taking any new trainees. He was then sent to the San Diego NTC, from there a delay in Chicago enroute to the Philadelphia, Navy Yard, from there to Lido Beach, LI, NY, and finally to Great Lakes Naval Training Center where it all began. He was released from duty on either January 13 or 16 (forgets).

He states that the disappointment of being sent all of those places instead of staying with his ship until decommissioning has never left him. He has always wondered what it would have been like to be there with the whole crew for the decommissioning and the taking of all the pictures, etc. Most of all he missed all of the "good-byes" he could have experienced. He was awarded several theatre ribbons and two stars.

He is now in the process of writing a book, an autobiography, which he had been urged by relatives to write for years. It is near completion. A great portion of the book includes all his Navy experiences as he recalls them.

On July 19, 1946 he met Eleanor Lucille Edgren. They married on Dec. 27, 1946, between two large Christmas trees in Cicero, IL. They have three sons and five grandsons, all whom live within 320 miles of where they live. He retired from the Broadway Stores (part of the Carter, Hawley, Hale Corp.) on April 1, 1988. He now lives in Banning, CA.

When he entered the Navy he had only two years of high school education, having dropped out at the age of 16, and again at age 17. In the Navy he took an Armed Forces Institute course in American History and eventually got his GED diploma in 1946. He has had a variety of jobs including a pilot's license; real estate license; a mobile home license; 17 years in wholesale auto parts; sold cars; armed bank guard; and large store's security manager; just to name a few.

He still likes to keep in touch with any of the ship's crew that he can, but has never been able to attend any of the reunions.

GEORGE SEEFCHAK, MoMM2/c, USS *Pettit* (DE-253), was born July 18, 1921 in New York, NY. Joined the USCG in April 10, 1941. Stationed at Ellis Island, NY, and on the USS *Pettit* (DE-253).

He remembers walking up the wrong gangway with three stars (flying), and meeting and working with a great bunch of guys. He states that war is Hell, but that they did have some good times.

He received the American Defense, American Theatre Ribbon, European Theatre Ribbon, and World War II Victory Medal.

He married Elma Lewis, they raised one son, Steve. He has lived in Florida for over 40 years. Retired from AF (Res) and the Postal Service. Enjoys watching the Miami Dolphins and doing a little fishing.

PAUL SEGAL, was born Aug. 11, 1914 in Philadelphia, PA. Joined the U.S. Navy Aug. 27, 1943. Stationed Bainbridge, MD; Mare Island, CA and Norfolk, VA in the States. He had attained the rank of water tender third class at the time of discharge.

A memorable experience for him was going into Leyte Gulf in the Philippines, they were told to make lots of smoke. In the aft fireroom they had a young fireman, Peter Binder from Philadelphia, PA; he thought that by removing the tips out of the burners, it would make lots of smoke, but little did he know that in doing this he caused a fire in the smoke stack and black smoke back fired into the fireroom. Of course they had to secure the fireroom, and the men were told to come to the forward fireroom where he was stationed. When the men came down the hatch, it was a sight that he says he will never forget, that even now he has to laugh to himself at their faces and clothing blackened with soot and unrecognizable.

He received a star for the consolidation of Solomon Islands, consolidation of Northern Solomon, Leyte Operation, Toem-Wadke-Sarmi Area Operation, and Philippine Republic Presidential Unit Citation Badge.

Married to Elsie, with two daughters, one son, three grandchildren with one on the way at the time of this writing. He is retired and resides in Philadelphia with a winter home in Florida.

EUGENE H. SHAFFER, SR., SM1/c, USS *Bostwick* (DE-103), USS *Thomas* (DE-102), enlisted in the U.S. Navy Feb. 10, 1945. Went to boot camp at NTS Bainbridge, MD. Joined the crew of the USS *Bostwick* at New London, CT, May 1, 1945. North Atlantic convoy, home Port Quonset Point Naval Air Station plane guard training pilots for carrier duty.

Green Cove Springs, FL, Nov. 15, 1945 and they decommissioned the USS *Bostwick* May 1, 1946. Then assigned to the USS *Thomas*, discharged July 16, 1946.

Received the European Theatre Ribbon, World War II Victory Medal, and American Theatre Ribbons.

Married to Marjorie Walterhoefer May 30, 1950. They have two children Christine and Eugene, three grandchildren, Elizabeth, Dennis and Candice. Worked 42 years as crane operator, 40 years as a Boy Scout leader, earned district award of Merit, Silver Beaver, and St. George Medal of Honor.

Eugene is a member of VFW Post 7472, American Legion Post 156, Maryland Charter DESA.

GEORGE LINDSAY SHARP, EM2/c, USS *Durik* (DE-666), was born at Perry Station, Jessamine County, KY on Jan. 3, 1924. He was sworn into the Naval Reserve on April 14, 1943, in Cincinnati, OH. Took his boot training at Great Lakes, IL. Next he was sent to Iowa State College Ames, IA for 16 weeks of Electrician School, he completed that and was sent to Norfolk, VA to await further assignment.

The *Durik* was being built in Pittsburg and he was in the crew made up for it. It was floated down the Ohio and Mississippi Rivers to New Orleans. The *Durik* arrived in March 1944. After dock and sea trails it was commissioned. They went to Bermuda on their shakedown cruise, next to Boston for assignment which was escorting a convoy to the Mediterranean Sea. With other DEs they put the convoy safely through the Strait of Gibraltar where it was taken over by other ships.

They steamed Southwest to Casablanca to await another convoy to escort back to the States. On each of their next runs they had several sonar contacts, shot some hedgehogs and dropped some depth charges, but saw no signs of enemy submarine damage. They never lost a ship while he was on the *Durik*.

Their next assignment was escorting six yard oilers from New York to the Mediterranean. It took them 24 days to get them through the Straits. They left the Mediterranean with a returning convoy, but after a few days they split off to the Azore Islands to escort another DE to the States whose fantail had been blown off by enemy torpedo.

Their next assignment, which was their last, was another convoy to the Mediterranean to Oran, North Africa. They were there a few days then escorted a tanker into the vicinity of the Canary Islands to refuel a sub killer group. When they arrived the killer group had just captured an enemy sub. They were sworn to secrecy about this capture, and when they arrived back to the States the sub was on public display. This capture occurred on on June 4-10 in 1945. Shortly after the war in Europe was over. Sent to school for one week at Northern Pump Co. in Minneapolis. After their return from school the war in Japan ended and they celebrated in Brooklyn, where their ship was at that time.

After his service duty, he did engineering and pipeline construction work for many years. He has been raising cattle for the last 15 years.

JAMES F. SHARRETT, was born Dec. 12, 1926 in Jeffersonville, OH. Joined the United States Navy Jan. 7, 1944 at 17 years old. Attended Key West Sound School at Great Lakes, IL. He was aboard the DE-354 for her commissioning and decommissioning. Served with the USNR from May 22, 1946 until Nov. 21, 1946, the USN from Nov. 23, 1946 until Nov. 21, 1952. He made several trips to the Mediterranean with the 6th Fleet on DDR-831. His last year in the Navy he was instructor at Fleet Sonar School in Key West.

Memorable experiences for him include the commissioning of DE-354, going to the Pacific, the big typhoon, and leaving his appendix on the USS *Medusa* in Leyte.

Married to Joan with one son and two daughters. From Nov. 23, 1952 until Feb. 28, 1991 he worked for Armco Steel Company and now retired and active in Ham Radio, his call number is WB8AWM. Now resides in Middletown, OH.

PLEZE E. SHAW, JR., EM2/c, was born April 4, 1923. On July 27, 1941 he went to work for C&P Telephone Co. Enlisted in the Navy November 1942. Went to Great Lakes, IL, Camp Perry for boot camp, then on to Purdue University for 16 weeks. He made third class electrician. He then to Norfolk, VA to make up part of electrician crew then to Mare Island, CA. He was put on the USS *Lee Hardy* (DE-20) to Pearl Harbor home port. They were in Gilberts at Tarawa. In Marshalls at Kwajalein and also Wotte. Back to Pearl Harbor then went on convoy duty with oil tankers, from Pearl Harbor to Ulithi. Traveled about 200,000 miles. Went to Seattle, WA for Gen. Overall. Left DE-20 when it went to sea.

Home on leave to Norfolk, VA, put on sea going tug, but he didn't stay long. He was sent to Treasure Island, CA put on yard mine sweep, to Pearl Harbor, then left ship with enough points to get out. On to Little Creek, Norfolk, VA where he was discharged January 1946 with the rank of EM second class.

After discharge he went back to C&P Telephone and retired March 2, 1982. He has been married to Nellie for 46 years, with one son, Bob, one daughter, Mary and three grandchildren. He is now travelling by motorhome and enjoying the countryside.

REV. MONROE SHEARER, JR., was born July 30, 1924 in York City, PA. Joined the service Feb. 25, 1943. Naval training at Bainbridge, MD, Radar School at Virginia Beach, VA. Served in the USNR on the USS *Doneff* (DE-49). He had achieved the rank of radarman third class at the time of his discharge on Jan. 20, 1946. All of his three years spent on the USS *Doneff* were memorable for him.

He received the American Theatre Campaign Ribbon, World War II Victory Medal, Asiatic Pacific Theatre Ribbon, and Points System.

Married to Thelma Zimmerman with five daughters, Edith, Joyce, Denise, Julie, Kay, and two sons, Monroe III and George. He is a retired minister doing oil paintings and making furniture in his spare time.

ARTHUR SHOOK, USS *Fiske* (DE-143), entered Naval Service Feb. 13, 1943. He took boot camp at Bainbridge, MD. Upon completion, transferred to Norfolk, VA for DE training and was assigned to the

USS *Fiske* (DE-143). The *Fiske* was commissioned in Orange, TX on Aug. 25, 1943. The *Fiske* made several trips escorting convoys to the Mediterranean and back to the U.S.

While on anti-submarine patrol with a Hunter-Killer team the *Fiske* was sunk by a German submarine. After a leave he was transferred to Newport, RI for pre-commissioning training and assigned to the USS *New Hanover* (AKA-73). The new *Hanover* was commissioned at Charleston, SC and assigned to the Pacific. He did duty aboard this ship until September 1945. The *New Hanover* returned to the U.S. and he was transferred to other ships and stationed in the Far East. Arthur retired February 1973 and resides in Tucson, AZ.

DONALD J. SHRADER, MM3/c, USS *William T. Powell* (DE-213), was born and raised in Berwick, PA. Graduated in 1943, enlisted in the Navy, December 1943. Basic in Sampson, NY. Continued Norfolk NOB Machinist School March 1944-July 1944. Was assigned as a machinist on board of *Powell* (DE-213) in charge of machine shop and responsible for engineering office July 1944-March 1946. Was hospitalized in Chelsea Hospital for seven weeks with gangrene. Ribbons earned were European Theatre, American Theatre, and World War II Victory Medal.

Married Navy sweetheart Dorothy E. Stump of York, PA on July 16, 1945. Had a son, Jim. Dorothy passed away July 21, 1953. Presently married to Donna Lanning, raised five children, Jim, Jeff, Diane, Dan and Lanette and are grandparents of seven.

In civilian life, was in administration in Berwick and Bloomsburg, PA area until becoming disabled with COPD in June 1986. Home is in Mifflinville, PA. Enjoys going fishing when able. Also looks forward to hearing from former shipmates.

E. ARTHUR SHUMAN, JR., was born July 2, 1906 in Boston, MA. Inducted into United States Navy in 1931. He had achieved the rank of captain at the time of his discharge in 1962.

He recalls (DE-159) rescuing survivors of USS *Frechtler* (DE-157) on May 5 and 6, September 5 until October 17 Korea with (APD-55), China, and Flagship ComudRonTwo.

Father, Boston, mother, Salem. He has a son who is a retired captain in the United States Navy, and a grandson who is an active lieutenant in the Navy. He is now retired.

BURTON M. SICKELSMITH, S1/c, USS *Bronstein* (DE-189), enlisted at the age of 17, on Aug. 27, 1943 at Lansing, MI. Attended boot camp at Great

Lakes, IL for seven weeks, Co. 1298. Was one of many from this company to be assigned to the USS *Bronstein*. Attended Destroyer School in Norfolk for gunners mate. Went aboard the *Bronstein* in November and she was commissioned Dec. 13, 1943. Made one trip on convoy to Bizerte, Tunisia. Most of their work dealt with anti-submarine warfare. They were credited with sinking three German subs and capturing 39 prisoners on their first trip, two on the same night. Also brought back part of $68,000,000 of Polands gold from Dakar, Senegal. Took the ship to Green Cove Springs, FL November 1945. Discharged March 19, 1946.

Campaign ribbons include the American Theatre, European African Theatre with four stars, Victory Ribbon and a Presidential Unit Citation.

He worked for General Motors 36 years and retired in January 1983 at the age of 56. He is married with three daughters and five grandchildren.

GEORGE DEWEY SIMON, TM3/c, USCGR, USS *Mosley* (DE-321), entered United States Coast Guard April 1943. Graduated U.S. Navy Torpedo School NOB Norfolk. Commissioned USS Mosley at Orange, TX. Made convoy runs to Casablanca, Bizerte, and Oran, including convoy UGS-38 April 20, 1944 in which the USS *Lansdale* and Liberty Ship *Paul Hamilton* sunk with loss of 580 Army

Air Force personnel in one massive explosion. *Mosley* credited with one plane. USS (DE-157) was sunk with USS *Menges,* Free French DE torpedoed on West bound return.

Later, Mosley credited with one Sub as part of Hunter Killer Group in American Theatre. Transferred June 1945 to 3rd Naval District Shore Patrol. Discharged October 1945. Enlisted USNR Lakehurst, NJ. 1948 in Squadron ZP 751 1948 as AOU2/c. Flew as flight rigger in K Class Blimps. Graduated Rider College in 1950.

Commissioned Ensign (SC) USNR, Air Wing ZP-75. Recalled to active duty August 1950. Attended Navy Supply Corps School. Served in U.S. Naval Beach Group 2 until release to inactive service as LT (jg) USNR, October 1952. Worked for IBM, RCA, Peat Marwick, Northern Telecom. Currently Director of Communications for Canadian Pacific Computers and Communication. Held commercial pilot and flight instructor certificates. Currently holds U.S. Coast Guard licenses as master and certified radar observer. He and his wife Joan hope to cruise the Caribbean. They plan to live part time in Florida and Canada.

PAUL THOMAS SINDY, Coxswain, USS *Wesson* (DE-184), entered the Navy June 1, 1943. Boot camp at Bainbridge, MD. From Bainbridge to Norfolk Naval Base for three months, then to the Federal Shipbuilding and Dry Dock Co. at Kearney, NJ where he was assigned to the USS *Wesson*. Ship commissioned Nov. 11, 1943 shakedown cruise to Bermuda and on to the Pacific.

Participated in the invasions of the Marshall Islands, Marianas, Guam, Saipan, Tinian, Southern Palau Islands, Formosa, Leyte, Luzon, Iwo Jima and Okinawa.

The *Wesson* was hit by a kamikaze April 7, 1944. Came back to Mare Island, CA for repairs, then back to the Pacific for the invasion of Tokyo.

Campaign ribbons were the American Theatre, Philippine Liberation Medal with one Engagement Star, and Asiatic-Pacific with seven stars.

October 31, 1945 Tokyo Bay boarded USS *Cape Johnson* (AP-172) for stateside. Discharged Nov. 13, 1945.

He retired from Celanese Corporation at the age of 62. Traveled extensively after retiring. Celebrated 52nd wedding anniversary with wife Delores, Dec. 25, 1990.

HERBERT C. SINN, JR. *(See page 744)*

ANDREW F. SISKA, ETM2/c, USS *Gillette* (DE-681), Flagship Comcort Div. 56, Atlantic Fleet, was born July 28, 1925. Graduated from high school in Johnstown, PA on June 3, 1943. Enlisted USNR July 22, 1943. Completed boot camp with Co. 418, Sampson, NY in September 1943. Assigned Radar Operator and Technical School, Virginia Beach, VA. Assigned precommission crew and plankowner of DE-681. Shakedown in Bermuda. Participated in search and rescue operations during hurricane storm off Bermuda. Assigned submarine shakedown group, West banks Balboa, Panama. Made public relations and coutesy calls to several Central, South American and Caribbean countries. (DE-681) was assigned convoy duty as flagship Comcort Div. 56, as such participated in research and development and improvement of radar, sonar, loran and radio control, deflection and jamming equipment. After several convoys, berthed Plymouth, England. Patroled the English Channel. Assigned Mediterranean Fleet escorting to various North American Ports entering the Bay of Tunis, Tunisia while heavy fighting was still in progress. Escort LCI and LSTs used in invasion back to the U.S. arriving in Brooklyn Navy yard in late December 1944. January 1945, transferred ETM School. Enlisted USN Nov. 5, 1945. Transferred Treasure Island, CA June 1946 for advanced ETM. October 1946 rate changed to ETM2/c and assigned precommission crew, plankowner and senior ETM Ice Breaker AG 88 Burton Island. Commissioned Dec. 6, 1946, ordered to South Pole (Little America) Dec. 26, 1946 under emergency conditions (no shakedown) due to late freeze.

Flagship Admiral Richard Byrd's 1946-47 expedition to South Pole (Operation Highjump). After public relations calls to Australia, New Zealand and American Samoa he returned to San Diego. May 1947 assigned Operation Deep Freeze re-supply expedition to North Pole region returning to San Pedro, CA in September 1947. Last person to be discharged under

terminal leave program Oct. 3, 1947 with discharge effective Nov. 5, 1947.

After discharge he participated in various civic, government and charitable organizations. Worked on research development like Polaris missile, atomic subs, atomic power reactors, USS *Kitty Hawk* and various other military and commercial aircraft programs. Semi-retired as design engineer November 1989. Presently living with wife of 26 years in Willoughby, OH.

He was awarded the American European African Middle Eastern, Mediterranean Theatre Ribbons, World War II Victory Medal and Good Conduct.

He would like to hear from plankowners on either vessel.

FRANK J. SKUBIS, was born Sept. 6, 1924 in Dunkirk, NY. Joined the service March 20, 1943. Boot camp at NTS Sampson, NY for eight weeks. Shakedown on two ships in Bermuda, the USS *Tomich* (DE-242) for six months, and USS *Wingfield* (DE-194) for two years. PSC Lido Beach LI, NY April 7, 1946. He had attained the rank of SC first class at the time of his discharge.

He remembers raising hell in New York City between convoy duty to England, North Africa and then through the Panama Canal to Hawaii and Marshall Islands.

He received the Good Conduct Medal, American Theatre, Asiatic-Pacific, European Theatre, and World War II Victory Medal.

Married to Nancy Russo on Aug. 16, 1947. They have one son, Joseph, three daughters, Lucy, Suzanne and Nancy, and eight grandchildren. He is now retired and a member of VFW Twin Village Post 463 and DESA in Buffalo, NY.

EDWARD D. SLATE, S2/c, USS *Hopping* (DE-155), (APD-51), enlisted in the U.S Navy Feb. 6, 1943 in Richmond, VA. Received boot camp training at Bainbridge, MD and additional training at Norfolk, VA Amphibious Base. Attended Signal School in Casco Bay, ME.

Assigned to the USS *Hopping* (DE-155), which was under construction in the Norfolk shipyard and was commissioned on May 21, 1943. After a shakedown cruise to Bermuda, the USS *Hopping* returned to Norfolk and was assigned to convoy duty between the east coast ports of Norfolk and New York to European ports in England and Ireland.

After traveling more than 85,000 miles doing convoy duty, the *Hopping* returned to New York Staten Island Shipyard for conversion to a high speed Marine transport (APD-51), which was completed Sept. 26, 1944. The *Hopping* and crew were then transferred to the Pacific Theatre of War where they were in on the

Liberation of the Philippine Islands, the Invasic Okinawa and the occupation of Japan.

Discharged from the U.S. Navy, active du 22, 1946, at the Norfolk Amphibious base.

Attended Virginia Polytechnical Institute enlisting and after discharge. Employed by the monwealth of Virginia, Department of Transporta obtaining the position of assistant division administrator overseeing all general services for the department. Retired July 1, 1991, after 44 years of service.

Married Mary Harrison, Aug. 12, 1949 in Thomasville, NC. Two children, Gilbert and Bobbie Elizabeth and four grandchildren. Member of Trinity Methodist Church, Masonic Lodge, DESA, VFW, American Legion and Willow Oak Country Club in Richmond, VA. Received the following medals: World War II Victory Medal, Asiatic Pacific with one star, Philippine Liberation, and European African Theatre.

PAUL SLATER, (SLATS), MoMM1/c, USS *Walter S. Brown* (DE-258), enlisted in December 1942. Born Jan. 8, 1924 in New York City. Boot camp at Great Lakes, then Diesel School. Assigned to (DE-258), then being completed, as one of plankowners.

Made all of the *Brown's* cruises, convoy duty in the Atlantic and Mediterranean, Hunter Killer groups, Bay of Biscayne. Navy Unit Commendation. Discharged February 1946.

Especially memorable times: Missing the ship as she left on shakedown (while on errand for engineering officer); convoy UGS-40 under air attack by 62 aircraft, three torpedoes heading for ship at the same time and meeting some his shipmates 45 years later, including the one that missed the ship with him! Remembers hurricane off Cape Hatteras, Sept. 13, 1944 watching sister ships being tossed about, wondering how they could survive (USS *Warrington*, USCG Cutters *Jackson* and *Bedloe* and YMS 409 lost) and realizing that his ship was enduring the same pounding.

Worked as mechanic, farmer, college teacher and now retired. Lives in Massachusetts with Miriam, his wife of 43 years, a history professor; has two nifty kids, Margaret, a veterinarian, and Leo, a research chemist.

CHARLES LEO SMITH, SM1/c 701, USS *Cockrell* (DE-366), was born in San Francisco, CA on April 29, 1921. Enlisted apprentice seaman, February 1942. Boot camp at San Diego, CA. Signal School same. Graduated SM3/c. Transferred Subchaser Training Center, Miami, FL. Thence Philadelphia Navy Yard. Plank owner SC-701. Escort duties in the Atlantic, Gulf, Caribbean. Weaponry updated Panama. Provided escort, eventually to New Caledonia. Early 1943 escort and picket duty New Hebrices. Guadalcanal, Tulagi areas. SM 2/C transferred to UCLA V-12. Requested transfer. Granted February 1944. Original participant 592 JASCO, U.S. Marine Base, Camp Pendelton, CA. Jungle training, harbor patrol, picket boat charge, HI. Designated Signalman for President Franklin D. Roosevelt fishing trip out of Kaneheo Bay Maine Base. Attached to Gropac nine for Peleliu invasion. SM1/c aboard the USS *Cohasset*, Kossol Pass preparing for invasion of the Philippines. Assigned Com DE Div. 65 aboard USS *Cockrell* (DE-366), retrieving survivors USS *Indianapolis*, leading 1st occupation landing Wakayama, Japan. Returned U.S.

anc hints via Okinawa typhoon, USS *Vicksburg*, San He sco. Discharged Oct. 10, 1945. F Married Ann, entered shoe business; developed in es; merged; retired in 1981, Clearlake, CA. They x children of whom two were Vietnam veterans. ive and well. 14 grandchildren. *(See photos, pg. 74)*.

DAVID E. SMITH, born Jan. 14, 1925 in Elwood, IN. Joined the USNR in June 1942. Atlantic convoy duty served with USS *Evarts* (DE-5), and USS *Garlies* (DE-271). Plankowner on USS *Evarts*. Achieved the rank of CEM at the time of his discharge Dec. 13, 1945.

His ship made 13 large convoy duty escort round trips to different European and African locations without a convoy loss. He was shipped to England with a group on the *Queen Elizabeth* to return a number of DEs that had been manned by the British Navy.

He was awarded a Battle Star for air battle in the Mediterranean.

Married to Dorothy E. Ledbetter in June 1950 and has two sons. He worked for IBM for 35 years in computer engineering with last 24 years connected with NASA space programs after receiving degree in electrical engineering from Southern Methodist University in June 1952. He enjoys traveling and gardening.

FLOYD L. SMITH *(See page 744)*

HAROLD GLEN SMITH, was born May 5, 1920 in Eros, LA, the son of Henry and Mae Smith. Seventeen year old Glen Smith had boot camp on the coast of Virginia. Seaman Smith served six months on the USS *Wyoming*, a battleship. Then on the USS *Enterprise* launched on Oct. 3, 1936. He was on the shakedown cruise under Capt. Newton H. White, Jr. On her first cruise the *Enterprise* sailed down the busy Caribbean. The *Enterprise* also sailed into Rio de Janero. Captain C.A. Parnell replaced Captain White. In April 1939 the *Enterprise* moved to the Pacific, being based at San Diego.

On Sept. 1, 1939, Hitler's armies invaded Poland and WWII began.

The USS *Enterprise* set sail for its new base at Pearl Harbor. Glen Smith was sent to San Diego to receive an honorable discharge.

Jan. 5, 1943 he reported to the USS *Submarine Chaser* 1043. Attached to and serving on board the USS Submarine Chaser 1043 when this vessel, under order of CTG 80.4, became an advance striking force for the purpose of carrying out diversion raids on the islands of Ventotene and Ischia in the Tyrrhenian Sea, northeast of Naples, Italy, five hours prior to launching of Allied invasion on Salerno, Italy.

September 9, 1943 he served on the USS *Submarine Chaser* 1043 when this vessel rejoined main allied assault forces in the initial invasion and occupation of Salerno. It is noted that from date of actual invasion until Sept. 23, 1943, a period of 14 days, this vessel's crew was summoned to man all battle stations 75 consecutive times and successfully sustained 29 actual air attacks by the enemy. The commanding officer is pleased to state that Smith performed his duties at his battle station in a highly commendable manner.

Reported to USS *Stewart* (DE-238) on Jan. 6, 1945. Receiving station New York, NY. April 16, 1945 he was granted seven days leave and two days travel time this date June 2, 1945. As a member of the crew on the USS *Stewart* (DE-238) while performing convoy escort duties in American and European waters is qualified for and authorized to wear the American Area Campaign and European African Middle Eastern Area Medals in accordance with G.O. 194.

The USS *Stewart* participated in training, convoy duty and anti-submarine exercises. One June 28, 1945, she headed for Pearl Harbor. On the trip a special message came that the war in Europe was over.

Glen Smith returned to West Monroe, LA.

JAMES RUSSELL SMITH, SC1/c, USS *Sloat* (DE-245), enlisted in Navy on March 16, 1943. Boot

camp at Bainbridge, MD. DE training Norfolk, VA. NOB. Assigned to USS *Sloat*. Was laid down by Brown Shipbuilding Co., Houston, TX. Commissioned on August 16, 1943 with Lt. Cmdr. E.E. Garcia in command. Sailed to New Orleans, then to Bermuda for shakedown. Then ran convoy trips, New York to Norfolk. Following convoy trips to North Africa, Casablanca, Algiers, Bizerte Tunisia. Was in convoy UGS-36, largest to enter the Mediterranean Sea. Was also in Submarine Hunter Killer Task Group TG22.4, largest A.S.W. operation in American history.

Spent next year all over the Pacific Ocean, Pearl Harbor, Saipan, Guam, Iwo Jima, Shanghai, China. Accepted Japan's surrender Sept. 17, 1945 at Waleai Atoll, the Caroline Islands. Campaign ribbons were American Theatre, European Theatre, one Battle Star, Asaitic Pacific, Good Conduct and World War II Ribbon.

Worked for General Electric Co. for 26 years. Retired in 1985. Married Dec. 30, 1946 to Mamie E. Bond. They have three daughters and five grandchildren and reside in Pulaski, VA.

ROBERT LEE SMITH, F1/c, was born June 28, 1925. Enlisted in the Navy Oct. 29. 1942. Discharged Feb. 11, 1946. Boot camp at Great Lakes, IL. Commissioned USS *Elmore* Feb. 4, 1944 for shakedown in Bermuda. Hunter Killer Task Group for convoy duty European African and Middle Eastern. Earned Service Medal and two Battle Stars. USS *Elmore* sank sub that sank Carrier *Block Island* and hit USS *Barr* in fantail. Towed *Barr* to Casablanca.

Commissioned Nov. 7, 1944, Orange, TX Shakedown Bermuda Asiatic-Pacific convoy duty, Leyte Gulf, Ulithi, New Caledonia, Manus, Saipan, Guam, Iwo Jima, Okinawa, Truk Island Harbor patrol and Station ship pending the occupation of that enemy post by U.S. forces.

Married Armilda, raised three children, Sandra, Micheal and Brenda. Retired Montgomery Ward, Baltimore, MD. Tractor driver for 25 years.

CHARLES ERVIN SNEDEGER, EM2/c, USS *Vammen* (DE-644), born neat Selman, OK Aug. 29, 1925. Entered U.S. Navy Nov. 26, 1943. Boot camp, San Diego, CA. Training in Electrical Engineering School, University of Kansas at Lawrence. Boarded the USS *Vammen* May 21, 1944. The rest of his service was on board the *Vammen* in the Pacific area Pearl Harbor, Hawaii, Philippines, Ellice Island, Marshall Islands, Leyte, Guam and Saipan in screening and escorting operations, and the invasion of Okinawa. At wars end he was discharged at Norman, OK Jan. 14, 1946.

After his discharge Snedeger lived in Lawrence, KS where he and his wife Jean (Chapman) now reside. They were married Aug. 10, 1944 in Vallejo, CA. They have two daughters, one son, and eight grandchildren. In 1990 he retired from the Kansas Public Service Company and sold his coin laundry business of 23 years to his son. He belongs to the DESA and the USS *Vammen* Association.

JOHN W. SNURE, was born Aug. 7, 1925 in Roosevelt, L.I., NY. Joined the U.S. Navy Oct. 14, 1943. Boot camp at NTS Newport, RI. Radio School at University of Chicago. Went aboard the USS *Cronin* (DE-704) just prior to shakedown in Bermuda.

He received the European Theatre Medal, Asiatic Pacific Theatre Medal, Philippine Liberation Ribbon, American Theatre Medal, and World War II Victory Medal.

Married to the former Sally P. Phillips of Port Washington, NY. After his discharge he continued working for the Department of the Navy as a civilian in the field of printing. At the latter part of his career he was the Director of the Defense Printing Service in the Pentagon in Washington from 1964 until 1977. He then transferred to Philadelphia, PA as the Northern Division Director of Navy Publications and Printing.

GEORGE SOLMS III, was born Jan. 11,1918 in Richmond Hill, NY. Enlisted in the USCG Sept. 11, 1940, CG Training Station, Ellis Island, NY. Assignment, CCGD3 New York, NY, CG Station, Fort Trumbull, New London, CT. Served on the USS *Ricketts* (DE-254), CGC Eastwind, Green Cove Springs, FL. He was discharged Nov. 27, 1946.

He later served in the USCGR, assignments CG Station Shinnecock, L.I., NY, CG Station St. Petersburg, FL, Coast Guard Training Station, Yorktown, NA. CCGD 9, Cleveland, OH. Final discharge Jan. 11, 1978, after achieving the rank of SKC. He received the Asiatic-Pacific, Defense Medal and others.

Married, and now retired from, Grumman Corp. He served 27 years in the USCG and USCGR. George is active in the VFW, Safety Harbor, FL and living in Clearwater, FL.

GEORGE P. SOTOS, Captain USN, born Dec. 11, 1919 in Chicago. Enlisted in June 1940 as a seaman in the Navy V-7, officer candidate program. Commissioned Ensign USNR in March 1941, was aboard the ammunition ship USS *Nitro* when WWII started. Served as executive officer on the PC 476 and 451 before reporting to the commissioning detail as gunnery officer for the USS *Willis* (DE-395) in December 1943. Willis's operations were primarily with the Bogue Hunter Killer group in the Atlantic, where she earned the Presidential Unit Citation with two Combat Stars. As commanding officer, decommissioned the *Willies* in October 1945. Subsequently commands, USS Colonel LSD 18, USS *Harlan R. Dickson* (DD-708), DER Squadron 5, which consisted of nine DEs converted to radar picket ships for mid-Pacific early warning duties, and USS *Tolovana* (AO-64).

Married to former Georgette Catsis, two sons John and George, both doctors. Currently employed as a senior official in the U.S. Department of Education.

ANDREW C. SOUCY, MM, USS *Barr* (DE-576), born Leonminster, MA. Joined the Navy, 1943. Attended Machinist Mate School, Ford Motor CO., Dearborn, MI; advanced school, Norfolk, VA. Part of the commissioning crew of USS *Barr*. Served aboard her until Nov. 1945.

USS *Barr* was part of Submarine Killer Group operating with USS *Block Island* and three other DEs. The *Block Island* sank during enemy encounter. USS *Barr*, heavily damaged, suffered many casualties, was towed to Boston for repair. Left Boston for Pacific. Took on underwater demolition team at Maui and operated with team until the end of the war. Ship was then used for evacuation of Allied prisoners of war traveling up and down the coast of Japan.

In civilian life employed by General Electric Co. in department manufacturing many turbine generator sets which were installed in the DEs during the war. Retired 1984. Wife Patricia died in 1979. Three children. Later married Catherine Osowski. Very active in reunions with *Barr* and other DEs.

GERMANY A. SOUDER, Phm 2/c, enlisted in the Navy November 1942. Boot camp and HC1/c at Great Lakes Naval Hospital. Assigned to the USS LST-286, sailed to England transferred to USS LST 400. Trained for invasion of Normandy, France, June 6, 1944. Shuttled back and forth to England with wounded prisoners. After Normandy invasion, transferred to Norfolk, VA for further duty. Assigned to the USS *Naifeh* (DE-352) September 1944 for convoy duty in the Atlantic and Mediterranean Sea. One trip in North Atlantic they encountered a severe storm and heavy seas damaged top side, gun turents caved in, etc. They enlisted more than 60 degrees. He believes the Lord

held their ship upright. They caught up with the convoy later.

After duty in the Atlantic, the *Naifeh* was assigned to the Pacific via Panama Canal for convoying and patrolling duty all over the Pacific Islands, including dogging torpedoes until the war was over. He was transferred to an APD for return to the States. He was discharged at Memphis, TN November 1945.

He has been active in the VFW since 1947, presently Quartermaster of Post 9629. Also DESA member.

He is married and a father of four children. He lives in Bluff City, TN.

After travelling to many countries, he states that there is no other country like ours. He truly believes that God set America aside as the protector of mankind.

KENNETH I. SOURS, RM2/c, enlisted Nov. 10, 1942. Boot camp at Great Lakes Naval Training Center. Radio Service School at University of Wisconsin. Commissioned the USS *Chase* (DE-158) at Norfolk, VA July 18, 1943. Shakedown off the coast of Bermuda. Rode out two Atlantic hurricanes. Convoy service in the Atlantic, Mediterranean and the Caribbean. Was on the outer convoy ring when Germans attacked from the air on April 20, 1944 off the coast of Algiers. Picked up a number of survivors from sunken ships. Returned to Boston, MA, and was converted to APD-54. On Jan. 8, 1945 married Kathleen Vaughn, hometown girl. After a short shakedown off the East Coast left for the Pacific on Jan. 25, 1945. Was in the invasion of Okinawa April 1, 1945. Served on picket line until disabled by a Japanese suicide plane on May 20. Returned to the States and was discharged Oct. 15, 1945.

Received the American, European and Asiatic Theatre Ribbons with two Battle Stars. Returned to home town of Luray, VA. After several places of employment started work at the Page Valley National Bank of Luray. Retired after 29 years as vice president and loan officer. In past years he has been very active in the work of Beth Eden Lutheran Church. Also a member of the Masonic Order. Enjoys gardening, travel and outdoor activities. He and his wife have one daughter and two grandsons.

MELVIN LESTER SPARKS, enlisted in the Navy on June 10, 1942, after graduating from high school. Was first stationed at Philadelphia Navy Yard. Was later transferred to NOB Norfolk, VA. After training in ASW, he was assigned to ships crew for the USS *Wileman* (DE-22). Put the *Wileman* in commission in California. After a shakedown they headed for Pearl Harbor and the Pacific. They were in the Naval forces for the Marshall Islands and the Gilbert Islands.

After some 10 months, he was transferred back to the States. Arrived back at the Philadelphia Navy Yard and went to Boiler School there. After graduation, was transferred to Miami, FL. He was assigned to the USS *Brock* (API-93). Put the *Brock* in commission at the Charlestown, SC Navy Yard. They went down through the Panama Canal and back to the Pacific. Served on board throughout the Philippine Campaign and also the Okinawa Campaign.

Transferred back to the States and later served on the USS *Lyon* (AP-71). He was discharged March 25, 1946. Was called back to duty on Aug. 10, 1950. Was stationed at Newport, RI for Recruit Training Command. Was discharged again at Bainbridge, MD in 1952.

He was in the trucking business. Sold out and retired in 1986. Still lives in the state of Delaware, where he was born and raised.

HENRY L. SPEARMAN, CGM, USN, born Oct. 20, 1918 in Harris City, GA. Enlisted April 24, 1940 in Macon, GA. Boot camp Platoon 70 Norfolk, VA. Aviation Ordinance School NAS Norfolk, VA. Assigned CV6 Enterprise February 1941 at San Diego. Home ported Pearl Harbor. Returning to Pearl Harbor from Wake Island when the Japanese attacked. Participated in 10 major engagements including invasion of Guadalcanal, second battle Coral Sea, Battle of Midway, also Doolittles Tokyo Raid. Transferred August 1943 to Electric/Hydraulic School Naval Gun Factory in Washington, DC. Transferred to Subchasing School Miami, FL October 1943. Assigned USS *Major* (DE-796) December 1943, which was commissioned Feb. 12, 1944. After shakedown in Caribbean they were assigned escort duty to North African Ports and Plymouth, England passed through Panama Canal Feb. 27, 1945 for escort and picket duty in the Philippines and Okinawa. Anchored Tokyo Bay Sept. 2, 1945 and observed Jap surrender on board *Missouri*. Returned to San Diego Dec. 17, 1945. Discharged May 10, 1946 Charleston, SC.

Married Mildred Hines at Newman, GA Aug. 9, 1946. They have two sons, one daughter and six grandchildren. Wife passed away April 17, 1977. Married to Mary Ellen Key since 1979. Presently employed as retail salesman of building materials.

CHARLES HENRY SPECHT, RM3/c USNR, USS *Rolf* (DE-362), born July 13, 1920 in Glendale, CA. Boot camp at Farragut, ID and Navy Radio School at Moscow, ID. Shipped to Hollandia, New Guinea where assigned to the *Rolf*. Did duty from Hollandia to Leyte. *Rolf* went to Manila, then to Subic Bay. Worked there with U.S. submarines. They were in Shanghai, China when they received orders to come home. Received honorable discharge February 1946.

Attended college on the GI Bill. Receiving teaching credential and taught high school physics. Retired in 1978. He and his wife are enjoying retirement in Bishop, CA. They have five children and several grandchildren and great-grandchildren.

ROBERT F. SPEES, Ensign, USS *Spangenberg* (DE-223), entered Navy V-6 Program in October 1943 at Olathe, KS NAS. Transferred to V-12 NROTC in March 1944. Commissioned ensign in June 1946, at Rice University, Houston, TX. Assigned to USS *Spangenberg* (DE-223) in July 1946 as gunnery officer. Operated on the East Coast of U.S. and Caribbean in 1946-1947 performing anti-sub and air intercept training missions. Plane guard for the escort carrier *Salerno Bay*. Participated in the last large scale Atlantic Fleet maneuvers in 1947. Transferred to inactive reserve in May 1947 and discharged as lieutenant (jg) in June 1961.

Graduated from University of Pennsylvania in 1951 with B.S. in economics. Employed by Atlantic Refining Co. in June 1951 at Philadelphia, PA. Developed pioneering computer oriented Material Management System for Arco Refineries. Papers on Materials Management published by ASME, and National Petroleum Refiners Association. Transferred to Alaska in 1977 as materials superintendent, Prudhoe Bay. In 1982 named materials manager for Arco Alaska, with headquarters in Anchorage.

Retired from Arco in 1985. Married 40 years and living with wife Emma in Eagle River, AK. Enjoy travelling, local history/genealogical research, politics and volunteer activities. Three sons and their families also live in Alaska.

WILLIAM R. SPOSA, MM3/c, USS *Jack W. Wilke* (DE-800), entered the U.S. Navy on September 1951. Upon completion of his basic training at Bainbridge, MD he was assigned to the *Jack W. Wilke* (DE-800) out of Key West, FL. Upon his tour of duty he spent his four years in the E. Div. and worked in the evaptor space. He also ran the eng. store room and ran the motor whale boat.

In August 1951 he was released from the Navy at Charleston Navy Yard. In the following years he was in the plumbing and heating business. In the later years of his life he received a license as a New Jersey State plumbing inspector.

In 1987 he received a call from Jim Hunter regarding a ship reunion. They made the plans for their first reunion. It has been great for him ever since.

He has been married for 38 years to his wife Marie. They have four children, Lynn, Cindy, Gerlyn and Douglas. They also have eight grandchildren.

LEE SPRAGUE, USN, USS *Hanna* (DE-449), was born April 12, 1932 in Scranton, PA. Joined the Navy April 1951. Served in the U.S. Navy on the USS *Hanna* (DE-449). Achieved the rank of ET2/c at the time of his discharge.

He is married with two sons. Now retired and living in Vancouver, WA.

KEN W. SPRINGBORN, RM1/c, was born July 29, 1924 in Shawano, WI. Enlisted in the U.S. Navy Sept. 4, 1942. Boot camp at Great Lakes, IL. Radio School at University of Wisconsin, Newport, RI, Norfolk, VA, Boston, MA. Served on the USS *Montour*, Japan acct point accumulation to the USS *Tennessee* for the trip back to the States leaving Japan the middle of October 1945, arriving via the Cape of Good Hope, Philadelphia, Dec. 7, 1945 for discharge.

Received the World War II Victory Medal, American Theatre, European Theatre, Asiatic Pacific, Philippine Liberation, Good Conduct Medal and later Occupation Medal.

At the end of the war the USS *Montour* took part of the U.S. Army 25th Div. off the Philippines to Japan for occupation troops.

Married to Isabel Caron 1942. Blessed with four daughters and three sons. Retired in 1984.

VINCENT EMENIO SQUILLANTE, son of Alphonso Squillante, served in the U.S. Navy. Aboard the USS *Bowers* (DE-637) March 26, 1944. He was killed in Okinawa on April 16, 1943. He had achieved the rank of F1/c at that time. *Survived by his father, Alphonso Squillante*

WILLIAM E. STAKES, was born Aug. 13, 1917 in Pungo, VA. Enlisted in the USCG Sept. 19, 1940 after several years at sea with the Merchant Marines. Boot camp at Curtis Bay, MD. Picked up ammo at Yorktown, VA on the USS *Champlain*; weather patrol then ship given to England. CGRS Ellis Island, NY. Silver Guard detail he ran shot gun on truck load of silver to West point, NY. Coast Guard Receiving Unit Manhattan Beach Training Station where he taught boots. Served on the USS *Wakefield*; USS *Galetea* as cook on coastal convoy, New York to Rebecca Shoals; USS *Pettie* BM2/c North Atlantic convoy duty for two years.

Memorable experiences for him were serving as seaman aboard the USS *Wakefield* beginning Nov. 10, 1941. They picked up British troops, the Royal Norfolks and the Fifth Suffolks, at Halifax, Nova Scotia, Canada. They passed into Mona Passage Nov. 15, 1941. They arrived in Singapore, Federated Malay States Jan. 29, 1942 and departed Jan. 30, 1942, with several assignments in between including crossing the Equator seven times. While unloading troops and taking on refugees they were bombed. The bomb entered the main deck and found it's way into Sick Bay losing all members there. Out of the seven Equator crossings only the first had a King Neptune ceremony. Sporting a full beard he was brought up before King Neptune's Court and shorn before the whole crowd. With dwindling humiliation he watched a British General lost half of his gorgeous red handlebar moustache. What a sight. What a laugh.

Continuing on his duty aboard the *Wakefield* they picked up U.S. Marines at port of embarkation and sailed through Panama Canal to Aukland, New Zealand. Discharged Marines, returned via canal to New York. Next trip, returning from England the *Wakefield* burned at sea some 700 miles off the coast. They had some civilians from Greenland aboard. He was rescued by the cruiser *Brooklyn*. Taken to Boston he volunteered with other crew members to return to their ship and tow her into Halifax from there into Boston, MA. The USS *Wakefield* made headlines in the *Norfolk Ledger Dispatch*: "Former USS *Manhattan* Burns at Sea!". Also in the *Chicago Tribune*: "USS *Wakefield* sails through 55,000 miles of Blood and Valor!"

He had achieved the rank of boatswains mate second class at the time of his discharge. Received the American Area Campaign Ribbon, American Defense Service Ribbon with Bronze "A", European African Middle Eastern Area Campaign Ribbon with Bronze Star.

Married with three children, two girls and one boy, and six grandchildren. Now retired and raking leaves!

CARL H. STARK, EM2/c, (Starkie), USS *Andres* (DE-45), was born April 9, 1923 at Lancaster, PA. Enlisted in the Navy Sept. 15, 1942. Sworn in at Philadelphia, PA. Boot camp at Lakehurst, NJ. Was assigned duty at Lakehurst in the 4th Div. and earned EM3/c during this time. Assigned duty as hydrogen plant electrician for several months, later requesting sea duty. Shipped out to Little Creek, VA. Served on a mine sweeper for a short time, transferred to SCTC Miami, FL and assigned to USS *Andres* (DE-45) in November 1943. *Andres* served as a school ship here until Nov. 28, 1944. Made three round trips to Gibraltar by May 28, 1943. After refitting, *Andres* sailed for the Pacific and while underway, the war ended. He was then raised to EM second class on this ship, with duties

included standing watch on main propulsion, main distribution, and after steering. He was discharged Jan. 11, 1946.

Married to Mildred Stehman, June 20, 1948. They have one daughter, Cheri, wife of Roger Kurtz. Retired from the electrical business after 39 years. Reside at Landisville, PA and still very busy.

WALTER A. STASIOWSKI,

was born Aug. 11, 192 in Milwaukee, WI. Entered U.S. Coast Guard Dec. 23, 1941. Received training at Jackson Park Coast Guard Station in Chicago, IL. Life saving small boat handling and good seamanship according to USCG tradition. There he did various guard duty, at Navy Pier and Chicago Canal locks.

August 1942: on board the CG *Semlogh*, 55 yacht Coast Guard took over, went across Great Lakes. Later ended up on Chesapeake Bay towing targets for the big battle wagons. Did offshore submarine patrol on the coast of Savannah, GA on CG 55019. They were equipped with one 50 caliber Browning machine gun and four depth charges.

April 1943, entered Navy Torpedo School at Newport, RI. Graduated as torpedoman third class (only 12 U.S. Coast Guard men to enter Torpedo School). Assigned to the USS *Lowe* (DE-325) November 1943 until June 1945. While on convoy duty N.A. and to Mediterranean, and North African ports he received two Battle Stars, American Theatre, and European Theatre. Sank submarine off coast of Newfoundland. Made torpedoman first class. He did gunnery work after torpedo tubes were removed. His rank was never changed although others were changed to gunners mates.

Discharged June 19, 1946. Later worked for American Can Co. in Milwaukee, WI for 32 years as a mechanic. Now retired, with two sons and four grandchildren. Amateur radio operator for 28 years as a hobby.

DANIEL V. STEEG, CMoMM (PA), USN,

was born Oct. 4, 1917 in Elizabeth, NJ. Enlisted March 1936 as apprentice seaman. Boot training at Great Lakes, IL. Then ordered to USS *Ranger*, CV-4, Bremerton Navy Yard. Upon completion of overhaul *Ranger* returned to the homeport San Diego and rejoined the Pacific Fleet. Then followed two fleet problems and a visit to Lima, Peru (Goodwill). Fleet problem XX took place in the Caribbean in 1939, War broke out in Europe. On completion of maneuvers, most of the fleet returned to the Pacific, except for the newly formed Atlantic Squadron, which included *Ranger*. They then attended the New York Worlds Fair. Then followed a busy year. American Defense. Cruised all over the Caribbean and the East Coast.

Completed four year enlistment in 1940, rating held was MM1/c. After a year out he re-enlisted for four years at same rate. Then followed four months aboard the Marine Transport USS *Barnett*.

He then volunteered for Surface Diesel School at New London, CT. On completion, ordered to P.C. 472 being built at Bay City, MI. Commissioned ship on Dec. 10, 1941. Next day departed for Boston. A Canadian Ice Breaker assisted then half the way. On completion of outfitting, roamed the Atlantic submarine hunting until convoys were started. On those first convoys, escort vessels were wooden SCs, a few steel PCs, steel eagle boats, left over from World War I. There were even yachts outfitted with depth charges. The Atlantic was a graveyard at this time.

Left the States on sealed orders in October 1942. Their task force consisted of eight PCs, eight SCs, eight mine sweepers, two tugs, one tanker and one light cruiser. Arrived in Casa Blanca, November 1942 to a harbor of sunken ships. One year spent leading and protecting convoys in and out of the harbor and convoying Collier's to Gibralter. Also patrolled off the Rock during the invasion of Italy. Made CPO while in Africa. Received orders to report to NOB Norfolk, VA. Transportation was via Pan American Clipper.

After 30 days leave, ordered to Sub Chaser Training Center, Miami. Next stop, USS *Carter* (DE-112) being built at Wilmington, DE.

Since commissioning on May 3, 1944 their ship had sunk one enemy sub, and participated in the capture of two U-boats. They had steamed over 80,000 miles. After Germany surrendered, *Carter* was sent to Mayport, FL for plane guard duty to the Aircraft Carriers *Guadalcanal* and *Mission Bay*. After Japan surrendered, departed from the Navy on points and expiration of enlistment.

He and his wife decided to stay in Florida. After about 10 years, he became a Master Plumber then operated his own plumbing business. Purchased the house where he still lives, in January 1948. They will celebrate their Golden Anniversary in 1992. Six children, two of their sons have taken over the business. Also have eight grandchildren and one granddaughter.

BRUCE R. STEELE, RM2/c, USS *Alvin C. Cockrell*

(DE-366), was born in Granville, IL on Feb. 3, 1924. Enlisted Recruiting Station at Chicago April 25, 1944. Boot camp and Radio Operators school at Great Lakes, IL. Boarded *Cockrell* Dec. 13, 1944 in Norfolk after shakedown, thence through Panama Canal to San Diego. Operated in central/western Pacific convoying carrier groups. Did anti-sub patrols off Marshalls, Guam, Okinawa plus air-sea rescues and participated in search for survivors of USS *Indianapolis* following its' sinking by a Japanese submarine. After Japan's surrender *Cockrell* was part of 5th Fleet which entered the Inland Sea along with mine sweepers, hospital ships and troop ships to remove war prisoners, first landing in Wakayama. They were privileged to view the sunken fleet at Kobe Naval Base as well as results of the atom bomb at Hiroshima. Rode out the famous typhoon of Sept. 17-18, 1945 which hit Okinawa and Japan, they being at Wakayama, Japan. Feb. 1, 1946 arrived in California and decommissioned the *Cockrell*. Discharged May 5, 1946.

Married Phyllis Buhn Feb. 2, 1947 with two sons, Robert, an attorney and James, a six year DE/Fast

Frigate (DE-1092) sailor (Vietnam War) and nuclear plant technician. They also have five grandchildren. Career was as a farmer and electrician, lived retired at Tonica, IL.

STAN STEFANICK,

was born June 11, 1919 in Detroit, MI. Enlisted in the Navy in January 1942. Boot camp at Newport, RI for two-three months. Radio School Boston Navy Yard for two months. Transferred to South Weymouth Naval Air Station April 19. Served there in radio operations. Took part in sport activities. Received orders in early November 1944 for sea duty aboard the USS *Robert Brazier* 345). Served in the South Pacific until December and discharged at Great Lakes, IL in January 19

Married to Ruth M. Lessnau May 8, 1952. Father of three sons and five daughters. Retired from Ford Display Exhibit in May 1986 after 33 years. Woodworking is one of his hobbies now. Constructs many wood toys and donates to various charities.

RICHARD T. STENGEL, (CASEY), SM2/c,

USN & USNR, was born in Allentown, PA on May 28, 1924. Joined the U.S. Navy Nov. 30, 1942. Boots and Signal School Newport, RI. DE School Norfolk, VA. Commissioned USS *Duffy* (DE-27) Mare Island, CA. Two years in Pacific, Tarawa, Kwajalien, Marshalls, Gilberts, Solomons, Saipan, Guam, Leyte, etc. Survived two typhoons off Samar in 1944. Had stern blown out of the water-premature depth charge explosion. Lost steering (and his breakfast). Two years as shore patrolman Tacoma, WA (1946-47). ADAK, USS *Virgo*, USS *Tanner* (Labrador). Left Navy Dec. 30, 1948 and joined the USNR. Called for Korean duty in 1950. Total service time 14 years, seven active and seven served in the Reserves. Navy boxing career-won 35 and lost one. Fifteen medals, three commendations, 14 Battle Stars, five boxing titles.

Married to Dorothy in 1957. They have six children, 11 grandchildren and three great-grandchildren. Retired as chief deputy coroner for Pierce County, WA. Now enjoy salmon fishing, hunting, family, retirement, locating old shipmates and DESA. Life membership with DESA, D.A.V, and Lodge #1450 B.P.O.E., and he still gets seasick.

ALEXANDER C. STERNBERG, MM1/c, USS

Salinas (AO-19) and USS *Buckley* (DE-51), enlisted in the Navy December 1941. Boot camp at Newport, RI, then assigned to the *Salinas*. Two trips on the *Salinas*, one to Iceland, and one to Greenland. Transferred to Sub-chaser Training Center Miami, FL, October 1942. After training assigned to the USS *Buckley* (DE-51), then under construction.

... commissioned the *Buckley* April 30, 1943. Made ... *Buckley* cruises, including special assignment as ... ... l ship, and a research trip to Gitmo, convoy duty in the Atlantic Ocean, and the Mediterranean Sea, hunter killer duty in the North and South Atlantic.

Two German boats to their credit, repelled air attacks in the Mediterranean. Awarded the Navy Unit Commendation and three Battle Stars.

After war ended in Europe, the *Buckley* was converted to a Radar Picket Ship DER-51 and was set to go to the Pacific Theatre when war ended with A-bomb. Discharged October 1945. Worked for UPS for 35 years. Retired in 1984. Lives in Clark, NJ with wife, Nancy. They have one daughter, Judy, and two grandsons Michael and Matthew.

BRUCE H. STICKROTH, EM3/c, was born Oct. 3, 1926 in Toledo, OH. Joined the U.S. Navy Reserves Sept. 30, 1944. EM School at Great Lakes, IL. Served on the USS *Oswald* (DE-767) and USS *Stanton* (DE-247).

Memorable experience for him was DE Squadron with baby flattop out of Miami, FL August-October 1945 Brooklyn Navy Yard, then to Jacksonville, FL and St. John's River for decommissioning in 1946. He received Good Behavior Award.

Married November 1947 with one daughter and four sons. Two oldest sons married, Mark has four sons and one daughter, Matt has a son and daughter. His first wife passed away and he married again in May 1974, she has two sons, one daughter and 11 grandchildren. He retired after four years from Dana Corp. after 37 years as checker in Engineer Department of Universal Joint Div. in Toledo, OH. Joined DESA in 1980 National in 1980 and Ohio Chapter later that year.

GORDON M. STREET, was born Oct. 17, 1913 in San Diego, CA. Attended Yale ROTC 1931-1935 as ensign. Active service in 1938. Attended Sound School Key West 1942 with "S" Co., PC-573; DE USS *Donnell* in 1943; hit S.W. of Ireland; London Task Force C.O. APD-122 Schribner in Pacific; Okinawa; 1946-1978 World Bank of D.C.

Remembers being torpedoed in North Atlantic and pursued by kamikazi-knocked some down in Pacific. He received Bronze Star, Gold Star, N.R. and various area medals.

Married for 55 years to Virginia with two children, Mark and Alison and one grandchild. Happily retired, enjoyed golf, travel woodworking, until severe stroke in 1991. He is slowly recovering.

ALBERT STRINGFIELD, was born Nov. 2, 1925 in New River, TN. Joined the service Oct. 21, 1943 at Chattanooga, TN. Served in the Navy. Boot camp at

Great Lakes, IL. Assigned to the USS *Bermingham* (DE-530). Shakedown at Bermuda then convoy duty to Oran, Africa several times and Ireland, England and when the war was over they pulled in to Charleston, SC to decommission ship. October 1945 he received 30 days ReHab. leave. After leave he went to Brooklyn, NY to pick up the USS *Portland* (CA-33) and went to LeHavre, France. December 1945 to pick up about 1,000 troops to bring home. Rank S1/c when discharged April 6, 1946 at Memphis, TN.

He received the American Area Ribbon, European African Middle Eastern Ribbon and World War II Victory Medal.

Married Pauline Scott Nov. 26, 1948. Have two sons, W. Randall and Douglas A., and one daughter, Marsha Gail. They also have seven grandsons and one granddaughter. Retired from Tennessee Highway Patrol September 1976.

MATTHEW C. STRONSKI, GM2/c, USS *Decker* (DE-47), joined Navy Sept. 27, 1942. Boot camp in Rhode Island. January 4, 1943 he was assigned to M.S. Texas Sun Armed Guard Unit. Made two convoy trips to Morcambe and Bristol, England. One trip to Australia traveling alone. Reported to the *Decker* after he shakedown cruise. Took most convoys to North Africa. Earned three ribbons the Asiatic-Pacific, European African Middle Eastern Theatre with Engagement Star. Discharged Dec. 3, 1945. Served in Naval Reserve and was called to serve aboard USS *Currituck* AV7 Sea Plane Tender May 8, 1951 to Aug. 7, 1952.

Now 69 years of age, married to a wonderful wife of 42 years. Retired from RCA Camden Engineering Model Shop, as a model maker after 43 years. He has three sons and five grandchildren.

JOSE ANGEL SUAREZ, JR., SM1/c, USS *Richey* (DE-385), USS *Theenim* (AKA-63), enlisted Coast Guard Oct. 28, 1942. Born and raised Aug. 31, 1922 in Ybor City, Tampa, FL to Aurora T. and Jose' A. Suarez, Sr. Boot camp CGTS Curtis Bay, MD. Signalman School at Manhattan Beach, NY.

Assignments include DCGO-5th N.D.; Currituck Beach LBS; Pilot boat Hampton Roads CGR 5189, Naval Training Station Norfolk; USS *Richey*; Coast Guard Rec. Sta. EINY; USS *Theenim* (AKA-63). (DE-385) for shakedown in Bermuda, returned to the States, practice off Portland, New London, New York Ammunition Depot, convoy to Oran; Bizerte; North Atlantic; Casablanca; Gibraltar; North Channel; Irish Sea; Belfast; Milville; and Londonderry, Ireland.

March 28, 1944 while on North Atlantic convoy sub contact foggy, rough cold night collided with convoy 4:55-bow damaged secured forward compartment-reported to Oran, clear collision problem. Moored to Germany, dry dock, that evening German scout plane dropped flares lit area. Ships shot at targets except they're shooting at enemy plane, they told officer on duty, they're shooting at enemy plane, he replied just practice. The next day they told commanding officer, next time, shot. Returned to States, arrived Brooklyn Navy Yard Sept. 5, 1944.

He was transferred with ten days leave, reported to district Coast Guard office third Naval District, New York City on Sept. 15, 1944. Assigned to USS *Theenim* (AKA-63). Boarded at Brooklyn Navy Yard Dec. 22, 1944, commission Dec. 23, 1944. Fifteen days later proceeded to Norfolk, shakedown in Norfolk, before crossing Panama Canal. First stop Pearl Harbor; Guadalcanal; Saipan; Okinawa invasion; Guam; Manus; Espiritu Santos; Leyte; Aomori; Tokyo Bay (Peace Treaty Ceremony) Yokohama; Manila; Portland Oregon; San Francisco; Subic Bay PI; to Norfolk, VA. Discharged April 30, 1946.

Married to Pauline Georgia Kalaboke Nov. 29, 1946 in New York City. Raised two daughters Susan and Joan. Retired from City University after 30 years service as senior supervising engineer. Member of VFW Post 364, Tappan, NY and DESA. Will eventually live in Florida.

TIM SULLIVAN, was born Feb. 25, 1925 in Gary, IN. Joined the U.S. Navy June 19, 1945. Stationed Great Lakes, IL, Norfolk, VA, Mare Island, USS *Rall* (DE-304). Achieved the rank of EM2/c at the time of discharge.

Remembers the typhoon, Iwo Jima and Okinawa. He received the American Theatre Ribbon, Philippine Battle, World War II Victory Medal, Asiatic-Pacific with four stars, Presidential Unit Citation.

Married to Rose Mary for 44 years, three daughters, Carol Klemz, Marti Hubble, Bridget Sullivan. Also has grandson Tim, Mike, Nelson, and Brandon Sulivan-Hulde. He is President and Business Representative for Teamsters Local Union 142. St. Helen's Parish Board member, Tradewind's Rehabilitation, Pirate's support group, Boy's and Girl's Clubs, N.W. Indiana Sons of Erin. Resides in Hebron, IN.

CARL JOSEPH SUNDSTRAND, born Dec. 31, 1925 in Philadelphia, PA. Inducted into U.S. Navy March 24, 1944 and started his recruit training March 25, at Bainbridge, MD Finished training April 25. Attended Electrician's Mate school at Bainbridge and completed Aug. 19, 1944. Went aboard the USS *Harding* Oct. 10, 1944. It was converted to Destroyer Minesweeper (DMS-28). On Jan. 6, 1945 they proceeded through canal to Balboa. Later on to San Francisco, Pearl Harbor, Eniwelok Atoll, Ulithi and Okinawa. Began mine sweeping operations in Okinawa March 23, 1945. Still mine sweeping March 26 while the invasion began. April 6, they had a near miss by a horizontal Japanese bomber, and attacked by a suicide plane tearing a huge gash in the ships side from keel to main deck when the bomb exploded. 14 men were killed, eight were missing in action and over nine wounded.

On Sept. 17, 1945 the *Harding* arrived in Norfolk, VA and was decommissioned Nov. 2 and sold for scrap. Dec. 13, 1944 he was transferred to USS *Snyder* (DE-745). Transferred later to Lido Beach, LI, NY for his honorable discharge. He received the American Theatre Medal, Asiatic Pacific Medal with one star, Victory Medal. Authorized to wear the Minecraft shoulder insignia.

June 18, 1946, was given his first honorable discharge and then re-enlisted for four years in the inactive Reserves as electrician's mate third class. Training at U.S. Submarine Base New London, CT. Served on the USS *Raton* and USS *Grouper*. He was given his second honorable discharge on June 18, 1954. He has never married, has no children and studies Astrology.

NELSON K. SUTTER, TM3/c, USS *Cockrill* (DE-385), enlisted in Navy on Oct. 1, 1942. Boot camp at Great Lakes, IL. Attended Torpedo school at Newport, RI. Then was assigned to USS *Cockrill*. Went from Norfolk to Bizerte once. Hawaii, Philippines, Solomon Islands and the Island of Mog Mog. The *Cockrill* collided with an oil tanker during the war which was a never forgotten incident.

Received Good Conduct, Philippines Liberation, American European and Pacific Medals. He was discharged December 1945.

Married to Florence Caplan. Graduated Bradley University, Peoria, IL June 1950 with a B.S. in business administration. Have one daughter, Sally. Worked as an auditor for the Illinois Agricultural Auditing Association for 25 years and retired December 1982 at the age of 58. Has had an accounting business for five years but is now fully retired and enjoying a life of leisure. He lives in Galesburg, IL and is no longer active but is a lifetime member of Post 2257 VFW. He is also a member of Cosmopolitan International.

CARROLL F. SWEET, USNR, commissioned ensign USNR in April 1939, lieutenant commander. Sweet drilled with a reserve unit in Grand Rapids, MI, until August 1940, participating in Great Lakes training that year aboard USS *Paducah*. On Sept. 7, 1940 he reported for active duty on USS *Ranger* (CV-4), an aircraft carrier, and was assigned C&R Dept. and Damage Control duties. He qualified as OOD watch

stander both port and sea and wrote and conducted many damage control drill problems. In June 1942, he was transferred to SCTC, Miami, Group 16, and became Lt. (jg). On completion ASW training, he was ordered to Nyack, NY, as prospective CO of USS SC-738. October 20, ship commissioned. Lt. Sweet in command, Ensign Robert Woodcock USNR, Exec., took ship to Australia for duty with Australian Navy, escorting shipping across Coral Sea between Townesville, Port Moresby and Milne Bay (New Guinea). June 1943, SC-738 was transferred to U.S. Amphibious Forces under Admiral Dan Barbey, based in Milne Bay, escorting landing craft to Buna and other forward areas. Though Sweet was ordered to SCTC for DE command training in September 1943, by then guns, which on Dec. 21, 1943, with ship under command of Lt. Woodcock, proved critical in defending attack by more than 65 enemy aircraft, at least six shot down with minor damage to SC-738 and crew.

On completion of DE command training, Lt. Sweet was ordered to duty as prospective Exec. of USS *Kyne* (DE-744) under construction in San Pedro, CA and became Exec. when ship was commissioned April 4, 1944. Ship reported to Pacific Fleet in June and on July 25 he relieved Commander Alexander Jackson USNR as commanding officer. Ship assigned to Palau invasion force; escorted supply ship to beachhead soon after D-Day. Then escorted USS *Dixie*, first station ship, to Ulithi lagoon. He became lieutenant commander in October. On November 10, while anchored at Manus, Admirality Islands, *Kyne* was slightly damaged and lost one man to flying debris from USS *Mt. Hood* explosion. January 1945, assigned to logistics support of fast carrier attack groups. While escorting replenishment tankers and carrier through Philippines' Surigao Strait route to rendezvous with Admiral Halsey forces in South China Sea, formation was attacked by enemy submarine, no damage to ship or convoy. Was ASW patrol at Iwo Jima on D-Day. With floating replenishment base of the fast carrier groups escorted replenishment tankers and carriers between the base and Ulithi and Guam. Survived violent hurricanes during this time. On completion Okinawa campaign, June 1945, loaned to Seventh Fleet to escort carrier support for amphibious landings at Balikpapan, Borneo. Then rejoined logistic force involved in air strikes on Japanese homeland. Lt. Cmdr. Sweet, on hearing of Japanese surrender, suffered sudden stress release disability; transferred to hospital ship.

USS *Kyne* became third ship to enter Tokyo Bay, but before surrender ceremony was sent out to escort USS *Pennsylvania*, which had been torpedoed by "die hard" Japanese cub commander. *Kyne* returned to California in October and was decommissioned and stored at Green Cove Springs, FL, but soon reactivated and, based at Fort Schuyler, NY, served as a reserve training ship for at least 10 years.

Returned to civilian status in January 1946, retired in 1991 after 45 years as a real estate developer and consultant. He is now a member of Destroyer Escort Commanding Officers (DECO) and had written a book-length report on this six-year Navy career.

ROBERT SWEITZER (See photos, pg. 744.)

HOWARD WILLIAM TAGLIABUE, SM2/c, was inducted into the U.S. Navy in July 1943 and spent the next six months at Newport, RI in boot camp and then Signal School. Upon completion of this training, he was

assigned to an outfit destined to man the Port of Cherbourg, France after it was taken from the Germans.

After several months of waiting in Scotland, he was detached and assigned to Commodore Campbell D. Edgar's "Flag" aboard the USS *Maloy* (DE-791) which was lead to a flotilla of LCIs across the English Channel on D-Day. During its stay at Omaha Beach, the *Maloy* shot down a German plane and captured its pilot.

When Cherbourg was finally liberated, he spent the next ten months as part of the Harbor control, serving on the several signal towers overlooking the harbor.

After V-E Day and a 30 day leave, he attended advanced Signalman/Quartermaster School for two months in Miami, FL. He then was assigned to the USS *Marengo* (AK-194). Further assignment took him to the USS YW-131, a yard water tanker aboard which he completed his Navy career delivering water daily to DEs being mothballed at Green Cove Springs, FL which was featured in a recent edition of the DESA NEWS.

He was discharged in April 1946, attended and graduated from Central College, in Pella, IA. He then worked the next 35 years in the Trust Department of the Chase Manhattan Bank in New York City and is now retired.

He has been married for 41 years and has four children, Nancy, Judy, Robert, John and two grandchildren.

EDWARD W. TALLAU, JR., EM2/c, USS *Frament* (DE-677-APD-77), was drafted into the Navy July 13, 1943 upon graduation from Columbia High School in Maplewood, NJ. After completing boot camp at Newport, RI he attended Electrician Mates School also at Newport. At Pier 92 in Manhattan he was assigned to (DE-677) on availability at the Brooklyn Navy Yard in the winter of 1944.

The USS *Frament* made regular round trips to Londonderry, Ireland and one trip to Gibraltar. While in Gibraltar the *Frament* was assigned to duty to escort an Italian submarine back to the U.S.

Upon completion of the modification to an APD in December 1945, the *Frament* was ordered through the Panama Canal and made the usual stops through Pearl Harbor, Eniwetok, Ulithi, and Leyte arriving in Okinawa in late May 1945 where she joined the outer patrol screen guarding ships off the island.

At the close of the war the *Frament* was one of the first ships into Shanghai serving until Jan. 1, 1946 when she sailed for the East Coast. In early April 1946 Tallau was released from the *Frament* when it was mothballed in Green Cove Springs, FL.

He married Gladys Mott in June of 1947. He worked in the casualty insurance business for 36 years retiring on Sept. 1, 1982 and still lives in Florham Park, NJ. Ed and Gladys have one son, two daughters and eight grandchildren. Ed is currently skipper of the Garden State Chapter of DESA.

GLEN TAYLOR, S1/c, USS *Smartt* (DE-257), entry into active service Nov. 12, 1943. Boot camp at Great Lakes Navy Training Center. Then assigned to USS *Smartt* (DE-257), February 1944 to October 1945. Made eight convoy trips from New York to Gibralter, Casablanca, Oran, Bizerte, and Sicily.

Was attacked by Japanese J.U. 88 German dive bombers on May 11, 1944. Served in American, European, African and Middle Eastern areas. Received one Battle Star. He was discharged April 27, 1946.

Married to Emogene Tipton on July 1, 1950. They have two daughters and two grandchildren. Retired in 1988 at the age of 63, after 31 years service with Holston Defense Corporation. Now living in Kingsport, TN.

ANTHONY A. TERRAMEO, Sr., was born Nov. 20, 1924 in Niagara Falls, NY. Joined the U.S. Navy March 20, 1943. Served on the USS *Swearer* (DE-186). He achieved the rank of electrician mate first mate. Received the Philippine Liberation with one star, Asiatic-Pacific with seven stars.

Married to wife Mildred with one son, Anthony and two daughters, Judy and Jane. Retired from Niagara Falls New York Fire Department. He now enjoys decoys carving.

KENNETH L. TETO, was born Sept. 28, 1925 in Fitchburg, MA. Enlisted in USCGR Sept. 15, 1943. Boot camp at Manhattan Beach, NY. Served on the USS PC-556 in Italian and French campaigns from March 1944 until October 1944. Ship was commissioned to French at Toulon France. Returned to New York and assigned to USS *Kirkpatrick* (DE-318) with convoy escort duty New York to France and England. (Skipper V.E. Bakanas).

He was transferred to USS *Poole* (DE-151) on June 4, 1945. Left New York City for Pacific duty for occupation of Japan. On Nov. 9, 1945 he left for U.S. on eventually to Green Cove Springs, FL to mothball USS *Poole*. Returned home for discharge April 6, 1946, with the rank of SM2/c.

After discharge he worked for Simonds Saw and Steel (Fitchburg, MA) for 30 years. Owned coin-op for 25 years. Married his high school sweetheart in 1948. They had two daughters, two sons and five grandchildren. He is now retired and in ill health (cardiac), but still goes out to sea on his 25 foot cabin cruiser during summer months at Newbury Port, MA.

W.A. THOMPSON, was born Jan. 7, 1924 in Xenia, IL. Joined the U.S. Navy Dec. 21, 1942. Boot camp at Great Lakes. Stationed Algiers Receiving Station, New Orleans, Norfolk, and USS *Sturtevant* (DE-239) for the duration of his service time. Made 11 round trips convoy to North Atlantic then through canal to Pacific. After the war he went back through canal to Charleston, SC and was discharged. He received the European Theatre, and the Asiatic-Pacific.

Married Sallie Thompson with two children Jerry and Vicki. They also have two grandchildren Sean and Jason. He retired after 40 years as an engineer at a television broadcast station.

REX A. THORNE, was born Jan. 21, 1926 in Huntington, IN. Joined U.S. Navy in July 1944. Boot camp at Great Lakes, IL. On to Norfolk, VA and Brooklyn Navy Yard. Served on the USS *Heyliger* (DE-510) in the Pacific and returned to the U.S. in January 1946 to Boston. Then to Green Cove Springs, FL where the ship was mothballed. He was discharged June 1946 with the rank of SK2/c.

Married Ruth Shutt Aug. 29, 1948. Graduated from Purdue University August 1950 as chemical engineer. They have two sons and two daughters. He is currently corporate director for Environmental Affairs for Union Camp Corp.

JACK A. THURMOND, M.D., was born Sept. 19, 1925 in Clearwater, SC. Joined the USNR in December 1942. Attended Bainbridge Training Station, Electrician's Mate School Newport, RI; Gyro Compass School; Brooklyn Navy Yard; Nucleus Crew, Orange, TX and on to the USS *Finch* (DE-328) Decem-

ber 1943-December 1945, USS *Albert T. Harris* December 1945-February 1946. He was discharged at that time achieving the rank of EM1/c.

Memorable experiences for him were rescuing POWs at Formosa in 1945, and the association with the great members of the *Finch* crew.

After discharge he graduated from college and medical school. He practiced medicine (ophthalmology) for 35 years before retiring May 1, 1990. Married to a fantastic wife Lois, with for wonderful children, three boys and one daughter. They also have three grandchildren.

DONALD R. TILLOTSON, was born April 8, 1926 in Hot Springs, SD. Joined the U.S. Navy June 6, 1943. Served 20 years mostly DDs, Sub Tenders and Stations.

Remembers the Suez blockade, Cuban Blockade and surviving a suicide hit on (DE-637). Also recalls VJ Day and VE Day.

He received the Asiatic-Pacific with four stars, five Good Conduct Medals, Philippine Liberation, World War II Victory Medal, National Defense, Armed Force Expert and American Campaign Ribbon. He had achieved the rank of ET1/c at the time of his discharge.

Married to wife "Irish" with two children, one son who has served in the Army for 24 years. He is now retired from Chief Central Service, VA Hospital in Hot Springs, SD.

JOHN A. TORDO, SR., was born March 7, 1942 in Wallingford, CT. Enlisted in the USNR Jan. 3, 1943. Served on DE-161/APD-57. Achieved the rank of BM2/c at the time of his discharge.

Married to Shirley Smith, with six children and five grandchildren. He retired after 26 years with Olin Corporation serving at Winchester Div. for 19 years, chemical division for seven years.

JAMES LELAND TREVOR, LT. CMDR., USNR, was born 1917 in Eagle Butte, SD, son of Spanish-American War homesteader; educated Avon, IL; graduated Knox College, Galesburg, IL in 1938; joined American Chicle Co., New York City 1941-Attended OTS, USS *Prairie State* moored Hudson River; Commissioned ensign December 1941. Communications School, Noroton, CT; assigned March 1942, USAT *Ernest J. Hinds,* liaison officer, Communications Group. *Hinds* manned by U.S. Maritime; mission was to transport military passengers. *Hinds* transited Panama Canal then delivered passengers to Galopagos, Hawaii, Alaska, Ulithi, Guadacanal, Noumea, Fiji; leaving Guadacanal for Tulagi *Hinds* maneuvered in uncharted waters to avoid submarine sighting. Destroyer in area (*Hinds* sailed without escort) made sonar search during which *Hinds* struck rocks and was pulled off by destroyer at high tide, next a.m. *Hinds* ordered to drydock, San Francisco where all Navy personnel (Armed Guard and Communications) were transferred, February 1943.

Trevor proceeded SCTC, Miami; used time granted for transfer to get married to Illinois sweetheart who recently had moved to West Coast. He then proceeded to Quincy, MA assigned as stores officer on new USS *Frament* (DE-677). September 1943, first of 14 convoy crossings, during which Trevor was promoted twice to Lt. (jg) and lieutenant. He took a turn at gunnery officer, then was named executive officer.

December 1944, the *Frament* was converted to APD-77, assigned to Pacific Fleet. Convoy duty in Western Pacific; picket ship at Okinawa, sent to Philippines to provide LCVP landing training for MacArthur's combat team. While so engaged, the war ended.

Frament was caught in September 1945 typhoon with convoy of mine sweepers headed for Korea, was obliged to perform 36-hour heroic bowing of rudderless survey ship, taking her to safety in Okinawa. *Frament* assigned duty as pilot ship in Yangtse River, entrance to Shanghai.

Trevor had acquired enough points to return to the U.S.A on board USS *Rockwall* (APA-230). After one rejoined American Chicle. In 1948 he was promoted to assistant sales and advertising manager, Chicle Adams, Sao Paulo, Brazil. Trevor spent five years in Brazil where four children were born; promoted to sales and advertising manager, then Commercial Director In 1949, Naval Attache, Rio de Janeiro notified Trevor of his promotion to lieutenant commander.

1953, he was promoted to assistant sales manager A.C. Co., USA. Moved to Irvington, NY. Two more children were born in 1955 and 1960. Promoted to manager, Product Development, then to Director of Sales. A.C. Co. acquired by Warner-Lambert Co. Trevor moved to Chatham, NY near their headquarters with the title of director of sales.

In 1979 he retired from Warner-Lambert. With four sons and two daughters, all college graduates, and six grandchildren to date. He is active in Kiwanis, and in constant contact with five former officers of the *Frament,* and a member of DESA for six years.

JACOB R. TRUXAL, enlisted in the U.S. Navy Jan. 20, 1942, entered active duty Feb. 22, 1943. Commissioned June 16, 1943. Attended Midshipman's School at Columbia University; Recognition School, Ohio State University; Damage Control and Fire Fighting School, Philadelphia Navy Yard; Sub Chase Training Command, Miami, FL. Joined the USS *Lloyd* (DE-209) at Charleston, SC. The (DE-209) was converted to (APD-63) June 29, 1944. At the time of his discharge he had achieved the rank of lieutenant senior grade (Deck).

He recalls the Battle of Ormoc Bay and the invasion of Mindoro. Received the American Theatre, ETO Theatre, Asiatic Pacific Theatre with three stars, Philippine Liberation with one star, and World War II Victory Medal.

Married to Frances Emogene Whitacre in 1948. He obtained a Master's degree from the University of Pittsburgh and a doctor's degree from the Pennsylvania State University. He is now in private practice. Retired

as a psychologist in 1980 from the Pennsylvania Department of Corrections.

BENEDICT A. TURGEON, was born Feb. 12, 1922 in Burke, SD. Joined the service Oct. 16, 1942. Boot camp at Great Lakes, IL; Diesel Schooling GMC Cleveland, OH; F-Morse Navy Pier 18 Mos DE 327 and the Pearl Harbor Navy Yard. Served in the Navy Engineering Department.

He had achieved the rank of MoMM1/c at the time of his discharge. He recalls making seven trips across the Atlantic. Docking in Cardiff, Wales in England, and going ashore in Naples, Italy. He received European Bars.

Married raised three sons, Thomas (40), Steven (37), and Brent (31). He also has one grandson Christopher (3). He worked in the direct sales field and is now semi-retired.

ADAM C. UMHOLTZ, QM2/c, enlisted in the U.S. Navy Jan. 9, 1943, Orlando, FL. Was unaware of minority enlistment because being 17, thus required to serve until 21. Attended boot camp at Bainbridge, MD, Co. 240. Completed boot training and attended Subchaser Training Center, Miami, April of 1943. Went to Gunnery School Norfolk, VA, May 1943. Completed Gunnery School, reported for duty aboard USS *Wileman* (DE-22), Mare Island, CA. Ship commissioned June 11, 1943. After shakedown San Francisco Bay and off San Clementi Island, San Diego, was formed as escort screen for group of Kaiser type cargo ships from San Francisco to Noumea, New Caledonia.

The *Willeman* served as anti-submarine escort with LSTs, supply ships, fleet tankers and hunter killer task forces from the Samoa Islands, Ellice Islands, Gilbert Islands, Marshall Islands and Marianas.

Honorably discharged March 9, 1946, Bainbridge, MD. Married high school sweetheart, Margaret "Midge" Shanley, March 31, 1943. Raised two sons and a daughter, Steven C., Michael A., and Tamara Del. They also have eleven grandchildren and one on the way. Attended University of Maryland and University of Florida from 1948 through 1952. Learned the electrical construction business. Opened own company Feb. 9, 1965, with Robert W. Behe as partner on a handshake. Twenty-six years later still there on the handshake. Plan to work until whenever—enjoying work but not the bureaucracy.

EARL D. UNDERWOOD, JR., joined the U.S. Navy June 17, 1940 in Little Rock, AR. Served on USS *Vammen* (DE-644). Achieved the rank of EM3/c at the time of discharge. Serving in Vietnam in 1961 was a very memorable experience for him.

He is the father of a son, Lt. Darryl Underwood. He resides in Los Angeles, CA and is working for Los Angeles Department of Water and Power.

MARCEL VAILLANCOURT, (VAL), was born July 4, 1923. Joined the Navy on August 1942. As a Navy first class seaman he toured in the Pacific Region on three ships the USS *Ibis* a mine sweeper, USS *Wesson* a destroyer, and USS *Bandera* apa. He was a cook on all three ships and everyone knew his as "Val". Had been to California and Hawaii while in the Navy. "Val" was discharged in Septmeber 1945.

Married to Rita Riel on Aug. 5, 1945 in Cohoes, NY. Raised six daughters and is now grandfather to 17 grandchildren. He was retired after 33 years from Al Tech Steel and is currently working as a chauffeur for New Médico Hospital in Troy, NY. He has been a volunteer fireman for Peck Hose Co. for 33 years and a member of the Cohoes Waterford Elks. Also a member of the Holy Name Society at St. Anne's Church in Waterford.

EARNEST J. VALLAS, RM3/c, shellback and plankowner of the USS *O'Toole* (DE-527). Enlisted in the Navy on June 15, 1943 in Norfolk, VA at the age of 17. Attended boot camp at Bainbridge, MD, and on completion, assigned to the Outgoing Unit (OGU) in Norfolk to await orders. Received orders to Charleston Shipyard in Boston, MA for the commissioning of the USS *O'Toole* (DE-527) (commissioned Jan. 22, 1944).

Following shakedown off Bermuda they served as a training ship for the Fleet Sonar School, Key West, FL. Detached in mid-July they sailed north to Casco Bay, ME and then to Norfolk to escort the Tripoli CVE-64 to Recife, Brazil. On their return voyage they escorted the Solomons CVE-67, arriving in Norfolk on Aug. 25, 1944.

In early September they stood out of New York Harbor awaiting their first escort convoy mission. Acting as communication liaison ship between CTG 27.5 and convoy NY119, they shepherded a small craft convoy to the Azores and then to Falmouth, England, arriving there in mid-October. In early November they departed for Reykjavik, Iceland to escort the *Abnaki* (ATF-96) back to Norfolk. Leaving Norfolk they proceeded to New York, where they rejoined Cort Div. 80 to escort convoy USG-64 to North Africa, returning Jan. 23, 1945. They completed another Mediterranean run with several ports of call in April.

They were en route from Algeria when the war in Europe ended. They arrived in New York on May 23, 1945 and then operated off the New England coast until mid-July, receiving orders to proceed to Miami for a brief tour as a schoolship. In September they sailed to

Charleston, SC arriving there on Sept. 10, 1945. The decommissioning of the USS *O'Toole* took place Oct. 18, 1945. He was then transferred to Camp Sheldon, VA to await discharge from the Navy.

Upon leaving the service they attended school in Chicago under the GI Bill, then hired on at Norfolk Naval Air Station-Overhaul and Repair Depot/Final Lab Test. Also during this period he served as a weekend warrior assigned to Navy Reserve Squadron VS-862 as an AT2/c with duty weekends once a month and a two week cruise once a year until 1955.

In February of 1955, joined the RCA Service Company as a field engineer assigned to the Mobile Electronics Technical Units under COMCRUDESPAC, with assignments in San Diego Long Beach, Treasure Island in California and Yokuska and Sasebo Naval Bases in Japan.

In June of 1959, he became employed by RCA Astro, as a systems engineer and leader, working on the Automatic Program Checkout Equipment (APCHE) designed to test the Atlas booster in support of the ICBM program. Assignments were at Vanderberg AFB, CA and Schilling AFB, NE. Employment remains with RCA (now GE Astro-Space) in Los Angeles, CA and currently managing the Technical Support and Services Contract of the Defense Meteorological Space Program (DMSP) in Los Angeles, CA.

GUS VALSAMEDIS, S1/c, USS *Underhill* (DE-682), entered Navy Feb. 21, 1944. Boot camp Sampson, NY. Gunners Mate School at Newport, RI. Assigned to the USS *Underhill* August 1944. Convoyed ships to Plymouth, England, Oran Algeria. Entered Pacific Theatre January 1945. Convoyed subs in the southwest Pacific area. Sunk in action July 24, 1945 by Japanese off coast of Formosa 1930 hours. One hundred and twenty-eight sailors went down with the ship and 112 survived and returned home in September 1945.

The war ended about that time. The USS *Underhill* successfully defended her convoy in keeping with the highest traditions of the Navy.

WILLIAM H. VANDIVER, was born in Winston Salem, NC. Joined the U.S. Navy August 1945. Boot camp Camp Peary, VA. From January 1946 until August 1949 he served on the USS *Currier* (DE-700). He was discharged in San Francisco, in August 1949 with the rank of radarman. He had many memorable experiences while he served in the Navy. He served four years from 1949-53 with the Naval Reserve.

He received the Good Conduct Medal, Navy Occupational Medal, World War II Victory Medal, and China Service Medal.

Married to Sally with one son, Mark Allen who is deceased. He is now retired.

JAMES A. VERTES, MM1/c, USS *Barr* (DE-576) (APD-39), enlisted in the Navy on June 21, 1943. Discharged April 22, 1946. Boot camp at Newport, RI. Attended mMachinist School at Dearborn, MI. After training was assigned to newly commissioned USS *Barr* (DE-576). Had their shakedown in Bermuda, then assigned to anti-submarine duty with the aircraft carrier USS *Block Island* (CVE-21). On May 29, 1944, the USS *Block Island* was hit with three torpedoes and sunk; the USS *Barr* (DE-576) took a torpedo in the stern but it did not sink. The USS *Elmore* (DE-586) attacked and sunk the German U-Boat. The USS *Block Island* was the only aircraft carrier sunk in the Atlantic.

The USS *Barr* was towed to Casablanca for repairs, then towed to Boston, MA and converted to APD-39. The USS *Barr* then proceeded to the Pacific Theatre taking part in the invasions of Iwo Jima and Okinawa with the underwater demolition team 13.

After the Japanese surrendered the USS *Barr* disembarked Royal Marines in initial landings at Yokasuka Naval Base, then proceeded to operate as part of TG 30.6 evacuating 1135 POWs. USS *Barr* was then assigned as base of operation ship to U.S. Strategic Bomb Survey at Nagaski, Japan.

The USS *Barr* returned to the U.S. and was put in the Mothball Fleet at Green Cove Springs, FL.

He and his wife, Gloria, live in New Jersey, and have three children, a son and two daughters.

Note: Lest we forget USS *Barr* (DE-576) was named after Marine Private First Class Woodrow Wilson Barr, killed in action at Tulagi, Solomon Islands, Aug. 7, 1942, was awarded the Purple Heart, Presidential Unit Citation in 1942, Asiatic-Pacific Campaign Medal in 1942, and the Silver Star.

MARTIN A. VESEL, MM1/c, USS *Gendreau* (DE-639), came from a family of 12 of which six served in World War II (five brothers and one sister). Five of them served in the Army and one served in the Navy. He was inducted into service June 1, 1943. He was born Jan. 4, 1924 in Soudan, MN. Went to boot camp at Farragut, ID. Machinist School at Wahpeton, ND and was assigned to the crew of the USS *Gendreau* (DE-639). Was plankowner of the ship which was commissioned March 17, 1944. Participated in convoy duty in the South Pacific, the Invasion of Okinawa and the Occupation of Japan.

Campaign Medal and Ribbons include the American Campaign, Asiatic Pacific Campaign with two stars, Japan Occupation, and World War II Victory

Medal. He was discharged from Minneapolis Naval Station July 5, 1946.

Married Margot Stoffel and raised two daughters Marcia and Margo. They have three grandchildren Paul, Sandra and Julie.

Retired from the Unites States Department of Justice Bureau of Prisons. Worked in the Education Department as a teacher.

VIRGIL W. VINSON, RM3/c, USS *Chester T. O'Brien* (DE-421), born in Atlanta, GA in 1923. Enlisted in the Navy early 1943. Boot camp Bainbridge, MD, then on to Radio School at Charleston, SC. Advance training at SCTC Miami, FL. Was sent to Galveston, TX to catch the *O'Brien*. Their shakedown to Bermuda was interrupted to escort the captured Italian sub *Mameli* to Portsmouth. Then convoy duty to Naples, Italy, back to Brooklyn Navy Yards for preparation for Pacific duty. They were at Manus, throughout the Philippines. Went to Hollandia to help protect the landing of reinforcements of Davao. They also helped in landing troops on Balut, an island controlling the Saragani Straits. He was in the typhoon off Okinawa. Discharged Dec. 31, 1945.

Married to Grace Morris with two sons, two grandsons and one granddaughter. After working for a large national company and several transfers the last being Tampa, FL. Retired 36 years. Their home is in Land O' Lakes, FL.

JOHN A. VIRUM, MM3/c, USS *Gendreau* (DE-639), born in Minneapolis, MN, March 27, 1924. Son of Hans and Emma Virum and brother to Margaret. Inducted into Navy June 4, 1943 in Minneapolis, MN. Had boot camp at Farragut, ID. Attended Machinist School at Wahpeton, ND State School of Science from September 1943 until January 1944. Was sent to Norfolk, VA where he was assigned to the crew of the USS *Gendreau*. Was plankowner of ship which was commissioned March 17, 1944 at San Francisco, CA. After shakedown cruise and convoy duty in the South Pacific, took part in the Invasion of Okinawa and the Occupation of Japan. Discharged from service at Naval Air Station, Minneapolis, MN April 16, 1946.

He received the American Campaign, Asiatic-Pacific Campaign with two stars, Japan Occupation, and World War II Victory Medal.

Retired after 40 years as a lumber, sash and door salesman. Married to the former Joyce Hollstadt. They have one daughter, Barbara, and one son Thomas. Now living in St. Louis Park, MN.

JOE VOIGT, RDM2/c, USS *Buckley* (DE-51), USS *Howard F. Clark* (DE-533), born Baldwin, L.I., NY

July 15, 1925. Enlisted in 1942. Attended boot camp at Newport, RI, patrol duty YP-213 off Rockland, ME. After commissioning and shakedown cruise USS *Buckley* (DE-51) Sonar training at SCTC, Miami then to commissioning and Pacific Fleet duty aboard the USS *Howard F. Clark* (DE-533).

Took part in the invasions of the Philippines, Iwo Jima and Okinawa and awarded a commendation letter during the typhoon off Okinawa for "Exposure beyond the ordinary hazards of the sea."

Following the surrender of Japan and the decommissioning of the Clark, Voigt took part in Operations Crossroads (1946) and Sandstone (1948) the atomic bomb tests at Bikini and Eniwetok Atolls. Also took part in "Highjump" Admiral Byrds Antarctic expedition aboard the USS *Brownson* (DE-868).

He is entitled to wear six campaign ribbons, three Battle Stars, a Philippine Liberation Commendation Medal and is a member of the "Horned Shellbacks" for rounding Cape Horn.

After teaching school in Aiken, SC, he and his wife Johanna retired to Edgewater, FL. They have four daughters, Joanna, Jeanette, Janice and Judy.

WILLIAM HOMER WADE, was born July 30, 1925 in English, WV. Drafted Oct. 29, 1943. Sent to NTS Great Lakes, IL for boot training, then he attended Sonar School at Key West, FL. After graduation he was assigned to NTS Norfolk, VA. Then assigned to USS *Richard W. Suesens* (DE-342) being buillt at Orange, TX. Served aboard as sonar man until end of the war.

Took part in the invasion of Leyte November 1944; Battle of the Philippines November 1944; invasion of Lingayen, Luzon January 1945; invasion of Luzon, January 1945; invasion of Kerama Retto, March 1944; invasion of Okinawa, March-July 1945; China Sea Operation, July-September 1945; Occupation of Korea, September 1945; Occupation of Japanese homeland, September-November 1945. They destroyed seven enemy aircraft and left several more burning.

He received the Good Conduct Medal, World War II Victory Medal, American Campaign Medal, Asiatic Pacific with three stars, Philippine Liberation with two stars, Philippine Presidential Unit Citation, and Navy occupation Service Medal.

He was dischargd as Som2/c at Camp Shelton, VA on April 10, 1946. He married Louise Daniel Nov. 28, 1947. They have two sons, Jeffrey and Steven and two grandchildren. They have been married for 44 years at this writing. He is retired from Norfolk and Western Railway, after 40 years service.

ROBERT F. WAGNER, was born Oct. 13, 1922 in Whitestone, NY. Graduated from U.S. Merchant Ma-

rine Academy Dec. 25, 1943. Commissioned ensign, USNR Jan. 15, 1944. Ordered to active duty Pacific Fleet on board USS *Victoria* (AO-46) as engineering officer until ship was decommissioned December 1945. Assigned USS *Malabar* (AF-37) as engineering officer until released from active duty Dec. 27, 1946.

Recalled active duty Feb. 8, 1951 as engineering officer on board USS *Silverstein* (DE-534). Ship recommissioned Feb. 28, 1951 U.S. Naval Station, San Diego, CA. Served eight months Korean Theatre of Operation. Released from active duty July 12, 1952.

Received bachelor science degree from U.S. Merchant Marine Academy. Served in various Staff Billets Naval Reserve MSTS until retirement Jan. 20, 1971.

Married to Miriam F. Dorfman on Dec. 7, 1946 and raised five children. Civilian life worked over 40 years for Union Carbide Corporation as sales manager.

WARREN HENRY WALKER, BM1/c, USS *Howard D. Crow* (DE-252), 70th Div. North Atlantic the day before D-Day their ship moved out in the middle of the night in Irish Sea. Where they were lame upon the USS *Nevada Battle Wagon,* and her flotilla. They became a part of the flotilla, and participated in German U-Boat patrol on the flank of invasion. USS *Howard D. Crow* was credited (suspicious) for  German U-Boat who would lay on Sand Bay going into the English Channel French side.

FRANCIS RICHARD WALSH, Lt., USNR, USS *Damon M. Cummings* (DE-643), commissioned ensign, Chicago, IL, December 1943, then on to ASW School, Miami, FL; and Recognition School, Ohio State University. Served aboard the *Cummings* from June 1944 until December 1945. Ship saw duty in the Solomons, Marianas, Philippines, Okinawa and many areas in between the above. From December 1945 until July 1946 he was stationed at U.S. Naval Ammunition Depot in Earle, NJ.

Later he graduated from Georgetown University Law School; member of the State Bar of California; presently a professor of law, Hastings College of the Law, University of California, San Francisco; also an arbitrator in labor and commercial cases. He and Ethel have been married to each other for 48 years, with one son, Jeffrey, an attorney in San Francisco.

CHARLES W. WARD, was born in Brooklyn, NY. Enlisted as seaman apprentice July 23, 1941. Served in the U.S Naval Reserves from 1941-1945, and the U.S. Navy from 1945-75. He served everywhere except for India and Australia. He had command of six

ships (two combat commands). He ended with assignment as Com. IUWG 2.

He received the Legion of Merit, Navy Commendation Meritorious Achievement and 18 other medals and awards.

Married to Trousdale S. Ward, two children (one girl and one boy), three stepchildren, six grandchildren, and four step-grandchildren. He owns and operates a fishing boat and assists his wife in horticultural pursuits.

HAROLD L. WARD, was born June 30, 1924 in Muncie, IN. Joined the U.S Navy June 23, 1943. Served on the USS *Gustafson* (DE-182) in the North Atlantic, Mediterranean, South Atlantic and Pacific. Achieved the rank of MoMM1/c at the time of his discharge.

While one convoy duty in North and South Atlantic they sank one German sub off Boston in April 1945. He was plankowner of *Gustafson* until his discharge.

Married June Schenck Oct. 27, 1946. They have one daughter, Janice. He is now retired and living in Peoria, IL. Enjoying travelling and three grandsons.

FRANK WARNER, SF3/c, USS *Engstrom* (DE-50), enlisted in the Navy Jan. 7, 1943. Went to Great Lakes Training Center and then on to Norfolk, VA. Was assigned to USS *Engstrom* (DE-50) at the Philadelphia Navy Yard. The ship was commissioned June 21, 1943. Left Philadelphia for a shakedown in Bermuda. Then on to San Diego, by way of the canal. Went on to the Aleutian Islands. Stayed for over a year. Then was shipped to San Diego, to attend the Fleet Welding School, where after graduation they were going to be sent to Pearl Harbor to work on ships but the was ended.

Since the war, Warner worked as a machine repairman for 35 years for ITT Higbie in Rochester, MI. He retired in 1980 after open heart surgery and is taking life easy now.

CHARLES DANIEL WATERS, FN, USS *Weeden* (DE-797), was born in Yankton, SD June 21,

1933. Enlisted in Navy Aug. 4, 1950, San Diego, CA NTS August-October 1950. Assigned to USS *Weeden* for duty with older brother. Attended Advanced Fire Training School. Ship assigned to reserve training status after Korean conflict and was stationed in Long Beach, CA 1952-1960, where it was later scrapped in Portland, OR.

Married since 1952, with three children, and three grandchildren. Lived in Anaheim, CA and was a fireman there from 1960 to December 1987 when he retired with the rank of captain. Member of American Legion Post #222, Masonic Lodge #207, and a life member of DESA. Now living in Laguna Niguel, CA with wife of 39 years and owns his own company, Waters Electrical Contracting.

DONALD E. WATERS, was born February 1926 in Yankton, SD. Joined the U.S. Navy in February 1942. Served on the USS *Weeden* (DE-797) from 1950-51, and the USS *Shiels* from 1951-52. He had achieved the rank of MoM2/c at the time of discharge.

He received the Pacific Theatre, World War II Victory Medal, Korea Conflict (1950-52).

He is the father of four children, two daughters and two sons. Now retired from U.S. Postal Service and living in South Dakota. He fishes a lot and loves it!

ROY EARL WEAVER, GM2/c, USS *Reeves* (DE-156), enlisted in the Navy, Nov. 3, 1942. Took boot camp at Great Lakes Naval Training Station in Illinois. Attended GM School at Great Lakes. Went aboard the *Reeves* as part of the nucleus crew, ship being commissioned June 9, 1943 at Norfolk, VA. Served aboard the *Reeves* during North Atlantic convoy duty between the States and foreign ports of Casablanca, Londonderry Eireland, Glasgow Scotland and Liverpool England.

Reeves crew rescued 85 of 86 crewman from a torpedoed tanker (Seakay). Endured 70 mph gale in Mid-Atlantic (Christmas Day 1943) and took into tow the USS *Donnel* which had been torpedoed by U-boat. *Donnel* was towed to Ireland. He was aboard the *Reeves* until it was decommissioned as a DE and recommissioned as the APD-52 in Philadelphia Navy Yard in September 1944. Attended Washington Naval Gun Factory for turret training. From there to board his second ship the USS *Ray K. Edwards* (APD-96) at Charleston, SC.

Left the *Edwards* in September 1945 at Pearl Harbor for discharge from service. Caught the USS *Mississippi* (BB) for the States and was discharged at the Naval Air Station at St. Louis, MO on Oct. 21, 1945.

He is married with three sons all whom are married and seven grandchildren.

BYRON E. WEED, was born June 18, 1938 in Ann Arbor, MI. Joined the USNR in 1955. Served on the USS *Daniel A. Joy* (DE-585). Stationed at Grosse Isle Naval Air Station and attended University of Michigan Naval Reserve Station. Achieved the rank of YN3/c at the time of discharge in 1963 after serving a total of eight years in the Reserves.

He recalls the days aboard ship on Great Lakes and Canada.

He is the father of two daughters Dalana (22) and

Anissa (20). Byron is a real estate broker and residential home builder. Now residing in Ann Arbor, MI.

ALVIN LOUIS WELCH, was born June 5, 1932. Joined Navy Reserve Jan. 7, 1949, and Regular Navy Jan. 7, 1950. Went through boot camp in San Diego, CA for three months. After boot camp was assigned to motor pool until June 25, 1950.

The Korean War started and he went aboard the USS *T.E. Chandler* (DD-717) on June 26, 1950 until March 25, 1951. Was in Korean War for nine months and returned to San Diego, CA. March 26, 1951, went aboard USS *Harveson*. Left San Diego for Newport, RI, via the Panama Canal. USS *Harveson* operated on East Coast and Caribbean Sea. It was an experimental radar ship.

He was discharged June 8, 1953, at Charleston, SC with rank of EW3/c. Received the Navy Occupation Medal (Asia), China Service, Korean Service with two stars, United Nations Service Medal and Korean Presidential Unit Citation.

He retired from Louisville Water Company March 1, 1991 with 31 years service, 10 years as plant electrician and 21 years as plant maintenance supervisor.

DAVID FIFE WELCH, was born Sept. 5, 1918 in Fort Wayne, IN. Commissioned ensign, USNR, May 15, 1941 at USNA through V-7 Program. Attended ASW School, Miami; General Line School, Montery; NAVWARCOL, Newport, RI; and NATO Defense College in Paris, France.

Served as commander, commanding officer, or executive officer for the following: CO USS PC-473; XO USS *Carter* (DE-112); CO USS *Ray K. Edwards* (APD-96); CO USS *Frybarger* (DE-705); CO UDT ONE; CO USS *Bausell* (DE-845); ComMinRon 8; ComDesRon 10; ComPhibTraLant; ComPhiGru 1; Commander Task Force 43, Naval Support Force, Antarctica (Operation Deep Freeze).

He was instructor, ASW Training Center, Key West; Staff Naval War College; Operation Division; CINCPAC Staff; OPNAV, 1) AAW Assistant, Surface War Division (OP-43), 2) Assistant VCNO (Logistics) (OP-04B); ACOS Logistics, Staff CINCUSNAVEUR; Head Requirements Section, Operations Division, Staff COMUSMACV, Saigon.

Married Mary Spalding Stewart, Dec. 7, 1949. They had no children. He retired as rear admiral, USN, July 1, 1972.

Honors and decorations include: Honorary Doctor of Laws, Franklin College of Indiana; Antarctica mountain range named Welch Mountains; minor planet (2504) named Welch; Silver Star; Legion of Merit with four stars; Bronze Star with Combat "V"; Navy Com-

mendation Medal; Presidential Unit Citation; NUC; and various area ribbons.

Civilian education include: Bachelor of Arts, Franklin College of Indiana; Master of Arts, George Washington University; Doctor of Education; the American University. As civilian he held the positions of Professional Lecturer at American University; assistant treasurer and administrative executive, Association of Universities for Research in Astronomy, Inc., Tucson, AZ; Advisory Council, Arizona-Sonora Desert Museum; Supervisory Committee, Pima Federal Credit Union; Docent, Arizona-Sonora Desert Museum.

Member of the Explorer's Club; The Army-Navy Town Club; The Antartican Society; Arizona-Sonora Desert Museum; AZAD; TROA; The Navy League; The Naval Institute; MOWW; Friends of the U of A Library; Arizona Historical Society; Adobe Corral of Westerners International; Tucson Committee on Foreign Relations; Tucson Lodge No.4, F & A.M.; Scottish Rite Bodies; York Rite; Sabbar Shrine.

DARYL E. WELTY, GM2/c, entered the Navy August 1942. After finishing a few weeks of boot camp at Green Bay, WI, he was assigned to the USS PC-496. This ship did convoy duty in both the North and South Atlantic, then was sent to the North African Campaign. There on Jan. 4, 1943, the 496 sank in two and a half minutes from a tremendous under-water explosion while escorting an ammunition ship. Five crew members were lost. The survivors spent several months with the U.S. Army in North African, picking up two Battle Stars.

He then was assigned duty on the USS *Bowers* (DE-637). In January 1944 the *Bowers* started her tour of duty in the Pacific where she picked up four major Battle Stars. On April 16, 1945 she was hit by a Val type kamikaze plane which demolished her superstructure and killed more than half of her crew.

After discharge in 1945, he went back to school to become a mechanical engineer. Most of his career was spent working for companies overseas. He retired in 1986 and is presently running his registered Hereford cattle ranch near Corning, CA. Even though he was wounded three times he still works 8 to 10 hours daily.

He has been married to his wife Jean for 46 years. They have four children, six grandchildren and three great-grandchildren.

ROBERT R. WHITE, MM2/c, USS *Fiske* (DE-143), was inducted in the Navy June 14, 1943, three weeks after his 17th birthday. Received boot training at Newport, RI and then to Diesel Training School in Richmond, VA. On September 11, after completing school was assigned to USS *Fiske*. After several convoys to Casablanca and Bizerte, the *Fiske* was assigned to Hunter-Killer duty with the USS *Wake Island*. While

on this duty on Aug. 2, 1944 the *Fiske* was torpedoed by the U-804 and sunk.

After survivors leave, he was assigned to the USS *Osage* LSV3 and put this ship in commission on Dec. 30, 1944. After shakedown they took the ship through canal and proceeded to Okinawa for the invasion of this last Jap stronghold on April 1, 1945.

He was discharged April 23, 1946 and went to work in the construction industry. He was a piping superintendent, throughout his working career. He married his wife Gerry in 1948, have been married for 42 years, they have four children and eight grandchildren. Retired in 1988.

GEORGE W. WICKIZER, was born Aug. 22, 1923 in Vincennes, IN. Enlisted in the U.S Coast Guard on Oct. 14, 1942. Training stations were in New Orleans, LA, St. Augustine, FL, Jacksonville, FL; Norfolk, VA; Brooklyn, NY; USS *Merril* (DE-392), San Pedro, CA, and Alameda, CA.

Served aboard the USS *Merril* and made 16 trips across the Atlantic on convoy duty. His most memorable experience was an air attack on the convoy on July 11, 1944.

Discharged March 1, 1946. Left the service as S1/c. His service ribbons are the American Theatre, European Theatre and Good Conduct Medal.

Retired from the postal service in 1985, and has pastored a church in Cresent City, CA for the past 20 years. Married Jerry Phillips of Mishawaka, IN. They have three sons and two daughters. He has eight grandsons, one granddaughter, two great-granddaughters and one great-grandson.

ROBERT WILKES (ED), S1/c, USNR, USS *Thomason* (DE-203), born Richmond, VA on Dec. 9, 1918. He has lived in Baltimore, MD since 1927. Entered Navy September 1943, discharged November 1945. Took boot training at Bainbridge, MD, discharged from Bainbridge. Was a plank sailor boarding the USS *Thomason* at Charleston, SC. Ship commissioned Dec. 10, 1943. Shakedown in Bermuda. Convoys between Charleston, SC, Norfolk, Newport, Rhode Island and Panama Canal. Entered Pacific waters March 21, 1944. Ship sailed 120,000 miles in 22 months.

Medals include the Asiatic-Pacific with one Bronze Star, World War II Victory Medal, Navy Occupation Service Medal with (Asia Clasp), Philippine Liberation, Philippine Republic President Unit Citation Badge.

Married Margaret Daniels April 7, 1941. They have two daughters and five grandchildren. Retired from Schmidt Baking Company, 1981, after 30 years of service.

Life member VFW Parkville Post 9083, American Legion, Catholic War Veteran, Knight of Columbus.

HAROLD E. WILLIAMS, was born Nov. 27, 1922 in Mansfield, OH. Joined the Navy Reserves September 1942. Served with the Supply Corp. Military locations and stations include Bayonne NSD, Harvard Supply Corp School, Depaun University V-12, USS *Swenning* (DE-394), Marquette University. He had achieved the rank of lieutenant (jg) at the time of his discharge.

He received the European American Theatre Ribbon, Asiatic Theatres, Unit Citation.

Married to Jean with three sons, David, Lawrence, Ted and four granddaughters. He is now retired and living in Tucson, AZ.

JOHN WILLIAMS, volunteered 1939, at outbreak of the war. Trained as ASDIC (Submarine Detector) operator. Served on HMS *Foxhound* (Destroyer) and saw action in Russian convoys, Malta convoys, bombardment of Tobruck and Bardia. Then to Bombay, Ceylon, Mauritius, Adu Attol, Madagascar landings, South Atlantic patrols and convoy to Bombay. Later on the *Ranchi* an Armed Merchant Cruiser from Bombay to Liverpool. 1943, Boston, Asbury Park, Key West (duties ASDIC Instructor). HMS *Bentley* (DE-74) in Bethlehem Hingham, working-up trials Bermuda, convoy to Londonderry, sub hunting in Atlantic, D-Day landing, escort subs to Belfast. HMS *Ardrossen* for mine sweeping operations, DE-mobbed 1946.

He received the Defense Medal, 1939-45 Star, Mediterranean Star, Italy Star, Burma Star, France and Germany Star, Atlantic Star and Clasp, North African Star, and Pacific Star.

After discharge he worked in road haulage, later as heavy goods instructor. Retired in 1985. Married to June Anne Elizabeth, with one married son and daughter. They have one grandson, Gareth. He joined DESA in 1990, dubbed... "The First American Limey."

ROBERT E. WILLIAMS, was born July 21, 1926 in Stony Creek, NY. Enlisted in the Navy Nov. 8, 1943. Went through basic training at Sampson, NY. After basic he was transferred to NTS Norfolk, VA for training.

Transferred to Houston, TX where the *Edmonds* was commissioned. Served aboard her until the war was over. He had achieved the rank of seaman first class at time of discharge. He received the American Theatre Medal, Victory Medal, Asiatic-Pacific Medal with five stars, and Philippine Liberation Ribbon with two stars.

After the war was over he worked for the U.S.

Government in the Department of Defense Police. He worked as a New York State Capital police officer for 23 years, retired in 1987. Now enjoys hunting, fishing and playing golf.

He and his wife Alice have three children and seven grandchildren. They have been married for 45 years.

RUDOLPH P. WILLIAMSON, ENC, USS *Brister* (DER-327), USS *Cromwell* (DE-1014), enlisted September 1944, boot camp at Great Lakes, IL. Attended Diesel School at Gulfport, MS and then served on four amphibious ships, fleet tug, yard tug, patrol craft. In December 1951, flew to Germany to receive two ice-breakers back from Russians. Recommissioned USS *Brister* (DER-327) in 1956. Operated in North Atlantic on dew line. Transferred to *Cromwell* (DE-1014) 1957. First squadron of DEs to enter the Mediterranean since World War II. Served on *W.A. Lee* (DL-4) and later tour in Vietnam as advisor to coastal junk force.

Retired in 1968, returning to Florida. Superintendent for shipping department at steel foundry in Jacksonville for 12 years. Now still working part-time for upholstery supply company.

ALEXANDER WITOSHYNSKY, whose parents came to the United States from the Ukraine section of Russia, was born in New York City on Nov. 1, 1921. He attended elementary and high school in NYC.

In the spring of 1941, Alex completed five trips on the SS *America* as a member of the National Maritime Union. When the United States entered World War II on Dec. 8, 1941, Alex enlisted in the U.S Coast Guard and was sworn in April 21, 1942. He served at Ocean City and Barnegat Light, NJ, Coast Guard Stations, and attended Electrician's Mate School at Samuel Gompers High School in Bronx, NY, graduating Aug. 6, 1943. Alex was then sent to Houston, TX, where he met other crew members assigned to the (DE-384) USS *Rhodes*, that was commissioned Oct. 25, 1943.

The 384s first duty was an escort for a convoy going to North Africa in January 1944. Two other North African-Mediterranean Sea trips followed, with air and submarine attacks a constant hazard. Eight escort duty voyages were later made to United Kingdom ports, crossing the North Atlantic route where rough seas and bad weather were added to the enemy's bombs and torpedoes.

After V-E Day, the *Rhodes* passed through the Panama Canal on June 18, 1945, and continued to Adak, in the Aleutian Islands, reaching there July 8. From Alaska, Alex returned home to New York City, and was discharged Nov. 23, 1945.

The *Rhodes* served in the Aleutians, and in the Pacific Theatre near Hawaii and China. It was scrapped Oct. 7, 1963.

Alex attended New York Technical Institute from 1951-1953. While on vacation in Miami, FL in June 1952, he met and married Gerry Ball, a New Hampshire native. They returned to New York City while he completed his courses. In the spring of 1953, the Witoshynskys returned to South Florida to make it their home.

In Miami, Alex worked as a boat canvas craftsman at the Scottie-Craft Boat Company, and was later employed by Jenkins and Frey Company and Bennie

LaPointe's American Marine Coverings. He also worked at the Aztec Boat Company for a time, before establishing the upholstery department at Bertram Yacht Company in 1972. He retired in 1989, after 17 years as department supervisor at Bertram.

They have four children, Mary (Dr. Jose Gabriel Lopez), John, Michael, (Ruth, daughter Leah) and Thomas.

In 1956, Alex and Gerry had a home built in the new Pembroke Pines subdivision in South Broward. They voted with their fellow residents in 1960 to incorporate their neighborhood into the City of Pembroke Pines, that now has a population of 65,000.

Alex (known to his shipmates as Woody and Whitney) now limits his boating activities to an occasional fishing trip with his sons, but recalls his oceangoing war-time adventures on the *Rhodes* as "the best days of his life". He attended the *Rhodes* re-union at Venice, FL on May 30, 1992.

CLARENCE H. WOLFF, S1/c, USS *Herbert C. Jones* (DE-137),

enlisted in the Navy September 1942. Was born April 6, 1923 in Baltimore, MD. Commissioned the *Jones* July 21, 1943 Orange, TX, for shakedown in Bermuda. Gibralter, Algiers and Algeria. Convoy duty in Mediterranean with Task Group 80.2. Oran, Algeria, Bizerto, Naples, Anzio Landings and Civitavecchia, Italy. San Raphel, invasion of Southern France. Convoy GUS-53 Oran, Algeria to New York October 1944. Assigned to escort Division Nine Submarine Killer Group North Atlantic, Jacksonville, FL. Guantanamo, Cuba. Pearl Harbor, Hawaii via Panama Canal. Eniwetok Marshalls Gilbert group, Wake Island. The *Jones* received three Battle Stars and the Navy Unit Commendation. He was discharged October 1945.

Enlisted June 1948. Assigned to the receiving ship Anacostia, WA Funeral details Arlington National Cemetery. Naval War College 1st District, Providence, RI. Discharged February 1950.

Married Frances Prietz, July 10, 1948 has three sons. Retired from Westinghouse in 1986. Currently resides in Baltimore, MD.

BENJAMIN JUDSON WOOD, JR., RDM3/c,

USS *Crouter* (DE-11), was born July 26, 1921 in Elizabeth City, NC. Enlisted in Navy Dec. 15, 1942. Boot camp at Bainbridge, MD Co. 104, Barracks 111. Trained as a radioman at Auburn, AL. Picked up ship at Boston Navy Yard. Ship had enough radiomen so he became a radar stricker. Ship was engaged in escort and screening duties in areas of Guadacanal, Espiritu Santo, Treasure Island, Munda, Efate, and Figi Islands. On the morning of April 29 he picked up a Jap Betty on radar off their starboard bow, pull GQ and it was driven off

by their machine gun fire. Battles of Saipan, Guadacanal, and Okinawa. Ship received one Battle Star. It escorted 69 convoys without loss of a single ship.

He was discharged Oct. 18, 1945 as RDM3/c.

He is now retired after working for the Westinghouse Electric Corporation 35 years as electronic technician Lg. 15. Married Alice Catherine June 20, 1959. They have three sons and three daughters. Member of American Legion Hamilton Post 20, and Parkville VFW Memorial Post 9083 both of Baltimore, MD.

RAYMOND A. WOOD, born Oct. 26, 1931 in

Cuthbert, GA. Joined the U.S. Navy Aug. 1, 1947. He served on the USS *Raby* (DE-698) for four years, two in the Pacific and two in the Atlantic. Achieved the rank of seaman first class at the time of his discharge in 1951.

During an Atomic bomb test on the *Raby* in 1948, they tracked an unidentified submarine, and saw three Atomic bombs go off. He remembers the experience of serving in the Korean War. Received the Good Conduct Medal.

Married Ann Patrick in 1953, and have three grown children, Ray, Vickie and Derek. They also have three grandchildren. He has owned and operated a gas station for 34 years. He is a member of American Legion Post 85.

RAYMOND K. WOODHOUSE, CETM, USS

Loy (DE-160), was born in New York City on March 7, 1918. As an amateur radio operator he was qualified in an important field. After enlistment on Feb. 9, 1942 as RM2/c, he spent two weeks in boot training at Staten Island, NY, then three months at Grove City College, PA prior to attending radio and radar training courses at Treasure Island, CA. He was promoted to RT1/c and then served as radar instructor at Submarine Chaser Training Center, Miami, FL.

He was a plankowner when USS *Loy* (DE-160) was commissioned in 1943. Duties aboard were maintenance and repair of radio, radar, and sonar equipment. He served aboard *Loy* during several runs into the Mediterranean on convoy duty. *Loy* was converted to (APD-56) at Boston and sailed to the Pacific for operations in the Philippines and at the invasion of Okinawa, carrying aboard UDT-4 and their landing craft and gear.

He left *Loy* in the Sea of Japan after the Okinawa invasion and surrender, and was discharged at Boston on Dec. 10, 1945. He remained in the electronics field until retirement, and recently celebrated his 50th wedding anniversary. They have three children.

V. MAURICE WOODS, Chief Yeoman, USS

Griswold (DE-7), born in Shenandoah, IA, Nov. 18, 1920. Enlisted in USNR at St. Louis, MO, Dec. 8, 1941. En route to San Diego troop train was involved in derailment neat Tucumcari, NM. Assigned temporary Ship's Company, personnel office, NTS, San Diego. Sent to RS, Bremerton, WA, and assigned temporary Ship's Company, USS *Nevada* (in dry dock being repaired account Pearl Harbor attack). Went by commercial steamer through Inland Passage to Kodiak, AL. Served there at NSB, NAS, NOB. Transferred to SCTC, Miami, FL, and assigned as a member of the pre-commissioning detail, USS *Griswold*. Ship com-

missioned at Charleston Navy Yard, Boston, MA April 28, 1943. Ship inspected by Secretary of the Navy Frank Knox at Boston, it was the first DE he had seen. The (DE-7) was the 3rd DE commissioned at Boston. Ship's shakedown cruise was to Bermuda. Upon return to Boston, painted Pacific Ocean color, went through Panama Canal, enroute to Bora Bora, Society Islands, and to Noumea, New Caledonia, where ship was inspected by Admiral "Bull" Halsey, also the first DE he had seen. The *Griswold* was the first DE in the South Pacific and the first DE to receive creditable recognition for confirmed battle action-sunk Japanese submarine off Guadacanal, Solomon Islands, Dec. 23, 1943. Promoted to chief in 1944. Left ship early in 1945, at Ulithi, Caroline Islands. Completed service as discharge yeoman personnel officer, NTS, San Diego. Discharged at St. Louis, MO Dec. 18, 1945.

He was awarded the World War II Victory Medal, Asiatic Pacific Campaign Medal with two Battle Stars, Good Conduct Medal and American Campaign Medal.

He returned to work for Wabash RR, and promoted to Personal Injury Claim Department. Retired from N&W Railway, Dec. 1, 1980, with over 41 years of railroad service. Married Betty Karnes at Moberly, MO, Nov. 15, 1946. They have two sons, Rodney and Steve (both of whom served in the U.S. Army), a grandson, and a granddaughter. Woody and Betty have resided in Decatur, IL since April 1958.

PERCELL LEON WORLEY, CMM, USS *Dennis*

(DE-405), graduated from high school in 1940, worked in defense plants, and joined the Naval Reserve Aviation Cadet Program in June 1943. Transferred November 1943, to Bainbridge, MD, for reassignment to SubChaser School, Miami, FL in December 1943. Transferred to Nucleus Crew March 1944, traveled to Houston, TX, for ship familiarization and commissioning in April 1944 at Brown Shipyard. After outfitting, sailed to Bermuda for shakedown. Then on to Boston and Norfolk for minor repairs prior to sailing though the Panama Canal en route to San Diego for boiler repairs.

The *Dennis* went to war in the Pacific Ocean, and was involved in the landings at Iwo Jima (where Worley witnessed the raising of the flag on Mt. Sirubachi, through binoculars), Okinawa and was in the Taffy III Task Group (air support) Leyte Gulf, covering the landings at Samar Island, Philippines. In this battle, the *Dennis* sank a Jap heavy cruiser, for which the crew received the Presidential Unit Citation. They also suffered substantial damage and had five crew members killed. Five of the 13 ships in this group were sunk and the *Dennis* rescued 434 survivors from the Aircraft Carrier *ST LO*. Returned to Alameda, CA, for repairs and back to the Pacific for more action. Also survived the Okinawa typhoon. After the war, the *Dennis* returned to San Diego for De-commissioning into the Mothball Fleet. Sold for salvage in 1973.

Worley was discharged in May 1946, at Bainbridge, MD. Returned to Hanover, PA, and York Corp. to begin his new career as a refrigeration and air conditioner field service engineer. He retired in 1981 after his wife of 26 years died, and lives in his hometown of Hanover, PA. Belongs to DESA, Susquenhanna Chapter DESA, Navy League, VFW and is active with the *Dennis* reunions and correspondence with *Dennis* shipmates.

FRANK L. WYCKOFF, was born Aug. 12, 1927 in High Bridge, NJ and passed away Dec. 3, 1987. Survived by his wife of 54 years, Mary Gladys and by one son, Louis O. both associate members of DESA. He was a retired iron molder/core maker and equipment operator. Enlisted in the U.S. Navy Feb. 22, 1943 and was separated from active duty Oct. 26, 1945. Served as a MoMM1/c on the USS *McConnell* (DE-163).

Awarded the World War II Victory Medal, American Theatre Medal, Asiatic Pacific Medal with three Bronze Stars, Philippine Liberation Medal with one Bronze Star, Philippine Presidential Unit Citation.

Joined U.S Navy Reserve located at Trenton, NJ in 1946. Volunteered for active duty June/July 1950, reported to Philadelphia Navy Yard and sent to Yokohama, Japan and boarded the USS *Lincoln County* (LST-898). Served at Inchon, Korea Sept. 15, 1950 and the area of the Korean waters, separated from active duty May 1951.

Awarded the Korean Campaign Medal with one Bronze Star, United Nations Medal, Japan Occupational Medal, National Defense Medal, and Korean Presidential Unit Citation. Awards came from his official awards and decorations page from his official Navy Service Record Book. One of his last wishes was that his son never have a photo published of him and his son states that he will always honor this request.

As an additional note according to Official Armed Forces Decorations and Medals chart, the Philippine Presidential Unit Citation and the Philippine Independence Ribbon was awarded to any person that received the Philippine Defense and/or Liberation Medal. Therefore the Independence Ribbon was not listed as it was not on his records. He always referred to the *McConnell* as she and that she was a fine ship with a great crew.

ROBERT O. WYLLIE, JR., was born Oct. 20, 1944 in Ithaca, NY. Joined the U.S. Navy in April 1963. Stations include Great Lakes, IL, and Newport, RI. Served on the USS *Hammerberg* (DE-1015). Achieved the rank of MM3/c at the time of his discharge.

Most memorable for him was his participation in the "Matchmaker Squadron" which was a NATO exercise involving his ship and three NATO ships from Canada, Great Britain and Holland, from February 18 to July 19, 1945.

Married to wife Louise for 23 years with one son, Bret (18). He owned and operated a dry cleaners in Ithaca, NY.

JOHN W. WYLLIS, was born in Jackson, MI on April 9, 1925. Enlisted in the Navy the day before his 18th birthday. Went to Great Lakes, IL for boot train-

ing, from there on to Northwestern University to Radioman's school. Transferred from there to Norfolk, VA where he was assigned duty to the USS *Stewart* (DE-238) just before Thanksgiving 1943. Except for transfer for an emergency appendectomy in August 1944 and RM School at Great Diamond Island, Casco Bay, ME. He spent his whole tour on the *Stewart*. He was transferred at Pearl Harbor to Military Government 3011 Yard.

Discharged in February 1946. Re-enlisted in October 1947, and spent the rest of his Navy career with the NAVSECGRU until he retired from active service February 1965. He is now retired and active in the American Legion and the Forty & Eight.

CARLETON W. WYSS, SM1/c, USN, he joined the Navy May 15, 1941, had recruit training at NTS Newport, RI. After finishing boot camp he was transferred to NAS Quonset Point, RI, where he spent a couple years. He then went to the NSB at Woods Hole, MA, where he was assigned to a degaussing range at the entrance of the Cape Cod Canal, Buzzards Bay, MA.

When the range was closed he then went out to the Pacific Theatre and was assigned to the USS *Dixie* (AD-14) in Purvis Bay, Solomon Islands, where he spent several months.

Later he was transferred to COMCORTDIV 73 aboard the USS *Gendreau* (DE-639) serving under Cmdr. Paul G. Hammond Commodore. Commander Hammond later was relieved by Cmdr. Roland H. Groff an experienced DE officer.

When the *Gendreau* was hit by a shore battery on June 10, 1945 the flag was moved to the *Paul G. Baker* (DE-642) where he stayed until the *Baker* returned to the States late November 1945. Being in the regular Navy he did not get discharged until June 1946 at NAS Squantum, MA.

Some memorable war experiences include serving on DEs and the invasion of Okinawa. It was also a thrill riding out a typhoon on a convoy from Okinawa to Saipan. Another memorable experience was seeing a kamikaze plane just miss them and sink a Sub-Chaser in the next screening station.

He was married in December 1945 to Joyce Shippee who presented him with two wonderful daughters that have given them five grandsons. He had several jobs before settling with New Jersey Bell Telephone Company, where he served for over 30 years until the breakup of AT&T. Then retiring from AT&T in 1984.

MERLYN E. YODER, born Nov. 26, 1920 in Haxtun, CO. Joined the U.S. Navy Feb. 13, 1940. Served on the USS *Tennessee* (DD-606), USS *Bowers* (DE-637), USS

Barton (DD-722) and M.S. *Mervine*. He had achieved the rank of CMM at the time of his discharge.

His most memorable experiences were Pearl Harbor, Korman Dorski, Okinawa and the A-bomb at Bikini.

He is married with five daughters and eight grandchildren. Now retired and living in San Lorenzo, CA.

ELMER J. YOUNG, JR., SM1/c, USS *Lyman* (DE-302), USS *General M. Randall* (AP-115), born Philadelphia, PA. Enlisted in the Navy Sept. 21, 1943. Boot camp at Sampson, NY. Commissioned *Lyman* Feb. 19, 1944. Sailed February 23, from Mare Island Navy Yard for Pearl Harbor and training. Left Pearl Harbor August 20, for forward areas. Took part in invasions of Palau Islands, Luzon, Iwo Jima, and Okinawa. Also Japanese Homeland Raid, July 1945. Five Battle Stars. *Lyman* was first DE to enter Tokyo Bay. USS *Missouri* is off *Lyman's* starboard bow for surrender ceremonies. Returned to States, October 1945. Was reassigned to *Randall,* sailing from San Francisco for Far East. Embarked 1st Marines from China. Returned to States and received honorable discharge May 5, 1946.

As civilian he was a Philadelphia police officer for 25 years. Raised a son and a daughter. Currently Chief of Security at U.S. Headquarters of a large corporation. Living near Wilmington, DE.

ALBERT J. ZIDLICK, enlisted 6th Battalion, 212th Fleet Div. Jan. 4, 1935. Served until 1940. Had two weeks active duty for training aboard four piper destroyers, BBs Texas and Wyoming. Nov. 25, 1940 he was ordered to active duty catching his ship in Brooklyn Navy Yard. Served on the USS *P.C. 509*. Two years in Panama, instructor for Sub-Chaser School in Miami. Beaumont, TX for precommissioning detail of the USS *Herbert C. Jones* (DE-137, after commissioning, had jammer gear installed along with sister ship USS *Federick C. Davis* (DE-136). Assigned to Mediterranean area to test effect of gear against German controlled glider bombs. It worked so good that two weeks temporary duty turned into two years, also invasions of Angio and Southern France. Also a few air-sea battles.

He received the Navy Unit Citation, American Defense Ribbon, European Ribbon with three Battle Stars, Navy Good Conduct, Navy Reserve Good Conduct, American Campaign and World War II Victory Medal.

Separated from active duty September 1945. He stayed in Navy Reserves until March 1974. Retired as gunner mate chief senior. After separation worked for Navy Publication and Printing. His wife passed away in 1986.

CASIMER WALTER ZIMAK, MM1/c, (T) Volunteer Reserve, USS *Alvin C. Cockrell* (DE-366), enlisted in the USNR Feb. 4, 1942. Subgroup III a machinist at the Navy Service School, Ford Motor Co. Ship was YP-445 a patrol craft. Inshore patrol, NOB St. Thomas, VI. Mined fields and Hurricane. Jan. 31, 1944, he was transferred to Sub-chaser Training Center in Miami, FL. Transferred to Orange, TX on board the USS *Alvin C. Cockrell* (DE-366), on board when commissioned Oct. 7, 1944. Escort Div. 86 encountered typhoon at Okinawa. They had both anchors dragging and turbine engines revolving slow against the wind to ride out the typhoon in the bay. Burial at sea for the dead from USS *Indianapolis* air-sea rescues. Task unit entered Wakanoura Wan and freed Allied POWs.

Two sailors looking from the top of a hill could see Hiroshima to the west and north, there was a Japanese battleship with a flightdeck covered over with netting

DESA, III Misc. Biographies

JACK L. BAKER *(See Bio, page 670)*

CLAUDE E. BRIDGES, MM 3/c, was born September 20, 1926, in Rockingham, NC, and joined the USNR in August, 1944, training at Bainbridge, MD and shipped to Miami, FL, where he was assigned to the USS *Donald W. Wolf (APD-129)* which was being built in Bay City, MI.

He was part of the nucleus crew and stayed with the ship which went from Chicago down the Mississippi River to Algiers, LA, for final rigging being commissioned in April, 1945. After a shake down cruise to "Gitmo," Cuba, they sailed to Norfolk, VA, for a check up then to San Diego, CA, where UDT 8 was assigned to ship. After 17 APDs formed a convoy, they went to Hawaii then to Okinawa. Later he learned that this was to be an amphibian operation for an invasion of Kyushu, Japan. (The war was officially over when they reached Okinawa.) They did screening duty for troop carriers into Jensen, Korea. His most memorable experience was riding out the Okinawa typhoon in

moored in the bay. From commission, stood #2 engine room watch, underway and throttle at general quarter. Crossed the International Dateline (180th Meridian), crossed the Equator initiated a shellback.

He was authorized to wear the American Area and Asiatic-Pacific Area Ribbon. Recommended for Good Conduct Medal.

Gave his last salute to ship in Tokyo Bay on his way the United States. Received honorable discharge Dec. 25, 1945. Returned to the house, where his mother welcomed him home. He is single, retired and living a relaxed life.

WILLIAM ZIPF, born Feb. 23, 1925 in Weehawken, NJ. Joined the USNR June 5, 1943. Stationed at New London, CT; Norfolk, VA; Mare Island, CA; and served on the USS *Crowley* (DE-303) plankowner; USS *Rowe* (DD-564),; and USS *Brownson* (DD-668). He had achieved the rank of EM2/c at the time of his discharge on Good Friday April, 19, 1946.

Remembers Typhoon "Cobra" Dec. 18, 1944, picking up downed carrier pilots, Okinawa landing, Iwo Jima, and Palau Islands.

Married to Delores in 1954. Worked for PSE & G Co, for more than 30 years. Attended Stevens War Industries School in Hoboken, NJ for seven years. He is now retired and enjoys travelling, camping. He likes all sports including baseball.

ERNEST DOMNICK ZUCCA, BM2/c, was born on June 2, 1923 in Vineland, NJ. Zucca enlisted in the

Navy December 1942. He attended boot camp in Bainbridge, MD February 1943. He then attended school in Norfolk, VA for submarine warfare. Zucca was assigned to the USS *Bebas* (DE-10) when it was commissioned in May 1943. After participating in some convoy duty in the Atlantic, the *Bebas* then took him to the Pacific where he took part in the following campaigns: Bougainville, Palau, Philippine, Okinawa and the initial strike on Japan. He remained with the *Bebas* until the wars end. Zucca was then transferred to the Philadelphia Navy Yard, where he stayed until he had enough points. He was discharged at Lido Beach, NY in January 1946.

He married Susie Arpino on Oct. 28, 1945. They have three daughters, Donna and twins Jane and Judy, and eight grandchildren. Today, Zucca, along with his brothers, owns and operates a bakery founded by his grandfather in 1896. He is moving toward full retirement.

September, 1945. *Wolf* was put out of commission in April, 1946, and he was assigned to USS *George W. Ingram (APD-43/DE-62)*. He was discharged on June 19, 1946 and joined the reserve after his brother talked him into it. He was called back to active duty in August, 1950, serving in the Mediterranean with the Atlantic 7th Fleet and was discharged in June, 1951, in San Pedro, CA.

He married on July 3, 1949, and has three children, four grandchildren. He retired from Exxon after 32 years. He enjoys woodworking as a hobby residing in Waxhaw, NC.

MAURICE P. CARTIER, Cmdr., USNR (Ret.), enlisted as recruit seaman on July 1, 1941, at Green Bay, WS, and trained as a apprentice seaman at Great Lakes, IL and as a gunners mate (striker).

He was assigned as a gunners mate 3/c on the USS *Kilty (DD-137)* at San Diego, CA. He attended aviation pilot training as aviation cadet V-5 aboard the *USS Wolverine 1x 64* (Carrier Training) in January, 1942. He was eliminated from the Navy Aviation Training due to an aircraft crash and injuries received. He was assigned to an "Old Rusty Bucket Merchant Ship" in Boston, MA, doing the Murmansk Run in February, 1943. On the return trip the ship was torpedoed and sunk by a German submarine. The sub fired on the convoy with deck guns and small arms. He and other wounded armed guard survivors were transferred to the *USS Bogue (CVE 9)* then taken to the Boston Naval Hospital. After two weeks of "basket leave," he reported for training in Washington, DC, at the Navy Yard Gun Factory where he was qualified as a diver 3/c and for explosive ordinance disposal (EOD). In May 1943, he was trained for underwater demolition team (UDT) operations at FT Pierce, FL. He was transferred

to Pearl Harbor, then to Aleutian Islands, Kiska, Attu, Atka, aboard the *USS Sante FE (CL-60)* as EOD Diver 3/c. He went to the Luriles Islands in September, 1943, on the *USS Richmond (CL-9)*; then to New Guinea, Langamak Bay, UDT aboard the *USS Kilty (APD-15)*; the Central Gilberts, Tarawa, Makin, Betio, UDT on the *USS Le Hardy (APD -20)* in November, 1943; the Southern Marshalls, Kwajalein, Wotje, Eniwetok, Senior EOD Diver 2/c, on the *USS Portland (CA-33)* in February, 1944; Admiralties, Kavieng, Manus, Rabaul, on the *USS Phoenix (CL-60)* in March, 1944; Southern Marianas, Saipan, Tinian, Guam, UDT, on the *USS Manlove (DE-36)* in June, 1944; Palau, Ulithi, Peleliu, Yap, Mortai, Gunners Mate 1/c, Senior EOD Diver 2/c, on the *USS Sante Fe (CL-60)*; Phillippines, Leyte, Surigao Strait, Samar Island, on the *USS Portland (CA-33)*. He went through the typhoon on December, 1944, on the *USS Wisconsin (BB-64)*. He went to Bonins, Iwo Jima, Higashi Iwa, in April, 1945, and Okinawa, Ryukus, Kermama Retto, in May, 1945, on the *USS Bates (APD-68)*. He went to Guam-Leyte on the *USS Indianapolis (CA-35)* in July, 1945. In February, 1946, he was on the *USS Willis (DE-395)* returning to U.S. for additional duties.

His awards include the Navy Commendation with "V," Bronze Star with "V," Philippine Republic Presidential Unit Citation, Philippine Liberation, Purple Heart, Navy Good Conduct, Silver Star, WWII Victory, Navy Occupation Service Medal (Asia Clasp), Expert Rifleman, Expert Pistol, American Defense (Fleet Clasp), American Campaign, and the European-African-Mid East Campaign.

He is currently retired residing in Casper, WY.

LUTHER JAY HESS, MM 2/c, was born October 4, 1925, in Berwick, PA, and entered the U.S. Navy on December 9, 1943. He went to Sampson Training Center, New York, and Norfolk Virginia Engineering School. He served aboard the *USS Jack Miller (DE-410)* which was named after 1st LT Jack Miller, USMC, who was born in Dallas, TX, on April 2, 1920 and died December 4, 1942, of wounds received in action at Guadalcanal being awarded the Purple Heart and Navy Cross Medals. Hess' memorable experience are many typhoons, kamikazes, and picket duty at Okinawa. He was in the Naval Reserve and served aboard the *USS Dortch (DD-670)* as the throttle man on #2 engine room turbines during the Korean War. He

went to Bermuda, Cuba (three times), and Guantanamo Bay on training exercises for atomic bomb and submarine attacks. His awards include the American Area, Victory Medal, Asiatic Pacific with two stars. He was discharged on May 26, 1946 at St. Louis, MO.

He married Gloria Knecht on March 6, 1947, and they have a 35 year old son, Douglas Jay, who is a geologist in Harrisburg, PA, and a 41 year old daughter, Lucinda Kishbaugh, who is an administrative assistant in the financial aid office at the university in Bloomsburg, PA. He is retired residing in Berwick, PA.

CARROLL L. JONES, was born July 20, 1922, in Three Rivers, MI. He attended elementary school in Phoenix, AZ, and High School in Jackson, MI. He enlisted in the U.S. Navy on January 17, 1942, being assigned to the Naval Training Station, San Diego, CA. He served aboard the *USS Sperry* and the *USS Connolly (DE-306)* and the *USS Connolly (DE- 306)*. His most memorable experience was Iwo Jima. He was discharged December 12, 1945, as Chief Commissary Steward.

His wife's name is Ruth and they have four children and 13 grandchildren. He resides in Des Moines, IA.

WALTER F. LYNCH, YN 2/C, USS *Tisdale* (DE-33), USS *Fleming* (DE-32), born in Philadelphia, PA on June 10, 1921, was one of four sons born to Walter A. and Mary J. (Doyle) Lynch.

He enlisted in the Navy on Sept. 19, 1942 and in August 1943, he was assigned to the commissioning crew of the USS *Tisdale* (DE-33) as Yeoman 2/C. Walter served on the *Tisdale* until Sept. 1944, when he transferred to the USS *Fleming* (DE-32). He served aboard the *Fleming* until Sept. 1945. He was discharged on March 13, 1946. He earned four ribbons: American Theatre, Asiatic Pacific with four stars, WW II Victory and Naval Good Conduct.

Walter and Mary (Carr) Lynch were married in Chester, PA in 1948, and have resided in Glenolden, PA since 1955. Their family includes three sons—Walter, James and John, and a daughter, Julie.

JOHN MITCHELL

HENRY J. RACETTE, Captain, U.S. Navy, was born on May 12, 1919, in Brooklyn, NY, and joined the service on August 24, 1938. He served on ten ships at numerous stations in the Pacific Theatre both ashore and afloat. He participated in the battles at Pearl Harbor, the Coral Sea and Midway. His awards and decorations include the Legion of Merit, Navy Commendation Medal (two awards), and the Navy Unit Commendation Ribbon (three awards). He was discharged on June 30, 1972 at the rank of Captain.

He married Mildred Nickels, and they have four children and six grandchildren. He currently resides in San Diego, CA and devotes himself to his family, community and church activities. *(See photos, page 721)*

HERBERT C. SINN, JR., RADM, says that he is a bit of a clown, but even clowns can cry. He enjoys his former shipmates thoroughly though they often make him weep. His beloved shipmate Roy Larick, the last CO of the *USS Deede*, died suddenly last February, 1991. Also, his life long friend, John Hamilton Luff,

CO of *AP Calso* took the deep six in February. They went to Lafayette together, then to North Western sub chaser training in Miami. They parted company until the war's end. His brother married his sister.

He spent three grand years restoring the warrant officer's mess room aboard the *USS Olympia*, moored at the Philadelphia Landing, as a memorial to the U.S. Navy Blue Angels.

His oral cancer is now in the sixth year of remission. Like he always says, "Old DESA sailors never die...they just sail away."

CHARLES LEO SMITH *(See Bio, page 728)*

FLOYD L. SMITH, MMOC 3/C, was born November 24, 1924, in Mulberry Canyon, TX He graduated from the Police Academy at Howard County Junior College, Big Springs, TX, and entered the U.S. Navy as a selective volunteer on April 5, 1943, receiving Boot Training at San Diego, CA, Class #133, and assigned to the *USS Island* Mail Merchant Marine Transport Ship

going to New Caledonia then to a tanker going to the Northern Solomon Islands. He was assigned to the *USS Cleveland* (No. 55) with Task Force 38 at Bourgainville.

He received DE training at Norfolk, VA and went the Mare Island Naval Yard for commissioning of the *USS Connolly (DE-306)* on July 8, 1944. He was in the 3rd Division assigned to the Forward Motor Room as Fireman 1st Class with battle station on a 20mm gun on the starboard side. They sailed to Honolulu for submarine and gunnery training, then went to the Marshall Islands in preparation for Iwo Jima. He was at Okinawa when a Kamikaze crashed 30 feet from the starboard side. The *USS Bowers (DE-637)* was hit and the *Connolly* picked up survivors. The *Connolly* was

decommissioned November 29, 1945 at Charleston, SC. He was discharged May 20, 1946. His decorations include American Area Campaign Ribbon, Asiatic-Pacific Campaign Ribbon, Philippine Liberation Medal, Presidential Unit Citation, and WWII Victory Medal.

He married Patsy Ruth (Tucker) on November 18, 1951, and they have a son, Joe Don, daughter-in-law, Pamela Ann, and grandson, Christopher Alan, He is the Criminal Investigator Deputy Sheriff for the Nolan County Sheriff Department in Sweetwater, TX, where he resides.

ROBERT SWEITZER

R.W. MILLER (Bob)

DESTROYER ESCORT SAILORS ASSOCIATION ROSTER

This is the roster submitted by the Destroyer Escort Sailors Association for inclusion in this publication. The Publisher is not liable for any errors or omissions contained herein.

- A -
Aagaard, William M.
Abbene, Louis F.
Abbott, Frank T.
Abbott, Mason
Abbott, Wilmer A. Jr.
Abbvato, Joseph W.
Abel, Brent
Abel, Richard A.
Abend, Leonard F.
Abenethy, Frank
Abernathy, Clyde
Abernathy, Denver
Ablamsky, Michael Jr.
Ablonsky, John
Abner, William R.
Abney, Manley
Aboff, Jack
Abrahamian, Paul
Abrahamsen, John P.
Abrahm, Bernard
Abrams, Arthur T.
Abrams, Benjamin L.
Abrams, Harold H.
Abrams, Robert H.
Abruzino, Joseph V.
Abt, Robert E.
Ackendorf, Robert B.
Ackerman, John H.
Ackerson, Charles F.
Ackert, Robert J.
Ackroyd, William B.
Adair, Robert
Adamczyk, Henry
Adamkiewicz, Matthew
Adams, Austin
Adams, Basil
Adams, Charles F.
Adams, Earl B. Jr.
Adams, Herman H. Jr.
Adams, Hugh C.
Adams, James E.
Adams, Kenneth F.
Adams, Paul J.
Adams, Paul R.
Adams, Ralph D.
Adams, Renee
Adams, Ronald C.
Adams, Roy A.
Adams, William S.
Adamshick, George
Adamson, Edward E.
Adcock, Albert Ray
Adcock, Jennings B.
Adcox, Duncan E.
Addison, William B.
Adesso, Anthony G.
Adkins, Aubrey V.
Adkins, Claude R.
Adkison, Ralph D.
Adler, Leonard
Ager, Richard A.
Agnew, Edwin J.
Agnew, John P.
Agnew, Robert B.
Ahearn, John V.
Aho, Aulis W.
Aicken, Francis H.
Aiken, George H.
Aja, Richard
Akers, Charles E.
Akers, John S.
Akey, Malcolm C.
Akin, Larry D.
Akins, Harvey W.
Alair, Charles N.
Albers, Paul
Albert, Anthony G.
Albertine, John
Albertine, Paul K.
Albrecht, Lawrence
Albrecht, William
Albright, Paul J.
Albritton, John A.
Alcorn, David S.
Alcott, George R.
Alder, Alfred F.
Alderman, Cecil
Alderson, George W.
Aldrich, Gordon E.
Aldrich, Harold D.
Aldrich, Thomas L.
Aldridge, Garet V.
Alekna, Edgar A.
Alesandro, Fabian J.
Alexander, Frank G.
Alexander, Joseph J.
Alexander, Paul J.
Alfano, Sam
Aliano, Salvatore J.
Allard, Rene E.
Allen, Arthur E. Jr.
Allen, Burl
Allen, Charles A.
Allen, Charles A.
Allen, Charles F.
Allen, David W.
Allen, Delos E.
Allen, Earl W.
Allen, Edward T.
Allen, Elmo S.
Allen, George C. Jr.
Allen, Gerald R.
Allen, Harry D.
Allen, Jack E.
Allen, Jack F.
Allen, James E.
Allen, James L.
Allen, Joe C.
Allen, John E.
Allen, Leonard Van
Allen, Ralph B.
Allen, Robert M.
Allen, Sheldon
Allen, Wyatt
Allenbaugh, William G.
Aller, Neal
Allgeier, Edward C.
Allgren, Mahlon
Allinger, Warren L.
Allison, B.F.
Allison, J.M.
Allwein, Robert C.
Alonge, Salvatore
Alpaugh, John G.
Alpaugh, Russell Jr.
Alsobrook, Thomas M.
Altemus, Thomas W.
Altimont, O.W.
Altman, Merle H.
Alvarez, Amando
Alves, Leo St. John
Amann, Leonard J.
Ambrose, Joseph E.
Ambrose, Michael J.
Ambrose, William D.
Ambruso, Dennis A.
Amelio, Rudy
Amendola, Salvatore
Ammendola, Anthony
Amorosa, Mario J.
Amory, Lloyd R. Jr.
Amos, Howard W.
Amsden, Milton L.
Anamier, Frederick H.
Andersen, Alex E. Jr.
Andersen, Eldon T.
Andersen, Harry T.
Andersen, John B.
Andersen, Kenneth E.
Andersen, Stanley S.
Anderson, Andy
Anderson, Bernard C.
Anderson, Bernie
Anderson, Bertle M.
Anderson, Carl A.
Anderson, Carl H.
Anderson, Carl K.
Anderson, Charles A.
Anderson, Delmar L.
Anderson, Ernest A.
Anderson, Frederick
Anderson, Frederick R.
Anderson, George B.
Anderson, George E.
Anderson, Harold G.
Anderson, Harold H.
Anderson, Harris R.
Anderson, Henry C. Jr.
Anderson, James E.
Anderson, John F.
Anderson, Joseph F.
Anderson, Marshall
Anderson, Parley G.
Anderson, Paul F.
Anderson, Paul L.
Anderson, Robert E.
Anderson, Robert J.
Anderson, Thomas J.
Anderson, W.P.
Anderson, William
Andleton, Paul F.
Andrew, Glenn N.
Andrew, Ralph E. Jr.
Andrews, Edwin S.
Andrews, Fred F.
Andrews, Lewis M. Jr.
Andrews, Louis H.
Andrews, Paul B.
Andrews, Paul S.
Andrews, Richard E.
Andries, Justin J. Jr.
Andriopoulos, Spiros
Andruskiewicz, John F.
Angelilli, Edward
Angelotti, Joseph V.
Angle, Richard W.
Angotti, Michael A.
Anlage, John G.
Annau, William E.
Annibale, Anthony
Ansart, Nicholas B.
Anterni, John J.
Anthony, Edward J.
Anthony, Joseph T.
Antoine, John S.
Anton, George A.
Antonakos, Basil
Antonellis, Anthony J.
Antonich, Michael Jr.
Antonio, Jimmie G.
Antonio, Roland D.
Antonucci, Vincent
Antosz, John J.
Antritt, John
Anuszczyk, Edmond
Anzalone, Joseph
Anzur, Edward C.
Apisaloma, Iakopo T.
Apple, Joseph M.
Applebury, Carl W.
Arcery, Nicholas J.
Archer, Robert J.
Archer, W.W.
Archer, W.W.
Arenberg, J.T. Jr.
Arens, Leo V.
Arent, David
Arft, Henry
Argenti, Benjamin
Argust, William G. Sr.
Arleth, Norman
Armbruster, Carl
Armillei, Manfred J.
Armin, Dayton C.
Armstrong, Carl Wm.
Armstrong, Henry J.
Armstrong, Richard E.
Armstrong, Willie
Arneson, Robert E.
Arnold, Charlie R.
Arnold, Clifford W.
Arnold, Frederick W.
Arnold, George W.
Arnold, Herbert Y.
Arnold, John R.
Arnold, Richard G.
Arnold, Robert M.
Arnold, Sam J. Jr.
Arnold, Sidney C.
Arntz, Robert A.
Aronoff, Bernard
Arr, Merle W.
Arrington, Asa W.
Arrington, C.C. Jr.
Arsenault, Frederick J.
Arterburn, Edward P.
Arterburn, Gary
Arthur, Harry E.
Arthur, Lewis R.
Artistic-West
Arts, Arthur A.
Aschendorf, Philip
Asetta, Charles
Ash, Oscar H.
Ashbaugh, Merlyn R.
Ashby, Elton E.
Ashby, Ward L.
Asher, Willard F.
Ashley, Hubert A.
Askew, Foster R.
Aslin, Gorty
Asmar, Henry C.
Asselmeier, Clifford C.
Astley, Arthur D.
Aston, Warren A.
Atfield, Fred C.
Atherholt, W.
Athey, Fredrick L.
Atkins, Edward H.
Atkins, Jack B.
Atkinson, Robert C. Jr.
Atkinson, William I.
Atterbury, G.R.
Atwell, Frederick W.
Atwood, Frank D.
Aucella, Anthony
Aucoin, Joseph F.
Audette, Roland D.
Auer, Norman
Auge, Roger J.
Auger, Raymond L.
August, Edward G.
Augustine, Howard A.
Augustine, P.R.
Augustyn, Frank
Aukamp, Gustav M.
Auld, James W.
Auld, William R. Jr.
Aulwurm, Frederick H.
Austin, Edward
Austin, George A.
Austin, Julius H.
Austin, Roy G.
Auth, Edwin F.
Autry, Joseph W.
Avanzato, Joseph A.
Avener, John W.
Averill, Jack E.
Averill, Merle C.
Avers, Willis C.
Avery, James D. Jr.
Avery, R.C.
Avery, Richard L.
Axelrod, Harry
Axtmann, Harry L.
Ayars, William F.
Aycock, Willie L.
Ayers, O.C.
Ayers, Perry R.
Aylsworth, David A. Jr.
Ayres, Charles R.
- B -
Baas, Joseph C.
Babb, Richard L.
Babb, Richard L.
Babcock, Dwight H.
Babcock, Robert R. Jr.
Baber, Ronald L.
Babineau, Raymond J.
Babnik, Richard A.
Bach, Orville E.
Bacher, James K.
Bachman, Robert C.
Bachorz, Raymond
Bacome, Tony A.
Badders, Charles E.
Badeaux, Joseph C.
Bader, David
Bader, Frank
Badowich, Raymond G.
Baehler, Leo C.
Baer, Eugene L.
Bage, Eddie V.
Baggott, Buel G.
Bailey, Edward H.
Bailey, Gerald
Bailey, John L.
Bailey, Johnny Ebert
Bailey, Joseph A. III
Bailey, Omer
Bailey, Radford R.
Bailey, Ralph
Bailey, Willard A.
Bair, Herbert N.
Bair, Howard J.
Bair, Lowell S.
Bair, Sheldon E.
Baird, Charles E.
Baird, Clayton D.
Baird, Joseph J.
Baity, Fred W.
Baker, Alan D.
Baker, Alton K.
Baker, Charles S.
Baker, Cleamon O. Jr.
Baker, Dale
Baker, Edward L.
Baker, Edward R.
Baker, Ellis R.
Baker, Harold L.
Baker, Harold W.
Baker, Jack B.
Baker, Jack L.
Baker, Malcolm E.
Baker, Paul H.
Baker, Robert E.
Baker, Roy C.
Baker, T.F.
Baker, Vernon B.
Baker, Willis W.
Bakke, Oscar Sidney
Balabuch, Francis
Balach, Steve J.
Balcom, George H. Jr.
Balcombe, Ralph
Baldauf, Albert A.
Baldock, Chester
Baldoni, Robert R.
Balducci, Geno A.
Baldwin, Donald R.
Baldwin, Fred H. Jr.
Baldwin, Wayne R.
Baldyga, Ladislaus A.
Bales, Clifford Jr.
Bales, Richard A.
Baley, Richard F.
Ball, Charles Jr.
Ball, Hubert J.
Ball, Ralph L.
Ballantine, Robert G.
Ballard, Wayne E.
Baller, Maxwell J.
Ballinger, C. Edwin
Balmer, Robert E.
Balsam, Neil R.
Balsly, Donald L.
Baltzell, William M.
Bamburak, Stanley
Bander, Edward J.
Bandy, Jesse D.
Bandy, Kenneth M.
Bankert, Charles M. Jr.
Bankovich, Jerome J. Sr.
Banks, Al
Banks, Charles E.
Banks, John M.
Banks, Orland Ray
Banks, Wilbur
Bannasch, Dennis
Banning, William Po.
Bannon, James R.
Bannon, John P.
Baranoski, Melvin L.
Barauskas, Al
Barbee, Dale L.
Barbee, William R.
Barber, Donald
Barber, Harold A.
Barber, Herman W.
Barber, James H.
Barber, John T.
Barber, Raymond
Barber, Robert C.
Barber, William F.
Barberi, James G.
Barbieri, Guy
Barbieri, Robert C. MD
Barclay, Victor F.
Barcone, Benito H.
Bardenwerper, H.W. MD
Bardon, Theodore J.
Barfield, Glenn L.
Barfield, Hill M.
Barger, Lyle H.
Barger, Robert
Bargert, Jack L.
Baric, Warren L.
Barker, Frederick P.
Barker, Howard L.
Barker, Kenneth R.
Barksdale, Henry R.
Barlow, Floyd T.
Barnes, Charles A.
Barnes, Charles E.
Barnes, Charles J.
Barnes, Joseph P.
Barnes, Kenneth
Barnes, Les
Barnes, Robert
Barnes, Robert F.
Barnett, William D.
Barnhardt, Roy L. Jr.
Barnhart, Ben A.
Barnhart, Richard E.
Baron, Leonard R.
Barone, Anthony C.
Barone, Dominic J.
Barr, Marlin W.
Barr, Paul J.
Barr, Rome E.
Barrett, Curtis D.
Barrett, Horace M.
Barrett, James L.
Barrett, Robert A.
Barrett, Robert D.
Barrett, Willard J.
Barron, Vincent J.
Barros, Ferando
Barrow, Winford W.
Barrows, Hubert O.
Barry, William
Bartels, Harold J.
Barthalomew, Eugene
Bartholomew, John
Bartimus, Charles V.
Bartkoski, Paul A.
Bartkus, Anthony
Bartlett, Armand G.
Bartley, Ray
Bartola, Chester
Bartoli, Henry P.
Bartolone, Nicholas J.
Bartolotta, Joseph
Bartow, Donald M.
Bartow, Stuart A.
Bartow, Stuart A.
Bartruff, Charles
Basche, Bartley B.
Basehart, Joseph R.
Bash, James R.
Baskin, Nathan
Baskin, Nathan
Baskovic, Joseph S.
Batchelder, Edwin Jr.
Batcheldor, Robert E.
Batchelor, John P.
Batchelor, Ralph E.
Bateman, Leonard E.
Bates, Aubrey L.
Bates, David
Bates, Ernest H.
Bates, Warren W.
Bates, Wayne W.
Batson, Marion E.
Battaglia, Carmello J.
Battista, John A.
Battle, John S. Jr.
Battle, Paul R.
Batzkall, Carl V.
Bau, Elaine
Bauer, Elvie L.
Bauer, Frederick H.
Baum, Kenneth
Baum, W. Russell
Bauman, Frank H.
Baumann, George A.
Baumgarn, Marvin A.
Baumgarner, Paul W.
Baumgarten, Rudolf C.
Baur, William T.
Bava, Nicholas A.
Bavier, Robert
Baxa, Russell
Baxter, Edward E.
Baxter, Robert F.
Baxter, William C.
Bayer, Frank J. Jr.
Bayless, Roy E.
Bayley, Roy C.
Bayliss, Bill
Bayne, Cleve J.
Baynes, John T.
Bazemore, Robert W.
Beach, Gerald L.
Beach, Glenn
Beach, Michael G.
Beach, Otto F.
Beacham, Curtis K.
Beagle, Clayton
Beal, Francis L.
Beal, Humbert H.
Beal, Robert M.
Beale, Jack
Beals, James B.
Beamer, Wallace R.
Bean, Ernest L. Jr.
Bean, Jay
Beard, C.E.
Beaton, M. Currie Jr.
Cockayne, Arthur J.
Beattie, Charles H. Jr.
Beattie, Henry C.
Beatty, Bruce L.
Beatty, Edward
Beatty, Lyman D.
Beaty, Thomas L.
Beaubien, Philip J.
Beauchaine, Lester
Beaudin, Rene E.
Beaudoin, Albert
Beauford, Dudley B.
Beaumier, George A.
Beauregard, Lawrence Dr.
Beauregard, Theodore J.
Beaver, Earnest J.
Beaverson, Lester R.
Beazley, C. Henry
Beccia, Nick A.
Becht, Paul F.
Beck, Henry C.
Beck, Kenneth E.
Beck, Rev. Glen
Beck, Richard E.
Beck, Warren S.
Becker, Gerald C.
Becker, Joseph J.
Beckett, Philip B.
Beckman, Donald J.
Beckstine, Willard F.
Beckwith, Neil M.
Becton, Julian F.
Beddow, Merle
Bednarczyk, Edward
Bedsaul, Bryant
Beebout, Mark W.
Beer, Guy R.
Beerman, Morris
Beerup, Leo L.
Beeson, Doyle G.
Beeson, Phillip
Beetel, William T.
Begley, John J.
Behmerwohld, James K.
Behr, William F.
Behrnes, Maurice H.
Beidelman, Curtis P.
Beiderbeck, Edward J.
Beine, Floyd J.
Belden, Richard D.
Beline, Thomas M.
Belkin, Robert M.
Bell, Arthur L.
Bell, Calvin O. Jr.
Bell, Cleveland
Bell, Donald A.
Bell, Donald E.
Bell, Frank J.
Bell, Harold E.
Bell, Keith E.
Bell, Lovelin A.
Bell, Orville W.
Bell, Paul A.
Bell, Robert H.
Bell, William P.
Bellairs, C.
Beller, Charles R. Jr.
Beller, George A.
Bellino, Vincent A.
Bellissimo, Frederick
Belloise, James W.
Belongie, Francis A.
Beltrani, Vincent J.
Benard, Armand A.
Bence, Robert L.
Bender, Edwin J.
Bender, Howard R.
Bender, James J.
Bender, Nicholas C.
Benderson, Ben
Bendit, Robert O.
Bendixen, James R.
Bendorf, Alfred L.
Benefield, Harvey Wm.
Benewiat, Michael
Benfante, Angelo A.
Benfield, Jesse E.
Benich, John A.
Benick, Charles
Benkert, Gerard G.
Benko, Edward J.
Benko, Edward W.
Bennet, William N.
Bennett, Arthur
Bennett, Ashby C.
Bennett, Charles
Bennett, Charles W.
Bennett, Clifton L.
Bennett, Clinton K.
Bennett, Dick W.
Bennett, Franklin O.
Bennett, John S.
Bennett, Samuel L.
Bennett, Scott
Bennett, Stephen D.
Bennett, Thomas
Bennett, William H. Sr.
Benoit, Charles E.
Bensfield, Nicholas E.
Bensilhe, Goldie C.
Benson, Leonard M.
Benson, Lyndon B.
Bentley, James F.
Bentley, Ray
Bentley, Wallace A. Jr.
Benton, Roy B.
Benz, H.L.
Benz, Rudolph G.
Berard, Arnold G.
Berbrick, Guyer C.
Berens, Robert C.
Berg, Paul L.
Berg, Robert G.
Berg, Ward D.
Berg, William J.
Bergantz, Walter S.
Bergen, Joseph J.
Bergen, Richard H.
Berger, Frances
Berger, Herman Jr.
Berger, James R.
Bergin, Donald J.
Berglund, Jack E.
Bergman, Donald
Bergren, Kenneth
Bergsma, Edwin M.
Berit, Henri P.
Berkemeier, Ernest L.
Berliss, Arthur D. Jr.
Bernard, Russell A.
Bernardini, Alfred
Bernays, Richard W.
Bernhard, Louis J.
Bernhardt, Roger E.
Berot, Bernard J. Jr.
Berres, Robert K.
Berrier, Paul H.
Berry, Cecil E.
Berry, Delbert W.
Berry, Glenn
Berry, Harry S.
Berry, John T.
Berry, Leon C.
Berry, Robert W.
Berryhill, Malcolm O.
Berryhill, Malcolm O.
Berryman, Robert E.
Berteau, Huey
Berthelson, Fenton
Bertiaux, Paul R.
Bertoncini, Alfred
Bertrand, Alex
Bertucci, Walter J.
Besanson, Clayton J.
Besaw, Gerald B.
Besemer, John
Beskind, Robert L.
Bess, John Q.
Best, Lawrence H.
Best, Marvin G.
Best, Richard V.N.
Best, William E.
Best, William W.
Beste, George F.
Bethel, Donald G.
Better, Frank
Bettner, G. William
Beutel, Leo E.
Beuther, Kenneth R.
Beveridge, George M.
Bewley, James F.
Bewley, William
Beyer, Frederic B.
Beyersdorf, Herbert
Bezark, W.S.
Bianca, Dominic
Bianco, John J. Sr.
Biase, Robert G.
Biasi, Charles A.
Bice, Grover F.
Bice, Grover F.
Bickel, Robert F.
Bickerstaff, Riley
Biedron, Henry S.
Biegelman, Leonard
Biel, Eugene J.
Bielinski, Paul E.
Bienhoff, Henry H.
Bierbach, Kenneth R.
Biermann, Frederick W.
Bifulco, Freddie
Biggane, Leon T.
Biggerstaff, W.E.
Biggs, Lloyd O.
Biglieri, Melvin J.
Bilbee, Francis M.
Bilderback, Arthur H.
Bill, David S. Jr.
Biller, Dorsey A.
Billigmeier, Robert
Billing, Robert A.
Billings, David P.
Billings, James P.
Billingsley, Ralph E.
Binford, William M.
Binner, John
Binninger, Charles
Birch, Clyde J.
Birch, Doug
Birch, Louis T.
Birchard, Edson A.
Bird, Darell I.
Bird, Grace E.
Birk, Joe S.
Bischoff, Harry W.
Bischoff, John J.
Bischoff, O.J.
Bischoff, Paul A.
Bischoff, Robert
Bishop, Edward C.
Bishop, Edward L.
Bishop, Frank M.
Bishop, John C.
Bishop, Robert L.
Bismarck, Calvin W.
Bissell, Harry E.
Bitoff, John W.
Bitterling, George A.
Bjorkman, Russell I.
Black, Delbert D.
Black, Edwin B.
Black, Gill R.
Black, Harold F.
Black, James E.
Black, Robert
Black, William J. Sr.
Blackburn, Robert J.
Blackburn, T.M.
Blackford, Donald L.
Blackhall, Allen H. Jr.
Blackley, Shem K. Jr.
Blackmon, Glen
Blackwell, Francis
Blackwell, Jack D.
Blackwell, John D.
Blackwell, Kenneth E.
Blackwood, A.L.
Blair, Bruce M.
Blair, Elzie H.
Blair, James A.
Blair, James R.
Blair, Leroy E.
Blair, Robert A.
Blair, Robert L.
Blair, William S.
Blaisdell, Raymond W.
Blake, Walter S.
Blanchard, Edward J.
Bland, Jess R.
Bland, William H.
Blane, Joseph J.
Blankenship, Carroll L.
Blankenship, James D.
Blankenship, John Jr.
Blanks, Alton R.
Blanton, Dwight J.
Blanton, Halton L.
Blastic, Richard
Blaszka, Otto F.
Blaszynski, Irvin
Blatt, Sol
Blattenberger, Richard
Blaze, Arthur N.
Blazek, Joseph L.
Blechl, Alvin J.
Blemberg, Peter P.
Bleyenberg, Frank A.
Bliss, Nate
Blissman, William T.
Bliznuk, June E.
Block, Walter R.
Blomgren, Vernon R.
Blood, Charles J.
Bloodgood, M.J.
Bloodworth, Dennis Jr.
Bloom, Jack
Bloom, Jack
Bloom, Leonard
Bloom, Robert
Bloom, Roy W.
Bloomquist, Alfred G.

Blose, Philip D.
Blosser, Lawrence
Blouch, Charles Mrs.
Blowers, William J.
Bloyd, Roy
Blue, Casper W. Jr.
Blue, Rhoderick R.
Blum, Stanford K. Jr.
Blume, Elmer M.
Blumenfeld, Milton J.
Blust, Richard
Bly, Elmer L.
Boardman, John M.
Boardway, Leon
Bobe, S.P.
Bocchieri, Albert
Boccitto, Anthony A.
Bock, James H.
Bockius, Peter L.
Boczany, William J.
Boday, Raymond L.
Boddy, George E.
Boderman, William
Bodley, Robert W.
Bodling, Paul F. Jr.
Bodnar, Annette M.
Boeck, Robert G.
Boedecker, Carl A.
Boehrer, Elmer G.
Boerner, Fred P.
Boesner, A. John
Bofinger, Harry W.
Bogan, Jack W.
Bogart, Floyd
Bogart, William G.
Boger, Vernis N.
Bogert, Walter M. Jr.
Boggess, Kenneth R.
Bogucki, Edward J.
Bogwald, Jack R.
Bohaczyk, Ted
Bohmann, Walter E.
Bohn, Robert M.
Bohnert, Robert J.
Bohr, Nick
Boisits, Gustave A.
Bojanowski, Wallace A.
Bolak, Frank
Boland, John F.
Boldosser, Richard G.
Bole, David C.
Boles, George F.
Bolick, Maude K.
Bolinger, A. Ted
Bolio, Robert
Bolt, Sam D.
Bolton, Edwin R.
Bolton, Jay H.
Bonacci, Michael J.
Bonacci, Nick
Bonaguidi, Robert
Bonas, Richard F.
Bonbrake, Benny J.
Bonbrake, Benny J.
Boncek, Edward J.
Bond, Edward A.
Bond, Eugene T.
Bond, Gerald
Bond, Kenneth F.
Bond, Thomas W. Jr.
Bongartz, Ferdinand
Bongiorno, Sebastian J.
Bonhag, Walter D.
Bonhamer, Arthur H.
Bonis, Donald
Bonito, Carmel
Bonnell, Oscar F.
Bonneville, Vern
Bonney, Harry H. Jr.
Bono, Charles J.
Bonomo, Conrad
Bontreger, Glenn D.
Bookbinder, A.G.
Booker, James P.
Boon, John
Boone, Charles A.
Boone, John Jr.
Boortz, J.J.
Booth, Franklin
Booth, Paul
Booth, Robert W.
Bordogna, Joseph
Boren, James H.
Boren, John F.
Boress, Dick
Borgrud, Marlin
Boring, C.H.
Borm, Roland
Boromei, Vincent
Borowiec, John R.
Borowski, Dennis
Borst, Kenneth W.
Bortscheller, Adam
Bortz, Ralph H.
Boruchowski, Thaddeus
Borum, Marion L.
Bos, B.E.
Boselli, Thomas S.
Boselli, Thomas S.
Bossert, William
Bossidy, Frank
Bost, E.L.
Bost, Harvey B.
Boswell, John C.
Bothwell, Hugh R.
Botkin, Grover F.
Botts, James B.
Boucher, Henry R.
Boucher, Paul
Boucher, Stephen R.
Boudreaux, John D.
Bouley, Francis E. Sr.
Boulrice, Robert G.
Bourne, Warren W.
Boutilier, David K.
Bouton, William
Bowe, James T.
Bowen, Charles H.
Bowen, Robert Lee
Bowen, Vincent J.
Bowen, Wm. H.
Bower, Dane W.
Bower, T.L.
Bower, T.L.
Bowers, Ben B.
Bowers, Clifford
Bowers, Donald W.
Bowers, Francis W.
Bowers, Wade M.
Bowes, William L.
Bowes, William L.
Bowie, James M.
Bowie, Kenneth J.
Bowie, Kenneth J.
Bowles, Ivan R.
Bowman, Dean P.
Bowman, Grafton E.
Bowman, Harold
Bowman, John R.
Bowman, Robert
Bowman, Wayne E.
Bowne, Edward L.
Boy, John B.
Boyack, Raymond O.
Boyce, Calvin K.
Boyce, Henry E.
Boyd, Al
Boyd, Alex W. Jr.
Boyd, Carl P.
Boyd, James H.
Boyd, Lee H.
Boyd, Robert W.
Boyd, Wilbur L.
Boydstun, Dorene/
Chastity
Boyer, Charles B.
Boyer, Claude P.
Boyer, David C.
Boyer, Irvin J.
Boyer, Paul A.
Boyette, Edward L.
Boykin, Gerald C.
Boylan, Vernon L.
Boyle, Carl M.
Boyle, Eugene V. Jr.
Boyle, Frank J. Jr.
Boynton, Ralph S.
Boynton, Robert L.
Bozanic, Milton
Bozee, Edward F.
Bozek, John F.
Braa, Wesley J.
Brabant, Paul
Bracelin, John F.
Bracken, Robert O.
Brackett, James L.
Brackett, James W.
Braddock, Jack
Bradford, Addison R.
Bradford, Russell R.
Bradley, Ralph T.
Bradley, Robert
Bradley, Robert G.
Bradley, William L.
Bradshaw, Walter L.
Bradsher, Harry E.
Bradsher, James R.
Bradtke, Don F.
Brady, David R.
Brady, Ennis R.
Brady, Robert N.
Brady, Thomas
Brady, William E.
Brady, William J.
Bragdon, Carlyle A. Jr.
Bragg, James M.
Bragg, Richard A.
Braham, Vernon J.
Bramble, Frank C.
Bramlett, Mary L.
Brancato, Joseph
Branch, Earl L.
Brand, Edward L.
Brand, John H.
Brand, Joseph F.
Brand, Robert M.
Brandalick, Joseph
Brandenburg, Paul D.
Brandl, Michael J.
Brandon, Richard H.
Brandow, Roy
Brandt, Melvin A.
Brandt, Robert
Brandy, William F.
Branham, Bill
Brannan, Jake M.
Brant, Floyd O.
Brantley, James J.
Brasfield, Ollie F.
Brashars, Ewell E.
Brasher, Clinton M.
Braun, Dan
Braun, Herbert
Braxton, Rayford E.
Bray, George E.
Bray, John L.
Bray, Leo T.
Bray, Sumner P. Jr.
Breagy, Tom
Brecko, Joseph J.
Breda, Oren H.
Bredernitz, Ormond R.
Breeden, William H.
Breeding, Roy L.
Breeling, Harold E.
Breen, Robert P.
Brehl, Bernard F.
Brehm, Benjamin F.
Brehm, Warren
Breidenbach, Frank
Breil, Richard J.
Brelia, Warren J.
Bremner, James M.
Brendza, Michael A.
Brennan, David
Brennan, David
Brennan, Edward C.
Brennan, Leo F.
Brennan, Robert F.
Brennan, Thomas F.
Brennan, Thomas J.
Brennan, Thomas M.
Brennan, William A. Jr.
Brenner, Joseph T.
Brenner, Lloyd R.
Bresee, Miles H. Jr.
Bresko, William J.
Bretherton, John P. Jr.
Bretzger, William J.
Brew, Hobart S.
Brewer, Alvia J.
Brewer, George R.
Brewer, Joseph A.
Brewer, Richard A.
Brewer, Robert W. Jr.
Brewer, Tom
Brewster, Harold
Brian, Harry A.
Brick, Gene
Brickner, Mark Q.
Brickser, H.C.
Bridges, Claude E.
Bridges, Gerard J.
Bridges, Luke M.
Briggs, Robert G.
Bright, Robert D.
Brindle, Ralph A.
Brindle, Robert E.
Brindle, William F. Sr.
Brine, Dexter D.
Briner, George W.
Brinkley, Roscoe Jr.
Brinkman, Henry J.
Brissey, G.T.
Britt, Franklin E.
Britt, Jack D.
Britton, James P.
Britton, Kenneth H.
Britton, William R.
Brixius, Albert H.
Broaddus, Nash T.
Broccolo, Vincent
Brock, Dale L.
Brockmeyer, Arlyn
Brodhacker, John
Brodie, David
Brodie, Francis R.
Brodie, George W.
Brogden, Thomas
Broich, Joseph W.
Broker, Donald J.
Bromley, Walter E.
Brons, Richard G.
Bronson, Edward J.
Brooker, Julian L.
Brooks, Alvin T.
Brooks, Arthur C.
Brooks, Eugene J.
Brooks, Herbert R.
Brooks, Ralph K.
Brooks, Wallace D.
Broome, Robert M.
Broomfield, Maurice O.
Brophy, Joseph H.
Brophy, Michael E.
Brosca, Anthony P.
Brosious, Robert W.
Brothers, Jack L.
Broughton, Julian H.
Browder, Raymond
Brower, Curtis M.
Brower, Donald L.
Brower, John E.
Brown, Allen R.
Brown, B.J.
Brown, Bernard K.
Brown, Carl H.
Brown, Charles A.
Brown, Charles A.
Brown, Charles E.
Brown, Charles E.
Brown, Charles K.
Brown, Charles R.
Brown, Clarence A.
Brown, Daniel M.
Brown, Eugene A.
Brown, George W.
Brown, Harold H.
Brown, Herbert M.
Brown, Howard H.
Brown, Hulon B.
Brown, Hunter N.
Brown, J.W.
Brown, James F.
Brown, James I.
Brown, James W.
Brown, Jasper M. Jr.
Brown, Joe E.
Brown, John A.
Brown, John J.
Brown, John T.
Brown, Joseph R.
Brown, Larry R.
Brown, Maynard D.
Brown, Mrs. Charles B.
Brown, Percy R.
Brown, Ralph B.
Brown, Raymond O.
Brown, Richard H.
Brown, Richard O.
Brown, Robert
Brown, Robert H.
Brown, Robert J.
Brown, Robert L.
Brown, Ronald E.
Brown, Roy D.
Brown, Ted C. Sr.
Brown, Tom A.
Brown, Ward
Brown, William H. Jr.
Brown, William L.
Brownawell, John O.
Browne, Jette
Browne, John A.
Brownfield, John C.
Browning, Arthur U.
Brownrigg, Daniel E.
Bruce, Donald M.
Bruce, Harold N.
Bruce, Thomas L.
Bruce, Wallace G.
Bruch, Walter P.
Bruck, Anthony E.
Brugger, Paul D.
Brummett, William J.
Brundage, Jerry
Brunk, Don L.
Bruno, Thomas W.
Bruns, Wilfred A.
Brush, Cyrus E.
Brush, George L.
Brusha, Oscar
Bryan, Ben F.
Bryan, Paul D. Jr.
Bryan, Woodrow A.
Bryant, Charles F.
Bryant, David F.
Bryant, E.C.
Bryant, Joe J.
Brzostek, Francis B.
Bubernak, Steve
Bubniak, Alexander L.
Buccieri, Frank R.
Buchan, William F.
Buchanan, Gordon D. Jr.
Buchanan, Lyle
Buchanan, Wellford N.
Buchanan, William H.
Buchmiller, Richard
Buck, Victor E.
Buck, Wesley T.
Buckler, William
Buckley, John N.
Buckner, Ralph
Bucko, Chester
Buckwell, Boyd V.
Buco, John
Bucy, Robert V.
Budd, Robert M. Sr.
Budd, Robert V.
Budias, Robert
Budzyn, Walter J.
Bue, William D.
Buerschinger, Wallace
Bugash, Andrew G.
Bugg, Winfred E.
Buhl, James
Buhrman, Edgar J.
Buice, Charles J.
Bulanowski, Emily S.
Bulfinch, Thomas
Bull, Carl E.
Bull, John A.
Bulla, John
Bullimore, Robert B.
Bullock, Joseph C. Jr.
Bullock, Robert T.
Bullock, Vernon O.
Bulwicz, Leonard A.
Bumford, Edwin J.
Bunch, James C.
Bunetta, Thomas J.
Bunkall, Robert D.
Bunker, George P.
Bunting, Barry S.
Buonforte, Louis
Burandt, Raymond
Burch, Donald R.
Burch, John R. Jr.
Burch, William R.
Burchfield, Burnell
Burchill, Edward
Burde, Gerald E.
Burdett, Lester C. Jr.
Burdick, Ronald F.
Burg, Robert R.
Burgdorff, Glenn E.
Burge, Lewis G.
Burger, Arthur F.
Burger, Sheran L.
Burgers, H.
Burgert, Harold C. Jr.
Burgess, George W.
Burgess, John A.
Burgess, Robert Dr.
Burgett, Loren A.
Burgin, Max N.
Burgon, Walter
Burgstahler, Edwin J.
Burgstahler, Edwin J.
Buring, Robert M.
Burk, Ray W.
Burke, Arthur F. Jr.
Burke, Clyde
Burke, Doyle L.
Burke, George W.
Burke, John J.
Burke, Paul P.
Burkel, Edward P.
Burkett, Richard P.
Burkholder, William R.
Burnett, Clifford F.
Burnette, Jesse
Burnham, John D.
Burns, Burton J.
Burns, Charles A.
Burns, Douglas C.
Burns, Joseph E. Jr.
Burns, Laurence C. Sr.
Burns, Leo
Burns, Martin E.
Burokas, Walter
Burris, Bill
Burris, Daniel M. Jr.
Burrows, Capt. J. Jr.
Burrows, Thomas J.
Burruano, Vincent J.
Bursack, Edward J.
Burtchin, Harry A.
Burton, George H.
Burton, James F.
Busch, Joseph P.
Buschmann, Wilbur J.
Buser, Fred J.
Bush, James W.
Bush, Marshall M. Sr.
Bush, Robert A.
Bushnell, David S.
Bushnell, Earl
Buss, Harold H.
Bussiere, Pamela
Butcher, Gerald J.
Butcher, James F.
Butchko, Thomas G.
Butchko, Thomas G.
Butler, Earl F.
Butler, Floyd A.
Butler, Ralph E.
Butler, Stanley H.
Butler, W.D. Pete
Butler, Wade L.
Butman, Harold W.
Butterfield, Joseph
Butterfield, Robert S.
Butterfield, William
Butts, John H.
Butvidas, Peter J.
Buy, Fletcher D.
Buy, Frank A.
Buza, Frank
Buzby, George W.
Bybel, William
Byers, Ray E.
Bylund, Edward L.
Byrd, Anderson M.
Byrd, John D. Jr.
Byrd, Marvin E.
Byrd, Zollie L.
Byre, Clay M. Jr.
Byrne, Clifford T.
Byrne, Francis J.
Byrne, John A. Jr.
Byrne, Wilbur L.
Byrnes, Frederick C.
Byrnes, Gordon M.
Byron, Harold J.
Byxbee, Robert L.
Byxbee, William E.

- C -

Cable, Paul J.
Caccamise, John S. Sr.
Cader, Casimer
Cader, Joseph S.
Caffarel, Carl J.
Cafferty, Edward
Caffrey, Donald
Cagle, Albert W.
Cagno, Frank M.
Cahill, John J.
Cahill, Joseph
Cahill, Richard J.
Caiafa, Albert
Cain, Clifford C.
Cain, John R.
Cairns, Julius
Calabrese, Joseph E.
Calandrino, Sam
Calcaine, Thomas
Caldarone, Harold Dr.
Caldeira, George Sr.
Caldero, Joe A.
Calderone, Albert R.
Caldwell, Roy L.
Caldwell, Rusty
Calef, Charles W.
Calfas, Jason G.
Calfee, Donald E.
Calish, Sydney R.
Calka, Walter J.
Calkins, Delbert A.
Call, John R.
Call, Joseph G.
Call,Gwyn
Callahan Arthur J.
Callahan, James L.
Callanan, James F.
Callow, Joseph V.
Calo, Anthony M.
Calvert, Franklin P.
Calyore, Joseph M.
Camarillo, Vincent Sr.
Cameron, John B.
Cameron, Tom
Camp, Frank D.
Camp, Richard J.
Camp, Willets C.
Campagna, Robert W.
Campana, Bill
Campanelli, Carmen J.
Campbell, Charles B. Jr.
Campbell, Earl
Campbell, Eugene L.
Campbell, Everett C.
Campbell, Everett E.
Campbell, Frank T.
Campbell, James M.
Campbell, James W.
Campbell, Julian
Campbell, Patrick J.
Campbell, Raymond H.
Campbell, Robert V. Sr.
Campbell, Stanley
Campbell, Thomas D.
Campbell, Thomas S.
Campbell, W. Cothran
Campfield, Glen M.
Campomenosi, Louis Jr.
Canady, Joy L.
Canally, Richard
Cance, Marvin S.
Cancilla, Pasquale
Caney, Loring M.
Cann, John R.
Cannan, Kenneth M.
Cannon, James A.
Cannon, James W.
Canter, Stanley
Cantera, David J.
Canterbury, Paul W.
Cantrell, Grady E.
Cantrell, William L.
Canulla, Francis D.
Canulla, Francis D.
Capalbo, Joseph
Capanear, Michael A.
Capasso, Joseph C.
Capen, Morris N.
Capone, Lucien Jr.
Capozzi, Dan
Cappello, Anthony J.
Capps, George
Capraun, Edward C.
Caracciolo, George
Caracofe, Wesley L.
Carameta, George
Carangi, Cosmo Gus
Carawan, Claud W. Jr.
Carazo, Edwin
Carbone, Michael P.
Card, Clarence F.
Carder, Edward E.
Cardinale, Cosmo
Cardinale, Raymond F.
Cardoza, Nelson M.
Carinci, Joseph
Carita, Frank
Carl, Joseph L. Jr.
Carl, Ralph R.
Carlisle, Harvey
Carlisle, N.L.
Carlisle, Robert
Carlsen, Merrill E.
Carlson, George W.
Carlson, Grant A.
Carlson, John A.
Carlson, Raymond A.
Carlson, Roger D.
Carlson, Roy
Carlucci, Victor
Carlyle, Wayne R.
Carman, Larry A.
Carmer, Robert L.
Carmitchel, Glenn N.
Carmitchel, Glenn N.
Carmody, Robert E.
Carmony, Warren E.
Carnevale, Frank J.
Carney, Frederick T.
Carney, James E.
Carney, James V.
Carney, William D.
Carnot, Laddie
Carnrick, Wesley S.
Carnright, Robert L.
Caro, Ned
Carolyne, Duane C.
Carpenter, Billy R.
Carpenter, Chris I.
Carpenter, Earl S.
Carpenter, Llewellyn F.
Carr, F.K.
Carr, Franklin M.
Carr, Wendell D.
Carraro, Louis G.
Carrico, Lee K.
Carrier, William O.
Carrigg, Gerald
Carro, Melvin J.
Carroll, Berlin R.
Carroll, Dyer E.
Carroll, Edward L.
Carroll, Eugene C.
Carroll, Hugh L.
Carroll, John M. Jr.
Carroll, William D.
Carroll, William E.
Carrow, Samuel L. Jr.
Carson, Ernest V.
Carson, Ramon E.
Carson, William J.
Carstens, Melvin J.
Cartano, John D.
Carter, Alton R.
Carter, Charles W.
Carter, Clint
Carter, David J.
Carter, David R.
Carter, David R.
Carter, Harold S.
Carter, James B.
Carter, James S.
Carter, Joseph E.
Carter, Marcus W.
Carter, Paul S.
Carter, Ralph
Carter, Raymond E.
Carter, Rex L.
Carter, Robert W.
Carter, William L.
Carter, Winford W.
Cartier, Maurice P.
Cartisano, James S.
Cartmell, Derwent D.
Carver, Darrell G.
Carver, Merton E.
Casagranda, Matt
Casale, Joseph J.
Casey, George W.
Casey, Kendrick A.
Casey, Ray
Casey, Stanley T.
Casey, Thomas J.
Cash, Albert
Cash, Ira D.
Cash, Russell O.
Cashier, Anthony
Cashin, Michael J.
Cashin, Russell W.
Cashman, Frank E. Jr.
Cassady, Robert E.
Cassar, Stanley J.
Cassells, David
Casselman, George E.
Casserly, Vincent M.
Cassese, Henry
Cassidy, B.F.
Cassidy, Jack R.
Cassleman, George W.
Castaldo, Richard V.
Castellucci, Paul
Castilla, Richard F.
Castle, Philip W.
Castleton, Arthur
Castonguay, Roland
Castor, Willard G.
Casucci, C.C.
Catalanotto, Stephen V.
Cataldo, Anthony R.
Cate, Paxton R.
Catelli, Alice
Catharine, Robert M.
Caton, Charles C.
Caton, Robert M.
Caton, Willard T.
Catozzi, Andrew
Cauley, Raymond E. Jr.
Caulfield, Frank K.
Caulo, Edward
Cavaco, Manuel
Cavaliero, Edward
Cavallo Margaret
Cavanagh, Charles A.
Cavanaugh, Paul V.
Cavanaugh, Wilfred F.
Cavnar, Wesley R.
Cavolt, Darrell V.
Caya, Albert Jr.
Cazaubon, Francis L.
Cebulski, Eugene
Cechnicki, John W.
Cecil, Gordon L. Jr.
Cecrie, Capt.
Ceelen, Henry R.
Cefaratt, Gil
Celli, Robert E.
Cenchitz, Frank J.
Cerbone, Nicholas C.
Cerda, Louis D.
Cerezo, Anthony
Cericola, Leo F.
Cerra, Edward J.
Cervenka, Jack
Cesta, Thomas G.
Cetkowski, Henry F.
Chabino, Kenneth V.
Chadonnet, Edward J.
Chadrjian, Jack
Chadwell, John D.
Chaffin, Chester Jr.
Chaisson, George J.
Chalk, Francis E.
Chalkley, William R. Jr.
Chambard, Alon C.
Chamberlin, Robert M.
Chambers, James R.
Chambers, William P.
Chambless, Ray
Champ, John A.
Champagne, Raymond L.
Champy, Anthony T.
Chandler, Robert E.
Chaney, William F.
Channell, Kenneth D. Jr.
Chapdelaine, Robert L.
Chapin, Robert S.
Chapman, Eugene A.
Chapman, Floyd E.
Chapman, Herman M.
Chapman, John P.
Chapman, Raymond J.
Chappell, Early Ray
Chaput, Eugene
Charbonnet, Wilfred H.
Charles, A.G. Jr.
Charles, Thomas J.
Charlock, Charles
Charlton, Leon J.
Charnisky, Thomas
Charvat, Roy J. Sr.
Charysz, John
Chase, Enoch D.
Chase, Frederick C.
Chase, Lewis A.
Chase, Phillip
Chase, William L.
Chastain, Norman F.
Chasteen, Robert F.
Chatman, Paul E.
Chaussy, Charles H.
Checchia, Joseph A.
Cheek, Royce E.
Chellis, Stephen W.
Chenault, James S.
Cheney, Daniel M.
Cherniack, Theodore
Cherry, Parker E.
Cherry, Walter L.
Ches, Bernard R.
Cheshire, Godfrey, Jr.
Chesky, Allan L.
Cheslock, Andrew
Chesnut, Francis
Chester, Alvin P.
Chester, Robert A.
Chester, Virginia Mrs.
Chestnut, Raymond Jr.
Chevallay, Leon C. Jr.
Chew, William B.
Chiamulera, Bruno J.
Chiarelli, Louis T.
Chickini, Alfred J.
Chicvara, George F.
Chieppa, Nicholas
Chilcott, Eugene C.
Childers, J.B.
Chinn, C.W.
Chiodo, Mike
Chips, Stanley D.
Chirichella, John
Chism, Edward J.
Chitester, Charles E.
Chittick, J. Robert
Chiusano, Rocco P.
Chmura, Edward F.
Chookazian, Roger
Christ, Robert H.
Christensen, John R.
Christensen, Walter V.
Christian, Joseph A.
Christian, William E. Jr.
Christie, Donald B.
Christie, Julian P.
Christmas, Vincent J.
Christo, Van
Christopher, Fritz Hugh
Christopher, Pete
Christy, Mac
Chrysler, Edward J.
Chrzan, Stanley P. Jr.
Chuba, Joseph A.
Chubet, Edward R.
Chupko, Frank
Church, Stanley E.
Churchill, Douglas A.
Churchill, Dwight W.
Ciaccio, Hugo
Ciaccio, Thomas J.
Ciano, Gustave F.
Cicero, Nunzio J.
Cierniewski, Frank G.

Cieslak, Leonard K.
Cifizzari, Pasquale J.
Cigno, Vincent C.
Cihy, Edward A.
Cimorelli, Emil H.
Clociolo, Frank J.
Ciresi, Anthony W.
Cisar, Paul J.
Cisternino, Andrew L.
Cluccoli, William B.
Civiello, Eugene J.
Clagett, Chester F.
Claggett, Donald S.
Clancy, Edward F.
Clancy, Robert F. Jr.
Clancy, Thomas M.
Clapp, Joseph H.
Clare, Frank
Clarhaut, Albert
Clark, Burnie C.
Clark, Cecil R.
Clark, Charles F.
Clark, Donald D.
Clark, Donald N.
Clark, E.W.
Clark, George L.
Clark, James B.
Clark, Jeremiah
Clark, John L.
Clark, Lindy L.
Clark, Reedie A.
Clark, Remous A.
Clark, Roland G.
Clark, W.P.
Clark, Wilbur
Clark, William A.
Clarke, Elmer O.
Clarke, Frederick H.
Clarke, Joe B. Jr.
Clarkson, Howard B.
Clarren, Ron
Clason, Richard L.
Clausen, Bill
Clay, Conway T.
Clayton, Johnny L.
Clayton, Kenneth E.
Clayton, Stanley B.
Claytor, Calvin P.
Claytor, Ernest R.
Claytor, Graham W.
Cleary, John
Clemens, Harold A.
Clement, Harold M.
Clements, Cabell F. Sr.
Clements, Cabell F. Sr.
Clements, Robert F.
Clements, William A.
Cliborne, Robert D.
Clifford, Edwin F.
Clift, Ray J.
Clifton, William D.
Cline, Carl J.
Cline, Kelly R.
Cline, Maywood
Clingerman, Ottis F.
Cloos, Charles C.
Close, Frank J.
Clouser, Clarence E.
Cloys, P.C.
Clyatt, Will
Coakley, Rollins W.
Coan, Donald J.
Coates, Edward J.
Coates, Robert
Coates, Robert S.
Coats, Roy I.
Coats, Thomas A.
Cobb, Howard L.
Cobb, Howell W.
Cobb, Jay
Cobble, Thomas H.
Coble, Thomas D.
Coblish, Edward J.
Coblish, Edward J.
Coburn, Edward W.
Coburn, Ralph G.
Cocchi, Robert V.
Cocchiola, Gerard
Coccia, Michael A.
Cocco, Joseph G.
Cochran, Jack C.
Cochran, James Jr.
Cochrane, Jack D.
Cochrane, James
Cockerham, Johnie C.
Coco, Anthony J.
Cocroft, Mason F.
Coda, Emil M.
Cody, Hiram S. Jr.
Cody, William R.
Coe, Arthur
Coe, Donald L.
Cofer, Mazie Davis
Coffee, Joseph D. Jr.
Coffey, Dennis M.
Coffey, Matthew J.
Coffey, Paul E.
Coffey, Richard E.
Coffin, Darrel
Coffta, Albin J.
Coggeshall, Timothy
Coghlan, John A.
Coghlan, John A.
Cohen, Harvey
Cohen, Herbert S.
Cohen, Stanley H.
Cohn, Sheldon R. Dr.
Coie, John E. Jr.
Coil, Ross A. Sr.
Colaizzo, Oronzo F.
Colangelo, Francis
Cole, Anson D.
Cole, Dr. T. II
Cole, Edward
Cole, Francis F. Jr.
Cole, Frank J. Jr.
Cole, Gordon J.
Cole, Lloyd David
Cole, Paul R.
Cole, Paul R.
Cole, Robert E.
Colegrove, Newton R.
Coleman, David
Coleman, David
Coleman, Edwin W.
Coleman, Frank R.
Coleman, Howard A.
Coleman, John A. III
Coler, Edward E.
Coler, Jack
Coles, Ray
Colesanti, Nicholas
Coley, Jack H.
Coley, Joseph P.
Colgan, Charles
Colihan, Hugh J.
Collar, Carleton H.
Colletti, Joseph A.
Colley, Paul W.
Collier, Royce O.
Collins, Alfred W.
Collins, Dale A.
Collins, Elmer F.
Collins, Fred
Collins, Harold V.
Collins, Jack O.
Collins, James
Collins, James S.
Collins, John J.
Collins, John L.
Collins, Neal
Collins, Robert M.
Collins, Stanley S.
Collins, Warfield
Colliver, Forrest W.
Collopy, Robert E.
Colo, Donald R.
Colona, Arthur N.
Colonna, Adrian S. Sr.
Colquett, John D. Jr.
Colson, Eugene C.
Colucci, Frank S.
Colvin, Bernard F.
Colwell, George
Combat Md. Veterans
Combs, Marvin L.
Comeau, Russell J.
Comer, Robert F.
Comer, Willard L.
Cometa, Charles A.
Comly, John A.
Comparet, Robert J.
Compton, Clay C.
Compton, Lloyd B.
Compton, Raymond Jr.
Conaway, Donald W.
Conboy, Michael J.
Conder, Bernard A.
Condit, Donald B.
Condit, Earl H.
Condon, James H. Sr.
Condrey, Floyd J. Jr.
Conkle, Henry
Conklin, Ray W.
Conley, Franklyn F.
Conley, James W.
Conley, Walter J.
Conley, William J.
Conmick, R.W.
Conn, Henry A.
Connell, Wallace J.
Connell, William C.
Connelly, Robert M.
Conner, D. Bruce
Conner, Janvier S.
Conner, William J.
Conners, Jerome P.
Connolly, Gerald F.
Connolly, James E.
Connolly, John
Connolly, John T.
Connolly, Lavetta
Connolly, Leo J.
Connor, John P.
Connor, Robert T.
Connors, Joseph E.
Connors, Thomas F.
Conover, Cameron H.
Conrad, Carlton S.
Conrad, Charles F.
Conrad, Donald A.
Conrad, Lewis L.
Conroy, Francis L.
Conroy, Frank E.
Conroy, John
Conroy, William J.
Conserva, Martin B.
Contreras, Cornelio
Converse, Francis C.
Conwall, James
Conway, Charles E.
Conway, Stanley A.
Conway, Stanley A.
Cook, Al
Cook, Al
Cook, Albert J.
Cook, Arthur G.
Cook, Charlie A.
Cook, Dale E.
Cook, Francis W. Jr.
Cook, Frank J.
Cook, Grace A.
Cook, Jess E.
Cook, John E.
Cook, John K.
Cook, Leland R.
Cook, Roy W.
Cook, Verdis O.
Cooke, Eldridge M.
Cooke, Norman I.
Cooksey, Albert R.
Cooley, Frank G.
Coombs, Richard L.
Coon, Jimmie L.
Cooney, Edward J.
Cooney, Peter
Coonradt, Nelson
Cooper, Edgar F.
Cooper, Eugene
Cooper, James N.
Cooper, Jimmie W.
Cooper, Ralph E.
Cooper, Robert T.
Cope, Robert W.
Copeland, Glenn M.
Copeland, Hariet
Coppel, Donald F.
Coppock, Robert M.
Corbett, Bernard F.
Corbett, Duane C.
Corbett, Harry M.
Corbett, John W.
Corbiere, Raymond J.
Corbin, Clyde W.
Corbin, Harvey R.
Corbin, J.R.
Corbin, James H.
Corbin, Maurice E.
Corbo, Nicholas J.
Corcoran, Daniel R.
Corcoran, William Jr.
Cordell, Daniel L.
Cordray, John A.
Core, Norman A.
Corliss, Francis J. Sr.
Cormier, Warren G.
Cormier, Warren G.
Corneau, Wilfred
Cornell, H. Edgar
Cornell, Merrill E.
Cornin, Edgar L.
Correll, Tom
Corrick, Darl E.
Corrigan, Bruce J.
Corrigan, James J.
Corsi, Alvin J.
Corwin, James A.
Cosco, John L.
Cosenza, John J.
Cosgrove, John P.
Cosner, Jonas A. Jr.
Costa, Alexander
Costa, Constantine
Costantine, Larry F.
Costello, Albert E.
Cote, Larry R.
Cote, Roland G.
Cotter, John T.
Cotter, Wm. D.
Cottle, Walter H.
Cottone, Vincent J.
Couch, Harry N.
Couch, Raymond B.
Couey, Duane E.
Coughlin, Lebeous W.
Coughlin, William P.
Coulombre, Raymond A.
Coulston, George W.
Coulter, Edward T.
Coulter, Monte C. Jr.
Coulter, Robert A.
Coupens, Jerome M.
Coursey, Thomas J.
Courtney, I.G.
Coury, Joseph F.
Coutts, H. Donald
Couture, Raymond R.
Coverick, William
Covert, Warren
Covington, Kenneth
Cowan, George E.
Cowan, Robert S.
Cowan, William W.
Cowardin, L.J. Sr.
Cowart, Harry F.
Cowden, Lewis M.
Cowell, Harold E. Sr.
Cox, Charles R.
Cox, Earl Jr.
Cox, H.E. Gene
Cox, Herbert
Cox, Hugo
Cox, James D.
Cox, James H.
Cox, John F.
Cox, Malcolm E.
Cox, Riley W.
Cox, T.O. Jr.
Cox, William C.
Cox, Winford F.
Coxwell, Robert E.
Coy, Charles R.
Coyle, Harry W.
Coyle, Joseph
Coyle, Raymond W.
Cozens, Roger W.
Craanen, John J.
Crader, James R.
Craft, Stuart S.
Crafton, Omer
Craig, Edward D.
Craig, Harold D.
Craig, Henry D. Jr.
Craig, John F.
Craig, Wm. B.
Crail, Chester B.
Cramer, Calvin K.
Cramer, Noel J. Jr.
Cramer, Peter N.
Crandall, Robert E.
Crandall, Stuart M.
Crandell, William R.
Crane, David D.
Crane, George
Crane, John H.
Cranford, H.B.
Cranford, Joseph L.
Crangle, William H.
Craven, Frank
Crawford, Cletus N.
Crawford, Frank R.
Crawford, Fred L.
Crawford, Fred W.
Crawley, Lowell B.
Crays, George E.
Creasy, Loxley P.
Creasy, Richard N. Jr.
Creech, William E.
Creel, Levon
Creel, Vance D.
Creighton, James A.
Crescione, George J.
Crilley, Thomas E.
Crim, Charles H.
Cripe, John R.
Critelli, Joseph
Crittenden, Carl A.
Croft, James A.
Cromer, Elmo
Cromer, Harold E.
Cromer, Richard
Cromer, Thomas W.
Crontz, Arthur T.
Croom, Milton M.
Crop, Earl M.
Cropp, Vince
Cropper, Leland D.
Croskey, Walter F.
Cross, Clifton J.
Cross, Eason Jr.
Cross, Vernon G.
Croteau, Thomas A.
Crotteau, Donald O.
Crouch, Allen T.
Crouch, Bonny F.
Crouse, Richard
Crouse, Robert L.
Crow, Edgar P.
Crow, Harold J.
Crow, Warren O.
Crowder, Neal J.
Crowe, Charles H.
Crowe, Leo C.
Crowe, Michael D.
Crowle, Leonard E.
Crowley, Robert F.
Croxton, Warren R.
Cruikshank, J.D.
Crum, Rodger J.
Crumpler, Robert A.
Crumrine, William E.
Cruser, John E.
Cryer, Charles P.
Cubberly, Howard B.
Cubler, Harry N.
Cucchiara, Angelo
Cuccia, John A.
Cullen, Paige C. Jr.
Culley, George B.
Cullinan, John F.
Culp, Clayton
Culver, Catherine
Culver, Ed
Culver, Irving
Cumbee, Jesse J. Sr.
Cummings, Thomas P.
Cummins, Robert A.
Cundiff, William B.
Cunliff, Edward H.
Cunningham, John J.
Cunningham, Reese A.
Cunningham, W. Frank
Cunningham, William P.
Cuppett, S. Dean
Cupps, William R.
Curan, James A.
Curnyn, James J.
Curran, Andrew J.
Curran, John J. Jr.
Curran, Mark L.
Current, John Wm.
Currie, Lenox J. Jr.
Currie, Robert N.
Currier, Gus S. Jr.
Curry, Alfred G.
Curry, Donald P. Jr.
Curry, George E.
Curry, James C.
Curry, Joseph B.
Curry, Richard L.
Curry, Warren H.
Curtice, Cooper G.
Curtis, Gordon W.
Curtis, Harold D.
Curtis, James H.
Curtis, James M.
Curtis, Robert L.
Curtis, Thomas A.
Cusanelli, Thomas V.
Cusato, Paul
Cushman, Douglas W.
Custer, William
Cuthbertson, M.D.
Cutler, Donald D.
Cutsail, William E.
Cutter, Dilver A.
Cuttrell, Michael W.
Cyr, Joseph H.
Cyr, Robert T.
Czech, Charles J. Sr.
Czwalga, Stanley J.

- D -

D'Agosta, Frank D.
D'Alvisio, Nicholas J.
D'Amico, Bill
D'Amore, James
D'Angelo, Laborio S.
D'Antino, Ben
Dabbs, James A.
Daddario, Raymond F.
Daeger, Alfred J.
Dagen, Richard
Dagle, Raymond G.
Dahlgaard, Roger C.
Dailey, Raymond J.
Dailey, Willis C.
Daily, Robert B.
Dake, Earl L.
Dakis, Milton J.
Daleo, George S.
Daleo, John
Dalin, Melford J.
Dalpoggetto, Newton
Dalrymple, Delbert W. Jr.
Dalrymple, Richard
Dalton, William H.
Daly, James C.
Daly, John D.
Daly, William G.
Daly, William James
Dammeier, W.H.
Damon, Monroe F.
Dampf, Warren F.
Damrell, Jack H.
Danaher, Jerold J.
Dance, Eugene E.
Dando, Thomas O.
Danforth, James R.
Daniello, Louis E.
Daniels, John W.
Daniels, Leonard J.
Danielson, Sam H.
Danik, Lawrence
Danner, Kenneth H.
Danthony, Pete J.
Daoke, Steve
Dardano, Joseph P.
Darling, Ernest J.
Darnell, Werth
Darner, W. Whitney
Dashevsky, Sid
Dast, Clare J.
Dato, Anthony J.
Datsis, James J.
Daum, Ralph
Dauphinee, C.E.
Daus, Vincent E.
Dausch, Donald L.
Davenport, William
David, Merrill O.
Davids, Robert J.
Davidson, Edwin N.
Davidson, Fred
Davidson, Harvey L.
Davidson, James F.
Davidson, P.K.
Davidson, Robert G.
Davidson, Robert O.
Davie, Reed C.
Davies, John C.
Davies, Robert C.
Davies, Thomas E.
Davies, William R.
Davignon, Arthur
Davis, Arthur L.
Davis, Carmen D.
Davis, Clark I.
Davis, Clyde E.
Davis, Edward J.
Davis, Frederick Jr.
Davis, H.M.
Davis, Harold C.
Davis, Harry S. II
Davis, Henry E.
Davis, James W.
Davis, Leroy E. Jr.
Davis, Leslie K.
Davis, Louis V.
Davis, M.T. Sr.
Davis, Martin
Davis, Paul J.
Davis, Preston L.
Davis, Raymond B.
Davis, Raymond C.
Davis, Reginald H.
Davis, Richard D.
Davis, Robert B.
Davis, Robert C.
Davis, Robert C.
Davis, Robert D.
Davis, Robert J.
Davis, Robert S. Jr.
Davis, Robert W.
Davis, Russell J.
Davis, Virgil E.
Davis, Virgil E.
Davis, Virgil O.
Davis, Walter J.
Davis, Wesley H.
Davis, William
Davis, William H.
Dawes, Marshall M. Jr.
Dawes, Thoams E.
Dawson, Cooper S. Jr.
Dawson, George R.
Dawson, John
Day, Charles E.
Day, Clayton E.
Day, Edward J.
Day, Ronald W.
Dayton, Roy O'Neal
Dazbaz, Walter
Deal, James E.
Deangelis, Robert W.
Deangelo, Joseph J.
Deany, Charles E.
Dearnaley, Ernest
DeBoer, Charles
DeBooy, Merle C. Mrs.
DeCarlo, Armando E.
Decker, Art
Decker, August J. Jr.
Decker, Earl L.
Decker, Jay W.
Decker, Loren J.
Decker, Walter L.
DeCorso, Carmen
DeCoudres, Dean
DeCristofaro, Joseph
Deebs, Thomas M.
Deeney, Delbert J.
Dees, Charles A. Jr.
Deeter, Calvin D.
Deeton, James D.
DeFanti, Edward A.
DeFiore, Anthony N.
DeFlin, Joseph R.
DeFreitas, Peter J.
DeFriest, Irad R.
Degnitz, Merlin W.
Degroff, Henry
DeHart, Robert H.
DeHart, Royal
DeHaven, Dwight G.
Deibler, Damon D.
Deichert, David K.
Deichgraber, Ernest B.
Deickman, Leslie
Deleso, Donald
Deisenroth, Herman E.
Deissler, Edward J.
Deissler, Joseph C.
Dekanich, William A.
Delamorton, Howard
DeLand, George
Delaney, John J. Jr.
Delaney, Raymond W.
Delaney, William F.
Delaware, Warren M.
Delchini, Lawrence J.
DeLeonardis, Dante F.
Delfoe, Joseph C.
Delgenio, Benny
Delgoda, Jim
DeLisle, Gerald F.
Dellert, William J. Jr.
Dellinger, Lawrence W.
Dellinger, Robert
Dellucky, Joseph S.
DeLouise, Warren J.
Deltuvia, Andy Jr.
Deluca, John J.
Delucantonio, Gerald D.
Deluke, Lewis A.
Deluzio, Charles J.
DeMarco, Charles Sr.
DeMarco, Eugene V.
DeMarco, Richard E.
DeMarco, Vincent
Dembowski, Ted
Demers, Eugene M.
Demers, Normand R.
Demeskey, Frank
Demeule, Edward A.
DeMille, Forest Ray
Demmy, Shirley M.
Demopoulos, Andrew J.
Demory, Ross E.
Demos, William H.
Dempsey, Kenneth
Dempski, Edward A.
DeNardo, Frank P.
Denault, Paul R.
Denham, Perry A.
Denitto, Anthony
Denney, Duane
Denney, Loren H.
Dennis, D.M. Jr.
Dennis, George
Dennis, Richard H.
Dennis, William
Dennison, Walter P.
Denniston, Robert P.
Denny, Arthur
Denny, William J.
Densmore, Russell
Denson, Howard K.
Dent, Emmore
Dente, Lawrence
Denton, H. Morris
Denuel, Paul J.
Denver, James H.
Denyes, Robert E.
DePaola, Joseph C.
Depaoli, Martin H.
DePape, Robert
DePaula, Julian S.
DePecol, Benjamin D.
DePecol, Mario
DePhillips, Louis
DePierro, Ronald M.
DePlasita, Jimmy G. Sr.
Deriscavage, George A.
Derk, Robert
Derwoyed, Donald
Desabatine, Arthur
DeSantis, George
DeSantis, Ralph Jr.
DeSantis, Raymond R.
DeSarno, Louis J.
DesForges, Raymond F.
DeSousa, John
Desser, Gary S.
Determan, William A.
Dettenmayer, Edward N.
Dettling, James H.
Detweiler, Paul B.
Detwiler, Beulah
Detwiler, Charles W.
Detwiler, Harry
Detwiler, Howard
Devault, Warren E.
Devencenzi, Victor A.
DeVeney, Richard J.
DeVine, Francis J.
Devine, Joseph J.
DeVito, James M.
Devitt, James
Devlin, James J.
Devlin, William J.
DeVore, Roy E. Jr.
Dewimille, Eugene C.
DeWinne, Albert R.
Dewitt, Fred D.
Dewitt, Keith G.
Dexter, Thomas S.
Diamond, C. Richard
Dianovsky, Ray
Diaz, Frank
Diaz, Vicente V.
DiBella, Frank R.
Dichter, Melvin M.
Dick, George
Dick, James E.
Dickerson, Charles F.
Dickerson, Joseph Jr.
Dickey, Bill
Dickey, Edward M.
Dickey, Paul Jr.
Dickinson, John R.
Dickinson, Robert V.
Dickson, Jerry V.
Dickson, Teresa M.
Didychuk, Nicholas
Dieckert, Eugene
Diegle, George R.
Diehl, Alfred
Diehl, Clifford P.
Diel, Fred H.
Diessner, Karl F.
Digaetano, Frank A.
DiGrandi, Dino R.
DiGraziano, Frank
Dilbert, Michael V.
DiLello, Mario
Dilg, Earl W. Jr.
Dill, E.Q. Jr.
Dill, J. Lamar
Dillard, Ben P.
Dillard, Earle S.
Dillard, Joe S.
Diller, Clifford
Dillingham, Dallas E.
Dillman, Leonard A.
Dillon, Robert V.
Dillon, Vincent
DiMeo, Alfred
DiMilla, Salvatore J.
Dimmitt, Donald K.
Dimuro, Mario P.
Dincesen, Robert
Dineen, Richard J.
Dinges, Donald
DiNofrio, Paul
DiNucci, John J.
Diomede, Vincent
DiPasquale, Frank
Dipietro, Henry
Dippre, Harold J.
Dircks, Lawrence
Director, Nathan
DiRenzo, Anthony
Direnzo, John J.
Dirian, William H.
Dirienzo, Armand
Dirkes, V. Douglas
Dirosa, Michael
Dirrim, Lysle R.
Disanzo, Edward
Discavage, Robert
Dispenza, Louis J.
Dittmar, William C.
Ditto, Paul W.
Ditty, Charles C.
Diventi, Ben
Divers, Charles W.
Divins, Grover C.
Dix, Thomas R.
Dixon, Archie
Dixon, Dewey W.
Dixon, Fred Cooper
Dixon, P.W.
Dixon, R.E.
Dize, Carl M. Sr.
Dluhosh, Arnold E.
Dluhy, Leonard A.
Dmytrasz, Daniel
Doar, W.T. Jr.
Dobas, Harlan P.
Dobbs, Chester
Dobbs, Henry C.
Dobkowski, Edward
Doblone, Frank
Doblosky, Henry J. Jr.
Dobrowolski, Sigmund
Dobsen, Richard H.
Docke, George J.
Dodd, Peggy Carr
Dodd, Ralph V.
Dodd, Ray W.
Dodge, Duane R.
Dodge, E.M.
Dodge, Richard W.
Dodson, Robert V.
Doherty, Edward
Doherty, Paul
Dohr, John
Doland, Ethan
Dolding, Walter R.
Dole, Richard C.
Dolk, Allan G.
Dollinger, Thomas K.
Dolzani, Robert E.
Dombrowsky, James L.
Domenico, Charles A.
Domingues, Gordon L.
Dominick, William H.
Donahue, Alphonsus
Donahue, Simeon J.
Donald, Richard J.
Donaldson, Earl W.
Donaldson, Francis X.
Donaldson, Robert
Donaldson, Thomas E.
Donall, Edmond G.
Donato, Nicholas J.
Doncarlos, Martial L.
Doney, R.G.
Donlan, Thomas V.
Donley, Harry B.
Donnellan, Edward G.
Donnolo, Thomas
Donohue, Thomas J.
Donovan, Daniel J.
Donovan, Richard F.
Donovan, William P.
Doody, William J.
Dooley, James S.
Doran, Francis M.
Doran, James A.
Doran, Raymond E.
Doranda, Edward J.
Dore, Charles G.
Dorman, Jack
Dornes, Chester L.
Dorr, Edward C.
Dorsam, Francis W.
Dorsey, Joseph M.
Dorsey, Laurent
Dorsey, Robert J.
Dosenbach, Milt K.
Doss, Billy E.
Doten, Alfred F.
Dotson, Emry M.
Dotson, William H.
Dotson, William S.
Doty, Robert
Doubler, Ralph D.
Dougherty, Richard J.
Dougherty, Thomas B.
Dougherty, Thomas F.
Dougherty, Walter L.
Douglas, Argean
Douglass, Kelly B.
Dove, Donald L.
Dow, Gordon B.
Dowd, Martin J.
Dowd, Robert
Dowell, Bruce R.
Dowell, Woodrow C.

Gaskill, H.S.
Gaskill, William E.
Gasper, William P.
Gass, Matthew
Gasser, Blaine E.
Gately, David E.
Gates, Charles W.
Gates, John W. Jr.
Gates, Raymond J.
Gatlin, William P.
Gattmann, James R.
Gattmann, James R.
Gaudet, Emil J.
Gaulin, Joseph
Gause, Carl H.
Gauthier, Robert E.
Gavel, Justin J.
Gavin, Dan James
Gavin, Richard P.
Gavitt, Leo C.
Gavitt, Philip S.
Gay, John T. Jr.
Gaykovich, John M.
Gaylor, Bobby C.
Gaylord, William H.
Gayman, Lee C.
Gearon, John
Gebauer, Elwin H.
Geden, Joseph H.
Geer, Carl E.
Geer, James W.
Gehring, Richard K.
Geier, Otto M. Jr.
Geigel, Clifford M.
Geis, Neil F.
Gelaides, Charles A.
Gelbin, Arnold J.
Geldhof, Alexander
Gelfat, Michael
Gellert, Theodore Jr.
Gelling, Joseph W.
Gellner, John H.
Genauer, Floyd
Gentile, Frank
Gentilesco, James V.
Gentry, Elbert
George, Donald H.
George, George J.
Gerba, Steven J.
Gerber, Roland C.
Gerber, Roland C.
Gerelus, Charles
Gerencser, Joseph S.
Gerner, Robert
Gerson, Gary R.
Gerson, Gary R.
Gerson, Joe
Gerstenberger, Richard J.
Gerus, Walter
Gessler, George A.
Gettler, Richard J.
Gettmann, Frederick D.
Gettys, John W.
Getz, Joseph T.
Getz, Robert H.
Geving, Robert L.
Gex, Virgil E.
Ghere, Roy D.
Giachino, Dante L.
Gialames, Michael D.
Giambelluca, Robert W.
Giancarlo, Frank R.
Giannattasio, Daniel
Gibbons, John J.
Gibbons, Thomas F.
Gibbons, Walter F.
Gibbs, William E.
Giblin, Charles J.
Giblin, Joseph P.
Gibson, Charles D.
Gibson, George E.
Gibson, Harold L.
Gibson, Homer F.
Gielniak, Joseph J.
Giering, August C.
Giffin, James F.
Gifford, Adam
Gigantino, James
Gilb, William H. Sr.
Gilbert, Cleon L.
Gilbert, David B.
Gilbert, Joseph H.
Gilbert, Ronald L.
Gilbert, W.H.
Gilbreath, Rex
Gile, Alden E.
Giles, Arthur H.
Giles, James A.
Giles, Robert W.
Gilkey, Robert D.
Gill, Frank J.
Gill, John S.
Gill, Robert C.
Gillaspie, Terry W.
Gillaspy, Edward F.
Gillbride, Maurice J.
Gillerstrom, Roger H.
Gillespie, Alexander Jr.
Gillespie, Russell L.
Gillespie, Thomas
Gillespie, William L.
Gillette, Earl H. Jr.
Gillette, Gordon D.
Gilliam, Walter E. Jr.
Gilligan, Harold
Gilligan, Harold
Gilliland, Charles L.
Gillissen, Albert P.
Gilmore, Harry E.
Gilmore, William E.
Gilpatrick, Max J.
Gilstrap, Jacob W.
Gimourginas, Constantine
Gingery, Don R.
Ginneman, Walter E.
Giordano, Louis Sr.
Gisane, Albert A.
Gish, Donald
Gittings, Theo B.
Gittins, Eric F.
Givens, Charles H.
Givens, Joseph R.
Gladding, Charles E.
Gladson, Donald M.
Glanton, Gene W.
Glaser, Donald A.
Glass, Fred E.
Glassman, Elliott
Glatts, John F. Jr.
Glavina, Frank J.
Glaze, Edward C. Jr.
Glazebrook, Y.W.
Gleason, Charles R.
Gleason, Roy G.
Gleason, Tom
Glebus, Francis R.
Glendenning, John K.
Glenn, Robert
Glessner, Theodore Jr.
Glidden, Robert Ned
Gliwa, Richard F.
Glorioso, Robert Jr.
Glover, Adam C. Jr.
Glover, Bryan H.
Glover, Timothy Jr.
Gluth, Edward A.
Glynn, William A.
Gnat, Edward A.
Gnatovich, George
Gnotcc
Gocella, Donald A.
Goddard, A.B.
Goddard, Earl W.
Godlin, Harold N.
Godsey, William L.
Godsoe, John E.
Godula, Regis F.
Godusky, Warren C.
Godwin, Ed
Goebel, Harvey E.
Goeckel, William F.
Goedde, Russell A.
Goedecke, Roy C.
Goettel, Frederick A.
Goetz, Dale H.
Goetzman, Wayne
Goff, Darwin K.
Goff, Ovia P.
Goggins, James
Goin, James D.
Goins, Eugene
Goins, Hubert M.
Goins, James C.
Golba, Jacob C.
Gold, Herbert
Goldberg, Norton R.
Goldberg, Samuel M.
Goldman, David
Goldrick, Edward F.
Goldrick, Louis J.
Goldsmith, Joseph K.
Goldstein, Daniel B.
Golibart, Richard S.
Golinski, Thomas D.
Golliher, Kenneth
Gollinge, Alexander
Gong, Kung W.
Gonsalves, Joe
Gonser, Ray W.
Gonzales, Joe
Gonzales, Manuel S.
Gonzales, Marion C.
Gonzalez, Ramon J.
Goodhand, Jim
Goodier, Elwood J. Jr.
Goodloe, Thomas C.
Goodman, James M. Jr.
Goodman, Leon
Goodnight, Olan R.
Goodrich, Judson E.
Goodrich, Robert
Goodrich, Vincent N.
Goodwin, Charles I.
Goodwin, Charles O.
Goodwin, Donald B.
Goodwin, Leslie
Goodwin, Norman
Goodwin, Russel E.
Goodwin, Stephen W.
Goodwyn, John W. Jr.
Goolsby, William W.
Gorby, Donald R.
Gordon, Ancil H. Jr.
Gordon, Bennett
Gordon, Clyde B.
Gordon, Denis
Gordon, Homer C.
Gordon, Leon
Gordon, Robert F.
Gorecki, Edward F.
Gorenflo, Raymond
Gorges, Clifford L.
Gorges, Frank
Gorman, Charles V.
Gorman, John P.
Gorman, Robert R.
Gormley, Ann M.
Gormley, Edmund J.
Gorniak, Frank J.
Gorrell, Clifford A.
Gorrick, Kenneth W.
Gorse, Edward J.
Gorse, Robert A. Sr.
Goshco, Victor
Gosoroski, Jim
Goss, Chester F.
Goss, Chester F.
Goss, Dave
Gosselin, Albert D.
Gosselin, Roland P.
Gossett, Robert R.
Goswick, Jay
Gotfryd, John M.
Gottshall, Charles
Goudie, John
Gould, Elwood H.
Gould, Lawrence
Gould, Louis A.
Gouloff, Ted M.
Goutink, Edward III
Gow, Robert B.
Gowing, Ned W.
Goza, Fremont L.
Grabau, Reuben
Grabowski, Roman A.
Grace, Robert F.
Grady, Myrl E.
Graeff, William G.
Graff, Arthur C.
Graff, Donald B.
Graff, Tracy
Graffam, Joseph F.
Graham, Albert J.
Graham, Basil R.
Graham, Carl M.
Graham, Claude L. Jr.
Graham, James J.
Graham, James O.
Graham, James W.
Graham, Richard C. Sr.
Graham, Richard H.
Graham, Robert F.
Graham, Robert W.
Graham, Roy E.
Grames, John A.
Grammer, Robert E.
Grandjean, James J.
Grandzel, Stanley
Grant, C.J.
Grant, Donald J.
Grant, Edmund G.
Grant, Frederick F.
Grant, Lewis C.
Grantham, Albert D.
Grantham, George W.
Grasek, Lou
Grasso, James
Grasso, Sebastian I.
Gratien, Edward L.
Graue, Harry J.
Graugnard, Casimir
Graulich, Raymond
Gravely, Samuel L. Jr.
Graves, Richard T. Jr.
Graves, Richard W.
Graves, Rodney J.
Graves, Swan Hubert
Gray, Calvin S.
Gray, David
Gray, Gaynel M.
Gray, Harold E.
Gray, Howard K. Jr.
Gray, James A.
Gray, John L.
Gray, Rex O.
Gray, Robert N.
Gray, William G.
Graybeal, David M.
Graybosch, Thomas G.
Graziano, Fred
Graziano, Gerald J.
Graziano, Philip A.
Grdina, Joseph J.
Grealish, James V.
Greatorex, Frederick A.
Greber, Alfred
Greco, Antoinette
Greco, Louis E.
Greco, Russell S.
Grear, George R.
Greeling, Wilbur
Green, Albert
Green, Alfred E.
Green, Avery G.
Green, Charles E.
Green, Chester R. Sr.
Green, Dale G.
Green, Dewey M.
Green, Earl A.
Green, Howard R.
Green, James E.
Green, Lawrence E.
Green, M.H. Jr.
Green, Philip E.
Green, Robert
Green, Suzanne
Green, William J.
Greenawalt, Robert K.
Greenbacker, John E.
Greenberg, Louis
Greene, Albert G. Jr.
Greene, Charles D.
Greene, Donald F.
Greene, Gene B.
Greene, Gene B.
Greene, George
Greene, Herbert E.
Greene, Jerry N.
Greene, Wendell J.
Greenhalgh, William R.
Greenough, Bernard J.
Greenspan, Louis
Greenstreet, Robert L.
Greenwood, Russell C.
Greer, James S.
Greeson, Ernest
Greff, Godfrey K.
Greger, George P.
Gregg, Henry A.
Gregg, Linn E.
Gregory, Joseph D.
Gregory, Julian W.
Gregory, Stephen S.
Gregory, Walter J.
Greiner, Harold E.
Greiner, Martin L.
Grennon, William J.
Grenon, Leopold J.
Gresham, Buddy Joe
Gretz, Robert J.
Grey, James R.
Gribble, Don C.
Grice, G.H.
Grider, George W.
Gridley, Kenneth R.
Grier, Howard F.
Grieve, Vivian
Griffey, James
Griffin, Frank M.
Griffin, George C.
Griffin, George W.
Griffin, Jesse L.
Griffin, Joseph B.
Griffin, Kenneth L.
Griffin, Phillip R.
Griffin, Robert W.
Griffin, Thomas B.
Griffin, Wilbur E.
Griffin, William E.
Griffin, William J.
Griffith, Harry L.
Griffith, Lloyd
Griffiths, Gerald
Griggs, James W.
Griggs, William L.
Grill, John W. Sr.
Grillo, Pat L. Cdr.
Grills, Albert J.
Grim, Burrel F.
Grimes, Charles Jr.
Grimes, James J.
Grimes, James O.
Grimes, John J.
Grimm, Leonard P.
Grimm, Zane E.
Grimmer, Henry P.
Grindal, Billy M.
Griner, Judson H.
Grinspan, Walter
Grinuk, Joseph
Griot, Lou E.
Grippando, James V.
Grissom, Holly C.
Griswold, Melvin K.
Groel, Otto R. Jr.
Groen, John Jr.
Groff, Harold H.
Grogean, Charles J.
Groncki, Thedore J.
Groncki, Walter
Grose, Kenneth G.
Groseclose, C.A.
Grosglass, Thomas R.
Groskopf, Richard A.
Gross, Clair
Gross, Clyde
Gross, Eugene
Gross, Franklyn W.
Gross, Ray Donald
Grosser, Hugo C.
Grossi, Elmer J.
Grossman, E.M. MD
Grossmann, Frank
Grote, William G.
Groth, Kenneth F.
Grothues, Maurice
Grout, Claude
Grover, Harold D.
Groves, Duane A.
Growden, Ellwood W.
Grubbs, David T.
Grubbs, Kenneth R.
Gruber, Clair T.
Gruber, Thomas J.
Grudzinskas, Charles A.
Grueter, Vincent C.
Gruhn, Ted E.
Grumblatt, Donald E.
Grun, William A.
Grundon, William R.
Gruner, William C.
Grunewald, Charles B.
Gspann, Charles J.
Gualdoni, Ambrose N.
Guard, Alan H.
Guarneri, Salvatore C.
Guarnero, Dante R.
Guernsey, Gerald Q.
Guerry, James A.
Guffey, Lee R.
Gugler, Richard G.
Guglielmo, Vincent
Guice, David A.
Guice, Stephen L. Jr.
Guidetti, David A.
Guilliams, John S.
Guinan, John F. Jr.
Guith, Ronald H.
Gullickson, Alfred T.
Gullickson, Ray A.
Gundelach, Charles H.
Gundina, Lloyd L.
Gunn, Herbert
Gunn, James P.
Gunnells, Ronald C.
Gunter, Doyle
Gurewich, Bernard F.
Gurrera, Nicholas C.
Gusovius, Kenneth
Gustafson, H.E.
Gustafson, Merwin J.
Gustafson, Robert H.
Gutenkauf, William
Guterding, Joseph T.
Gutmann, Stephen P.
Guyer, Robert A.
Guyn, Ward H.
Guziak, Joseph A.
Gwaltney, James E.
Gwynne, Howard

- H -

Haas, Charles E.
Haas, Ernest L.
Haas, George R.
Haas, Joseph A.
Haas, William L.
Haase, Alfred W.
Habegger, Glenn B.
Haber, Sam
Haberstroh, Herbert
Habiger, Walter
Habina, Andrew T.
Hack, Robert R.
Hackenberg, Ray L.
Hacker, Harry W.
Hacker, Henry C.
Hacker, John J.
Hackett, Joseph D.
Hackler, Wm. W.
Hackney, Joseph Z. Jr.
Hadaway, Dalton L.
Haddock, William J.
Haddon, Edward J.
Haddox, Robert A.
Haeberle, Fred S.
Hafer, Al
Hagan, Marion J.
Hagar, James W.
Hage, Warren
Hageman, John
Hagen, Charles A.
Hagen, Merle Capt.
Hagenbuch, Richard N.
Hagerty, Charles M.
Hagopian, Ardash A.
Hagopian, John
Hagosky, Anthony J.
Hagstrom, Winton
Hagy, Donald E.
Hagymasi, Andy
Hahn, Harold H.
Hahn, Vern
Haight, Harold E.
Hailey, Larry G.
Haines, William
Hair, Maurice E.
Hajek, Eugene V.
Hale, David P.
Hale, George E.
Hale, Harry T.
Hale, John A.
Hale, Norman B.
Hale, Ralph M.
Hale, Samuel E.
Haley, Clarence
Haley, Joe C.
Haley, Joe C.
Hall, Arthur A. Jr.
Hall, Arthur R.
Hall, Charles
Hall, Charles E.
Hall, Charles James
Hall, David T.
Hall, Eugene S.
Hall, Gordon J.
Hall, Jack A.
Hall, Keith B.
Hall, Lyle D.
Hall, Raymond C.
Hall, Raymond G.
Hall, Richard D.
Hall, Richard L.
Hall, Robert D.
Hall, Robert H.
Hall, Robert II
Hall, Roscoe B.
Hall, Russell R.
Hall, Val J.
Hall, W.W.
Hall, Walter M.
Hall, Wilbur E.
Hall, Wilfred H.
Hall, William C.
Hall, William L.
Hall, William L.
Hallaman, Robert H. Sr.
Halleck, John P.
Haller, George
Haller, William D.
Hallett, Gilbert
Hallett, Thomas L. Jr.
Hallisey, Francis P.
Hallman, Curtis A.
Halpen, Frank B.
Halsey, Macdonald
Halstead, Alan F.
Halterman, James R.
Haman, Robert W.
Hamann, Carl H.
Hamaty, Nicholas
Hamby, Frank Jr.
Hamby, William R.
Hamel, George G.
Hamilton, Alex B.
Hamilton, Charles J.
Hamilton, Harry L.
Hamilton, Herbert M.
Hamilton, Hudson B.
Hamilton, Issac F.
Hamilton, James E.
Hamilton, Joseph W.
Hamilton, Louis
Hamilton, Robert C.
Hamilton, Thomas L.
Hamlin, Charles A.
Hamlin, Charles G.
Hamlin, Donald W.
Hamm, William O.
Hammer, Karl L.
Hammermeister, Robert
Hammond, Cecil W.
Hammond, Charles L.
Hammond, John M.
Hammond, Kenneth
Hammond, Lynn C.
Hammond, Walter D.
Hammond, William J. Sr.
Hamner, Herschel L.
Hampton, Carroll B.
Hampton, Russell S.
Hampton, Russell S.
Hampton, William E.
Hamski, Ray J.
Hanbury, Louis F.
Hancock, Clyde E.
Hancock, Frank H.
Hand, Isaac J.
Hand, Leroy Jr.
Handley, Darien H.
Handley, Richard W.
Handly, Robert S.
Hanenberg, Thomas W.
Hanes, Grover G.
Hanes, Grover W. Jr.
Haney, Corliss
Hanft, Warren A.
Hanke, Russell K.
Hankins, Wm. M.
Hankosky, Stanley
Hanley, Frank A. Capt.
Hanlon, Arthur
Hanlon, Donald W.
Hanlon, Francis X.
Hanna, Donald C.
Hanna, Richard Lee
Hannah, James B.
Hannah, Richard C.
Hannan, Kenneth H.
Hannigan, Mike
Hanning, Richard G.
Hannmann, Horst H.
Hanschu, Kermit L.
Hanscom, Ray E.
Hansen, Gerald H.
Hansen, John F.
Hansen, Robert E.
Hansen, Wilbur R.
Hanson, Daniel W.
Hanson, Duane W.
Hanson, Kenneth I.
Hanson, Ralph A.
Hanus, Bennie L.
Hapke, Wayne L.
Haralson, Thomas J.
Harapat, Vernon J.
Haraz, Robert
Harbert, Ned D.
Harbison, Joseph F. Jr.
Harbuck, Wiley C.
Hardee, Thomas E.
Hardegen, Lawrence H.
Harden, Max N.
Harden, Robert M.
Hardesty, Roger A.
Hardick, Francis A.
Hardifer, Daniel W.
Harding, Ed
Harding, Elmer
Harding, Hobart D.
Harding, Ralph L.
Hardy, David
Hardy, Jack A.
Hardy, John B.
Harford, James E.
Hargest, Thomas S.
Hargis, Joseph A.
Harkey, Cletus B.
Harless, Chester H.
Harman, Carroll F.
Harman, Norman E.
Harman, Richard D.
Harmon, Eston
Harmon, Raymond F.
Harmon, Robert R. Jr.
Harmon, William J.
Harmonay, George F.
Harmony, Frederick A.
Harms, Herbert A.
Harner, James L.
Harner, Robert L.
Harner, Robert L. Sr.
Harner, Stewart D. Jr.
Harner, Stewart D. Jr.
Harney, William F.
Harp, Clifford F.
Harpel, Donald E.
Harper, George A.
Harper, Maynard
Harper, Preston Earl
Harrell, Earl H.
Harrell, James A.
Harrell, James A.
Harrell, Tom W.
Harrick, Charles E.
Harrill, Earl A.
Harrington, Charles N.
Harrington, Charles P.
Harrington, J.J.
Harris, C. William
Harris, Carey
Harris, Dale E.
Harris, Dennis D.
Harris, Elmer J. Jr.
Harris, Geo. L. Jr.
Harris, Hubbard
Harris, James T.
Harris, Joe E. Sr.
Harris, Kenneth P.
Harris, Milton A.
Harris, Robert F.
Harris, Robert L.
Harris, Robert S.
Harris, Robert W.
Harris, Russell M.
Harris, Sherman M.
Harris, Verlyn L.
Harris, W.C. Jr.
Harrison, J.T.
Harrison, Joseph F. III
Harrison, Joseph F. Jr.
Harshbarger, James
Hart, Arlis T.
Hart, Frank C.
Hart, Frank M.
Hart, Harold V.
Hart, Lawrence
Hart, Ralph E.
Hart, Robert H.
Hart, Shelby C.
Hart, Thomas J.
Hart, William J. Jr.
Hartley, Terrell S.
Hartlieb, Paul L. Jr.
Hartman, Fred C.
Hartman, Jack M.
Hartman, James C.
Hartman, Warren
Hartmann, William H.
Hartmeyer, Clarence B.
Hartnett, J.H.
Hartwig, Donald E.
Hartzler, Elinore
Hartzog, Harry E.
Harvey, Charles E.
Harvey, James A.
Harvey, James W.
Harvey, John C.
Harvey, Joseph J.
Harwell, Avery W.
Harwick, Forrest D.
Haselgard, Carlton S.
Haskett, Joseph R.
Haskin, Herbert E.
Hass, Ralph L.
Hassel, Walter B.
Hassell, Harold M.
Hassler, Edward E.
Hastings, Paul A.
Hastings, Robert D.
Hatch, A. Frost
Hatch, Charles K. Jr.
Hatcher, Henry C.
Hatfield, A.J.
Hatfield, Harry
Hatfield, Robert T.
Hatfield, Tennis H.
Hathcock, William G.
Hatsell, Wilbur
Hatstat, Leslie Jr.
Hatt, Norman J.
Hauck, Albert
Hauck, William F.
Haugen, Earl S.
Haughenberry, Chauncey
Haun, Frank F.
Haupt, John F. Jr.
Hauschild, Arthur J.
Hauser, Emmett M.
Hauser, Frank W.
Hauser, George
Hausman, Conrad Hnrbl.
Haveman, james H.
Havens, Charles E.
Havens, Jack L.
Haverkamp, Lewis H.
Haverstick, Russell J.
Hawk, Dusty
Hawkins, Andrew R.
Hawkins, Donald J.
Hawkins, Gordon S.
Hawkins, Howard R.
Hawksworth, John S.
Hawthorne, Raymond G.
Hawthorne, Robert W.
Hay, Adrian
Hayden, Mrs. Robert A.
Hayes, Charles R. Jr.
Hayes, Dale M.
Hayes, Edgar W.
Hayes, Glenn A.
Hayes, Leonard D.
Hayes, Robert E.
Hayes, Tom
Hayes, William E.
Haymes, Robert
Haynes, Richard
Hays, Kenneth C. Jr.
Hays, Otho E.
Hays, Robert
Hayward, Tom R.
Hazlett, Claude C.
Heacock, William B.
Head, Robert M.
Headland, E.H.
Headman, Thomas
Healey, John F.
Healey, Lawrence P.
Heaney, Lawrence
Heard, James H.
Hearn, James W.
Hearn, Joseph D.
Hearne, James F.
Heater, Jack
Heath, Raymond G.
Heath, Richard
Heather, Robert F.
Hecht, Joseph E.
Heck, Joaquim L.
Heckart, Francis D.
Heckel, Roy Jr.
Heckler, C. Derwood
Heckman, Fred W.
Heckman, Harold H.
Heckman, LeRoy G.
Hector, Carl S.
Hedberg, Harry
Hedglin, David S.
Hedrick, Elwood J.
Heffner, Irving
Heffner, Kelly B. Jr.
Heffron, James
Hegfield, Robert W.
Heidelmeier, William J.
Heidrich, William A., Jr.
Heiler, Frederick J.
Heilman, Charles J.
Heim, Dallas W. Jr.
Heim, Paul K.
Heimann, Bernard A.
Heindselman, Clifford
Heinisch, George J.
Heinmiller, Thomas A.
Heinrich, Walter A.
Heins, John N. Sr.
Heintz, Theodore W.
Heinzman, Jack S.
Heitland, John
Hejny, Orval A.
Helberg, James D.
Helgren, Ronald
Helinski, Raymond J.
Helle, Dwight E.
Hellein, William G.
Heller, Frederick C. Jr.
Heller, John F. Jr.
Heller, Ray
Heller, Richard C.
Helm, Frederick J.
Helm, Leonard L.
Helmer, Jim
Helminger, Joseph A.
Helsley, Leonard
Heltzel, Emerson
Helwig, Frederick C.
Hemenway, Earle E.
Hemenway, Robert D.
Heminger, Raymond R.
Hemphill, Gerald H.
Hempstead, Douglas
Hemree, David J.
Henaghan, Patrick F.
Hench, Dale M.
Henderson, Clinton
Henderson, Glenn W.
Henderson, James L.
Henderson, June E.
Henderson, Norman E.
Henderson, Ray
Henderson, Thomas C.
Henderson, Tom W.

Henderson, Wallace B.
Hendley, Edwin E.
Hendricks, John J. Jr.
Hendricks, Malcolm R.
Hendrickson, Aldon M.
Hendrickson, George I.
Hendrickson, James
Hendrickson, Jim
Hendrickson, Leroy
Hendrickson, Leroy
Hendrix, Charles E.
Hendrix, David C.
Hendrix, George D.
Hendrix, Merl E.
Hendron, Frank
Hengel, Lawrence J.
Hengel, Lawrence J.
Henick, Joseph R.
Henkel, Richard D.
Hennefer, Fred R.
Hennies, Robert S.
Henning, Raymond E.
Henriques, Charles B.
Henry, Alexander Jr.
Henry, Cranford J.
Henry, O.A.
Henry, Thomas B. Jr.
Henschel, Harold L.
Hensel, John F. Jr.
Henslee, William M.
Hensler, Harold E.
Hensler, Phillip J.
Hensley, Clifton
Hensley, Lucius
Henson, George E.
Henson, Sidney
Hentges, Robert J.
Hepinstall, George
Herberger, Raymond F.
Herbster, Bob B.
Herdy, Herschel Hugh
Herens, James E.
Herens, James E.
Herking, Frank S.
Herlihy, James F.
Herman, Clemence
Herman, Ed
Herman, Norman
Herman, Walter
Hermann, George III
Hermes, Frederick W.
Hernandez, Robert J.
Hero, James E.
Herr, Charles L.
Herr, Raymond H.
Herrera, Adolph Z.
Herrigel, A. Warren
Herring, Harold E.
Herring, M.B.
Herron, Robert L.
Herron, William H.
Hertwig, Frank O.
Herzig, Theodore R.
Heseltine, Robert G.
Hesen, Louis M. Jr.
Hess, Fred L.
Hess, Harry J. Jr.
Hess, Luther J.
Hess, William M.
Hessek, Edgar L.
Hessek, Robert F.
Hesselbarth, Keith R.
Hessemer, Philip F.
Heston, Herman M.
Hetrick, Alfred L.
Hetrick, John G.
Hetzel, Earl L.
Heuer, Carl H.
Heuser, Stanley W.
Heuss, Fred H.
Hewitt, Maurice B.
Heyart, William E.
Heyer, Frank N.
Hibbs, David L.
Hickey, Doris M.
Hickey, Gerald L.
Hickey, Norman W.
Hicks, Benjamin D.
Hicks, Bert S.
Hicks, Curtis H.
Hicks, Raymond J.
Hicks, Richard H.
Hicks, Robert C.
Hicks, Rodeheaver H.
Hicks, Wesley W.
Higby, Jack B.
Higgens, Joseph C.
Higgins, Curtis C.
Higgins, Donald O.
Higgins, George G. III
Higgins, Howard
Higgins, James A.
Higgins, James F.
Higgins, John W. Jr.
Higham, William A.
Highbaugh, Karl
Hight, Jordan M.
Higley, Raymond Rev.
Hilbert, Albert T.
Hilbert, Goodwin
Hilbert, Robert E.
Hildebrand, Virgil E.
Hildebrandt, Richard
Hile, William
Hill, Charles E.
Hill, Charles M.
Hill, David
Hill, Elwood
Hill, Fraser L. Jr.
Hill, Harold H.
Hill, John J.
Hill, Kenneth W.
Hill, Martin W.
Hill, Robert F.
Hill, Ronald E.
Hill, Thomas
Hill, Vernon W.
Hill, Warren M.
Hill, William Smith
Hiller, John J.
Hillpot, Richard
Hillyer, Richard B.
Hilmer, Herbert H. Jr.
Hilsabeck, James R.
Hilton, E.S.
Hilton, James V.
Hilton, Robert
Hilton, Robert J.
Hilton, Robert P.
Hiltz, Larry
Himmelberger, Mark
Hincks, Donald D.
Hindes, Wayne F.
Hine, Charles M.
Hines, Alfred
Hines, Bernard L.
Hines, John N.
Hines, Lisle T.
Hines, Ronald C.
Hines, William
Hinkle, Truman
Hinton, Herman D.
Hinton, W. Boyd
Hipke, A.R.
Hipp, Cletus
Hipp, James V.
Hipple, Dale E.
Hirsh, Martin
Hirst, Forrest R.
Hirt, Homer B.
Hirtle, Walter W. Jr.
Hissam, Barbara
Hissong, Terry W.
Hitchcock, Philip A.
Hiteshew, R.F.
Hixson, Chalmer G.
Hixson, Donald D.
Hlista, Julius R.
Hoag, Leo P.
Hoagland, D.L.
Hoanzl, Frank
Hoback, Ernest E.
Hobbie, John E. Sr.
Hobbie, John E. Sr.
Hobbs, Earle B.
Hobbs, John H.
Hobbs, Julius M.
Hobel, James A.
Hobson, Allard D.
Hock, Earl S.
Hock, Irving A.
Hockensmith, Rev. C.H.
Hocking, William J.
Hockstad, Paul
Hodash, Leon
Hoddinott, Charles J.
Hoden, Joseph
Hodges, George
Hodges, Newton K.
Hodges, Robert E.
Hodskins, Morgan B. Jr.
Hoeglund, Milton A.
Hoelderlin, Walter W.
Hoellen, John J.
Hoelzel, Marvin C.
Hoelzle, Raymond J.
Hoerling, Robert W.
Hofele, Earl E.
Hofeller, Ed
Hoff, James E.
Hoffer, Terry
Hoffman, Carl W. Sr.
Hoffman, Charles
Hoffman, Harold K.
Hoffman, Murray
Hoffman, Paul H.
Hoffman, Richard R.
Hoffman, Wilbur
Hoffman, William V. Jr.
Hoffmann, Alfred E.
Hogan, Robert F.
Hogan, Thomas A.
Hogan, William B.
Hogg, Bruce B.
Hoggins, Thomas M.
Hogue, Louis L.
Hoinski, Alex
Hoisington, Russell F.
Holbert, Herbert R.
Holcomb, Leonard Jr.
Holcomb, Russell F.
Holdcroft, Shirley
Holden, Charles F.
Holden, James P. Jr.
Holden, Roger W.
Holden, William
Holder, John T.
Holder, Rev. Richard C.
Holdridge, Floyd T.
Holifield, Robert W.
Holko, Edward C.
Holladay, John B. Jr.
Holland, Jack H.
Holland, James E.
Holland, William D.
Holler, Gerald D. Sr.
Holler, Harold J.
Hollern, Daniel F.
Hollett, Norman Jr.
Holley, William S.
Holliday, Garnett
Holliday, Horace
Holliday, Robert L.
Hollier, Alice
Hollingsworth, Edward
Hollingsworth, George Sr.
Hollins, Edwin L.
Hollis, Fred
Hollis, John M.
Hollister, Gordon L.
Hollister, John W.
Holloran, John W.
Holloway, Everett T.
Holloway, Lowell Radm.
Holman, Donald L.
Holman, Robert E.
Holmberg, Douglas V.
Holmes, Charles E.
Holmes, Clifford L.
Holmes, Clyde W.
Holmes, Edward J.
Holmes, George
Holmes, Harvey L.
Holmes, Howard L.
Holmes, James K.
Holmes, Kenneth B.
Holmes, Lowell D.
Holmes, Paul M.
Holmes, Robert M.
Holmquist, Robert R.
Holsinger, George W.
Holsonback, Edward E.
Holstius, Albert E.
Holstrom, Forrest A.
Holt, Arthur G.
Holt, Harry W.
Holt, Leslie R.
Holthe, Fred H.
Holtyn, Henry L.
Holtzman, Harry E.
Holub, John M.
Holzem, Francis L.
Holzman, Russell
Homan, Leonard R.
Homberger, Kenneth E.
Homer, Albert
Homer, Ray F.
Homovec, Joseph W.
Honeycutt, Earl
Honse, John W.
Hooft, Jacobus W.
Hoogerhoud, Nicholas Jr.
Hoogerwerf, Clarence
Hook, John G.
Hooke, Robert L.
Hooks, Delbert
Hooper, Robert C.
Hooven, Robert C.
Hoover, Harold N.
Hopfgarten, Edwin F.
Hopkins, Al
Hopkins, Arthur J.
Hopkins, George E.
Hopkins, Robert L.
Hopper, Eugene M.
Hopps, Darrell R.
Horan, George P.
Horban, Walter C.
Horch, Charles
Horgash, Joseph J.
Horine, Perry
Horn, Alvin J.
Horn, Frank J.
Horn, Richard I.
Horn, Walter H.
Horne, Simon Jr.
Horner, Robert W. Jr.
Horner, Thomas O.
Horning, Chester A.
Hornsby, Herbert
Hornyak, John M. Jr.
Hornyak, John M. Sr.
Horovitz, Frank W.
Horowitz, Leonard E.
Horrigan, James O.
Horst, William J.
Horstman, Harold
Horstmann, Gerard G.
Horton, Clinton O.
Horton, Dewey
Horton, Edmund G.
Horton, Robert G.
Horton, William H.
Horvath, Charles
Horvath, Charles F.
Horvath, George
Hosbach, James D.
Hosbrook, Theresa V.
Hotchkiss, Stuart T.
Hott, George H.
Houchins, Max
Houde, Robert F.
Houghton, Thomas F.
Houk, George H.
House, Fredrick W.
House, Hubert L.
House, James O.
House, Leonard J.
House, R.A.
Houser, Joseph C.
Houser, Thomas S.
Houston, Corinne
Houtkooper, Charles M.
Hove, Alfred T. Jr.
Howard, Daniel J.
Howard, David T.
Howard, Denver
Howard, Everette H.
Howard, Gilbert E.
Howard, Herbert J.
Howard, Kenneth A.
Howard, Sanford A.
Howe, C. Thomas
Howe, George
Howe, James N.
Howe, Lenard L.
Howe, Milton B.
Howe, Richard C.
Howe, Robert H.
Howell, Albert
Howell, Eddie W.
Howell, John E.
Howell, Norman
Howell, Richard A.
Howell, Robert J.
Howerton, James G.
Howey, John H.
Howisey, Robert W.
Howison, William A.
Howko, Alex
Howland, David G.
Howlett, Daniel R.
Hoyer, William C.
Hoyt, John W.
Hoyt, Lewis A.
Hoyt, William A.
Hrabchak, Joseph M.
Hreben, Frank N.
Hrodey, Robert H.
Hron, Rudolph H.
Hruska, Stephen A.
Hubbard, B.R.
Hubbard, Don E.
Hubbard, John E.
Hubbell, Lester E.
Huber, Lawrence H.
Hubler, Gene R.
Huck, John J.
Huddleson, Preston
Hudgins, R.B.
Hudock, John J.
Hudson, James D.
Hudson, Jesse Jr.
Hudson, Kover M. Jr.
Hudson, Luther W. Jr.
Hudson, Samuel E.
Hudson, William J.
Huebner, Earl F.
Huebner, Robert P.
Huebner, Wilbert E.
Huemmrich, George J.
Huey, Dorothy
Huff, Lether E.
Huffer, Jacob B. Jr.
Huffman, James I.
Huffstutler, Bill
Huggins, John E.
Hughes, Alton M.
Hughes, Charles F.
Hughes, Floyd J.
Hughes, Joseph
Hughes, Richard W
Hughes, S.J.
Hughes, Thomas S.
Hughes, Warren G.
Huiet, James F.
Hull, Charles A.
Hull, Fred John
Hull, John
Hull, Robert B. Jr.
Hulsmann, Robert H.
Humble, Qurlie
Hume, John E.
Hume, Kevin C.
Hume, Marvin E.
Humechick, Metro
Humes, Donald F.
Humienny, Bill
Hummel, Charles R.
Humphrey, Donald
Humphrey, Matilda W.
Humphries, James W.
Hunchberger, Earl R.
Hundley, Andrew
Hundley, Clyde L.
Hundsrucker, John E.
Hungerford, George
Hunt, Donald Jr.
Hunt, Floyd B. Jr.
Hunt, John
Hunt, William J.
Hunter, C.T.
Hunter, Dana L.
Hunter, Francis C.
Hunter, Glen E.
Hunters, Shark
Huntington, Floyd A.
Huntington, John
Huntley, Arthur V.
Huntley, Ira H.
Huntzinger, Oliver E.
Hunziker, Clayton C.
Hupenece, Edward
Hurd, Charles
Hurd, John G.
Hurdle, Robert R.
Hurdzon, Nick
Hurlbert, Charles H.
Hurley, Frank J.
Hurston, Frederick E.
Husen, Carl C.
Hush, Melvin T.
Husman, Lloyd J.
Huston, Gordon T.
Hutchings, Frederick Sr.
Hutchins, D.C.
Hutchinson, Calvin L.
Hutchinson, Donald
Hutchinson, James F.
Hutchinson, Lester
Hutchinson, Louis H.
Hutchison, Gerald D.
Hutton, James B.
Huza, Frank J.
Hvizd, Andrew
Hyatt, Daniel F. Jr.
Hyde, Benjamin D.
Hyde, Frederick J.
Hyde, Harold T.
Hyde, Latimer
Hyduke, B.F.

- I -

Iannucci, Joseph
Iannuzzi, James
Ibbs, John W.
Iden, Robert V.
Ignatczuk, Adolph
Igo, William T.
Ihler, Amos A.
Ilgen, Lenard
Illig, Frank J.
Illingworth, S.G.
Iltz, Marvin
Imeri, Arthur J.
Imms, John W. Jr.
Indri, Alfeo
Ingalls, Joseph F.
Ingalls, Maurice T.
Ingano, Eugene P.
Ingham, J. Gerald
Ingle, John P. Jr.
Ingles, Fred C.
Ingman, Maurice
Ingraham, Robert B.
Ingram, Charles Allen
Ingram, L.O.
Ingram, Victor H.
Inman, Richard T.
Insko, M.D.
Introini, Dante
Ireland, Jack R.
Ireland, James E.
Irish, John H.
Iron, Raymond E.
Irons, Charles L.
Irvin, Daniel G.
Irvin, Kenneth P.
Irving, Joseph A.
Irwin, Harry A.
Irwin, William
Irwin, William K.
Irwin, William W. Jr.
Isaacson, Arthur
Isaacson, Myron E.
Isabell, George E.
Isackson, Ralph J.
Isakson, Robert A.
Iselin, Sally Cary
Isom, Tom H.
Iversen, Harold
Iversen, John B.
Iverson, Harold O.
Iwancio, Carolyn

- J -

Jabaut, Ron
Jablonski, Henry
Jablonsky, Michael R.
Jacke, Stan
Jackson, Alexander Jr.
Jackson, Charles
Jackson, Edward J.
Jackson, Frank A.
Jackson, Harry R.
Jackson, J.T.
Jackson, John H.
Jackson, John R.
Jackson, Kermit
Jackson, Omar M.
Jackson, Ralph A.
Jackson, Raymond E.
Jackson, Robert M.
Jackson, Robert M.
Jacob, Robert
Jacob, Robert
Jacobs, Clayton R.
Jácobs, Gaza
Jacobs, James M.
Jacobs, M.P.
Jacobs, Marlin F.
Jacobs, Thomas E.
Jacobson, Howard
Jacobson, Howard W.
Jacobson, Roy V.
Jacoby, Walter H.
Jaderborg, Hilding A.
Jaeger, Dolph
Jaeger, Douglas T.
Jaeger, George G.
Jaeger, Robert F.
Jaeger, Tobias L.
Jagielko, Edward
Jago, Allan L.
Jakubowski, Marion R.
James, Clinton M.
James, Harry E.
James, John W.
James, Mort
James, Ralph
James, Raymond A.
James, Sidney D.
James, Talmadge G.
James, W.G. Jr.
James, William J.
Jameson, K.R.
Jamison, George K.
Jamison, Ralph F.
Jamison, Walter K.
Janes, William H.
Jankowski, Dave
Jansen, Leo H.
Janvskevich, Joseph P.
Jaquith, Edwin G.
Jarema, John J.
Jarigese, Frederick J.
Jarlsberg, Robert
Jarnell, Edward F. Jr.
Jarrett, W.D.
Jarriel, Edwin C.
Jaskoviak, Boyd F.
Jatho, Jake L.
Javornicky, Lewis
Jeamel, John B.
Jeanot, Paul
Jefferies, Mark D.
Jefferis, Lawrence R.
Jefferis, Richard W.
Jeffers, Alfred E.
Jeffries, Aubrey E.
Jeglinski, Lucien G.
Jeisy, Robert V.
Jenkins, Charles W.
Jenkins, Clayton E.
Jenkins, Henry A.
Jenkins, Henry C.
Jenkins, Hugh Dee
Jenkins, Robert G.
Jenkins, Robert R.
Jenkins, Wm. Jack
Jenner, Carroll W. Jr.
Jennings, Grant U.
Jennings, Joseph F. Sr.
Jennings, Kenneth
Jennings, Paul H.
Jensen, Carl
Jensen, Charles R.
Jensen, Don A.
Jensen, LaVern H.
Jensen, Richard
Jensen, Ronald J.
Jentzsch, Karl H.
Jerard, Thomas J.
Jeremiah, David Adm.
Jernigan, Lee E.
Jernigan, Roy
Jessen, Martin D.
Jessen, Warren L.
Jesso, Harold E. Jr.
Jessogne, Russell J.
Jobes, William A.
Jobson, James H.
Johanson, Wallace D.
John, Alfred E.
Johnson, Adron C.
Johnson, Alfred
Johnson, Allen V. Jr.
Johnson, Armand L.
Johnson, Arnold E.
Johnson, Arthur B.
Johnson, Augustus P.
Johnson, Azel M.
Johnson, Bernt C.
Johnson, Bill
Johnson, Boyd C.
Johnson, Carl W.
Johnson, Cecil C.
Johnson, Charles A.
Johnson, Charles R.
Johnson, David
Johnson, David H.
Johnson, Donald M.
Johnson, Douglas W.
Johnson, Earl F.
Johnson, Edgar H.
Johnson, Edward J.
Johnson, Edwin
Johnson, Edwin R.
Johnson, Ernest C.
Johnson, Erskine
Johnson, Erskine
Johnson, Francis E.
Johnson, Francis S.
Johnson, George E.
Johnson, George L.
Johnson, George O.
Johnson, Harry B.
Johnson, Harry E.
Johnson, Harry I. Jr.
Johnson, Herbert M.
Johnson, Hugh E.
Johnson, Irving L.
Johnson, Iver
Johnson, J.F.
Johnson, J.F.
Johnson, James C.
Johnson, James R.
Johnson, James W. III
Johnson, John A.
Johnson, John R.
Johnson, K.L.
Johnson, Leach M.
Johnson, Lee G.
Johnson, Leland K.
Johnson, Lloyd
Johnson, Luther J. Sr.
Johnson, Marvin D.
Johnson, Noel C.
Johnson, Norman H.
Johnson, Paul E.
Johnson, Porter
Johnson, Ralph H.
Johnson, Ray J.
Johnson, Raymond J.
Johnson, Richard H.
Johnson, Richard H.
Johnson, Robert E.
Johnson, Robert L.
Johnson, Robert M.
Johnson, Rolf Eric
Johnson, Santford C.
Johnson, Stanley E.
Johnson, Thomas F.
Johnson, Thomas J.
Johnson, Thomas M.
Johnson, Walter A.
Johnson, Walter E.
Johnson, Warren D.
Johnson, Werner E.
Johnson, Wilbur A.
Johnston, Donald L.
Johnston, Edward M.
Johnston, George W.
Johnston, Ray
Johnston, Richard E.
Jolley, Clare F.
Jolley, Everett M.
Jolley, Paul R.
Jolly, Bill
Jonas, Leroy
Jones, Barton M. Jr.
Jones, Billy D.
Jones, Bob
Jones, Buford F.
Jones, Calvin C.
Jones, Calvin M.
Jones, Carroll L.
Jones, Claude O.
Jones, David E.
Jones, Denny
Jones, Donald J.
Jones, Ernest B.
Jones, Floyd A. Jr.
Jones, Floyd C.
Jones, Fred G.
Jones, Gordon T.
Jones, Harry B.
Jones, Harry E. Jr.
Jones, Irving E.
Jones, James C.
Jones, Jamie E.
Jones, John R. Sr.
Jones, Malcolm C.
Jones, Marion
Jones, Mervin E.
Jones, Richard W.
Jones, Robert H.
Jones, Robert L. Sr.
Jones, Santos Basillo
Jones, Theodore E.
Jones, Tom C.
Jones, Willard H.
Jones, William B. Jr.
Jones, William S.
Jones, William V.
Jontow, Lawrence
Jontz, Jack D.
Jordan, David
Jordan, E.G. Jr.
Jordan, Edward M.
Jordan, Paul L.
Jordan, Richard H.
Jordan, Robert K.
Jordan, Thomas
Jordan, William B. Jr.
Jordan, William Jr.
Jordan, William Jr.
Jorgensen, Edward L.
Jorpeland, Ole
Joseck, Harry C.
Josefiak, Merle F.
Joslin, Robert K.
Joslin, William D.
Jouas, Richard
Joy, Benedict A.
Joyce, Donald A.
Joyce, Frederick E.
Joyce, John J.
Joyce, Raymond S.
Joyce, William E.
Joye, David B.
Joyner, Frederick
Joyner, T. Eli Jr.
Judd, Feldie M.
Judd, Feldie M.
Judkins, William R.
Judson, Charles S.
Julian, John
Julien, Daniel J.
Julnes, N.S.
Jung, Howard V.
Juracek, Joseph
Juraschek, John F.
Jurkiewicz, Joseph H.
Jurs, Frank A.
Justice, Clarence
Juttner, Arthur J.

- K -

Kabat, Raymond J.
Kabbes, Charles Mrs.
Kadison, Stuart L.
Kahler, Donald K.
Kahn, Carroll J.
Kahrs, William H.
Kain, Charles I.
Kaiser, Raymond S.
Kaiser, Raymond S.
Kaiser, William
Kalal, Frank W.
Kalb, George M.
Kalb, Joseph G.
Kalbaugh, Jack C.
Kalch, Lester W.
Kale, William E.
Kaleta, William S.
Kalinofsky, Henry A.
Kalivas, George
Kalogeros, Arthur J.
Kamerson, Robert L.
Kaminski, Frank F.
Kamp, Andrew J.
Kampa, Carlton J.
Kamradt, J.B.
Kana, Edward A.
Kana, John
Kanady, Robert W.
Kanavel, Raymond T.
Kandres, George C.
Kane, Carl L.
Kane, John A.
Kane, Patrick H.
Kane, Robert A. Jr.
Kane, Robert J.
Kanellis, Dave
Kanenbley, Charles H.
Kaney, Jack D.
Kanikula, Harry J.
Kanoza, Cyril J.
Kantor, Walter B.
Kapeler, Frederick A.
Kapp, Eugene
Kapplor, George D.
Karahalios, John N.
Karan, Leonard F.
Karas, Nick
Karban, John
Karetka, Peter E.
Karl, Fred J.
Karl, Henry T.
Karmel, Charles L.
Karthas, Nicholas G.
Kaspar, Gerald D.
Kasper, Francis
Kastelic, John M.
Kaszycki, Joseph
Kauffman, Charles J.
Kaufman, John R.
Kaufman, Robert M.
Kaufmann, Fred
Kaufmann, Joseph G.
Kauppi, Robert
Kausch, Winfred R.
Kavanagh, Jack J.
Kaverman, Charles J.
Kavich, Walter J. Jr.
Kayman, Sidney
Kayse, Robert O.
Keally, John B.
Kean, Douglas
Keane, Thomas A.
Keaough, Gerald E.
Kear, Robert G. Sr.
Kearn, Warren F.
Kearney, Joseph W.
Kearney, Richard L.
Kearney, William R.
Kearns, Donald J.
Kearns, Frank J.
Kearse, Douglas W.
Keasling, Jack
Keating, Donald F.
Keck, James C.
Keck, Robert H.
Keddy, Norman B.
Kee, John
Keefe, Eugene F.
Keefe, John F.
Keefer, Wilbert P.
Keeler, William H.
Keene, Henry C. Jr.
Keene, Roland
Keener, Bruce III
Keener, Carl E.
Keeney, Wayne M.
Kehlenbeck, Henry G.
Kehrberg, Luther M.
Keilholtz, Kenneth W.
Keim, Norman Dale
Keith, William H.

Keitz, John
Kelleher, Benjamin Jr.
Kelleher, Gerald J.
Kelleher, William K.
Keller, Francis J.
Keller, George R.
Keller, Raymond L.
Kelley, Arthur F.
Kelley, Charles R.
Kelley, Clyde
Kelley, Hugh J.
Kelley, James O.
Kelley, Marion F.
Kelley, Richard E.
Kelley, Russell H.
Kelley, Scott R.
Kelley, Thomas F.
Kellogg, David M.
Kelly, Clifford O.
Kelly, Edward J.
Kelly, Henry E.
Kelly, James A.
Kelly, James M.
Kelly, James P.
Kelly, James Wilson
Kelly, John R.
Kelly, John W.
Kelly, Joseph J.
Kelly, Joseph P.
Kelly, Martin D.
Kelly, Thomas P.
Kelly, William D.
Kelm, William
Kelso, Albert E.
Kelso, Leo G.
Keltner, Melvin E.
Kemmis, Richard J.
Kemmler, R.E.
Kempe, Robert A.
Kempf, Valentine
Kempler, Bernard J.
Kempski, Chester F.
Kendall, Roy J.
Kendig, Ellsworth Jr.
Kendrew, Thomas J.
Kendus, Stanley W.
Kenna, William
Kenna, William
Kennard, Gordon Sr.
Kennedy, Charles D.
Kennedy, Edward C.
Kennedy, Frank
Kennedy, John R.
Kennedy, Raymond F.
Kennedy, Richard J.
Kennedy, Richard R.
Kennedy, Thomas E.
Kennedy, Vernon H.
Kennedy, William
Kennedy, William J.
Kenney, James P.
Kenney, Phillip L.
Kenney, Ross J.
Kennicutt, Herb V.
Kenny, Patrick F.
Kenton, E.S.
Kenward, William F.
Kerber, Leander P.
Kerby, William T.
Kerka, W.A.
Kern, Ralph
Kern, Walter R.
Kerner, Leroy E.
Kerns, Hamilton Y.
Kerns, Hugh
Kersen, Frank N.
Kersey, George Mrs.
Kersten, Herman J.
Kertes, Al
Kessinger, A.G.
Kessinger, Gene L.
Kessler, Harold H.
Kessler, John R.
Kessler, Robert
Kessman, Ralph L.
Kestranek, Joseph R. Jr.
Kettelhut, Glen T.
Ketterer, R. Owen
Keyes, Bernard F.
Keys, Charles H.
Keys, Lewis C.
Keyte, Mack L.
Kichar, Martin C.
Kicinski, Alfred F.
Kidd, Stanley R.
Kidd, Thomas L. Jr.
Kiddy, William F.
Kieckhafer, Donald E.
Kiefer, Robert G.
Kieff, John H. Jr.
Kienzler, Rudolph
Kier, Charles D.
Kiesewetter, John J.
Kilberg, Raymond L.
Kilburn, J.W.
Kilchenman, William Jr.
Kilchenstein, Francis W.
Kilday, Francis J.
Kilgore, James H.
Kilgore, William
Killian, James D.
Killion, Buck P.
Kilmer, Jack
Kilmurray, John A.
Kilpatrick Robert G.
Kilpatrick, Albert E.
Kilpatrick, George G.
Kimball, Albert W.
Kimball, Donald L.
Kimble, John
Kimbrell, Ollie H.
Kimler, Wayne D.
Kimmell, Vern
Kimmelshue, George E.
Kincaid, James C.
Kindt, Eric H.
King, Albert D. Sr.
King, Atkins H. Jr.
King, Byron C.
King, Charles R.
King, Charles W.
King, Curtis A.
King, Donald E.
King, Edward A.
King, Edward A.
King, Francis
King, George T.
King, James Anderson
King, John J.
King, John L.
King, John R.
King, Keith C.
King, Maurice R.
King, Oliver C.
King, Oscar E.
King, Ralph H.
King, Richard T.
King, Robert J.
King, Robert W.
King, Ross C. Jr.
King, Seth T.
King, Tasker D.
King, Warren R.
King, William L.
Kingsbury, Stanley L.
Kingsley, James F.
Kingston, Eugene J.
Kingston, George W.
Kinnane, John R.
Kinney, Sheldon H.
Kinnish, Walter N.
Kinnison, Hurshell L.
Kinsley, Dick
Kinsley, Frederic W.
Kinter, Robert C.
Kippax, Lynn
Kirby, David J.
Kirby, Edward F.
Kirby, Eugene J.
Kirby, Frederick T.
Kirchherr, Walter G.
Kirchner, Samuel J.
Kirk, Austin J.
Kirk, Baylor C.
Kirk, Earl
Kirk, John W.
Kirk, Kenneth D. Jr.
Kirk, Robert W.
Kirk, William
Kirkhuff, Larry A. Jr.
Kirkley, Allen T.
Kirkpatrick, E.H.
Kirkpatrick, Jack
Kirkpatrick, Jerry J.
Kirkpatrick, Leroy H.
Kirsch, Michael
Kirtley, Malcolm B.
Kiselak, Joseph M.
Kisil, William R. Sr.
Kiska, Thomas P.
Kitchen, Donald C.
Kitchener, Charles J.
Kitchens, M.A.
Kitchens, Stanley R.
Kitzler, Robert F.
Kizziah, Sterling D. Jr.
Klaiber, Robert D.
Klaila, William J.
Klane, Charles H.
Klarecki, Edwin A.
Klarman, John
Klasic, Emil
Klass, Harold J.
Klause, Robert G.
Klein, George W.
Klein, Marvin B.
Kleinhagen, George
Kleinman, Paul H.
Kleintop, Richard M.
Klementovic, Fred J.
Klemm, Frederick R.
Kleopfer, Elmer K.
Kleponis, John A.
Klepper, James L.
Klevanosky, Paul
Kline, Eugene M.
Kline, Marvin G.
Kline, Robert C.
Klingele, Cyril J.
Klinger, Calvin E.
Klinger, Carlos G.
Klitz, Harry L.
Klobnak, Andy R.
Klocek, James L.
Kloepfer, Elbert
Klonowski, Thomas J.
Klope, Allen G.
Kluck, Raymond T.
Klug, Erwin E.
Klukos, Henry
Klunder, Stanley A.
Knapp, James W.
Knapp, Ralph E. Dr.
Knaus, Harry E.
Knause, Francis H.
Knecht, Harry B.
Knecht, Raymond L.
Kneeland, Ray
Knepp, Orville T.
Knickerbocker, Douglas H.
Knight, Andrew J.
Knight, D.A.
Knight, Earl R.
Knight, James A.
Knight, Robert K.
Knighten, W.J.
Kniptash, William R.
Knobloch, Erich
Knode, Charles F.
Knollmeyer, Eugene A.
Knopf, Fred
Knopp, Roy L.
Knott, John A.
Knott, Robert W.
Knowles, Harold
Knowles, William B.
Knowlton, Timothy J.
Knox, Paul W.
Knox, William C.
Knurek, Casimir W.
Knutson, Trygue K.
Koban, Andrew
Kobek, Alex
Kobela, Andrew J.
Kober, Francis E.
Kobriger, Dallas J.
Koca, Frank J.
Kocevar, Richard
Koch, Alfred J.
Koch, Berthold F.
Koch, John J.
Koch, Junius A.
Koch, Stella
Koehler, Earl G.
Koehler, Karl F.
Koehn, Walter J.
Koelker, Robert W.
Koenig, Carl F.
Koerner, Bernard H.
Koetsch, Robert
Koffman, James
Kohl, George M.
Kohler, Charles L.
Kohn, Ann Marie
Kohrt, Lawrence E.
Kokoszka, Edward A.
Kokura, John
Kolanko, Harry A.
Kolar, Roland F.
Kolb, Albert W.
Kolb, John H.
Kolb, Raymod C.
Kollath, Harry J.
Kolody, Russell
Komsisky, Francis
Koncal, Irv
Koneski, George W.
Konrad, Henry R.
Kontzen, Joseph
Kooiker, Vernon G.
Koon, Huey D.
Kopel, Howard F.
Koppen, Donald G.
Koppenhaver, Dean S.
Koral, Joseph G.
Korbut, Walter J.
Korcal, Lawrence R.
Kordus, Arthur R.
Korfman, Walter
Korinek, John R. Sr.
Koripsky, Joseph
Korleski, Vernon A.
Korman, Sinclair
Kornacivich, John L.
Kornegay, P.R.
Kornmiller, Harry
Korpi, George O.
Kortbawi, Albert G.
Korte, Clay E.
Korth, Donald W. Jr.
Kos, Anthony R.
Kosey, Roy A.
Koski, Arden
Koskinen, Carl W.
Koskinen, Carl W.
Koslicki, Daniel E.
Kossakoski, Richard C.
Kost, Stanley G.
Koster, Allen T.
Kostibos, Jack F.
Kostoff, Chris
Kostoroski, Paul
Koteras, Raymond
Kotik, Wallace
Kott, Stanley P.
Koundakjian, Richard C.
Kovach, Peter
Kovacs, George W.
Kowalczyk, John P.
Kowalczyk, Stanley J.
Kowaleski, John A.
Kowalewski, Eugene M.
Kowalewski, Richard J.
Kowalski, Edward J.
Kowalski, Stanley F.
Kozachek, Walter
Kozar, Edward
Kraft, Victor
Krajick, John J.
Krakowski, Walter
Krall, Albert R.
Kralovec, Earl A.
Kralt, Frank Jr.
Kramber, John E.
Kramer, Joshua
Kramer, Le F. Roy
Kramer, Valentine G.
Krammes, Stanley R.
Krantz, John
Kranz, John W.
Krasinski, Joseph J.
Krasney, Abe
Krasulak, Frank V.
Krattli, Daniel L.
Kraus, Henry I.
Krause, Edward
Krause, James T.
Krause, William J.
Krauskopf, Charles J.
Kravitz, Albert
Krawczyk, Frank P.
Kreiger, Ted
Kreinberg, Leo E.
Kreisel, Conrad W.
Kreitzer, Martin L.
Krekel, Forrest G.
Kreps, Joseph T.
Kress, Paul Jr.
Kress, Robert G.
Kretschmer, Eugene W.
Krick, Gerald
Krieg, Eric
Krile, Robert L.
Krisher, Willard B.
Krisko, Peter
Krisza, Charles W.
Kroch, Carl A.
Krol, Edward J.
Krolikowski, S.
Kronemyer, Robert E.
Kropp, Frank C.
Krostag, Edward
Krothe, Walter R.
Krueper, Louis
Krug, George R.
Kruger, Paul
Krukow, Kenneth W.
Krull, Frederick C.
Krumenacker, N.A. Jr.
Kruse, Donald J.
Krystof, Joseph A.
Kszepka, Henry
Kubelsky, Victor
Kubik, William M.
Kughn, James C.
Kuhach, Joseph
Kuhn, Gerald H.
Kuhn, Robert G.
Kuhn, William H. Jr.
Kujawa, Fred E.
Kukelhan, Walter
Kulikowski, Albert
Kulis, Melvin R.
Kull, Henry E.
Kull, Merle C.
Kulnis, Ed
Kumpus, Felix G.
Kundich, Donald M.
Kundis, Pauline
Kunkel, Elmer M.
Kuntz, Frank
Kuntz, W.E.
Kunz, Walter S., Sr.
Kupczyk, Richard
Kurnyta, John
Kurtz, Myron H.
Kusek, James J.
Kushner, Edward
Kutner, David H.
Kuykendall, David H.
Kuzma, John
Kuzmicz, Frank M.
Kwiatkoski, Joseph
Kyle, Burton
Kyte, Jewell T.

- L -

Labarge, Raymond W.
Labarr, Raymond A.
LaBauve, Clarence A.
Labedz, Raymond
Laber, Earl
LaBorde, George P.
Laborde, Alden J.
Laborde, Ellis T.
Labosky, Steven A.
Labrier, William A. Jr.
Labriola, Eugene W.
Lacasse, Lawrence
Lacey, Malcolm
Lackey, Fred H.
Lacko, Lester M.
LaComb, Frank A.
Lacomb, Daniel A.
Ladre, Bert O.
Lafayette, Kenneth W.
LaFevers, Herman L.
Lafferty, Charles F.
Lafferty, Frank T.
Laflamme, Joseph R.
LaFleur, Robert
Lagana, Anthony E.
Lagemann, Richard H.
Lagerquist, A. Lloyd
Lagess, Thomas F.
Lagomarsino, Victor Jr.
Lagsdin, John E. Jr.
Laidley, W.S.
Laidman, Sanford
Lain, John W.
Laing, Freddie
Laird, Charles H.
Laird, Chess
Laird, Galen W.
Lajoure, Gerald A.
Lake, Floyd J.
Lake, Ralph W.
Lake, Timothy D.
Lake, Walter F.
Lakey, Raymond M.
LaMarre, J.G.
Lamartine, Frank J.
Lamb, Dennis W.
Lamb, Robert K.
Lambert, Edward E.
Lambert, Murray
Lambert, Nelson V.
Lambert, Richard B.
Lambertson, Robert E.
Lambiase, John E.
Lamie, Howard H.
Lammon, Bertram
Lamont, Lester
Lampe, Emil C.
Lampe, John B.
LaMunyon, John T.
Lancaster, Chauncy C.
Lancaster, Ted M.
Lance, Donald
Lance, Theron M.
Landauer, Fred
Lander, William A.
Landers, Gene Louie
Landfried, Erling C.
Landing, William
Landis, Paul E.
Landrum, Emmett B.
Landrum, Thomas C.
Landry, Edward W.
Landry, Joseph E.
Landry, Milton E.
Lane, Arthur S.
Lane, Hubert R. Jr.
Lanfranchi, Charles
Lang, Bernie
Lang, Elvin R.
Langdale, John
Langdon, Robert K.
Lange, Earl
Lange, Henry G. Jr.
Langenahn, Tim M.
Langill, William H.
Langone, Michael C.
Lanham, Billy G.
Lanham, Robert F.
Lanier, Roland V.
Lanno, Frank Sr.
Lanspery, Michael J.
Lantaigne, Robert A.
Lantz, Ira L.
Lantz, Kenneth H. Jr.
Lapham, Harold A.
Lapham, Ralph R.
Lapierre, Lorenzo
Lapinta, Joseph A.
Lapointe, Rodney E.
Laporta, Philip
Lappala, Ernest
Lappe, Charles A. Jr.
Laquatra, Michael Jr.
Lareau, Raymond L.
Larkin, Ernest W.
Larkin, William R.
Larner, James R.
LaRocca, Salvatore
Larosa, Joseph S.
LaRose, Leroy R.
Larrisey, Raymond J.
Larsen, Leland M.
Larson, Gene
Larson, Harlan S.
Larson, Lawrence A.
Larson, Luther T.
Larson, Neal E.
Larson, Orel
LaRue, John W. Jr.
Larue, Allen
Larue, Robert
LaSata, Charles J.
Lasek, John F.
Lash, Melvin E.
Lasher, Harry
Lasher, Robert E.
Lashmet, Franklin
Lashuay, Gerald
Laskey, Floyd J.
Lasky, Ralph
Lasseter, Thomas M.
Last, Arthur F.
Latham, James F.
Latham, William F.
Latorraca, Nivo D.
Lattanzio, Dominick J.
Latterell, Bernard A.
Lattimer, John H. Rev.
Latus, George
Lauer, E.H.
Lauer, Herbert E.
Lauffer, Dale E.
Launi, Joseph
Lauritano, Eugene J.
Lautz, Harry J.
Lauzon, Joseph B.
Laval, Robert W.
LaValley, Theodore J.
Laverdiere, Gaston L.
Lavigne, Joseph F.
Lavin, George H.
Lavine, Bill
Lavine, Bill
LaVoie, Thomas
Lavoie, Albert J.
Lawicki, Melvin E.
Lawler, Frank A.
Lawless, Ralph
Lawrence, Charles R. Jr.
Lawrence, James B.
Lawrence, Richard C.
Lawrence, Richard T.
Lawson, Bud W.H.
Lawson, Frank E.
Lawson, George T. Jr.
Lawson, Quinton Y.
Laxton, Thomas C.
Lay, Douglas H.
Layman, George E.
Lazar, Stavis P.
Lea, Warren Y.
Leach, Douglas E.
Leach, Fernley P. Sr.
Leach, Howard M.
Leach, Jimmie W.
Leach, Russell
Leach, U.H.
Leady, Charles E.
Leal, Ben
Lear, Robert G.
Leathers, Eugene L.
Leatherwood, G.T.
Leavitt, Lester C.
Leavitt, Luther C.
Leazer, George L.
Lebeau, Ernest W.
Leber, William S.
Lebert, Gordon
LeBioda, Edward A.
Leboutillier, Philip Jr.
Leclair, Louis G.
Ledbetter, Homer C.
Ledonne, Alfred R.
Lee, Coleman W.
Lee, Donald R.
Lee, Ernest F.
Lee, Gerald E.
Lee, James F.
Lee, John D.
Lee, John S.
Lee, Paul J.
Lee, Raymond E.
Lee, Robert E. Jr.
Lee, Warren
Lee, William C.
Lee, William T.
Leeper, Chauncey L.
Leeper, Ronald E.
Lees, Jim
Lefever, Charles F.
Lefever, Vaughn R.
Lefevre, O.C.
Lefeyre, Rene F.
Leffler, Thomas L.
Lefker, Raymond P.
Lefort, Lawrence
Legault, Eugene P.
Legum, Edgar
Lehan, Joseph F.
Lehardy, Clement D.
Lehman, John F. Jr.
Lehmann, Gerald E.
Lehner, Gerard M.
Leigh, Byron R. IV
Leigh, Byron R. IV
Lein, S.
Leinbach, Elwood J.
Leippe, Harry M.
Leitl, L.J.
Leitl, L.J.
Lelito, Walter J.
LeMaster, Floyd A.
Lemasters, Kenneth C.
Lemieux, Maurice
Lemihan, John J.
Lemke, Karl H.
Lemker, Elmer H.
Lemm, John C.
Lemon, Edward
Lemongello, Gerard J.
Lemstrom, Donald A.
Leneave, Vance
Lennick, Leo
Lennox, Daniel H.
Lenox, Joseph P. Jr.
Lentner, Arthur
Lents, Paul B.
Lentz, Elmer Jr.
Lentz, Milton
Lentz, Noel V.
Lenz, John E.
Lenz, William H.
Leonard, Arthur H.
Leonard, Raymond A.
Leone, John R.
Leonhardi, Willis A.
Leonhardt, Alfred J.
Lepore, Gerardo J.
Lepore, Rev. Daniel
Lera, Paul
Lermack, Howard
Lerner, Richard J.
Lesko, Steve
Leslie, Carl B.
Leslie, Gordon S. Jr.
Lesnett, Samuel A. Jr.
Lesniak, Edward L.
Lesnikowski, Donald H.
Lessard, Richard A.
Lessner, John H.
Lester, Brooks
Lester, Clifford W.
Letterman, Joseph E.
Levaas, John B.
Levan, Robert L.
Levasseur, Ivan G.
Levine, Bernard
Levine, Lester A.
Levine, Robert E.
Levitzki, Francis J.
Levy, Harold
Levy, Howard E.
Levy, Morris E. Sr.
Levy, Samuel Earl
Levy, Simon
Lewczyk, John J.
Lewis, Allen E.
Lewis, Charles H.
Lewis, Donald E.
Lewis, Fred C.
Lewis, Homer H. Jr.
Lewis, James C.
Lewis, James E.
Lewis, Joe E.
Lewis, John L.
Lewis, Robert E.
Lewis, Roger
Lewis, Russell
Lewis, Sam
Lewis, T.M.
Lex, Frank
Libb, Edward
Libby, James O.
Libecki, Arthur
Liberto, Joseph V.
Liberto, Oliver R.
Libman, Arthur
Lichty, Girard E.
Liddell, Kenneth W.
Lieb, Mathias J.
Lieberman, Burton L.
Liepper, Alex
Lightfoot, Paul E.
Lightowler, Frank E.
Liguori, Robert J.
Liljeblad, George I.
Lilljander, M.S.
Lilly, Frederick R.
Linane, Richard J.
Lincicome, Calvin L.
Lincoln, Edward J. Jr.
Linde, Arthur T.
Lindley, David D.
Lindquist, Robert
Lindquist, Roy N.
Lindsley, J.E.
Lindstrom, Buzz
Lindstrom, Evert
Linkus, Bonaventure
Linn, Daniel W.
Linn, Oscar M.
Linneman, Jack R.
Linton, Paul W.
Linville, Edwin W.
Lippert, Ernest
Lippiello, Constantino
Lippincott, William
Lischwe, Herbert J.
Lisica, Charles E.
Lisle, Robert W.
Listerud, M.B.
Litinger, Martin
Little, Clinton B.
Little, Norman D.
Little, William M.
Littmann, Jack H.
Livernois, Rochel L.
Livesay, John O.
Livezey, William T.
Livingston, Charles A.
Livingston, Marshall D.
Livingston, Robert D.
Liwosz, Jerome J.
Lizotte, Edward H.
Lloyd, Bill
Lloyd, Charles A.
Lloyd, Edward J.
Lloyd, Ellwood J.
Lloyd, Karl A.
Lloyd, Richard H.
Lloyd, Walter
Lloyd, William E.
Loats, William L.
Lochrie, Roy
Lochtefeld, Elmo
Lockard, Orlyn
Lockhart, James E.
Lockwood, Robert G.
Lodge, Winthrop D.
Loeper, Bernard J.
Loerzel, Willard G.
Loewith, Marvin S.
Lofgren, Robert E.
Lofton, Jack
Logan, Donald A.
Logan, Fred J.
Logan, Odus T.
Logue, Carroll R. Sr.
Lohr, Earl E.
Lohr, Raymond E.
Lohr, Robert A.
Lohr, Robert F.
Loiselle, Paul A.
Lollar, Herbert S.
Lollar, James D.
Lombardi, Daniel P.
Lombardi, Joseph A.
Lombardo, Frank T.
Lombardo, James S.
Lombardo, Salvatore
Lonas, Ralph S.
Londy, Harold Wm.
Long, Edward
Long, Edward L.
Long, George
Long, James A.
Long, John W.
Long, Lester M.
Long, Marvin K.
Long, Neil D.
Long, Otis
Long, Percy J.
Long, R.B. Jr.
Long, Richard M.
Long, Robert B.
Long, Robert L.
Long, Robert R.
Long, Wilbur A.
Long, William C.
Long, William R.
Longello, Peter S.
Longi, Joseph A.
Longley, John H.
Longnecker, Benjamin F.
Longo, I.J.
Longstreet, Albert M.
Longuillo, Alphonse
Lontz, Edward J.
Look, Robert G.
Lopez, Robert G.
Lord, Truman B.
Lorenson, Charles Sr.
Lorentson, Adrian V.
Lorenz, Donnell L.
Losievsky, Stefan
Loss, Adolf A.
Loss, Esther
Loss, Vincent
Lott, James S. Jr.
Lotz, William
Loughrey, Ernest J.
Louthian, Landon Jr.
Loutrel, Louis F. Jr.
Love, Henry J. Jr.
Love, Hugh E.
Lovegren, H. Eugene
Lovell, Justin J.
Lovell, William R.
Lovenberg, Richard Lee
Loveridge, G.W.
Lovin, Dayton R.
Lowe, Charles W.
Lowe, James A.
Lowe, Joseph W.
Lowe, Robert L.
Lowe, Robert S.
Lowenthal, Murray
Lower, Herman D.
Lowman, Charles L.
Lowman, Joseph L.
Lowman, Tom F.
Lown, Raymond C.
Lowry, William M.
Loy, Fredrick
Loy, Jack L.
Lubas, Edwin J.
Lubeck, Charles F.
Lubick, Clarence
Lubinsky, Francis
Lucas, Fred
Lucas, James C.
Lucas, Jay Paul
Lucca, Francis S.
Lucci, Armando
Lucci, Pasquale
Luce, Philip T.
Lucie, Alfred L.
Luckey, Joe Jr.
Ludwig, Andrew C.
Ludwig, Myles G.
Ludwig, Russell L.
Ludyga, Raymond J.
Lueck, Francis J.
Luedecke, John F.
Luerssen, Eugene
Luesbrink, Leonard R.
Lugo, Manuel B.
Luiz, Gilbert
Lukacs, Norbert
Lukens, H. Bradford
Lukosius, Zenon B.
Lumpkin, Joseph A.
Lund, James R.
Lundbeck, Paul J.

Lundeberg, Philip K.
Lundy, Lee T.
Lunsford, Ralph M.
Lunt, Les
Luoma, Marvin J.
Lupica, Cosmo M.
Luptak, Andrew
Lusk, Charles T.
Lusk, Hugh F.
Lusk, Robert R.
Lutes, Edward W.
Luthman, Nels W. Sr.
Luthy, C.L.
Luttrell, Willie G.
Lutz, John W.
Lutz, Noah C. Jr.
Luzius, Donald H.
Lyberg, Andy
Lyberg, Andy
Lyche, Bill
Lydecker, Richard A.
Lydon, Joseph P.
Lynch, George A.
Lynch, Jim
Lynch, Jim
Lynch, John J.
Lynch, Robert L.
Lynch, Walter F.
Lynch, William A.
Lynk, Gerald
Lynn, Martin R.
Lynskey, Joseph T. Jr.
Lyons, Francis E.
Lyons, Kenneth L.
Lyons, Lynn F.
Lyons, Richard J.
Lyons, William S.
Lyons, William W.
Lytle, Thomas V.

- M -

Mabray, Robert B.
Macaulay, Robert E.
MacBlane, John V.
Maccarey, John C.
Macchia, Donald
Maccubbin, Harry E.
MacDonald, Archie F.
MacDonald, George A.
Macdonald, Bruce A.
Macdonald, H.T.
Macdonald, James L.
Macdonald, Richard J.
Macdonald, Robert B.
Macdonald, Walter S.
Macdougall, Robert D.
MacFarland, William F.
MacGibbon, John E.
Mach, Bernard
Macholz, Edward S.
Machovina, Edward
Machulsky, William
Maciag, Theodore S.
Maciag, Theodore S.
Macintosh, Hiram P.
Mack, John W.
Mack, Laurence E.
Mack, Mearl
Mack, Newton C.
MacKenzie, Carroll A.
Mackenzie, William
Mackey, C.R.
Mackey, David L.
Macko, John
Maclean, Malcolm
Macmillan, Jack W.
Madden, Robert
Madden, William P.
Maddox, Homer E.
Maddux, Donald E.
Madill, Franklin R.
Madison, James P.
Madison, John E.
Madison, Richard J.
Madsen, Robert W.
Magee, Capt. W.
Magee, John C.
Magee, LeRoy
Magee, William
Magera, George E.
Maggio, Frank G.
Maggio, M.G.
Maginnis, James B.
Maglione, Dominic J.
Magnusson, John S.
Magoffin, Frank J.
Maguire, Paul
Maguire, Paul
Mahaffey, Ernest J.
Mahan, Donald F.
Maher, James P.
Mahler, Al
Mahlman, Kermett
Mahon, Thomas J.
Mahoney, George W.
Mahoney, Joseph M.
Maier, Paul E.
Maier, Raymond
Maikner, Emil J.
Mailloux, Leonard
Maimone, Albert M.
Maimone, Anthony P.
Main, Francis E.
Mainock, Richard
Maio, Tony
Maiorana, Philip
Major, Donald J.
Maki, Edward A.
Maki, John M.
Makin, Herbert C.
Malat, Michael M. Sr.
Malchiodi, Tony
Malcolm, John
Malec, Paul F.
Malen, Eli
Malinchok, William
Malinowski, Theodore A.
Maliwick, Walter
Mallers, William C.
Mallett, Elmer K.
Mallin, Anthony
Mallon, Stephen J.
Mallon, William E. Sr.
Malloy, William E.
Malone, Glenn
Malone, Jack R.
Malone, Odell
Maloney, Denis F.
Maloney, John F.
Maloney, John J.
Maloney, John J.
Maloney, Thomas P.
Mals, Chester S.
MaMahan, William
MaMahon, Thomas G.
Mamoliti, Jasper J.
Manack, Phil
Manchak, Eugene
Mancinelli, Bruno
Mancini, James
Mancuso, Paul
Mancuso, Raymond L.
Mandrackie, Andrew J.
Manduke, Arthur R.
Manes, Jesse D.
Maneskjold, Erik O.
Manganello, Felix C.
Manghan, Joseph L.
Mangiacapra, Joseph
Mangrum, Thomas F.
Manire, James M.
Mankin, Harold A.
Mann, Anderson R.
Mann, Pat
Mann, William
Mannarelli, Joseph
Mannel, Kenneth O.
Manni, Luigi V.
Manniello, Saverio
Manning, Charles E.
Manning, D.C.
Manning, George W.
Manning, William T.
Mannon, Robert
Manseau, Raymond M.
Mansell, C.B.
Mansfield, Martin A.
Mansfield, William B.
Mantella, Biaggio
Mantis, Theodore
Manzetti, George
Mapes, Ernest Dale
Marazo, Angelo
Marble, Warren E.
Marcewicz, Stanley J.
Marchese, Anthony S.
Marchino, Carolynn
Marcone, Louis
Marcotte, Gerard L.
Marcus, Carl
Marczyk, Joseph S. Jr.
Marek, J.F. Jr.
Marek, Joseph D.
Marek, Stanley J.
Mari, Robert
Marian, Charles
Mariano, Anthony J.
Marie, Eugene N.
Marinaro, Anthony S.
Marinello, Ralph
Marinez, Vincent
Marini, Ettore J.
Marino, Anthony
Marion, Norman E.
Markham, Charles R.
Markowitz, Mae
Markowski, Clarence R.
Marks, Archie P.
Marks, Donald L.
Marks, John A.
Marks, Joseph A.
Marks, Richard H.
Markward, Gerald A.
Marler, Kenneth J.
Marochi, John G.
Maroney, James E. Jr.
Maroukis, Manuel J.
Marquardt, Robert
Marr, William R.
Marriner, Arnold V.
Marrocco, Louis
Marrow, Ned J.
Marschlowitz, Walter H.
Marsh, Edward D.
Marsh, Gary A.
Marsh, William E.
Marshall, Bruce R.
Marshall, Elmer D.
Marshall, Homer Jr.
Marshall, Robert T.
Marshall, Rolland E.
Marshall, William S.
Marsilii, Joe
Marsland, James Jr.
Martel, George E.
Martens, Warren G.
Marth, George J.
Martin, Antero J.
Martin, Calvin D.
Martin, Clarence
Martin, David O.
Martin, Dell L. Jr.
Martin, Donald W.
Martin, Douglas D.
Martin, Frederick E.
Martin, Gene
Martin, Harlen J.
Martin, Homer M.
Martin, Howard B.
Martin, Jack A.
Martin, James R.
Martin, John P.
Martin, John W.
Martin, Joseph R.
Martin, Ken
Martin, Maynard S.
Martin, Paul J.
Martin, Robert D.
Martin, Stokley
Martin, Thomas M.
Martin, Willard G.
Martin, William C.
Martin, William F.
Martin, William F.
Martin, William L.
Martina, Nicholas A.
Martines, Nicholas J.
Martinez, Frank
Marttila, William
Martucci, Vito W.
Martz, Bill D.
Martz, Carl B.
Marusiak, Henry C.
Marvel, Charles C.
Marvin, George
Marx, William
Mascaro, John J.
Mascaro, William T.
Masek, Marjorie Hayter
Maser, George R.
Masiello, Frank
Masker, Raymond E. Sr.
Maslanka, Stephen
Maslen, William O.
Mason, Charles M.
Mason, Peter
Mason, Raymond H.
Massagli, Pete
Massette, Sam L.
Masson, Alfred N.
Massoni, John
Mastandrea, Peter J.
Masten, John
Masters, Reynold
Mastro, Michael J.
Mastrovaselis, John G.
Mather, Carl D.
Mather, Dan
Mathews, Arthur Earl
Mathews, C. Allan
Mathews, Charlie Joe
Mathews, Charlie Joe
Mathews, Clyde E.
Mathews, Joseph P.
Mathews, Ronald P.
Mathias, Donald E.
Mathias, Elbert C.
Mathias, James C.
Mathieu, Kenneth A.
Mathis, Howard D.
Mathis, Leroy T.
Mathisen, Chris
Matt, John A. Sr.
Matthews, Budd C.
Matthews, Cannon W.
Matthews, David J. Jr.
Matthews, George H.
Matthews, Ira J.
Matthews, J.W. Jr.
Matthews, James D.
Matthews, W.G. Jr.
Mattie, Steve P.
Mattison, Roy
Mattmueller, Fred C.
Mattox, Emmett
Mattox, Roy E.
Matuck, George T.
Matwichuk, Walter H.
Matys, William E. Jr.
Maude, James W.
Mauger, Kenneth P.
Mauldin, James E.
Mauldin, Richard C.
Mauney, C.B.
Mauney, Hugh P.
Maupin, Harold J.
Maupin, Wade E.
Maurer, Ben L.
Maurer, Harold L. Sr.
Maurer, Louis N.
Maurizio, Michael J.
Mauro, Alexander
Mauro, Domenic
Mawer, Howard B.
Mawn, Gerald S.
Maxey, Cecil H.
Maxwell, A.L.
Maxwell, Bernard J.
Maxwell, Edward A.
Maxwell, Harry E.
Maxwell, John H. III
Maxwell, Kenneth R.
Maxwell, Richard
Maxwell, Robert W.
Maxwell, Walter U.
Maxwell, William H.
May, Claude T.
May, Claude T.
May, Daniel H.
May, James R.
May, John J.
May, Robert H.
May, Victor Keith
Maychek, William G.
Mayer, Clarence
Mayer, Earl J.
Mayer, Robert A.
Mayes, Frank W.
Maynard, Donald
Maynard, Judson E.
Mayne, Harold R.
Mayne, Wiley E.
Mayo, Donald W.
Mays, Alva J. Jr.
Maze, Richard R.
Maziarka, Edward M.
Maziarz, Joseph J.
Mazmanian, George
Mazzari, Richard F.
Mazzola, Adam F.
McAdam, Allan T.
Mcadams, S.C. Jr.
Mcaleer, William R.
McAloney, Gilbert
McAnn, Ethel
Mcauley, Fred M.
Mcbrayer, Jack D.
McBride, Frank J.
Mcbride, Gregg
Mcbride, John
Mcbride, Thomas M.
Mcbride, William H.
McCabe, Frank M.
McCabe, John G.
McCabe, John R.
McCabe, Lee
Mccabe, Donald C.
McCadden, Robert D.
Mccafferty, Edward R.
McCall, Robert F.
McCall, William F.
Mccall, Roy C. Jr.
Mccallen, Robert R.
Mccallum, Hubert A. Jr.
McCammon, Allen L.
Mccandless, Addison S.
McCanless, A.W.
McCann, Daniel H.
McCann, Raymond R.
Mccann, David
Mccarley, William W.
Mccarter, Grady
McCarthy, Jerry
Mccarthy, Charles Jr.
Mccarthy, George D.
Mccarthy, John R.
Mccarthy, William L.
Mccartney, Lawrence J.
McCarty, Earl Lester
McCarver, Clinton W.
McCauley, Donald F.
Mccauley, Robert L.
McCaulley, Jules P.
Mcclafferty, Bernard
Mcclaid, Sherman D. Jr.
Mcclain, Kirby L. III
Mcclain, W.A.
McClellan, Charles J.
McClellan, Thomas L.
Mcclintock, H.W.
Mcclintock, Walt
Mccloskey, Cordes W.
Mccloud, Billie E.
McClung, John N.
Mcclure, Bob R.
Mcclure, Douglas A.
Mcclure, George W. Sr.
Mcclure, Warren C.
McCombs, Dale E.
McCombs, Ivan W.
Mcconkey, James R.
McConnell, William N.
McCool, Fred R.
McCormick, Vincent J.
Mccormick, Horace R.
McCown, James
McCoy, Robert A.
McCra, Joseph
McCrabb, Harold J.
McCracken, James A.
Mccreadie, Charles H.
McCroskey, William T.
McCrudden, Andrew J.
Mccullar, George L.
Mccullough, Edward J.
Mccullough, James M.
Mccullough, John E.
Mccullough, Robert L.
Mccullough, Robert W.
McCully, Richard
Mccune, B.F.
Mccurdy, Ralph D.
McDade, Thomas M.
Mcdaid, Ray
Mcdaniels, Paul E.
McDermott, Fred J.
Mcdermott, Edward J.
Mcdevitt, Edward J.
McDonald, James P.
McDonald, Louis D.
Mcdonald, Alfred F.
Mcdonald, Allan D.
Mcdonald, Buford A.
Mcdonald, Chalres J.
Mcdonald, Jack
Mcdonald, Lloyd J.
Mcdonald, Robert E.
Mcdonald, Robert E.
McDonnell, Charles R.
Mcdonnell, H.
McDonough, Michael G.
Mcdonough, Robert E.
Mcdonough, William C.
Mcdonough, William J.
McDowell, Raymond R.
McDuffie, Jesse T.
McElrath, Edward L.
Mcentire, Thomas
McFadden, Robert R.
Mcfarland, Charles H.
Mcfarlane, Walter D.
Mcgarr, Frank J.
Mcgarr, Robert E.
McGarvey, Robert G.
Mcgarvey, Roy
McGavghey, Guy E. Jr.
Mcgee, Howard W.
Mcgee, Joe C.
McGhee, Donald L.
McGhee, Kenneth B.
Mcgill, Edwin E.
McGimpsey, Frank J.
McGinn, O.C.
McGinn, O.C.
McGinnis, Henry N.
McGinnis, Paul H.
McGirt, Burnell S.
Mcgivern, Kenneth A.
Mcglashan, Peter R.
Mcglothin, Elmer R.
Mcglothlin, Ellie A.
Mcgoff, George P.
Mcgonigle, Joseph G.
Mcgough, Leo I.
McGovern, William J.
Mcgovern, John H.
Mcgovern, Patrick
McGowan, Thomas C.
McGrath, Edward T.
McGrath, John R.
McGrath, Robert L.
Mcgrath, Ralph N.
McGraw, Donald C. Jr.
McGraw, Richard J.
Mcgraw, Edward J.
McGuire, Kenneth J.
Mcguire, William C.
Mchail, Rex R.
Mchale, Eugene A.
Mchale, George
Mchenry, Donald E.
McHugh, John T.
Mchugh, Donald H.
Mchugh, George J.
McIlvaine, Joseph F.
Mcilvaine, Robinson
McIntosh, Theresa
McIntosh, Vincent J.
Mcintosh, James A.
McIntyre, Thomas F.
Mcintyre, Donald
Mcintyre, Ralph J.
McKay, Donald R.
McKay, Edward R.
Mckean, Gordon C.
McKenna, Thomas E.
McKenna, William G.
Mckenna, Kenneth
Mckenzie, Joseph A.
Mckenzie, Paul M.
McKeown, Kevin
McKernan, Francis J.
McKibben, Milton S.
Mckillip, Alvin A.
Mckinlay, Doanld Jr.
McKinney, A.J.
McKinney, Benjamin J.
Mckinney, Donald R.
Mckinney, Harry D.
Mckinney, William
McKnight, Joe
McKnight, John M.
Mcknight, David P.
Mckosky, Clarence
McLain, Arnold Lee
Mclain, W.J.
McLaney, Harry W. Jr.
McLaughlin, Gilbert H.
Mclaughlin, Charles
Mclaughlin, Harry R.
Mclaughlin, Robert V.
Mclaughlin, Robert W.
Mclawhorn, Charles W.
McLellan, John
McLeod, Frederick E.
McLeod, Robert W.
Mclernon, James
McLinden, Peter J.
Mcloughlin, Thomas J.
McMahon, Aaron
McMahon, Bernard P.
McMahon, Robert L.
Mcmanamy, John V.
Mcmanmon, James P.
McManus, Bernard J.
Mcmanus, George F.
Mcmaster, Wayne
McMullen, Donald P.
McMurtry, Jack W.
McNally, Tom
McNamara, Edward T.
Mcnamara, Arthur D.
Mcnamara, James F.
McNamee, Thomas X.
McNary, Charles E.
McNeal, Pernell
McNeely, Bill
Mcneill, Alex C.
Mcnelly, Don
Mcnulty, Eugene P.
Mcnulty, Patrick F.
Mcnulty, Willard J.
McPhail, David
Mcpherson, George A.
Mcphillips, James F.
Mcphillips, John W.
McRae, Charles M.
McRae, Kenneth L.
McReynolds, Robert B.
McRorie, Johnson W.
Mcsherry, Francis X.
Mcsloy, John J.
Mcspadden, Henry
Mcsweeney, Brian
McTaggart, Loren M.
McTiernan, James A.
Mcwhorter, John H.
Mcwhorter, Kenneth D.
Mead, Lawrence D.
Mead, Richard
Meador, Aubrey R. Jr.
Meador, William L.
Meagher, James F. III
Mealey, Dana L.
Meals, Fred W.
Meals, Robert
Means, Richard G.
Mears, Verl E.
Mears, William G.
Meddings, Walter Sr.
Medford, Cecil G.
Medina, Mario
Medlock, Ronald N.
Meehan, Philip F.
Meehan, Samuel
Meeker, Jack A.
Meekins, John E.
Meese, Arthur F.
Megyesi, Charles B.
Mehling, William A.
Mehringer, Jerry
Meier, Joseph B.
Meier, Ralph F.
Mekarski, Stephen A.
Mekeel, Lewis F.
Melby, Arthur
Meleta, Mike
Melillo, Consantino
Meliski, Joseph J.
Mellinger, Rush M.
Mello, Augustine L.
Mello, Edward
Mellott, Harry E.
Meloan, Wade
Melton, Harry
Melton, Harry
Melton, Herman L.
Melton, Herman L.
Melton, Roland W.
Melton, Vivian J.
Melusky, Thomas A.
Menchella, John A.
Menees, Ben W.
Menees, Ben W.
Menicos, Donald
Menius, Charles L.
Mensen, Raphael A.
Mentgen, George J.
Meny, Clifford J.
Meoni, Andrew J. Jr.
Mercer, Richard E.
Mercereau, Donald M.
Meredith, Victor W.
Mericle, Donald
Mermingis, Charles
Merrill, Norman N.
Merrill, Philip A.
Merring, Robert H.
Merritts, Kenneth S.
Merryman, Sam B. Jr.
Mertes, William M.
Mertz, Claude O. Jr.
Mertz, James M.
Mesarcik, Anton L.
Mesaros, Frank
Mesiano, Dominic
Mesick, Ralph L.
Mespell, Howard
Messere, Austin
Messick, William F.
Messinger, Irving M.
Metz, Howard L.
Metz, William B.
Meyer, August L.
Meyer, C.E.
Meyer, Gerhardt E.
Meyer, Glenn W.
Meyer, Johnny W.
Meyer, Lester F.
Meyer, Paul W.
Meyer, Raymond G.
Meyer, Robert
Meyer, Thomas J.
Meyer, Walter F.
Meyers, Arthur T. Jr.
Meyers, Arthur T. Sr.
Meyers, Bobby
Meyers, Boby
Meyers, Frank A.
Meyers, Harold T.
Mical, F.W.
Micciulla, Virgilio G.
Michaelis, Edwin
Michaelis, Mervyn G. Jr.
Michaels, Andrew J.
Michaelson, Carl W.
Michaelson, Earl J.
Michalski, Edward H.
Michel, Moe
Michels, Herbert E.
Mick, George
Micklish, Willard R.
Middlebrook, William T.
Middlebrooks, Charles E.
Middlebrooks, Evann
Middleton, Ned
Mierkowski, Clarence
Mietz, Donald T.
Might, Paul E.
Migliorino, Frank A.
Mikels, Jack W.
Mikelsen, Arthur
Mikos, Stanley A.
Mikosz, John
Miladin, Steve W.
Milam, Thomas S.
Milardo, Joseph E. Sr.
Milcic, Richard H.
Miles, Dean J.
Miles, L.M.
Miles, Paul J.
Miles, Raymond L.
Miles, William A.
Milewski, John J.
Milewski, John J.
Miley, Thomas W.
Milhoan, Melvin L.
Militello, Peter
Millar, David M.
Millat, Henry E.
Miller, Albert J. Jr.
Miller, Bob G.
Miller, Charles E.
Miller, Charles Wm.
Miller, Donald E.
Miller, Donald E.
Miller, Earl J.
Miller, Edmund M. Jr.
Miller, Edward A.
Miller, Elizabeth K.
Miller, Emory P.
Miller, Eugene H.
Miller, George A.
Miller, George A. Sr.
Miller, George E.
Miller, Gerald B. .
Miller, Gerard
Miller, Harry J.
Miller, Herbert W.
Miller, Jack R.
Miller, James M.
Miller, John F. Jr.
Miller, Joseph S.
Miller, King K.
Miller, Larry A.
Miller, Leo G. Sr.
Miller, Leon
Miller, Marcus J.
Miller, Maurice G.
Miller, Max R.
Miller, Paul L.
Miller, Paul R.
Miller, Ralph Wayne
Miller, Randell L.
Miller, Randy
Miller, Raymond J.
Miller, Richard K.
Miller, Richard P.
Miller, Robert C.
Miller, Robert D.
Miller, Robert D.
Miller, Robert E.
Miller, Robert G.
Miller, Robert L.
Miller, Robert M.
Miller, Robert T.
Miller, Robert W.
Miller, Robert W.
Miller, Russell S.
Miller, Thomas A. Jr.
Miller, Thomas B.
Miller, Thomas J.
Miller, Tilman C.
Miller, Vernon J.
Miller, William H.
Miller, Wisdom W.
Millman, Paul L.
Mills, Edwin S.
Mills, Robert A.
Mills, Robert E.
Mills, William F.
Millward, Joe L.
Milner, Delbert R.
Milner, Donald G. Sr.
Milota, Roy F.
Milstead, Jimmie S.
Milstead, John F.
Miner, Frank E. Jr.
Minerd, Robert E.
Mingus, Joel A.
Minich, Joseph C.
Minich, Joseph C.
Minichino, Benedetto
Mink, Robert J.
Minnery, Robert T.
Minutello, Richard A.
Minuti, Frank A.
Miracle, Herb
Mirek, Emil J.
Mirolli, Arthur D.
Misal, Charles A.
Miscioscia, Richard
Miskill, Thomas G.
Misko, Walter J.
Mismas, Joseph A.
Mistrette, James A.
Mitas, Leonard E.
Mitchell, Chalon S.
Mitchell, Dewey T.
Mitchell, Donald R.
Mitchell, James R.
Mitchell, John J.
Mitchell, John M.
Mitchell, Lawrence O.
Mitchell, Linden R.
Mitchell, Nick W. Sr.
Mitchell, R.B.
Mitchell, Robert E.
Mitchell, Robert E.
Mitchell, Robert F.
Mitchell, Robert S.
Mixon, Claude L. Jr.
Mizell, Charles
Mizell, Joe P.
Mocan, John P.
Moe, H.L.
Moe, Ralph S. Jr.
Moehrle, James A.
Moenius, Charles J. Jr.
Moffett, Glenn C.
Moffett, Tommy H.
Mogen, William G.
Mogiulski, William J.
Mohn, Arthur I.
Mohn, George B.
Mohr, Armin F.
Mohr, Henry J.
Molinari, John
Molino, John J.
Molkup, Joseph J.
Mollica, Isadore
Mollohan, Perry
Molnar, Daniel F.
Molnar, Peter
Molnar, Steve
Molstad, Donald S.
Molten, Robert H.
Molyneaux, Dawson E.
Molyneaux, Dawson E.
Monack, Raymond F.
Monaco, Peter J.
Monaghan, Vincent J.
Monahan, Albert E.
Monahan, John J.
Monahan, William C.
Monce, Raymond E.
Mondor, Bernard G.
Mondy, Harvey G.
Mongillo, Joseph
Monichetti, John H.
Monk, Robert A.
Monopoli, Salvatore
Monroe, Henry
Monsky, Stanley J.
Montagne, Earl B.
Montagne, Monty E.
Montague, Robert D.
Montague, Robert W.
Montaldi, Serafino
Montaquila, Peter A.
Monteith, Arnold L.
Montes, Eddiw
Montgomery, Arthur P.
Montgomery, Everett, G.
Montgomery, George E.
Montgomery, James F.
Montgomery, James S.
Montgomery, John L.
Montgomery, Joseph
Montgomery, W.W.
Montgomery, William T.
Monusky, George J.
Moody, Russell
Moody, William D.
Moon, Frank F. Jr.
Mooney, John
Mooney, John
Moorad, Alex
Moorcroft, John W.
Moore, Alvah J.
Moore, Charles E. Jr.

Moore, Claude H.
Moore, E.T.
Moore, Harry F.
Moore, Harry R.
Moore, Harry V.
Moore, James A.
Moore, James E. Jr.
Moore, James H.
Moore, Jessie W.
Moore, John C.
Moore, Joseph S.
Moore, Lewis
Moore, Moe
Moore, Otis S.
Moore, Sidney R.
Moore, T.P.
Moore, Thomas Cee
Moore, W.J.
Moore, Walter M.
Moore, Wellford H.
Moore, William H.
Moorman, Otto J.
Moosegian, William
Morck, Sophus J.
Morea, Frank
Moreau, Ivy P. Jr.
Morehouse, John C.
Morelle, Pierre J.
Moreno, Robert
Morenzi, Americo F.
Morgan, Arthur
Morgan, Berrey O.
Morgan, Edward B.
Morgan, Francis S.
Morgan, Herbert F.
Morgan, Irvin C.
Morgan, Jack E.
Morgan, Jack M.
Morgan, John C.
Morgan, John H.
Morgan, John J.
Morgan, Joseph
Morgan, Paul E.
Morgan, Russell B.
Morgan, William C.
Morgan, William J.
Morgan, William M.
Morin, Joseph C.
Morio, George A.
Morley, Robert C.
Morlock, Ray
Moros, William H.
Morrill, Linwood E.
Morris, Albert F.
Morris, Clyde E.
Morris, John E.
Morris, Joseph W.
Morris, Llewellyn
Morris, Robert A.
Morris, Walter G.
Morris, William H.
Morrison, Donald R.
Morrison, Edward R.
Morrison, James R.
Morrison, Lejeune
Morrison, Robert A.
Morrison, Vincent R.
Morrissey, Donald M.
Morrow, Sidney R.
Morse, Allan D.
Mort, Robert L.
Mortensen, Lars S.
Mortenson, Stanley
Morton, Edward
Moscarello, Michael S.
Moscato, Charles J.
Moscinski, Edwin J.
Mosconi, James A.
Moseley, Al
Mosessian, Kosta
Mosley, William R.
Moss, Billie Lee
Moss, Carl L.
Moszkowicz, Isidore
Motsinger, Edward A.
Mottram, Leo A. Sr.
Motz, James A.
Mouer, Philip L.
Moul, Ron
Mouledous, Alex P.
Moulton, Harold A.
Mountford, Russell F.
Mounts, Carl W.
Moust, Bernard S.
Mover, Eliot S.
Moxley, Ralph P.
Moyer, Thomas F.
Moyer, Thomas F.
Moylan, J. Dudley
Moynihan, Daniel J.
Moynihan, John V.
Mrazek, Bob Cong.
Mrohaly, Clayton J.
Mucci, Pasquale A.
Mucha, Edward
Mucha, Eugene H. Sr.
Mudge, George R.
Mueller, Armin E.
Mueller, Charles F.
Mueller, Ferd F.
Mueller, Myron
Mueller, Wayne A.
Muench, Joseph
Muennink, Kyle E.
Muffly, Robert E.

Mulcahy, Thomas L.
Mulcare, James J.
Mulderig, John
Muldoon, Paul J.
Muldrew, William H. Jr.
Mulholland, William B.
Mullady, Robert S.
Mullahy, Jack
Mullen, Graham P.
Mullen, Ross
Mullen, Warren
Muller, Earl E.
Muller, Richard G.
Mullett, Ralph
Mulligan, Thomas Jr.
Mulligan, William J.
Mullin, John C.
Mullings, Marshall E.
Mullins, Francis L.
Mulqueeney, John M.
Mulready, John J.
Mulrey, John J.
Mulski, John H.
Mulvaney, Joseph S.
Mulvey, Bernard J.
Mulvey, Robert J.
Mundis, Elwood L.
Mundzak, Edward F.
Mungall, Andrew W.
Munger, John F.
Muni, William B.
Munley, Paul F.
Munley, Thomas J.
Munn, Joe C.
Munroe, James S.
Munzer, R.J.
Mura, Robert J.
Murchie, Richard T.
Murdoch, Don
Murnan, David J.
Murphey, Wesley T.
Murphey, Wesley T.
Murphree, James O.
Murphree, Louie A.
Murphy, Arthur P.
Murphy, Charles A.
Murphy, Donald E.
Murphy, Gil
Murphy, Glenn E.
Murphy, Henry D.
Murphy, Ivy Joe
Murphy, James J.
Murphy, James J.
Murphy, John F.
Murphy, John J.
Murphy, Joseph M.
Murphy, Robert R.
Murphy, Ross G.
Murphy, Thomas D. Jr.
Murphy, Thomas P.
Murphy, William J.
Murray, Donald L.
Murray, John P.
Murray, Michael
Murray, Michael D.
Murray, O.A.
Murray, Thomas
Murray, Thomas
Murray, Thomas F. Jr.
Murray, William H.
Murtaugh, T.P.
Murtha, James J.
Musall, Otto K.
Musarra, Joseph F.
Muscato, Russell J.
Muschietty, James A.
Musial, Frank J.
Musicaro, S.A.
Musumeci, Frank
Muth, Theodore A.
Mutulo, Philip John
Muzic, Charles H.
Myatt, Joe E.
Myers, Clifford J.
Myers, Gerald E.
Myers, Jack K.
Myers, James E.
Myers, Kenneth C.
Myers, Paul B.
Myers, Richard H.
Myers, Terry L.
Myers, William W.
Myreng, Jack H.

- N -

Nabb, George F. Jr.
Nace, Thomas L.
Nadolski, Frank
Nagel, Edwin
Nagel, William G.
Nagy, David L.
Nagy, David L.
Nagy, George A.
Naiman, Martin
Nakis, William C.
Nance, Gettis A.
Nance, James K.
Nance, William M.
Napier, Curtis L.
Napierala, Robert
Nardello, Salvatore
Nardini, Robert F.
Nash, Louis V.
Natale, Anthony R.
Nathan, Duffy
Nathanson, Stan

Naunas, Robert Ash
Navarre, Leo F.
Navy U.S. Magazine
Naylor, Arthur E.
Naylor, John B.
Neal, Nathaniel L.
Neamtz, Charles E.
Nease, Karl W.
Nebelsick, John H.
Necca, Anthony
Nee, William
Need, Donald R.
Needham, David C.
Needham, George H.
Needham, Gordon A.
Neff, Carl E.
Neff, Robert A.
Negosian, Louis G.
Neil, Kenneth B.
Nelson, Albert F.
Nelson, Albert M.
Nelson, Bob
Nelson, Donald W.
Nelson, Dwight D.
Nelson, George P. Jr.
Nelson, George Z.
Nelson, Harry J.
Nelson, Hugh G. Jr.
Nelson, James
Nelson, James Jr.
Nelson, Jesse E.
Nelson, John
Nelson, John F.
Nelson, John F.
Nelson, Joseph B. Jr.
Nelson, Marion C.
Nelson, Ralph W.
Nelson, Richard A.
Nelson, Robert C.
Nelson, Robert H.
Nelson, Roy E.
Nelson, Sidney H.
Nelson, Wesley E.
Nemec, Joseph W.
Nesseth, Donald J.
Neth, Richard N.
Nettles, Jack E.
Nettleton, John F.
Nettleton, John F.
Netwig, Clarence L.
Neubeck, Elwood A.
Neufer, F. Earl
Neumann, Richard A.
Neumen, Walter J.
Neuschwander, James E.
Newberry, Robert G.
Newbill, Mathis Jr.
Newcomb, Donald H.
Newell, Charles R.
Newell, Lajoy G.
Newman, Beulah M.
Newman, Don J.
Newman, Earl T. Sr.
Newman, Eileen A.
Newman, Frank E.
Newman, George E.
Newman, Marvin
Newman, Mitchell J.
Newport, Thomas
Newren, Robert W.
Newswander, Wally E.
Newton, Charles V.
Newton, Dean W.
Newton, Eugene F.
Newton, Johnny
Newton, Joseph E.
Newton, Mack A. Jr.
Newton, Ralph A.
Newton, Wilburn A.
Newton, William
Ney, Charles
Niafeh, Robert N.
Nicholas, Donald B.
Nicholls, Elton J.
Nichols, Jack E.
Nichols, John W.
Nichols, Steward O.
Nichols, Thomas C.
Nichols, Warren R.
Nichols, William E.
Nicholson, Fred L.
Nicholson, Lee
Nicholson, N.H.
Nicholson, William J.
Nickerson, R.L.
Nickerson, Robert
Nickle, William A. Jr.
Nicklus, Edward
Nickolus, Nick
Nicodemus, Robert W.
Nicolas, Robert L.
Nicolaus, Nelson A.
Nicotera, Arthur J.
Niedentohl, Merle E.
Niehaus, Melvin J.
Nielsen, Chris
Nielsen, Martin L.
Nielson, William S.
Nieman, Edwin C.
Niemzyk, Philip A.
Nienaber, George L.
Nienau, Albert H.
Niepp, Fred A. Jr.
Niese, Albert G.
Niewinski, John P.

Nigro, Anthony C.
Nikirk, Ohla C. Jr.
Niles, Harry O. Jr.
Ninesling, Stephen A.
Nisen, Carl
Nissley, Guy L.
Nitz, William E.
Nix, Kenneth W.
Nixon, Andrew F.
Nixon, Christopher C.
Nixon, Robert H.
Noah, J.D.
Nobbs, Frederick S.
Noble, Dan
Noetzel, Justin R.
Nohowec, Milton J.
Nolan, John
Nolan, Louis H.
Nolan, Thomas N.
Nolan, Timothy J.
Nolbert, Richard A.
Nolen, Lewis W.
Noletti, Umbert P.
Nolte, Richard Sr.
Nolte, Robert E.
Noon, Reginald
Noone, Paul W.
Nooney, Thomas J.
Noort, Albert J.
Nordeen, George G.
Nordhaus, Earl R.
Norgaard, Henning
Norgaard, Rollo N.
Norling, Paul K.
Norman, Harold E.
Norman, Ralph
Norquist, E.G.
Norris, Claiborne C.
Norris, Isaac E.
Norris, Jospeh E.
Norris, Lathan H.
Norris, Marshall F.
Norris, Melvin J.
Norris, Robert L.
Norton, Ernest A.
Norton, Paul E.
Norton, Robert
Norton, Vernon P.
Notaro, Anthony P.
Nottingham, Charles D.
Novak, Benjamin S.
Novak, Paul Leon
Novello, Salvatore R.
Novotny, Richard R.
Nowacki, Edward J.
Nowrey, John A.
Nugent, Marland E.
Nunally, Dell S.
Nunes, Augustine J.
Nuneville, Gray D.
Nunham, Ernest L.
Nunnenkamp, Wayne E.
Nussbaum, Arthur E.
Nutt, Earl R.
Nuttman, William
Nyberg, Kenneth A.
Nyberg, Lawrence T.
Nygren, Bernard L.
Nyquist, Dawson E.

- O -

O'berne, Leslie
O'Brien, Edward F.
O'Brien, Francis B.
O'Brien, Frank
O'Brien, Michael J.
O'Brien, Raymond C.
O'brien, Allan J.
O'brien, Claude Lee
O'brien, Herbert J.
O'brien, Joseph
O'brien, Paul E.
O'Connell, Thomas A.
O'connell, Edward
O'connell, Edward J.
O'Connor, Lawrence W.
O'Connor, Michael
O'Connor, Richard V.
O'connor, James V.
O'day, Robert M.
O'dell, Gerald H.
O'dell, Hugh Dale
O'dell, William B.
O'donnell, Luke B.
O'donnell, William J.
O'donoghue, Denis P.
O'driscoll, John T.
O'dwyer, Edmund P.
O'Gee, Russell C.
O'grady, Walter V. Sr.
O'Hagan, John J.
O'hagan, Charles
O'Hanlon, Eugene C.
O'hanlon, David B.
O'Hara, Thomas A.
O'Keefe, William
O'keefe, James W.
O'keefe, Michael F.
O'Leary, Frank R.
O'Leary, George D.
O'Leary, Walter J.
O'leary, Edward F.
O'leary, John E.
O'leary, William G.
O'meara, John R.
O'Neal, Joe T.

O'Neal, Russell A.
O'Neil, James D.
O'neil, George J.
O'Neill, Bartholomew F.
O'Neill, Eloise
O'Neill, James D.
O'Neill, Matthew
O'Neill, Robert
O'neill, Charles J.
O'neill, Janie
O'neill, William J.
O'rear, Marvin K.
O'reilly, Joseph M.
O'rourke, Charles L.
Oas, Roy E.
Oates, Richard J.
Obbink, Leland M.
Ober, Charles E.
Oberbillig, Harlow
Oberg, Carl W. Jr.
Obermeier, Clayton G.
Obern, E. George
Oblath, Leo
Ochoa, Henry P.
Ochonicky, Jerry
Odle, James L.
Oertel, Henry V.
Oeser, James F.
Oettel, Joe
Oettinger, Ernest J.
Oettinger, Joseph R.
Offill, Doyle M.
Ogiba, Frank A.
Ogle, Malcolm C.
Ogle, Owen L.
Oglesby, David E.
Oglesby, Theodore R.
Ogno, Nicholas
Ogrodnik, Joseph
Ohland, George T.
Ohnemus, Robert A.
Olberg, Ralph S.
Oldham, Neild B.
Oldham, Robert J.
Olejkowski, Stanley F.
Olenick, Casimir S.
Oleska, Anthony J.
Olhasso, John J.
Olinger, Robert T.
Oliphant, Fred J.
Oliveira, Gilbert C.
Oliver, Frank J.
Oliver, James E.
Oliver, Robert A.
Olivier, William R.
Olle, Erwin H.
Olsen, Alfred S.
Olsen, Donald F.
Olsen, Earl A.
Olsen, Gerard
Olsen, Richard F.
Olson, Arden
Olson, Bernard E.
Olson, Clare S.
Olson, Dewey G.
Olson, Gary A.
Olson, George E.
Olson, Herbert E.
Olson, James E.
Olson, John
Olson, John W.
Olson, Raymond M.
Olszewski, Stanley J.
Oltz, Edgar E.
Omohundro, George A.
Omohundro, George A.
Oneto, James S.
Onufer, George M. Jr.
Onusko, John Jr.
Onyx, Raymond C.
Oostdyk, Jacob F.
Opiekun, Andrew J.
Opitz, Fletcher R.
Oponik, Joseph
Oppenheimer, Jerome
Opromollo, Martin V.
Opsal, John L.
Orefice, Frank J.
Orenstein, Arnold
Origer, Emil J.
Orlando, Joe A. Jr.
Orlando, Mario J.
Orr, David F.
Orr, George A. Jr.
Orr, Thomas J.
Orr, Warren D.
Orr, William
Orr, William H.
Orrell, Richard E.
Orrison, Rex Wesley
Orrs, William L.
Orsborn, Herman G.
Ortolani, John B.
Ortt, Paul K.
Osborne, Clyde M.
Osborne, Donald C.
Osborne, George E.
Osborne, John J.
Osborne, Joseph P.
Osborne, Richard C.
Osborne, Thomas
Osborne, Thomas J. Jr.
Osborne, Vernon L.
Osenni, Daniel
Oser, George J.

Osman, Felix J.
Osman, Felix J.
Osman, Harry R. Jr.
Ostaszewski, Stanley J.
Osteen, Jack H.
Osten, Joseph W.
Ostergaard, Homer L.
Ostergren, Robert N.
Osterling, Walter J. Jr.
Osterson, Woodrow W.
Ostman, Albin J. Jr.
Ostrander, Raymond L.
Osvai, Edward A.
Ott, James Wm.
Otto, Earl P.
Otto, Robert O.
Ouellette, Albert L.
Oufnac, Lester
Overacker, Arthur L.
Overdorf, Jack M.
Overmyer, Dale O.
Owen, Albert T.
Owen, Billy A.
Owen, Bruce A. Sr.
Owen, Robert J.
Owen, Thomas H.
Owens, Dewitt C.
Owens, Grover C. Jr.
Owens, Kelton L.
Owens, Marvin E.
Owens, William
Oxford, George T.
Oxley, Joseph C.

- P -

Paar, Charles N.
Pace, Ben H.
Pace, John E.
Pace, Lloyd A.
Pacheco, Adrian J.
Pacheco, Henry W.
Paciorek, Richard L.
Pacitto, Joseph R.
Packard, Lee S.
Paddock, Stephen
Padgett, Gilmer T.
Pagano, Samuel J.
Page, Austin J.
Page, Ernest F. Jr.
Page, Glen C.
Page, Glenn A.
Page, Harold E.
Page, James B.
Page, L.N.
Page, Lowell E.
Page, Oren W. Jr.
Page, Robert H.
Pagh, Eric
Pahel, Harry E.
Paholski, John J. Sr.
Paige, Earl T. Sr.
Paige, John W.
Paine, Max
Painter, Aubrey L.
Paisley, Robert H.
Paladino, Anthony
Palazzo, Michael J.
Palczewski, Andy
Palermo, Loreto A.
Palermo, Nicholas D.
Palermo, Sam
Palko, John J.
Pallagut, Joyce
Pallone, Felix M.
Palm, John W.
Palmer, Arthur M.
Palmer, Floyd B.
Palmer, George W.
Palmer, Glenn R.
Palmer, Harold
Palmer, Horace
Palmer, Kenneth R.
Palmer, Mark I.
Palmer, Ulon
Palmer, Walter C. Jr.
Palmer, Walter J.
Palmeri, Fiore R.
Palmore, William M.
Paluch, Roman G.
Palumbo, James P.
Palumbo, Joseph
Palumbo, Vincent
Panasuk, Alec J.
Panda, Chester
Panetta, John Mrs.
Panfil, Edmund J.
Pangburn, Ernest S.
Panger, Wilma
Panich, Joseph M.
Panichella, Anthony A.
Pankake, Paul S.
Panko, John F.
Panowitz, Edward A.
Paolini, Armon
Paolini, Primo T.
Papa, Ralph J.
Papa, Ralph J.
Papke, Alanson C.
Papp, Frank
Pappano, Albert E.
Paquin, Wilfred E.
Para, Edward J.
Paradis, Clement R.
Pardo, John
Parent, Arthur N.
Parent, Robert F.

Parent, Robert P.
Parine, Leonard J.
Parine, Leonard J.
Paris, Al
Paris, William J.
Parise, Frank
Parisi, Frank J.
Parisian, Anthony E.
Parizek, Norman E.
Park, Oliver W.
Park, S.R.
Parker, Charles A.
Parker, Dale A.
Parker, Frank E.
Parker, George J.
Parker, Harold
Parker, Harry L.
Parker, Henry S. Jr.
Parker, Howard S.
Parker, James D.
Parker, Jesse J.
Parker, Jewell K.
Parker, Raymond A.
Parker, Robert C.
Parker, Robert W.
Parker, Thomas R.
Parkman, Henry
Parks, Leroy W.
Parks, Sheridan A.
Parlon, Thomas N.
Parmer, Dan G.
Parnell, J.C.
Parr, Robert A.
Parrish, David E.
Parson, Wayne W.
Parsons, William T.
Partenheimer, Harold P.
Partin, Donald
Partington, Eugene T.
Partington, George J.
Parzyk, John A.
Pasada, John W.
Pascento, Phillip P.
Paslowski, Ray
Pasquale, Anthony G.
Pasquinelli, Fred A.
Pasquini, Elio
Pastor, Charles R.
Pastula, John S.
Patafio, John J. Jr.
Pate, Paul A.
Pate, Paul N.
Pate, Thomas E.
Paterson, Thomas J.
Patience, Donald
Patin, Roland R.
Patrick, William
Patrick, Willis W.
Patterson, Elmore C.
Patterson, Hugh C.
Patterson, James
Patterson, James H.
Patterson, Jewel E.
Patterson, Paul A.
Patterson, Thomas S.
Patterson, W.M.
Pattison, Abbott
Patton, Ben Jr.
Patton, Kent Wm.
Patton, Richard H.
Patton, William F.
Pauek, John S.
Paugh, Richard
Paul, Harrell M.
Paul, Horace E.
Paul, James
Paul, John H.
Paulet, Lawrence D.
Paulsen, Emil R.
Paulson, William L.
Pauly, Melvin F.
Pautke, Walter
Pavey, Donald E.
Pavkovich, Chester F.
Pavlik, William G.
Pavlock, Cornelius F.
Pawlenty, Edward F.
Pawlowicz, Henry
Paxton, Claude E. Jr.
Payne, James R.
Payne, Louis
Payne, Teddy H.
Payton, James E.
Pearce, Albert E.
Pearson, Albert W.
Pearson, Arthur
Pearson, Karl Harry
Pearson, W.T.
Pearson, William
Pease, Lester H. Jr.
Peck, Bud W.
Peck, Curtis R.
Peck, Gerald
Peckham, Gordon E.
Pecora, Joseph M.
Pedersen, Raymond
Peduzzi, Reno J.
Peed, Charles A.
Peed, Jerry E.
Peek, Richard E.
Pell, Arthur B.
Pelletier, Raymond
Pelletier, Vernon D.
Pellittiere, Mike
Pelton, Gerald W.

Peluso, Joseph
Pemberton, Harold D.
Pence, Chester D.
Pence, John Jr.
Pender, Teddy H.
Pendleton, Morton E.
Penge, Pasquale F.
Penman, David Y.
Penn, Warren C. Sr.
Pennacchia, Dante A.
Pennell, Clyde R.
Pennell, George L.
Pennell, John H.
Pennell, Laxton C.
Pennell, Walter F.
Pennell, William L. Jr.
Penney, Hubert L.
Penney, Robert J.
Penning, Jacob
Pennington, Charles H.
Pennington, James W.
Pensiero, Larry R.
Pentony, James J.
Penwell, Joseph E.
Pepa, John J.
Pepera, Michael J.
Pepper, Frank T.
Peralta, William A.
Percer, O.G.
Percival, Frank B.
Percival, Lawrence A.
Perdo, Thomas A.
Perez, Herman
Perina, Frank L.
Perkins, Elmer E.
Perkins, Frederick B.
Perkins, R.N.
Perlak, Arthur
Perle, Arthur
Perlman, Sam
Perlstein, Michael
Perna, Anthony
Perrella, Frank
Perren, Lawrence A.
Perreten, Paul F.
Perrino, Raymond L.
Perry, Frank E.
Perry, Hoyt Jr.
Perry, Robert N.
Persinger, Henry R.
Persinger, Oscar A.
Pertzborn, James E.
Pesek, Paul E.
Peters, Arthur C.
Peters, George S.
Peters, Gerald S.
Peters, Grover C.
Peters, Hubert K.
Peters, Larry A.
Peters, Ralph E. Jr.
Peters, Van R.
Peters, Vernon L.
Petersen, Laurence C.
Petersen, Orville B. Sr.
Petersen, Peter R.
Petersen, Richard L.
Petersen, Sigurd
Peterson, A.C.
Peterson, Arthur Jr.
Peterson, Charles R.
Peterson, David J.
Peterson, Donald L.
Peterson, Donald N.
Peterson, Duane C.
Peterson, Ernest F.
Peterson, Harry M.
Peterson, Jimmie G.
Peterson, Katie Carr
Peterson, Lee G.
Peterson, Maurice J.
Peterson, Norman A.
Peterson, Oliver O.
Peterson, Pauline M.
Peterson, Raymond D.
Peterson, Richard K.
Peterson, Richard W.
Peterson, Vernon G.
Peterson, Walter
Petit, John B.
Petit, John M.
Petit, William A.
Petrasek, Edwin
Petrequin, Harry J. Jr.
Petricco, John
Petrino, James Jr.
Petrogallo, Joseph
Petrosky, Edward F.
Petrowski, Richard F.
Petrozza, Michael J.
Petruzzella, Constantino
Petruzzella, Constantino
Pettigrew, Grover C.
Pettine, Joseph
Petton, Charles O.
Petty, A.J.
Pettyjohn, Hershell P. Sr.
Petzold, Paul O.
Petzold, Richard A.
Pfeffer, Martin C.
Pfeifer, Henry
Pfeiffer, Edward F.
Pfeil, John C.
Pfiel, Russell C.
Phair, John L.
Phelan, Thomas J.

Phelps, Charles R.
Phelps, Homer A.
Phelps, William H.
Phernetton, Robert F.
Philbin, Martin
Philipps, Richard C.
Philippy, Basil H.
Phillips, Billy G.
Phillips, Denzel
Phillips, Donald F.
Phillips, Donald R.
Phillips, Emmett J.
Phillips, George A. Jr.
Phillips, George E.
Phillips, J. Anthony
Phillips, James P.
Phillips, John J.
Phillips, Joseph E.
Phillips, Leighton Jr.
Phillips, Sam M.
Phillips, Wendell Jr.
Phillips, William F.
Phillips, William G.
Phillips, William O.
Phipps, William J.
Photenhauer, Jack
Piantedosi, Michael
Piatek, Daniel A.
Piazza, George Della
Piccirillo, Joseph A.
Picinich, Robert S.
Pick, Alan E.
Pickels, Wayne M.
Pickett, Paul E.
Pickett, Wayne R.
Pidgeon, Wayne M.
Piechota, Stanley F.
Pierce, Edward E. Sr.
Pierce, Greer C.
Pierce, Harry W.
Pierce, Leora I.
Pierce, Walter E. Jr.
Pierpont, Nathan M. Jr.
Pierson, W.H. Jim Jr.
Pierz, Harold W.
Pieszak, Frank A.
Pietron, Valoise M.
Pietrzak, Edward A.
Pietrzak, Edward A.
Pietrzak, Ray
Pietrzak, Ray
Pigg, William J.
Pigman, Donald S.
Pignone, Anthony J.
Pihlkar, Daniel W.
Pike, Chester
Pike, Clarence L.
Pike, Sammy J.
Pilecki, Benny P.
Pilgrim, J.B.
Pilkington, A.D.
Pill, Richard D.
Pilling, Joseph R. Jr.
Pinchuk, Walter
Pinckard, W.G.
Pinkston, Bert M. Jr.
Pinney, S. Calvin
Pino, Michael J.
Pinto, William G. Jr.
Pinzel, John G.
Piotrowski, Clemens F.
Piotrowski, Ladislaus
Pipa, Michael
Piper, Earnest M.
Pipkin, John L.
Pippen, Vaughan C.
Pippin, John B.
Pippitt, Charles H.
Pisani, Joseph E.
Piskorowski, Stanley A.
Pistner, Richard
Pistorino, William L.
Pitcher, A.L.
Pitleck, John F.
Pitman, Robert P.
Pitt, Karl B.
Pittman, George H.
Pittman, James T.
Pittman, Robert D.
Pittman, Vincent J.
Pitts, Gail W.
Pizie, Donald B.
Pizzacar, Vincent A.
Pizzolato, Anthony S.
Plage, Henry L.
Plage, W.R.
Plageman, James W.
Plamondon, Theodore Jr.
Planche, David
Plate, Valentine W.
Platek, Arthur
Platt, Merle
Pleasant, James E.
Plessing, Walter
Pletkovich, John
Pletman, Jack
Plettner, Bert
Pletz, Charles
Plewa, Frank B.
Plomos, Kore
Plough, James G.
Plucinski, Arthur
Plueddemann, Arthur H.
Plumb, Raymond E.
Plumer, Bernard J.
Plumley, William D.
Pochmann, Henry A.
Podolak, Steve
Podorski, Joseph I. Jr.
Poe, David G.
Poetker, Murl E.
Pohlman, Louis F. Jr.
Poister, William
Pokorny, Edward S.
Polakoski, Carroll A.
Poland, David
Poland, Harold
Polanskey, R. Walter
Polanski, M.F.
Polewczak, Stanley
Poling, Howard D.
Poling, Robert L.
Polito, Salvatore T.
Polk, Lamar H.
Polk, Monnie
Pollak, George
Pollard, Riley T. Jr.
Polley, Raymond T.
Pollock, William A.
Poloha, Steve
Polozzolo, Tony
Polsky, Irving
Polson, Hardin W.
Polvinen, Eino E.
Poma, Nicholas
Pomerantz, Irving
Pomeroy, Jack S.
Pona, James F.
Ponder, Paul L.
Pongrat, Glen A.
Pontius, Paul E.
Poole, Allen M.
Poole, Edward L.
Poole, Grover Q.
Poole, John H.
Poole, Julius R.
Popadak, Michael P.
Pope, C.E.
Pope, Joseph A.
Pope, Mary Green
Porambo, Joseph S. Sr.
Porter, Arnold T.
Porter, Charles
Porter, Edward F.
Porter, George N.
Porter, John F.
Porter, Robert E.
Posipanko, Stephen J.
Post, David L.
Post, Harvey J.
Post, Harvey L.
Postlewait, John
Postma, E. Herbert
Poteat, Johnnie J.
Poteet, Paul
Potochniak, Anthony
Potratz, Clifford
Potter, Curtis
Potter, David B.
Potter, Jack B.
Potter, James G.
Potter, John
Potter, Lloyd A.
Potter, Raymond W.
Potter, Thomas A.
Potts, Edward S.
Poulin, Joseph
Poulton, Lloyd E.
Pouncey, Oliver K.
Powell, Franklin E.
Powell, James H.
Powell, Larry J.
Powell, William H.
Powers, Edmund J.
Powers, Norman J.
Powers, Raymond C.
Powers, William A.
Powers, William F.
Poweski, Harry S.
Pracht, Richard E.
Pracht, Richard E.
Prager, Theodore E.
Prainito, Fidele
Prais, Bernard A.
Prall, John S.
Prather, James A.
Pratt, Donald W.
Pratt, Frank B.
Pratt, Harley W.
Pratt, John D. Jr.
Pratt, Kenneth A.
Pratt, Robert W.
Prawdzik, Stan
Prebish, George J.
Preble, Dennis H.
Precie, Anthony A.
Prehoda, John Mrs.
Preiner, Frank
Preisendorfer, Robert
Prentiss, Robert G.
Prescott, George Jr.
Prescott, Richard
Preseren, Michael
Presley, George
Presley, Orville
Presnell, A.P. Jr.
Presson, Richard N.
Preston, Charles G.
Preston, Marion R.
Prewett, Mercer B.
Prezikowski, Clemens A.
Price, Earl A.
Price, Frank A.
Price, Fred A.
Price, Henry L. Jr.
Price, Lloyd L.
Price, Norman I.
Price, Robert E.
Price, Robert I.
Price, William E.
Price, William T.
Priest, Clifford M.
Priest, Clyde M.
Priest, Kindred C. Sr.
Prillaman, Herman N.
Printz, Ferdinand
Prio, Peter S.
Prisch, Robert M.
Prisco, Joseph H.
Pritt, James R.
Prock, John D.
Proctor, Roland J. Sr.
Proehl, Henry
Prosser, Sweney Jr.
Proudfoot, Wilbert D.
Proudfoot, William P.
Proue, Herbert J.
Proulx, Roger J.
Provenza, John J.
Prucha, Lad L.
Prumachuk, Fred
Prusia, George E.
Pryor, Edward G.
Prys, John A.
Przybyl, Edward
Psomiades, William
Psoras, Sam
Puelicher, John A.
Pugh, James E.
Pugh, James N.
Pukajlo, Chet
Puknat, Albert Jr.
Pulaski, Dan J.
Pulaski, Edward J.
Puliatti, Dan
Pulley, R.B.
Pullig, Vernon L.
Pundt, Mrs. Lee
Purcell, James B.
Purcell, Thomas F.
Purdy, Paul S.
Purgason, Fred W.
Pursell, Jack W.
Pursell, Warren
Purvis, Frank G. Jr.
Purvis, Joseph L.
Pusateri, Joseph G.
Puso, Fred
Putnam, John G.
Puzin, Robert S.
Pyke, Earl W.
Pyles, Earl K.
Pylypciw, Max
Pynn, Verne H.
Pytlik, Walter E.

- Q -

Quackenbush, William C.
Quality Inn
Quartararo, Phil
Queen, Averill W.
Queen, James O.
Quesenberry, Stanley M.
Quick, Elmer E.
Quick, George M. Jr.
Quick, William E.
Quicke, Arley M.
Quidley, William L.
Quigel, Bert E.
Quiggle, Howard J.
Quigley, George W.
Quigley, Robert F.
Quimby, Donald R.
Quincy, Samuel B.
Quinlan, Edna
Quinlan, Thomas E.
Quinn, Curtis R.
Quinn, George A.
Quinn, James Jr.
Quinn, James V.
Quinn, John P.
Quinn, William
Quinonez, Peter P.

- R -

Raab, George W.
Raak, Raymond
Rabinowitz, Frnak
Racette, Henry J.
Racicot, Lionel E.
Rackov, John
Raddell, Ludwig F. Jr.
Rader, Bill L.
Rader, Harry A.
Rader, Robert F. Jr.
Radford, Eugene P.
Radis, Robert P.
Radkovich, Daniel M.
Radocy, Stephen
Rae, Morris B.
Rafferty, Thomas W.
Ragan, Stuart
Rahmer, Eugene E.
Raike, Douglas Jr.
Rainen, Arthur O.
Rainone, Joseph D.
Rajinicek, Steve J.
Rak-Rock, John
Rakocy, Francis A.
Ralston, Howard E.
Ralston, Wayne
Ralston, William I.
Ramey, Paul M.
Ramirez, Paul Ray
Ramisch, Frank L.
Rammler, Harold J.
Ramos, Thomas J. Jr.
Rampy, Robert E.
Ramsay, John S.
Ramsden, Frank A.
Ramsey, Amos O.
Ramsey, Gilbert D.
Ramsey, Ralph A.
Ramsey, Rev. Victor
Ramsey, Robert N.
Ramstad, Marshall
Ranalli, Fran V. Sr.
Rancourt, Arthur E.
Randall, Charle H.
Randall, David S.
Ranelli, Louis
Ranieri, Mario V.
Rankin, John Henry
Ranniko, Toivo R.
Ranta, S.C.
Rapoza, Manuel
Raschke, John F.
Raskopf, Jack
Ratajczak, Walter J.
Ratcliffe, William F.
Rathburn, James G.
Rathmanner, Ralph E.
Ratledge, Warren G.
Ratner, Manney
Ratner, Nathaniel
Ratner, Robert C.
Raucci, Peter
Raunch, E.L.
Rauschenbach, John
Rauseo, Arthur J.
Rawls, Thomas B.
Ray, Robert M.
Rayburn, Robert E.
Raymond, James E.
Raymond, Joseph F.
Raymond, Louis
Rayside, Charles
Read, Garth H.
Read, Robert E.
Reader, Jack T.
Reames, William C.
Reames, William C.
Recio, Joseph
Reck, Joseph W.
Rector, Charles H.
Rector, Ernest A.
Reddish, Robert G.
Reddy, T. Joseph
Reddy, Thomas F. Jr.
Redinger, Robert H.
Redler, John
Redmayne, Richard B.
Redmon, Robert E.
Redwine, Crowell L.
Reed, David H.
Reed, Jack
Reed, Morton L. Jr.
Reed, Philip R.
Reed, Robert F.
Reed, W.G. (Bill)
Rees, George A.
Reeves, Howard
Reeves, John D.
Refer, Donald W.
Regan, Robert E.
Regester, Jack
Register, Walter G.
Regot, Alvin
Rehak, Rudy
Rehmus, August H.
Reich, Gene E.
Reichard, Earl R.
Reichert, Walter
Reichhart, Norbert J.
Reid, Alfred L.
Reid, Carl S.
Reid, Donald J.
Reid, Frank L.
Reid, James R.
Reid, Joseph L.
Reid, Robert W.
Reid, William T.
Reierson, Paul D.
Reierson, Ronald M.
Reifert, Timothy
Reiff, John T.
Reilly, David E.
Reilly, Eugene T.
Reilly, Hugh J.
Reilly, James A.
Reilly, John
Reilly, Richard F.
Reinhagen, Robert C.
Reinhold, Robert N.
Reinoehl, Robert U.
Reish, Paul E.
Reiss, Wilbur R.
Reitan, Henry M.
Reitano, Domenic S.
Reith, Herbert W. Jr.
Reitz, Bruce W.
Reitz, Elton G.
Relf, Joseph E.
Relyea, Audrey P.
Remley, Reginald S.
Renaud, Clifford
Rendon, Joseph S.
Renfro, Stanley
Rennie, David C.
Rennie, Don R.
Reno, Robert B.
Renzulli, John O.
Repasy, Andy J.
Repka, Frank
Rescott, John W.
Reska, Walter F.
Ressel, Dale
Retcho, Joseph
Rettkowski, Herbert A.
Retzl, Rudolph
Reuter, Harold J.
Reuter, Kenneth
Revelle, Donald J.
Rever, Carl R.
Rexroat, W.E.
Rexrode, Ercil V. Jr.
Rey, William J. Jr.
Reynolds, Alfred H.
Reynolds, Barry L.
Reynolds, Charles Jr.
Reynolds, Francis
Reynolds, Harold I.
Reynolds, Joseph J.
Reynolds, Paul I.
Reynolds, Vernon
Reynolds, Winton G.
Reysack, Henry D.
Rezendes, Lawrence
Rhoads, Norman C.
Rhodes, Harold J.
Rhodes, Opha E.
Rhodes, Richard
Rhodus, Hollis W.
Rhudy, Harold C.
Riach, Robert R.
Ribich, Edward F.
Riccio, Andrew
Rice, Charles Jr.
Rice, Irwin R.
Rice, Jack H.
Rice, James A.
Rice, Ralph E.
Rich, James A.
Richards, Bobby H.
Richards, Jack L.
Richards, John H.
Richards, Philip W.
Richards, Philip W.
Richards, Robert L.
Richards, Roland H.
Richards, Russell V.
Richards, William C.
Richards, William J.
Richardson, Emery P.
Richardson, Frank C.
Richardson, Harris Jr.
Richardson, J.T.
Richardson, James E.
Richardson, Lawrence
Richardson, Norman L.
Richardson, Norman L.
Richardson, Ralph
Richardson, Ronald D.
Richardson, William W.
Richl, Thomas E.
Richman, Alan
Richman, Donald
Richman, Philip S.
Richmond, Stanley
Richter, Harold W.
Richter, John G.
Richter, Matthew
Richter, Reinhold A.
Richter, William A.
Richwine, John
Ricker, Darlington
Ricker, Robert A.
Rickett, Burrell O.
Rickett, Walter W.
Ricketts, Vance O.
Rickman, Herman L.
Ricottone, Mike P.
Riddle, Donald
Riddle, William H.
Ridenour, J.R.
Ridgway, Keneth R.
Ried, William V.
Riel, Francis J.
Riemer, William B.
Riester, Wilfred J.
Riethman, Clarence P.
Rife, Robert C.
Rigg, Luther E.
Rigger, Robert J.
Riggle, Arthur L.
Riggle, Richard
Riggleman, Clair L.
Riggs, Larry T.
Rigter, Joel A.
Riley, Doyle L.
Riley, Edwin J. Jr.
Riley, Robert L.
Riley, Walter S.
Riley, Wendy
Riley, William J.
Riley, William W.
Rinaldi, Anthony J.
Rinaldo, Frank
Rindge, Frederick H.
Rinehart, John
Rinklin, John G. Jr.
Rinn, Paul X.
Riordan, Dennis A.
Riper, Robert J.
Rippeon, Otis N.
Rippeon, Otis N.
Risman, Rudy
Risner, Eric
Ritchey, J.F.
Ritchie, Grace P.
Rittberg, Russell L.
Ritz, H. Glenwood Jr.
Ritz, John A.
Rivard, Leland G.
Rivera, Radames
Rivette, Gilbert H.
Rivinius, Harold J.
Rizzi, John
Rizzo, Anthony
Rizzo, Dominic G.
Rizzo, Henry
Rizzo, Salvatore
Rizzuto, Timothy C.
Roaf, George
Roark, W.D.
Roark, William H.
Robb, Hallack F.
Robb, Marlen
Robb, Ralph W.
Robb, Robert F. Dr.
Robbe, Theodore R.
Robbins, David F.
Robbins, Leroy W.
Robbins, Orren B.
Robbins, Raymond R.
Roberge, Kenneth
Roberge, Ralph F.
Roberge, Walter L. Jr.
Roberge, William F.
Roberson, Hubert G.
Roberts, Alfred R. Jr.
Roberts, Charles E.
Roberts, Clyde C.
Roberts, Clyde M. Jr.
Roberts, David W.
Roberts, Donald G.
Roberts, Dubiel O.
Roberts, Edwin J.
Roberts, Eva
Roberts, Everett E. Jr.
Roberts, James S.
Roberts, John E.
Roberts, John P.
Roberts, John P.
Roberts, Leonard J.
Roberts, Ralph S.
Roberts, Ronald W.
Roberts, Walter F.
Roberts, Wesley E.
Roberts, William L.
Robertson, Duane E.
Robertson, Harley R.
Robertson, Jack
Robertson, James M.
Robertson, Lloyd
Robinson, Alden F.
Robinson, Bronnie P.
Robinson, Clarke
Robinson, Donald M.
Robinson, Dwane
Robinson, Edwin K.
Robinson, Frederick I.
Robinson, James E.
Robinson, Malcolm P.
Robinson, Marvel Ike
Robinson, Owen J.
Robinson, Ransom C.
Robinson, Ray G.
Robinson, Roger M.
Robinson, Vere
Robinson, William C.
Robishaw, Robert J.
Robison, Andrew A.
Robison, Vernon D.
Rocco, Rocky
Roche, Frank P.
Rochner, Wm. E.
Rock, Michael J.
Rockwood, Paul L.
Rodgers, Odell
Rodgers, Robert V.
Rodi, Merton P.
Rodman, Murray
Rodwell, Robert J.
Roeder, Eugene F.
Roeder, Richard E.
Roehm, Al
Roesener, Wayne W.
Roeser, John M.
Roessler, Paul J.
Roever, Horace J.
Rogers, Ben A.
Rogers, Carl T.
Rogers, Charles H. Jr.
Rogers, Charles W.
Rogers, Clenton R. Sr.
Rogers, Clinton M.
Rogers, Dennis G. Sr.
Rogers, James Jr.
Rogers, Jim
Rogers, John H.
Rogers, Ollie
Rogers, Robert E.
Rogers, Stanford J.
Rogers, Stuart E.
Rogers, Wendell H.
Rogina, Paul V.
Rohde, Richard K.
Rohloff, Arthur K. Sr.
Rohnke, Oscar C.
Rohrer, Harry W.
Rohrlack, Arthur W.
Roksiewicz, A.E.
Roksiewicz, A.E.
Roll, Albert J.
Roll, Frank C.
Rollar, Chris
Romann, Leonard R.
Romano, Aldo J.
Romano, Dominic
Rome, Irvin L.
Rominski, Leo W.
Romme, George H.
Ronk, Rex J.
Ronk, Robert L.
Rooks, Theodore
Root, Robert W.
Roppel, Edward B.
Rosa, John J.
Rosa, Orlando A.
Rosati, Alfred A.
Rosati, Frank J.
Rose, Durwood G.
Rose, Edward J.
Rose, Erlon
Rose, Forrest D.
Rose, Frank J.
Rose, Henry W. Jr.
Rose, Milton
Rose, Stuart M.
Rose, Wilfred J.
Rosen, Charles P.
Rosen, George
Rosen, Irving
Rosen, Ollie F.
Rosen, William M.
Rosenbloom, Jerry H.
Rosencrans, Philip W.
Rosengren, Chris J.
Rosenhaus, Stanley
Rosick, Joseph A.
Roslonowski, Alfred
Rosner, Albert
Ross, Charles
Ross, Charles D.
Ross, Donald L.
Ross, George
Ross, George E.
Ross, Harlan F.
Ross, Keith A.
Ross, Keith A.
Ross, Leonard
Ross, Ronald E.
Ross, William V.
Rossi, Arthur P.
Rossi, Rudy
Rossi, Salvatore
Rossley, Edward F.
Rotella, Edward F.
Roth, Dale J.
Roth, Harold B.
Rothardt, Robert W.
Rothbell, Jerry
Rothlauf, George H.
Rotolo, Pat M.
Rotondo, Charles
Rotondo, Natale
Rotschild, Harvey
Roux, Philip
Rouxel, Walter L.
Rowan, Hartley D.
Rowe, Chester A.
Rowe, John P.
Rowe, Robert J.
Rowe, William
Rowland, Philip T.
Rowland, William
Rowles, Fred
Rowley, James R.
Rowsemitt, Aaron
Roy, Arthur J.
Roy, Raymond
Royal, Raymond
Royer, Delbert A.
Royle, Larry S.
Rozanski, Raymond
Rozga, James T.
Rubash, Roy N.
Rube, James L.
Ruberg, Arthur J.
Rubin, Myer
Ruckdeschel, Charles
Rucker, A.M. Jr.
Ruda, Norbert T.
Rudder, Jack L.
Rudesyle, John
Rudisill, Franklin E.
Rudisill, Lawrence Jr.
Rudnick, Walter W.
Rudolph, Burton B.
Rudy, Lee H.
Ruebsamen, Darrel D.
Ruen, Richard W. Sr.
Rugani, Joseph
Ruggles, Steven J.
Ruh, Arthur W.
Ruhle, Berdette A.
Ruhlman, Lee C.
Rumens, William
Ruml, Francis R. Sr.
Runaldue, Martin R.
Runalls, Norris B.
Rund, David M.
Runge, Robert L.
Rupert, Wendell E.
Rupnik, Walter
Rupp, Roberta E.
Rupprecht, Herbert A.
Rusch, Frank R.
Rush, Juanita Carr
Rusin, Frank J.
Rusnak, Thomas C.
Russ, Eugene M.
Russ, F.A.
Russell, Charles B.
Russell, Curtis P.
Russell, Herbert
Russell, Jack
Russell, James A.
Russell, John V. Sr.
Russell, Richard B.
Russell, Robert A. Dr.
Russell, Robert W.
Russell, Wesley
Russell, William H.
Russer, Donald E.
Russo, Ernest
Russo, Jack M.
Russo, John S.
Rust, Arnold E.
Ruth, Philip F.
Rutkowski, Anthony
Rutledge, Vincent A.
Ruzanka, Edward
Ryan, Charles E.
Ryan, Erwin V.
Ryan, Francis A.
Ryan, Gary A.
Ryan, George G.
Ryan, James F.
Ryan, John
Ryan, John
Ryan, Peter Vincent
Ryan, Robert G.
Ryan, Tom
Rybecky, Martin J.
Rybka, Phillip J.
Ryburn, Harry E.
Ryder, John J.
Ryder, Robert W.
Rydstrom, Olaf F.
Rydzefski, John A.
Rynearson, Leo E.
Rzutkiewicz, Justin F.

- S -

Sabatini, Remo
Sabatini, William
Saber, Charles K.
Sabin, William I.
Sabol, Lawrence B.
Sachs, Edward
Sachtleben, William W.
Sackellares, James
Sackman, Joseph
Sadler, Woodrow A.
Saeli, Joseph F.
Sague, Henry
Sailer, Elmer A.
Sain, Katherine
Sak, Lillian
Sakay, Albert
Saker, Peter R.
Sale, Gordon A.
Saleck, Robert J.
Saliba, John
Salisbury, George A.
Salman, Donald R.
Saltalamacchia, Anthony
Salter, Hugh
Saltzer, Joseph M.
Salvail, Arthur J.
Salvatore, Dominico P.
Salvoni, Francis H.
Samborski, Frank C.
Sammito, Santo G.
Sampson, Charlie Sr.
Sampson, David S.
Sams, J.M.
Samson, Edward
Sanborn, Alfred N.
Sanchez, Carlos F.
Sanchez, William G.
Sanders, Henry R.
Sanders, Norman P.
Sanders, Phillip P.
Sanders, Victor
Sanderson, John Q.
Sandifer, G.N.
Sandrin, Joseph
Sandrock, William J.
Sands, Leo T. Sr.
Sandstrom, Arthur E.
Sandstrom, Edward
Sanford, Maurice W.
Sanford, Maurice W.
Sanley, Richard D.
Sanmarco, John
Sanphilipo, Joseph M.
Santacroce, Robert
Santelli, Patrick
Santini, Rinaldo A.
Santo, Michael

Santo, Michael
Santouosso, Anthony J.
Sanzone, Joseph J.
Sapolosky, Joseph
Sapp, Anson B.
Sapp, Mitchell
Sarslow, Anchor H.
Sarvey, William E.
Sarvis, Edgar C.
Sasal, Robert
Sauer, Albert L.
Saulenas, Frank V.
Sauls, Joseph C.
Saunders, David H.
Saunders, George
Saunders, Grace E.
Saunders, K.W.
Saunders, O.E.
Saurer, Russell F.
Sauter, George W. Jr.
Sauvageau, Leo J.
Savage, Richard R.
Savaiano, David
Savedge, Richard A.
Sawchuck, Joseph
Sawley, Elbert W. Jr.
Sawyer, John Mitchell
Sayles, Charles L.
Saylor, Samuel L.
Scala, Frank A.
Scales, James S.
Scalise, Anthony J.
Scalzo, Michael H.
Scamell, Ralph B.
Scandlyn, Tom
Scanlon, John H.
Scanlon, Ray
Scannell, Raymond J.
Scarcello, Joseph J.
Scarl, Robert C. Sr.
Scatchard, Wm. L.
Scattergood, John T.
Schaab, Eugene H.
Schaaf, Ben R.
Schaber, Lloyd
Schade, Gerald D.
Schaefer, William M.
Schaeffer, Charles Jr.
Schaen, William G.
Schaeppi, Joseph J. Dr.
Schallmo, Nelson J.
Schanbacher, Marie
Schank, Robert V.
Schapker, Paul P.
Scharf, Francis J.
Schattenberg, Donald B.
Schatz, Roland E.
Scheer, Robert W.
Scheer, Wilbert W.
Scheer, Wilbert W.
Scheff, Martin
Scheideler, Stanley E.
Scheirer, James S.
Scheld, George
Schell, Robert J.
Schenk, Elmer H.
Schepers, Levi H.
Schermerhorn, Estel D.
Schiavoni, Joseph S.
Schick, Virginia S.
Schiffbauer, Ben
Schiller, Herbert Jr.
Schilling, Paul J.
Schillings, Thomas J.
Schimmel, Robert D.
Schindler, William B.
Schineller, Lawrence
Schipper, Alvin
Schkolenko, Walter
Schlagnhaufer, G. Jr.
Schlamp, John J.
Schlawiedt, Herbert W.
Schlemmer, Jack D.
Schlimme, Edgar W.
Schlotfeldt, George E.
Schmalbach, George Jr.
Schmaltz, Anthony J.
Schmehl, Robert A.
Schmidt, Bruno G.
Schmidt, Edward A.
Schmidt, Ejlif
Schmidt, George C.
Schmidt, Joseph G.
Schmidt, Maurice J.
Schmidt, William A.
Schmidt, William G.
Schmitt, Frank A.
Schmitt, William F.
Schmitz, Marie M.
Schmocker, Daniel A.
Schnapp, Robert J.
Schneider, Clifford P.
Schneider, Eugene F.
Schneider, Frank F.
Schneider, Kenneth
Schneider, Sylvester
Schnelle, Charles L.
Schnetzer, Charles J.
Schnurstein, Robert B.
Schoen, Philip J. III
Schoenheider, Warren G.
Schoenrock, Ordwin
Schrader, E.N.
Schrader, Edward J.
Schrader, Max
Schrader, Rodney
Schramm, William L.
Schraut, George T.
Schrautemeier, Marvin
Schreck, Clarence W.
Schreiber, Alfred E.
Schriner, Charles T.
Schriver, Edward T.
Schroder, Charles J.
Schroeder, William J.
Schroeter, Charles W.
Schronk, Edward
Schubert, R.E.
Schuchman, N.W.
Schuh, Nicholas J.
Schuh, Nicholas J.
Schuhler, William J.
Schuller, Joseph V.
Schulte, Louis O.
Schultz, Albert H.
Schultz, Douglas C.
Schultz, James F.
Schultz, James R.
Schultz, Paul A.
Schulz, Dale R.
Schulze, Irene Carr
Schumacher, Victor
Schumann, Clyde M.
Schuster, Jean T.
Schuster, Louis
Schutt, Raymond C.
Schutty, Robert A.
Schwab, Charles P.
Schwan, Robert W.
Schwartz, David B.
Schwartz, Leo
Schwartz, Samuel
Schwarz, F.K.
Schwedock, Arnold
Schweiberger, Frank R.
Schweitzer, Dale H.
Schweitzer, Thomas A.
Schwennsen, Robert
Schwer, Dr. William E.
Schwimmer, Richard A.
Schwingen, Robert
Scobee, Stanley E.
Scoles, Peter
Scott, Adis B.
Scott, Garland E.
Scott, Louis P.
Scott, Robert C.
Scott, Robert E.
Scott, Robert R.
Scott, William L. Jr.
Scroggin, Isaac W.
Scudder, Elbert C.
Scudder, Jack B.
Scudder, John W.
Scuderi, Carmen
Scull, Stanley L.
Scussel, Mario A.
Seabrook, Archibald F.
Seacord, William E.
Seaholm, Lawrence R.
Sealise, Frank Jr.
Sealscott, Doyle M.
Sealy, Bill Q.
Seaman, Earl T.
Seaman, George B. Sr.
Searfoss, George R.
Searle, Richard J.
Searles, Robert
Sears, John
Seaton, Edward E.
Seay, Ray
Seay, Russell E. Jr.
Seboda, Earl F.
Secory, Albert W.
Sedlack, Edward T.
Sedlak, Michael G.
Sedory, John
Sedrowski, Stanley A.
Seeger, Ronald C.
Seegers, Henry
Seemour, Robert E.
Segler, Vincent E.
Segobiano, Sabino
Segulin, Joseph M.
Seib, John J.
Seiberling, Donald G.
Seidler, Ted Donald
Seidlitz, G.R.
Seidman, David
Seidman, Monroe L.
Seifert, Lucille
Seifert, Robert G.
Seigal, Travis
Seisser, Max
Seitz, Robert E.
Selby, Lester Max
Selby, William E.
Self, J.W. Jr.
Selivonchik, Walter
Sella, Tony
Sellers, Elisha Jr.
Sellers, George W. III
Sellers, Walter Paul
Sellers, William W.
Seltzer, Arnold F.
Seltzer, Claire
Seltzer, Thomas G.
Selvitella, Jerry G.
Seman, Andrew
Semans, Frederick L.
Semjkal, Longin J.
Semke, Charles R.
Senet, Leslie E.
Senn, William F.
Senna, Charles J.
Senninger, Earl J. Jr.
Senor, S.C.
Sensor, John R.
Sensor, John R.
Sepich, Louis M.
Seruntine, Alex, Jr.
Sevde, O.M.
Severin, Edward G.
Severson, Gordon
Sevinor, Philip
Seward, Floyd L.
Seward, Joseph G.
Seward, Marston E.
Seward, Roy E.
Sewell, Charles L.
Sewell, Charles L.
Sexauer, Evan C.
Sexton, Elton N.
Sexton, John
Seymour, Chip
Seymour, John F. Jr.
Sgammato, Nicholas
Shafer, Steven H. Jr.
Shaffer, Eugene H. Sr.
Shaffer, George W.
Shaffer, Julius J.
Shaffer, Marvin C.
Shaffer, Richard C.
Shalline, Paul
Shallman, James H.
Shambach, James E.
Shamberger, Harold J.
Shambroom, William D.
Shane, Fred L.
Shanklin, Robert G.
Shanley, Walter
Shannahan, John M.
Shannon, James F.
Shannon, Robert M.
Shapiro, Jacob M.
Sharer, Donald C.
Sharp, George L.
Sharp, James M.
Sharp, Russell V.
Sharrett, James F.
Shashy, Edmund T.
Shattuck, James
Shaub, Walter
Shaughnessy, John R.
Shaver, A.L.
Shaver, Judy
Shaver, Reginald M.
Shaw, James Ray
Shaw, Kenneth C.
Shaw, Leslie W.
Shaw, Maurice O.
Shaw, Pleze E.
Shea, Daniel J.
Shea, John D.
Shea, Robert G.
Shealy, Grover L.
Shearer, Richard A.
Sheba, George A.
Shedlock, Andrew J. III
Shedlock, Andrew J. Jr.
Sheehan, John J.
Sheehan, John J. Sr.
Sheets, John E.
Sheets, Robert M.
Sheiner, Hy
Shell, Roland G. Jr.
Shellenberger, Mahrle
Shelly, Willard M.
Shelton, Donald L.
Shelton, Glenn M.
Shelton, Ken H.
Shelton, William G.
Shepard, Kenneth H.
Shepard, Lea
Shepard, Montgomery L.
Shepard, Thomas R. Jr.
Shepard, Warren C.
Shepherd, John W.
Shepherd, Louis A. Sr.
Sherer, Edward
Sherfey, Euell K.
Sheridan, Courtney J.
Sherman, Bill
Sherman, Edward C.
Sherman, George B. Jr.
Sherman, George E.
Shersick, John
Shersmith, Ralph
Sheruc, Edmund S.
Sherwood, Clarkson
Sherwood, Donald H. Jr.
Sherwood, Harold D.
Sherwood, Willodean
Shields, Bill L.
Shields, Roger D.
Shiflet, Robert L.
Shimp, John R.
Shimp, Neil Dr.
Shiner, George W.
Shipe, Guy C.
Shipley, Howard H.
Shipley, Kenneth E.
Shipman, Howard
Shires, Orlin H.
Shirey, Keoster E.
Shirk, Robert L.
Shirley, W.J.
Shirrell, Ray A.
Shockey, John H.
Shoffner, Harold I.
Sholley, Duke
Sholtis, George A.
Shonerd, David A.
Shonkwiler, Douglas C.
Shook, Arthur Q.
Shook, James W.
Shope, Grover Lee
Shores, Harold C.
Shoup, Willis R.
Shovan, John R.
Shover, C.J.
Showalter, Samuel J.
Shrader, Donald J.
Shrader, Richard R.
Shreve, Andrew
Shreve, Carl
Shreves, James M.
Shrieves, Robert F.
Shuda, William
Shugart, Calvin L.
Shull, Arthur Jr.
Shumaker, Vernon O.
Shuman, Arthur E. Jr.
Shumar, Samuel L.
Shumate, William V.
Shumway, Conrad
Shumway, Lewis K.
Shunney, Frank
Shutan, Robert H.
Shute, Howard E.
Sibbing, Roy J.
Sibley, John P.
Siboloski, Norman F.
Sicard, Robert L.
Sicilia, Louis A.
Sickelsmith, Burton M.
Siderio, Francis P.
Sides, Donald R.
Sides, Neal O.
Siedlecki, Henry
Siegel, Arnold R.
Siegwart, Richard E.
Siek, Chester J.
Siemon, Martin O. Jr.
Siepiela, John F.
Sieracki, Raymond
Sierp, Charles
Sievert, Robert N.
Sieviec, Theodore J.
Sifford, Stanhope A.
Signer, Robert W.
Sikora, Chester J.
Sikora, Edmund J.
Sikora, Ralph S.
Sikowitz, Bertram
Silance, Paul T.
Silleck, Robert B.
Silva, Frank
Silva, Manuel F.
Silver, Dan W.
Silverman, Elliot
Silverstein, Jerome W.
Silvia, John
Simeone, Joseph
Simiensyk, Fred
Siminski, Thaddeus
Simler, Francis L.
Simmen, Cliff
Simmons, Charles A. Sr.
Simmons, Dorothy L.
Simmons, E.W.
Simmons, Harold B.
Simmons, Horace Jr.
Simmons, Ira K.
Simmons, Robert W.
Simmons, Roy L.
Simon, David
Simon, William
Simonds, Philip H.
Simonetti, Vincent J.
Simons, Joseph M.
Simons, William E.
Simpson, Herbert R.
Simpson, Robert
Simpson, Robert L.
Sims, Emery S. Jr.
Simsak, Martin A.
Sindy, Paul T.
Siner, James W.
Singer, John D.
Singer, Monroe J.
Siniak, Michael J.
Siniscalchi, Ralph
Sinn, Herbert C.
Sipes, Donald C.
Sirls, Wilkes M.
Siry, William F.
Sisco, Herbert L.
Sisco, Leamon E.
Sisinger, John
Sisson, Earl L.
Sist, Joseph L.
Sitarski, Edward J.
Sites, George F.
Sitman, William D.
Sittre, Joe H. Jr.
Sivco, Charles E.
Sivia, Joseph A.
Sixour, George E.
Skalsky, Bill
Skebe, Stanley G.
Skeen, Joshua W.
Skelton, Guy
Skerven, Hildegard M.
Skiba, Leo
Skidmore, John H.
Skiles, Clarence
Skillman, Arthur D. Jr.
Skinner, Paul J.
Sklodowski, Joseph W.
Skoczen, Chester W.
Skoko, Thomas
Skorvanek, William R.
Skubis, Frank J.
Skyles, Alvin
Slack, Neil R.
Slanczka, Eugene
Slate, Edward D.
Slate, Merrill E.
Slater, Donald E.
Slater, Elam A.
Slater, Paul
Slater, William F.
Slaughter, D.C.
Slavin, Charles P.
Slavin, Walter M.
Slavinsky, Albert
Slaymen, Edward
Slayton, John A.
Sliben, John T. Jr.
Slizik, William
Sloan, Clyde C.
Sloan, Howard L.
Sloan, Randle L.
Slocum, Willard W.
Slokom, Sam
Slomczewski, Thomas B.
Sloper, Roger B.
Slovak, Michael J.
Sluzas, Ted
Smale, John R.
Smales, Allan B.
Smallwood, Frederick
Smanko, George J.
Smathers, David J.
Smead, Ralph L.
Smeathers, Harmon D.
Smedley, Gordon L.
Smeltz, Jack E.
Smeltzer, William O.
Smiddy, Michael L.
Smigel, Harry S.
Smiley, Billy L.
Smiley, Carl W.
Smith, A.Q.
Smith, Alfred J. Jr.
Smith, Alvin J.
Smith, Alvin L.
Smith, Alvin N.
Smith, Arthur E.
Smith, Arthur R.
Smith, Ben H. Jr.
Smith, Bernard F.
Smith, Billy J.
Smith, Bradford A.
Smith, Carl O. Jr.
Smith, Carl W.
Smith, Cecil V.
Smith, Charles C.
Smith, Charles Leo
Smith, Chester E.
Smith, chester G.
Smith, Clarence S.
Smith, Dallas R. III
Smith, Dan C.
Smith, David E.
Smith, Donald E.
Smith, Donald F.
Smith, Donald N.
Smith, Earnest T.
Smith, Edward H.
Smith, Edwin F.
Smith, Elbert B.
Smith, Ernest D.
Smith, Ernest D.
Smith, Floyd R.
Smith, Frank A.
Smith, Frank A.
Smith, Franklin C.
Smith, Frederick G.
Smith, Frederick G.
Smith, George
Smith, George G.
Smith, George W.
Smith, Glenn A.
Smith, Harold G.
Smith, Harold J.
Smith, Harold W.
Smith, Howard
Smith, Howard D.
Smith, J.E.
Smith, Jack L.
Smith, James D.
Smith, James H.
Smith, James L.
Smith, James P.
Smith, James R.
Smith, James W.
Smith, John J.
Smith, John M.
Smith, John P.
Smith, John W. Jr.
Smith, Joseph S.
Smith, Leonard
Smith, Leonard J.
Smith, Lewis B.
Smith, Louise
Smith, Louise
Smith, Lucien C.
Smith, Lyle P.
Smith, Marshall
Smith, Martin H.
Smith, Maurice B.
Smith, Merritt M.
Smith, Morris B.
Smith, Morris R.
Smith, Norfleet E.
Smith, Norman L.
Smith, Pat
Smith, Paul C.
Smith, Paul H.
Smith, Paul H.
Smith, Paul P.
Smith, Philip R.
Smith, Ralph E.
Smith, Ray E.
Smith, Ray L.
Smith, Raymond H.
Smith, Raymond H.
Smith, Raymond V.
Smith, Raymond V.
Smith, Richard G.
Smith, Richard H.
Smith, Roalin E.
Smith, Robert A.
Smith, Robert B.
Smith, Robert E.
Smith, Robert E.
Smith, Robert L.
Smith, Robert L.
Smith, Robert Lee
Smith, Robert M.
Smith, Robert M.
Smith, Robert W.
Smith, Roy R.
Smith, Samuel L.
Smith, Scott E.
Smith, Sherrill J.
Smith, Stanton D.
Smith, W.L.
Smith, Walter L.
Smith, Walter V.
Smith, Wilbur E.
Smith, Willard S.
Smith, William A.
Smith, William J. Jr.
Smith, William K.
Smith, William R.
Smith, William R.
Smith, Willie E.
Smits, C.J.
Smock, Robert L. Jr.
Smoller, Kenneth R.
Smook, Norman
Smothers, Donald C.
Smuda, William J.
Smyth, John M.
Snapp, John C.
Snapp, Leslie F.
Snavely, Michael
Snead, George C.
Snedeger, Charles E.
Snell, Forrest H.
Snellen, James R.
Snellgrove, John W. Jr.
Snider, Robert T.
Snipes, Samuel J.
Snow, Arnold K.
Snuggs, Charles L.
Snure, John W.
Snure, Robert
Snyder, Charles N.
Snyder, David H.
Snyder, Donald D.
Snyder, Donald E.
Snyder, Donald J.
Snyder, Edward
Snyder, Mark
Snyder, Robert L.
Snyder, William H.
Soares, Stephen Sr.
Sobeck, Eugene G.
Soboslay, Steve
Sofuolis, Ernest A.
Sokol, Peter E.
Solari, Peter B.
Solis, August L.
Solms, George III
Solomon, Louis S.
Solomon, Max
Soltis, Joseph J.
Solum, Floyd K.
Somerville, Robert D.
Sommer, Robert
Sones, Chester H.
Sonnabend, Joel S.
Sonsalla, Roy T.
Sorensen, Howard W.
Sorkin, Morton
Sorrell, James E.
Sorrick, Paul W. Jr.
Sotos, George
Sottile, Chester
Soucy, Andrew C.
Souder, Germany
Sourbeer, Patricia R.
Sours, Kenneth I.
Southard, Russell A.
Souza, Leo J.
Spagna, Joseph R.
Spain, Albert E.
Spain, Robert E.
Spaman, Henry J.
Spangenberg, Catherine
Spangler, Dick
Spangler, Duane L.
Spannbauer, Robert B.
Spano, Louis L.
Sparacino, Nick J.
Sparano, Charles
Sparks, Barney V.
Sparks, Charles E.
Sparks, Harold A.
Sparks, Melvin L.
Sparks, Rufus Jr.
Sparr, Richard H.
Sparrow, Robert G.
Spear, Robert R.
Spearin, Frederic W.
Spearman, Henry L.
Spears, Harold D.
Spears, Phil H.
Speas, Walton M.
Specht, Charles H.
Spees, Robert F.
Spees, Robert G.
Spenard, George J.
Spence, Raymond
Spence, Wayne J.
Spencer, George V. Jr.
Spencer, George V. Jr.
Spencer, Harold L.
Spencer, John H.
Spencer, Mary A.
Spencer, Melvin L.
Spencer, William A.
Spencer, William C.
Spengler, Martin F.
Spera, John A.
Sperduto, Vincent J.
Spicer, Sherman S.
Spicer, Timothy J.
Spies, Harvey A.
Spillane, Joseph A.
Spiller, Robert W.
Spillman, Thomas F.
Spindler, Donald C.
Spinelli, Gene
Spinicci, Bruno
Spinks, Oswell H.
Spiridis, George M.
Spiridon, John
Spiro, Frank
Spitsen, John R.
Spittel, James M.
Spolar, George A.
Sposa, William R.
Sprague, Lee
Spratt, James
Spray, William R.
Sprayberry, Bruce A.
Sprecher, William P.
Spreckelsen, Marvin R.
Spring, George N. Jr.
Spring, William S.
Spring, William S.
Springborn, Ken W.
Springer, Edward L.
Sprinkle, Mike
Sprinkle, Robert B.
Sprinkle, Thomas M.
Sproles, Mckinney J.
Spuhler, Karl L.
Squilanti, Guswin P.
Squire, Henry H.
Squyres, Max E.
St. Charles, Louis Jr.
St. Denis, Thomas A.
St. George, Louis C.
St. Jean, Albert R.
St. Jean, Arthur
St. Jean, Richard A.
St. John, Clayton E.
St. Yves, Edmond B.
Staab, John G.
Staack, Charles D.
Stacey, Charles G.
Stachowiak, Harry W.
Stack, Arthur
Stack, Margaret M.
Stackman, Edward W.
Stacy, Gordon P.
Stadvec, A.R.
Stafford, James J.
Stahl, Byron E.
Stahl, Ervin H.
Stahl, Lee R.
Stahl, Morris
Stahr, Donald D.
Stahr, Richard
Stakes, William E.
Stalder, James R.
Staley, B.R.
Staley, Roger
Staley, Thomas A.
Stalliviere, Bart M.
Stalo, Robert W.
Stalo, Robert W.
Stambach, Robert L.
Stambaugh, Robert R.
Stampahar, Raymond J.
Stanek, Joseph Jr.
Stanford, John A.
Stanley, Barclay L.
Stanley, Clifford E.
Stanley, Gene K.
Stanley, Jessie L.
Stanley, Lawrence R.
Stanley, Tom J.
Stannard, Ralph L.
Stanner, Wendell C.
Stanoski, Walter J.
Stanowski, Peter
Stanton, Charles R.
Stanton, George E.
Stanton, Stanley A.
Stanus, Leo J.
Staples, Horace H.
Stapleton, James A.
Starbuck, Raymond B.
Stark, Bruce E.
Stark, Carl H.
Stark, Joseph L.
Stark, Paul F.
Stark, Peter A.
Starkel, Walter
Starkey, James E.
Starkey, John V.
Starrett, Edwin B.
Starrett, Nathaniel Jr.
Starsoneck, Edward H.
Stasch, William J.
Stashkevetch, Joseph
Stasiak, Walter C.
Stasiowski, Walter A.
Statile, Daniel A.
Statler, Kenneth C.
Staub, Charles E.
Staude, Richard
Stauder, Anne
Stauffer, Francis T.
Stauffer, Raymond G.
Staula, Dom
Staut, Harry W.
Stauth, Ward
Staveski, Albert G.
Stavinoha, Werner J.
Stawski, Albert
Steadman, Thomas J.
Steadman, William T.
Steady, Eugene
Stearns, Walter E.
Stechschulte, Harold
Steco, Michael
Stedman, Lynn G. Jr.
Steeg, Daniel V.
Steel, Francis P.
Steel, Robert W.
Steele, Bruce R.
Steele, Carl J.
Steele, Edward J.
Steele, Lloyd E.
Steele, Robert R.
Steele, Wallace O.
Steelman, Ellwood A.
Stefaniak, John
Stefaniak, W.J.
Stefanick, Stan
Steffen, Edward J.
Steib, Curt F.
Stein, Karl E.
Stein, Milton A.
Stein, Morrie
Stein, Paul D.
Steinbeck, Gary L.
Steinberg, Richard M.
Steinberg, Sidney J.
Steiner, Joseph
Steinhaus, Edward T.
Steinhauser, John A.
Steinmeyer, Theodore J.
Steinway, Gerald
Stell, Roy W.
Stellick, Roland G.
Stelzer, Stanley J.
Stendall, Carl P.
Stender, Roy W.
Stengel, Raymond
Stengel, Raymond
Stengel, Richard T.
Stepanek, Tony
Stephan, Joseph L.
Stephan, Ken
Stephan, Philip
Stephens, James E.
Stephens, Jane
Stephens, John B.
Stern, Maurice
Sternberg, Alexander Jr.
Sterner, John W.
Sterner, Maynard W.
Sterrath, Donald
Sterrett, D.H.
Stetler, William H.
Stetz, John S.
Stevens, E. Seward
Stevens, John J.
Stevens, Madison R.
Stevens, Robert L.
Stevenson, George W. Jr.
Stevenson, Robert L.
Stevenson, Thomas Jr.
Stevenson, Thomas R.
Steward, L.W.
Stewart, Allen N.
Stewart, Carl W.
Stewart, James E.
Stewart, James W.
Stewart, John H. Jr.
Stewart, Maxey H. Jr.

Stewart, Robert E.
Stewart, Ronald E.
Stewart, Samuel R.
Stewart, William A.
Stewart, William G.
Stewart, William K.
Stewart, William M.
Stice, Billy E.
Stickles, Martin R.
Stickley, William W.
Stickroth, Bruce H.
Stiehl, Jay G.
Stierheim, Francis B.
Stiffler, Charles S.
Stilley, Levi G.
Stillwell, George
Stinson, Leo F.
Stipp, Thad P.
Stirsman, Elmon R.
Stites, John
Stitt, Robert G.
Stiver, Herman A.
Stocker, R.A.
Stocker, Ralph
Stocks, Kenneth M.
Stockton, James E.
Stockwell, Dorwin D.
Stoddard, George H.
Stokes, William L.
Stolarczyk, John S.
Stoll, George Rives
Stoll, Harley F.
Stoll, Harold W.
Stoll, Ralph
Stollak, Julius
Stolte, Lawrence
Stombaugh, Miles E.
Stone, Chas. M.
Stone, Paul M.
Stone, Roy M.
Stone, Ted
Stone, W.J.
Stonebraker, Keith E.
Stoner, James E.
Stonerock, Harold A.
Storer, Roy U.
Storrick, Robert W.
Stotmeister, Francis L.
Stottrup, Bruce
Stout, Donald C.
Stout, William J.
Stovall, James C.
Strachan, Thomas D.
Strand, Donald Elmer
Strand, Merlin A.
Strate, Hermond O.
Strathearn, R.G.
Strause, Leon V.
Straw, John J.
Strawa, Helen
Strawser, Robert S.
Street, Gordon M.
Street, Ross L.
Streeter, Donald
Streeter, Leslie W.
Streeter, Warren
Stricek, Peter J.
Strickland, William D.
Stricklen, Jack C.
Strickler, Elmo E.
Stride, Calvin P.
Strike, Robert R.
Stringer, Gerald N.
Stringer, Roy F.
Strode, Elbert W.
Stroh, Alan E.
Stroh, Lewis R.
Strong, Donald J.
Strong, Norman W.
Strong, Thomas M.
Stronski, Matthew C.
Stroo, J.W.
Strot, Richard P.
Stroud, Robert
Stroup, Charles C.
Strube, Alfred C.
Stuart, Carl W.
Stuart, Walter E.
Stubblefield, Kemble L.
Stubblefield, Marcus H.
Stubbs, Hibbard C.
Stubelek, Walter H.
Stuckey, Bythel
Studdard, Arthur B.
Studley, Joseph L.
Stull, Donald
Stuller, Joseph L.
Stultz, Raymond W.
Stumpp, Earl E.
Sturdivent, Walter B.
Sturgis, Buddy
Sturtevant, James M.
Sturzyk, Joseph V.
Stusick, Steve S.
Stuski, Benjamin J.
Stuvengen, Charles G.
Styer, Lester C.
Suarez, Joe A.
Suchar, Florian M. Sr.
Sudvary, John
Suessmann, James R.
Sufczynski, Joseph F.
Suffel, Harold
Suffern, George E.
Suiter, John J.
Sujdak, Harry
Suleski, Stephen J.
Sullivan, Bernard A.
Sullivan, Byron R.
Sullivan, Daniel E.
Sullivan, Daniel E.
Sullivan, Donald E.
Sullivan, Edward F.
Sullivan, Ezra D.
Sullivan, John J.
Sullivan, John P.
Sullivan, Joseph
Sullivan, Louis P.
Sullivan, Patrick J.
Sullivan, Patrick L.
Sullivan, Robert F.
Sullivan, Roy S.
Sullivan, Thomas P.
Sullivan, Timothy E.
Summerford, Kenneth T.
Summers, George R.
Summers, James P. Jr.
Summers, Wallace D.
Summerville, Carl W.
Summerville, P.G. Jr.
Sumner, Thomas
Sundberg, John A.
Sunderland, Ray
Sundsback, Birger L.
Sundstrand, Carl J.
Sunstrom, Willard A.
Suravage, Dominic A.
Surig, Ted
Surrett, Harold C.
Susa, Raymond F.
Susin, Adam
Sussman, Meyer
Sutcliffe, John R.
Sutherland, Austin
Sutherland, Lewis F.
Sutherland, Woodrow C.
Suttelle, D.A.
Sutter, Nelson K.
Sutton, Fred I. Jr.
Sutton, Herschel C.
Sutton, Joe E.
Sutton, Paul M.
Sutton, Robert H.
Suzdak, Stanley
Svejda, Edmund W.
Svendsen, Edgar N.
Svihovec, William J.
Svitak, Annetta
Swall, James M.
Swan, Merril A.
Swaney, Edward R.
Swansfeger, Oscar F.
Swanson, Alfred
Swanson, Arnold C.
Swanson, Axel Frederick
Swanson, Carl J.
Swanson, David R.
Swanson, Loren A.
Swanson, Lowell J.
Swanson, Marlin R.
Swanson, Norman W.
Swanson, Vernon C.
Swanson, Warren A.
Swanton, Elmer A.
Swartz, Kenneth W.
Swartz, Ralph C.
Swartz, Robert L.
Swearingen, Wayne W.
Sweeney, Austin W.
Sweeney, Edward F.
Sweeney, Robert E.
Sweet, Carroll F.
Sweet, Robert E.
Swegel, Valentine
Sweigert, Richard
Sweitzer, Robert C.
Swengel, Robert T.
Swenson, Merle
Swenson, Paul C.
Swierczynski, Raymond
Swietochowski, Ted
Swift, Charles G.
Swift, Charles S.
Swift, Harold V.
Swigert, Max R.
Swihart, Harry L.
Swisher, Harold D.
Sydney, Clifford E. Jr.
Sylak, Frank
Syme, Barbara M.
Symmonds, Edward N.
Synos, Edward
Sype, Warren D.
Syrek, Stanley
Syverson, Harry C.
Szajko, Frank
Szczepanek, Walter F.
Szypa, William

- T -

Tabone, Salvatore M.
Tadych, Marcel F.
Taggart, Alvin F.
Tagland, Arthur H.
Tagliabue, Howard W.
Tahamont, David
Taillon, Norman J.
Takemire, Wilbur L.
Takemire, Wilbur L.
Talbert, Harley D.
Tallau, Edward W. Jr.
Talley, Alfred
Talley, Richard E.
Tally, William J.
Talton, Gordon E.
Tambling, John R.
Tamulevicz, Bron J.
Tangney, Donald J.
Tanguay, Walter
Tanner, James A.
Tannich, Ted T.
Taormina, Dominick
Tapfer, Eugene
Tapscott, Robert L.
Taranovich, Joseph
Tarnaski, Ray A.
Tarrant, George M.
Tashman, Nathaniel
Tasker, Alvin R.
Tate, George R.
Tate, Hayward L.
Tate, James M.
Tate, John A. Jr.
Tatosian, Michael Jr.
Tattan, John R.
Tatum, Virgil
Taub, Raymond P.
Taulelle, Paul A.
Taussig, Joseph K. Jr.
Taylor, A.F.
Taylor, Allen J. Capt.
Taylor, Alvin Ray
Taylor, Carl F.
Taylor, Daniel
Taylor, Daniel
Taylor, Glen
Taylor, James J.
Taylor, Joseph C.
Taylor, Kenneth W.
Taylor, Morton J.
Taylor, Norman C.
Taylor, Raymond F.
Taylor, Richard E.
Taylor, Robert O.
Taylor, Thomas B.
Taylor, Thomas L.
Taylor, W.P.
Taylor, Walter T.
Taylor, William L.
Taylor, William L.
Taylor, Willis H.
Teagle, Edward F.
Teague, Buret A.
Teague, Lewis E.
Teasley, Warren
Teat, Virgil
Tecza, Thaddeus W.
Tedesko, Frank W.
Tedford, J.L.
Teepen, Vincent
Teichmiller, William F.
Telford, Jack K.
Teman, Harold
Tempany, Edward J.
Temple, Alvin D.
Temple, James
Tener, Donald
Tenney, William R.
Tennie, Alfred C. Jr.
Tennihan, Ralph E.
Tennis, Peter J.
Tente, Paul
Terhaar, Jerome H.
Terhune, Johnnie J.
Tero, Robert J.
Terrameo, Anthony A.
Terrian, Louis J.
Tessenear, James R.
Testudine, Joseph
Teter, Gordon S.
Teto, Kenneth Loren
Tetreault, Albert F.
Tetrick, James E. Sr.
Tetrick, Robert E.
Tewfell, Frank
Thacher, Carroll
Thaete, William E.
Thalen, Warren R.
Thayer, Frederick G.
The Lone Sailor
The War Memorial Comm.
Thede, Orville J.
Theis, Kenneth W.
Theriault, Eugene L.
Theriault, Harry R.
Thibodeau, Maurice L.
Thiede, Elmer W.
Thiede, Loren C.
Thielke, Gordon G.
Thiergartner, Leonard
Thifault, Charles E.
Thiroway, Patrick J.
Thobe, Richard
Thoennes, John
Thole, Howard F.
Thomas, Carlton A.
Thomas, Clarence
Thomas, Clarence
Thomas, Elmer
Thomas, Emil J.
Thomas, Ernest
Thomas, Fred L.
Thomas, Fred L.
Thomas, George A.
Thomas, Gerald C.
Thomas, Helen N.
Thomas, James E.
Thomas, James H.
Thomas, James V.
Thomas, James W.
Thomas, John L.
Thomas, Les A.
Thomas, Rex L.
Thomas, Rodney Y.
Thomas, Roland E. Jr.
Thomas, Tillman C.
Thomas, Van
Thomason, John C.
Thomasson, Bernard O.
Thomasson, John R.
Thomison, William
Thompson, Archie R.
Thompson, Charles E. Jr.
Thompson, Charles R.
Thompson, Charles W.
Thompson, Edward S.
Thompson, Garland C.
Thompson, Hal L.
Thompson, Herbert K.
Thompson, Howard
Thompson, James A.
Thompson, Lemuel A. Jr.
Thompson, Leonard M.
Thompson, Paul W.
Thompson, R.M.
Thompson, Ross B.
Thompson, W.A.
Thompson, W.L.
Thompson, William F.
Thompson, William J.
Thomspon, Jack C.
Thorbeck, George
Thorbjornsen, Melvin
Thorbjornsen, Melvin
Thorburn, Kenneth E.
Thorn, Raymond C.
Thornberry, George I.
Thorne, Edwin
Thorne, Rex
Thornhill, Jerry F.
Thornton, Charles Jr.
Thornton, James
Thornton, William M.
Threet, Jewel M.
Thul, Charles E.
Thurlo, Emmett H.
Thurmond, Jack A.
Thurston, Ned E.
Thyen, Ed
Tibben, Marvin L.
Tibbetts, Harry E.
Tibbetts, Willard H.
Ticken, John G. Jr.
Tidwell, Otis
Tiedemann, Howard M.
Tielsch, Paul
Tiger, Gordon M.
Tillotson, Donald R.
Tilton, Harold W.
Timmerman, Francis
Tindall, Gary W.
Tindall, Herbert L.
Tindle, Coy J.
Tingwall, Ralph E.
Tinkham, Alvah L.
Tinsley, Richard S.
Tippins, Robert G.
Tipton, David W.
Tipton, David W.
Tipton, James R.
Tisdale, James Henry
Tisi, Rocco
Titlow, Albert
Titone, Gaspar A.
Titus, Donald A.
Titus, Joseph P. Jr.
Titus, Lowell M.
Tiwald, Herman J.
Tober, Richard C.
Tobin, Richard T.
Tobin, Tom
Toczylowski, Edward J.
Todaro, Thomas J.
Todd, Franklin W.
Todd, John E.
Todd, John L.
Todd, Marion
Todd, Philip A.
Todd, Robert W.
Todd, Von E.
Todd, Walter J.
Todhunter, Paul D.
Toft, James C.
Tolan, Robert T.
Tolbert, Jesse J.
Tolleris, Ralph
Tollerson, Lyle P.
Tolowitzki, William
Tolson, Albert C.
Tomalko, George
Tomasak, William
Tomberg, Ernest W.
Tomcho, Leonard J.
Tomczak, Richard C.
Tomkinson, Philip K.
Tomkovitch, Sigmund
Tomkowiak, Florian J.
Tomlin, Larney W.
Tomlonovich, Anthony
Tomlonovich, Anthony
Tommie, Joe D.
Tompkins, Kenneth H.
Toms, Earl E.
Toms, Robert H.
Tomsic, Joseph W.
Toner, Edward J. Jr.
Tonkiss, Ace J.
Toombs, Curtis
Topley, Steve
Tordo, John A. Sr.
Torick, John
Torkelson, Richard A.
Tormey, William D.
Tornatore, Sal R.
Torrey, James H.
Tortora, Carl
Tortorelli, Joseph
Tortorello, Carmine
Toth, Joseph
Toth, Stephen A.
Toth, William H.
Totilo, Anthony T.
Touchinski, Richard
Touzell, Charles W.
Tow, Vernon V.
Towell, Clyde L.
Towers, Chester W.
Towne, Kenneth R.
Townley, Jack
Townsend, Frank H.
Townsley, Jack W.
Toy, Max E.
Tracey, Patrick J.
Tracy, Thomas E.
Trader, Leo E.
Traft, Richard J.
Trainor, Peter J.
Trantalis, George W.
Trapp, Kenneth W.
Trasser, Louis W.
Travers, John R.
Travillian, Harold W.
Travis, Darrell E.
Traynor, Francis M.
Treadwell, William H.
Treanor, Joseph
Treantafilos, Charles
Treece, Richard F.
Treem, Richard
Trefry, James C.
Tremlett, Lawrence R.
Trench, P.W.
Trent, John M.
Trevor, James L.
Trexler, Robert E.
Tribbitt, Sherman W.
Trignano, Nicholas A.
Trilla, John M.
Tringali, Anthony J.
Triplett, George V.
Triplett, John R.
Tripp, Warren C.
Trippanera, Robert A.
Troha, Jos
Trott, Rosemary
Trotz, William L.
Troutman, John P.
Troutman, Lee Rosco
Trovato, Charles J.
Trudeau, Lawrence
Truelsen, Kenneth
Truhe, John
Trull, Ellis G.
Truman, Joseph J.
Truman, Kenneth G.
Trusheim, Philip N.
Truxal, Jacob R.
Tschupp, Harvey C.
Tubbs, Warren G.
Tubergen, Harry F.
Tuchalski, Carl R.
Tucker, Albert S. Jr.
Tucker, Buford A.
Tucker, George R.
Tucker, Harvey T.
Tucker, James J.
Tucker, John F.
Tucker, Kenneth
Tucker, Paul E.
Tucker, Roy L.
Tucker, Sterling W.
Tufo, Ferdinand G.
Tufte, Elster J.
Tulimiero, Joseph R.
Tully, William C.
Tumey, Charles E.
Tumminia, Frank
Turacy, John T.
Turcotte, Gene
Turcotte, Joseph E.
Turek, Robert J.
Turgeon, Benedict A.
Turgeon, Eugene L.
Turinese, Alfred
Turman, Jerry N.
Turnbull, George
Turner, Dave
Turner, Harold
Turner, John W.
Turner, Joseph E.
Turner, Kebbie J.
Turner, Kella D.
Turner, Lee R. Jr.
Turner, Lonnie Harold
Turner, Neal J.
Turner, R.L.
Turner, Sullivan H.
Turso, Dominick A.
Tushaus, Kenneth
Tuttle, Charles F.
Tuttle, Jack B.
Tuttle, Richard G.
Tuttle, William L.
Tuxward, Howard
Twait, Leroy C.
Tweed, Harry L.
Tweedie, Richard D.
Twist, Carroll E.
Tylander, William H.
Tyler, Marvin W.
Tyler, Roger
Tymjack, Dan E.
Tymon, Charles J.
Tyra, Stanley
Tyrie, Ralph
Tyrrell, Francis J.
Tyrrell, James F.

- U -

Uhl, John H.
Ulkloss, William W.
Ullman, Karl H.
Ulrich, John H.
Umbarger, James R.
Umberger, William R.
Umholtz, Adam C.
Umile, Benjamin E.
Umstattd, Eugene I.
Underhill, A.E.
Underwood, Donald C.
Underwood, Earl D. Jr.
Underwood, Ed
Underwood, Norfleet Jr.
Unkert, Leonard E.
Unkle, Edward H.
Upham, Harry E.
Upshaw, Charles F.
Upton, Cynthia
Upton, King
Uravic, Nickolas
Urban, Arthur
Urban, Arthur
Urban, William A.
Urbanski, Eugene J.
Urick, Mike
Utvich, John

- V -

Vacca, Anthony
Vaccarella, Leonard
Vaillancourt, Marcel
Vaillant, Ovide V.
Valdez, Joseph I. Jr.
Valente, Thomas
Valentine, Thomas E.
Valentino, Joseph Jr.
Valeri, Robert M.
Vallas, Earnest J.
Vallette, William J.
Valls, Luis A.
Valsamedis, Gus
Valunas, Walter J.
Vanallen, William K.
Vanaman, Clyde Dr.
Vanasco, Roy G.
Vanatta, Theodore L.
Vanauken, Bradford
VanCourt, Roger M.
Vandegriek, Thomas
VanDerbeck, Donald W.
Vanderbie, George R.
Vandermeer, Albertus W.
Vandermeer, Douglass D.
Vandermeulen, Charles
Vandersanden, George
Vanderscors, Robert L.
Vanderslice, Elmer C.
VanDerWerff, Robert
Vanderzee, William E.
Vandiver, William H.
Vandre, Gilbert
Vandriel, Henry J.
VanDussen, Cornelus
VanDyke, Donald
VanEpps, Dahlman F.
VanFleet, Robert V.
VanFossen, Carl M.
Vangelakos, Harry
Vanhook, Richard E.
VanHousen, E.I.
Vanhoy, Chuck
Vanlear, Guy B.
Vanlear, Oney A. Jr.
Vanmaele, M.J.
VanMeter, Benjamin F.
VanNest, Richard B.
VanNostrand, Roy
Vannoy, James L.
Vannucci, Alfred F.
Vanorden, Walter A.
VanSickle, Melvin J.
Vansyoc, Thomas L.
VanValkenburg, Dalton
Vanwinkle, Nick
VanWoert, Gail F.
Vanyo, Adam M. Sr.
VanZandt, Larry K.
Varisco, Andrew A.
Varner, Robert L.
Varroso, William A.
Varvara, Peter
Varwig, William H.
Vasco, John P.
Vasile, Francis X.
Vasko, Dennis L.
Vasquez, W.A.
Vassallo, Daniel M.
Vassalluzzo, Dominic P.
Vaughan, Elwood J.
Vaughan, Henry L.
Vaughan, William N.
Vaughn, James H.
Vautier, William B.
Vaver, Edward
Vavreck, Joseph B.
Vavruska, William C.
Veatch, Homer D.
Velky, Paul J.
Venema, Harry G.
Ventullo, Patrick S.
Ventura, Joseph T.
Vercolio, Pete D.
Verdelotti, William R.
Vermeersch, Albert W.
Vermette, George J.
Vermillion, I.G.
Verna, Nick
Vernachio, Ernest
Vernetti, Ameul D.
Vernon, Otis L.
Versnik, Lewis V.
Vertes, James A.
Vertifeuille, Bert
Vescovi, Anthony F.
Vesel, Martin A.
Vestal, Tula W.
Vetter, Joseph
Vetter, Robert L.
Vezina, Harvey J.
Viani, John A.
Viebrock, Harold W.
Viggers, Veryl
Vilardi, Alfred
Villalva, Trinidad
Villanella, Joseph T.
Vinci, Daniel P.
Vinson, Virgil W.
Virgili, Edmond P.
Virgilito, Tony
Virtue, Ray W.
Virum, John A.
Vistinis, Anthony
Vitale, Cosmo A.
Vitale, Dominick
Vitiello, Aldo
Vito, Frank
Vlasich, Nick
Voelker, Robert J.
Voelzke, John W.
Vogel, Charles E.
Vogt, Floyd
Vogt, Joseph J.
Voigt, Joseph
Vojtecky, Frank B.
Volker, Carl C.
Vollbracht, Ralph L.
Vollbrecht, Frederic
Voloshik, James J.
Voluse, Charles R. Jr.
Vondohre, Arthur J.
Vondras, James J.
Vondrey, James B.
VonHolten, Jeffrey
VonHone, Walter A.
VonLumm, Edward J.
Voorhes, Fred R.
Vore, Allen E.
Vorenkamp, Capt. R.
Vorholy, Joseph M. Jr.
Vorholy, Joseph M. Jr.
Vormbrock, Bernard J.
Vosier, Douglas D.
Voss, Kenton J.
Voss, Robert W.
Vrabel, Dorothy
Vreeland Milton R.
Vreeland, Kenneth
Vytlacil, George C.

- W -

Wachter, Andrew J. Sr.
Wachter, Robert C.
Wachter, Robert M.
Wadas, Rudolph J.
Waddell, David M.
Wade, Walter E.
Wade, William H.
Wadel, Wesley E.
Wadsworth, Edward M.
Wadsworth, Floyd E.
Waesche, Russell R.
Wagenknecht, Richard M.
Wager, Berl Wm.
Wagner, Albert Van
Wagner, Charles R.
Wagner, Ernest J.
Wagner, Glenn G.
Wagner, Louis K.
Wagner, Otto A.
Wagner, Richard L.
Wagner, Robert F.
Wagner, Rod
Wagner, William D.
Wagner, William Jr.
Wagner, William L.
Wagoner, Robert G.
Wahl, Ralph H.
Wainscott, Guy Jr.
Waite, Douglas W.
Wakefield, Duane A.
Walburn, Richard F.
Walck, Ralph M.
Walden, Carl W. Jr.
Walden, Vernon E.
Walden, Wyatt
Waldman, Samuel
Waldmiller, Cletus A.
Waldron, Edwin B.
Waldron, Edwin B.
Waldron, John
Waldrop, George R.
Waldrop, John D.
Walker, Danny N.
Walker, Donald C.
Walker, Donald F.
Walker, Donald F.
Walker, Earle
Walker, Elmer R.
Walker, Frank M.
Walker, Hallam
Walker, Harold B.
Walker, Hilton L.
Walker, Hubert G.
Walker, James E.
Walker, John D.
Walker, Kenneth J.
Walker, Kenneth W.
Walker, Raymond R.
Walker, Richard H.
Walker, Robert
Walker, Samuel W.
Walker, Warren H.
Walker, Willis L. Sr.
Wall, Billie M.
Wall, Donald
Wall, Keith D.
Wall, Keith D.
Wall, Kenneth H.
Wall, Kenneth H.
Wall, Paul E.
Wallace, D.E.
Wallace, Franklin L.
Wallace, Gerald J.
Wallace, James C.
Wallace, John R.
Wallace, Lewis B.
Wallace, Richard
Wallace, Robert
Wallace, Robert T.
Wallace, Ulen A.
Wallace, William Jr.
Walley, Yancy D.
Walsh, Alice M.
Walsh, David H.
Walsh, Francis R.
Walsh, Francis R.
Walsh, John L.
Walsh, Mark
Walsh, Raymond J.
Walter, Richard L.
Walters, Charles A.
Walters, Eddie D.
Walters, John R.
Walters, Kenneth A.
Walters, Leonard G.
Walters, Norman P.
Walters, Roland E.
Waltman, Leonard H.
Walton, Alfred Jr.
Walton, Carl R. Jr.
Walton, Nelson C.
Wamser, Edward J.
Wamsley, William C.
Wander, Donald P.
Wapinsky, James A.
Ward, Arnold H.
Ward, Charles W.
Ward, Edward D.
Ward, Harold L.
Ward, John M.
Ward, John T. Sr.
Ward, John W.
Ward, Raymond P.
Ward, Robert W.
Ward, Thomas F.
Ward, Thomas J.
Ware, Roy O.
Wareham, Donald O.
Warehime, Joseph C.
Warford, K.C. Sr.
Wargo, Peter
Wark, John T.
Warming, Leonard T.
Warneke, Thomas C.
Warner, Edward A.
Warner, Frank E.
Warner, Frank W.
Warner, Worthy J.
Warnock, Frank K.
Waro, E.M.
Warren, Alfred J.
Warren, Eugene
Warren, Frank F.
Warren, Victor M.
Warring, Carl C.
Warrington, Edward
Warshaw, Murray
Warunik, Charles R.
Warwick, Loren
Washburn, George
Washick, Metro
Wasilewski, John H.
Wasilewski, Joseph A.

Wasylyk, George M.
Waterbury, Merlin
Waterman, Chester
Waterman, Clifford W.
Waters, Charles
Waters, John M.
Waters, Norman R.
Waterworth, Doyal I.
Watkins, Albert R.
Watkins, Eldon
Watkins, James E. Sr.
Watkins, Thomas H.
Watkins, Willard W.
Watlington, Elijah L.
Watson, Artemus
Watson, Cordell M.
Watson, Don
Watson, Frederick E.
Watson, George H.
Watson, George M.
Watson, Jack L.
Watson, John L. Jr.
Watson, Lewis A.
Watson, Robert D. Jr.
Watson, Roy G.
Watson, Ruth
Watson, Thomas W.
Watson, Veto W.
Watson, William
Watt, Harry L.
Watt, Reginald R.
Wattam, Clifford R. Jr.
Watts, Arthur L.
Watts, Bob
Watts, Edward H.
Watts, Edward Jr.
Watts, George E.
Watts, Lester J.
Waxman, Arnold L.
Waymire, Donald M.
Weafer, James E.
Weakland, George
Weal, Richard
Wear, Dale E.
Wease, Flay
Weathers, E.L.
Weaver, Frank A.
Weaver, Garland W.
Weaver, Norman
Weaver, Roy Earl
Weaver, Wes
Weaver, William W.
Webb, Aldon J.
Webb, Clifton L.
Webb, Harry D.
Webb, Jack G.
Webb, John R.
Webb, R.D.
Webber, Irwin H.
Webber, Robert
Webeck, James E.
Weber, Alban
Weber, Curtis G.
Weber, Ernest W.
Weber, George C.
Weber, William E.
Webster, Charles D.
Webster, Donald E.
Webster, Gayle A.
Webster, Leonard O.
Webster, Richard M.
Wechsler, George W.
Weddle, Donald G.
Wedemayer, Walter E.
Wedig, George A.
Wedinger, Frederick C.
Weed, Byron E.
Weeks, F.C.
Weeks, Harry S. Jr.
Weeks, James L.
Wefer, Herbert G.
Weible, William W.
Weick, E.C.
Weidman, Catherine M.
Weidman, George W.
Weidner, Frank E.
Weimer, Raymond J.
Weinand, Richard
Weiner, Abraham A.
Weinert, James J.
Weinland, Bernard T.
Weinroth, Jack
Weinstein, David M.
Weinstein, Joel
Weir, Donald E.
Weir, Hollis L.
Weis, Kenneth F.
Weise, Burton H.
Weisman, Robert F.
Weiss, Albert L.
Weiss, Henry M.
Weiss, Hymen
Weiss, Jerome
Weissman, George
Weisspfennig, Walter W.
Weisswasser, Barry G.
Weist, James J.
Weitze, Frederick W.
Wejner, Bernhard J.
Welch, Alvin L.
Welch, David F.
Welch, George M.
Welch, James R.
Welch, Joseph J.
Welch, Norman D.
Welcome, Leigh H.
Welker, Clifford E.
Well, John P.
Wellborn, Johnson
Weller, Jack
Weller, Joseph F. Jr.
Weller, Milburn R.
Wells, Alford W.
Wells, Belvin M.
Wells, Donald R. Sr.
Wells, Howard E. Jr.
Wells, Jack W.
Wells, Leotha
Wells, Louis J.
Wells, Robert E.
Welsh, Charles
Welsh, James L.
Welsh, John H.
Welter, Thomas L.
Welton, Norris A.
Welty, Daryl E.
Welty, Karl F.
Wendel, George H.
Wendeler, Henry
Wendell, Douglas C. Jr.
Wendells, Arthur T.
Wengland, Charles E.
Wengler, Donald E.
Wengryn, Michael
Wenrich, James
Wentworth, Harold R.
Wenzel, William H.
Wenzel, William H.
Werley, Al
Wermuth, Robert P.
Werner, Ralph J.
Wernersbach, Ralph E.
Wernicki, Michael F.
Werstein, Kaspar J.
Wert, Blake H.
Werthmuller, Frank L.
Wertman, Charles G.
Wertz, Frank H.
Wescott, Harry L.
Wesenberg, Donald R.
Wesley, Eugene
Wessel, Wayne L.
Wessner, Peg
West, Hersey W.
West, Homer Dennis
West, Mary C.
West, Oscar E. Jr.
West, Paul Franklin
West, Robert F.
West, Ronald W.
West, Thompson B.
West, Walter L.
Westbrook, Glendon
Westergaard, Clarence
Weston, Frank H.
Westwater, Joseph J.
Wetmore, Eugene S.
Wetzel, Leo D.
Wetzler, Robert J.
Weyer, Richard W.
Weyl, Paul J.
Whaley, Daniel
Whaley, Harrison L.
Whaley, Mel
Whaling, Herman
Wharton, Heyward M.
Wheat, Charles F. Sr.
Wheat, Edwin
Wheeler, Alan K.
Wheeler, D.R.
Wheeler, Frederick A.
Wheeler, Harry L.
Wheeler, Kenneth A.
Wheeler, Stephen M.
Wheeler, William J.
Wheeley, Wilton B.
Whelan, Richard T.
Wheldon, John W.
Wherritt, George
Wherry, John D.
Whipp, Donald V. Jr.
Whitaker, Walter
Whitbeck, James F.
White, A.C. Jr.
White, Alvin L.
White, Arnold M.
White, Arthur L.
White, Austin J.
White, David L.
White, Donald
White, Edwin
White, Elsie H.
White, Floyd A
White, Frank
White, Franklyn
White, George A.
White, Henry H.
White, James B.
White, John E.
White, John R.
White, Joseph J.
White, Lee E.
White, Marion E.
White, O. Frank
White, Paul E.
White, Robert C.
White, Robert R.
White, Roy E.
White, Russell A.
White, Scott
White, Wallace
White, Walter B. Jr.
White, William
White, William D.
White, William F.
White, William G. Jr.
White, William J.
White, William S.
White, Yale
Whitebeaver, Ruben
Whitebread, Donald B.
Whitehead, Gerald J.
Whitehill, George L. Jr.
Whiteley, John R.
Whitely, Robert Q.
Whiteside, James W.
Whitley, George S. Jr.
Whitley, John H.
Whitmore, James F.
Whitmore, L.E.
Whitmore, T.E.
Whitney, Burton F.
Whitney, Donald G.
Whitney, Frank J.
Whitney, Glenn K.
Whitney, J. Malcolm
Whitney, Lewis A. Jr.
Whitt, Sidney G.
Whittaker, Walter W.
Whittier, Willard H.
Whittington, Joseph M.
Whitton, Robert E.
Whittredge, Nelson L.
Whyte, Gordon
Wichers, Cyrus L.
Wichser, C.F.
Wichta, A.J.
Wicinski, Martin
Wickizer, George W.
Wickson, Robert
Wiebush, Joseph R.
Wieczorek, Joseph A.
Wiedeman, C.F. Jr.
Wiedenheft, Robert F.
Wiedman, John M.
Wiepert, Louis R.
Wiese, Fred
Wiesen, John W.
Wiess, Paul F.
Wigley, Jack E.
Wigmore, Walter J.
Wigo, John W.
Wilbur, William L. III
Wilcox, Donald W.
Wilcox, Philip M.
Wilcox, Robert
Wilcox, Robert
Wilcox, William L.
Wildasin, Emory B.
Wilde, Kip William
Wilde, Robert L.
Wildemann, Paul H.
Wilder, James D.
Wildes, F.L.
Wilhelms, Robert G.
Wilkerson, Billy V.
Wilkerson, Charles B.
Wilkes, Paul E.
Wilkes, Robert E.
Wilkie, John C.
Wilkin, William R.
Wilkins, Clyde E.
Wilkins, D.E. Jr.
Wilkins, Donald K.
Wilkinson, Fred
Wilkinson, Norman J.
Wilkinson, William C.
Willadsen, W.A.
Willard, Barry F.
Willard, Joseph F.
Wille, Chris H.
Wille, Robert W.
Willey, Addison
Williams, Clarence R.
Williams, Donald L. Sr.
Williams, Earle C.
Williams, Edward A.
Williams, Edward T.
Williams, Edwin A.
Williams, Fred W. Jr.
Williams, Frederick G.
Williams, Gary W.
Williams, George M.
Williams, Glenn E.
Williams, Harlan E.
Williams, Harold E.
Williams, Harold E.
Williams, Harper G.
Williams, Harrison
Williams, Henry
Williams, Henry N.
Williams, Hoyt O.
Williams, J. Elliott
Williams, James E.
Williams, James H.
Williams, James M.
Williams, James P.
Williams, James R.
Williams, Joe B.
Williams, John B.
Williams, John R.
Williams, John T.
Williams, Leo H.
Williams, Nelson E.
Williams, Richard E.
Williams, Robert C.
Williams, Robert E.
Williams, Robert E.
Williams, Robert J.
Williams, Robert R.
Williams, Vergle E. Jr.
Williams, W.A.
Williams, Wilbur A.
Williamson, Charles R.
Williamson, Darvie F.
Williamson, Grover A.
Williamson, John A.
Williamson, Melvin G.
Williamson, Robert Jr.
Williamson, Rudolph P.
Willis, Robert A.
Wills, Charles E. Sr.
Wills, Joseph G.
Wilmarth, Jay E.
Wilmer, John W.
Wilsey, Richard T.
Wilshire, Paul E.
Wilson, Allan M.
Wilson, Alvin C.
Wilson, Arthur
Wilson, Arthur G. Jr.
Wilson, Arthur L.
Wilson, Billy A.
Wilson, Charles W.
Wilson, Claude V.
Wilson, Clifford E.
Wilson, David
Wilson, Dickerson W.
Wilson, Donald R.
Wilson, Edith Carr
Wilson, Edward J.
Wilson, Edwin C.
Wilson, George
Wilson, George R.
Wilson, Glenmarr
Wilson, Hayden D. Sr.
Wilson, Herbert C.
Wilson, James A.
Wilson, James S.
Wilson, James T.
Wilson, James W.
Wilson, John
Wilson, Maurice P.
Wilson, Norman L.
Wilson, Robert C.
Wilson, Robert C.
Wilson, Robert F.
Wilson, Testing O.
Wilson, Walter L.
Wilson, Wilbert
Wilson, William A.
Wilson, William H.
Wilson, William W.
Wilson, Woodrow
Wiman, Kenneth G.
Wimer, Denson A.
Winand, Richard S.
Winans, Charles B.
Winchester, Lorimer
Windeler, Carl W.
Windham, Asa
Windham, John A.
Windle, Ray D.
Windom, James Ray
Windstrup, Richard E.
Winebarger, James E.
Winesett, J.C.
Winfield, Joseph C.
Wingate, V.R.
Wingerter, Joseph G.
Wingren, Robert E.
Winkelspecht, Charles
Winkelspecht, Edward P. Jr.
Winkler, Kenneth R.
Winling, Ernest
Winn, William L.
Winnar, Eric O.
Winnie, Donald G.
Winoker, Lester G.
Winsett, Walter
Winston, Arthur
Winston, Henry
Winters, Colin G.
Winters, Ira J.
Winters, Willard W.
Wintrode, James A.
Winzen, Mathias A.
Wirzfeld, R.W.
Wisber, Peter F.
Wischerth, Louis J.
Wisdo, John J.
Wise, Charles E.
Wise, Edward J.
Wisecup, Roger J.
Wiseheart, Paul W.
Wisenall, Jacob H. Sr.
Wismer, Charles H.
Wisner, Roy M.
Wisniewski, William P.
Wissinger, Raymond E.
Withington, Nelson T.
Witmer, Lyle
Witoshynsky, Alexander
Witt, James E.
Wittel, Allen L.
Witten, Charles H.
Witting, Joseph A.
Wittman, Elmer H.
Wittrock, C. John
Wix, John
Wlodyka, Henry J.
Wnek, Frank A.
Wocoski, Joseph E.
Woehler, Gordon
Woeltje, Marvin C.
Woerner, William C.
Wohlsen, Robert S.
Woidke, Norbert J.
Wojciechowski, Jerome
Wojcik, Joseph
Wojtkowski, Mieczyslaw
Wolbert, Adam E.
Wolcott, Gerald H.
Woleyer, Eldon B.
Wolf, Alois
Wolf, Carl W.
Wolf, George E.
Wolf, Jerome D.
Wolfarth, John
Wolfe, Clarence
Wolfe, Donald L.
Wolfe, Henry J.
Wolfe, Robert M.
Wolfe, William G.
Wolfer, Alfred J.
Wolff, Clarence H.
Wolff, Herbert J.
Wolfford, Liles
Wolford, Kenneth E.
Wolfskill, Arnold L.
Wolner, Andy W.
Wolsky, Nat
Woltjer, Hubert H.
Woltz, Clifton W.
Womack, Charles
Womersley, George
Wood, Benjamin J. Jr.
Wood, Charles K.
Wood, Edwin B.
Wood, Fred
Wood, Mason T.
Wood, Raymond A.
Wood, Richard L.
Wood, Robert E.
Wood, Warren W.
Wood, William
Wood, William D.
Wood, William H.
Wood, William P.
Woodall, Everett M. Jr.
Woodard, Tressye Carr
Woodbridge, Dudley E.
Woodbury, Clarence C.
Wooddy, Lynn R.
Woodhouse, Raymond K.
Woodland, Robert B.
Woodman, Claude R.
Woodman, Leroy A.
Woodruff, Charles L.
Woods, David L.
Woods, Virgil H.
Woods, William Lee
Woodward, John D.
Woodward, Mark A.
Woodward, Robert G.
Woodward, W.J.
Woolard, H.C.
Wooten, George
Wooten, George W.
Worden, Delbert W.
Worden, Gordon W.
Worden, Harry S.
Worden, Ithiel M.
Workman, Brenda
Workman, Earl W.
Workman, Jack
Worley, Percell L.
Wormer, Roland
Worms, Earl F.
Worsham, Roy W.
Worsley, Ernest E.
Worth, Larry
Worth, Larry
Worthington, Daniel Jr.
Wranek, Joseph N.
Wrase, William A.
Wray, Bob R.
Wright, James E.
Wright, Laverne C.
Wright, Lloyd Bud
Wright, Raymond B.
Wright, Robert H.
Wright, Ronald
Wright, Roy J.
Wright, W.A.
Wright, William K.
Wroten, Max
Wuckert, A.E.
Wudarski, Al
Wulf, Paul A.
Wulf, Robert W.
Wulff, George J.
Wunschel, Frank
Wurlitzer, Rymund
Wurzbach, William M. Sr.
Wurzel, Leon
Wuslick, George C.
Wyatt, Shelford S.
Wyckoff, Andrus M.
Wyckoff, Frank M.
Wyckoff, Gladys
Wyckoff, Louis Jr.
Wyckoff, Robert
Wydick, George
Wydra, Wallace
Wydronkowski, Francis
Wykoff, William O.
Wylde, Neil
Wyllie, Robert O. Jr.
Wyllie, William V.
Wyllis, John W.
Wylot, Henry E.
Wlota, John
Wynd, Robert H.
Wynn, Thomas W.
Wynne, John J.
Wysocki, John F.
Wyss, Carleton W.

- Y -

Yager, Michael S.
Yaggi, Fred A.
Yampell, Arnold
Yanarella, John J.
Yancovich, Norman J. Sr.
Yanez, Marcelino
Yanish, Edward O.
Yankee, Nelson R.
Yankow, Russ
Yarbrough, Herman R.
Yarusi, Frederick M.
Yasus, Vytold C.
Yates, Charles G.
Yates, Charles L.
Yates, Russell P.
Yates, Sanford A.
Yates, William B.
Yazzo, Frank
Yeager, Lewis W.
Yeargan, Willie R.
Yent, Rufus W.
Yeoman, Hugh E. Jr.
Yingling, Elmer E.
Yoder, Merlyn E.
Yon, Charles L.
York, Leonard E.
York, Peter F.
Yost, George J.
Yost, Paul A. Adm.
Young, Bob
Young, Conrad
Young, Conrad
Young, Edward T.
Young, Elmer J.
Young, Eugene A.
Young, Jack E.
Young, Jack S.
Young, James B.
Young, Joe L.
Young, Joseph V.
Young, Kenneth E.
Young, Kenneth W.
Young, Leroy M.
Young, Maynard F.
Young, Norman
Young, Raymond J.
Young, Richard C.
Young, Robert D.
Young, Robert R.
Young, Russell J.
Young, Warren B.
Young, William C.
Young, William H. Jr.
Youngman, Frank N. Jr.
Yount, Charles I.
Youtz, Charles B.
Yusen, Jack

- Z -

Zabroski, Charles R.
Zacherson, Bruce K.
Zahn, Warren A.
Zalec, Stephen J.
Zalewski, Stanley J.
Zambelli, George R.
Zamorski, Edward
Zane, Clarence J.
Zane, Levi
Zangari, Louis J.
Zapalski, Emil J.
Zarcone, Michael J.
Zarem, Ronald W.
Zayac, Edward
Zbikowski, Arthur R.
Zdanowicz, Vincent
Zeigler, Gordon L.
Zeiller, Don
Zelazo, Edward S.
Zell, James W. III
Zeller, Andrew P.
Zeller, John E.
Zelzer, Louis F.
Zembrzuski, Edward
Zensen, Allen R.
Zepp, Leonard S.
Zepp, Reginald M.
Zera, Angelo D.
Zeronda, Joseph T.
Zeuch, Ralph C.
Zevnik, Francis C.
Zgoda, Jerome S.
Zidlick, Albert J.
Ziegler, George
Ziegler, Norval
Ziemba, Joseph
Zimbardo, Carmen
Zimmerman, Donald
Zimmerman, Elmer C.
Zimmerman, Harry A.
Zimmerman, John R.
Zimmerman, Michael W.
Zimmerman, Robert I.
Zimmerman, Samuel
Zinni, Richard
Zinski, Jack
Ziolkowski, John J.
Zipf, William
Zips, Edward J.
Zitkus, Peter
Zito, Jack D.
Zoglio, Angelo
Zola, George
Zolla, Armand A.
Zook, Morgan
Zotian, John M.
Zubak, Paul J.
Zubik, Edward L.
Zucca, Ernest D.
Zugelder, Don
Zuhn, Walter E. Jr.
Zukovsky, Frank T.
Zumpfe, Donald
Zwierzchowski, Henry
Zydowicz, Edward P.

USS Keith (DE-241), June 22, 1944. (US Navy photograph courtesy of Robert C. Sweitzer)

DESTROYER ESCORT SAILORS ASSOCATION INDEX, VOL. I-III

The index was compiled using available information. The Publisher is not responsible for errors or omissions.

General arra

Courtesy of Tom Freeman